PIMLICO

687

BLOOD KINDRED

W. J. Mc Cormack is Librarian-in-Charge, at the Edward Worth Library, Dublin. Until 2002, he was Professor of Literary History and head of the English Department at Goldsmiths' College, University of London. His publications include *A Festschrift for Francis Stuart* (1972), *Sheridan Le Fanu and Victorian Ireland* (1980, 1991 and 1997), *Ascendancy and Tradition in Anglo-Irish Literary History* (1985), *From Burke to Beckett* (1993), *Fool of the Family: A Life of J. M. Synge* (2000) and *The Silence of Barbara Synge* (2003). He is also the author of a number of volumes of poetry under the name Hugh Maxton. *Poems 2000–2005* will appear in 2005.

BLOOD KINDRED

W. B. Yeats
The Life, The Death, The Politics

W. J. McCORMACK

PIMLICO

Published by Pimlico 2005

2 4 6 8 10 9 7 5 3 1

Copyright © W. J. Mc Cormack 2005

W. J. Mc Cormack has asserted his right
under the Copyright, Designs and Patents Act 1988
to be identified as the author of this work

First published in Great Britain by Pimlico 2005

Pimlico
Random House, 20 Vauxhall Bridge Road,
London SW1V 2SA

Random House Australia (Pty) Limited
20 Alfred Street, Milsons Point, Sydney,
New South Wales 2061, Australia

Random House New Zealand Limited
18 Poland Road, Glenfield,
Auckland 10, New Zealand

Random House South Africa (Pty) Limited
Endulini, 5A Jubilee Road, Parktown 2193, South Africa

The Random House Group Limited Reg. No. 954009

A CIP catalogue record for this book
is available from the British Library

ISBN 0-7126-6514-5

Poetry, Drama and Prose by W. B. Yeats is reproduced by kind
permission of A. P. Watt on behalf of Michael B. Yeats.
Letters by W. B. Yeats are reproduced by kind permission
of Oxford University Press.

Every effort has been made to trace and contact
copyright holders. The publishers will be pleased to correct any
mistakes or omissions in future editions.

Papers used by Random House are natural,
recyclable products made from wood grown in sustainable forests.
The manufacturing processes conform to the environmental
regulations of the country of origin

Typeset by Deltatype Ltd, Birkenhead, Merseyside

Printed and bound in Great Britain by
Mackays of Chatham

For Lucinda Thomson and Hugh Hartnett

Think where man's glory most begins and ends
And say my glory was I had such friends.
The Municipal Gallery Re-visited, 1937

It's quite true what philosophy says, that life must be understood
backwards. But then one forgets the other principle, that it must be
lived forwards.

Søren Kierkegaard

No reasoning forward ever gives me a conviction.

W. B. Yeats
Letter to Ethel Mannin,
24 May 1937

Contents

Acknowledgments

My first and warmest acknowledgment must be to Warwick Gould, a better Yeats scholar than I shall ever be, an excellent colleague while I was employed in the University of London, and an ever-constant irritant to my assumptions about political wickedness. Without his affable discouragement, *Blood Kindred* would never have been written. My second, no less heartfelt acknowledgment names Will Sulkin, who commissioned the book while we were both much younger. The last gentleman in London publishing, he has remained confident that the thing would be done, until now when 'tis done he has appointed Rosalind Porter to see it into print with sympathetic diligence.

Though work was concluded in the hospitable environs of the Bruno Kreitsky Haus and the Sigmund Freud Museum in Vienna, extensive preparations were laid down in the National Library of Ireland: once again, I happily acknowledge the dedication and skill of Tom Desmond, most resourceful and obliging of the librarians in Kildare Street. Ciaran Brady, Alan Kramer, Eunan O'Halpin and Bill Vaughan in the School of Modern History, Trinity College Dublin, provided advice and direction on points of common concern; Katherine Simms kindly advised on points of medieval Gaelic Irish history, and Jane Maxwell clarified matters of College registration. Dr Seamus Helferty, of University College Dublin, assisted me in locating some obscure material relating to several minor members of the Blood Kindred. At the Military Archives, in Cathal Brugha Barracks, Commandants Patrick Brennan and Victor Laing were especially helpful to one whose project seemed at first remote from the material for which they are responsible. Staff at the Public Record Office (Kew) were expeditious as ever in finding bayonets in their haystack.

I am grateful to Dr Judith Priestman, of the Bodleian Library in Oxford, for her kindness in answering a last-minute enquiry.

Years before this book was set in motion, John Gray, librarian at the Linen Hall in Belfast, encouraged me to follow up the Ulster background of Yeats's Victorian forebears. Even earlier, the late

Rodney Green fired in me an enthusiasm for relating economic and industrial history (his discipline) with the loose baggy monster which then was Irish literary history. Iconoclasts both, they were under no obligation to like the consequences or to approve the conclusions reached. I make no claims to expertise in the field of industrial history – I just think one should make efforts to acknowledge the breadth and depth of the field in which literature grows.

Although *Blood Kindred* is intended to serve as a political biography of its subject, it may also be profitably read as a moral essay on method. In the latter sense, it resembles those Venn-diagrams once beloved of school-book illustrations: that is, certain material is shown to belong in more than one category or discussion and consequently comes into view more than once. This critical double attention is suggested in micro-form, devised to refute the doctrine of limited liability by post-romanticism and retail scholarship. If the effect is inelegant at this point or that, I apologise for not completing the task suavely.

Anyone who sets out to write about Yeats must feel sympathy with undergraduates in Tony Blair's New Labour Britain: it is fated that one begins the work burdened with debts. I should at the outset apologise to the thousands of commentators on Yeats whose articles, books, dissertations, editions, essays and other publications I have not read. Among the elite on whom I have relied I want to thank Terence Brown, Roy Foster, Warwick Gould (again), Derry Jeffares, Peter Jochum, John Kelly, Brenda Maddox, David Pierce, Deirdre Toomey and Tim Webb. All are known personally to me: indeed, though I differ sharply from one or two in the list, I count all as friends.

In Aarhus, Ane Line Søndergaard; in Bambery, Cecilie Roppelt, in Berlin, Bettina Schültke; in Cologne, Astrid Gerber; in Dublin, Jackie Blackman, Joe Collins, Ann Dolan, Rebecca Hayes, Tony Jordan, Carla King, Alan Phelan, Rosalinde Schut and Ronnie Wallace; in Frankfurt, Sylvia Goldhammer, Brigitte Klein, Steffi Lamla, Michael Lenarz and Konrad Schneider; in Galway, Basil Fenton and Hermann Rasche; in London, John London, Fiona Macintosh and Wim van Mierlo; in Rockcorry, Philip Clarke and Brian McDonald; in Vienna, Monika Wittmann and Mica Niculescu – all assisted in giving me access to, or insight into, material beyond the range I previously felt comfortable with. Margaret and Jennifer Fitzgibbon cheerfully tolerated the dying stages of the project when we might all have gone tobogganing. To all of these I owe debts of gratitude.

Ciaran Brady, Justin Keating, Mary King, Ferenc Takács and Dennis Tate read all or most of a near-final version. I am deeply grateful to each for the time spent, the patience exhibited and the assistance provided. The errors that remain are clearly ones to which I am attached.

Finally I should like to thank Michael Yeats for answering some unpalatable queries with great courtesy at the commencement of this work.

List of Illustrations

Part One
The Death

In the Catacombs

'The work is done,' grown old he thought,
'According to my boyish plan;
Let the fools rage, I swerved in nought,
Something to perfection brought';
But louder sang that ghost, 'What then?'
                              'What then?', 1937

Where shall the case be heard? Where shall judgment be given? These questions serve to underline the extent to which William Butler Yeats (1865–1939) employed questions as a vital part of his poetic style. They also recall the tone of earlier debates about his politics – the clash of prosecution and defence, quarrels about evidence, appeals for a higher hearing. Without (I think) exception, biographers have accepted that the context in which he should be considered is Irish, defined in such a way as to hold together a cultural nationalism at home and a socio-professional career in England. In other words, they have accepted Yeats's own definition of his world.

With appropriate derogations for individual circumstances, that is our world also. Some readers of the poetry may never have set foot in Ireland, others may deplore nationalism, others again laugh at the coterie of titled nonentities with whom he associated in his last two decades. But all agree that his achievement should be measured by the standards or codes of these 'places of interpretation' which can be located on everybody's map, located and revisited imaginatively or actually. An ordinary universe.

But Yeats did not restrict himself to this world, these ideas. For example, he held strong views on life and death. While few – if any – may share all of these, it would be a foolish biographer who ignored them totally. His sources were diverse and his allegiance far from unconditional. But for much of his life, he professed what is generally regarded as a spiritualist belief in the afterlife. His dynamic of theories, experiences and desires gave prominence to a Vision of the Blood Kindred. According to Emanuel Swedenborg (1688–1772),

3

whose views Yeats used in devising his own system, the soul immediately after death is not aware of its new condition, but sees the familiar world and familiar persons as in life. This is not a permanent condition, for it leads into a complex reorientation of the soul – or dreaming-back – towards its original purity, towards what the poet called 'radical innocence'.

Yeats came to this view early in his poetic career, and it never left him. There is a canonical statement in *A Vision* (1925), the first version of his quasi-official or public philosophy. 'At death the man passes into what seems to him afterwards a state of darkness and sleep; there is a sinking in upon fate analogous to that of the individual cones at Phase 22. During the darkness he is surrounded by his kindred, present in their simulacrae, or in their Spirits when they are between lives, the more recent dead the more visible.'[1] There is a second passage in *A Vision* that transfers the idea away from post-mortem dynamics into a future politics: 'this thought must find expression' among elites of learning and wealth and rank, and 'those kindreds [*sic*] once formed must obey irrational force and create hitherto unknown experience, or that which is incredible'. As Roy Foster notes, these words were written in Mussolini's Italy.[2]

To this unfamiliar notion, let us add another borrowed from musicology – borrowed through an unexpected agency. In *Freud and the Non-European* (2003), Edward Said speaks of *Spätstil* or late style, instancing 'the intransigence and a sort of irascible transgressiveness' of Beethoven's final compositions. In offering a specifically political Life of Yeats, I am aware of the extent to which the topic has been conditioned by the author of *Orientalism* (1978). His recent appropriation of Yeats to the post-colonial cause seems perverse in the extreme, but his extraordinarily broad sympathies as literary critic, political activist and pianist earn him unusual respect.[3]

Yeats's 'late style' can be dated from *circa* 1930 – that is, from the very different work that followed *The Tower* (1928). Perhaps one could point to a second phase, or intensification, commencing in mid-decade and involving surgery as well as poetry. One way or another, body and spirit engaged in a renewal of those struggles usually observed in early manhood. In the poem 'The Tower', Yeats declared, 'It is time that I wrote my will', but in practice he tore up rule-books for old men. His 1934 decision to undergo the 'Steinach operation', in pursuit of sexual renewal, has several political aspects. A desire to put

4

the clock back emerges as a sometimes covert, sometimes dominant, theme.

Within Yeats's corpus of poetry, drama and prose, the most accessible exploration of this arcane idea is to be found in his play 'The Words Upon the Window-pane' (published in 1934). This is a point of reference to which I return several times, for it handles a great deal of material with biographical implications. The outward circumstances are not auspicious. A shabby Dublin lodging-house provides the setting for a *séance* at which the voice of Jonathan Swift (1667–1745) is heard in purgatorial anguish. But the great Augustan satirist is accessible only via a series of mediations through which the violent twentieth century and the timid-polite Victorian age play their parts. I want to write my political life of Yeats with these preoccupations of his in mind, neither accepting nor dismissing them. They constitute not only a spiritualist credo, but also a theory of history. For this reason, and others, they necessarily have a strong political character, not least with reference to notions of free will, social participation, class (democracy versus breeding), sexuality and 'the body'.

Yeats sets the dead Swift amid commonplace listeners – a horse-racing enthusiast, teashop proprietor, gospel preacher and Cambridge student. It seems legitimate to wonder: amidst what unlikely figures might one (with privilege) encounter the dead Yeats? Or, to pose the question from his point of view, what former associates and 'blood kindred' did the soul of Yeats see when released from the body in January 1939? In dying, he had been comforted by a small group of intimates, of whom his wife was the most central to his career. But there is little further to be learned from envisioning these predictable angels. The processes of dreaming-back allegedly involve shocks of recognition, rather than reassurances. The underlying true character of the life is gradually unfolded, laying bare much that has been concealed or repressed. My organising conceit in these preliminary pages requires the identification of Yeats's political unconscious, and the investigation of affinities largely denied in the life – and denied even more assiduously in the many Lives of the poet published to date. But I have no wish to shock for shock's sake; on the contrary, I want carefully to discriminate between coarseness and subtlety, opportunism and self-denial. If at first Yeats is thrown among unsavoury characters, and shown to be of their world, the ultimate objective is to explain biographically how the poet *came about*.

A Sub-Fascist Underground

He did not die at home in bed, but in southern France, a distant and warmer clime good for the health of an ailing man. One consequence of this off-screen obit has been the recurrent use of over-familiar directions to get him back in focus. Yeats has been successively located in the historic cartography of an Anglo-Ireland he helped to invent, of a nationalist Ireland he found alluring and infuriating, and of a domestic-professional milieu very tightly defined. All very good.

When serious reflective commentary on the poet began after the Second World War, the social condition of contemporary Ireland did not attract much attention. Its less attractive aspects were ignored in favour of generalised approval. So too with the other literary figures who had done so much to attract the world's attention. Augusta Gregory (1852–1932) was stringently benign, J. M. Synge (1871–1909) a martyr, James Joyce (1882–1941) a genius. Most critics who chose to write about Yeats did so from a position that was sympathetic and approving from the outset. Thus R. M. Kain's *Dublin in the Age of William Butler Yeats and James Joyce* (1962), described by Peter Jochum as 'the intelligent reader's Baedeker to Irish literature and literary Dublin', scarcely went below the surface of the city's Georgian squares and dull suburbs.[4] The fault was not just one of unfamiliarity. Home-based Irish historians had not by the late 1950s begun to excavate *mentalité* or to document latter-day subversion. Approaches to the poet were, in various senses, positivistic.

Much has changed. By the beginning of the twenty-first century, even Yeats's last days have been absorbed irrevocably into the past, to be denied nostalgia's bonus. Conjuring a 'Vision of the Blood Kindred', we will call up ruffians and victims whom the Yeatsian tableau has not previously accommodated, figures all too characteristic of the time in which he and they lived. Habits of thought condition the way in which judgments are expressed and contextualised. These enclose 'figures of the age' who may become less familiar if loosened from habitual contexts. In the ordinary-language discussion of modern history, one of the most pervasive modes of periodisation has emphasised the distinctive character of successive decades. A dominant moral or other characteristic is frequently inferred: the Naughty Nineties, the Roaring Twenties, etc. Implicit in this simplified sense of historical movement is a series of qualitative changes occurring at ten-year intervals. Occasionally, major events underscored this sense of drastic change. The commencement of war in September 1939 undoubtedly assisted the configuration of the 1930s – which W. H. Auden memorably christened 'a low dishonest decade'. Yeats died in the last January of peace. Looking back, too many have sought to preserve the memory of peace at the expense of historical truth.

Local, or small-scale, maps are required. To find our way back to the city over which Yeats has distantly presided, a ground plan of that largely mythic zone known as The Catacombs would be useful. There a few hardy specimens of Dublin's literary Bohemia lived in Georgian pantries and wine-cellars, to achieve a flickering immortality in J. P. Donleavy's novel, *The Ginger Man* (1955), and Anthony Cronin's splendid memoir, *Dead as Doornails* (1976). There indeed was heard 'porter drinker's randy laughter' – but not heard by Yeats. The Catacombs post-dated him, yet also can serve to mark off his neo-Augustan old age from contemporary reality. A ruinous eighteenth-century house appears, disappears and reappears in Yeats's work, as if the building itself were an uneasy spirit. As literary undergrounds went, the 'institutional' Catacombs was a small holding which, by its allusion to the inhabited burial tunnels of Rome, evoked a coexistence of the quick and the dead. Those living therein were not always quick.

An ideological map of the same imaginative territory is likewise difficult to cipher, being older and more wrinkled with frustrated use than any Rough Guide to the Catacombs. Panoramas of right-wing politics in 1930s Ireland have been sketched primarily in terms of the Blue Shirts, whose nickname was designed to acknowledge continental models. The Army Comrades Association – to use their original cognomen – was bitterly opposed by the Irish Republican Army which was, for the most part, no less right-wing than its foes. On 28 February 1934, John A. Costello (1891–1976) advised Dáil Eireann: 'The Blackshirts were victorious in Italy and the Hitler Shirts were victorious in Germany as, assuredly, the Blueshirts will be victorious in the Irish Free State.' Confusion was not limited to parliament. When the IRA split along supposedly right/left lines, the dissidents reconstituted themselves as Republican Congress; they notably included Frank Ryan (1902–1944), a charismatic figure who ended his days as a less-than-reluctant bosom comrade of the Nazis. Irish paramilitary politics has displayed a steady right-wing bias, even when the rhetoric was socialistic.

The at once colourful and drab uniformity of this subversion against the Irish Free State persisted even after Eamon de Valera's somewhat republican Constitution was adopted in 1937. As an old oath-bound member of the Irish Republican Brotherhood (IRB), Yeats found himself divided between his psychological hunger for order and his ideological allegiance to rebellion. The appeal of fascism lay in its witch's cauldron: the psychological and the ideological swapped places in a bubbling stew, with order and outrage for interchangeable salt and pepper. By contrast with its British cousin, Irish fascism lacked pedigree: there were no Anglo-Irish or 'ascendancy' Mitfords, nor could the demi-Republic boast of anything like Edward VIII, crony of Nazis and conniver in fascist hauteur. Passingly noted in 'Parnell's Funeral', Yeats's disappointment with the Blue Shirt General Eoin O'Duffy (1892–1944) found consolation in a bad poem about the abdication crisis of 1936. From papers released in 2003, we gather that the security services in Britain had the means of ridding their king and country of Mrs Simpson, but chose to dispose of him, so great was the risk posed by his associations and behaviour.

Deprived of such a monarch, but willing to elegise Edward's Russian cousins two decades after their deaths, Yeats had needs to look high. Division, in so many ways vital to the Yeatsian aesthetic, cropped up in his politics with all its gross actuality. You could find action in Ireland, yet have to look eastwards for breeding. As Samuel Beckett (1906–1989) put it, writing of Jack Yeats's art, the problem lay in 'the being in the street when it happens in the room, the being in the room when it happens in the street . . .'[5] Whereas Ireland was Yeats's native land, English was his native tongue. Whereas he had devoted himself to the common people of Ireland in their rural and traditional garb, he loathed the urban mob, amongst whom ideas of fascism might yet be sown.

Yeats's self-proclaimed disillusion with the Blue Shirts has been taken as sufficient evidence of his disengagement from extreme politics. Two factors complicate this otherwise convenient rehabilitation. The first, as already indicated, was the absence of any politically active cohort amongst the class to which he aspired. Apart from a very few landowners and businessmen appointed with him to the first Irish Senate, no member of the so-called Anglo-Irish ascendancy played a significant role in national politics. Nor could there ever be a party to represent their interests or to nurture anti-democratic reaction in their favour. It was therefore necessary for Yeats to look abroad for stimulation in this regard – first to Mussolini's *fascisti*, to L'Action française in the mid-1920s, and after 1933 to Hitler's Germany also. In considering his attitude towards Italy after 1920, one needs to pay an historian's attention to changes within the fascist regime, especially those of 1926–27 when Mussolini was demanding a uniquely fascist culture to complement a uniquely fascist state.[6]

Yeats's interest survived that radicalising campaign. A further 'reform' occurred early in 1928, when Il Duce's Council of Ministers drastically modified the country's vestigial electoral system to authorise the Fascist Party's 'designation' of public representatives: later that year Yeats resigned from the Irish Senate and by November had acquired an apartment in Rapallo. Ill-health took him out of Ireland; the choice of destination was his own. Spanish authoritarianism proved less attractive because of its Catholic populist rhetoric, a fact deftly deployed to suggest his distaste for all variants. Before acquitting Yeats of any further interest in fascism after 1934, one should additionally factor into the argument the petit-bourgeois nature of the movement in its local Irish manifestations. One could despise the Blue Shirts in the name of a Higher Fascism.

The classification of the Army Comrades Association, Coras na Poblachta, the Irish Friends of Germany, the People's National Party, and even phases of IRA activity under the common name of fascism raises problems of definition. Some who regarded themselves as communists were willing to rub shoulders with admirers of Hitler, even after the Soviet Union was attacked. 'The national question' provided common ground, it seems. In addition to political theory, ordinary criminal activity deserves consideration. In the larger context of continental politics, purists have treated German Nazism as an amalgam of fascism and gross lawlessness, with the original Italian movement regarded as a model only partly imitated elsewhere.[7] With violence forming an intrinsic part of fascism in action and in theory, the distinction is far from absolute. In Yeats, active violence bred envy, whether the exemplar was Patrick McCartan (1878–1963, IRB man turned medic) or Adolf Hitler (1889–1945, painter turned successful megalomaniac). Theories of violence informed Yeats's philosophical writings, often through the notion of 'terror'. It is worth enquiring if Nazism's ability to legitimate (or at least institutionalise) violence in unprecedented extremes did not constitute its fundamental appeal for Yeats who, characteristically, held back from an open endorsement of his inner needs and desires.

If terror had patrolled back-street and small-farm Ireland during the Troubles of 1919–23, a decade later Irish society was wracked by less concentrated – that is, more pervasive – forms of violence. There was of course the inherited violence endured in poverty, to which de Valera (1882–1975) turned some attention after the electoral success of Fianna Fáil in 1932. The arrival of his reformed republicans in government consolidated the State in the long run, but bred immediate factional conflict, an increase in the use of capital punishment, and heightened debate about relations with the old enemy, Britain. In this context Yeats's divisions came to possess what Lucien Goldmann termed a structural homology. That is, the literary corpus of poetry and imaginative prose presents in symbolic form the structuring conflicts and tensions characterising Irish society and its relations to the material world.[8] We will have little time to expand on this relationship, except to stress that *Yeats matters*: his work is an essential part of a national history and, beyond that, part of an international crisis also.

Herein lies the quality distinguishing Yeats's relationship to fascism from that of – say – George Russell (1867–1935, known as 'AE') on the one hand and Maud Gonne (1866–1953) on the other. In the early 1920s, AE evinced considerable interest in Italian developments, contributing an introduction to Odon Por's book on *Fascism* (1923). His novel, *The Interpreters* (1922), had absorbed something of Mussolini's politics in an effort to classify and stabilise the dangerous flux (as he saw it) of Irish society in the aftermath of 1916, 1917, 1918, 1919, etc. While Russell is often regarded as the secular saint of the Irish literary movement, and his journalism as a bastion of liberal tolerance, he too can be found positively responding to the appeal of fascism.[9] The novel just mentioned certainly influenced Francis Stuart (1902–2000), who proved more vulnerable or susceptible to the pathological side of what were loosely termed the new movements in Europe. Yeats might seem to lack the palingenetic or 'born-again' commitments that characterise Roger Griffin's definition of fascism, but he did intermittently embrace the new, as with George Antheil's new music, new para-psychological theories of identity, and (more crucially) the idiom of birth, death and rebirth. In the 1937 'Introduction' written for a never-published collected edition of his work, he predicted that in two or three generations it will be known that natural and supernatural are knit together. Meanwhile to escape a dangerous fanaticism, 'we must study a new science'. If the avoidance of fanaticism sounds admirable, the further prediction (in 1937) of Judaism's disappearance from the historical background of Christianity does not.[10] He certainly longed for a new order, if not the New Order.

For Maud Gonne, the central theme was racial, as befitted an English colonel's wealthy daughter in denial. Hard on the heels of her anti-English conversion came the anti-Dreyfusard or anti-Semitic bile, in which latter Yeats signally had not supported her. Gonne's irredentism after 1921 has less to do with political theory, or the definition of a republic, than it has to do with perpetuating areas of conflict in which her native land and first allegiance can figure as the Evil One. Psychologically, she exemplifies the element of resentment that propelled figures like Oswald Mosley (1896–1980) to the British extreme right. Together with Yeats, she exerted a baleful influence on young Stuart while simultaneously resisting his marriage to her daughter. The dynamics of the ghost family – Gonne-Yeats-Stuart – tell us much about the self-wounding and self-justifying masochism that forms part of the fascist psyche (see 'Marital Politics', pp. 201–225).

Gonne and Stuart outlived Yeats by many years. Indeed, in some bizarre attempt at the cancellation of his own generative history, Stuart outlived nearly all his children – and certainly wished to. These cruelties or callous amoralities gloss at the domestic level his more notorious wartime residence in Berlin. In Stuart's *Blacklist, Section H* (1971), the manipulative figure of Yeats – dubbed Yardley in the first draft, after the cosmetics manufacturer – is superseded by a strangely distant Hitler. Published as the Troubles resumed in Northern Ireland, Stuart's best-known novel might claim to be the last word in Irish anarcho-fascism, though its analytical dimension should not be overlooked in the rush to condemn its content.

Yeats's death in France in January 1939 cannot be taken as a terminal date to this context. The war for which he prayed in 'Under Ben Bulben' obliged in September, and the eugenic theories he studied during his final years did not lose the name of *achtung*. Ireland, under de Valera's canny rule, dropped out of sight to provide a darkroom for the blotchy development of a few Nazi plots involving people Yeats had known at whatever remove. In 1943, the first biography of the poet appeared, while his most assiduous admiring critic (Richard Ellmann) was serving in the American forces, and his early amour (Gonne) consorted with German agents. Only in 1948 was the poet's body repatriated by an Irish inter-party government jointly led by the aforementioned Costello and Maud Gonne's son, Sean MacBride (1904–1988).

Throughout the war years, the open alliance of Nazi Germany and the IRA moved from tragedy to farce and back again. While there is no reason to be surprised at the attitude of a Sean Russell (1893–1940) or a Joseph McGarrity (1874–1940) – the very term 'physical-force men' is sufficient – a different approach is required in the cases of Helena Moloney (1884–1967) and Kathleen Lynn (1874–1955). Both had been associated with the socialist, even Marxist, element of Irish insurrection in 1916, and both were committed to feminism. Their embroilment in the Gonnes' protection of the spy, Hermann Görtz (d. 1947), is some indication of the intellectual and moral confusion that characterised Irish politics at the time. Indeed, the nest of gentlewomen that harboured the Nazi cuckoo constitutes a remarkable instance of the erotic as a component of fascist/radical dialogue. Iseult Stuart (1895–1954, née Gonne) not only sheltered Görtz in Laragh but had an affair with him, while her husband sent the housekeeping from Berlin.

In plays such as 'The King of the Great Clock Tower' (1934/35), 'Purgatory' (1938) and 'The Death of Cuchulain' (1939) Yeats explored themes of decapitation, polluted blood and betrayal. His recurrent emphasis on authority invested in status dramatised both a needy desire of fascist-style solutions and a brilliant defence against them. At the time of his much-trumpeted break with the Blue Shirts, Yeats had declared that he would rewrite his marching songs till nobody could sing them. This yearning for a greater extreme, beyond articulation, did not prevent his acceptance of a Nazi literary prize in June 1934. It signalled his frustration at failing to find in Ireland an allegiance to satisfy his needs without wounding his dignity. The leaders whom he had been able to name in 'Parnell's Funeral' – Kevin O'Higgins (1892–1927), W. T. Cosgrave (1880–1965), Eoin O'Duffy and Eamon de Valera – were either dead or compromised by their links to the popular mob. Yeats's last-minute intervention into the 1936 controversy over Roger Casement's diaries usefully re-established his patriotic credentials while attaching him to perhaps the least democratic of the executed 1916 leaders. (Nor had Yeats taken any interest in Casement's African and South American campaigns for native human rights.) In contemporary Ireland, the enemies of promise were deplorably vulgar. As proof of Yeats's lack of congenial allies, one has only to look at the men and women who, a year after his death, came together as the People's National Party (to be called PENAPA for short), kindred of a decidedly bloody kind.

Introducing the Blood Kindred

Yeats was a great man in life; in death he was greeted by his epigones. Let us pick out one or two among the posse for closer consideration. Among these we might choose the swashbuckling fascist and Higher Hindu, Dermot Arthur Maurice MacManus (1891–1974?), were it not for the difficulty in establishing his complex sense of identity.[11] This difficulty will become a characteristic among the Kindred. Take another epigone, less attention-seeking. In 1939, the police believed that Patrick Moylett reached Dublin from Galway in around 1930. In their eyes, he and/or younger members of his family had been involved in petty crime. Together with a brother, Moylett became engaged in the confectionery trade; both professed a politics that merged right-wing and racist views with anti-imperialism. In July 1940, Patrick Moylett came to the attention of the Garda in connection with the activities of Liam Walsh, a convicted embezzler of Irish Army funds, a political maverick and low-level employee of the Italian Legation. Their associates included George Griffin and his wife, veterans of the Irish Friends of Germany. Griffin held that 'propaganda regarding the German cruelties and the persecution of the Catholics were [sic] nothing but a fabrication of lies'.[12] There was some uncertainty about Moylett's other activities; he was 'suspected' of contributing to the *Catholic Standard* in the late 1930s. The sudden rise of PENAPA in the latter half of 1940 may have been assisted by external funding, though a refusal to pay hoteliers and printers helped to balance the books. Back in August, a garrulous Mrs Griffin told a police infiltrator that PENAPA was 'purely Nazi in outlook [and] out to overthrow the Government'.[13] Its putsch a distant prospect, the party was quickly suppressed, not least for the grossness of its racialist propaganda. Yet before this armageddon, Moylett had been expelled on 10 October for allegedly siphoning off party funds.

In Moylett, anti-Semitism and financial greed were united to an extent that would have fitted Theodor Adorno's most astringent analysis of prejudice, for he practised what he preached against. A regular activity in Dublin was to oppose the renewal of licences held by Jewish traders, including money-lenders. On this basis, Moylett collected subscriptions from rival traders, while his colleague ingratiated himself with a bigoted minor judge. On 4 October 1940, Moylett confided to Griffin that a number of PENAPA letters had been held by the postal censor because the word Jew appeared in them. If this was an attempt to curry favour with a party leadership as much concerned with petty cash as gross prejudice, it was doomed to failure. In a police interview of mid-November, Moylett 'stated that no general meeting of the "People's National Party" had ever been held, but before the split Griffin and himself intended calling one with a view to electing officers'. A sequence of events at the Westbrook Hotel drew further attention to his independent ways. Having attended the first meeting on 29 October – apparently after his expulsion from PENAPA – he failed to turn up in November, perhaps because the proprietor had not been paid.

After that debacle, Moylett gravitated towards Coras na Poblachta, a bigger outfit, which sometimes gave the impression that it was the IRA's political arm. A Gaelic National Socialist Youth Movement was also mooted with the name of Gerald Callinan, who had fled from Britain in 1939, mentioned in police enquiries. The band of 1939 *arrivistes* included specimens of ideological confusion whom we will encounter in various contexts. Their collective escape from the bodily rigours of war against Nazism, with (for consolation) refuge in Catholic Ireland, follows Yeats's own passage from the earthly body to the reception rooms of the Blood Kindred. By comparison, Moylett had skiffled gracefully between Brixton and Ballyhaunis in 1920. Now his exit from PENAPA virtually coincided with the Garda's decision to intercept his post, and a warrant for this purpose was issued in October 1940. The financial basis of that organisation had been frail, with nothing to justify hints of subvention by Joe McGrath, sponsor of *The Forged Casement Diaries* in 1936. In contrast, Coras na Poblachta was to attract several hundreds of people at its public meetings.

In May 1941, a meeting of the new movement heard a paper from Roger McHugh (1908–1987) on the evils of Freemasonry, the speaker being a member of the English Department at University College Dublin. Moylett observed that he had been put out of business by the masons, while Father Alexander Carey complained that the same element controlled the Aliens Section in the Department of Justice.[14] By October 1941, young-ish McHugh – soon a Yeats scholar of some distinction – was interned on the Curragh. The more experienced Moylett steered between extremes of street action and rural sequestration by weaseling his way into the management of Coras na Poblachta. On 18 June 1941, the *Irish Independent* reported his election as treasurer of a south Dublin branch.

Meetings in June 1941 dramatically indicate how confused, or thoroughly varied, opinions held by members and sympathisers of Coras were. At a private session, one member 'agreed with Herr Hitler and his policy' on democracy. A week later, Nora Connolly-O'Brien gave a public lecture on her father (James Connolly), under the same auspices. It says much for their acumen that de Valera's party was seen as a spent force in Irish politics. Meanwhile, the Coras line bore a strong resemblance to Nazi propaganda of ten years earlier. Native enterprise was being undermined by foreigners, amongst whom all Jews were lumped. Conspiracies by the same Jews, and by Freemasons, were detected even behind the private finances of a government member. Tactics resembled those of *Kristallnacht* (in November 1938) – the distribution of intimidating leaflets, anti-Semitic graffiti in public places, leading on to the smashing of shop windows. Coras was able to capitalise on the publicity that Moylett and Griffin had generated through opposing the renewal of business licences to Jews. When McHugh spoke at a public meeting in the Portobello district, on the control exercised by foreigners over ground rents, the proximity of Dublin's Jewish quarter in Clanbrassil Street, of the synagogue on the South Circular Road and of a new Jewish school even closer to Portobello acted as his megaphone. At Terenure, where better-off Jews were moving, a crowd estimated by the police to number 300 heard a Coras speaker denounce government tolerance of English and Jewish firms that allegedly controlled sections of Irish industry. There was no mention, we may be sure, of Franz Winkelmann, a Nazi party member who was a senior employee in the Irish Glass Bottle Company, while the name of Mendel Waltzmann (a glass-blower in the same firm) prompted different reactions. Even less reference was made to the equally foreign Budina brothers, who had run the Kilmacurragh Hotel in Wicklow until, in 1939, they chose to run instead to Berlin. There was a physio-psychic link between the Budinas and Yeats: at the end of the 1920s, the house had been rented by Mrs Lucy (the 'Lion') Phillimore (née Fitzpa-trick), a wealthy and argumentative writer with whom Yeats had a blazing row about politics on 1 September 1929. The speaker at the Terenure meeting of Sunday, 27 July 1941 was almost certainly McHugh again, who later edited Yeats's correspondence with Katharine Tynan (published in 1953) and with Margot Collis (1970).

August was the cruellest month for these petty fascists. Father Carey's disciples daubed slogans on the walls of Trinity College and planned to wreck Louis Wine's shop in Grafton Street. A Special Branch man reported Moylett exposing Jewish plans to clear the debts of a Fianna Fáil minister (never named), and delivering yet another talk on 'foreign' control of industry. This was impressive in someone the Garda had regarded as 'a man whom no party wanted'. But the financial motive recurs at least as often as the evidence of Moylett's pro-Germanism. Associating him with yet another subversive group (An Cumann Náisiúnta) in July 1940, Special Branch officer M. J. Wymes believed Moylett to be 'the type of person who would engage in dangerous activities if he was sure of profiting therefrom'.

Similar details allow one to construct a plausible sociology of Moylett's money-shrewd extremism. Members of the family had been active in Dublin during the campaign against the sale of 'Bass' beer and English-manufactured confectionery between 1931 and 1934. Hostility to Bass was based on the connivance of the brewer (Lord Carrington) in English support for the Free State's attack on republicans who had seized the Four Courts in 1922. The campaign was thus a republican animus rather than a broad nationalist resistance to product imperialism. Opposition to the sale of imported sweets and confectionery, on the other hand, touched directly on the family's economic base. Patrick Moylett's brother was a manufacturing confectioner, based in north Dublin. Moylett was employed as a commercial traveller, a role that facilitated political agitation among shopkeepers. In 1940, when the father was thought capable of dangerous activity if profit were to accrue, two sons were found guilty of larceny at a tennis club, an offence that carried a whiff of sectarianism.

In the autumn of 1940, Wymes believed Patrick Moylett to be engaged full-time in PENAPA business. Both he and Griffin were in 'very affluent circumstances'. This hardly accords with his complaint of being ruined by Freemasons, and questions arise about the source of Moylett's income. His business in O'Connell's Street had benefited from a start-up grant of £1,200, and with his brother as supplier of goods Moylett enjoyed advantages envied by his competitors. Failing to mind the shop while attending full-time to the PENAPA, he may have quietly topped up his cashflow from the latter. But the resources to which he had access were very limited unless, of course, the party had private sponsors or external support. Moylett's contacts with the Reich's representatives in Dublin cannot be shown to have brought benefits. Trade-oriented rather than specifically ideological, they nonetheless failed to satisfy the Special Branch.

The comparison of a Nobel Prize winner's dying utterances with the manoeuvres of a petty criminal must outrage admirers of Yeats and his work. Yet such was the complex relationship between Yeats's thought and the social reality of independent Ireland that the grubby, the squalid and the violent inevitably find a place in the former as in the latter. Naturally, there were mediating agencies, both institutional and philosophical. On at least two occasions within a year, the security authorities noticed Moylett visiting the German Legation in Dublin. Early in October 1940, he tried to make contact with a view to business. Unfortunately for him, Army Intelligence had bugged the legation's telephone, and duly recorded the findings in a sardonically named Toilet Counter Report. On Monday, 9 June 1941, Moylett was seen entering the premises. 'It is unlikely that Moylett would have any legitimate business at the German Legation,' Wymes commented in his weekly report.

A Sketch-Map of Jewish Harold's Cross

What were McHugh and Moylett fighting for and against? Did Yeats have any remotely similar concerns? In so far as the PENAPA campaigns opposed foreign business activity in Ireland, they could be dignified as economic protectionism, a doctrine traceable in Ireland through Arthur Griffith (1871–1922), Isaac Butt (1813–1879) and others back to the philosopher-bishop George Berkeley (1685–1753). Both Yeats and Moylett knew Griffith personally; Yeats's father had a long romantic affair (platonic maybe) with Butt's daughter, Rosa, and Butt himself had been an acquaintance of the poet's grandfather and namesake, the Revd William Butler Yeats (1806–1862) of County Down. Berkeley, of course, became one of Yeats's spiritual ancestors, an anti-Whig immaterialist. In part woven of assumptions, the fragile chain desires to bind. Abstruse metaphysics and crude prejudice are its twin components. Moylett and Griffith were anti-Semites, and PENAPA opposed the Jews in Dublin.

The social map by which most readers reach Yeats even today was drawn along coordinates that highlighted Butt and Berkeley, and which cast Moylett – with the anti-Semitic side of Griffith – into outer darkness. But if Yeats can communicate with the aristocratic dead, perhaps his plebeian contemporaries are not totally beyond the pale. The poet was highly selective in his choice of company, yet also chose to live in actual communities rather than retire permanently to a tower or cell. Contemptuous of politicians, he kept up a running battle with them, as if they could not be trusted to remain contemptible in his absence. The anxiety underlying this sustained engagement in diurnal brawling might be translated upwards into Berkeley's theory of vision, or downwards into a history of social resentment and insecurity experienced across Europe since 1848. Yeats's portmanteau word in these contexts is the 'mob'. And whatever threatened to become uncontrollable, unpredictable and in that sense revolutionary, he either addressed with all his powers of mind and imagination – or he ignored it utterly.

There had been no continuous Jewish presence in Ireland of the kind found in England or France. Geographic isolation and the lack of a centralised power may have discouraged immigrants. But successive waves of Jewish migration had arrived, settled and gradually dispersed. In Joyce's *Ulysses* (1922), the schoolmaster Deasy reveals the secret of Ireland's immunity to the Jews' pernicious influence – 'she never let them in' – an explanation that presupposes an Irish executive power quite as imaginary as the subversive Hebrew. When Joyce's novel was published, the Jewish population of the Irish Free State was about 3,600, or 0.1 per cent of the total. For the most part, it was based in Dublin, with a sizeable second community in Cork. (Limerick Jews had dispersed after the pogrom of 1904.) Numbers increased between the censuses of 1926 and 1946, and thereafter declined, though the falling off was less marked than that of Methodists. The proportion has never risen above 0.1 per cent. These are the ghostly victims in my imaginary Blood Kindred.

As Roger McHugh and his associates knew in choosing Portobello as their site of protest at foreign rents, the Jewish community in Dublin was based on the South Circular Road, close to the point where Clanbrassil Street emerged from the old city into the suburb of

Harold's Cross, with Terenure lying further out. Yeats had been ashamed of his family's three-year sojourn at what is now No. 418 Harold's Cross Road (then No. 10 Ashfield Terrace), describing it in 1914 as 'a villa where the red bricks were made pretentious and vulgar with streaks of slate grey'.[15] Eight years later, when he was well over fifty and about to become a Senator, he confided to Lady Gregory his residual fear of having to live in such a place of 'crowding & indignity'.[16] Close by is Kenilworth Park, where I grew up in the 1950s and where, during Moylett and McHugh's heyday, a sizeable proportion of Dublin's Jews lived. In 1943, more than 10 per cent of households were Jewish, exceeding the Protestants by a whisker. Names like Feldman, Lapedus, Steinberg and Woolfson threatened what Moylett regarded as the national being and what Yeats termed Unity of Culture. These are names I remember, names of the kids I played with. *Pace* Joyce's Mr Deasy, there was an Irish Jewish community to be persecuted or protected in the 1930s.

By 1934, the Geneva-based High Commissioner for Refugees, Jewish and Other, was in touch with the Irish authorities about the needs and welfare of Hitler's victims in flight. Through the League of Nations (as a council-member since 1930), the Irish Free State had obligations; by virtue of its status within the British dominions, some of these were routed through Downing Street, the Foreign Office and Whitehall. Most applications for residence permits and/or work permits came from Jews who had already reached England and were visiting Ireland. Applications from the Continent tended to originate with professional people, doctors and so on, for whom conditions had not yet become intolerable in Germany. Enquiries also came from Austria, Poland, Romania and elsewhere within the expanding Nazi sphere of influence. The Department of Justice's record in processing these applications is one of almost unbroken intransigence, recorded in language of petty self-interest, prejudice and occasional viciousness. The Minister for Industry and Commerce, Sean Lemass (1899–1971, sometime Fianna Fáil moderniser and *saint läique*), repeatedly gave jobs for the boys as Ireland's answer to the international crisis.

The official attitude was softened whenever a case reached the attention of Eamon de Valera, who held the External Affairs portfolio in addition to being head of government. A memo from the Department of Justice to the Secretary of External Affairs claimed with some pride that 'only one case has come to notice in which it has been ascertained that the nationality of a former German subject had been cancelled'.[17] That was in the summer of 1936. Less than two years later, the Minister for Justice informed a parliamentary member of his own party – Robert Briscoe, who was Jewish – that 'the Jewish community in this country should not be increased by way of immigration'.[18] When the name of Louis Steinberg, of 98 Kenilworth Park, featured once without annotation in the wartime intelligence files, assisting illegal migrants was probably the offence suspected.

A few cases reached relatively happy conclusions. After two years' (1936–38) deliberation, the Irish authorities allowed Madame Margulies and her family to join her German-Jewish husband in Dublin.[19] Dr Vaas, originally from Austria (a country that had ceased to exist), was admitted in 1938. The case of another former Austrian, the Viennese analytical chemist called Bacher, was under prolonged discussion while he languished in a concentration camp. This last fact, de Valera finally opined, should not be treated as a reason in itself for refusing a work permit. Bacher was approved in the end, but Professor Dermot Keogh, inexhaustible historian of this chapter in the moral history of our country, has been unable to discover whether the prisoner ever arrived.

If this was the moral climate in which Yeats lived out his last years and yearnings, where exactly does the great poet fit in? Why should my Jewish neighbours of old feature in his Vision of the Blood Kindred, with sad accusing stares? They constituted a case in which he chose to ignore, or not to see, what might become a difficult and unpredictable situation. As if it were not already a difficult situation. Albert Einstein, whose relativity Yeats found compatible with the emerging *Vision*-philosophy in June 1923, quickly found himself an object of special execration.[20] After de Valera, Yeats was the most influential Irish public figure who moved upon an international stage. He was a Nobel Prize winner, and German-Jewish holders of the same distinction were being forced to resign their academic posts, resign their birthright and homeland in considerable numbers. Yeats's intervention on behalf of such an applicant for refuge would have commanded respect, even in the Department of Justice. His local support of Louis Steinberg would have helped to legitimise what was always morally justifiable. A public statement from Yeats, on the issue of persecution and protection, would have made headlines from Sligo to Sydney. A rebuke to Moylett might not have been personally efficacious, but it would have gained a wider reception among demoralised veterans of the IRB. It is true that Moylett and McHugh only took up their cause after endorsement by the Wehrmacht, but it is unlikely their opinions were formed *ab ovo* on the eve of Hitler's Polish campaign. They had studied hatred while Yeats still lived.

Orientalism in Action

Yeats was of course dead when Poland fell, but he too had supped with the Devil or, at the least, sipped tea. Sometime in September 1938 he accepted a copy of *Germany Speaks,* an English-language anthology of propagandist essays by more than twenty Nazi experts in such areas as education, health, land, race and women's affairs. The donor was Eduard Hempel (1887–1972), minister at (i.e. head of) the German Legation in Ireland, and Hempel's inscription spoke of 'an unforgettable afternoon' which the two men had spent together that month.[21] It has been suggested by the Yeats scholar Warwick Gould that Maud Gonne's house at Clonskeagh may have been the venue for this encounter, yet the effect is hardly to mitigate the symbolism of the gift. The MacBrides were hand-in-fist with the German Legation, and not only through the association of Helmut Clissmann (1911–1997, an Abwehr agent in Ireland) with Sean MacBride, recently an IRA chief of staff. In the early summer of 1940, both Maud Gonne and her daughter Iseult Stuart were rightly suspected of assisting the German spy, Görtz; indeed, Mrs Stuart was tried in July and miraculously acquitted.

The moment of Yeats's introduction to Hempel can be identified with some precision, the agents of it with surprising ease. In 1965 Josephine MacNeill, widow of the last Governor-General James MacNeill (1869–1938), wrote to the *Irish Times* about 'Yeats's Nazism or Fascism or whatever they like to call it'.[22] Her principal contribution to a debate then heating up was to reveal how, in the summer of 1937, she had organised a tea-party to assist Yeats in the search for an objective discussion of Nazism. Apart from the poet, her guests were the Reich's representative and his wife. After some chat about the poet Stefan George (1868–1933), whose last collection was entitled *Das neue Reich* (1928), Yeats delivered a lengthy and incomprehensible monologue. Mrs MacNeill recalled no details, but perhaps the general thrust had been rehearsed in May 1937:

At this moment all the specialisms are about to run together in our new

Alexandria, thought is about to be unified as its own free act & the shaddow [*sic*] in Germany & elsewhere is an attempted unity by force.[23]

As Hempel was mightily impressed by stuff like this, the hostess thought the occasion a notable hit. Younger brother of the historian and Volunteer leader Eoin MacNeill (1867–1945), Josephine's husband (also present) had ceased to represent the Crown in Ireland on 1 November 1932: in retirement he was beyond any criticism of assisting a foreign representative to advance his masters' cause. Earlier in his career, James MacNeill had worked in the Indian civil service, where he acquired an interest in orientalist matters. Hempel had spent time in Asia before the Great War; his wife Eva (formerly Ahlemann) pursued her own orientialist interests during their years in Ireland.[24] Yeats himself was currently engaged in a translation of the *Upanishads*. The objective discussion of Nazism never arose, though Hempel was doubtless content that his eminent new acquaintance would raise no pointed questions. The venue was Woodley Park, Dundrum; when the tea-party took place is less easily established. The Hempels had arrived in Dublin early in July 1937. Yeats was in England from 8 June to 21 July, and again from 9 September to 1 November. Thus Mrs MacNeill's initiative can be assigned to the six-week period with the month of August at its centre, a quiet spell in international affairs. Within two months, the Nazis' representative had been introduced to Yeats by the wife of George V's former representative. A few days before his own death in January 1939, he wrote a letter of condolence to Josephine MacNeill, having just heard of her husband's death the previous month.

By comparison, the German Legation may have despised Patrick Moylett's overtures. There was a hierarchy of strata through which one could move upwards through back-room anti-Semitism, paramilitary subversion, social intercourse, and finally arrive at a civilised tea- or garden-party. Hempel's personal physician was Victor Millington Synge (d. 1976), in whom the astute diplomat respected not a kinsman of Yeats's co-director at the Abbey Theatre, but someone the police thought 'very anti-Jewish'.[25] Synge's car was used on occasion to transport despatch cases from the legation. In July 1942, Army Intelligence (or G2) requested information on the Elpis Nursing Home where, in 1909, J. M. Synge had died. G2 suspected that Hans Marschner had spent a fortnight there, evading detection after his escape from Mountjoy Prison. As Elpis was in part owned by a kinsman of Victor Synge's, the authorities were keen to check out the place. Hospitable collaborators were also found among the Gael and pseudo-Gael; Marschner was put up by the Brugha family, and by Donal Joseph O'Sullivan of Ballybrack.[26] The latter, a distinguished researcher into eighteenth-century Irish folk music, had been Clerk to the Senate during Yeats's second term. Even closer to the Yeatsian gyres, there were other well-born raparees. Hempel's deputy, Henning Thomsen (?1905–), had known an Irishman called Chalmers Edward Fitz-John Trench (d.2005) at Cambridge: Trench's father had been professor of English at Trinity College Dublin – beating Yeats for the job – and a minor poet. Young Trench attended 'Friends of Germany' events at the Red Bank restaurant, and was tracked by the authorities both in Northern Ireland and the southern state. (His friend Thomsen was thought to belong to the SD, the SS's own security service: he held the rank of SS-Untersturmführer.)

Beyond these flowers of the Anglo-Irish professional classes, the Stuarts and Maud Gonne MacBride provided Yeats with a more personal access to the legation. Or, to be fair, through them the German minister reached Yeats, who was thus added like top dressing to that geology of corruption. Dublin's strange Bohème encouraged some children of the comfortable middle classes to reclassify themselves as revolutionaries, for the Bohème was irreducibly middle-class. A rather tougher 'revolutionary' network – the MacBrides, Clissmann, Marschner and Görtz – saw to it that the roots of Nazi cultivation passed down again to General O'Duffy's roughs, to Coras na Poblachta, PENAPA and the rest of that underworld.

Though he died before the War to End All Wars resumed, Yeats fully understood the role that action and violent action played in the hidden formation of his art. His generation's best gift was prophecy, and in Yeats's case there was no element of the self-fulfilling. Freudian terminology was anathema to him, yet he knew the processes of sublimation by which civilisation sought to control and conceal its origins in conflict. Yeats scholars have too often engaged in a parody of these painful insights, denying that the poet ever entertained the reanimation of violence, especially that presenting itself in the 1920s and '30s through various kinds of fascism. Evidence of his interest in Nazi Germany has been written down as an aggravating enthusiasm, but it may have revived memories of his efforts to find for the youthful Iseult Gonne a place in the London School of Oriental Studies in 1918, less than two years before she married Francis Stuart. The very symbol of the Third Reich proclaimed its orientalist credentials, and theories of Aryanism underpinned racialist practice.

Publishing in 1943, the biographer-scholar V. K. N. Menon noted the sinister side to Yeats's visionary philosophy, and an Indian commentator might be allowed some insight into the poet's appropriation of Asian wisdom. Certainly George Orwell thought so, reviewing *The Development of W. B. Yeats* for *Horizon*. In mid-war, neither man had time to resurrect the longer history of 'Aryanism' and related nineteenth-century theories of race, as they attracted followers in France, Germany and the United Kingdom (including Ireland). From the vast corpus of ancient myth and scripture, and the intimidating wealth of scholarship and appropriation, one text can serve to illuminate the larger context. The narrative locus of the *Bhagavad Gita* is the eve-of-war discussion between a reluctant warrior and his spiritual adviser. The coming conflict will set cousin against cousin, and the taboo prohibiting the killing of kin has to be overcome. The doctrine of 'action without attachment' is presented as a means of persuading Arjuna to take part. Spiritually, it may be read as a path towards release from the self, and in this regard commended itself to Mahatma Gandhi; philosophically, it implicates issues known in the West through concepts of free will and determinism and has been discussed by Ted Honderich and other philosophers. But the work does not exist in motionless amber. In the view of Simon Brodbeck, the *Bhagavad Gita* is an accretion of texts rather than a credal statement, its origins extending over a lengthy period of exposition and modification. 'In such a disrupted world, creators of successful stabilising texts advanced their own interests so that the text is rhetorical and ideological rather than philosophical.' If its concerns with tribal decay, pollution and conflict may have recommended it to Yeats thematically, as he himself composed those late poems and plays in which such themes occur, its manifest urging of 'action without attachment' made it germane to debates about German philosophy and its relationship to the 'disrupted world' of fascism.

One could pursue this topic with reference to the sociologist Max Weber (1864–1920), the novelist Ernst Jünger (1895–1998), or half a dozen other prominent German thinkers. More grossly, one has to note the insistence of German fascism – as distinct from the Italian version – on the Aryan origins of racial purity. As once-respectable academic disciplines, Sanskrit scholarship and Indology found themselves inducted into a rhetoric of Hitlerite myth, and Hindu writings as commended by the wife of a Nazi diplomat did not exist *in vacuo*. While Messrs Griffin, Moylett and their rougher associates may have regarded the Schutzstaffeln (or SS) as a model way of dealing with Dublin's 'non-Irish' small traders, others were aware that the SS had its *Ahnerbe* (or Ancestral Heritage Office) directly answering to Heinrich Himmler (1900–1945). The Sicilian Julius Evola (1898–1974), who fed into this occult division of Nazism, published *Erhebung wider die Moderne Welt* in Stuttgart in 1935.[27] Savatri Devi (born in Lyons of mixed French and Greek background) regarded the SS Einsatzgruppen on the Eastern Front as latter-day commissioners of the *Bhagavad Gita*'s warrior code – precisely quoting for her authority the text of Chapter 3:19, 'Perform without attachment that action which is duty . . .'

In 1937, Yeats was visited by an Indian professor, Abinash Bose, who politely requested a message from the poet to his country. 'Let ten thousand men of one side meet the other. That is my message to India.' Relating this incident, Richard Ellmann described how Yeats then seized a Japanese sword and shouted, 'Conflict, more conflict.'[28] Insufficient is known about the scholarly achievements of Iseult Stuart and Frau Eva Hempel during the Emergency, meeting in Maud Gonne's home at Roebuck House or in the Stuarts' County Wicklow nineteenth-century castle. According to Sean MacBride's daughter, quoting Iseult's own daughter, the Nazi agent who arrived into her castle-yard seemed 'an incarnation of some figure of her imaginings with whom she could discuss not only Nazism in an idealistic "cosmic" way, but share a deep interest in Eastern philosophies'. To add perspective, Mrs MacBride White observes that 'probably not since her friendship with Yeats had she been able to discuss so well the spiritual dimensions of ideas and philosophies'.[29] Yeats had been dead fifteen months, and Görtz the spy would eventually commit suicide in 1947 after release from an Irish prison.

By the end of the war, the Hempels and Iseult shared a particular interest in the *Bhagavad*. The interest of Army Intelligence was fixed on more mundane questions – IRA links with Nazi Germany, Francis Stuart's activities in Berlin, the German Legation's relations with these aristocrats of republicanism. On 30 July 1941 a Garda memo noted that 'Dr Hempel has always been a frequent visitor to the McBrides'. Ever since his arrival in Dublin in the summer of 1937,

Eduard Hempel and his wife had befriended Maud Gonne and her family, including Sean MacBride, who reciprocated with political advice. Iseult was frequently in her mother's house when the Hempels were received as guests, and in time she opened Laragh Castle to the German minister.

Laragh Castle and Roebuck House formed the rural and suburban poles of an Irish collaborative axis. If some of the local participants were near-naïve, hidden influences were close by, if not in space then certainly in the blood-line. Frau Hempel's brother, Georg Ahlemann (b. 1911), served in the SS as part of the guard unit ('Deathshead-Standarte') in the concentration camp at Dachau in 1937–38. Her husband, often euphemised as a non-Nazi, was in effect disadvantaged by his status, which he emended by joining on 1 July 1938.[30] Sometime in September 1938, Hempel presented Yeats with his volume of propaganda essays. Roebuck was probably the venue. In Leonard Robert Edwards, the London publishers (Butterworth) had an Irish representative who associated with Carlheinz Petersen, press *attaché* at the legation. Petersen's Irish mistresses were believed by G2 to include a Gate Theatre actress who was bridesmaid at the wedding of Count John McCormack's son. As Cyril McCormack was then serving in the Irish Army, G2 feared German penetration through Petersen's Irish sally. There were points where trade and propaganda intersected, likewise propaganda, theatre and poetry. These points did not spring into existence with Yeats's death: they preceded it.

Let us assume that a Vision of the Blood Kindred lasts an earthly year at least, and therefore the figures whom the dead Yeats strode among were obliged to confront the war. Security issues became sharper after the outbreak of hostilities and Francis Stuart's return to Berlin. G2 monitored Iseult Stuart's incoming post, while plain-clothes detectives shadowed her movements. To some extent these attentions were offered as tributes to her mother and her brother. Additionally, Francis Stuart was clearly a matter of concern, but he was beyond observation. As a result, files devoted to the couple contain far more information about Mrs Stuart than about her husband. After the summer of 1940, when she was arrested and tried for assisting Görtz, surveillance was vigorously maintained, even though she was deliberately acquitted in the Special Criminal Court. It was natural that mother and daughter should visit each other frequently. Roebuck was celebrated as a chapel royal of comfortable republicanism. Hempel's use of the side entrance (as noted sardonically in July 1941) was linked in the mind of young Ion Stuart with the minister's willingness to collect Maud Gonne's post for delivery in the Reich. Playing in the neighbourhood, the boy exclaimed, 'That's the man who comes for my Grannie's letters.'[31]

To whom was Maud Gonne writing in terms that required improper use of the diplomatic bag? Hardly her novelist son-in-law, whom she had never liked and whose links with home could be adequately maintained by Iseult. Back in late 1939, there had been a flurry of literary activity between the Gonne-Stuart households and Berlin. As a consequence, G2 advised External Affairs on 10 November 1939 that Maud Gonne's agent in Berlin for the purposes of publishing a German edition of her autobiography was Ruth Weiland. Six weeks earlier Weiland had been in touch with the recently arrived Francis Stuart about plans for a German version of W. J. Maloney's book, *The Forged Casement Diaries* (1936). 'The Irish Embassy seems very much interested in a German version of these documents reveiling [*sic*] the procedure of British policy and of the British secret service. I shall have a talk with Dr Thielke of the Ministry of Propaganda one of the next days.' That this letter survives in a typed copy prepared by the Garda suggests that she had been writing prior to Stuart's departure from Ireland at the beginning of September, and that a proposal to translate Maloney was in place from the outset. In the event, Maloney unexpectedly refused permission, and *Der Fall Casement* appeared under a Hamburg imprint and Stuart's own name in 1940, with much of the work done by Weiland herself. During the remainder of the war, she published translations of three novels by Stuart. According to Madeline Stuart, Weiland was a member of the Nazi party.

The security authorities took considerable interest in the Stuart household's finances. At one point, a detailed list of moneys sent regularly from Germany to Laragh was drawn up. Though Maud Gonne had considerable – if diminishing – wealth in her own right, and the Stuarts now occupied an ersatz-castle which she had bought for them in 1927, Iseult Stuart had difficulty making ends meet. Ion was educated at St Gerrard's private school in Bray, and later at Glenstal, the Benedictine establishment outside Limerick. His sister, Kay, attended similar places, and eventually went up to university – to study German. These were expensive investments in respectability, and it is not clear that the parents directly footed the bills. In June

1942 Iseult gave up the telephone line for reasons of economy. Wicklow Gardaí noted that, following a visit by Minister Hempel on Sunday, 28 June 1942, her financial situation visibly improved. Local bills were paid, debts cleared and affairs brought into a more prosperous condition. Though the police admit that money may have come from Francis Stuart, the legation seems an unlikely route for him to use, given the continuing effectiveness of ordinary banking channels used in the past. G2 clearly wondered if Mrs Stuart was not, somehow, in the pay of the Germans. After all, she had protected Görtz for months two years earlier. When Hempel visited Laragh on 29 November 1942, he complained that the accompanying police-car parked too close to the castle instead of remaining on the distant public road. The lengthy report on Stuart's remissions to his wife dates from as late as July 1943. The Hempels continued to visit the Gonnes, mother and daughter, even after the fall of Berlin and German surrender.

The pre-war and pro-war orientation of the *Bhagavad Gita,* a shared interest of Frau Hempel and Mrs Stuart in 1945, acquired a nostalgic or consolatory significance. For some combatants soon to face prosecution for crimes against humanity, it had been the case that the spiritual damage normally caused by committing atrocious deeds can be averted if those deeds are performed in a non-attached manner. Catch phrases – the 'acte gratuit', 'only obeying orders', automatism, frenzy – cast kaleidoscopic light on a problem that is as much psychological as it is philosophical. The English philosopher Ted Honderich, writing of determinism in the traditions of both East and West, identifies the search for 'the compensation of an escape from a mordant kind of self-dislike and self-disapproval'.[32] If this resembles a diagnosis of the authoritarian personality in some of its variants, it also – quite independent of intention on Honderich's part – sheds light on the character of W. B. Yeats and the character of his politics.

One could go further in interpreting Iseult Stuart's devotion to the *Bhagavad* during the months that brought liberation to the survivors of Belsen and Auschwitz. She has been presented as a somewhat pathetic figure, abandoned in Wicklow while her husband ate caviar on the Kurfursterdam. Yet as an emblem of the problematic 1930s and '40s, she is far from uninformative. Rather than treat her as a naïf whom an Irish military court properly acquitted, one should recognise *naïveté* as amongst the most dangerous attributes the innocent might possess in the low dishonest decade. She too earns a place with the Blood Kindred, an especially poignant assignment, given Yeats's feelings for her. Nor should *naïveté* be presumed in the absence of a guilty verdict at the trial of July 1940. From the uncertainties of her setting forth, as her mother's so-called 'niece', until her death in 1954, Iseult Stuart's relationship with Yeats was political in one sense or another. Though she occupied a place off the map of his native city, she represented aspects of his life that are central, if not always clearly marked.

An emphasis on relatively unfamiliar figures in Yeats's last years results from more than a desire to avoid predictable casting. By 1939 Yeats had already lost many of his closest associates in literature – Standish O'Grady (d. 1928), Augusta Gregory (1932), George Moore (1933), George William Russell (1935). Others, most notably Shaw, O'Casey and Joyce, were living abroad. The decade was one of increasing barrenness for Yeats, relieved by episodes of almost frenzied creativity. Politically, the party to which he related more easily than any other had slipped from power, to be replaced by the inscrutable de Valera. The elegiac tendency, powerful in Yeats himself, has persuaded biographers to place him amid these well-established shades, ignoring lesser figures, contemporary realities and pretty awkward questions.

On the Edge of a Communal Fosse

Few things could be more awkward than the circumstances of Yeats's burial. A temporary resting-place, it is best approached through the avenues of his final compositions. Hempel's kind gift of *Germany Speaks* may not have affected the poet's political attitudes, but there were practical considerations. Still in Dublin on 12 September 1938, he was keen to get away. Much depended on his English aristocratic friend, Dorothy Wellesley's movements; 'but it is no use writing till after Hitlers [*sic*] speech for till that's over she will be very unsettled not knowing when, if ever, she can go to her villa in the South of France'.[33] On 15 September, the Führer declared his intention to annex the Sudetenland, scarcely the weather desired by holiday-makers. The luckless British premier, Neville Chamberlain, paid a working visit to Munich, and on 30 September declared, 'This is the second time in our history that there has come back from Germany to Downing Street peace with honour. I believe it is peace for our time.'

As an allusion to the Book of Common Prayer it is scarcely more accurate than Yeats's 'Send war in our time, O Lord'.

The poem in which he ascribed the latter travesty to John Mitchel (1815–1875) is 'Under Ben Bulben'. Jon Stallworthy establishes that work had begun in mid-August, that F. R. Higgins heard an advanced version of the complete poem in late October (on the evening before Yeats's final departure from Ireland), and that in France on 26 January 1939 (two days short of his death) Yeats dictated some corrections to his wife.[34] A starting point appears to have been an essay on Rainer Maria Rilke's 'conception of death', or at least Yeats referred to such an essay in a letter of 15 August to Wellesley.[35] James Pethica's meticulous volume in the Cornell Yeats series of manuscript facsimiles and transcriptions reproduces seventeen pages of the poet's drafts and six of annotated typescripts of the poem.[36] From these, the following lines are here and now uncritically culled:

9) the newly dead show themselves

12) I believe that there is nothing to fear

16) armed philosophers seeking each other

These are taken from the first draft as enumerated in Pethica's schema. Most of it is crossed through, though one should read this not as cancellation by Yeats, but as a signal that a second draft has superseded. From the second draft let us note:

8) let the bombs fall – let them destroy the
9) hateful cities –

Care in reading these words is required. They cannot be taken as embodying the poet's considered opinions, for they exist in an evolving poetic text subject to his revisions and reworkings. It is worth noting that the prompt had been consideration of a *German* poet, resulting in a *rejection* of the German poet's attitude towards death. Against this, however, one should equally note that Yeats's interim title for the poem was 'His Convictions'; the words quoted have a textual existence not only within a process of composition, but also as the product of the composing mind.

The complex evolution of 'Under Ben Bulben' will be traced by Warwick Gould, who is writing a textual biography of Yeats. Here, in *Blood Kindred*, we can concentrate on two interrelated factors.

One is the pervasive mixing of sexual and military imagery in the evolving poem; the other is the company Yeats chose to keep as he moved through this, his elegy for himself, towards death in France. In the second draft, a second section to the poem opens:

13) And this is what I beleive [*sic*] that
14) ~~Ma~~ man stands between two
15) eternities, that of ~~this family~~, his
16) race that of his soul. Further
17) I declare that man serves these
18) sword in hand ~~or with armed~~
19) ~~mind~~ & with an armoured mind. That
20) ~~a race is born~~ only so armed does
21) man pick the right mate . . .[37]

And from the third section:

35) What matter though the skies
36) drop fire – children take hands
37) & dance

It is only in a much later draft that an echo of the Book of Common Prayer is dimly audible. Preserving Yeats's spelling, but simplifying the physical disposition of words on the page, we find the lines:

> You that ~~heard~~ John Mitchell prey
> That God might send war ~~in his day~~ before he died

This draft is dated by Yeats himself, 4 September 1938. From this it might seem reasonable to conclude that the shaping of Mitchel's prayer into its final form was prompted by Neville Chamberlain's different recourse to the Anglican litany at the end of the month. In fact, a virtually final text was sent to Dorothy Wellesley on 7 September, with the liturgical version of Mitchel's prayer.

One further group of lines might be noted:

39) So whats the odds if war must come
40) ~~From Moscow, from Berlin & Rome.~~
41) From London, Moscow, Berlin, Rome.
42) ~~Let~~ So children should an aero plane
43) Some neighbouring city pavement stain,

31

44) ~~Or~~ Should the deafening cannon sound
45) ~~Lay hand in~~ Clasp hands and dance ~~a ro~~ in a round.
46) The passing moment makes it sweet
47) When male & female organ meet

Once again, the provisionality of such writings cannot be exaggerated, their casual use of grammar an indicator of the astonishing speed at which Yeats's poem emerges on to the page. Nevertheless, certain interpretive claims relate to these lines in themselves, quite independent of their subsequent development.

In *Yeats, Ireland and Fascism* (1981), Elizabeth Cullingford made much ado about Yeats's omitting Nazi Germany from his climactic poem, 'Politics'. According to her, 'Berlin was excluded not solely for reasons of euphony', but because 'Yeats's curiosity about fascism ... did not long survive Hitler's accession to power. For him the essential political antithesis was between Russia and Italy.'[38] Even if Yeats had never approved the Nuremberg Laws, and never accepted an award from Oberbürgermeister Krebs, his drafts for 'Under Ben Bulben' destroy the happy Cullingford thesis of political liberalism. Berlin and bombing were among Yeats's chosen themes in August and September 1938. These should be recognised as proof of Yeats's 'profound understanding of the age in which he lived' (Auden's phrase). But there is a problem of tone.

Chamberlain's return from Munich justified a resurrection of John Mitchel praising the Czar. Yet this is a professional point, a tiff among professors. More disturbing is the virtual pornography of Yeats's associating the bombing of children with a dance 'when male & female organ meet'. This bombing, one should note, would only *stain* a neighbouring city pavement, though quite what it should stain the pavement *with* is left unspecified, perhaps because it is after all only a *neighbouring* pavement not to be directly confronted. If the dance of children is taken as a traditional symbol of harmony and innocence (as in William Blake's *Songs*), the price paid is the lives of the children concerned: their chances of survival are Ground Zero. None of this will reach the finally published, the canonical version of 'Under Ben Bulben', and it is legitimate to say that the process of writing was, for Yeats, a purification of his thought. What the drafts reveal is the extent to which purification was in order, both technically and thematically. The problem cannot simply be dissolved by invoking a well-wrought urn, nor indeed would Yeats have stooped to New Critical manoeuvres to prevent us seeing what his urn contained – Bandusian crystal or blood for the ghosts. In the first of the drafts, three of the poem's twenty-eight lines begin 'I beleive . . .', surely in conscious if misspelled imitation of the Trinitarian creed. And the credal line 9 – 'the newly dead show themselves' – is worked up into, rather than out of, the final poem. So too with the other disturbing matter: it is not excluded but assimilated.

One further example of this matter, relevant to the issue of Yeats's company in his final weeks, can be briefly considered. The fourth section of 'Under Ben Bulben' alludes to Michelangelo's Sistine Chapel ceilings:

> Where but half-awakened Adam
> Can disturb globe-trotting Madam
> Till her bowels are in heat,
> Proof that there's a purpose set . . .

In Pethica's reading, an early manuscript had read:

> Where his homo-sexual Adam . . .

This temporary line never reappears, but an awareness of its existence alters our response to the poem's repeated insistence on choosing a mate, on filling the cradles right, on condemnation of 'base born products of base beds' and, finally, on Yeats's Sligo ancestry. Stallworthy diplomatically omitted the line, and generally aimed for a reassuring account of 'Under Ben Bulben': 'it is not only children who discover peace at the centre of conflict, but also lovers and soldiers'.[39]

With the poem more or less finished, Yeats left Dublin in late (25 or 26) October 1938, travelling to England en route to France. In the course of the month, he wrote sixteen letters – roughly one every second day, despite lumbago, toothache, his more serious illnesses and the rigours of boat, train and motor-car. Of these sixteen, five might be described as business letters, including an amusing and biting letter about Maud Gonne addressed to his wife. (There was also some communication, via his London agents, with the German publisher, Gustav Kiepenheuer.[40]) One letter to an Indian friend, Shri Purohit Swami (1882–1941) dealt with the mental and medical condition of Margot Collis (1907–1951), an actress whom Yeats had 'befriended' in London and Majorca. Four were directed to Dorothy Wellesley, three to Edith Shackleton Heald (1885–1976) and three to

Ethel Mannin (1900–1984). Yeats had sexual relations with all three of these women, two of whom were lesbians.

As the seventy-three-year-old smiling private man approached what he knew to be his last months, he planned something of a regal visit to his English lovers. Having left his wife behind in Dublin (to follow later), Yeats had intended to stay first with Dorothy Wellesley at Penn in the Rocks in Sussex, and then to progress to Steyning in the same county, where Edith Shackleton Heald occupied a pleasant sixteenth-century house. Since Brenda Maddox published *George's Ghosts* (1999), it is difficult to know where the line of decorum can be laid down in the matter of Yeats's sexual behaviour. Yeats's rejuvenation in the 1930s can be considered in that context. Quite what his 'Steinach operation' did for him physically is not clear. Without doubt it released him psychically, though conventional genito-penetrative heterosexual intercourse does not appear to have featured. What is relevant here is the political aspect of his relations and the bearing of that upon the circumstances of his death.

Let us return to the scene of death, like revenants, pilgrims or detectives. It was a European event, in both literary and literal senses of the phrase. Yeats died in the South of France on 28 January 1939, a Saturday afternoon. He had been in declining health for several years. His English wife, and some friends, were with him at the end. Born Bertha Georgina Hyde-Lees in 1892, she was now a relatively young widow who had tolerated her husband's sexual adventures as one further expression of his genius. Among those present at the burial in Roquebrune cemetery was Heald, a journalist and lesbian. The Irish painter Dermod O'Brien and his wife, who moved in an outer circle, scarcely knew who these attendant angels were. Though it was intended to bring Yeats's remains back to Ireland, and the French government offered to provide a naval destroyer for the purpose, the outbreak of war led to an extended delay. Only in September 1948 did it prove possible to convey his body to Drumcliff churchyard in County Sligo. Even the solemnity of this final repatriation has been profaned. Rumour occasionally suggests that the wrong corpse had been disinterred from a mass grave used for what had been thought of as a temporary resting-place.

This uncertainty has generated some ribald comment in recent years, obscuring the more compelling uncertainty of the sea-borne corpse destined for burial in sacred territory.[41] Conceived in these terms, the plans for Yeats's final interment hark back, if not to

Homer, then to a Tennysonian pastiche of the archaic and heroic last journey. Yeats's own debt to the foundation myths of European civilisation – was there another Troy for him to burn? – might turn out on closer examination to be yet another short-term loan from the far more recent, Victorian circumstances of his birth. Whether in poetry or drama, modern tragedy (of which he was truly a master) stands with its heels insecurely placed on the immediately pre-contemporary period. The vessel that conveyed the dead bard to Drumcliff was neither iron-clad, nor iron-age; it was the product of a nineteenth-century industrial civilisation that he detested and damned.

Despite Georgie Yeats's efforts to tidy up her late husband's personal and philosophical legacy, an aura of disreputable unconventionality has never quite lifted from his Olympian shoulders. Negotiating this, she was aided by dutiful biographers – first Joseph Hone (1943), then Richard Ellmann (1948) and A. N. Jeffares (1949). These naturally played down the irregularity of Yeats's sexual behaviour, not least because the numerous other parties were still alive. But, for reasons that differed in each case, they also played down the poet's political views and activities. In this, they took their lead from Mrs Yeats, who had quickly set about editing her husband's controversial prose works even before the Second World War had begun. Yeats's reputation has benefited more from her generous (if not always honest) engagement with his late writings than from the advocacy of any critic or academic commentator.

Tolerant of his strange infidelities, she sought to regularise his political relationship with Ireland. Though English-born, and a cosmopolitan by upbringing, she continued to live in Dublin until her death in 1968. By her example, she suggested an attachment to Irish democracy that was quite different from Yeats's own position. Not that she was a paragon of suburban virtue: given to drink, she was suspected of mild hydrophobia in matters of personal hygiene. Nevertheless Mrs Yeats was a revered figure in post-war Ireland during her last years, and she succeeded in conferring some of her better qualities on her husband's reputation.

When, in 1965, the first serious challenge to his accepted status as a nationalist in the tradition of (somehow) both C. S. Parnell and Patrick Pearse was mounted, it seemed appropriate that the iconoclast was a resident of west Africa. Conor Cruise O'Brien lived far off the map of accepted Irish opinion, and his quotations from the poetic oeuvre were sufficiently imprecise or inaccurate to confirm his marginality.[42] Nevertheless, allegations of the poet's authoritarianism provoked responses that were strangely excessive. Indeed, the debates that revolved round Yeats were in all respects larger than diurnal life. R. P. Blackmur, Denis Donoghue, G. M. Harper, T. R. Henn, Kathleen Raine – critic after critic found confirmation of a reality beyond the senses buried in Yeatsian metaphor and stanza. Quickly, however, the resumption of 'the Troubles' in Northern Ireland brought seemingly different issues to the fore. Elizabeth Cullingford's *Yeats, Ireland and Fascism* (1981) was a determined attempt to redirect enquiries into more fashionable areas. Yeats was now a proper subject of study in American universities, a valuable potential export to the Third World.

Three factors strongly argue against any complaisant acceptance of this biographic image. First, the women with whom Yeats associated during the 1930s are by now all dead, and offence cannot reasonably be taken by any living person if his conduct is scrutinised. Feminist approaches to Yeats's poetry have redefined the conventions within which his sexuality can be considered, though the benefits have registered more in areas of ambiguity – his 'affairs' with lesbians – than in those heterosexual lives (Ethel Mannin, Margot Collis, and others) where he also made his presence felt.

Second, the conclusion of the Troubles (at least for the moment) has allowed for a broader assessment of Irish nationalism than had been possible at any time since the 1920s. The political orthodoxy to which Yeats was assigned by his considerate followers is no longer seen as the 'natural' state of Ireland: in the course of three decades, nationalism has been contextualised by a dozen other ideologies with which it has had to contend since 1968. These include American globalisation, British imperialism, Catholic social teaching, Civil Rights agitation, fundamentalist Protestantism, Marxist socialism, modernisation theory, Orange loyalism, republicanism, secularisation, terror, Trotskyism and so forth. The old Blue Shirt Dermot MacManus decided in January 1972 that the Provisional IRA were 'internationalist and atheist Marxists in with Russia', a judgment consistent with his political advice to Yeats forty years earlier. Some of the confusingly new ideologies overlapped in a few people's experience, whereas others impacted with the spectral force of conversion to the utterly unknown. In this latter-day context of constantly debated positions, it would have been impossible even for a uniquely gifted man to declare (as Yeats did in 1937), 'I am no Nationalist, except in Ireland for passing reasons.'[43]

The virtual containment of 'the Troubles' within Northern Ireland, coinciding with this intensive ideological consciousness, brought a new awareness of that region, its geography, history and political boundaries. Books proliferated. Side by side with the Yeats Industry there developed an almost equally productive Ulster Studies Industry. Unfortunately, these have rarely – if ever – overlapped, such has been the mystique of Sligo and the west of Ireland perpetuated by Yeats himself in his lifetime and confirmed by the reinterment of 1948. In 1981, Margaret Thatcher and Charles Haughey ruled their distinctive roosts, while the IRA embarked on an unprecedented hunger-strike campaign, ending with ten deaths and a greatly exacerbated public opinion. In the same *annus horribilis,* three studies of Yeats's politics were published, one as neglectful of the continuing northern problem as the other.[44] Yet long before the famous words 'Cast a cold eye / On life, on death. / Horseman, pass by!' were blazoned on the Drumcliff tombstone, a tablet in Tullylish parish church, County Down, commemorated the Reverend William Butler Yeats, rector there from 1836 until his death (in Dublin) in 1862. Whereas the poet posthumously inscribed his own self-composed epitaph, his namesake and grandfather is remembered on a marble tablet inscribed with ornamental rubric lettering.[45]

It is a principle in this present biography of W. B. Yeats that these oblique northern traces deserve more attention than they have ever received. Perhaps it has taken the turbulence of thirty years to bring Ulster into focus to this extent. But the relevance of Victorian Tullylish for the life of a poet dying near Monte Carlo in 1939 emerges also from other altering perspectives. The war that began seven months after his death not only delayed his reburial: its greater imposition on the appreciation of Yeats's peculiar genius has only begun to lift within the last few years. The collapse of the Soviet Union, and the resurgence of extreme nationalism in the Balkans, may seem events remote from Sligo and Tullylish. Yet it is through these twin developments that a fuller appreciation of European fascism – its classic regimes, its imitative opponents and its vicious grandchildren – becomes possible. Parts of Europe that were relegated to obscurity in the Cold War scenario now demand attention. Romania, in which Hitler conducted dangerous experiments, is disclosed with all the horrific evidence of its post-fascist dictatorship. Czechoslovakia, from which the Provisional IRA obtained a reliable supply of Semtex explosive, has split revealingly in two, mimicking a partition that the Provos sought to obliterate. Yugoslavia, once a model of federal balance and non-alignment, inflicts genocidal savagery on one portion of its people after another. In Germany, xenophobia notches up a weekly toll of violent (often fatal) attacks on migrant workers and (more discreetly) Jewish monuments. Even closer to home in France, the motherland of all modern republics persists in giving representation to an expressly racist and anti-Semitic party. If we can now study the authoritarianism (Roy Foster's preferred term) with which Yeats entered into compact seventy years ago, some benefits flow both from the final break-up of a World System derived from opposition to fascism, and others (less welcome) from the recrudescence of micro-fascisms in what had been hidden corners of Europe. The theoretical framework of Fascism vs Communism has dissolved, but cruising amid the wreckage are a few practices no less vicious and inhumane than those of Nazi stormtroopers.[46]

Meanwhile the ordinary Irish became enthralled by a succession of revelations which have 'shaken the foundations': wholesale corruption in the beef trade, a celibate bishop and his bastard son, the tax-withholding perjured head of government, nuns who abused orphans. Occurring under the cover of Northern Troubles, these evinced a strikingly similar morality in a demi-establishment of the South, based on ruthless exploitation of opportunities and the abandonment of 'victims'. Fraud and terror alike proclaim that absence. All of this may seem entirely irrelevant to the biography of Yeats, who had, however, asked in 'Church and State' in 1934, 'What if the Church and the State / Are the mob that howl at the door!'

What made these scandalous events possible was the reign of Charles Haughey, happily acquitted of a conspiracy charge in 1972, late head of Ireland's largest political party, speculator in land and patron of the arts. Financed by his unwitting citizenry, Haughey lived in eighteenth-century splendour, occupying a house built by John Beresford, who had flogged Dublin's Jacobins to deathly silence in the 1790s. For primitivist balance, he has also colonised a depopulated western island, republican monarch of all he suborned. On discovery of these facts, the mob did not quite howl at the doors of Church and State. But there has unquestionably been a reduction in the degree of legitimacy conferred on the agencies of Church and State by the sovereign people. We read Yeats today, profoundly altered in our sense of what his legacy has become.

Is it really necessary to preface a biography of Yeats, the author of 'Beautiful Lofty Things' and 'The Lake Isle of Inisfree', with such weighty and incriminating summaries of recent history? In 1981, Elizabeth Cullingford proclaimed that the poet's interest in Mussolini – and surely there was no question of Hitler attracting him? – arose out of his interest in the Irish Augustan age. That the eighteenth century was a proper object of admiration was tacitly assumed, despite Yeats's own view of his heroes (Jonathan Swift, Oliver Goldsmith and Edmund Burke) as oppositional figures, in no sense representative of their time. Oblivious to Haughey's revival of eighteenth-century corruption, Dr Cullingford was able to insist that Yeats's view was (in any case) not different from the post-war anxieties of many admirable Europeans, such as Winston Churchill.

The record is less reassuring. As late as August 1938, the *Irish Independent* reported Yeats publicly approving the Hereditary Farm Law of 1933 – a prologue to the infamous Nuremberg code of 1935 – by which Jews were systematically ejected from their homes so that these might be repossessed by Aryans.[47] The phrasing is oddly indirect for a man who by then proclaimed the merit of outrageous frankness. 'In Germany,' he had said during a debate in the Abbey Theatre, 'there is special legislation to enable old families to go living where their fathers lived.'[48] This matter had been the subject of press comment in Britain by September 1935.[49] It is striking that Yeats should recall this early Nazi provision and approve it, without reference to subsequent and far more virulent racial provision. For example, on 14 June and again on 6 July 1938, the Reich legally tightened control of Jewish trade and business, especially with reference to real-estate and loan agencies, in effect closing off the means whereby German Jews might secure themselves a living independent of the state-pervaded public sector. Landless but law-di-daw, Yeats took an emulous interest in hereditary property, and on this basis was open to suggestions of Nazi thoughtfulness.

He may not have noticed the new decrees as publicised in newspapers, or he may have preferred to invoke the fundamental code of 1935. Joseph Hone's parallel comment in the biography of 1943 is less evasive, while wholly omitting any reference to the Jews:

someone told Yeats that there was 'a new law in that country whereby ancient and impoverished families can recover their hereditary properties'.[50] The question was: from whom? This, though it has been scrupulously ignored by Yeats's latter-day apologists, is not all. Among the essays that the widow prepared for publication between January and September 1939 one finds the bluntest endorsement of biologist eugenics, enthusiastic anticipations of war, and an utter contempt for democracy. Though she released *On the Boiler* after Britain and France had responded to the invasion of Poland by declaring war on Germany, it is likely that Mrs Yeats had earlier intervened to tone down the violence of her husband's posthumous testament: a second issue was already being planned when Yeats died but, in the event, only one ever appeared. The collective arrangement of his prose works, in a series of volumes issued by Macmillan between 1955 and 1962, had the further effect of diffusing Yeats's political statements, not least by omitting some of the more outrageous. One can hardly blame Mrs Yeats, given her personal respect for Irish democracy and her love for the poet in whose literary achievement she had invested much and found everything to admire. By the time his body was brought home on board an Irish naval corvette – for the French fleets had been sunk in 1940 – the full consequences of the Nuremberg housing policy were unmistakable. Yet Yeats had never been (seriously) anti-Semitic or even (in any grave sense) racist in his views.

So what was going on in the Riviera household over Christmas 1938 and into January 1939? For the most detailed answers we must await John Kelly's magisterial annotation of the poet's *Collected Letters* – say, twelve further years. Long before the final volume appears in print, we can still trace the lineaments of apocalypse. Michael Yeats's cold-eyed memoirs report that he and his father had 'some emotional discussions on the politics of central Europe' but more adult concerns were preferred in the public domain.[51] *The Times* of London was prompt in its commemoration, printing an anonymous obituary on 30 January. On the same day, further to the east, Adolf Hitler delivered an epochal speech to the first Greater German Reichstag, in which he warned Jews that, whereas they had reacted scornfully to the prophecies of his youth, he believed 'the roaring laughter of those days already had stuck in Jewry's throat' and now he promised 'the annihilation of the Jewish race in Europe'.[52] This

was widely reported, with varying degrees of outrage and complacency. The times were exceptional, but were they filled with anything
more ominous than bombast?

The anonymous Yeats obituary was strikingly out of date even
within its own terms. And so, exceptionally for *The Times,* a post-
obit followed some days afterwards – and after the Führer's genocidal
threat – over the initials D. W. It revealed a Yeats who was much
closer to contemporary events:

> Those who have been privileged to discuss with him in recent years the
> questions of poetry and life which have occupied his mind will bear
> witness to his passionate interest in the new ideas now at work in Europe.
> He had latterly been studying eugenic authorities, and had embodied his
> ideas on the vital importance of quality as distinct from quantity of
> population in an informal prose essay ... He sought everywhere for
> firsthand information about the spiritual and poetical ideas from which
> the new movements derived. Little more than a fortnight ago he was
> eagerly discussing with Austrian and German acquaintances the philoso-
> phy of the poets Stefan Georg [sic] and Rilke. He was following with
> sympathetic interest and shrewd practical advice the plans of a group of
> English friends for giving concrete expression to ideas of a constructive
> democracy in Great Britain.[53]

This appeared on 9 February, its author Dorothy Wellesley, a leading
figure in Yeats's emotional world. Whatever Yeats had been discussing in the previous two to three weeks, and with whom, the
discussions had taken place in the South of France. Only someone as
dottily right-wing as she was could mistake the Irish poet's politics
for 'the plans of a group of English friends for giving concrete
expression to ideas of a constructive democracy in Great Britain'.
Yeats gave not a fig for Britain, nor for democracy, however
'constructive'. Yet Lady Wellesley was unquestionably right about
the eugenics and the 'informal prose essay', which, in Mrs Yeats's
hand, became *On the Boiler.* There is no doubt that 'the new ideas
now at work in Europe' were political, authoritarian and – quite
simply – fascist. In 1937 Wellesley had asked Yeats who Oliver
Cromwell was, and considered Hitler 'better' than Mussolini, so we
are in the company of distinguished minds.[54] *The Times* under the
editorship of Geoffrey Dawson was strongly pro-appeasement: as late
as 31 January 1938 a leader-writer could refer moderately to the
Nazis' *outlawry* of the Jews and, even after the Munich farce and the

invasion of Czechoslovakia, it audibly yearned for a return to appeasement.[55]

If the discussions in the Hôtel Idéal-Séjour involved Austrian and German acquaintances, this takes them beyond the circle of Wellesley and Heald. Confirmation of the Teutonic presence can be found in an unlikely place – the literary supplement of the *Berliner Börsenzeitung*, or stock-exchange gazette. In general, the Reich's newspapers were lavish in their coverage of Yeats's death.[56] On Thursday, 2 February 1939 – a full week before Wellesley's piece in *The Times* – the gazette's *Volk und Kultur* section printed an account of Yeats's life and work on its front page. Much of the detail was commonplace (birth, parentage, publications, senatorial career) together with a brief comparison of Yeats and Stefan George (1868–1933). The German poet had been assiduously cultivated by the Nazis in their coming to power, but when Hitler offered George presidency of the new Dichter-Akademie, he refused the position, withdrew to Switzerland and died. What is striking in this German obituary is not the allusion to George as such, but rather its anticipation of Wellesley's unexpected reference to him.[57]

The Berlin obituarist moves confidently into areas of Yeats's last days, for which public sources of information were insufficient: '*im vorigen Jahr veröffentlichte er noch zwei neue Spiele, Monologe eines alten Mannes, der auf sein langes Leben zurückblickt*' (In the last year, he published/announced two new plays, monologues of an old man looking back on his long life). The plays are clearly 'Purgatory' and 'The Death of Cuchulain', neither of which had been published before 2 February 1939. It is true that 'Purgatory' had been performed in August 1938; indeed, that occasion led to Yeats's commendation of Nazi law. But he was still working on 'The Death of Cuchulain', which more closely resembles a monologue, when he reached the South of France. *Last Poems and Two Plays*, which includes both, was not published until July. We may therefore suspect that the Berlin notice was written by someone who was in Yeats's presence in the last week or so of his life.[58]

How did the Nobel Prize winner of 1923, the noble elegist of the brave in 1916, the defender of J. M. Synge in 1907, the swooning admirer of Maud Gonne in the 1890s, get himself into such company? A predictable response invokes the idea of manipulation. Accordingly, the great man did not deliberately associate with Nazi journalists or sympathisers, but – while communing with Cuchulain –

he had his ear bent by dubious figures such as Walter Starkie or Dorothy Wellesley. This defence relies on a rigorous distinction between the inspired poet and the vulnerable man in his armchair, a distinction which thrives also on the belief that the elderly are particularly prone to this kind of manipulation. Standard biographies, which commence brusquely at the beginning and work rapidly into a person's achievements, connive with this convenient idea of manipulation.[59]

Instead, we shall 'go on backwards', like Mr and Mrs Rooney in Samuel Beckett's *All that Fall* (1957). If the title of this seemingly slight comico-tragedy is recognisable to good Irish biblical Protestants – see Psalm 145:14 – its allusiveness ranges from Dante to Sir Edward Grey (1862–1933). As Foreign Secretary in 1914, Grey had observed that 'The lamps are going out all over Europe. We shall not see them lit again in our time.'[60] Yeats's politics contributed to that darkness or blindness, partly through his high occultic disdain for the mere dead of the Somme. More disturbing is the rarely examined record of Yeats's 'brushes' with the Thousand-Year-Reich designed to reignite the world.

A Troubled Mirror

The Irregulars took care of our property and even moved a Russian icon of my wife's from a dry wall to a dry shelf, but after they had gone the country people stole all the mirrors. They left the blankets and such humdrum property but evidently found a novelty not to be resisted in the large mirrors. The same has happened elsewhere, men even stealing mirrors that would not fit into the thatched houses and had to be left outside to be charged by enraged cows.

To Thomas Sturge Moore, 18 August 1923

If this is more than just another life of William Butler Yeats, the important initial move must be to get thoroughly outside one's subject. Then, the important second stage must be to stay thoroughly outside him. The objective is understanding without sympathy, achieved through intimate knowledge gained without compromise.

Some lives of Yeats achieve a roughly similar effect by default. Previous biographies have not neglected his politics, but they invariably distribute the material through numerous chapters so that it never achieves critical mass in any one chapter. And as the biographers have been drawn exclusively from admirers of his poetry – no change in that respect with *Blood Kindred* – each chapter of the previous biographies has had plenty to distract it from the political issue.

Some readers may fear that I am striving to perpetuate an obsession with ideology that characterised the 1980s. Others may suspect a degree of insensitivity to his poetic work itself. In reply, I want to say that Yeats is probably the greatest poet in the English language since John Milton, and certainly the greatest since Wordsworth. What follows is a personal as well as professional undertaking, a brief account of which is unavoidable. The objective of understanding without sympathy can only be pursued after a frank admission of one's own historical situation and the efforts made at self-understanding.

I take my place in a disturbed and interrupted history. Yeats was not always a Brahmin untouchable, though those who directly

44

opposed him mostly came off second best. The critic John Eglington was a case in point. Another, more accomplished in literary terms, was George Moore, who mocked Yeats's disdain of his own middle class, poking fun at the poet's fur coat. Closer to today, Seamus Heaney is diplomatically right when he argues that *Hail and Farewell* was 'finally more of a testimony to Yeats's genius than a worrier of it'. I hope that, like Heaney's Moore, my enquiry can be 'corrective, accurate in its own way'.[1] Necessarily there will be worry about the task, and worrying of Yeats (especially of his silences), but there will be appreciation also. The dreadful decades place one under an obligation to look closely and aim at telling the truth.

Little Belfast

During the 1967 Yeats International Summer School, a 'Union Jack' was burned in the streets of Sligo in protest at remarks made by Dr Tom Henn, the school's director. Though displeasure had been formally registered that evening by the Sinn Féin mayor of Sligo, the incident symbolised a wider unease, which had for its focus Henn's own local origins and his grand presentation of these. One visitor at the summer school enquired innocently where Irish republicans got a British flag at short notice. The matter was taken seriously in Dublin, however, whence issued a senior theoretician to pour oil on shadowy waters. Roy Johnston, part of a new, avowedly Marxist leadership in Sinn Féin and the IRA, duly attempted to placate the mayor and educate the international students so as to 'advance the cause of peace and socialism'. Earlier in the year, the Northern Ireland Civil Rights Association had been founded in Belfast, with the same new-style republicans leading from behind.

It may seem that a summer school offered little preparation for the onslaught about to fall on the Civil Rights people in their quest for a single universal franchise in Northern Ireland. Yet the poet had been admitted as a member of the Irish Republican Brotherhood some time in the late 1880s, when Sligo's streets witnessed a repetition of sectarian riots that had broken out in Ulster. Despite a recent sedulously nurtured reputation for pastoral beauty, Sligo in those days was known as Little Belfast, such was the intensity of its communal hatreds. We might indeed pause to ask how important the western port was for the future Nobel Prize winner. For the poet had been born in Dublin (not the west of Ireland). His father, the painter J. B. Yeats, had been born in County Down (in the north-east), where *his* father was rector of a parish closer to 'Big' Belfast than to the hamlets and country houses celebrated by his grandson-namesake. Sligo was, to a degree, an acquired and not an immediate background. Indeed, in 1887 when the future poet was twenty-two, he admitted that the place had 'no flesh and blood attractions'.[2]

If Yeats had been in Sligo that August evening in 1967, he would not have sided with the inheritors of his IRB. They looked east to Moscow rather than west to Boston and New York. Johnston was a scientist, whose father had been an Ulster Protestant, an ancient historian turned economist and (like Yeats himself) sometime a member of the Irish Senate. Johnston's chief of staff was Cathal Goulding (1927–1998), born into the extended Behan family, later a long-time resident of Her Majesty's prisons. (Brendan Behan's mother had been a serving maid in the household of Maud Gonne, as if to symbolise a link between the Dublin working class and the gentry republicanism intermittently manifest in the poet's own social milieu.) By 1967 Goulding, charming and intelligent, had become a thoroughgoing Marxist whose attempts to take the gun out of republicanism had not dimmed his reputation as 'a hard man'. Class matters: for all Yeats's lifelong anti-English animus, he would have taken the Cambridge professor's arm rather than that of fellow-republicans.

The Exploding View

Sligo lies only a few miles west of the Irish border with the United Kingdom; 1967 was just two years short of the outbreak of serious communal violence across Northern Ireland and a recommencement of the Troubles. The three decades that followed government-approved attacks on Civil Rights marches in 1968 brought fundamental changes in popular and critical attitudes to Yeats. A Polaroid image of these could be obtained by taking a quick look at the magazine *Atlantis.* Conceived in the autumn of 1969, with Seamus Deane, Derek Mahon and the present writer as its editors, the first number appeared in March 1970, with Conor Cruise O'Brien listed among six patrons. In the editorial Deane asked provocatively, 'Adorno died last August. Who cares?' The first substantive article was O'Brien's T. S. Eliot Memorial Lecture on 'Burke and Machiavelli'. The second number of October 1970 included an extract from a new novel by Francis Stuart, while the fourth (September 1972) opened with a review article by Roy Johnston. Together with fiction by John Banville, Brian Moore and William Trevor, poetry by Donald Davie, Seamus Heaney and Derek Mahon, and criticism by Stephen Heath amongst others, *Atlantis* was a remarkable (if distinctly male) gathering of talents. Oddly enough, Yeats was nowhere discussed.

It could not last. The price of paper rocketed as a result of the oil crisis. The editors were obliged to seek more gainful employment, two of them leaving Dublin. And the North of Ireland continued to erupt. The impact of political instability can be traced in the subsequent ideological movements of notable participants. Cruise O'Brien, whose 1965 essay 'Passion and Cunning' had impressively dissected Yeats's authoritarianism, quickly became the heavy governmental hand keeping the airways free for debates that excluded the principal villains. Seamus Deane, who had briefly affiliated to Roy Johnston's Wolfe Tone Society, was soon heading in the opposite direction: deploring the universalist agenda of Marxism, and increasingly hostile to modernity, he has become the nationalist intellectual *par excellence*. Francis Stuart, born in 1902 and virtually forgotten in 1970, resurrected himself with *Blacklist Section H*, an autobiographical fiction that prominently featured Maud Gonne and Yeats. Johnston, by the fourth issue of *Atlantis* already listed as a *former* member of Sinn Féin, resumed academic life in Trinity College Dublin.

While this scattering of the magazine's personalities was typical of Irish literary and intellectual life once the Troubles took hold, Yeats in their altered and contrasting careers deserves closer attention. Seamus Deane's evolving views are traceable through certain important publications. Beginning with 'The Literary Myths of the Revival; A Case for their Abandonment' (1977), he has sought to replace the positivist and consensual approaches of Ellmann, Jeffares, Kain *et al.* with an agenda difficult to distinguish from that of Sinn Féin.[3]

Moving in the opposite direction, Conor Cruise O'Brien (b. 1917) had advanced in life as if by magic propelled. A brilliant (if wayward) student at Trinity College, he joined the Irish civil service and was seconded to the United Nations. There a trenchant critic of British and Belgian duplicity, he became a liberal academic serving in

Conor Cruise O'Brien

succession as Vice-Chancellor of the University of Ghana and as Albert Schweitzer Professor in New York University. When he published 'Passion and Cunning; an Essay on the Politics of W. B. Yeats' in 1965, the vehicle for his damaging analysis was a volume of centenary essays. As the book clocked up reviews deploring his impudence, Cruise O'Brien was gaining a reputation among liberals in America. 'Passion and Cunning', however, had been written in a different kind of ferment, that of problem-ridden, newly independent Ghana under Dr Nkrumah. The essay concluded with a promised second instalment in which Yeats's four last great poems would be analysed. We continue to wait. Meanwhile, Seamus Deane has reviewed the second and final volume of Roy Foster's authorised biography – *W. B. Yeats; a Life: II, the Arch-Poet (2003)* – with unexpected pleasure. The republican and the revisionist concur, perhaps even the nationalist and the unionist. No enemies on the centre-right, no left in view.

What appalled readers of Cruise O'Brien's essay in 1965 was not simply the accusation of pro-fascist views on Yeats's part. That, certainly, outraged Denis Donoghue, Terence de Vere White, Arland Ussher and other contributors to the *Irish Times* in the summer of 1965. In the Letters column, Anthony Cronin averred that:

> Whatever else a fascist may be he is someone who approves the limitation of other people's rights of expression and inquiry. To say that Yeats was a fascist is, with a sort of ugly hindsight, to say that he would have approved of the intimidation, suppression and murder of many fellow artists.[4]

The logic taking us from the first to the second of these sentences speaks for itself. At the time, feeling ran high. Official Ireland was erecting commemorative plaques all over County Sligo while intellectuals vied with each other in the newspapers to give the game away. Grattan Freyer, hard on Cronin's heels, declared, 'the bald statement "Yeats was a fascist" is clearly nonsense and I doubt if anyone has really said this.' His elaboration of the point fell short of vindicating the poet:

> But it is a fact that Yeats sympathised with that wide stream of European thought and feeling which reacted against nineteenth-century rationalism and liberalism, and of which varying manifestations were Fascism, Naziism, and the ethos of D. H. Lawrence.[5]

Dermot MacManus, writing modestly as 'an old and very dear

friend of W. B. Yeats', conceded that the latter was 'certainly no democrat', but one whose 'predilection was for a benevolent authoritarianism like that of Dr Salazar in Portugal'. On the question of political movements, he had this to add:

> Ethically, one organisation, like a machine-gun, is quite neutral, neither good nor evil, but both ideals and methods can be anything – good or bad.[6]

In advance of the Troubles, this prospect of the Thompson or Kalashnikov as a glorified fowling-piece had its charms. Objectors to Cruise O'Brien's essay felt an injury to their sense of fair play. Citation of the poet's private correspondence to prove the fascist allegation struck some as indecent. In 1954, *The Letters of W. B. Yeats* had appeared in a large, annotated volume: though very far from complete (and doctored in some crucial areas), it revealed more than its editor, or the poet's widow, may have realised at the time. For example, access to a letter of Yeats's, written in July 1933, compromised any polite assumption of the poet's consistent decency. He had written:

> It is amusing to live in a country where men will always act. Where nobody is satisfied with thought. There is so little in our stocking that we are ready at any moment to turn it inside out, and how can we not feel emulous when we see Hitler juggling with his sausage of stocking[?]. Our chosen colour is blue . . .[7]

This had been written months after the persecution of Jews had begun throughout the Reich with a national boycott of Jewish businesses, and after the suppression of Germany's trade unions. Now, with the *Letters* thus cited ostensibly in celebration of the poet's birth, the cat-o'-nine-tails was out of the bag. We were reminded in swinging 1965 that Yeats, who had supported harsh measures during the Irish civil war, was not wholly averse to Hitler's more comprehensive use of violence.

The Cruise O'Brien whom *Atlantis* had chosen as a patron was the recent author of such incisive iconoclasm, not yet the emergent government minister and censor of television news. The last issue (no. 6, winter 1973/74) divided itself between contemporary poetry from Northern Ireland and a selection of writing in translation from Central and Eastern Europe. As editor of an *Atlantis* now visibly sinking under the waves of insurgent violence and repressive authority, I tried to suggest that the examples of Johannes Bobrowski

(Germany), Titel Constantinescu (Romania) and Daniil Kharms (Soviet Union) might provide some illumination of our predicament in Ireland. Comparatism did not prove attractive in a renewed battle of the books fought out between essentialists and revisionists, nationalists and reformers. With few exceptions, Ulster Unionists opted out of the literary battle. With assistance from leading members of the Dublin government, the Marxists were purged from the IRA, and the Provos emerged from the carapace, financed unwittingly by the southern taxpayer.

'Passion and Cunning', with its attendant calculated outcries, had appeared in the summer I left secondary school. In the evolving crisis Yeats had come to fascinate me. While teaching in Derry in 1971–72 and researching a critical biography of the Victorian Irish novelist, Sheridan Le Fanu, I organised home rehearsals of Yeats's one-act play, 'The Words Upon the Window-pane'. Using the distinctly pre-war interior of a flat within firing range of both British Army and Provisional IRA, I even thought to have the results filmed. Nothing came of the larger project, but the publication of Liam Miller's *The Noble Drama of W. B. Yeats* (1977) later revealed how the intrusion of Jonathan Swift into the play's twentieth-century *séance* had its own origins in Yeats's private reading of Victorian Irish authors. Potentially, a coherent historical narrative was discernible behind the high-relief of Yeatsian categories. The 'Augustan Tradition' which he had successfully imposed on generations of readers was neither a fact of collective self-begetting on the part of Swift and Goldsmith, Berkeley and Burke, nor was it a brilliant fiction dreamed up by the latter-day poet. Transitional nineteenth-century figures of little appeal to academic giant-killers deserve recognition as the personnel of larger significant cultural transmissions and mediations, people like Isaac Butt and Le Fanu who had worked on the *Dublin University Magazine* (1833–77) together with – it is said – the Revd William Butler Yeats, rector of Tullylish, County Down.

No Victorians in motley occlude the view of Swift as a significant ancestor of the poet in Joseph Hassett's *Yeats and the Poetics of Hate* (1986). But the preternatural clarity of this perspective is itself illuminated in Hassett's opening paragraph: 'In 1916 Yeats set about acquiring his tower, Thoor Ballylee. Seven years later, Carl Jung began constructing a tower on the lake above Zurich at Bollingen. Jung sensed the presence of his ancestors congregating about his tower.' Jungian doctrines of the collective unconscious, and his later compliance in the Germanising of psychoanalysis (out of existence), are matter for extended discussion some other day. But the presence of Jung as a presiding spirit, at the outset of a conscientious academic vindication of Yeats's use of hatred, cannot be noted without reference to the background of continental anti-Semitism of which Yeats was complicitly unaware.[8] We will chart Yeats's use of the word hatred in due course.

Metaphors for Politics

At the risk of seeming to have been more in control of my career than was ever possible, I should record that the present book is the third in a sequence of biographies that explore Irish literary history while paying appropriate attention to the politics of the day. Its evolution has been complicated by a host of problems, ranging from literary copyright tightly controlled to the commodification of Yeatsian phrase in journalistic book-titles such as Ulick O'Connor's *A Terrible Beauty is Born*. Mr O'Connor, one might add, has written a biography of Yeats's friend, Oliver St John Gogarty, unspoiled by that medical gentleman's anti-Semitism.[9]

I had thought to call this book *Yeats, an Exploded View*, taking a lead from Michael Longley's collection of poems written in 1968–72 and using the same pathologist's or car-mechanic's term for title. Under that kind of verbal image or illustration, I could have shown how – somewhere between the spleen and the bile-duct – nodules of fascism had been located, or how (from an early age) the raised right arm was linked by muscle and nerve to the seat of the emotions. But I did not want to see Yeats (like Bunbury in *The Importance of Being Earnest*) 'quite exploded', for it would suggest that the poet whose life had been narrated by Joseph Hone, Richard Ellmann and A. N. Jeffares had been a dramatic fiction. True, I feel that the man we encounter in those early biographies has been trimmed of his epaulettes, his mind softened. The task, however, is to see the inner relationships of mind and brawn, imagination and cold blood, without leaving the external world of other bodies, social actions and unannounced explosions.

Yeats devised his own metaphors to account for this need to relate opposites. The Mask, the Anti-Self become recurrent terms of organisational reference as he strives with unprecedented dedication to bring philosophy and art into the one focus. The process involves gain and loss, claim and denial. Violence is admitted as the logically necessary conjugal partner of love, though love is often discounted and relabelled passion or friendship, desire or memory. A post-Hone and post-Ellmann school of Yeatsian scholars has embraced the supernatural apparatus from which much of this is suspended, ignoring (in most cases) the determinist implications. In *Heaven and Hell* (1758), one of Yeats's lesser instructors in the system had described how, after death, a soul's gradual association with other spirits reveals the true worth (or otherwise) of his conduct in the earthly life. The soul is, so to speak, no longer protected by self-deception, pretence or hypocrisy from acknowledgment of its own condition. This is especially true of pious men and solitary thinkers. In writing Yeats's biography, I materialise these vapours by taking them as metaphors of denied community, or of the moral-social world in which he lived but which he acknowledged principally through conceits of the Anti-Self. In other words, the affable Irregulars, swashbucklers, bitter and violent men, whom he envied but never emulated. If these are a myriad bit-parts in the story of one man, it is because he projected himself mightily.

I fix on a remark Yeats made in 1917 when he was about to embark on the study of his wife's automatic writing. Excited by the flood of information emanating from the spirit world, he offered to devote the remainder of his life to the study of that wisdom. No, the spirits obligingly replied. That's not what we have in mind. 'We have come to give you metaphors for poetry.'[10] Though the experiments that followed, and the philosophical treatise that resulted (*A Vision*, 1925), have excited voluminous commentary, few efforts have been made to compare Yeats's use of automatic writing with that of other writers. Back in the nineteenth century Victor Hugo had tried similar ways to communicate with Dante and Shakespeare, but Hugo was living in exile on Guernsey at the material time and did not found his subsequent literary practice on desperate remedies. More immediate comparisons might involve the Surrealists, or relate Yeats's recourse to this route towards composition to well-established Freudian practices. In the latter connection, we might find that Yeats's brief engagement with psychoanalytical ideas arose in a sexual and emotional context from which his marriage in 1917 constituted a deliberate flight. As for comparisons with Surrealist poets such as Robert Desnos, Pierre Reverdy (in 1918), André Breton and Philippe Soupault (see *Les Champs magnétiques*, 1919/20), it is clear that the

Yeatses were not tapping the unconscious, but charting an allegedly objective spirit world populated by historical or pseudo-historical figures. The contrasting political affiliations of Breton and Yeats hardly need emphasis.

Confronted by less elevated yet elusive antagonists, I still require metaphors for politics. For it has become clear over the last twenty years or so that to argue the case for regarding Yeats as fascist, or pro-fascist, or even merely as sympathetic to fascism, is to surrender from an attitude of reflective complexity into court-room logic. (The word 'as', in the phrase 'Yeats as fascist', is perhaps more difficult to analyse than 'fascist', though both will require thought.) Decisions, decisions, my interlocutors insist, while at the same time advising that I go down some additional avenue of enquiry to search slowly for a real clincher. What would count as a genuine smoking gun? Perhaps Yeats's admiring entry in the visitors' book at some obscure concentration camp. Had he not refused in 1936 to help Carl von Ossietzky, who in Sonnenberg or Papenburg-Esterwegen suffered his leg to be broken, repeatedly?

Yeats scholars, those judicious communicators who demand my smoking gun, raise their eyes in wearied tolerance. There he goes again, they murmur, always choosing the wrong avenue, barking up another ill-chosen stinkwood. But it keeps him occupied in his ill-bred preoccupations. Others who have revelled in astral bodies, studied Berkeley, hiked to Byzantium or camped it up in Drumahair find a critique of fascist politics too crudely recherché for their taste. So having advised one highly commended commender of Yeats's liberalism that she wholly ignored his admiration for part at least of the Nuremberg Laws against Jews, I try again.[11]

Comparison with other writers or intellectuals offers an obvious way forward. It is striking that critics and commentators who have attended to Yeats's politics – notably Conor Cruise O'Brien and Elizabeth Cullingford – have not ventured into a consideration of Ezra Pound's activities in Italy during the war, or pursued T. S. Eliot's strange gods. Back in 1966, John Harrison treated Yeats, Wyndham Lewis, Pound, Eliot and D. H. Lawrence as reactionaries, partisans of an anti-democratic intelligentsia, though his book had been unable to draw on Cruise O'Brien's explosive article of the previous year. Much later and with little by way of comparison, Grattan Freyer approvingly linked Yeats to an anti-democratic tradition. In short, attention to Yeats's politics has rarely adopted a comparative perspective; he is to be *sui generis*, it seems.

Admittedly, comparable figures are not easily identified, if the emphasis is to rest on Yeats the Irish poet rather than – say – Yeats the yogi. Walter Starkie (1894–1976), like Yeats a director of the Abbey Theatre, was a member of the Centre International d'Etudes sur le Fascisme, based in Brussels and Lausanne between the wars. In March 1936, he contributed to the *Irish Independent* seven or more articles written from Italian-occupied Abyssinia. At least one volume of his autobiographical writings – *The Waveless Plain* (1938) – was subsidised by the Mussolini government. Yet Starkie remains a minor figure, a musicologist of dubious ability, who crops up infrequently in Yeats's correspondence.

In due course I will introduce other Irish writers of the period, with undeniable links to fascism. The most notable of these is Francis Stuart, who married the daughter of Yeats's difficult muse. As a novelist, Stuart remained an apprentice during Yeats's lifetime: indeed, his development was hampered and nurtured by the older man's interest. Nothing like comparability between them can be entertained, though the extent to which the younger man carried out in wartime Berlin something of a programme hinted at by the elder deserves consideration.[12] In the hands of Yeats's vindicators, Stuart has become a jockey's whip to beat anyone questioning the poet's fundamental decency in politics. Meanwhile little attention is paid to the anti-Semitic utterances and pro-Nazi activities of Gonne, an English-Gaelic Pasionaria of the dishonest decade. Virtually talentless as a writer, she nonetheless offers a comparative basis for measuring Yeats's attitudes to race.

There were other fascist sympathisers in Ireland both before and during the Second World War, not forgetting a few 'wild geese' who found refuge in Berlin or Rome. Viewed as intellectuals or artists, none of these assists in understanding the author of *The Tower* (1928), one of the finest individual collections of poetry published since the days of the Romantics. Investigating some – Ruairi Brugha or George Griffin, for example – we quit Olympus for the smoky cellars of petit-bourgeois prejudice. The absence of any traced connection between Patrick Moylett and Yeats, or again between the Abwehr agent Helmut Clissmann and Yeats, can be readily seized on as evidence of the poet's remoteness from Nazi contagion. To mistake this absence of evidence for evidence of absence would, however, oversimplify the relationship between the writer and 'the new movements in Europe'.

Yeats's interest in fascism did not arise simply or solely from his disappointment at the course of Irish politics in the 1920s and '30s. From the outset, it had a broader context and a longer historical pedigree. After his disillusion with the Blue Shirts (Ireland's tribute to the black and brown legions), he found more congenial company in a few great and some lesser houses, in England. Instead of Eoin O'Duffy he now favoured Lady Dorothy Wellesley, who opened up for him a rarefied world of aristocratic acceptance and sexual adventurism. Wellesley was – in the weasel phrase – a published poet. Yet despite her new friend's inclusion of her in *The Oxford Book of Modern Verse* (1936), she did not inhabit the same spheres as the Christian T. S. Eliot, while the Marxist-inclined younger poets – W. H. Auden, Cecil Day Lewis and Louis MacNeice – lay even further out in outer space. In Britain, Yeats was in some ways isolated, but he surprised many by his talents as a radio speaker on the British Broadcasting Corporation. As a seventy-year-old, he took to an unfamiliar technology with relish, technology linked to aristocracy.

If Yeats's correspondence with Wellesley removed him from the grubbier side of his inheritance as a Fenian in plus-fours, the significance of his altered behaviour in the later 1930s goes beyond class preferences. Far from establishing his interest in fascism as a purely contemporary phenomenon, his letters indicate the continuity of his thought at least from – say – 1912 onwards. It is a truism that the roots of fascism lie in the Great War and the profound social disturbances that immediately resulted – mass unemployment, the breakdown of traditional regimes, the challenge of Marxism and so forth. Literary Modernism has been seen as resulting from a traumatic breach with the past; indeed, this diagnosis was supported by Richard Ellmann, one of Yeats's earliest and most sensitive biographers. Despite this persuasive argument, notable Modernists – Eliot, Faulkner, Pound, and Yeats certainly – are regarded as preoccupied with the past, the past as the better part of a comparison with the fury and the mire of modern times. In each case, history and myth both contend for supremacy. No one would want to confuse Mussolini's invocations of ancient Rome, or Hitler's Teutonic fantasies, with the Celtic Revival fabric of Yeats's early poetry and drama. But in February 1934 the new regime in Frankfurt-am-Main chose a fresh production of 'The Countess Cathleen' (1892, dedicated to Maud

Gonne) as their way of celebrating Goethe's centenary. And in October of the same year the playwright spoke at the Fourth Congress of the Alessandro Volta Foundation in Rome.

Germany, Not Just Italy

It is fitting that what we know of Yeats at the Volta Congress, we learn from Walter Starkie who accompanied him. The judicious communicators will respond, predictably, that here I am confusing associations with affinities. For the moment, we are still engaged with the animating theme. Yeats in Italy, Yeats declining an invitation to Nazi Germany, serves to emphasise his relative indifference to contemporary European culture. Though he travelled several times to Italy in the 1920s and '30s, and also convalesced in Spanish Majorca, Yeats had little or no contact with writers of his own generation or younger. Like any good Victorian of limited means, Europe for him was France, known since early manhood. As a consequence, he appears to have had no knowledge of such Italian poets as Giosuè Carducci (1835–1907), Giuseppe Ungaretti (1888–1970) or Eugenio Montale (1896–1981). Writers to whom he does refer – Gabriele D'Annunzio (1863–1938) and Luigi Pirandello (1867–1936) – were not only closer to him in time, but regarded fascism with approval. This may suggest a generational factor at work in directing certain writers towards totalitarianism. In the case of Yeats and Italy, it also underlines his preference for men of ideas rather than literati – the philosopher Benedetto Croce (1866–1952) features more often than any poet.

As for Germany, Yeats never set foot in the place, knew little or nothing of the language, and limited his reading to mystics like Jakob Boehme (1575–1624) or the classico-romantic Johann Wolfgang von Goethe (1749–1832). He does not appear to have known anything of R. M. Rilke until a decade after the Prague-born poet's death in 1926. Despite this apparent handicap, Yeats publicly endorsed German racial legislation in August 1938, a time when the character of the regime was beyond doubt or redemption. His declaration followed some assiduous 'wooing' by the Nazi regime – in 1934 when he was awarded the Goethe Plakette, and the next year when his seventieth birthday was celebrated in the Reich press. In some regards, the course of German history in Yeats's lifetime moved in mirror-reversal to that of Ireland. These particular regards – notably the relationship between effective power and representative democracy – were important for Yeats. A moment of intersection between two national 'destinies' had come in 1916, when Roger Casement sought support in Berlin for an Irish rebellion and was tried for treason as a consequence. Yeats's busy but ambiguous attitude towards the condemned man in mid-war is resurrected twenty years later, *entre les guerres*, in the emergence of a forgery theory to explain Casement's homosexual diaries. If the dead Casement had a lasting influence on Irish-German relations, Yeats helped to keep the axis well oiled.

On this last topic, the ghostly Casement will join the lesbian Wellesley in keeping the poet awake, though neither is recruited here to serve with the Blood Kindred. Behind the continuities of Irish nationalist complaint, Germany provides a figure of Yeats's own stature with whom he may properly be compared. Thomas Mann (1875–1955), winner of the Nobel Prize in 1929, will contribute valuably to the assessment of Yeats's political values. Yeats rarely mentions the novelist by name, though in his last years he sprinkles occasional references to thinkers such as Hegel and Husserl, with whom he had at best a nodding acquaintance of the Homeric kind. It will be a central proposition of *Blood Kindred* that, as Nobel laureates whom the public recognised, Yeats and Mann engaged in an undeclared but traceable duel for the conscience of European literature in the second quarter of the twentieth century.

For obvious reasons, Germany witnessed some of the most painful and complex exchanges between fascism and the profession of literature and of culture generally. From the moment of Hitler's accession, distinguished exiles from the Reich began to arrive in Britain, Denmark, France, the Soviet Union, Switzerland and the United States. Their names are well known, including Hannah Arendt, Bertolt Brecht, Marlene Dietrich, Thomas Mann, Stefan George, Ernst Toller, Bruno Walter and hundreds of other, scarcely lesser, names. The time-servers who took their places are happily forgotten. There was, however, a third category of German intellectuals who, finding Nazism inimical, nevertheless opted to remain inside Germany. These included at least one writer whom Yeats knew personally – Gerhart Hauptmann (1862–1946). Among musicians, Wilhelm Furtwängler (1886–1954) claimed that his staying at home gave some comfort and protection to Jewish members of his orchestra, though the behaviour of Richard Strauss (1864–1949) has attracted a more critical response. While its publication lies outside the period covered by *Blood Kindred*, Thomas Mann's last great novel, *Doktor Faustus* (1947), presents its allegory of Germany's descent into political madness through the biography of a musical genius, the fictional Adrian Leverkuhn. As with Yeats's play, 'The Countess Cathleen' (produced in Frankfurt in 1934), Mann's novel takes as its central motif the willingness of a human being to enter into a compact with Satan for what appears to be a good cause.

Alongside the stay-at-home musicians were figures of considerable international stature in other spheres of cultural activity. Apart from the elderly Hauptmann, the most distinguished writer who remained was Gottfried Benn (1886–1956). Far more influential both inside and outside the Reich was Martin Heidegger (1889–1976), whose *Sein und Zeit* (1927) marked a turning point in twentieth-century thought. While Heidegger could hardly be regarded as a figure generally comparable to Yeats – different as chalk and Cheshire cheese – the philosopher's relationship with fascism has been the subject of exacting analysis. In the context of Germany's public debate in the 1980s on the topic of historical revisionism, Jurgen Habermas moved to counter the tendency among some historians and politicians to relativise the unprecedented crimes against humanity committed by the Nazis. While the obvious differences should be respected, certain points in his account of Heidegger's philosophy, his behaviour during and after the Reich, and his subsequent reputation can assist in illuminating what is obscure in Yeats's political life.

Heidegger's major contribution to philosophy was published when he was only thirty-seven. The apex of Yeats's poetry came with *The Tower* in 1928 when he was approaching sixty-three. In the period immediately following, both men experienced a turning in their outlook and mode of expression (as did others in the same years). Habermas relates his countryman's altered attitude to the economic crisis of 1929 and the collapse of the Weimar Republic. In Yeats's case, the public causes might be identified in the assassination of the Irish government minister, Kevin O'Higgins (in July 1927), and his own resignation from the Irish Senate in September 1928. Of course, cause and effect often work contrarily, and so we might see in the resignation an effect rather than a cause. In the event, the invocation of eighteenth-century dignity that provides one of the organising principles of the title-poem ('The Tower') will be replaced by a more passionate, not to say frenzied, style in poems written shortly afterwards. Ceasing to be an Irish member of parliament, Yeats moved to Rapallo in Mussolini's Italy for the winter.

Heidegger's 'turning' involved a specific distortion or reorientation of the philosophy laid down in *Sein und Zeit* and implicit in his general position as a German thinker. In March 1929, he spoke dismissively of Goethe and eighteenth-century German Idealism, much to the surprise of his colleague, Ernst Cassirer. Installed as Rector of Freiburg University a few months later, he embarked on an audacious reformulation of the philosopher's role, which led in time to a purging of Jews from the academic staff. Having joined the Nazis in May 1933, he had no difficulty in identifying Hitler as the leader whom he must (philosophically) lead. Apocalyptic catastrophe loomed, and it behoved them to avert it by all means available, including technology. This last was to be understood as – simultaneously – 'mystery, security, danger'. Any sophisticated sense of history, or of a long-evolving complex human society, was replaced by doctrines of immediacy, crisis and action.

In fact, Heidegger resigned from the rectorship in April 1935, and apparently became disillusioned with Nazi policy or at least its implementation. In Habermas's words, he had to 'demote fascism and its leaders into symptoms of the disease they were originally supposed to heal'.[13] Habermas also contests the actuality of this, demonstrating the philosopher's repeated approval of Nazism in pronouncements dating from the mid-1930s well into the war years. A renunciation that affirms is not impossible in German dialectics; Hitler's mistake in the summer of 1934 had been to purge the true radicals – led by Ernst Röhm – from the movement, and thereafter he could only aspire to mortal glory. Yeats's own brief correspondence with Nazi Germany occurred in the run-up to this Night of the Long Knives on 30 June 1934.

More significant, however, is his own parallel disillusionment with Röhm's pale Irish imitators. The Blue Shirts acquired political focus through a new party, Fine Gael, which failed to make an impact in local elections held during the summer of 1934. Having written songs for the Shirts, Yeats declared himself unimpressed and sought to rewrite them, but in a manner that would prevent their easy exploitation. The intention was not disengagement, but an intensified search for 'unity of culture':

If any Government or party undertake this work it will need force, marching men; (the logic of fanaticism, whether in a woman or a mob is drawn from a premise protected by ignorance and therefore irrefutable) ... There is no such government or party today; should either appear I offer it these trivial songs and what remains to me of life.[14]

That was in April 1934.

There remains one final question on which Habermas's account of Heidegger can be helpful in beginning to understand Yeats's political career – racism. 'In spite of Heidegger's sustained relationship with one of the leading Nazi theoreticians of race, he was himself no racist; his anti-Semitism, so far as it can be confirmed at all, was rather of the usual, culturistic, breed.'[15] It is debatable whether a distinction between the two kinds (or generations) of anti-Semitism was of any practical use to any Jews in Germany and (later) Occupied Europe. Certainly, Ireland knew little or nothing of the newer anti-Semitism, at once 'scientific' and political. A comparison of Yeats with his friends T. S. Eliot, Maud Gonne and Oliver St John Gogarty would go a long way towards clearing him of having an *a priori* charge to answer. Yeats's occasional comments on Jews in Ireland can be considered in due course, together with the absence of any comments on Jews in trouble elsewhere. Heidegger's attitudes in this area included a '*neo-pagan turn* that pushed Christian themes into the background in favour of a mythologising recourse to the archaic'.[16] In this connection too, one can in due course notice a similar (if lesser) turn in Yeats's attitudes during the 1930s. Finally, one notes that both Yeats and Heidegger were enthusiastically taken up by coteries of Japanese admirers in the decade that saw fascism acquire its most powerful Asian ally.[17]

Mind and Loins

Blood Kindred is not to be concerned disproportionately with the 1930s, nor will it concentrate on fascism to the exclusion of other political interests and commitments. But of the – say – five decades in which Yeats was active in some political sense or other, the 1930s undeniably was the most tumultuous, and his utterances the most vigorous. This last phenomenon is directly connected with his pursuit of sexual renewal through surgery, and (in its own arcane way) his cult of the body. Right at the end of his life, he told Maud Gonne that 'for the first time I am saying what I believe about Irish and European politics'.[18] An explanation of this lifelong self-imposed embargo can only be pursued by first examining the circumstances in which it is lifted, and then by tracing back to its origins the repressions and drives that led to its establishment in his psyche.

In advance of that progressive retreat into Yeats's mid-Victorian origins, some further comparisons should be sketched in. If German instances have taken on an unexpected prominence in the *dramatis personae*, the reason may lie in the limited opportunities afforded by contemporaries closer to hand and comparable in achievement or intelligence. While Eliot (English or American) had been active in London, the crucial difference between them arises from their dates of death, not their national origins or affiliations. Eliot's way of dealing with contemporary politics was a variant on repression. That is, he chose to assign to other sources those aspects of fascism that he appropriated or approved. Later in life, he suppressed *After Strange Gods* (1934) with its explicit anti-Semitism, though this did not inhibit him from contributing a strange preface to *The Dark Side of the Moon* (1946).[19] In a volume dedicated to Poland's wartime history, the absence of any reference to Auschwitz, the Warsaw uprising or Jews of any kind constitutes a major achievement of the *suppressio veri* kind. Discussion of Eliot's politics has drawn in Christopher Ricks and Tom Paulin, with characteristic passion on each side of the argument.[20]

The ferocity of disagreement between Modernist writers has largely been lost sight of, as they congregate happily on academic syllabuses in a bizarre afterlife. Eliot's principal antagonist in *After Strange Gods* had been D. H. Lawrence, with whom Yeats might be usefully compared, especially on the topic of the Great War. But Lawrence's death in 1930 curtailed his passionate irrationalism to the period before Yeats's 'turning'. To judge from surviving correspondence, Yeats only got down to reading Lawrence's novels in the autumn of 1932 while staying at the Netherland Plaza, Cincinatti, Ohio. He was enthusiastic, but worried that boredom might set in.[21] William Faulkner (1897–1962), whom Yeats seems never to have read, may prove to be a more revealing comparison (see 'Second-Hand Tragedy', pp. 377–407).

There are manifest limitations to the comparative method, useful though it is in directing one's attention outside the self-defining parameters of the writer's individual world. Yeats's personality has endless fascination for biographers, though Terence Brown is the first to register an understandable distaste for some of his subject's antics and attitudes. Others have, for the most part, been persuaded that the scale of Yeats's literary genius prohibits minor complaints about snobbery, bullying or a tight purse. If a contradiction is highlighted here, perhaps it is not a unique one. Yeats himself wrote at length about conflict within the self, about rival selves, masks, and the like. One wonders at times if the cumbersome sophistication of his presentation is not itself a mask designed to repel those keen to understand. In such a case, the enquirer may learn more by turning away and looking elsewhere.

Eugène Delacroix (1798–1863) is remote enough from both Dachau and Drumcliff, yet Yeats paid him the compliment of citation in 'A Nativity' (August 1936). Delacroix's celebrated 'Liberty Leading the People' (1832) would hardly have done in either place, while his Algerian and other exotic scenes no doubt constitute orientalist crimes.[22] Charles Baudelaire (1821–1867) saw Delacroix as the last great artist of the Renaissance and the first modern. More particularly he characterised him as man with a passion for passion. Behind the characteristically Baudelairean paradox lies the implication that strong feeling in Delacroix existed to the power two, but at second remove. Together with intensity, there was calculation or at least ratiocination.[23] Yeats's 'A Nativity' appears to recruit the French painter to arrange the draperies at some further Second Coming. Draperies both conceal and keep the cold out or, with dextrous management, both reveal and expose. In a late letter to the English novelist Ethel Mannin, Yeats noted a comparable contrivance in his own emotional make-up. 'Because I want to live without automatic love & hate, I find that I must play my part in life as if in a charade.'[24]

A cold-eyed Yeats had much to offer. A certain southern Irish ability to stomach atrocities committed (elsewhere) by the Provos took nourishment from the apparent endorsement given by Yeats to their *soi-disant* precursors. But not for long. The nervousness, still evident among some leading Yeats scholars in Britain, at the corrosive impact of Provo 'thought' (on academic debate, the media and public opinion generally) may be excessive. To be fair, the temptation that has unfocused a few is *suppressio veri* rather than its companion, *suggestio falsi*: that is, Yeatsians have occasionally been willing to hide what is indecorous in the master's thoughts, words or deeds, out of – let us suppose – a fear that he might be mistaken for a rough beast, an affable Irregular, or one of those German U-boat commanders of the Great War whom he praised on the eve of its resumption.

The violence that links these three potential alibis is not something now imposed upon by Yeats in the aftermath of a longer bloody conflict in Ireland than any witnessed in his lifetime. In a phrase that Roy Foster had wisely highlighted in the Introduction to his two-volume biography, Ezra Pound had acutely diagnosed its centrality to his friend's character. 'Yeats knows life, despite his chiaroscuro, and his lack of a certain sort of observation – He learns by emotion, and is one of the few people who have ever had any, and who know what violent emotion really is like; who see from the centre of it – instead of trying to look in from the rim.' That was December 1915, after a year of slaughter in France, and four months short of the Dublin insurrection led by the secret society of which he was a (largely inactive) member. Yeats's own assessment of his personality acknowledged its violence, though in more complex ways than Pound allowed for. Late in his life, he admitted, 'All my life it has been hard to keep from action, as I wrote when a boy, – "to be not of the things I dream." '[25]

Baudelaire's analysis of Delacroix, and Yeats's own dichotomising of dream and action, accord strangely with the phrase that Cruise O'Brien chose as the title for his impressive article of 1965 – 'Passion and Cunning'. Cruise O'Brien's credentials as literary critic and political commentator have taken a battering since then, partly at his own hands. And the term 'cunning' is too emotive exactly to match what the splenetic Parisian saw in Delacroix. Nevertheless, if it were possible to design a double-helix representing the mind and loins coiled round each other – and drawings from *A Vision* might suggest models – then such a DNA diagram would approximate to the genius of Yeats.

Provocative as it was, Baudelaire's conceit was original only in its formulation. The relationship between thought and emotion, mind and body, has been a major theme of western philosophy since ancient times. At the beginning of the nineteenth century, romantic Idealism favoured the mind in theory, but liberated the body in the practice of notable individuals. Among Yeats's early heroes, Percy Bysshe Shelley achieved martyrdom as a philosophical atheist and victim of drowning. Divergent genealogies of 'the modern' give the palm to the French generation of which Baudelaire is the best known; or, in the English-speaking world, to Eliot, Pound and Yeats. While a third chronology is implicit for Germany, which before 1871 lacked the centralised confidence of a nation-state, the rock round which these modernist waves broke was evolution. The anxieties of

Tennyson and of Victorian England are well known; across the Channel, a literary avant-garde had raised its war-cry before *On the Origin of Species* (1859) challenged all assumptions about mind and body. These contrasting timetables had political implications, partly as a consequence of Chartism, 'the year of revolutions' (1848) and the *coup d'état* of Louis Bonaparte. But in Ireland, it was different again.

We know Yeats's own assessment of his own inheritance, and his early dreams of escape:

> I was unlike others of my generation in one thing only. I am very religious, and deprived by Huxley and Tyndall, whom I detested, of the simple-minded religion of my childhood, I had made a new religion, almost an infallible Church of poetic tradition, of a fardel of stories, and of personages, and of emotions, inseparable from their first expression, passed on from generation to generation by poets and painters with some help from philosophers and theologians. I wished for a world where I could discover this tradition perpetually, and not in pictures and in poems only, but in tiles round the chimney piece and in the hangings that kept out the draught.[26]

Here is no mere record of a Victorian religious crisis ingeniously resolved. Yeats claims to have made a new religion of elements inseparable from their unique primary expression, yet one which is also passed already through successive generations. Having made it, he wished for a world where he could find it. The Transcendental Self (or subject) is simultaneously a shivering object, and an empty-handed alchemist in the ingle-nook.

Characteristically, Yeats adopts this perspective on his youthful crisis of belief, not in the first volume of autobiography, but – as late as 1920, when he was fifty-five and married – in the second. Its title echoing a fable of the 1890s, *The Trembling of the Veil* (1922) appeared in the modernist *annus mirabilis* of *The Waste Land* and *Ulysses*. Among the Anglophone writers, Yeats dedicated a sizeable portion of his creative time to writing his own life. The obligation to weave the past into the present, and to establish a narrative across seismic breakdowns, discontinuities, gaps and – of course – aporias was zestfully maintained by the Nobel Prize winner. If, as Michael Longley has sought to remind readers of Irish poetry, the ancient Greeks located the future *behind* us, the future in 1920s Europe formed a darkening background to brilliant experiments in literature, music and painting. Oswald Spengler (1880–1936) had published *The Decline of the West* in 1918: within half a decade, its vaporously gloomy prophecies had become commonplaces. By the middle of 1925, even Yeats was paying attention to translated excerpts in *The Dial*. His conviction grew with his enthusiasm. Spengler had 'lit on a number of the same ideas as those in my book ... the introduction ... might have been a chapter of "A Vision" ... his thought & mine differ in nothing'.[27] By late summer, he was reading *The Decline* in his tower as he worked on *A Vision*. The past was now moving round so as to be located ahead of us.

One of the most poignant allusions in Yeats's poem, 'The Tower', draws upon the work of a great precursor, the author of 'Il Penseroso'. Few would deny that Milton was a political poet, even by the stratagem of counter-arguing that he was – but on separate occasions – a poet and a politician. In Yeats's generation, Milton's work had been denigrated by Eliot, who found in him a too-powerful instance of that 'dissociation of sensibility' which allegedly fell upon culture in the seventeenth century. It is some indication of Eliot's grasp on culture that, seeking to illustrate what 'the ordinary man' might thoughtfully do, he proposes the reading of Baruch Spinoza.[28] What is needed is 'unity of culture' so that falling in love and reading Spinoza would have something to do with each other. For that we need 'unity of culture'. Eliot says so, Yeats says so, and Heidegger says so.

We know what Heidegger's preferred reformers had in mind, and we shall see very shortly what Yeats thought of their early strivings. One reason for pressing on with this supernumerary life of the poet is that their past still lies ahead of us, unfinished, unsatisfied. An apprehension of this radical continuity came to me one evening in the 1990s, when I visited Francis Stuart in the Meath Hospital, Dublin. The ninety-year-old novelist and son-in-law of Maud Gonne had broken his hip at home, and was recuperating with the aid of Heidegger's *Introduction to Metaphysics*. Of all the Meister of Messkirch's texts, this is the most plainly Nazi, amalgamating 'being' (*Dasein*) with the being and mission of the German people under Hitler.[29] Stuart, of course, was fond of provocative display. No such explanation springs to mind when one finds Dr Ella O'Dwyer employing this Heidegger text *and no other*, this one philosophical text and no other, in her reading of Irish history and post-colonialism from Wolfe Tone to Chinua Achebe.[30] Against such militant partiality, the need to analyse, to clarify, and to reflect becomes all the more urgent.

O'Dwyer quotes Edward Said in her support. Said, in the passage quoted, is striving to illuminate Yeats's predicament as he writes 'the poetry that culminates in *The Tower*', yet has oddly chosen to see 'the Anglo-Irish conflict [as] a model of twentieth-century wars of liberation'.[31] Odd, because few of these have taken place within a unitary state with parliamentary democracy operating throughout. Odder still is Yeats's role at the point referred to as a member of an Irish democratic parliament, albeit a member increasingly authoritarian in his politics, reading Spengler and recommending L'Action française. As a life of Yeats, *Blood Kindred* has a double obligation. It should persuade readers who see Yeats solely as the author of magnificent poetry and drama that his 'occasional foray into public affairs' was not such a mere thing, that politics animated the poet as poet. But it should also (at least seek to) persuade those who see Yeats as a champion of the oppressed, an example to the Third World and a paragon of post-colonialist virtue that he was indeed a political animal, but not their political animal – or Aristotle's, either.

Flirtation and Hatred

In 1911, years after Thomas Hardy had abandoned fiction for poetry, he turned to an essentially novelistic theme which, true to his self-denying ordinance, he treats in dramatic monologue form. A man who hires a younger man to woo and then abandon the hirer's beloved is forced to kill (in Venice) the too-successful wooer, then marries his woman at home in England and begets a son. The child comes to consciousness believing that his false father has murdered his true, and the mother drowns herself (in echoes of Venice). In the words of perhaps the only critic to review this obscure poetic fiction, Hardy's grim texts reveals 'the murderous competitive beast in man, engendering anxieties over romantic faithfulness that congeal into a cross-generational curse'.[32] Hardy called it 'The Flirt's Tragedy'. Did he name it well?

If the Nazis wooed Yeats, they certainly did not woo James Joyce or Sean O'Casey. (G. B. Shaw is a different matter again.) The behaviour is inseparable from the language employed. The study of literature is said to train the mind in assessing language against action, as when we wonder if Hardy named his 1911 monologue aptly, or ironically, or provocatively ... or whatever. And the study of literature prompts questions of comparative measurement, if not judgment, sometimes within the literary domain and sometimes beyond any metaphor of 'domains'. Close to Hardy's time, the German philosopher Georg Simmel (1858–1918) wrote about flirtation as an essentially metropolitan activity, though he also regards it as a female art aspiring to 'the simultaneity of consent and refusal'. In this reading, does Hardy's plot resemble any Yeatsian drama?

Among the metaphors for politics repeatedly applied by critics and biographers of Yeats in this regard, none has been more tenacious than his 'flirtation' with fascism. Perhaps alliteration is to be blamed, but the mental tic is to be heard in many different quarters – Cleanth Brooks, Terence Brown, Anthony Cronin, Robert Fisk, Grattan Freyer, Marjorie Hawes and Anthony J. Jordan are just some contrasting instances. In Roy Foster's conclusive second volume of *W. B. Yeats, a Life*, it is the baptismal name under which the subject is rescued from original sin.[33]

It is a suggestive word suggesting suggestiveness – its polite euphemism covers a multitude or a solitude. Flirtation appears to be a great deal, but does nothing, or so its adepts suggest. Flirtation suggests an interest that is ultimately unsustained, indeed one that has no intention of sustaining itself. While describing Yeats's interest as 'transient', Foster repeats the denial through a further 200 pages. If indeed Yeats's relationship to fascism was simply of this kind, then it would hardly deserve more consideration than a passing interest in blood-sports. But 'flirtation' has its reflex aspect also: it connotes a desire to provoke a response and to observe that response from the security of the flirter's knowing that s/he intends no ultimate commitment. At this level it is both reciprocal and exploitative, a privileged manoeuvre. Thirdly, it is an emotional initiative rife with bodily potential: the origins of the word lie in the verb to throw suddenly, or to cock the nose, or to move with a springing action. In Dashiell Hammett's *The Glass Key* (1931), the anti-hero 'flirted a hand at Madvig', by way of greeting.

Simmel before the Great War was less concerned with the sociology of flirting than with new patterns of neurotic behaviour. But the seriousness of flirtation, its significance as a phenomenon in modern life, can be judged by his association of its playfulness with part of Immanuel Kant's famous definition of art, its 'purposiveness without purpose'.[34] When in the 1930s Yeats was engaged in what he *never* calls, but his defenders *invariably* call, a flirtation with fascism, the autonomy theory of art was itself under attack from both left and right.

These levels of meaning deserve more than a casual glance. Most users of the metaphor in connection with Yeats and fascism are consciously or semi-consciously discounting the seriousness of his interest or commitment: nevertheless, they simultaneously confirm the central position of the body in fascist ideology – the insistent saluting, massed demonstrations balanced with eugenical zealotry, the cult of physique and (not least, the counterpart of glorified physique) the systematic use of torture. Louis MacNeice, who did not opt for the metaphor of flirtation, is an early observer of Yeats's sadomasochism.[35] In the idiom adopted by some of the poet's recent academic admirers, fascism is 'a gender question'. In Yeats, we notice his practice of corresponding with women to discuss extreme politics, while looking to men for an embodiment of it.

Yeats did not merely flirt with Italian and German fascism, he pursued those interests with passion. I would say, however, that his engagement began in something like the attitude of the flirter. Then, as he discovered by rigorous self-examination that he lacked the power that sustains 'flirtation', he sought that power itself by maintaining, even heightening, the interest in fascism. Perhaps he was disappointed. Certainly others (to adapt J. M. Keynes) all ended up dead in their millions.

Why should Yeats be so categorically difficult? Or, to put the question more sharply, why should critics and readers be so anxious to deny or distort the political aspect of Yeats's vision? The answer to the last question provides an explanation for the shape of the present book: during the 1930s Yeats acquired a contagion he despised in others, and it is through an understanding of that period that we must look for a key to his particular conjunction of politics and poetry. In defiance of the normal decencies, this biographical study does not begin at the beginning (Dublin, 13 June 1865), but instead seeks to understand Yeats's effective origins in Victorian Ireland through a series of retrospections. Biographical narrative requires, as the King of Wonderland insisted, that one should begin at the beginning and go until he comes to the end. Biographical enquiry may thrive on different priorities. Lewis Carroll was not an author Yeats valued early or late in his life.

Edmund Burke was, at times. There is a remark attributed in various forms to him. 'For evil to triumph, all that is necessary is for the good man to do nothing.' Yeats's interest in the eighteenth century had many sources, including the work of his younger friend and biographer, Joseph Hone. While the Yeatsian tradition of Augustan Ireland is usually dated to his last decade or two, the theme can be traced earlier. In 'The Tables of the Law' (1896), the fictional character Owen Aherne declares that 'Jonathan Swift made a soul for the gentlemen of this city by hating his neighbour as himself.' Not only the name of Swift, and the emotion of hatred, will recur: Yeats's concern with class collectivity – in this case, the urban gentry in George II's time – will play its part in the development of his politics. Not only politics, but great poetry is affected.

In the third section of 'Nineteen Hundred and Nineteen', Yeats conjures his most sublime image of the imagination. It begins with the uncharacteristic acknowledgment of a debt:

> Some moralist or mythological poet
> Compares the solitary soul to a swan;
> I am satisfied with that.
> Satisfied if a troubled mirror show it,
> Before that brief gleam of its life be gone,
> An image of its state ...

Reading these lines, one happily concedes Yeats's incomparable greatness as a poet of the modern age. The troubled surface is at once the lake upon which the bird moves subject to 'those winds that clamour of approaching night' and the ordinary life of the poet upon which the imagination seeks to bear itself. That life vexes as well as supports, it troubles and supports ... So far, this analysis has kept to the conventional procedures of summarising and approving what the poet has said, demonstrating his genius by the inadequacy of the summary. But the troubled surface is declared to be a mirror, and one is immediately caught in less readily negotiated exchanges. Is the mirror troubled because it truthfully reflects the trouble besetting that which it reflects? Or is the mirror troubled *qua* mirror? If the latter – for the former seems too trite to be Yeatsian – then are we entitled to translate further and to see in reflection an image for a broader category of representation?

These are, or can be shown as, political implications, with theories of representation at their heart. But before moving to consider related issues in Yeats's use of discursive terms, we owe the admired poem more time. The word 'it' in the fourth line quoted above has for referent the noun 'swan' – surely? There are problems in such a reading, unless we are prepared to accept that 'it' refers also to the solitary soul; and to do that involves allowing that the solitary soul and the swan are both comparable and identical, a thing not desirable either in logic or theology. Yeats has moved from a poetry of the loosest simile – borrowed simile – to one of enacted metaphor, and the implications are profound and profoundly disturbing. We would not want to return to the trite reading, but we should be chilled by the right reading.

Traditionally, swans are invoked for their delayed gratifying death-sound, the incomparable song they make at the end. Additionally, they are presented as those rare birds which, though powerful, are also demure. Their heads are lowered, protective of their young or intent on the element they move on. After life, the soul is no longer solitary, but is gathered to its proper company – gentlemen of a celestial city, to use inadequate Church of Ireland clichés. But another part of Yeats's imagery refers us – wittingly or otherwise – back to the previous poem in *The Tower*. This is 'Meditations in Time of Civil War' in whose penultimate section the poet pleads with bees lodged in the loosening masonry of his own house that they should 'Come build in the empty house of the stare'.

The poet's own commentary on these lines relates them to a period of isolation which he and his family experienced at the tower in County Galway during the violence of 1922. No news seeped through, though explosions were heard and coffins observed in passing motor-cars. Sound and sight, aspects of the emblematic swan, but now presented by Yeats in his summary as prompting a desire 'not to lose all sense of the beauty of nature'. By the end of the poem/section, the bees in the masonry have become 'honey-bees', an unlikely transformation – unless, of course, Yeats has transferred his plea to a different species of bee. His knowledge of natural history was not extensive or accurate, and his explanation that 'the stare' is 'our West of Ireland name for a starling' has surprised many from that part of the world. There is another knowledge, however, transcending such quibbles. 'Presently, a strange thing happened. I began to smell honey in places where honey could not be.' Transcendental knowledge.

While 'Meditations in Time of Civil War' draws on such psychic resources, it also notes with admirable frankness the deterioration resulting because 'We have fed the heart on fantasies'. Mildly echoing Swift, Yeats notes 'More substance in our enmities / Than in our love'. Then, in the climactic final section of the poem, he presents its cavalry charge of apocalyptic images. The section is named 'I See Phantoms of Hatred and of the Heart's Fullness and of the Coming Emptiness' but, with the poem's two-and-a-half closing lines, the high futurism of this is cancelled and folded back into time past:

> The abstract joy,
> The half-read wisdom of daemonic images,
> Suffice the ageing man as once the growing boy.

How had the growing poet, if not still a boy, reflected on such themes? Though the dying cadences of the poem suggest a closure of argument, the words mutely invite an enquiry into questions of earlier attitude. To forward our understanding of the poem we need to look back. This is not to accept that the 'haughtier age' recalled in the first section possessed Golden qualities befitting an arcadian or Edenic condition from which man – especially Irishman – has fallen. And if the invitation were taken to enquire into where one might (speculatively) locate those 'great chambers and long galleries lined / With famous portraits of our ancestors', the answers might prove embarrassing rather than enhancing. We shall poke into one or two adjacent corners of these impressive architectural frames in the chapter devoted to Yeats's Victorian Kindred.

These minor matters aside, the final lines of 'Meditations in Time of Civil War' powerfully suggest a congruence in the responses of ageing man and growing boy alike, a response compacted in the diplomatic verb to 'suffice'. Hatred, envisaged in the poem's last section-title, strikes a different note. As we shall see, the word is stamped into each of the last four of ten stanzas in 'A Prayer for My Daughter', written in the first half of 1919. Indeed, it can be traced like the hoof-marks of an errant thoroughbred crossing the well-trimmed lawns of poetry and the herbaceous beds of private correspondence. Yeats is not always opposed to hatred; sometimes he prides himself on possessing that emotion, at other times he harnesses it to a suitable partner emotion. The word, with its cognate verbs, also occurs casually as in anybody's personal letters – hating a fuss, and so forth. However, there are occasions when hatred seems to be in charge of its rider, and not the other way round. And, as in 'A Prayer', Yeatsian hatred accumulates.

I see it as an emotion that cannot be feigned, cannot be worked up through imitation into the real thing. It is primary, even perhaps more so than love, though love may precede it. In 1900, when considering who from the Irish literary movement might tour the United States of America, Yeats remarked to Augusta Gregory how changeable in attitude George Moore was: 'his look changes & he becomes perfectly hateful'. Moore, at these moments, is not hate-filled by himself, but hated by Yeats, though the level of animus between them will increase greatly with the years. In the same letter, he expounds a political objective that replaces one political vocabulary with another, with hatred as the new centre:

> To transmute the anti-English passion into a passion of hatred against the vulgarity of a materialism whereon England found her worst life & the whole life that she sends us has always been a dream of mine.[36]

Six years later, Yeats was in touch with Florence Farr and transcribed for her songs from his play, 'The Unicorn from the Stars' (1908):

> O, they hurl a spell at him
> That he follow with desire
> Bodies that can never tire
> Or grow kind, for they anoint
> All their bodies joint by joint
> With a miracle working juice,
> That is made out of the grease
> Of the ungoverned unicorn;
> But the man is thrice forlorn
> Emptied, ruined, wracked and lost
>
> That they follow, for at most
> They will give him kiss for kiss
> While they murmur 'After this
> Hatred may be sweet in the taste.'
> Those wild hands that have embraced
> All his body can but shove
> At the burning wheel of love
> Till the side of hate comes up.

In the letter Yeats helpfully added, 'The hero had been praising an indomitable kind of woman and the chorus sing of her evil shadow. The Unicorn in the little play is a type of masterful and beautiful life but I shall not trouble to make the meaning clear . . .'[37] The quoted lines may not amount to great poetry, but they certainly convey an erotic charge along which 'hatred may be sweet'. Unconnected in substance, the letters of June 1900 and February 1906 share a common interest in the relationship of politics to sexuality. Yeats's difficulties with Moore had centred notably on Moore's disrespectful attitude towards Maud Gonne, the 'indomitable kind of woman', with Moore adding malice by asking Yeats why he had not slept with her.

Hatred and hate could be tracked through other textual paths in the years that follow. More than two decades later, and writing to a lover steadier and more enduring than Gonne or Farr, Yeats enthused about Wyndham Lewis's *Time and Western Man*: 'he has found an expression for my hatred – a hatred that being half drunk has half poisoned me'.[38] It is not clear whether this hatred is half-consumed or itself half-intoxicated, and the ambiguity suggests uncertainty or lack of full control on Yeats's part. His enthusiasm reverses an earlier opinion of 1918 when he felt that Iseult Gonne, sharing a flat in London with Lewis's mistress (Iris Barry), was moving into dangerous company. His request to Olivia Shakespear is directed even further back, to an era preceding his own boyhood. Can she establish if Mrs Wyndham Lewis, a widow whom Benjamin Disraeli married, is in any way related to the author of *Time and Western Man*, vorticist painter and Hitlerite? The urge to root in the Victorian past emerges almost unnoticed; nor should we miss the even-handedness by which Disraeli's Jewish origins are left uncommented upon, just like Wyndham Lewis's fascist politics.

The politics of hatred will be acted out in *On the Boiler* (1939), but it receives an early formulation in 'Four Philosophical Positions', which Yeats wrote out for his friend, Desmond FitzGerald, a former government minister. In the accompanying letter, he insisted that what he thought most important was 'to preserve the dynamic element of Fascism, the clear picture of something to be worked for'. The first of the four positions related to Kant; the second to Hegel:

> Hegel believes that he has solved the antinomies with his dialectic. Thesis, its negation anti-thesis, their combination synthesis. Being, non-being, becoming. Practical result, Communism.
>
> Each epoch and class is denied or refuted by a succeeding epoch or class. All the epochs and classes of a civilisation give way to a final synthesis which is so complete that it can have no successor. This is a classless, nationless condition. The individual is lost in the whole. The past is criminal. Hatred is justified.

Yeats was probably unaware of the extent to which his account of the dialectic came, not from Hegel, but from Marx's partner and heir,

Friedrich Engels. Not pausing, he outlined a third position, Italian in origin, with fascism as its 'practical result'. In this philosophical perspective, 'Every epoch or class is positive. Every civilisation reaches a final condition where the virtues of all are for all. Mankind rests in itself as shaped by history. The individual is preserved as a process of the whole without which the whole could not exist. The past is honoured. Hatred is condemned.'

One may wonder whether any close attention to the actualities of fascism, even if limited to the Italian version now augmented in March 1933 by the consolidation of Hitler's street-hurling regime, informed this synopsis. Hatred has been disposed between two abstract dispensations – one Marxist, which condemns past society and justifies hatred in this enterprise; the other fascist, which views all eras as one, and in which hatred is condemned (though quite what will efficaciously condemn hatred remains unspecified). In any case, there is a promised Fourth Position in which 'the Fascist philosophy is accepted but there is something <else> in man, which, lying deeper than intellect, is not affected by the flux of history'.[39]

For the moment we are following the spoors of hatred where they have been found in the idiosyncratic dialectic worked up between Hegel/Engels and Vico/Croce. The terms of this are not Hatred and its Opposite (e.g. love, forgiveness or redemption), but Hatred and its Condemner. Yeats's remarks on Lewis five years earlier remain relevant for, with whatever philosophical vagueness, what both pursue is a strong anti-realist position. And whereas Yeats to Olivia Shakespear had appeared to suggest a deleterious effect of hatred, to Sturge Moore a month later he expressed matters differently: *Time and Western Man* 'has given me, what I could not, a coherent voice to my hatred'.[40]

Writing to Shakespear a year later, he had another schema that related hatred to a philosophy of history, this time illustrated with lines from a poem in progress, 'Ribh Denounces Patrick'. The poem vigorously asserted supernatural begetting, while the schema associated each of the four elements with an epochal phase in man's culture. Water was equated with chivalry, 'an armed sexual age', while fire stood for 'the purging away of our civilisation by our hatred'. Since the formulation of his Four Positions for Desmond FitzGerald, Yeats had assigned to hatred a more integrated and necessary role, though, in writing to his lover of many years before, he was prepared also to provide a deeply personal agenda. 'Strange that I should write these things in my old age, when if I were to offer my self for new love I could only expect to be accepted by the very young wearied by the passive embraces of the bolster. That is why when I saw you last I named myself an uncle.'[41]

The final sentence resumes a theme of reassigned familial relationship – kindred – which played a central, and perhaps catastrophic, role in Yeats's dealings with Iseult Gonne between 1916 and 1924. As for offering himself for new love, in July 1934 he was on the brink of wholesale acquisitions in that regard, with Ethel Mannin, Dorothy Wellesley, Margot Collis and others. Politically, he has moved beyond FitzGerald and the local excitement of the Blue Shirts. Some have tried to see this as an end to the 'flirtation' with fascism: in reality, flirtation has been replaced by something more thoroughly organised, an activated desire in which love and hatred are alike required and for which we might substitute the sublunary names of sex and politics.

A year brought controversy and cross-party intercourse. The erstwhile communist Ethel Mannin intervened in a newspaper dispute about literature and political affiliation, with the unexpected consequence of a reconciliation between Sean O'Casey and Yeats. The latter was grateful to his new and left-wing love, commenting benignly, 'though your defense of propaganda has had this admirable result do not let it come too much into your life. I have lived in the midst of it, I have been always a propagandist though I have kept it out of my poems & it will embitter your soul with hatred as it has mine. You are doubly a woman, first because of yourself & secondly because of the muses whereas I am but once a woman.'[42]

Yeats's view that, when inspired by the Muse, he becomes a woman (in some sense or other), may have ancient roots, but his particular cultivation of it is a hybrid, an instance of that distinctive twentieth-century radicalised tradition of which he was the master. (Picasso was another.) The ancient roots lay deep. By the time of the great Roman poets, Virgil and Horace, inspiration in this classical sense is already a matter of conscious dedication rather than of possession by an external power. With the western Renaissance came a renewed interest in Platonist thought and the transmission of arcane knowledge of the True and the Just which, in turn, was tapped by certain figures in the Romantic Age – notably, in England, Percy Bysshe Shelley. But the individualism of post-Renaissance thinking found a place for the Muses only among other tropes and conventions.

Personal qualities of imagination, sincerity and originality superseded the older virtues or qualifications. Had Yeats known more of German Romanticism – through Coleridge, if not more directly – he might have constructed his pocket-book version of Hegelian Idealism with less debt to Engels and with a greater appreciation of how opposition, requiring negation, drives the dialectic. Instead conflict, drawing upon hatred, thrives in his late philosophy.

Alongside the hate-filled utterances just quoted, one must remember Yeats's own idiosyncratic supernaturalism. Olivia Shakespear held similar views, indeed their early intimacy had sprung from adventures among the spirits as well as the bed-springs; in 1914 her daughter married Ezra Pound, eventually to see him through his most anti-Semitic phase and into a pretended lunacy. Desmond FitzGerald was made of more orthodox stuff, being a good Catholic in search of additional weapons to fire into the English gutter-press (by which he was inordinately shocked) and into the clamorous, confused ranks of the Irish left. As for Ethel Mannin, her conversion to full-blooded irrationalism came only after the Second World War when – amongst other manoeuvres – she flirted with a fervent Catholicism that left her free to seek (unsuccessfully) to seduce Francis Stuart. Yeats's confidantes in the 1930s inspire little confidence in his judgment of character.

By what route did he reach the kind of political oracularism that gave increasing prominence to hatred? Quotations from personal correspondence are open to the charge that the writer trims his comments to suit each recipient in turn, not necessarily modifying or moderating them but, in one case or another, exaggerating them to achieve a desired response. The short history of hatred attempted above can plead innocent of any such charges, on the grounds that its findings are drawn not only from letters but also from quasi-formal documents that Yeats conveyed in or with letters. A more informal word – sincerity – should be researched with as much, if not greater, care.

Yeats in the late 1880s and '90s approved numerous minor Irish writers for their sincerity. In part this was an expression designed to acquit them of stage-Irishry or commercialism. Few of the names now register with literary historians. Writing to the abstemious Fenian, John O'Leary, in 1889, he mentioned an unexpected visitor at the Yeatses' Bedford Park home: 'Pat Gogarty, the Clondalkin shoemaker called ... the very day I came down [to Oxford] – he is over for a few days. He has really sent one or two capital studies of peasant life as far as substance & sincerity go but written in an old fashioned clumsy way.' Yeats's business in Oxford was to transcribe an Elizabethan text – 'a dull old aligory' [*sic*] – for a London publisher. 'I copy 6½ hours a day at it, never taking pen from paper except for a dip of ink. Covering so much paper gives one a fellow-feeling for the wandering Jew. Certainly he covered miles & years & I but foolscap sheets but then he walked fast & the years did not matter to him.'[43] Rosa Kavanagh and others earned similar weary plaudits for their 'sincerity'.

Some of these tributes were offered in public, through the columns of newspapers and propagandist magazines where a national literature might be encouraged. But newspaper oratory could drive the young Yeats into a fruitful perversity. To the editor of *The United Irishman*, he nervously recommended the prayer, 'O God, if this be sincerity, give us a little insincerity, a little of the self-possession, of the self-mastery that go to a conscious lie.' The argument that he developed reads oddly in the light of his later, hate-invoking opinions:

> Is not our social life ruined by the oratorical person? Whether his subject be the sins of the Parnellites or the anti-Parnellites, protection, the liquor laws, literature, or philosophy, all worthy and kindly converse dies when he enters a room. We all know his vehement intolerance – for how can he be tolerant whose world contains none but certainties? – his exaggerated opinions – for how can he be moderate who must always have a profound conviction? – his scorn of delicate half lights and quiet beauty – for how can he[,] who is ever affirming and declaring[,] understand that the gentle shall inherit the earth?[44]

By 1938, Yeats had acquired other views on inheritance, views that harmonised ironically with his easy identification of himself as scribe with the Wandering Jew. In the course of becoming a great man of letters, he had been able in 1916 to assist James Joyce, whom he recommended to Sir Edward Marsh for a Civil List pension. The letter is a model of stingy praise, with the conventional term 'sincerity' functioning almost as a slight:

> His work has a curious brooding intensity. I think one of his poems at any rate a thing of great beauty & great tecnical [*sic*] accomplishment. If I compiled an anthology of English or Irish Poetry I would include it. 'Dubliners' is like a first work of a great novelist. The background is too exclusively studied perhaps. 'The Portrait of the Artist' I have only seen in fragments but I saw enough to know that it has great intensity and

sincerity. I think him a possible man of genius, just such a man as it is well to help.[45]

Reading this, one can hear below the grumble of magnanimity a faint kiss of betrayal mixed with astuteness. Two years later, at a time of general war fatigue, and dismissing Swinburne from serious consideration as a poet, Yeats will ascribe to him the sincerity of a *Times* leading article.[46] His asperity grew in the succeeding years. Invited to attend a Great War veterans' fund-raising event in January 1921, he did not so much plead a need to defend his own sincerity as exempt himself from contributing. 'A Tribute from me would lack all sincerity. Though I might try to think of men, who served in France or Italy with a good conscience & who now perhaps need help, I would think instead of certain other ex-service men called "Auxialliary [*sic*] police" who in my own country rob & murder without hindrance.'[47] To be sure, the argument fitted his nationalist priorities, even though the veterans who disgraced civilisation in Ireland were many times outnumbered by the needy survivors of trench fever and mustard gas.

There were observers of Yeats's linguistic conduct. In March 1924 Lady Dunsany's private journal recorded her feelings on the poet's 'ingenious excuses for murder', conceding that his was a great mind. 'It makes for tolerance no doubt but also for insincerity.'[48] Behind this difference of opinion, one might read the outlines of Yeats's concern to weld all Irish classes into an acceptance of a new reality inevitably forged in violence. His invocation of an exclusively Irish politics, cancelling any other interests or obligations, was not without its exceptions. In the mid-1920s he publicly commended L'Action française in the Dublin press and quoted Mussolini with approval; a decade later, he took an active interest in Nazi propaganda and commended part of the Nuremberg code. Hatred played its part in this evolving politics, together with altering evaluations of sincerity as an artistic virtue. In 1933, an unidentified correspondent sought his advice on translating *A Vision* into French. There were certain phrases that Yeats sought to explain. 'The idea underlying "saved us from a dream" is that the ugliness of objective man and of his world inhibits the subjective dream. Think of the insistence of certain artists on ugliness, an insistence necessary to their pursuit of sincerity.'[49]

Here was Idealism that dealt with sincerity as a factor appropriate only to the relationship between objective man and his ugly material world. It is at best the in-side of a mask, the shape through which objective man looks outwards. But the world is not to be fully comprehended under aesthetic headings, and in the years of Yeats's maturity it was not only ugly but violent, riven by conflict and persecution. Perhaps it was and is always so, to one degree or another. Yeats's distinctive outlook brought together an inherited romantic aestheticism and an emotive psychology, which later highlighted hatred as its dynamic. Alfred Adler's defection from Freud's school of psychoanalysis in 1911 resulted from a related emphasis on *the motive to power*, a concept that embodies a doubled (and in extreme cases, an insatiable) need or drive.

The sources of Yeats's personal psychology are naturally diverse, almost beyond number, scarcely to be thought of as items to be gathered together or totted up. Parents made their contribution, likewise the nurture of schools and non-schools. While the shorthand term of *Zeitgeist* is crude, it summarises a perspective too often overlooked in the Irish approach to literary history, or indeed to biography of any kind. In Yeats's time, and in the actuality Yeats termed Spirit, economies and ideas were in spate. They flooded together through mill-race, forcing-house and combustion chamber; flooded through each other like air and water in steam; flooded each *as* the other, economic drive as intellectual reflection, mental event as labour process.

'All that is solid melts into air,' Karl Marx noted in a metaphor which did less than justice to his central preoccupation with constant change – think of the paradox, change that is constant, constancy that is change. That, so to speak, is a marker set down at Yeats's birth. In Samuel Beckett's first novel *Murphy*, written while Yeats was still alive, the wheelchair-bound father of Celia releases a handful of kite-twine – 'say the industrial revolution' – in a more self-consciously inadequate trope for play, for history. If twine could be adequate for one of these two, then could it be adequate for the other? If adequate as metaphor for one and the other, could it possibly *be* both?

Metaphors eventually break down like prisoners under interrogation. Yeats built poems entirely from questions – 'No Second Troy' (1908) is the best example, treating a woman who 'hurled the little streets upon the great', yet possessed beauty that was 'high and solitary'. Maud Gonne, thus imaged, is emotive and aesthetic, but only in so far as she remains a grammatical subject of interrogation. Did Yeats 'defect' from sincerity to hatred? Was the only sincerity available to him, shifting from late Romantic to proto-Modernist, hatred? Answers are not to be found exclusively within the terms of their questions. We shall look at the bleaching-greens of County Down during Yeats's grandfather's part-absentee tenure at Tullylish, a hidden Ireland pushy with factory girls and with Presbyterian leaders of the crowd. We cannot hope to link this Ulster Victorian industrialisation to the discovery of oil in the Middle East, to energy-economics and changing British attitudes to Jew and Arab. But we can note Yeats's textual shiftings from tent to tent, in his letters and plays. As he lay dying, the great powers geared up to renew the Great War, and some who were near his heart threw their little weight against the Jew. Years after Sligo 1967, did the ghost of Yeats interrogate its masks among the dead with a seminar-teaser like this:

> Did I rhyme verbose aplomb
> With nothing but a Provo's bomb?

Biography is the life one spends amongst others, especially those for whom one does nothing. Uncomfortably, there is also a chorus of Blood Kindred, the non-others whom even subjective man cannot swish away.

Some Paper Tigers

From an Aegean prison now
a Greek poet consults the sky
where sleepless, cold, computed stars
in random sequence light the bars;
and the United States, whose swell
intentions pave the road to hell,
send in the CIA to make
Cambodia safe for Dick Van Dyke.

Derek Mahon, 'Beyond Howth Head', 1970

Coventry and W. H. Auden

One of the living who conventionally responded to Yeats's death was his fellow-poet, W. H. Auden (1907–1973). The tribute involved poetry and commentary, in a manner that Yeats had practised in *The King of the Great Clock Tower*. The lesser of Auden's offerings addressed contemporary anxieties. 'The Public v. the Late Mr William Butler Yeats' appeared in the spring 1939 issue of *The Partisan Review*, in those days still robustly partisan. In it, Auden employed a court-room scenario to articulate a prosecution-and-defence account of the dead master. The younger poet was on the point of abandoning Chamberlain's Britain for the greater honesty of New York, and a dialogue between Prosecutor and Counsel for the Defence allowed him to state positions without adopting them. Of course, both statements contain acute and heartfelt judgments: it is, however, the equivocation of the form that is striking – and habit-forming among Yeats's most devoted followers.

In his final sentence, Counsel declares that 'the diction of *The Winding Stair* is the diction of a just man, and it is for this reason that just men will always recognise the author as a master'. Here may be something close to Auden's private view, though 'just' is hardly more than the cant of 1930s' politics (unless of course a Dantean justice is meant). Stridently masculinist, Counsel refers to a single collection published in 1929, that is, before Hitler troubled the age.[1] Nothing better than a 'not proven' Scottish verdict could be expected.

The Public Prosecutor opened with a claim, later argued by George Orwell with specific reference to Yeats's politics, but as yet unsubstantiated, 'that there is a close connection between the personal character of a poet and his work, and that the deceased was no exception'. The silent substitution of 'personal' for 'political' may augur a new tendency in Auden's own ideological affiliations. For the moment, his argument shifts uneasily from assertions that Yeats was an ardent neo-feudalist to insinuations that he sat on fences. 'Easter 1916' is the main exhibit. 'To succeed at such a time in writing a poem which could offend neither the Irish Republican nor the British Army was indeed a masterly achievement.' In response, Counsel for the Defence argued that Yeats's nationalism did not depend on the use of arms (at least personally) and that, in any case, 'Nationalism is a necessary stage towards Socialism.'[2] As National Socialism geared up its panzers on the Czech and Polish borders, Counsel's argument cannot be taken as Auden's.

His poem 'In Memory of W. B. Yeats' aimed far ahead of contemporary judgments. Written in February 1939 immediately after the death and obituaries, a two-part version appeared in the American *New Republic* on 8 March; the following month, the now-canonical three-part version was published in *The London Mercury*. What happened just before or in between to require so self-divergent a text? No single event will account for Auden's decision to add the present second section, with its renowned declaration that poetry makes nothing happen. But in the first three or four months of the year, the relationship between politics and poetry as Yeats knew and practised these was changed by the commencement on 16 January of an IRA bombing spree in Britain. Targets in Birmingham, London and Manchester were hit more or less simultaneously.

The Army Council which had approved the campaign was composed of men deeply critical of the previous chief of staff, Maud Gonne's son, Sean MacBride. Its members were obscure figures, though one, Máirtín Ó Cadhain (1906–1970), would subsequently become the most innovative and influential prose writer in modern Gaelic. Yeats knew MacBride and had discreetly concerned himself for the young man's welfare at the time of Kevin O'Higgins's assassination. Now MacBride resigned from the IRA, to begin his well-provendered long march towards the Lenin Peace Prize. Of Ó Cadhain, Yeats knew nothing, though the Connemara man came from a family of traditional story-tellers of the kind dear to the younger Yeats; he was a folklore collector, a school teacher dismissed by his bishop, and a gunman bent on overthrowing the State. In other words, the very paradigm of Yeats's romantic revolutionary. Before the end of 1939, he had published his first collection of short stories, *Idir Shúgradh agus Dáirire*.

The widespread and sustainable character of the campaign was soon evident. On 19 January, three days after the English bombings, an attempt on the life of Francis Chamberlain, the Prime Minister's holidaying son, was made in north Kerry. On 1 February, the Nazis sent a liaison officer (Oscar Pfaus), whose views on the Jewish Question satisfied Maud Gonne.[3] Yeats was above this kind of enterprise, yet no historian could wholly separate gross effect from self-declared cause, despite the ministrations of English ladies in Rivieran exile. When James McCormack and Peter Barnes were executed for explosions in Coventry killing five people and injuring seventy, the English did not shoot them, but hanged them after trial. Nevertheless, certain questioning lines from 'The Man and the Echo' of Yeats remained appropriate:

> Did that play of mine send out
> Certain men the English shot?

Yeats was dead, and Auden's 'In Memory' published, by the time of the Coventry bombing, yet the early impact of Sean Russell's IRA initiative is registered in Auden's meticulous, additional emphasis on 'mad Ireland' as the prompt to great poetry and on the exonerating principle (which Yeats himself could scarcely endorse) that 'poetry makes nothing happen' – especially in Coventry. Russell was financed from Berlin, and later died on a U-boat bound for an Ireland languishing in the thralls of a democracy Yeats detested. While both speakers in 'The Public v. the Late Mr William Butler Yeats' wish to admit that poetry does make something happen, the new middle section of 'In Memory' introduces an urgent clearance of suspicion, which allows the final lines of the poem – 'Teach the free man how to praise' – to seem less than mere hortation.

A Bridge Too Far

Two poets – Auden and Louis MacNeice – were to the fore in shaping Yeats's reputation in wartime, with MacNeice's *The Poetry of W. B. Yeats* appearing in 1941. The biographers were not slow to counter-attack, opening up a second front of interpretation. A two-sided image of the poet has long been in circulation. The young writer who venerated folklore and what he called 'the book of the people' became by degrees a mandarin figure scornful of popular opinion. In 1943, Joseph Hone issued what was, in effect, an official life, proposing an account of the poet most likely to harmonise any unavoidable disparities. Hone's task was not easy in wartime, especially if the political theme was maintained to the final pages.

Yeats's most sensitive biographer, Richard Ellmann, soon joined up. He found it necessary to write, in quick succession, two books to account for the complexities of Yeats's life – *Yeats, the Man and the Masks* (1948) and *The Identity of Yeats* (1954). Though Ellmann's explanation of the poet in terms of his overcoming insecurity and shyness no longer holds sway as it once did, Ellmann's own integrity as a biographer is universally acknowledged. In a new preface to *The Man and the Masks*, written in 1978, Ellmann quite bluntly records an unflattering account of Maud Gonne: 'Her passion for her adopted country was in many ways admirable, but it was adulterated by a fanatical quality which led her from the time of the Dreyfus case to anti-Semitism, and from the accession of Hitler to pro-Nazi sympathy. Hitler was to carry out the attack on Britain for which she had always longed.'[4]

When Ellmann first published his biography in 1948, Maud Gonne was still alive and, indeed, her son was Minister of External Affairs in Ireland's first inter-party government. At home and abroad, the political situation was complicated by post-war adjustments. The horrors of Auschwitz were still sinking in, and out of sight; the effect in Ireland is well caught in Thomas Kinsella's poem, 'Downstream', published in 1962 but written earlier. Ellmann had come to his task as biographer with all the alertness of a US Navy man attached to the Office of Strategic Services in London. Being a Jew, he was additionally sensitive to the unprecedented catastrophe of the Holocaust. Yet his biography steers round rather than through the topic of Yeats's politics in the 1930s, avoiding any reference to the poet's acceptance of a Nazi award in 1934 or to his public endorsement of Nazi legislation in 1938. As acute a critic as he was a biographer, Ellmann fully realised

Yeats's greatness, but somehow at that time could not come to terms with the details of such 'flirtations' with fascism.

The first so-to-speak professional biographer of Yeats, Ellmann had not been first in the field. As noted above, Hone's *W. B. Yeats 1865–1939* had been published by Macmillan of London early in 1943. Hone, who had distant family links with the Yeatses and was a friend of many years' standing, had managed to squeeze acknowledgment of the 1934 Goethe-Plakette into a footnote. The wartime circumstances in which he completed the book discouraged further elaboration. These circumstances were not yet in place when the poet had died and, while decorum and due reverence characterised the public obsequies, a different light was visible here and there.

Lurid light can blind as well as reveal. The Vision of the Blood Kindred has served its purpose as a metaphor for politics, at least in the short term. Confrontation in virtual unreality with unsought allies was an ordeal imposed on the recently dead poet which need not be perpetuated. Earthly powers greeted his demise with respect, even reverence. His close engagement with events leading to the establishment of an Irish Free State less than twenty years earlier ensured that the government in Dublin paid attention. It was an occasion of national mourning in all but official name.

Despite his stature, Yeats has not always fitted into the Irish view of things. A controversy over the naming of new public facilities in the town of Sligo illuminated the extent to which his reputation was resisted, even in the place most intimately associated with him. Decades ago a new bridge crossing the River Garravogue was diplomatically named after his contemporary, Douglas Hyde (1860–1949), a Protestant by origin like Yeats, but one closely associated with the Gaelic League, who served as the nation's first President. A few local people found the decision evasive at the time, but held their peace. When a second bridge downstream was necessitated some years later, deliberations as to its name were interrupted by one councillor who declared pointedly that, if it was not to be Yeats Bridge, then it must be Jekyll Bridge.

Looks Like Carelessness

Yeats died full of honours, at the height of his powers: proofs lay close to his hand. *The Times* obituary evoked a far older, almost Edwardian figure, an effect generated by the paper's practice of keeping obituaries on file, without always bringing them up to date. Thus, it was not unreasonable that a post-obit should make amends on 9 February 1939, with Dorothy Wellesley as its author. The crucial passage had read, 'Little more than a fortnight ago he was eagerly discussing with Austrian and German acquaintances the philosophy of the poets Stefan Georg [sic] and Rilke. He was following with sympathetic interest and shrewd practical advice the plans of a group of English friends for giving concrete expression to ideas of a constructive democracy in Great Britain.'

At first glance, Wellesley seems to be reporting a comprehensive political review by the dying poet, one that embraced the German and the British spheres, the poetic and the practical, together. Considered more closely, the two sentences emit quite distinct, even contradictory, activities. The two German poets were dead, R. M. Rilke from as far back as 1926. George – to give him his proper name – died in 1933, having gone into Swiss exile immediately on Hitler's coming to office. Death posed no barrier in itself. Both poets had been Symbolists, like Yeats himself, though German Symbolism was if anything more arcane than the Anglo-Irish instance where mixing it with the world of events remained possible. Neither Rilke nor George could be invoked as encouraging a politics either constructive or democratic. But it will be possible to identify some of Yeats's German or Austrian acquaintances with whom he spoke during the final weeks in the South of France.

Constructive democracy and the sentence devoted to it by Wellesley pose very different problems. Taken as a catch-phrase, the term probably derives from papers published in the wake of a conference held in July 1937 at Ashridge in Kent, where the Conservatives had a party 'college'.[5] Participants had included Lord Halifax (Tory Foreign Secretary), Arthur Bryant (historian), Ernest Simon and William Beveridge (civil servants), Clement Atlee (Labour Party leader), and so on – that is, spokesmen for middle-of-the-road England, supported by a few Oxford tutors. Two contributions might be thought especially appealing to Yeats, those by Sir Alfred Zimmern (on learning and scholarship) and Moritz J. Bonn. A Munich-based historical economist of Jewish background, Bonn had met Yeats in 1897 at Lady Gregory's Coole Park, and he returned to Ireland in 1903.[6] To judge from Yeats's extensive correspondence, he was not in touch with any other of these figures, and never mentioned their names in his letters. Nor does the published version of *On the*

Boiler (1939) indicate an interest in conventional British politics at that time.

But by the beginning of 1939, Ernest Simon's invocation of Constructive Democracy was taken as a rallying cry for some who were alarmed at the drift of international affairs towards extremism and conflict. Roy Foster assures us that Dorothy was an anti-appeaser, while failing to indicate when she abandoned her partiality for Hitler and instead adopted 'constructive democracy'. Her political volatility screened from comment, the effect of her post-obit was to suggest Yeats's links with *both* German culture *and* British democracy. These were the rival terms of a profound dispute which pre-dated the Great War and found notable expression in Thomas Mann's *Betrachtungen eines Unpolitischen* (1918).[7] In other words, the Irish poet bridged the extremes like a colossus, rendering them amenable to each other.

This was a clever elucidation of Yeats's recent political utterances, if indeed Wellesley was capable of cleverness. Nowhere in their intimate correspondence, which certainly discussed politics, does Ernest Simon's initiative feature; nor, frankly, is there any independent corroboration of Wellesley's claim. A different construing of Constructive Democracy, closer to her known views, would see it as a programme for consolidating the existing political system but with reduced, even minimal, reference to parliament and its tendency to criticise superior wisdom.[8] A British version of the corporate State as devised by Mussolini for Italy never found active expression, but its attractions for those enamoured of authority, power and tradition were obvious. In Yeats's back-yard, Eamon de Valera had stiffened his democratic constitution of 1937 with a corporativist aspect to the new Senate. More grandly, T. S. Eliot's essays on society and culture looked in that direction, despite the lamentable existence of Jews and other obstacles.

There was an American angle behind Eliot's concern with European civilisation. With Parke Godwin (b. 1816) and William Ellsworth Smythe (1861–1922), Constructive Democracy had its origins in a liberal (even radical) nineteenth-century New England from which Eliot had removed himself. The 'little lander' experiments of Smythe had some resemblance to the cooperativism later advocated in Ireland by Sir Horace Plunkett and Yeats's lifelong friend, G. W. Russell. But the terms of frontier self-sufficiency were readily translatable and updatable into German *Lebensraum* – the demand of the Reich to recover territories to the east; in proto-fascist Hungary, the American 'wild west' was taken up as a positive metaphor for social underdevelopment on the Great Plain. Despite Sir Ernest Simon, Constructive Democracy did not achieve a permanent place in English political debate, though the Scottish religious philosopher John MacMurray (1891–1976) published two lectures under the same title through Eliot's Faber & Faber in 1943. Like the volume prefaced by Simon in 1938, MacMurray's writings were explicitly anti-Nazi in purpose and content.

Though Wellesley's post-obit amounted to little more than a footnote to an assumed biography of the poet, according to which his occasional outbursts were inconsequential, it exemplified divisions in the mind of the genius it commemorated. 'Why should not old men be mad?' Yeats had asked in a poem written in January 1936, but unpublished until *On the Boiler* in September 1939 when the Great War resumed. By six days the IRA had anticipated Hitler's eastward aggression in Poland, launching its own blitzkrieg on Coventry. In Ireland, de Valera confirmed his country's neutrality in the world conflict. But Clissmann and Görtz, Moylett and Maud Gonne had other ideas. Each at his or her own speed would slouch towards Berlin. There was point in emphasising Yeats's more complex and anguished politics as the German war at last got under way.

A Late German Contribution

Like the dead whom Yeats respected, the issues refuse to lie down. If career-post-colonialism must take some responsibility for the confused state of American opinion regarding Yeats's politics, other theatres of interest occasionally bid to seize centre-stage in a manner not unlike Lady Wellesley's. For this reason, it is necessary to examine Yeats's German connections in two distinct stages, taking (first) the manner of their recent disinterment.

In 2002 *The Yeats Annual* published an article by K. P. S. Jochum, now retired from the University of Bamberg in southern Germany. This replied to a piece by myself called 'Samuel Beckett and *The Negro Anthology*', in which Yeats's political conduct in the 1930s was compared with that of his young fellow-Dubliner.[9] In the course of the argument, I had referred to Yeats's winning the Goethe-Plakette in February 1934 and to his manipulation by the Nazi authorities. Professor Jochum's intent was to defuse the Goethe-Plakette issue in advance of any more extensive discussion. To this end, he transcribed and published a short letter, written by Yeats to Friedrich Krebs (1894–1961), Oberbürgermeister of Frankfurt-am-Main, on 4 June 1934.[10] The Irish poet gratefully acknowledged receipt of a plaque – he spelt it 'plague' – by means of which the city of Frankfurt had conferred an award in the name of Johann von Goethe, the anniversary of whose death had occurred a full two years earlier. Scholars and general readers remain indebted to Peter Jochum for unearthing this item, in addition to his herculean achievements as the bibliographer of criticism devoted to Yeats.

Unfortunately, Professor Jochum abandoned the customary detachment of bibliographers and editors to engage, on that occasion, in personal invective and dubious historical justification. In doing so, he demonstrated the impulsive reluctance which afflicts many who delve into the question of Yeats's political interests in the 1920s and '30s. The pattern was established as far back as 1965 with Cruise O'Brien's lengthy and detailed tracing of an authoritarian strand in the poet's attitude towards politics, from the late nineteenth century through to the months preceding his death in January 1939. Though O'Brien was assailed by outraged poetry-lovers, in practice he understated the case, perhaps because he had written his article in west Africa, where access to sources was limited. Amongst the issues he omitted were: a) Yeats's acceptance of this award from a Nazi body in 1934, b) Yeats's public approval of some Nazi legislation in August 1938, and c) Yeats and anti-Semitism. Peter Jochum's excavations in the Frankfurt archives were conducted explicitly to 'clarify' the first of these, and implicitly to bury the second. The third awaits our attention (see 'The Unspeakable Question', pp. 100–131 below).

It is rarely a good idea to go in search of a hypothetical document which, if found, will answer an editor's non-editorial needs. The business of interpreting what (if anything) is found has already been compromised. Peter Jochum – a kind and generous host – had taken exception to the remark 'that Yeats was manipulated by German diplomacy during the 1930s', declaring that 'Mc Cormack does not quote any sources for this scurrilous allegation'. There are two problems here. Quite why an allegation directed at Nazis should be scurrilous remains unclear, unless (of course) Professor Jochum senses danger in any consideration of the poet with regard to the Reich. Thousands of people – great and small, high and humble – were so manipulated, and it would be naïve to suppose complete immunity even in so distinguished a figure as the Nobel Prize winner of 1923. This apprehensiveness in Professor Jochum was evidenced in a declaration that no sources had been quoted to support the idea of manipulation.

Secondly, one enters upon a delicate aspect of editorial practice - selective quotation. Had Jochum transcribed a crucial sentence to its end, his readers would have learned that 'it is also reasonable to assume that Yeats was manipulated by German diplomacy during the 1930s, even up to the last months of his life when he publicly approved aspects of Nazi legislation dealing with hereditary property'. The attached footnote directed readers (not excluding Peter Jochum) to details of Yeats's active engagements with Nazism, and of his passive involvement also by refusing in 1935/36 to assist Carl von Ossietzky (1888–1938), the pacifist journalist held in a concentration camp under barbarous conditions. That campaign had the support of Albert Einstein, Romain Rolland and Virginia Woolf; the approach to Yeats was made by Ethel Mannin (with whom he was having an affair) and Ernst Toller (the German Expressionist), but to no avail. On the question of Yeats's 1938 declarations, his speech was printed in the *Irish Independent* of 13 August 1938, reprinted in substance in Donald Torchiana's *Yeats and Georgian Ireland* (1966) and again in A. N. Jeffares and A. S. Knowland's *A Commentary on the Collected Plays of W. B. Yeats* (1975).

These numerous and accessible republications have not discouraged the late Edward Said, Elizabeth Cullingford, Declan Kiberd and others committed to a lucrative post-colonial Yeats from ignoring the evidence, even to the point of pretending it is not there. In some ways, their misguided politicisation of Yeats was preferable to the apolitical model offered during the Eisenhower era and after. Into this high-stakes academic racket, Peter Jochum stepped forward as a witness. What he had to say about me and Professor David Pierce was of little import compared with his characterisation of Nazi attitudes towards foreign artists and towards theatre in particular. Here a new opportunity to look comparatively at Yeats in a continental context arose.

Instead, there was a reversion to Yeats's own ideal approach to biography – its transformation into myth. That is to say, any reflection upon the hero is to be reflected back as brilliance, as vindication and celebration. The moment where Yeats outlines his

essential theory of biography has its own chilling attendant projec-
tions:

> I imagine new races, as it were, seeking domination, a world resembling
> but for its immensity that of the Greek tribes – each with its own
> Daimon or ancestral hero – the brood of Leda, War and Love: history
> grown symbolic, the biography changed into a myth.[11]

The paper-trail had begun in 1943. Joseph Hone, who had done
much to direct Yeats towards Mussolinian Italy, published his
biography in which the Goethe-Plakette business occupied an
awkward footnote: Gerhart Hauptmann was exempted from responsibility – 'nothing to do with the matter'.[12] This may have been
designed to console an old man in wartime Germany, but the denial
drew attention to itself and still requires explanation from the
historical biographer. It certainly eliminates one of the few non-Nazi
Germans who feature in the tale. But Hone's successors tended to
turn a blind eye to the award, for it finds no echo in Ellmann (1948)
or Jeffares (1949). Disinterred to illustrate a point about Samuel
Beckett's attitudes, it has become an embarrassment to professional
Yeatsians, a clanger dropped by Banquo's ghost. *The Arch-Poet*, Roy
Foster's conclusive second volume, longs for the last word on this
wretched Plakette, and wisely chooses Jochum's article in the *Yeats
Annual* as 'comprehensively' rebutting 'attempts to identify this
episode as a recognition by the Nazi state of a distinguished fellow
traveller'.[13] No such attempt had been made, which makes the rebuttal
all the more intriguing.

The award specifically cited a performance of 'The Countess
Cathleen' in German translation. Here was material for the mythologising of biography and history in double measure. Yeats's relations
with the new German regime demanded a theoretical justification that
would indemnify him from anything but aesthetic consequences,
while the play chosen explored a Faustian descent into total
commitment which is finally absolved. The moment was quintessen-
tially 1930s, the play was costume Late Victorian. Nevertheless,
diehards may protest that successful manipulation has yet to be
proven. Some relevant evidence is preserved in the National Library
of Ireland, a copy of *Germany Speaks* (1938) with an inscription that
now deserves a full reading:

Eduard Hempel, German Minister to Ireland gave this book to W. B.

Yeats in remembrance of an unforgettable afternoon he spent with him in September 1938.

That seems close enough to the poet's August approval of Nazi legislation depriving Jews of their property, of which the German minister approved. Yet Hempel, who joined the party on 1 July 1938, cannot have been an influence on Yeats in 1934 because he had not yet arrived in Dublin. On the issues raised in late summer 1938, one might pose speculative questions. Did the poet meet Joachim von Ribbentrop in any of the Great Houses which they both loved to visit? Who sent Yeats an uncorrected proof copy of Rudolf Frercks' *German Population Policy* (1937), published in English by Terremare of Berlin? Did Yeats adopt his friend Dorothy Wellesley's view that Hitler was a better man than Mussolini? Some of these questions are purely factual, and any attempt to vindicate Yeats might reasonably be expected to address them. With regard to Ribbentrop and Frercks, answers are more likely to turn up in German archives, if these were searched non-selectively. Certainly, in relation to the February performance of 'The Countess' in Frankfurt-am-Main, a detailed inquiry is essential (see pp. 332–337 below).

In Ireland, there are equally accessible contexts of enquiry. Maud Gonne, the zealous anti-Semite, entertained the Hempels at her home in south Dublin. Her daughter, Iseult Stuart, was close to Mrs Hempel, to Clissmann and to the Nazi spy, Hermann Görtz. She also made Laragh Castle available as a holiday retreat for the German military attaché and his wife. Other figures in the Irish political demi-monde – the family of republican Cathal Brugha (killed in action 1922), for example – were equally hospitable. It may be that a garden party at Maud Gonne's home, or drawing-room discussion of the *Bhagavad Gita* between Frau Hempel and Mrs Stuart, provided a scented context for the minister's planting of *Germany Speaks* on the ageing poet. Foster keeps Hempel entirely out of sight, as if poet and diplomat never met and the signed evidence in the National Library never existed.

From the Goethe business onwards, Yeats tolerated his own envious sympathy, despite *Kristallnacht* and a few other violations of decency. In August 1938, after the premiere of 'Purgatory', he reaffirmed his passing sympathies by commending Nazi laws against Jewish ownership. 'Emulous' had been a perfumed word in 1933; five years brought a change of air. In an interview of 12 August 1938,

Yeats spoke about his play, for which he provided an unmistakable ideological context:

> I know of old houses, old pictures, old furniture that have been sold without apparent regret. In a few cases a house has been destroyed by a mesalliance. I have founded my play on this exceptional case, partly because of my interest in certain problems of eugenics, partly because it enables me to depict more vividly than would otherwise be possible the tragedy of the house.
>
> In Germany there is special legislation to enable old families to go on living where their fathers lived. The problem is not Irish, but European, though it is perhaps more acute here than elsewhere.[14]

Foster regards this as 'unforgivably myopic', which, as he proceeds promptly to forgive, might seem unforgivably myopic in a biographer. Concerning 'Purgatory' he suggests 'it is worth remembering that Coole haunts the play as it did WBY' – an inelegant zeugma, surely. The sale of Lady Gregory's domestic possessions by her daughter-in-law may have angered the playwright, but his work cannot be simply diagnosed as a bad case of Connacht spleen. Then there is the proffered mitigation that the little play found its plot in the remote history of the St George and St Lawrence families in the neighbourhood of Coole almost 200 years earlier. If 'these Irish obsessions drive *Purgatory*, rather than any ill-digested notions about Nazi legislation', are there not some massive misjudgments of scale at work here, in the moral and in the aesthetic spheres? Some St George filly may have been mounted by a stable-lad in the sour by-and-by, but son-killing with anti-Semitic legislation 'vaguely' invoked seems a bit thin.

There was not much time left for Yeats to reboot his mind, for the 'passing' of his 'sympathies'. Sean Russell's bombs insolently echo Yeats's drafts for 'Under Ben Bulben', but they find no rebuke. Dorothy Wellesley published her post-obit in *The Times* on 9 February 1939. Who were Yeats's German acquaintances? What was Wellesley's idea of 'constructive democracy'? Little light is shed on these neglected eleventh-hour questions by whitewashing the activities of Oberburgermeister Krebs in 1934, or of Hempel in 1938. Yet the most pressing question remains to be asked, and it resists formulation. It concerns the implications of Yeats's accommodation of Nazi honours for our understanding of him as a poet and dramatist.

It may be helpful to note his commitment to tragic drama, yet to deny him the dignity of being a tragedian or tragic poet. Here critical and aesthetic judgments are called for. But perhaps he was instead a tragic figure, in so far as that might be possible in the twentieth century, less Lear than Coriolanus, more tragic victim than master. Even this argument clings to an academic view of tragedy which the century had overthrown and liquidated. If, as Auden's Public Prosecutor suggested, Yeats may have possessed 'a profound understanding of the age in which he lived'; and if that age had already manifested degrees of barbarism and mechanised violence inconceivable in 1900 – then does it not follow that Yeats's understanding absorbed something of those characteristics? To answer positively is not to confuse thought and action, the Marquis de Sade with Dr Mengele. The positive answer, however, acknowledges that the mind is not immune to thought, nor the eye to attraction.

Foreign Bodies in the Library

These are large issues, of a kind avoided by biographers. Detail, on the other hand, does not condemn one to the minutiae of a man's life; it can illuminate the penumbra in unexpected ways, and especially in the case of one whose actions are (virtually by definition) mental and intellectual. The books that Yeats owned at the time of his death cannot be taken as a comprehensive index of his reading, yet there is scarcely an item which has no story to tell. For example, all that he possessed of Hugo von Hofmannsthal (1874–1929) was his *Electra*, in an English version of 1908 by Arthur Symonds. Nevertheless, the Austrian dramatist's example in bringing Greek classical drama into the contemporary theatre will bear fruit with Yeats's version of the Oedipus plays in the 1920s when Hofmannsthal was advocating a Conservative Revolution (and not only in the arts.) In contrast, Yeats possessed no traceable volumes by Rilke, though he took a keen interest in the latter's view of death during his last months.

Two lesser items surviving in Yeats's library likewise serve to illustrate the range of his response to reading matter. As the more recent of these has not (as far as I am aware) been the subject of any comment by biographers or scholars, it deserves a word or two of introduction. The Italian author Lauro de Bosis (1901–1931) had welcomed the fascist revolution at the outset, but during the 1920s came to despise its brutality and vulgarity. Despite the difference in age, de Bosis and Yeats had much in common. Each wrote a version of Sophocles' *Oedipus at Colonnus* in the 1920s. Each studied James Fraser's *The Golden Bough*; indeed, the Italian had edited and translated a three-volume abridgement in 1925. De Bosis aspired to be a lyric playwright, and his *Icaro* won critical acclaim in 1927: an English translation was published by Oxford University Press (New York) in 1933.[15] But one day in 1932, after long planning, he launched a protest against the regime in the hope of directing others towards the light. From his own aeroplane, named Pegasus, he scattered antifascist leaflets over the city of Rome, flying so low that people feared he would crash on the Spanish Steps. He was never seen again, evidently shot down (perhaps in the western sea, heading for France) by Mussolini's men and spirited away. In 1933, Faber & Faber published the text of his protest, together with a brief introduction in English, as *The Story of My Death*. Yeats's copy, however acquired, is listed as Item 255 in Edward O'Shea's *Catalog*.

Item 655 has a somewhat similar title. But *On Life After Death* by Gustav Theodor Fechner (1801–1887) is a short nineteenth-century spiritualist work, resembling Emanuel Swedenborg's system, but expounded in a more casual fashion. Yeats possessed a copy of the third English-language edition, published in Chicago in 1914. It is extensively annotated in pencil. On at least two occasions, the marginal jottings mention Dreaming Back, that stage of the posthumous existence that Yeats turned to dramatic advantage in 'The Dreaming of the Bones', 'Purgatory' and elsewhere.[16] Here he inscribed words quoted elsewhere in *Blood Kindred* – 'If two spirits of the dead meet (on earth) their nations also meet'. It is instructive to note the passage by Fechner so annotated by Yeats:

> Now, whenever two kindred spirits meet on earth, growing into one through their common qualities, and influencing and enriching one another through their different qualities, the communities, nations, or generations, to which they formerly belonged individually, enter into spiritual communion as well.[17]

On the immediately previous page, one finds a passage annotated by Yeats with two similar single words and a simple diagram:

> The higher spirits living as they are not in an individual man, but each living and acting in many, are spiritual bonds between those persons, uniting them all in the same belief, the same moral or political tendency. All the persons who have any spiritual fellowship between them belong to the body of one spirit.[18]

The annotations appear in the right margin. Opposite the phrase 'moral or political tendency', Yeats has marked a long narrow Y, his own initial, signifying the coming together in unity of what previously (so to speak) had been numerous (the two upper stems of the letter conjoined in the lower one). It is never clear what reality time has in Yeats's 'afterlife', consequently it remains unclear how one can speak of sequence or consequence: despite this, he insists on a strongly historical framework in presenting the figures of his Vision. It is as if one could conceive of history without time.

But let us return to the pages of *On Life After Death*. In amplification of this crude Y illustration, Yeats inscribes the word 'cones', suggesting a fully three-dimensional symbol or verbal embodiment of the spiritual process. Opposite the phrase 'body of one spirit', the word 'covens' is entered in the margin. The similarity of the two words is bewitching, to the point that one is in danger of missing the early evolutionary stages of Yeats's Vision-vocabulary ('cones') and its closeness in the margin to the term ('covens') for witches in conclave. The latter is cognate with 'convents' (from the Latin *convenire*).

Why should these two items – the Italian of 1933 and the German of 1914 – be abstracted from the catalogue of Yeats's library at death? In a very crudely political sense, they mark the commencement of crises in Europe: outbreak of the Great War, consolidation of German fascism. Such readings have nothing whatever to do with the authors, Fechner being long dead and de Bosis living under an Italian, not a German, regime. The books cannot have arrived in Yeats's possession before the dates (of publication) in question: they mark acts of reading, not of writing. Is it possible to write the biography of a reader?

The Italian item seems unhelpful, for it is so nearly pristine in condition as to challenge the claim Yeats had opened it. It would be the act of a desperate Counsel for the Defence to argue that the book's undamaged condition proved the owner's innocence of its contents. Preserved under his roof until Yeats's death, *The Story of My Death* lies doggo among other books, awaiting recognition as 'An Italian Airman Foresees His Death'. Given that the original Airman (Robert Gregory, 1881–1918) had died in Italian air space when just a few years older than de Bosis, and died like him as the consequence of 'friendly fire' (sharply defined), it would take Counsel more skilled even than Sean MacBride to persuade a jury that Yeats never opened

The Story of My Death. Its publication by Faber was almost certainly arranged by the dead author's fiancée, Ruth Draper, an American whose family claimed Henry James among their friends and Henry Adams among their kin, WASPs whom T. S. Eliot could not resist even in the year of *After Strange Gods*. Yeats was at home in Ireland when de Bosis died, having spent time the previous summer in the company of a different kind of Italian, Mario Rossi. In 1933, when the book was published, he was engaged in 'trying to work out a social philosophy for Ireland based on his "Four Philosophical Positions",' in turn based on his appreciation of fascism.[19] If it is accepted that Yeats opened de Bosis's posthumous book, then it follows that he consciously chose not to annotate it, as he had annotated Fechner's *On Life After Death* and sundry other books. Yet was not the publication of *The Story of My Death*, likewise *The Golden Book of Italian Poetry*, an instance of de Bosis's life after death, a form of literary immortality for which Roman Horace and John Milton had settled?

In contrast, the German item remains open to scrutiny and interpretation. The English text is somewhat rambling in style, lacking the systematic rigour of Swedenborg in organisation, just as it fails to anticipate the vigorous intelligence of its most famous reader. The Instructors who brought automatic writing and other benefits to Yeats and his wife instructed them to 'Read Fechner', and they did. As the Instructors rarely gave orders which their subjects could not easily obey, it seems likely that the little volume was already in the possession of either the poet or his new wife. The annotations, carefully preserved, cry out to be dated, echoing as they do several phrases relevant to the composition of 'The Dreaming of the Bones' in 1917, during which year Yeats was close to Iseult Gonne before marrying George Hyde-Lees. Of course, the annotations may have been entered on different occasions, separated in time. The style differs in one striking instance. Beside words which might be read as a truism banal or brutal – 'a child, which has been alive only for a moment, can never die again' – Yeats has added not words, but just an approving tick, a schoolmaster among souls.[20] What prompted the pencilled nod of approval: some recollection of Maud Gonne's infant son or news of Iseult's daughter dying in 1921?

Such bodies of sub-literature in the library challenge the biographer. Fechner stands for Yeats's willingness to subordinate the events of our mundane world to accounts of spirit-movements which most people believe to be unverifiable at best and plain incredible in the vast majority of cases. Judgment is to be based upon a reality which itself is beyond reach. To complain of this central and organising feature of Yeats's thought is not to dismiss everything that fails to meet A. J. Ayer's minimalist criteria for meaningful statements. Religious belief, aesthetic value, passionate desire, intimations from the past, hunches, rituals, communal expressions – a host of non-rational or unverifiable things have their value. But the subordinating of systems of broadly shared acceptance to arcane, occult and exclusivist belief leads to conflicts of ethical, social and political value.

To take a historical example – the scientific work of Robert Boyle and Isaac Newton in the seventeenth century is in no way compromised by residual commitments to alchemy or astrology: these latter retained a place in the loose consensus of beliefs, practices and living metaphors of the time. Or to take another example – the Euro-centrism (cf. orientalism) of Montesquieu or the liberalism of John Stuart Mill was strictly limited in effect by the technology of their respective times. A commitment to alchemy on the part of John Maynard Keynes, or to irrational views of ethnicity on the part of Werner Heisenberg, would be quite another matter.

Fechner, we are tempted to say, was harmless: looked at in a more scientific light, he had something to offer Sigmund Freud. A close examination of what Yeats writes by way of annotation suggests that what was harmless in its day can be mobilised to different and kinetic effect in altered conditions. When the German alluded to 'communities, nations, or generations' among the dead, the term 'nation' did not yet have the potential which, in Yeats's middle years, is already exploited. When the German spoke of 'political tendency' and went on to declare that 'all the persons who have any spiritual fellowship between them belong to the body of one spirit', it would be absurd to detect proto-fascism: it would be equally myopic to ignore the potential for a transvaluation of these words in the era of actually existing fascism.

De Bosis, we are tempted to say, was incorrigibly romantic, given also perhaps to a naïve belief in gesture ('a lonely impulse of delight') as propaganda. In Yeats's library, however, the body of the Italian airman, spirited away by Mussolini's alchemists, stands for Yeats's refusal to acknowledge the mundane world's exits, his occasional absolute limitation of interest to the other world. If a young writer sharing so much with the Nobel Prize winner could elicit not a word of marginal regret or indignation, what could be hoped by mere millions of nameless others?

The Unspeakable Question

Better France perish than one man suffer injustice.
                              Yeats on the Dreyfus case, c.1894

And the jew squats on the window sill . . .
                              T. S. Eliot, 'Gerontion', 1920

Let me begin with a story from 1940 in Dublin. Sabina Wizniak (b. 1920), a Jewish girl with a four-week visa to visit a (non-existent) dying aunt, has outstayed her permitted welcome. She will be deported for lack of authorisation as a resident. An official from the Department of External Affairs directs her to Amiens Street railway station, where she must board the train for Belfast (in the United Kingdom). The two meet as arranged. The official, presumably touched by her innocence in keeping the appointment, advises her to get out at the first station and make her way back to Dublin. Then, throwing caution (and perhaps career) to the wind, he tells her to start walking, he will 'let on' that he saw her board the train.

The story does not quite end there, though the prospect of External Affairs providing a happy ending is unexpected. Sabina takes a room on the South Circular Road (which crosses Clanbrassil Street). After some happy weeks, she discovers that her landlady's husband is a policeman. Packing her bags for fear of embarrassment, she meets Mr Stapleton. Are you not happy here? he asks. I love it here, she replies. The guard winks. You can only leave, if you don't like it.

With reference to the Holocaust, my point is that the nameless and disobedient official, together with Guard Stapleton, did more for humanity than Yeats ever did. And, for the very reason that Sabina can be multiplied by 6,000,000, their action is qualitatively superior, not merely a cipher. Does absorption in poetry, dedication to the making of poetry, absolve one all day and every day from active human sympathy with the victims of brutal tyranny? I went to national school with Sabina's sons.

Yeats's keen interest in, even sympathy with, totalitarian politics has been conceded by his most liberal admirers who, in turn, concede a degree of agreement with him consistent with their own habitation of more progressive times and institutions. The best excuse usually turns out to invoke *folie de grandeur* or any other self-indulgence of the elderly great. Yet as consensual opinion has gradually found it necessary to substitute 'authoritarian' for 'liberal' in its characterisation of his position, so there has been a reluctance to visit the remoter sites of his rhetoric. These few outhouses of the Yeatsian *polis* threaten to invade the familiar public squares and decorated monuments, and deserve attention lest their number and scale be exaggerated.

So central to the ideology of twentieth-century totalitarianism was anti-Semitism that any account of the poet's life must address the matter sooner or later. In order to avoid any suspicion of *parti pris*, I should at the outset point to the extensive evidence of Russian anti-Semitism under Stalin and his heirs. Nazi Germany had no monopoly, nor indeed were its pathological hatreds without antecedent. Yeats, however, concerned himself very little with the Soviet Union, and scarcely more with communism, which he hated sight unseen. His practical engagements with totalitarian regimes were Italian and German. Again, care should be taken in distinguishing between the policies of Rome and of Berlin towards Jews. While the fate of Italian Jews was ultimately no less tragic and brutal than that of their German co-religionists, the longer pre-war existence of Mussolini's regime allowed for an early phase in which anti-Semitism was not a major concern. A favourite observation of apologists for Italian fascism was to remind its critics that the Chief Rabbi had been a member of the party.

Argument by exception quickly collapses into evasion. Certainly, by the time of Yeats's death, racial laws (1938) in Italy marked out a doomed minority. During his earlier visits to Rome and Rapallo, he had perhaps made no direct observation of prejudice or persecution, though the trumpetings of his friend Ezra Pound loudly proclaimed the threat posed by Jews and Judaism to what the American regarded as a civilised society. Placing Yeats in some sliding scale of prejudice on which Pound and T. S. Eliot also feature can only enhance the general opinion that he was innocent of their gross hatred and calculated indifference. Though he was personally closer to Pound – having shared a house with him before the Great War – Yeats is closer in tone to Eliot. *After Strange Gods* (1934) provided doctrine and chapter where 'Gerontion' (1919) had settled for a verse, a line, a lower-case contemptuous initial in the word [j]ew. 'Reasons of race and religion combine to make any large number of free-thinking Jews undesirable.'[1] Though Eliot's anti-Semitism was relatively open, and shored itself up with the visible traditions of Christianity, it also had its darker and unofficial side.

The Yellow Spot

Tom Paulin has been challenged in his attributing to Eliot of a short anonymous book-review in July 1936.[2] The item under scrutiny was *The Yellow Spot*, published by Victor Gollancz in London.[3] Though the book presented itself as 'a collection of facts and documents relating to three years' persecution of German Jews, derived chiefly from Nationalist Socialist sources, Brave Anon dismissed it as 'an attempt to rouse moral indignation by means of sensationalism'. By the summer of 1936, the Nuremberg Laws were fully operational, while the nature of 'concentration' camps like Dachau was plain to see – even at a distance. In its third month of operation, May 1933, twelve men were tortured to death or simply murdered outright: one was a thoroughly fit young Jewish lawyer from Bamberg, who lasted less than five days.[4] Unperturbed, *The Criterion*'s reviewer proceeded to mock any claim to 'a moral dictatorship of the world' by which these enormities might be checked – 'there is not the least prospect of our being able to exercise it'. Insufficiently convinced by his own self-proclaimed moral impotence, he continued with a nervous dissection of Gollancz's publication:

> it is noticeable that the jacket of the book speaks of the 'extermination' of the Jews in Germany, whereas the title page refers only to their 'persecution'; and as the title page is to the jacket, so are the contents to the title page, especially in the chapters devoted to the ill-treatment of Jews in German concentration camps.[5]

Though the coldness of this schoolboy logic may recall Delacroix as commemorated by Baudelaire, nothing so openly callous can be found in Yeats's commentary on the plight of Jews in the 1930s. Indeed, nothing so open as commentary on their plight can be found anywhere in his writings, private or public. The nearest he came to revealing a firm attitude was in the final stages of a letter to his young mistress, Ethel Mannin. 'I am not callous, every nerve trembles with horror at what is happening in Europe.'⁶ This was written a few weeks, if that, before Eliot's exercise in turning a blind editorial eye. The two poets were in correspondence between January 1935 and late 1937 about Indian mystical texts in part translated by Yeats. The July 1935 issue of Eliot's *Criterion* carried an essay by Yeats on the Mandookya Upanishad and, in April 1937, Faber & Faber (with Eliot as managing director) published *The Ten Principal Upanishads, put into English by Shree Purohit Swami and W. B. Yeats.* Though the substance of these publications and collaborations is not without political interest, they indicate more clearly than any other evidence that Yeats attended to Eliot's activities as publisher and editor.

In the business debated with Mannin in the late spring of 1936, the same issue arose as would be dismissed by the anonymous reviewer of *The Yellow Spot.* The international campaign to rescue Carl von Ossietzky from a Nazi concentration camp will be described later, together with the biographical context in which Yeats encountered it. For the moment, we should concentrate on his excuse for doing nothing. The campaigners aimed to have the prisoner awarded the Nobel Prize for Peace. Yeats told Mannin, 'if the Nobel Society did what you want it would seem to the majority of the German people that the Society hated their government for its politics not because it was inhuman . . .'⁷ As with Eliot and German Jewry at large, so with Yeats and this one prisoner (not a Jew).

His refusal to offer public support for a Gentile victim of Nazism provides a standard against which Yeats's attitude towards 'the Jewish question' can be measured. In the simplest terms, he can be generally acquitted of anti-Semitism though, in this connection, the inappropriateness of legal metaphor may work against him. Nevertheless, one can note his acceptance without comment of Moritz Bonn as a fellow-guest at Coole Park in 1897. More significant was his reliance on the gynaecologist, Bethel Solomons, during the crisis in Iseult Gonne's marriage to Francis Stuart in 1920. Solomons, of course, had been an amateur actor with links to the Abbey Theatre.

These domestic relations between the Irish poet and notable Jews whom he met at home in Ireland reflected a vague sense of affinity between the two nations as victims of history. The eighteenth-century antiquarian, Charles Vallencey, had laid down a shaky philological path towards some such theory, and there were other prompts. The general ground for mutual tolerance became specific in some enclaves of Victorian Irish Protestantism which were theologically philo-Semitic, emphasising the role of 'historic Israel' in the eventual Last Things. Yeats encountered this line of thinking through his friends W. K. Magee and J. M. Synge. The broader affinity was apparent to outsiders like Matthew Arnold and Ernest Renan in the nineteenth century, also to Arnold Toynbee, whom Yeats quoted on the topic in 1937.[8]

After 1918

Moritz Bonn and Bethel Solomons notwithstanding, different tonalities become audible in Yeats's attitude towards Jews as European fascism gains ground. A turning point can be discovered in that wonderful collection of poetry, philosophical prose and personal correspondence, *Per Amica Silentia Lunae* (1918). The seventeenth numbered section of 'Anima Mundi' reads as follows:

> Each Daemon is drawn to whatever man or, if its nature is more general, to whatever nation it most differs from, and it shapes into its own image the antithetical dream of man or nation. The Jews had already shown by the precious metals, by the ostentatious wealth of Solomon's temple, the passion that has made them the money-lenders of the modern world. If they had not been rapacious, lustful, narrow, and persecuting beyond the people of their time, the incarnation had been impossible; but it was an intellectual impulse from the Condition of Fire that shaped their antithetical self into that of the classic world. So always it is an impulse from some Daemon that gives to our vague, unsatisfied desire, a meaning, and a form all can accept.[9]

In certain ways, this passage turns common prejudice on its head. Where the Christian Church proclaimed the wickedness of the Jews as evidenced in and resulting from their rejection of Jesus, Yeats suggests that Jesus would not have been divine without their prior wickedness (rapacity, lust, etc.). It remains prejudice, of course, and projects itself into contemporary society by postulating an innate Jewish genius for money-lending. (Pound will make more of this.) On the other hand, while touring the United States early in 1920, Yeats publicly supported the Palestine Restoration Fund, launched to establish a permanent Jewish homeland.[10] Such a gesture may have been no more than an endorsement of the Balfour Declaration, that is approval of British imperial policy. Perhaps it owed something to the

parallel histories of the Irish and the Jews, though it also accommodated the idea (later influential in Germany) that the best one could
do for the Chosen People was to be rid of them, whether to
Madagascar, Palestine or elsewhere. Indubitably, Yeats's American
statement lacked any anti-Semitic coloration.

Where does the need for a theory relating the Incarnation to Jewish
lust arise? Both essays in *Per Amica Silentiae Lunae* are concerned
with the danger of poetic sterility, and Yeats pointed to William
Wordsworth 'withering into eighty years, honoured and empty
witted'. Poetic sterility, symbolised in bodily decrepitude, will later
be outwitted when Yeats undergoes surgery for the renewal of his
sexual life. Thus two politics engage in preliminary dialogue in these
essays published as the Great War ends – that of race and that of sex.
For the moment they are contained in what Terence Brown calls 'this
strangely beautiful, haunted text'.[11]

Haunted by whom? If Yeats was troubled by ghosts of the Great
War, he did not say so. That episode in human history figures little in
his meditations, in keeping with other ethical economies. His
approval of L'Action française in 1924 was silent on its direct descent
from the anti-Dreyfusard fury of the 1890s, though at the time Yeats
had not followed Maud Gonne into that cause. Yeats's rudeness to
Erich Gottgetreu in August 1928 should perhaps be omitted from any
list of his significant misdemeanours, on the grounds that no
surviving evidence establishes that the (fellow-) guest at Coole was
known to be Jewish and, in any case, things were to get much worse
for Germany's Jews. Yet the 'turn' of political attitudes was indeed
perning in its gyre.

On Christmas Day 1933, Yeats sent Gonne an account of more
recent experiences – 'a social disaster' at the PEN Club in London:

> Blood pressure was very high & as a result I was very cross. I looked
> round, saw several Indian authors & a lot of refugees from Germany, got
> the impression every woman there was a Britannia and was suckling a
> little Polish Jew. Result I devoted my speech to denouncing the Indians
> for writing in English ... As I looked round the room I saw a few
> delighted faces – all others glum – the delighted faces were those of Polish
> Jews. Much as they hate Germany for baiting Jews they hate it more for
> putting down the Polish language.[12]

Maybe this is simply awkward humour, maybe Yeats is playing to
Gonne's prejudices. It is difficult to feel that anyone at the end of

Hitler's first year in power found Jew-baiting in Germany less hateful than the alleged relegation of Polish at some unspecified period.[13] And – lest we unconsciously accept Yeats's word for it – were the vigorously if unsystematically persecuted Jews of pre-war Poland not persecuted at least in part because of their unpatriotic addiction to a form of German, namely Yiddish? The passage opens up issues that spill over the political and verbal – for example, were these refugees from Germany or Poland? Yeats seems undecided. What is striking in Yeats's anecdote is the image of bodily intimacy between 'every woman' and a little Jew. Having observed this (to him) noteworthy phantasm, he sought to divert his own attention by concentrating on the Indians who (like Yeats himself) wrote in the language of empire. The result of this manoeuvre, or rather the result in his account of the episode, is pleasure seemingly brought to the Jews, at least to Yeats's satisfaction.

Yeats had anti-Semitic friends, Maud Gonne always their *doyenne*. Few subjects of the biographer's art have combined limelight and whitewash so harmoniously. In Nancy Cardozo's portrait, there is no sign of the anti-Semitism which prompted G2 – the Irish Army's intelligence unit – to open one of its earliest files on Madame, even before the war began. While the evidence post-dates Yeats's death, it illustrates a series of ideological positions that Maud Gonne had been practising for decades. Her autobiography, entitled *A Servant of the Queen* with splendid ambiguity, had appeared in 1938, covering the years of her intimacy with the author of 'The Countess Cathleen', 'The Land of Heart's Desire', and so on. The publisher, Victor Gollancz, who later adopted her son-in-law Francis Stuart as a post-war novelist, was of course Jewish. But a German translator, Ruth Weiland, was at work by May 1939, and the resulting publication (on 3 October) had sold a quarter of a million copies by the end of 1943.[14] Dr Weiland, a Nazi party member, was looking forward to a promised second volume of Gonne's memoirs.

Madame was busy in correspondence with Oscar Pfaus, the German spy chosen to contact the IRA early in 1939. Pfaus was the Hamburg chief of an organisation called the Fichte Bund, whose ambition (bannered in English) was 'Union for World Veracity'. Under this motto, they debated Jewish responsibility for the partition of Ireland, with Pfaus insisting that 'most of the British propaganda which is flooding Eire is coming from British-Jewish sources in

Belfast', and Gonne in return seeking hard evidence of 'Jewish interference in this matter'. She continued:

> Of course the Jews, to a large extent are in control of the cinema industry & in spite of a supposed censorship get away with a terrible amount of British propaganda, both in the pictures & the news reels. Occasionally the IRA go in & destroy some films which improves things for a short while, but they soon get bad again. Then too the Jews have bought a great deal too much land in & around Dublin.[15]

Perhaps she had my father's neighbours on Kenilworth Park in mind. While her comments display neither literary talent nor even political ingenuity, they parallel Yeats of eleven years earlier: 'Young men stop trains, armed with automatics and take from the guard's van bundles of English newspapers ...'[16] The passage of time, the intervention of a degrading decade, led Gonne to approve what Yeats condemned, with the added difference that now the offenders were not British foreigners, but Jews of Irish residence or otherwise.

There were lesser figures who held similar opinions. Joseph W. Fowler, who ran a bookshop at 34 Wellington Quay, produced a booklet sufficiently impressive for Gonne to send Pfaus a copy. In journalistic circles, Lia Clarke (born Cornelia Cummins) was a colourful and eccentric minor writer, who had briefly studied medicine in Vienna. (In December 1920, she married the poet, Austin Clarke [1896–1974], though the marriage lasted a matter of days.[17]) She published some poetry as Margaret Lyster, worked for German news agencies in the 1930s, and mixed with Dublin's home-bred Nazis. In August 1939, Lia Clarke issued a crudely anti-Semitic statement on behalf of 'The Celtic Professional Societies' or 'Celtic Confederation of Occupational Guilds'. Mussolini's ideas of the corporative state provided a cover for hard fascism in Ireland where Roman Catholicism might make anything Italian seem respectable. But Mrs Clarke's attitude to the Jewish Question impressed Pfaus who responded to her overtures. According to her statement, circulated in English and German, a Mr Magee believed that Irish culture as presented to the world was 'nothing more than a pattern of Jewish and Freemason interest dressed up in green clothing'. Support for Nazi Germany was strongly urged, backed up with a quotation from Roger Casement. Among the lesser attendees at these gatherings was Chalmers Trench, whose background was closer to Yeats's: he worked for the Three Candles Press. Trench may not have been an anti-Semite, but he danced with German shepherds.

Commending Gogarty, Jewishing Beckett (1937)

Apart from the enigmatic Trench, these figures constituted a typical petit-bourgeois clique of the kind to be found in many British, French or Danish cities of Dublin's size. Throughout the 1920s and '30s, fascism attracted such disgruntled and largely ineffectual individuals. In contrast, Walter Starkie was a *bon-viveur* fascist whom Trinity College kept on its payroll even after he had taken up work in Madrid. Oliver St John Gogarty was another, personally far closer to Yeats than Lia Clarke. Surgeon, senator, poet, he marred his autobiographical work, *As I was Going Down Sackville Street* (1936), with offensive references which led a Dublin Jewish family named Sinclair to sue for libel. In May 1937, Yeats gave Dorothy Wellesley a progress report, in part an excuse to revel second-hand in Gogarty's colourful experience:

> In his book he has called a certain man a 'chicken butcher', meaning that he makes love to the immature. The informant, the man who swears that he recognised the victim [,] is a racketeer of a Dublin poet or imatative [sic] poet of the new school. He hates us all – his review of the Anthology was so violent the *Irish Times* refused to publish it.
>
> He & the 'chicken butcher' are Jews ... Two or three weeks ago Gogarty & the chicken butcher were drinking in our 'poet's pub' laughing at the work.[18]

Again, the recipient of this letter may be responsible for the derisive attitude towards Jews which her correspondent adopts. The facts of the matter are recoverable. Morris Harris (d. 1926) had been a Jewish antiques dealer with an address at Nassau Street, Dublin, duly noted by James Joyce in *Ulysses*. His daughter married a Protestant Gentile, who became vice-president and treasurer of a Jewish organisation in the city; their twin sons were brought up in the Jewish faith. The brothers, Harry and William Sinclair, were also libelled, and the case was finally taken in Harry Sinclair's name (William having died in the meantime).

Yeats confidently informed Lady Wellesley of the principal witness's literary failings, though he failed to name him – Samuel Beckett.[19] 'The anthology' was Yeats's *Oxford Book of Modern Verse* (1936), with copious representation of both Gogarty and Wellesley – and no Wilfred Owen, no Hugh MacDiarmid, no Austin Clarke. Examined textually, his letter scarcely goes further than to paraphrase Gogarty's libellous comments. The implicating of Beckett can confidently be attributed to Gogarty, who sometimes drank in the same pubs and would have seen in the young man the amanuensis of James Joyce, creator of 'Buck Mulligan'.[20] Its avid reception and transmission to Wellesley were solely Yeats's doing. If, as Yeats contends, 'chicken butcher' was a recognised term for paedophile, then the anti-Semitic animus is intensified, for both chicken-meat and kosher regulations for slaughter were trademarks of Jewish cuisine. Yeats is, perhaps, going no further than repeating Gogarty, except to envy him. Considered psychologically, this imitative behaviour harmonises with the anticipation of Wellesley's responses. That anti-Semitic prejudice of a highly vulgar kind should provide the occasion for this revealing passivity reinforces the unease experienced in reading Eliot and Yeats's protestations of helplessness the previous summer when concentration-camp conditions were drawn vividly to their attention. As German background to the Gogarty trial, and its echoes of ritual-murder accusations, consider two exhibitions then current, one devoted to *Der Ewige Jude* (The Eternal Jew) and the other (in Munich) to Degenerate Art.

Yeats's published work carries few, if any, indications of vacillation on the Jewish Question. One play – 'The Resurrection' (1931), just after the turn begins – deals directly with the relationship between Judaism and the origins of Christianity. Its type-characters are The Hebrew, The Greek, The Syrian, Christ, and Three Musicians. The beliefs about Christ assigned to The Hebrew would have been termed Unitarian in the nineteenth century – that is, they deny the divinity of Christ while stressing his excellence as perfect man. Historically, they might be associated with Jan Hus's pre-Reformation ideas in the early fifteenth century. The 1420 massacre of Vienna's Jews was in part justified by suspicions of an allegiance with Hussites, just as the latter were sometimes accused of reverting to Judaism.[21] Taken on its own, or in these learned contexts, 'The Resurrection' was no more anti-Semitic than the average Sunday morning sermon. But, as Louis MacNeice noted in 1941, the play embodies Yeats's philosophy of history.[22] No mere fable or tableau, it was also adaptable to changing conditions.

In a general introduction to his work, which Yeats wrote in 1937 for a major new collected edition, he summarised and invoked this philosophy. The PEN Club event of 1933 was recalled without any reference whatsoever to the Polish Jews who had so captivated him when reporting to Maud Gonne – perhaps the German exhibitions had now borne in upon him. Instead, the event (in retrospect described as a dinner party given in his honour) served to illustrate his attitude to Gaelic, which 'is my national language, but it is not my mother tongue'.[23] Freudians may be tempted to see the maternal/linguistic reference displacing the suckling Britannias of the earlier version, but Freudians should be patient. In this public account of the occasion, Yeats assailed the Indian writers present in order to *avoid* discussion of the 'political refugees' and any consequent praise of England as 'the protector of liberty'. Once again William Wordsworth is a scapegoat perhaps because his names anticipate Yeats's own first name and his high valuing of words. This time he is singled out as 'that typical Englishman' in the general introduction, and condemned for preferring 'a Santo Domingo negro', Toussaint L'Ouverture (c.1743–1803), to the Irish rebel Robert Emmet (1788–1803) as a subject for poetry. This is not the last dismissive reference to Negroes we shall find.

Quite apart from elision of the Jews, the 1937 recollection of Yeats's 1933 performance enacts a complex historico-political manoeuvre. The successful slave-leader Toussaint's death in 1803 had been followed by the further success of his cause when Haiti became independent in 1804. Of this pre-post-colonial triumph Yeats had nothing to say, preferring to excoriate Wordsworth for neglecting the unsuccessful Irish rebel. Emmet's brief and futile rebellion had been marked by a degree of brutality that disgusted its leader. Yet Yeats oddly merged neglect of this violence with neglect of government violence a few years earlier: the Lake Poet had 'remembered that rebellion as little as the half-hanging and the pitch-cap which preceded it'.[24]

On the surface, Yeats in 1937 reminds us of his IRB credentials, being always ready to invoke the sufferings of the Irish people down through the ages. Offstage, he is elected to the Athenaeum Club in London and broadcasts several times from the BBC. Between these conflicting loyalties, the Jews get lost from the 1937 version of events. The private and public accounts also differ in Yeats's sense of his own emotional responses. At the close of his Christmas message for Maud Gonne, he had written, 'I have been ashamed of myself ever since, just as if I were a cat and had eaten the canary.'[25] In the introduction of four years later, he was 'unrepentant and angry'.[26] Putting the two together may generate more sense than either manifests on its own:

shame without repentance is not an unheard-of condition. The outcome tends to be a state of paralysis.

The general introduction that Yeats wrote in 1937 did not appear until 1961. Frustration at the delay in seeing into print the New York *Collected Works* for which it was intended may have contributed to the increasing intemperance of Yeats's late prose. *On the Boiler* (1939) brought its own frustrations, as the author placed management of its printing in the hands of another, rather than entrust it to the Yeats sisters' Cuala Press. Delay in this project resulted in posthumous publication of a text that appears to have been toned down by his widow. Like the Ossietzky affair of 1936, *On the Boiler* requires scrutiny in the fuller context of Yeats's attitudes and behaviour throughout the 1930s. Nevertheless, its comment on the Jewish Question can be noted here.

There was no comment. In a series of provocative and highly original essays, written in the year of *Anschluss* and *Kristallnacht* and absolutely explicit threats of extermination, essays addressing eugenical, political, religious and constitutional issues and invoking Hegel and Husserl, Yeats had nothing to say about German or Austrian Jewry.[27] He did, however, cite Ninette de Valois (1898–2001), Dublin-born choreographer, who 'protested the other day because somebody had called the theatre the province of the Jews and the Irish. "The Irish," she said, "are adaptable immigrants, the bigger and emptier a country the better it pleases them."' The Jews, once again disappearing from Yeats's argument, are by silent implication not adaptable immigrants. Since the 1920s, *Mein Kampf* had argued along similar lines, but we should be slow to seek out this dancer in a Berlin cabaret. As the diligent editor of the *Later Essays* cannot supply a source for Dame Ninette's observation, it cannot be taken *tout court* as her considered view on anything. Yeats's acceptance of its sentiments, however, is amply demonstrated not only by its inclusion, but by its compatibility with another remarkable exaggeration in a portfolio of excess: 'Forcing reading and writing on those who wanted neither was a [*sic*] worst part of the violence which for two centuries has been creating that hell wherein we suffer . . .' Literacy as violence? The Great War: compare and contrast.

Embarrassingly inept comparison in this case may arise from Yeats's declared wish to shock. More than six years after his death, the same moral inversion came easily to Maud Gonne. Germany lay in ruins. The camps had been opened to the appalled eyes of the victors. Millions of displaced persons roamed through Central and Eastern Europe. The Allies struggled to circulate food and provide shelter in Germany, with mixed success. In a letter to the *Irish Press* of 10 December 1945, she wrote, 'It is hard to assess degrees of horror, but such conditions in peace time shock me more even than the horrors we read of in war-time concentration camps, though both are inexcusable.' Inexcusable seems feeble in the light of Auschwitz, Buchenwald, Dachau and Treblinka, especially as the Nuremberg Trials were in progress as she wrote. (Then we note the veiled qualifications of even that feeble word for, while the horrors the Allies mismanage are real, the concentration camps are just things 'we read of'.) Behind these veils, the Jews have disappeared again. Yeats, we might say in the spirit of Maud Gonne, was well dead and so under no obligation or suspicion in these circumstances. Perhaps her sudden post-war dropping of the Jews from her rhetoric did owe something to her friend's discretion in the 1930s.

There yet remains the question of Yeats's literary writing, distinct from the introductions and essays. If 'The Resurrection' stereotyped its Hebrew character in 1931, the larger arena of European culture was about to witness radical reassessments of Christian origins and the Christian contribution to western culture. Friedrich Nietzsche is generally blamed, though Nietzsche was no anti-Semite. The Nazis, commandeering Nietzsche's reputation, encouraged a German Christianity, a creed stripped of its Jewish inheritance and (at least as important) deprived of any power to rival the State. We know Yeats was aware of this strategy, because in 1935 he recalled the young AE as a premature exemplar of the German Christian, a Vox Clamans in Kildysert. (See note 10 to 'In the Catacombs', p. 435–6.)

Yeats's relationship to Church or doctrine was never close, despite his grandfather's holy orders. The incarnation took its place in his philosophy of history, as if he were a comparativist, not a believer. His general introduction spoke of Indian mysticism, and then looked forward two or three generations: 'at that moment Europeans may find something attractive in a Christ posed against a background not of Judaism but of Druidism, not shut off in dead history, but flowing, concrete, phenomenal'.[28] If this remark is generously taken in a philosophical sense, then echoes of Husserl and even Heidegger are audible.[29] On the other hand, as an exegesis of 'The Resurrection', its desired elision of Judaism (into 'dead history') is entirely consistent with Yeats's correspondence. Desired elision in itself resembles a form of repression, in which the erotic and the negative are to be reconciled.

The process, so cumulative in Yeats's allusions to the Jews from the early 1920s onwards, is suddenly reversed in a poem published a month before he died. Written in July 1938, when the British reported 800 attempts at suicide by Viennese Jews 'within a few days', and when Nazi claims on Czechoslovakia were endorsed by a British statesman, 'John Kinsella's Lament for Mrs Mary Moore' purports to be a ballad of the traditional kind. In keeping with this, its situations and emotions are conventional.[30] The second stanza virtually recounts the Gogarty libel in the name of a dead girl:

> Though stiff to strike a bargain,
>   Like an old Jew man,
> Her bargain struck we laughed and talked
>   And emptied many a can . . .

It is not just the Gogarty libel that is echoed here, but Yeats's letter to Wellesley in which convivial drinking signifies reconciliation between aggressor and victim. The echo is self-referential, a low mimetic version of that state in which the imagination turns in upon itself, as recommended by Yeats here, and deplored somewhere else. The sexual politics of their correspondence and of their relationship generally has yet to be addressed. Meanwhile, the Jewish Question presses. At the end, the unmentionable forces its way into Yeats's work through imitation of the outmoded. No foreign refugees in a ballad of the Irishry, no Polish (or is it German?) refugees, no polymath Solomons, just the age-old pedlar in the late summer and autumn of 1938. Like Wilhelm Aron of Bamberg, he won't last long, but at least he made it into the script.

The Ossietzky Case

Even in England, the island-fortress, Hitler's arrival in power provoked thought. Innumerable protest groups rose and fell, unable to match the enormity of the evil they opposed and feared. Inevitably Irish names occur among the membership of British lobbies. These include several with whom Yeats was familiar – the classicist E. R. Dodds, the poet C. Day Lewis and the medievalist Helen Waddell. Dodds had not only moved easily in Dublin literary circles after graduation from Oxford, he later sat on the council of the Society for Psychical Research to which Yeats addressed himself on numerous occasions. Louis MacNeice was an executive committee member of the Association of Writers for Intellectual Liberty (from December 1938) and read a paper about Yeats to the association on 1 March 1939.

The contradiction between a desire for peace and a resolute position on fascism was never resolved. Such failures of the decade accommodated Yeats's adroitly passive manoeuvres. Rearmanent, which could only be construed as an active response to German policies, was opposed by many sincere anti-fascists on grounds of pacifism. Quite apart from his increasingly authoritarian political utterances, Yeats was psychologically attuned towards violence, had been so since childhood, and acknowledged the inner struggle to control 'action'. Not all action involves bodily motion, or a kinetic chain of physical reactions. Words themselves constitute action in certain circumstances, as when the clergy say, 'I pronounce you man and wife.' Performative language of this kind characterises the style of Yeats's late poetry. In the six sections of 'Under Ben Bulben' (September 1938) we find that a verb in the imperative mood initiates sections I, IV and V. The third and perhaps best-known section adopts a more complex and elusive mode of address:

> You that Mitchel's prayer have heard
> 'Send war in our time, O Lord!'
> Know that when all words are said
> And a man is fighting mad,
> Something drops from eyes long blind ...

The main problem is to identify 'You'. If hearing a prayer is understood in the strong and active sense, the You is God. This would involve Yeats in an unprecedented act of *lèse-majesté*, proceeding to remind the Almighty of just how things stand. On the other hand, if 'You' is whoever has [over]heard John Mitchel's prayer, then the verb to 'know' may be an imperative, according to which Yeats insists on declaring what it is the hearers shall know. This is a performative sentence. Significantly, what it would perform is a complete transcending of language ('all words are said') after which wisdom is intensified by violence, which in turn is to be made manifest in sexual selection.

We are a long road from the discussions that preoccupied the International Association of Writers for the Defence of Culture in which Aldous Huxley and Virginia Woolf were uneasily active.[31] The language of progressive political agitation may have been repellent to

Yeats, but he possessed the intelligence to know that words may not always convey the full significance of their context. Fuzzy liberalism (E. M. Forster) and gendered pacifism (Virginia Woolf) may not have articulated a short and easy way of defeating the rough beast of Berlin but, by that inadequacy, they left room for greater concentration and sharper focus. Yeats, in contrast, moves to close off any debate or any possibility of debate. The 1930s were replete with opportunities to test these opposing theories against brute reality.

Within a year of its coming into existence, the Third Reich had entered into a compact with Yeats, however passive (though grateful) his own responses may have been. The award to him of a Goethe-Plakette in February 1934 is the theme of the next chapter. The relationship was bound to alter, in one direction or another. As the plight of German intellectuals – to mention no other victims – deteriorated, so writers and artists in the democracies became involved in defence or rescue operations, protests and petitions. Exiles such as Bertolt Brecht and Thomas Mann provided a focus for these activities, while the continued presence within Germany of Gottfried Benn, Gerhart Hauptmann, Ricarda Huch, Ernst Jünger, Emil Nolde and others generated a heated debate abroad about the relationship between the collective tyranny and their personal integrity.

The calculated enthusiasm of New Germany for Yeats's work can be gauged by the response to a selection of plays translated by Henry von Heiseler and published in 1933, sometime before June. The date is significant in that one can assume publication was under way – certainly the ten plays had been translated – before Hitler came to power. *Irische Schaubühne,* however, was privately printed in Munich in a limited and numbered (250) edition, with marbled endpapers and other refinements. It was, in effect, a collector's item, scarcely a commercial product. Nevertheless, three reviews appeared in Germany (and a fourth in Switzerland). The earliest was published in the *Berliner Tageblatt* of 11 February 1934, a full seven months after publication, but just a few days before a Goethe-Plakette was awarded to Yeats in Frankfurt. In June 1934, an excerpt from Heiseler's translation of Yeats's 'Deirdre' appeared in the *Deutsche Zeitschrift*, together with some poems and excerpts from essays translated by a different hand: this was the month Yeats formally accepted the Plakette. Two reviews of *Irische Schaubühne* were tied to the celebration of Yeats's seventieth birthday in June 1935.[32]

Although Carl von Ossietzky (1889-1938) was not an original writer in the sense that meant so much to Yeats – he was not an *artist* – his work as editor of *Die Weltbühne* had established him as a major influence in a sphere of artistic endeavour with which Yeats virtually identified himself in Stockholm – theatre. (In addition, the highly regarded magazine had published several articles on James Joyce between 1927 and 1932.) As the Abbey had proven time and time again, theatre was a point where art and politics undeniably met. In 1907, riots over Synge's 'Playboy of the Western World' had obliged the directors to call in the Dublin Metropolitan Police. The Lord Chamberlain's refusal to license G. B. Shaw's 'The Shewing Up of Blanco Posnet' two years later, and the several controversies about Sean O'Casey's work in the 1920s, had given Yeats plenty of experience in this area. Occurring in 1929, the last of these revolved round O'Casey's 'Silver Tassie', its perceived revolutionary debt to German Expressionism, and its opposition to war. It was hardly to be expected that, in Nazi Germany, theatre and its supporters would go unmolested.

Ossietzky had been born on 3 October 1889 into an impoverished Silesian petty aristocratic family. His father had worked as a clerk in a Hamburg lawyer's office. The family had never been landed, consisting instead of a succession of officers, clergy and minor officials. In this respect, his social background was not unlike that of the Yeatses in the early nineteenth century, more attached to Dublin Castle than to ancestral acres, advancing through clerical appointments rather than marriage into the dynasts. As a young man, Ossietzky was influenced by the work of the Darwinist Ernst Haeckel and the social democratic politics of August Bebel (who was twice imprisoned before his death in 1913). The Ossietzky family illustrates the variety and relative modesty of social ranking consistent within the *Junker* class, just as the Irish Protestant Ascendancy sported fewer venerable aristocrats than self-aggrandised merchants. If the Yeatses illustrated a similar case of social misprision, the two sons of these families diverged strikingly in response to their situation, the German moving steadily to the left (in the political spectrum of the time), the Irishman to the right. Their views of science and Darwinism in particular might be taken as conclusive evidence in this regard. Ironically, the societies from which they came – twenty-five years apart – were to diverge in the opposite fashion, so that each of them found himself strangely placed as non-representative of a national culture for which he nonetheless felt obliged to speak.

In 1913, Ossietzky married an Englishwoman, Maud Hester Lichfield Woods (1888–1974?), whose subsequent alcoholism caused him great pain, but which may have protected her from retribution under the Nazis (she outlived her husband). During the Great War, he published a series of articles later collected under the title *The Advancement of the New Reformation* (1919). By now he had moved to Berlin, and became secretary to the German Peace Society, from which he seceded to form the Peace League of War Veterans. Ever busy, Ossietzky had troubled the authorities by 1913, and as a journalist he developed an uncompromising style in attacking militarism under the Kaiser, the Weimar constitution and its successor. Essentially, he was a pacifist with distinct liberal commitments politically.

As the Nazis came closer to achieving power, he broke from the narrow position of many German liberals and socialists, to recommend a comprehensive alliance with the communists. Not that his only opponents were those as yet to triumph: in November 1931, Ossietzky was tried for treason in connection with an article published in *Die Weltbühne* two years earlier. Sentenced to eighteen months, he entered prison on 10 May 1932, but was released under a Christmas amnesty at the end of the year. On 30 January, Hitler was declared Chancellor, and on 27 February Ossietzky was rearrested and held in Spandau prison in Berlin. From there he was transferred first to Sonnenburg, newly converted into a concentration camp, and the following year was moved again, this time to Papenburg-Esterwegen in the boggy north-western region of Germany. His legal sentence had of course long since expired, and he himself was not far short of the same fate.

'A shaking, deadly pale something, a being which appears to have lost all feeling, one eye swollen, his teeth apparently smashed, dragging a broken and badly mended leg.' This was the description of Ossietzky provided by a Swiss Red Cross official, Carl J. Burckhardt, who had overcome great difficulties to visit the prisoner. At about the time of his transfer from camp to camp, an exiled journalist gave Thomas Mann in Switzerland a 'shattering' account of conditions in these places. In his diary for 13 February 1934, Mann recorded an image to freeze the blood of all stand-aside liberals:

Mute, frozen, a film over his eyes, unable to communicate: endlessly, crazily apologising. People who have been to visit the pacifist Ossietzky claim he is insensible to anything said to him or asked of him, but simply marches in goose-step around the room, saluting and shouting 'Yes sir'.[33]

Mann's source for this cameo was Friedrich Gübler, who had been, until recently, editor of the *Frankfurter Zeitung*. The following day, Yeats was fêted in Frankfurt-am-Main, his name celebrated in the Nazi press. The front page of what had been Gübler's paper led the applause.[34]

International concern for Ossietzky's welfare had begun in January 1934, when Wickham Steed published a letter in the London *Times*. The Reich was just one year in existence, and an unrealistic belief in the outer world's ability to reason with Hitler still prevailed. In June of that year, an international campaign to have the Nobel Peace Prize awarded to Ossietzky was launched, its more limited objectives being his release first from detention and then from Germany itself. Albert Einstein, Aldous Huxley, Augustus John, Romain Rolland and Virginia Woolf were among the distinguished supporters of the cause.[35] But progress was fearfully slow. The Nobel authorities were not anxious to give offence to a new regime at the first opportunity, and no award was made in the year 1935. While the world knew what was going on in Germany, moral obtuseness did not melt away. As time passed, the support of men and women who had already been awarded Nobel Prizes was deemed important in persuading both the prize committees and public opinion. Yeats was among those who were approached, as late as 1936.

The Archives of the Friends of Carl von Ossietzky are preserved in the Internationaal Institut voor Sociale Geschiedenis, Amsterdam. From these, and from the several publications issued by supporters in Britain, France and elsewhere, it is possible to reconstruct a great deal of the campaign.[36] But there is no reference whatsoever to Yeats. The organisers do not appear to have placed much faith in the chances of his support. More significant, however, is the absence of Ethel Mannin's name, left-wing novelist though she was at that time. And even Ernst Toller, German dramatist and fervent anti-fascist, does not feature extensively in the records. From these details, one can deduce that the approach to Yeats, made jointly by Mannin and Toller, was an impulsive and amateur act of recruitment.

Since the end of 1934 Yeats had been having an affair with Mannin – and other young women whom he met principally in London.[37]

One of their common interests was the Sexual Reform League of which she was a member; she was also a friend of Norman Haire, who had performed a limited vasectomy on the poet the previous spring, with a view (evidently successful) to reviving his erectile manhood. Perhaps the confusion of sexual and political interests was typical of Yeats at this time; it certainly did Ossietzky no good. London was the Irish poet's happy playground, where he tolerated no hard-luck stories. In many ways he was a provincial lad belatedly sowing his wild oats. Reminders of the brutal world beyond the restaurant, the club-room or the hotel suite sent him into a mental retreat to those four green provinces he half-despised himself for quitting.

In the meantime, Yeats had achieved his seventieth birthday, on 13 June 1935. His health gave cause for concern, but his sexuality had been reactivated, an episode yet to be considered in its political aspects. He was truly a great man unrivalled as a poet in the English language (perhaps any language), a former member of parliament, a Nobel Prize winner, and a fastidious cultivator of his own image. The birthday brought congratulations – in Germany as well as elsewhere. The *Berliner Tageblatt* (14 June) gave Walter F. Schirmer nearly one-third of a page in which to celebrate the Irish poet (or rather dramatist) whose work was a protest against the spirit of the nineteenth century. Karl Arns, who had been writing about Yeats since the mid-1920s, marked the occasion with a piece in the *Hamburger Fremdenblatt* (12 June). Unlike James Joyce or T. S. Eliot, Yeats was himself a trophy whom the Nazis wished to claim: his 'mystical' and folklore interests were manifestly compatible with their ideology, and it was a natural propagandistic step to translate compatibility as concurrence. The articles effecting this compact scarcely amounted to a satanic embrace, but they contributed to the anaesthetising of the poet at a time when other views of the Reich were brought to his attention.

Mannin has left a memoir of those days, rather vague as to dates, but suggesting that Yeats was inclined to sleep during some of his dinner engagements. This was a double disappointment for her, a man-eater of appetite. One evening in early 1935, she had met Ernst Toller at a Soviet Embassy reception where they drank deeply, despite her arrangement to dine later with Yeats. The German dramatist was at this point living in British exile, devoted to the Ossietzky cause. An American left-wing journalist, Louis Fischer, was also in town. From the embassy, Mannin and Toller departed by taxi for the Savile Club where she had arranged to meet her Celtic Lion, for Toller had decided to recruit Yeats to the Ossietzky campaign. Women were not admitted to the club premises, so the trio retired to Claridge's down the rain-sodden street, where Ossietzky's hopes of survival vied with the orchestra.

As the prime mover of this hopeless solicitation, Mannin is strikingly unrepentant in recollection:

> I knew before Toller had finished that Yeats would refuse. He was acutely uncomfortable about it, but he refused. He never meddled in political matters, he said; he never had. At the urging of Maud Gonne he had signed the petition on behalf of Roger Casement, but that was all, and the Casement case was after all an Irish affair. He was a poet, and Irish, and had no interest in European political squabbles. His interest was Ireland, and Ireland had nothing to do with Europe politically; it was outside, apart. He was sorry, but this had always been his attitude.
>
> Toller and I looked at each other. Toller's eyes filled with tears. Perhaps, he said, with emotion, perhaps one felt differently about these matters if one had been in prison oneself. This, he urged, was not a political matter; it was an affair of life and death, a question of a man's life. He, too, was a poet, but life was bigger than all the poetry ever written.
>
> ... Yeats no less stubbornly persisted that he knew nothing about Ossietzky as a writer; that he could not be involved in a matter of this kind; that it was no part of an artist's business to become involved in affairs of this kind. He was sorry. He was very sorry.[38]

Perhaps this exemplifies Yeats's classic liberal detachment, but it is a wobbly assertion of the principle. It may also be a statement of his Irish nationalist priorities; in this regard, too, Yeats's logic is of dogmatic silence rather than articulation. At a deeper level, the attitude towards Ossietzky exemplifies a view of language and silence explored in 'Under Ben Bulben' a few years later, a view that is not unconnected with those of Martin Heidegger. Of the writers who have chosen to write books about the poet's politics, only the late Geoffrey Thurley notes the Ossietzky case.[39] Thurley was refused permanent employment in Dublin's two universities.

To Mannin at least, Yeats later indicated a softening of his attitude – but not towards Ossietzky. He read Toller's *Seven Plays* (1935), and declared the author a greater technical innovator even than Pirandello. After Easter, he hoped to persuade the Abbey to stage 'Mrs Eddy'. As for the evening on which Mannin had brought Toller to meet him, Yeats had been unable to explain himself at the time because of a false impression founded on a very bad performance of an early Toller play. There was no mention of the prisoner in Germany, and there was no Dublin production of Toller's 'Mrs Eddy'.[40]

Thomas Mann and Archibald MacLeish

Patrick O'Neill and Heinz Kosok have some observations on the background to the publication of plays by Yeats in German translation, which also illuminate the manner in which the Irish poet was managed in the Third Reich. A contrast of misfortune and opportunism is once again evident. Henry von Heiseler had found himself induced into a Russian army towards the end of the Great War. Arriving back in Germany in 1922 with little but a manuscript in his possession, he was distressed to discover that authorisation to translate certain plays by Yeats had been acquired by another during his enforced absence. The legitimate but stylistically challenged owner, Herbert E. Herlitschka, saw to it that von Heiseler's *Irische Schaubühne*, made up of ten plays, was confined to its private edition of 250 copies. That was in 1933, when questions of copyright were not pressing. However, once the decision to honour Yeats early in 1934 was put into practice (without his prior consent), this de-luxe edition was reviewed more extensively than such items usually are with the effect of giving prominence to the dramatist's name in literary journals and newspapers.[41] Compared with the slowly emergent academic response, and the problems raised by editors, it was all very positive, very gratifying – incomprehensible to the man himself, but gratifying.

On a virtually global scale, Yeats in his later years became the object of extensive comment. Some of this he found flattering, much of it he ignored. Rarely did literary criticism affect his judgment as a poet, nor did he often respond in poetry to personal attacks or plaudits. When we come upon a poem which, by his own account, arose out of his reading of a critical essay, it deserves close attention, not least because of its political theme. One of the editorial decisions to which he devoted thought and time during his last weeks was the order in which his final writings should be printed. In the event, *Last Poems and Two Plays* (Cuala Press, June 1939) was issued under his sisters' private imprint in Dublin, and the war complicated the subsequent commercial publication of a new *Collected Poems* by Macmillan of London. By a decision agreed before his death, priority – that is, last place – was given to the following untypical poem:

POLITICS

'*In our time the destiny of man presents
its meanings in political terms.*' – THOMAS MANN

How can I, that girl standing there,
My attention fix
On Roman or on Russian
Or on Spanish politics?
Yet here's a travelled man that knows
What he talks about,
And there's a politician
That has read and thought,
And maybe what they say is true
Of war and war's alarms,
But O that I were young again
And held her in my arms.[42]

The first version of this had been written in May 1938, and the inspiration for it was Cora Hughes, a red-headed young woman of strongly left-wing views, whom Yeats had encountered on O'Connell Street in Dublin. The following month he left Ireland to stay at the Chantry House, in the village of Steyning, Sussex. His hostess was Edith Shackleton Heald, with whom he (at the age of seventy-two) had been having an affair since the previous year. During several sojourns in his lover's well-appointed home, Yeats wrote the desolate one-act play 'Purgatory', the premiere of which later provided him with a platform for his views on eugenics and German law. The plot arises from an act of what Yeats terms *mésalliance*, a sexual union deemed inadvisable on grounds of class, and his developing this theme in the house of his lesbian lover should be accounted a triumph among Yeats's liberal inconsistencies. The play and the poem were not the sole products of his remarkable late poetic fecundity, but they share preoccupations that render them especially valuable in this present study. In contrasting ways, both are concerned with desire in the past, and its disruptive presence in the writer's mind.

The sense of a disjunction, even what French theorists ungallantly term a rupture, between title and poem is literally inscribed in the epigraph that appears between them. Such intrusions or interventions are extremely rare in Yeats's poetry. Thus the epigraph to 'Politics' possesses a unique, if also ambiguous, status. Attributed to Thomas Mann, it reads, 'In our time the destiny of man presents its meanings in political terms.' When Yeats transmitted a draft to Dorothy Wellesley in May 1938, he evidently got the German novelist's remark slightly, but significantly, wrong. In the letter, Mann is quoted as referring to the destiny of man presenting its meaning (singular) in political terms. Conventionally, Yeats's source for the epigraph has been identified as an article entitled 'Public Speech and Private Speech in Poetry' by the American poet Archibald MacLeish. More often gestured at nowadays than critically examined, this had appeared in the *Yale Review* of March 1938, and it seems likely that its author – a competent poet and critic who was to become head of the Library of Congress in 1939 – had sent a copy directly to the poet. In his correspondence with Wellesley, Yeats represented it as dealing with his work more or less exclusively: 'the only article on the subject which has not bored me for years'.[43] In fact, of MacLeish's twelve pages only three paragraphs (amounting to little more than a single page) deal at all with Yeats. A far larger proportion treats what is termed 'a poetic revolution', by which English literature had liberated itself from an effete inheritance.

It is true that MacLeish opens his commentary on Yeats's poetry by remarking that it represents a new forthrightness:

> Yeats, who is the best of modern poets, may be taken in this as the most characteristic. Not in his capacity as a man of politics or as the director of a theatre but in his capacity as poet, Yeats has refused the customary costume. He is no self-conscious genius exploiting his difference from other men – and inventing differences where none exist. He is quite simply a man who is a poet. And his poetry is no escape from time and place and life and death but, on the contrary, the acceptance of these things and their embodiment.[44]

This constitutes the entirety of MacLeish's first paragraph on Yeats, and the second proceeds to make a distinction – it would now be deemed a hackneyed one – between the vagueness of the early poetry and 'the strong presentness, the urgent voice, of such a poem as "Byzantium"'. This is a paragraph of commendation, arguing that Yeats's poetry is the first in generations 'which can cast a shadow in the sun of actual things – men's lives, men's wills, men's future'. The paragraph concludes by declaring that 'writing as Yeats writes, a man need not pretend an ignorance of the world, need not affect a strangeness from his time, need not go mooning through an endless attic with the starlight clicking on the roof'.[45] The imagery of the last sentence clearly demonstrates the legacy of Victorian, or American-Victorian, poetic lumber that MacLeish was still renouncing. It is obvious how Yeats assists the exercise, but the influence of T. S. Eliot is also present.

The third paragraph devoted to Yeats is a great deal more critical – and urgent – than Yeats's own summary would lead one to believe. To Dorothy Wellesley, he had remarked loftily that the article had gone on 'to say that, owing to my age and my relation to Ireland, I was unable to use this "public" language on what it evidently considered the right public material, politics'.[46] MacLeish, however, had argued rather more precisely, writing that:

> The later poetry of Yeats, because of Yeats's somewhat isolated situation in Ireland and because of Yeats's age, has not been called upon to employ the results of the poetic revolution at the point where those results may prove to be most useful. Yeats has moved only briefly and unwillingly at the point where the poetic revolution crosses the revolution in the social and political and economic structure of the post-war world, which so deeply concerns our generation in this country. But it is precisely at that point that the greatest victories of modern poetry may be won.[47]

A number of points emerge from a fuller reading of MacLeish's article. First, Yeats had been wrong in supposing that it referred to his 'relation to Ireland' as an obstacle to the employment of a public poetic language on a public theme. What MacLeish had stressed was Yeats's 'isolated situation [by being] in Ireland', not (so to speak) his isolated position within Ireland. It is worth noting that Yeats had glossed 'isolated situation' as relating to him rather than to Ireland; his sense of dislocation from the nation or the state was unclouded by any suspicion that the nation or state was itself isolated.

The second, and more substantial point, arises from the paragraph succeeding that just quoted. Dismissive of historical determinism, MacLeish nevertheless finds himself obliged to invoke coincidence, because it is very difficult otherwise to explain the fact that:

> the revolution in the art of poetry which enabled poetry to re-enter the actual world, took place ten years or so before the social and economic and political revolution which to-day requires poetry either to re-enter the actual world or to perform a final bloodless suicide upon its laurel mountain. Thomas Mann, who has reason to know, says of the nature of our time, that in our time the destiny of man presents its meanings in

political terms. A political world and a destiny presented in political terms are a world and a destiny with which nineteenth-century poetry is impotent to deal. They are perhaps the world and the destiny to which modern poetry is best adapted.[48]

It should be noted in passing that MacLeish summarises more than a biographical career; within the limitations of a magazine article, he attempts to outline an epochal shift, from mid-Victorian tonalities to the distinctive contemporary anxieties of the 1930s. This synchronises with Yeats's career, but is far larger than it. A sudden revelation dawns, I believe, on the latter-day reader who reaches this point of MacLeish's argument. Having first alluded to 'the revolution in the social and political and economic structure of the post-war world', MacLeish now shifts his key term into a more concentrated arena. For, by 'political revolution' he has not signified some general turmoil in western civilisation, embracing the Great War, Mussolini, the Depression, Uncle Joe Stalin and all. Nor has he endorsed the then-familiar, if strained, argument that Roosevelt with his New Deal might be assimilated into a universal revolution, or pantheon of strong leaders, riding roughshod over constitutional niceties. On 2 January 1934, the *Irish Times* (a local example) headlined 'Roosevelt Reports to Congress on His Dictatorship'. This is not MacLeish's point. On the contrary, he now means fascism and, more specifically, he means German fascism. That is the only sense by which the timetable of a poetic revolution preceding a political revolution by ten or so years can be specified. *The Waste Land* and *Ulysses* had been published in 1922, the year of Mussolini's triumph; Hitler assumed power in January 1933. In any case, the prominent citation of Thomas Mann, Hitler's most formidable literary opponent, confirms this timetable. Closer to George Orwell than to Conor Cruise O'Brien, MacLeish had raised the question of how modernism in literature relates to authoritarianism in politics.

In 1938 when the article appeared, this matter was crystal-clear in readers' minds. Revolution was at least as often applied to the experiments of the Italian and German fascists as it was to those of Stalin and his rival, Trotsky. When Yeats wrote fervently in favour of 'Tomorrow's Revolution' in his lengthy pamphlet, *On the Boiler*, his fellow-travelling (if any) did not head leftwards. And when the Nazis at war chose to translate 'Ireland after the Revolution' (from the same pamphlet), they harboured no anxiety as to his possible Bolshevik leanings. Indeed, one of the effects of reading MacLeish's article afresh is that it requires a reconsideration of the context in which Yeats's very late political utterances should be read.

Yeats indirectly claimed to have found the epigraph for 'Politics' in this source. To be more precise, the words employed as epigraph (and therein ascribed to Thomas Mann) may be found in the article that Yeats certainly, but not so carefully, read. It may seem finicking to argue that the poem's epigraph attributes *verbatim* to Mann an opinion or utterance that can only be traced as MacLeish's brief paraphrase of the German's notion of the *Zeitgeist.* If we attend closely to MacLeish, and bear in mind that Yeats gives no indication of any other source, then the words cited take on a deeper complexion. Isolating them as a vatic utterance, Yeats apparently urges either an embrace of the political or, in stark opposition to that attitude, a scornful dismissal of a new dogma.

Evidence from the *Yale Review* refuses to endorse this reading by Yeats.[49] For a start, the epigraph as initially supplied in the letter to Wellesley has distorted the phrase by rewriting the plural 'meanings' as unique 'meaning'. Though the Cuala Press edition and its proofs suggest correction and counter-correction by one hand or another, the one-volume *Collected Poems,* which Macmillan kept in the bookshops from 1950 until the (temporary) expiry of copyright in 1990, perpetuated the singular 'meaning'. In this (distorted) form, the epigraph emphasises an absolute condition in which contemporary destiny is said by Thomas Mann to present its meaning – *entire, unqualified and exclusive* - in political terms. Embraced or dismissed, this would constitute, or at least synopsise, a veritable totalitarianism, with which it is impossible to associate Mann's name. But the restored reading is plural – 'meanings' – and with it the problem alters.

Politically, these divergent readings are dynamite. Neither of them is anywhere shown to be Mann's *ipsissima verba*; indeed, it is difficult to see how they could be, given that he wrote in German. Yet we do not want to accuse MacLeish also of some underhand exercise in strong reading in which he has, even earlier than Yeats may have, taken liberties with the German novelist's utterances. So we should ask what MacLeish's sources might have been, should ask in effect what *other* text by Mann has MacLeish paraphrased? I have to report that I have not identified any single, recognisable occasion on which Mann uttered words of which MacLeish's subordinate clause is a – so to speak – *oratio obliqua* version, but I can't pretend to have followed up Mann's original speeches and writings in every detail. Perhaps we might consider a sentence or so in a brief letter that Mann had sent for publication in the *Yale Review* in an anniversary issue of 1936, one sentence of which might be translated, 'The problem of Mankind today lies in this – that it is not easy to distinguish literature and the spirit from political and social matters.'[50] From this, it seems a reasonable induction that, in 1938, MacLeish translated-cum-paraphrased a sentence of Mann's which had appeared earlier in the same journal.

Mann published a great deal of material, isolated at first, but gradually cohering into a body of political expression from 1936 onwards. *Order of the Day* appeared in 1942, but the subtitle 'Political Essays and Speeches of Two Decades' indicates the extent to which the once-Olympian novelist had, in the course of the late 1920s and '30s, stooped to conquer the political, social and moral problems of the fascist 'revolution'. It is useful to take the longest of the pieces in *Order of the Day* as representative. 'The Coming Victory of Democracy' was written in 1937 while Mann was still an exile living in Switzerland; printed in German in Stockholm, it was the first of his political addresses intended for an American audience. In this brief litany of place-names it is possible to discern a degree of dislocation with which the Yeatsian dispute with de Valeran Ireland can offer no comparison. Yet several themes explored by Mann are considered (albeit under a different light) in *On the Boiler*.

A telling point of more substantial comparison between *Order of the Day* and *On the Boiler* may be found in the attitudes towards education evinced in each. In this regard, it is as well to emphasise the distinctly patrician and disengaged notion of culture which Mann had espoused during and after the Great War.[51] Now, in the essay already quoted, we find an insistence on democracy considered as thought, as 'thought related to life and action'. Moreover, 'democracy wishes to elevate mankind, to teach it to think, to set it free. It seeks to remove from culture the stamp of privilege and disseminate it among the people – in a word it aims at education.'[52] Yeats, on the other hand, links an educational fundamentalism to political and (by implication) military apocalypse. In the section entitled 'Ireland after the Revolution', he assumes:

> that some tragic crisis shall so alter Europe and all opinion that the Irish government will teach the great majority of its school-children nothing but ploughing, harrowing, sowing, curry-combing, bicycle-cleaning,

drill-driving, parcel-making, bale-pushing, tin-can-soldering, door-knob polishing, threshold-whitening, coat-cleaning, trouser-patching, and playing upon the Squiffer, all things that serve human dignity . . .[53]

Beyond this cynical humour, and keeping to an appropriately imperative mood in grammar, he continues, 'Teach nothing but Greek, Gaelic, mathematics and perhaps one modern language.' Latin is rejected for its 'feminine tricks', and a page later it is no surprise to read that 'armament comes next to education'. Falstaffian jokes about 'playing upon the squiffer' evidently relate to what might be done after 'some tragic crisis', without any attention to what might be entailed during the crisis. By such evasion, and by other bold declarations, On the Boiler is posited on the need for, desire of, war. And so desire is presented as necessity.

The Yale Review was not, however, the only publication that was pressed on Yeats's attention at this time. The wartime biography admitted that 'he had read a great number of popular books on Hitler's Germany', but understandably flinched from recording what these were or how Yeats had responded to them.[54] Edward O'Shea's Descriptive Catalog of Yeats's library operated under no such inhibitions. Here are preserved details of pamphlets from Terramare Publications of Berlin, including Fritz Edel's German Labour Service and Rudolf Frercks's German Population Policy (both 1937). In the latter case, what Yeats possessed and preserved was an uncorrected proof copy, evidence that certainly exempts him from the charge of spending money on such propaganda, but which, by the same token, establishes that he was a privileged recipient of Nazi material perhaps even in advance of its publication.

It is possible to argue that he was the passive recipient of these tracts – likewise a copy of Il Frontespizio (no. 6, Bologna, June 1938) with a contribution by Grattan Freyer. Yeats's biographers and political critics had their own agendas – still have – and one should not assume that he subscribed to Terramare Publications, even though he preserved their pamphlets. Nevertheless, passivity as a defence rapidly wears thin, especially in one clamouring for war. One of the less odious of these publications was Christmas Carols of Germany, a twelve-page item (with illustrations and facsimiles) prepared for the foreign reader in 1936 by Geraldine M. de Courcy, possibly an Irish name.

The relevance of this material to Yeats's work on On the Boiler is neatly encapsulated by the cataloguer who summarised Herr

Frercks's work: '[this] addresses the problem of the falling birth rate among "families hereditarily endowed with the highest qualities" and the rising rate among "families with a large number of social unadaptable elements." '[55] Given that Nazi sterilisation laws had been introduced as early as July 1933, the problem had not been left unattended. In the abstract, Nazi eugenics might be propagandistically summarised in terms of 'the best bred of the best', but the unavoidable corollary in practice was racialist persecution, as extensive reports of German official treatment of Jews and gypsies confirmed week after week. Yeats, who deplored propaganda, had a distinctly selective policy in ridding his library of it, and a distinctly myopic view of the concomitants of Nazi eugenics. Yet even so thorough an investigator of Yeats's sources for *On the Boiler* as David Bradshaw has acquitted him from using the Terramare pamphlets, preferring to stress the influence of the Eugenics Society in London and the work of Raymond Cattell.[56] The choice implied by Bradshaw is an artificial, indeed non-existent one. Yeats's German contacts were wider than a researcher into *On the Boiler* alone might deduce.

Underlying these interests and sympathies was an occult philosophy that endorsed the irrational. In his copy of G. T. Fechner's *On Life After Death* (1914), Yeats at some point marked a passage which taught that 'if two spirits of the dead meet (on earth) their nations also meet'. Late in 1938, Yeats (still quite alive) met Eduard Hempel, and not for the first time. Joachim von Ribbentrop (1893–1946) had become Hitler's Foreign Minister in February 1938: a frightful snob who had cultivated British high society, he ended his first year in office when Yeats died. It would be quite in keeping with his notion of the Reich's priorities in Ireland that Hempel should seek out Yeats so that their nations might meet.

The German minister has been fortunate in his commemorators. For years, his (admittedly late) affiliation as a Nazi party member was either unknown or diplomatically ignored. His manners were accounted evidence of his good feeling, and his success in winning de Valera's respect was at once a professional accomplishment and a personal insurance against final calamity. If he persuaded Berlin not to exploit Irish internal divisions beyond the creation of nuisance for the British, and kept his distance from the harder Nazi elements, he was also – from the outset – a shrewd innovator in the diplomacy of culture, including popular culture. In October 1937 he issued an

Aide-Mémoire about the showing in Dublin of 'The Road Back', an anti-war film based on the novel by the German writer Erich Maria Remarque (1898–1970). He applauded the film's official concern for world peace, but deplored its depiction of demoralised German troops and the troops' hostility towards their officers. The Irish authorities appreciated Hempel's cultivated approach, so different from the shrillness of his Italian counterpart. During the war he was able to have a playscript drastically rewritten before the Peacock Theatre staged it.[57] On the eve of war, he renewed his association with Yeats.

The occasion is commemorated in Yeats's copy of *Germany Speaks* (with a preface by von Ribbentrop) now preserved in the National Library of Ireland. Among the twenty-one contributions 'by leading members of party and state' there is a lengthy account of 'The Act for the Prevention of Hereditary Diseased Offspring' and of the provision (28 June 1935) abolishing 'the maxim according to which no offence can be punished unless it is specifically mentioned in the existing code' of law. As O'Shea's catalogue demonstrates, little of this was new to Yeats. Apart from the inaccurate citation that appears as the epigraph to 'Politics', there is no mention of Thomas Mann in Yeats's correspondence.

Yeats's concern with education did not arise from any very happy recollection of his own schooling. The brief period he spent in Dublin's High School was significant for the encounter there with other pupils who shared his interest in occultic matters. He was inclined to associate those years with social humiliation, principally because the family had been obliged to move into a suburban semi-detached house between Harold's Cross and Terenure. Nevertheless, at the end of his life Yeats was approached by the editor of *The Erasmian*, High School's magazine. The great man contributed a poem, 'What Then?', which gently mocks his own driving ambitions. A much younger ex-pupil 'recalls a teacher at High School in the 1940s boasting of the two sixth-year school trips he had organised to Nazi Germany, presumably with school sanction'.[58] From March 1934 onwards, High School had enjoyed cordial relations with the German educational representatives in Dublin, of whom Helmut Clissmann was a leader. Scholarships and reproduction paintings were made available. On 7 August 1936, thirty Dublin schoolboys arrived at Berlin's railway station in a party led by two teachers from the High School. They were met by a 'storm-troopers' band' who escorted them amidst a parade of Hitler Youth. Their German itinerary included the Olympic Games, the Czech border, and sundry provincial cities. 'All seemed happy and healthy, glorifying in their "New Germany".' Not all the pupils came from the High School, though A. N. Jeffares is seated in the middle row of the group photograph. In the same issue of the school mag, reporting this mission, Jeffares published a science fiction prophecy of 'High School – 2000 AD', complete with telespiritualist Latin classes offering 'introductions to the girls down at Carthage.' The following issue carried Yeats's poem, 'What then?'

The cultivation of links between Yeats's alma mater and the Reich was sustained the following year. Young Jeffares wrote up an account of the return visit by German boys in 1937, the highlights of which were lunch in the Shelbourne with Minister Hempel, a trip to the Aran Islands, and a reception in Glendalough at which we can assume the Stuarts were present, or at least Mrs Stuart. Even in 1938, the plucky Dubliners mounted a second trip to Germany, to find air-raid precautions in a high state of alert. 'Dresden, in particular, being (at the time of our visit) only thirty miles from the Czech frontier, had great need for adequate protection from enemy bombers.' (The phrase in parentheses has the oddest effect, in retrospect, of suggesting that Dresden – not the border – might have to be moved.) It is worth noting that the President of the Old Boys Union in 1937–38 was Rupert Jeffares, whose years in High School had overlapped with Yeats's.

Of course, the German in the end proved pluckiest of all. In 1939, in the face of imminent war, a party of schoolboys arrived in Dublin and were entertained by – *inter alia* – Dr Joseph Raftery of the National Museum, a loyal follower of Adolf Mahr, director of the museum and chief man of the Nazis in Dublin. Even the earliest of Yeats's experiences will become entangled in the Nazi catastrophe.

'My Frankfurt Honour'

[IN MEMORIAM LUITPOLD ROPPELT, 1908–1971, OF BAMBERG]

At Lucan District Court yesterday, before District Justice Reddin
... Lionel McGill, Lucan, charged Thomas McEvoy ... with
having assaulted him at Lucan on the 13th January, and with using
bad language towards him. After hearing the evidence, the Justice
said Mr McEvoy was known as 'The Burgomaster of Lucan', and as
such, should not use a four-grained fork as his mace. (Laughter.) He
adjourned the charge of using bad language generally, and for the
assault imposed a nominal fine of 1s, and 21s costs.

Irish Times, 14 February 1934

Was it for this the wild geese spread
The grey wing upon every tide ... ?

'September 1913'

Yeats in the German-speaking world before 1945 is no rich topic for
enquiry, for all Roy Foster notes that the poet had a devoted
following there. Some early work was translated, mainly from his
folkloristic publications or from literary works reflecting that interest.
Between the Anglophilia of one audience and the Celticism of
another, he fell uneasily. Quite outside these unexciting circumstances, Germany between the wars forms an unavoidable station on the
Yeats scholar's *via dolorosa*. Independent of the man and his work,
the Weimar Republic brought culture and politics into dialogue like
nowhere else, with economic catastrophe ever audible in the
background. For film, music, painting, sculpture, theatre – never
mind the silent sisters of lyric poetry and fiction – it was the showcase
(or disgrace) of Europe. It chose eclectically from American and
Soviet rival visions of the future, with chaotic but stimulating results.
Its impact spilled into London, Paris and Vienna. Through Ernst
Toller, if no other, its passions reached Dublin and Yeats. In a
pamphlet written for T. S. Eliot's *Criterion Miscellany*, Joseph Hone
(Yeats's future biographer) made a direct, if highly formal comparison

between the 'Liberal and Modern State' in which he lived and Weimar Germany: 'Saorstat in Irish can mean both Free State and Republic, just as Reich to a German can still mean old Empire as well as new Republic.'[1]

Not everyone in the new republic embraced democracy as the reward for loss of territory and prestige in 1918. There was a strong conservative movement, distinct from the violent right that would take over in 1933. This remained influential in areas of the civil service, especially the Foreign Office (even after Hitler's accession). In cultural circles, the heritage of Bach, Goethe and Kant was revered in Weimar even as it was despaired of. German spirituality and German Enlightenment (*Aufklärung*) were defended by theologians, critics and philosophers nonetheless fully aware of the historical chasm existing between past and present, thinkers nursing no glib ambitions to recover tradition simply by invoking it. Cities with strong cultural associations – Frankfurt and Leipzig, for example – sought to study the example of great men from their past.

Like many Anglophone writers of his generation, Yeats knew relatively little about classic German literature. The influence of Coleridge had never generated a philosophic idealism native to the English language. Mid-Victorian admirers of German thought (such as George Eliot) diverged markedly from the Romantic heritage. If English philosophy in the persons of F. H. Bradley (1846–1924) and Bernard Bosanquet (1848–1923) developed its own versions of Hegelianism, the literary response was registered mainly through the Shakespearean criticism of A. C. Bradley (1851–1935, brother of the philosopher) and the early work of T. S. Eliot. German poets such as Friedrich Hölderlin (1770–1843) were known only to a few. Contemporary novelists, amongst whom Theodor Fontane (1819–1898) was the late-flourishing master, and Thomas Mann (1875–1955) the precocious renovator of tradition, remained untranslated for years. The drama travelled somewhat better, especially in the case of Gerhart Hauptmann (1862–1946), whom Yeats met in Italy in the 1920s. Of course Yeats read Friedrich Nietzsche (1844–1900), or at least Havelock Ellis's essays on Nietzsche in *The Savoy*. But the author of *Zarathustra* was a dangerous guide to German cultural history – too unique, too ironic. Yeats's father was not taken in.

Despite this meagre preparation, allusions to Johann Wolfgang von Goethe (1749–1832) appear throughout Yeats's *Autobiographies*. The most specific of these is linked to the disputes about Parnell at and after his death. Yeats repeats a remark of the German poet much quoted in Irish newspapers in 1891, 'The Irish seem to me like a pack of hounds, always dragging down some noble stag.'[2] Goethe, musing on Catholic Emancipation in 1829, was a figure from the past for Yeats, admirable but remote.

The Goethe Centenary (1932)

In 1926, the Oberbürgermeister (mayor or chief administrator) of Frankfurt, Ludwig Landmann (1868–1945, a baptised Jew) inaugurated a Goethe-Preis specifically to commemorate the liberal and universalist aspect of the great poet's many-sided genius.[3] Only German speakers/writers were to be considered, but German nationality was not a prerequisite. The centenary of Goethe's death would occur in 1932, and the city authorities were keen to prepare the way for appropriate ceremonies and to pre-empt any attempt by extreme nationalists to co-opt him to their cause. The first award was made in 1927. Early recipients included the poet Stefan George, the theologian Albert Schweitzer (Alsace-born), Sigmund Freud (an Austrian who needs no introduction) and Ricarda Huch (the only woman until 1940), a novelist.[4] Oddly enough, Thomas Mann, who spoke at the centenary celebrations at Weimar in March 1932, was not given this major award despite his Nobel Prize. By the end of 1933 he was living in Swiss exile, planning a Faust novella because 'an abstract symbol of this sort for the character and fate of Europe might perhaps be not only more promising but also more accurate than a literary accounting' for the inmates of concentration camps.[5] It is important to emphasise that this Goethe-Preis is *not* the award that Yeats was given in 1934.

In 1932, the Goethe-Jahr, a second award-scheme was created. Once again Landmann was in charge, together with the city's chief of police, Ludwig Steinberg, whose involvement indicates the struggle to control commemoration as Germany lurched towards political disaster. The initial purpose of this second, and decidedly second-rank, award was to honour individuals who contributed positively to the great open-air stage productions and spectacles that marked the centenary. The number of Plaketten was initially large, and after the close of 1932, participation in the centennial events was not a requirement. Indeed, continued issue of the award beyond February

1933 was a Nazi decision, with a consequent shortage of ironwear by 1935, if not earlier.

All of this is relevant to Yeats, because he will be announced as co-winner of the Plakette with the novelist Hermann Stehr (1864–1940) in February 1934. It is also central to any reassessment of Yeats's biographers, some of whom have manifested more silent embarrassment than pride in their hero's Frankfurt honour, by others noisily pronounced kosher-clean. One could analyse the list of early recipients to show how considerable literary achievement (Hauptmann and Mann) and administrative dedication (Ernst Beutler, 1885–1960, director of the Goethehaus; also Alfons Paquet, 1881–1944, secretary to the Goethe-Preis committee) were equally rewarded in 1932.[6] But in June 1933, the granting of a Plakette to Hans Hinkel, the new Staatskommissar and soon a bright impermanent light in the Nazis' cultural heaven, indicates how promptly the scheme was appropriated by Hitler's people. Most crucial in assessing Yeats's status in 1934, and in assessing the treatment of this matter by Roy Foster and Peter Jochum, is the fact that Stehr and Yeats were not the only recipients of the Plakette that year, though they were the only two notified to the London *Times*. A third award was made to Ernst Krieck (1882–1947), a thoroughgoing ultra-racist Nazi involved since 1931 in Alfred Rosenberg's Kampfbund für Deutsche Kultur. Since May 1933 Krieck was also Rector of Frankfurt University, which is to say he purged Martin Buber (1878–1965), Karl Mannheim (1893–1947), Paul Tillich (1886–1965) and other (mainly) Jewish professors from the faculty. Not all the expelled were Jewish or even liberal: Kurt Riezler, who had protested at the 1930 award of the Goethe-Preis to Freud ('pregnantly un-Goethean'), was dismissed on grounds of 'national unreliability'.[7] Rektor Krieck was nothing if not thorough, and for this he was rewarded in the same coin as Yeats. Heidegger went about similar business in Freiburg, though the two zealots were rivals rather than allies in their desire to philosophise the new leadership.[8] A fourth award, though poorly documented (see illustration number 13), is listed against the name of Joseph Goebbels, the well-known diarist.[9]

At the timely celebrations in 1932, Schweitzer had spoken eloquently of the threat to individualism and individual liberty posed by the rising tide of street violence. Frankfurt quickly discovered the truth of his prophecy. On 30 January 1933, a party of SA men stormed the municipal theatre to mark Hitler's appointment as

Chancellor; another took over the Institute for Social Research. It is often argued that little was known of events in Germany, that this was particularly true in the early days of the Nazi regime, and all the more significant in remote Ireland where access to first-hand information (supplied by refugees) was difficult. Yet the *Irish Times* had lost no time in taking the measure of new, Führer-backed developments. By March 1933 it was already using headlines like 'Jewish Untouchables: Nazi Minister Describes Stories of Torture as Lies' (27 March), and 'German Jews Face Ruin' (30 March). Cultured victims, whose predicament might be supposed to have attracted Yeats's attention, were specifically named. The issue of 18 March had noted the ban imposed on the conductor Bruno Walter, and an attack on the novelist Lion Feuchtwanger's home. Not that Yeats was a recluse in Dublin. Early in May he visited London on business: during his stay, the press publicised the escape to Britain from Berlin of a Rabbi Frankel and his daughter, together with the brutal treatment they had received at home in Germany. One does not imagine that the poet read the *Daily Express* of 5 May, but it would be sanguine to believe that, if he had read its account of the Frankels' experience, his dealings with Frankfurt's new Oberbürgermeister Krebs would have been any different.

By March 1933 seventeen Jewish employees in the Schauspielhaus were blacked. Among these was the director of music Hans-Wilhelm Steinberg (1899–1978), whose kindred may have included some residents of Kenilworth Park. The April issue of *Das Literarische Echo* listed the Plakette awards to Krieck, Stehr and Yeats, a fact that eliminates any possibility that the first of these got the award late in the year, independent of the literary duo.[10] The ideological blitzkrieg was on time and relentless. At the theatre in May, Herbert Graf (1903–1973, Freud's 'Little Hans'), who had premiered Arnold Schoenberg's 'Die Glückliche Hand' (Vienna Volksoper, 1924), was given his marching orders, together with actors Lydia Busche, Kurt Katsch, Lothar Rewalt and the theatre's artistic director, Alwin Kronacher (1883–1951). They were all Jews. As stage-manager Fritz Peter Buch was guilty of *'undeutsche'* artistic tendencies, he went with them. There were others.[11]

Some victims of the new order survived through emigration. Steinberg made his way to Hamburg where, for a while, he played in one of those compulsory all-Jewish groups which the Nazis exploited while peace lasted: in 1936 he escaped to Palestine, thence to America where (as William Steinberg) he became conductor of the Pittsburgh Symphony Orchestra. Others did not survive *Kristallnacht* (11 November 1938): many were eventually deported and murdered. Moses Slager, a member of the theatre orchestra who had voiced the un-Nazi opinion that 'whoever is guilty of nothing has nothing to fear', was killed in Auschwitz some time during 1942. Richard Breitenfeld (1869–1942), a singer 'retired' from the Frankfurt theatre, was murdered that December, though the new artistic director (1933–1944) had taken the economic precaution of cancelling Breitenfeld's pension once the 'Jew transport train' had left for Theresianstadt the previous summer. Nothing more cynical indicates the one-way ticket these actors and musicians were given. Breitenfeld, Slager and Steinberg are all traceable through personal files in Frankfurt's Municipal Archives, though these do not seem to have been conned by Professor Jochum, who also missed ten Brown Shirts on the roof in 1933.[12]

The climate in which Yeats's play was produced in February 1934 derived immediately from these dismissals and the power-struggle between rival Nazi groups. By late 1933 Frankfurt was entirely run by Hitler's functionaries, notably the newly appointed chief of police, von Westrem (an SA man), and the Nazi street-leader turned Oberbürgermeister, Friedrich Krebs (1894–1961). Landmann had been forced out as soon as the Nazis took over. A less well-known figure than his counterpart in Cologne (Konrad Adenauer), he still attracted attention abroad. His 'resignation' was reported in the *Irish Times* of 14 March 1933, in an article that proceeded to detail prompt Nazi 'Theatre Cleansing' in Berlin and Darmstadt. Two months later, on 10 May, the notorious book-purge in German university quads and town squares was reported throughout the civilised world. Yeats met Jewish refugees in London in December 1933, two months before the Frankfurt premiere; indeed, he entertained them by mocking Indian subservience to the English language.

Yeats's involvement in the Goethe-Plakette awards cannot be conflated with a decision to stage 'The Countess Cathleen' in translation at the Schauspielhaus. The latter had been advertised in the seventeenth edition of the *Frankfurter Theater Almanach* in a programme finalised by autumn 1933. Given the sudden manner in which Yeats was notified of the Plakette in February 1934 – he apparently read about it in the press – the clear conclusion must be that the production was decided before the award. Yet he knew nothing of either, prior to his (presumed) reading in the *Irish Times* of 16 February 1934 that:

> Dr W. B. Yeats has been awarded the Goethe Plaque of the City of Frankfurt. The Municipal Prize Office point out that, contrary to the practice of the 'old regime', the plaque is now given only in exceptional cases to persons distinguished in cultural life, and that it was therefore a rare distinction for Dr Yeats and for the German poet [*sic*], Herr Hermann Stehr, who received the award at the same time.[13]

This appeared in the same paper that reported the fracas in Lucan, County Dublin. Indeed, the issue of that date was rich in cultural stories emanating from the Reich. Yeats's honour was reported on page seven; on page four, Herr Clissmann was noted for his theatrical endeavours with Trinity College undergraduates, while on page six a lecture by Tomás O Cleirigh of the National Museum was summarised in its two main themes: the achievements of Adolf Hitler and Germany's contribution to Celtic Studies. Back from a visit to Berlin, O Cleirigh was not uncritical of the Führer, and a comparison of the latter's platform antics to 'the battle fury of Cú Chulainn' was not intended to flatter Yeats's theatrical hero.

A version of the official press release, appearing in the London *Times*, additionally mentioned 'The Countess Cathleen' and its 'excellent reception'. The discrepancy is odd because it can only arise from one of two causes: a) either the Frankfurt municipal press office carefully prepared different press releases with a (naïve) view to keeping Dublin ignorant of the stage production; or b) someone in the *Irish Times* edited out this substantive piece of news. It is only with Yeats's own letter to a certain Frau Arndt on 27 March 1934 that the playwright reveals any awareness of the stage production, his letter principally being an acknowledgment of press cuttings sent by her from Frankfurt. With a financial interest in performance rights, Yeats might have thought himself entitled to some further explanation.

For many months I was prepared to accept that Frau Arndt would remain a cipher. However, the assistance of the city's Institut für Stadtgeschichte brought some progress. It is possible that she was Anna Babette Arndt (1899–1984), an active figure in municipal politics. Born Stünz, the daughter of strongly Social Democrat parents, Betty married Konrad Arndt in 1922.[14] All of these people were directly involved in the political life of Frankfurt, their story providing a useful insight into the tense local struggle surrounding the award of Goethe-Plaketten. In March 1934, Frau Arndt was in a perilous position. Not only was she a stubborn and effective member of the now-overthrown legitimate left, banned since June 1933, but her husband was languishing (if that is the word) in a remote concentration camp at Esterwegen, her brother and sister known to be involved in resistance activities. In these circumstances, it would be quixotic to assume that she could write as a free agent to Yeats, inviting a foreigner to stay in her house, should he choose to collect his Plakette in person. Indeed, the notion of Yeats actually visiting Frankfurt adds, in March 1934, a new dimension to the honours available to him. Fortunately, he had other plans for the weeks ahead.

Instead of illuminating any Arndt link, the documents Jochum chose to translate make it plain that the poet had quickly contacted the German Legation (not Embassy) in Dublin to ask 'when he might expect the sending of the medal and of the certificate'.[15] That is what was transmitted to Berlin, though, as no certificate had been mentioned in either press release, we must conclude that the legation's role had not been simply a passive one of forwarding Yeats's message. There were no questions about theatre cleansing, the burning of James Joyce's books (amongst others) or the persecution of Jews. Nor does this speedy response square with Foster's insistence that Yeats was uncertain about 'the provenance' of the Plakette. He was just keen to get his hands on it.

There were difficulties. The German minister, Georg von Dehn Schmidt (d. 1937), had arrived in Dublin as Consul General in 1924: wholly the product of Weimar's first efforts at diplomatic representation, he was without any links to the Nazi party. By February 1934 the Nazis had their agents in Ireland, including Helmut Clissmann and Adolf Mahr (Ó Cleirigh's boss). An old-style diplomat walked warily in ignorance of their objectives – not warily enough in Dehn Schmidt's case, who ended up suspiciously dead following denunciation by Mahr. In Frankfurt, three months' delay in sending the 'plague' (Yeats's spelling) might suggest that there was never any serious intention of presenting a trophy, merely of parading the recipient's name through the German and world press. Eventually, the Plakette (made by Harold Winter,[16] an obscure sculptor or metal-worker from the nearby village of Oberursel) was forwarded to Dublin. Acknowledging this, Yeats wrote to Oberbürgermeister Krebs:

I thank you for the great honour you have done me and for the beautiful plaque with the powerful head of Goethe upon it. I have read much Goethe, alas only in English translation, and certain thoughts that have accompanied me through life are from 'Wilhelm Meister'. A few weeks ago I was reading a translation of 'Faust' with my daughter who is fifteen years old but has been studying German for five years and is intelligent enough to understand something of the tale. My son, who is younger, will I hope pass the plaque on to his son as an heirloom.[17]

How do we understand these facts and sparse documents? Concentration on Yeats's own activities will reveal little or nothing extra. What he did not do – complain about dismissals in the Schauspielhaus, demand some control over the production of his work, return object and certificate in protest at the persecutions general in Germany – can only be assessed if the wider contexts of the production and the award are examined. Peter Jochum chose to concentrate on the role of the Foreign Ministry in transmitting messages to Dublin and to the Frankfurt authorities, with the effect of focusing on what happened in March 1934, rather than on the decisions that had borne fruit in February. The Auswärtiges Amt was politeness itself compared to the boys in brown whose *coup de théâtre* had marked Hitler's triumph. On local conditions, Jochum informs us that the three principal officials involved in the Yeats production were Friedrich Krebs (Oberbürgermeister), Hans Meissner (1896–1958, General-intendant, or artistic director) and Friedrich Bethge (1891–1963, Chefdramaturg, or executive producer). By Jochum's own admission, in 1934 all three were 'convinced Nazis and pursued a policy of strong anti-Semitism . . .' However, he proceeds to declare that 'they were certainly not the worst of the lot'.[18]

The SS-Untersturmbahnführer as Executive Producer

The only evidence to support this special 'comparativist' pleading is the claim that Krebs fell out with an unnamed Gauleiter who sought his execution near the end of the war. (And who was then the gentleman?) A Frankfurt Nazi since 1924, Krebs rose effortlessly from the rank of party Ortsgruppenleiter before 1933 to become the city's chief administrator, a man who hurled the little streets upon the great. On 14 February, the Oberbürgermeister was officially present in the theatre, to emphasise the political nature of the event. In later years Krebs was Landesleiter for Alfred Rosenberg's Kampfbund für deutsche Kultur and, in March 1941, he was the principal speaker at the inauguration in Frankfurt of Rosenberg's notorious Institute for Research into the Jewish Question. On the strength of his peasant origins and legal qualifications, he also became a leading light in the Reichsmusikkammer. All in all, his career demonstrated the fascist wish to give the masses the best mediocrity going. With three years' detention in an American camp at Darmstadt, Krebs survived the war to embrace the Deutsche Partei. His ambitions in the city council were frustrated by protests from the SDP, which forced his resignation in 1952.[19]

As for Hansi Meissner, the consolation for Jochum lay in his opportunism, a Social Democrat (like Betty Arndt) before 1933, who would turn Catholic after 1945. In the Frankfurt theatre, he sought to cut back the number of foreign productions during his first season at the helm, 1933–34. Only three reached the public – an operetta by the Hungarian Szilághy, a play about Napoleon co-scripted by Mussolini, and Yeats's 'Countess'. Later, in 1935–36, Shaw and Wilde would strut their stuff, the latter vaunted as a social critic, the former as a German-friendly Irishman.[20] Friedrich Bethge appears to have persuaded Meissner to relax his prohibition on foreign authors in 1933–34 because Yeats was for him (Bethge) a *Lieblingsautor*. Whether in the company of Krieck and Stehr (with Goebbels perhaps), or that of Mussolini and the complaisant Szilághy, Yeats was packaged in unflattering terms. Krebs played his part in assembling one of these trios, Meissner the second. Meissner is buried at Oberreifenberg outside Frankfurt under a tombstone reading with unintended irony: *Nulla crux, nulla corona.*

Bethge deserves closer attention if only because we are told he 'seems to have been genuinely fond of Yeats's plays' – part of the devoted German following. But what was it about Yeats's drama that attracted his admiration? His own work for the stage explored every nuance between monumental dullness and dull monumentality, nothing remotely imitative of his Irish favourite. Publicity for 'Gräfin Cathleen' invariably described it as a mystery-play and, in 1939, it was linked to Richard Wagner's medievalism. Perhaps Bethge found sublimity in the mix of nationalist and religious themes. Peter Jochum's evidence for the producer's partiality rests on an unsuccessful bid to stage 'The Golden Helmet' (a negligible piece) six years after 'Cathleen', in 1940. This gaffe may explain his failure to rise on the greasy *Hakenkreuz* further than the rank of Reichskultursenator, which he reached by June 1944. Such is the basis for the 'one good apple in a barrel' defence of Yeats's Nazi promoters in 1934.

We can discover a great deal more. Friedrich Franz Heinrich Bethge left behind a curriculum vitae (November 1936) from which additional detail may be absorbed into his biography. He was born in Berlin on 24 May 1891, the son of Dr Richard Bethge, a Germanist or academic specialist in literature and language. The background was staunchly Prussian-Protestant. Wounded eight times as a soldier in the Great War, young Bethge became a clerk in civilian life, but joined in the suppression of the Spartacus Rising. Though he gives generous dates for this left-revolutionary cause (1919–23), the Berlin communists had been crushed within a matter of months, and the wider German revolution soundly defeated before 1919 was over. (Hermann Görtz had also cut his teeth on Spartacus.) In 1923, Bethge was awarded a prize for lyric poetry, joined the People's Party (Volkspartei) for a year, but went over to the National Socialists under Hitler in May 1932. In his CV, Bethge claimed to have worked with Ernst Jünger on *Das Antlitz des Weltkrieges* (1930), dealing with the front-line experience of German soldiers.[21] When the Nazis came to power, he was patronised by the Culture Department (under Hinkel, a 1933 Plakette winner) and Rainer Schlösser, who became president of the Reichstheaterkammer. Active in the Dichterkreis (Poets' Circle), Bethge was directly employed by Joseph Goebbels in 1934 before being transferred in 1935 to the Reichskultursenat. It was thus during his time with Goebbels that he carried out his Yeats production in Frankfurt.[22]

Jochum tells us that the producer was doubly involved in the arrangements to honour Yeats, for Bethge's approval as Gau-Kultur-wart für Hessen-Nassau was additionally required: 'Bethge handled the whole thing more or less single-handedly.' Or, in short, distinctions between independent theatre and political power had been abolished.[23] We can in practice go much further in tracing Bethge's many-sided involvement in the political arts: he became 'Kurator' of the Goethe-Plakette panel (in other words, he chose the winners) and for his fiftieth birthday (in 1941) he won the award himself! That bonus lay in the future, compensation for the failure to stage 'The Golden Helmet'. More promptly in the Frankfurter Schauspielhaus, on the heels of 'Gräfin Cathleen', came Bethge's own iron-clad drama 'Reims', directed by Meissner with designs by Ludwig Sievert (1887–1966), a genuinely creative figure.

These clerkly accomplishments of Bethge's have a bearing on our understanding of Yeats in 1934. The executive director was not wholly unknown in the world of theatre and poetry. He was an educated man with a minor literary prize to his name. Enquiries, once instituted, would have produced for Yeats considerable information about Bethge's taste in drama, his position *vis-à-vis* the new regime and the theatre in Frankfurt, his general standing with the profession. Something similar could be said of Krebs; his predecessor Landmann had been sufficiently well known to earn newspaper coverage when run out of house, homeland and public office; the same Landmann had treated with authors whom Yeats read (certainly Stefan George and Sigmund Freud), not to mention his distinction as the first civic administrator to honour the author of *Faust*. Neither Bethge nor Krebs (nor indeed Meissner) was beyond enquiry, though we are asked to believe that no hesitation whatever crossed Yeats's mind about their unannounced embarking on a production of his first and much-renowned play. Did he know, or when did he know, about their activities and proclivities?

He could have asked advice of Hone, who recently (late in 1933) wrote an introduction to Julius Pokorny's *Short History of Ireland*. The author was an unworldly scholar of Celtic matters, a speaker of modern Gaelic, and successor in the Berlin chair to Yeats's admired acquaintance Kuno Meyer (1858–1919). Within months of Hitler's accession, Pokorny was suspended because of a Jewish grandparent, but reinstated after diplomatic representations by Eamon de Valera, Douglas Hyde and other internationally known figures. Hone commented sympathetically on the case in his Introduction, while demurring at the Celticist's embrace of Irish nationalist separatism. Pokorny's contrariness illustrates the merit of a biographer staying thoroughly outside his subject (in my case, Yeats). Mildly anti-Semitic in the 'culturalist' manner described by Jürgen Habermas, he was apparently shocked by the New Order's delving into his ancestry. Diligent in anthologising poetry by Yeats in German translation, he reaped no return in the hour of crisis. Both men had their weaknesses.[24] And perhaps Yeats did ask advice of Hone, who knew more of the matter ten years later than he cared to reveal.

Ireland was not without eruptions resembling, in character if not in scale, events in Germany. On 30 March 1933, the *Irish Times* reported at length an attack on Connolly Hall in Dublin by an anti-communist mob, which put thirty-three individuals into hospital with injuries including gunshot wounds. It is in this context that one should read Yeats's letter of early April in which he tells Olivia Shakespear, 'At the moment I am trying in association with [an] ex-cabinet minister, an eminent lawyer, and a philosopher, to work out a social theory which can be used against Communism in Ireland – what looks like emerging is Fascism modified by religion. This country is exciting.'[25] A year later, with 'The Countess' running in Frankfurt, Yeats was rushing his Blue Shirt ballads into print through the London-based *Spectator*. In January 1934, his arch-Blue Shirt friend, Ernest Blythe, was appointed to the Irish Senate, while the leader (Eoin O'Duffy) shuffled between the law courts (defendant) and the party congress (elected President). This was not a moment of Blue Shirt reversal; prominent members drew attention to European analogies, while Yeats sought the high ground in London for his immediate outlet of political verse. In Paris, rioters took over the streets; in Austria, the civil war unfolded.

Had Yeats wanted to bring the local and the continental perspectives into a different focus, he could have recalled how in May 1933 the newly elected Irish leader, de Valera, had met a Dublin Jewish delegation and (separately) the President of the World Zionist Organisation, all seeking Ireland's intervention with the German government on behalf of hard-pressed Jews (like Steinberg and Graf). There were reasons for believing that the German government might listen to Irish representations or enquiries, even if it intended little in response. Yeats might not have known that the *Völkischer Beobachter* (editor Alfred Rosenberg) considered de Valera himself to be half-Jewish, but he knew something of how Irish government departments gathered information and advised citizens.[26] He was long familiar with 'theatre business, management of men'. He had cited Weimar's theatre policy in seeking government funding for the Abbey; he also had the Abbey's limited resources and high reputation at his service.

As for the newly installed executive director in Frankfurt, there were sides to Bethge about which even Professor Jochum prefers not to speak. Citing Bettina Schültke's magisterial *Theater oder Propaganda? Die Statischen Bühnen Frankfurt-am-Main 1933–1945* in his lengthy footnotes, Jochum cannot be unaware that Bethge, a member of the SS, was in the habit of wearing his uniform while at work. We are told the SS-Dramaturg appeared at the opening performance to announce the Plakette award, and (we now know) in black uniform, to declare that Yeats 'was particularly close to our [*sic*] world of ideas'. Nor is Jochum's good apple enhanced by a photograph of Bethge (in full regalia) alongside Hitler and Goebbels (see illustration 14). The double image of the producer on stage in jackboots, and the demon-merchants made up with caricature Jewish noses (see illustration 9), should put to rest any qualms about Yeats being manipulated.

I am, however, moved by Terence Brown's distinction between manipulation and exploitation – at least, moved enough to measure the shortest distance between two problems. Exploitation, in Brown's view, is or can be a wholly one-sided affair, whereas manipulation involves some reciprocity from the 'passive' party. As Yeats knew nothing (we assume) about the *papier-mâché* noses of the demon-merchants in 1934, he was merely exploited. But as he did nothing whatsoever to learn any such detail, or (later) to assist those exploited in the facial make-up, he was successfully manipulated. No help for Pokorny in 1933, no enquiry about Bethge, no help for Ossietzky later. Yeats actively did, as the Intendant intended, nothing.[27]

Bethge's achievements the following year included another epic play called *Marsch der Veteranen* (set in Napoleonic Russia), for which he was awarded a prize in 1937. He took the time in June 1935 to write congratulating Yeats on his seventieth birthday.[28] Finally, after a dip in his fortunes early in the war, the good apple sought to exploit the execution of Ermin von Witzleben (of the July Plot to kill Hitler), claiming that he had foreseen 'the rebellious field-marshall' and his 'treason' in one of his own plays. Bethge's inglorious career as Nazi Kultursenator is of little import for us after 1934, nor should we enquire too sympathetically if *Marsch der Veteranen* came back to haunt him after Stalingrad. But the defence mounted by Jochum as if to relieve Foster, involving suppression of Krieck's Plakette and Goebbels's and Bethge's boots onstage, is just one of those unforced overstatements of innocence that arouse suspicion or, rather, the hermeneutics thereof.[29]

February 1934 in Detail

The Goethe-Plakette was to be awarded at the first performance of Yeats's play, 'The Countess Cathleen' in (it is said) Ernst E. Stein's translation.[30] Playbills and posters made no acknowledgment of the translator. In fact, there had been a very early translation in 1903 (in *Bühne und Welt*), and ownership of performance and translation rights in Germany was a complex issue. Something of a local tradition was recalled in Frankfurt of producing Yeats; or, more modestly, there had been several Irish Evenings in the theatre during March 1919. On that occasion, Frieda Weekley (née von Richtofen, aka Mrs D. H. Lawrence) had contributed to the German versions.[31] With the passage of time, matters had been tightened up. Herbert E. Herlitschka, having acquired certain rights, produced deplorable playtexts. His legal position now blocked other efforts, notably those of the minor poet Henry von Heiseler, whose superior translation of ten plays was released in 1933. Though Stein had published his 'Gräfin' back in 1925, printed on Japanese vellum it too was scarcely a commercial item, demonstrating that, if Yeats had a following in Germany, it was more coterie than fan-club.[32] Even if Bethge and Meissner used Stein's text for their production, alterations were made, resulting in a performance now difficult to reconstruct. It is possible that Stein modestly declined to have his name used. We know of alteration from Yeats's telling Frau Arndt amiably that he had 'no doubt the theatre was entirely right in its cuts in The Countess Cathleen. The play is a very early work.'[33] Yeats would scarcely give such licence to Lennox Robinson in the Abbey, and would not have allowed an unknown producer in London or New York to devise a text without prior consultation.

What might Bethge and Meissner have cut? At that moment Yeats was alert to 'The Countess' and, for the 1934 Collected Plays, had prepared a reading (not acting) text. It was 'an early work' yet lively in the writer's present thoughts. The final scene was crucial for the redemption of Cathleen, but difficult onstage. The theatre authorities were committed to a short run, and cannot have worried too much about niceties of copyright. Lines in that final scene may have been sacrificed to stage economy, though German reviewers liked it. Other parts were indispensable. In the first scene, a character reports a sighting of unnatural shapes – 'a man who had no mouth, / Nor eyes, nor ears; his face a wall of flesh' – these perhaps being famine victims themselves or evil portents of worse to come.[34] With the Nazi takeover, a new audience was falling into place; experienced theatregoers were reduced in number by the reluctance of Jews and others to appear in public. Opponents, even former allies, were denounced by Hitler as 'dwarfs' in application of his physiological theories to their liquidation. In what frame of mind did the new audience respond to these lines? On 1 January 1934, the new Law to Prevent Diseased Offspring came into force, aimed at the compulsory sterilisation of mental defectives, victims of genetic damage (evidenced sometimes in disfigurement) and eventually anti-social elements, schizophrenics and the work-shy (*Arbeitsscheue*). In a uniformed Nazi director's hands, 'Gräfin Cathleen' gestured to Goethe's version of the Faustian theme, while suggesting the entire *Reichsprogramm* of social hygiene, mobilisation of the workforce and stigmatisation of foreign (i.e. Jewish) gold.

Unlike the acting-script, the cast-list and the names of others involved in the production can be recovered. There is little to be said about them, apart from noting the absence of Busch, Katsch, Rewalt, etc. Bettina Schültke has shown how the purging of Jewish actors created difficulties that were met by short-term importations. One successful music director, Georg Ludwig Jochum (1909–1970), got his break through the Jewish expulsions; he arrived in 1934 and stayed till 1937, ending his post-war career with the Bamberg Symphony Orchestra.[35] Kurt Böhme (1908– ?; 'Ein Älterer Mann' in the Yeats production) was officially a singer with the Dresden Opera, who later enjoyed a distinguished musical career. By contrast, Rewalt ended up playing Nazi soldiers in Broadway's 'Stalag 17'. The Demon-Merchants were Paul Verhoeven (1901–1975) and Franz Schneider (1886–1968).[36] Hamburg-born Luise Glau, who played the countess, survived the war to record 'talking-books' in old age. Musical arrangements were provided by Bruno Hartl, whose resistance to research today strongly indicates he was not a long-standing Frankfurt staff member. The stage-designer was Ludwig Sievert, the stage-manager Richard Salzmann. The former had been distinguished in his profession since the mid-1920s. To judge from his designs for Verdi's 'Macbeth' early in 1932, he knew what was coming and conjured a death's-head population over whom the usurper-tyrant would rule. Together, Sievert and Salzmann had been responsible for one of the 1933/34 season's most topical productions – 'One Hundred Days', based on the writings of Benito Mussolini. By 1937 Sievert appears to have been in decline or retreat, with only two productions (Ibsen and Hauptmann) to his credit.[37]

Second Prize?

Honours were in some fashion to be divided with Hermann Stehr, a Silesian novelist of the *völkisch* kind and a party member. There was no reference in the English-language papers to Krieck or Goebbels.

His work mixing naturalism and vague mysticism, Stehr had counted among his friends Martin Buber, the Jewish philosopher just dismissed from the local university by Krieck. We can thus be reasonably sure that the author of *Ich und Du* (1923) was not in Yeats's Frankfurt audience. Stehr can have done little to comfort Buber, for the Silesian quickly became a minor official of the Reichsschrifttumskammer, a subdivision of the Cultural Chamber set up in September by Goebbels. Nevertheless, efforts at mollification were possible, even from within. According to a long-standing advocate of Stehr's work, on 19 February 1934 Stehr wrote in protest to Hitler about the terror waged by a police and SA Obergruppen-führer in Silesia.[38] The date is significant because it fell just days after the official celebration of the Goethe awards. Though there had also been some ceremonial with the Oberbürgermeister on Wednesday 14 February, presentation to Stehr had taken place on 16 February because it was his seventieth birthday. His letter to Hitler, however, went unanswered. In parallel with the new law of 1 January, and its purely physical remedies for that remnant of blemishes upon the new Body Politic, Stehr had been gelded with his own mental Plakette.

He could still run a lap of honour. In a collection of miscellaneous writings published in 1936, Stehr printed the text of an address he gave in acceptance of a Goethe honour in 1933 from the city of Frankfurt.[39] Actually, Stehr won both Plakette and Preis and a few other Goethe trinkets as well, to compensate him for the loss of Buber and Hauptmann as friends. It is a clear indication of Krebs's way with awards that his reason for issuing the Plakette to Stehr was that Stehr had already won the Preis! The published address is an unremarkable eulogy of the great eighteenth-century poet; there is no reference to sharing an award, and no reference whatever to Yeats. If, as Hone suggested, Yeats's name had emerged unexpectedly in 1934, by 1936 it was being quietly withdrawn. It is equally true that Hone quietly suppressed Stehr. And, although the official notice made no reference to any particular work by Yeats, Hone chose to specify 'The Countess Cathleen', knowing of the play production he did not mention.

Hone's hints and silences look shifty but hardly suspicious. The biography – authorised by the widow – is dated 1942, the year of Montgomery's great victory over Rommel at El Alamein. The German defeat at Stalingrad followed in January of the New Year. It was only in February 1943 that *W. B. Yeats 1865–1939* was finally issued – by Macmillan of London, which had been Yeats's principal publisher since March 1916. The dates in the title confirm the historical character of the poet's death, not just the Victorian moment of his birth. It was in a footnote, oddly displaced from the chronology of his subject's life, that Hone carried out his minor revelation: 'It may be mentioned here, although Hauptmann had nothing to do with the matter, that in 1934 Yeats quite unexpectedly, as author of *The Countess Cathleen,* received the Goethe Plakette from the Oberbürgermeister of Frankfort.'[40]

Who had something to do with the matter? Gerhart Hauptmann cannot be ruled out as easily as Hone wished. Certainly he was the most influential German literary figure whom Yeats had met (in Rapallo, where the ageing playwright's appetite for champagne excited envy). He had won the Nobel Prize back in 1912 and, in the year of Goethe's centenary, he won the Goethe-Preis (Landmann's initial scheme, founded in 1927) and picked up his own Plakette in the first batch of twelve or so in 1932. A fellow-Silesian, Hauptmann was a far greater figure than Stehr, with whom he had been on amiable terms. Hauptmann was no Nazi, and indeed some of his late work effectively allegorises the monstrous horrors of the Reich. Unlike Brecht, George and Mann, he did choose to stay throughout the entire war in Hitler's Germany, where he was tolerated despite his defence of a Jewish publisher. He also wrote a play as a moving requiem for another Jewish friend, Max Pinkus, who died in the year of the Stehr-Yeats awards – it remained unpublished, of course.[41] Hauptmann passed most of the war at Agnetendorf, less than 200 miles west of Auschwitz. His home was eventually liberated by the Red Army, who treated him with decency and respect, perhaps with a view to his taking up some significant role in the Soviet zone of a partitioned Germany.

If not Hauptmann, who? The first Goethe-Preis winner had been Stefan George, who evidently read Yeats with enthusiasm. But he was dead by the end of 1933, and can hardly have influenced (from Swiss exile) what looks like a last-minute decision to give Yeats a Plakette. Other candidates for the honour of slotting Yeats's name into the cultural dog-fight of Frankfurt's once-proud theatre are lesser figures. They might include Charles Bewley (1890–1969, maverick head of the Irish diplomatic mission in Berlin and an admirer of Nazism), Helmut Clissmann (a registered student in Frankfurt University while also subverting in Dublin under Adolf Mahr's watchful eye), and Bethge (Goebbels's fixer in the Schauspielhaus). Bettina Schültke favours Bethge as culprit, but she was probably unaware of Clissmann's undercover activities in Irish-German affairs. Jochum does not investigate the statement by Reichspropagandsminister Goebbels, with which the 1933/34 season of plays (including 'Gräfin Cathleen') was formally inaugurated, or even disclose its availability.

A factor in deciding among these possible sponsors is the plainly inferior status of the new Plakette compared with the Preis. There was no financial award, there was no invitation for the overseas winner to attend any ceremony (unless, in Yeats's case, this was contemplated in March through the Arndt manoeuvre). Under Landmann's scheme, Albert Schweitzer received the award in person in 1928. When, in 1930, Freud had been similarly honoured, he was represented in Frankfurt by his daughter, Anna: his address (as read in public by her) was published. The Plakette was a virtual event or pre-postmodern chimera – no cash, no personal appearance, just publicity, especially for the publicists. The motivation for its continuance after January 1933 may have been short-term. Literary prizes were already under fire in February 1934, and by the end of May Dresden would host the first fully Nazified Theatre Festival. Bethge seems the favourite in any quiz to name the prime mover in giving Yeats the Plakette, though Bewley or Clissmann might be suspected of an advisory role. Early in 1934 the latter was rehearsing a German one-act farce with the Modern Languages Society of Trinity College Dublin, to open on 19 February in the Gate Theatre.[42] On the same day, Bewley updated de Valera's government on new prohibitions against Jews practising in many professions.[43]

Some outline has already been provided of Yeats's options to distance himself from the double honour bestowed on him. The timetable for such a response begins on the day (in autumn 1933) when 'Gräfin Cathleen' was listed for production in the coming season; it runs until the moment Yeats cheerfully acknowledged receipt of the plaque from Oberbürgermeister Krebs (4 June 1934). While it is very unlikely that he studied the *Frankfurter Theater Almanach* each October, it must be remembered that he had friends and acquaintances who did closely follow German political and cultural developments. These individuals ranged over a spectrum of views – Maud Gonne, Gerhart Hauptmann, Joseph Hone, Walter Starkie, Iseult and Francis Stuart. The legation itself presumably scanned the German press for Irish references. In addition, there were prompters in the wings – the genial Clissmann, the uncongenial Mahr. Certainly, Yeats came to possess German propaganda later in the 1930s, from sources that remain unidentified.

The conventional perspective on the poet amid these issues places him in an aesthetic bubble of inaction. While this resembles respectable doctrines of 'art for art's sake' or (even better) artistic detachment from mundane affairs, it is closer to grotesque parody. In the 1890s, Wilde held strong political views and made no bones about them. If the divine Oscar finally realised that he had mistaken his life for art, Yeats risked similar hubris and fall in a more lethal decade. If he held that poem and play were neither produced nor apprehended by fundamentally extra-aesthetic agencies, but were the pure work of imagination conceiving itself, it did not follow that all his utterances and actions were born in the same manner. In practice, he moved effectively and eloquently in many non-literary spheres – the Irish Senate, the American lecture-circuit, London clubs, *séances* and board meetings. He took up positions in relation to Irish politics, while generally drawing the line at European affairs. Nationalism provided a rationale for this selectivity, though (carefully scrutinised) his record reveals many instances of British engagements, interventions in British debates, appeals to British organs of opinion. He even wrote to the press in support of Lady Rhonnda in her dispute with printers, his motive being as much detestation of trade unions as of censorship.[44]

On the German question, there was no shortage of opinion. In the course of 1933/34, numerous paeans emerged from the academico-intelligentsia to commend the regime – books by Gottfried Benn, Walter Darré, Martin Heidegger, Alfred Rosenberg and Carl Schmitt, for example. Benn was a poet, Darré celebrated a rebirth of the peasantry. Resistance, or at least non-compliance, was possible. Among significant writers who tried 'internal emigration', the Great War veteran Ernst Jünger declined nomination in November 1933 to a revamped Academy of Poetry and, in May 1934, also protested at unauthorised republication of his work in the *Völkischer Beobachter*. He was able to refuse Nazism by invoking battle-front experience, an area in which Yeats was spectacularly ignorant. If the comparison is extended to August 1938 and his public approval of Nazi racial legislation, the Irish prize winner might be observed (in the German cliché dating from February 1934) 'working towards the Führer'.[45]

There were also exile voices, notably Thomas Mann's. In the early days of the Reich, intellectual refugees tended to stay on the Continent (in France, the Netherlands or Switzerland), with the result that the debate was not conducted in English, while attracting the attention of a few English and American commentators. Yeats did not read or speak German, but in D. A. Binchy's important article on Hitler he had access to an Irish diplomat's considered view of the new Germany, its objectives and methods. Like Pokorny, Binchy was a Gaelic scholar of the highest order, learned in disciplines Yeats respected but never mastered.[46] When the moment came for a practical decision about the Plakette, Yeats ignored any advice his own (nationalist) government might have provided, choosing instead to consult the Reich's chief representative in Dublin. Naturally, Yeats was reassured and unreserved. It was 'my Frankfurt honour', 'the great honour' conferred on him.

Once and Never

The early months of 1934 found Walter Benjamin (1892–1940) in Paris. The least predictable Marxist of the latter-day 'Frankfurt School', he had left Berlin the previous March. Now he wandered near-penniless into Sylvia Beach's shop and studied the photographs of British writers, including James Joyce. In February Benjamin published a short essay in a Swiss journal, drawing extensively on Leon Trotsky's recollections of his father at work in the fields with a sickle, recollections not unlike Seamus Heaney's in 'Digging'. There is no link between Trotsky and Heaney, and precious little between Benjamin and Yeats – except Frankfurt.

The essay is about human labour, as distinct from warfare, games and school tests. These latter operate on a 'once and for all' basis. But the experienced worker recommences his task in the field as if he had not begun before, 'what he has done seems to evaporate under his hands and to leave no trace'.[47] This theme may represent Benjamin's pessimistic view of the political situation in Europe, or it might equally resemble a doctrine of artistic autonomy. Goethe's birthplace studied both at close quarters. On 30 January 1933, those Brown Shirts had stormed the citadel of enlightenment, inaugurating not just drastic change, but a hectic period of many changes. It was the 'Black Shirt' SS officer, Bethge, who was despatched from Berlin to take over the municipal theatre of a city with a proud liberal tradition and a largish (5 per cent) Jewish population. Behind the relative public calm of early 1934, tension between Ernst Roehm's now very numerous roughneck radicals (many of them veteran-suppressors of Spartacus in 1919) and the ferociously disciplined SS broke on 30 June with the Night of the Long Knives and the liquidation of Roehm and his lieutenants. The period forms one context in which an anti-Semitic, yet ultimately soothing 'Gräfin Cathleen' was showcased, with Bethge and Krebs in attendance.

The Brown influence was institutionalised in the name of the theatre's new journal, *Der 30. Januar: Braune Blätter der Städtischen Bühnen Frankfurt a. M.* The twelfth monthly number (February 1934) carried an article about Yeats by Ludwig Wagner (1896–1945).[48] Thoroughgoing coordination, if not manipulation, characterised the theatre's local treatment of its Irish dramatist. Five years later, when Yeats died, Wagner translated 'The Mask', a poem of 1910, in the same journal (no longer styled *Braune*), alongside an article on religious aspects of his work contributed by Reinhold Lindemann.

'Das Religiöse bei W. B. Yeats' opens with an allusion to Goethe on 'strong ages', nods approvingly towards Paul Claudel, and moves rapidly to concentrate on 'The Countess Cathleen' as an exemplary modern mystery-play. A regrettable lapse in political correctness threatens when Lindemann describes the heroine as 'somebody like an Irish Elizabeth'. He has in mind, however, not the Virgin Queen of England but Heilige Elizabeth (1207–1231) who appears heavily romanticised in *Tannhäuser* (revised version 1861). Thus Frankfurt marked Yeats's death by recalling its own production of 'Gräfin Cathleen' and assimilating the dramatist into Wagnerian neo-medievalism.[49]

Details of the February 1934 production, and the personalities behind it, are open to excessively minute interpretation if the larger and longer context is ignored. Nazi policy towards drama was complex and at times contradictory. As the contributors to John London's excellent *Theatre under the Nazis* demonstrate, a Judocidal regime sanctioned for its own 'reasons' a public Jewish theatre at least until the declaration of war in 1939, though Steinberg's *Jüdische Kulturbund* in Hamburg may not have had so long a leash. Furthermore, one of Hitler's favourite Anglophone dramatists was Shaw.[50] Theatre was a window of propaganda, not just for showcasing *völkisch* drama, but for demonstrations of 'liberalism' to impress the world. The relationship between fascism and theatre has long been recognised as potent, and our understanding of this is not enhanced by attempts to simplify the Meissner-Bethge production of 'Gräfin Cathleen' as politically innocuous. The year 1934 brought massive propagandist enterprises, including the first 'New Order' Nuremberg rally with Leni Riefenstahl's film, *The Triumph of the Will*, serving as liturgical script and Eucharist. Comprehensive theatre legislation (May 1934) completed the programme. In practice, from 1934 onwards virtually none of the permitted 'serious drama' was set in the present, while foreign authors were tolerated amid a famine of acceptable local work.[51] In immediate terms, Yeats unwittingly assisted the streamlining of Germany's theatrical repertoire and the overcoming of Brown by Black.

These conditions fitted 'The Countess Cathleen' (and vice versa), though choice of the play was explicitly linked to the Nazis' assimilation of Goethe to their pantheon. Coincidentally, it took him back to powerfully motivating inaugural moments: his passion for Maud Gonne, his commitment to theatre, his cultural nationalism and preoccupation with religio-cultic victimage. If he recollected a Dublin discussion of January 1909, whether a soul may not sacrifice (even to the point of losing) itself for a good end, he would have recalled also the suggestion of one participant that 'it is a further problem whether a nation may make this sacrifice'. Yeats had certainly recognised that as the issue at stake in his 'Countess Cathleen', and Lindemann concurred in 1939.[52] In February 1934 such an allegorical production of the foundational drama of modern Irish consciousness was to be revamped, while the 'sacrifice' of a different nation commenced in the orchestra pit. The German philosophy of sacrifice, invoked in 1909 by Dean Bernard, was no longer interpreting, but changing, the world.

Yeats's plot was essentially Faustian, with the additional 'merit' of a folk idiom. Casting merchants as the Devil's agents, the play readily (if you like, unwittingly) dramatised the radical ('Brown') aspect of Nazism as a critique of capitalism (especially Jewish capitalists). Was it coincidental that the moment in January 1909, when Yeats associated the play with a theory of sacrifice as applicable to individual or nation, had begun with a discussion of wealthy influence? He could still cite the German originator of that theory, Eduard Hartmann (1842–1906), in 1928.[53] For the production team in 1934, the play's performance in Goethe's birthplace enacted an '*Anschluss*' of past and present, native and foreign, high and popular elements; in other words, it fitted the fascist bill to perfection. Yeats was not to be alone in this manipulation of non-German art. Noel Coward and Somerset Maugham were played throughout the 1930s. And the socialist Shaw. Of his plays, only 'Arms and the Man' was prohibited, while 'Geneva' (with its blatant lampooning of Hitler) was positively fireproofed by Goebbels himself: it held its place on the German stage even after the war had begun.[54] This is an aspect of Shaw's record which some of his posthumous minders have been denying until very recently. Their evidence of Shaw's virtue – that his income from Germany allegedly fell after 1933 – depends on a range of financial records, which have failed to materialise on my request. In the month of Yeats's death, Shaw had refused to support a League of Dramatists' fund for Jewish refugees, writing, 'I am not in the camp [sic] of the Anti-Sheenies; but what of our members who are?'[55] If Yeats was politically myopic, he was not the only Dubliner to suffer from the condition.

The production, which ran for seven non-consecutive nights, was not repeated. The delay in sending Yeats his plaque provided opportunities for reflection; indeed, it provided numerous reports of further outrages in Germany which might have prompted a demurral. A biographer is supposed to establish what his subject was doing, where his subject was staying, when such tributes were being paid. Nothing quite so police-efficient will be attempted here, in the absence of Yeats's passport. At the end of February 1934, the poet was certainly in residence at Riversdale, outside Dublin, confiding to his former lover Olivia Shakespear on the topic of the Blue Shirts, Ireland's wannabe fascists. He and his wife, the English-born Georgie Hyde-Lees, differed on the subject, though he could be sardonic as well as approving, whereas she was four-square hostile. Blue Shirts, Yeats wrote, 'are upholding law, incarnations of public spirit, rioters in the cause of peace, and George hates Blue Shirts'.[56] That was two weeks after the Frankfurt celebrations, at which we can conclude Yeats was not present, because Goebbels would have flashed the Nobel laureate's picture around the world within minutes – as a rebuke to Thomas Mann, if nothing else.

For the Frankfurter Schauspielhaus, the purge was not over. With the Nuremberg Laws of 1935, a further forty or more people were dismissed, not necessarily because they were Jews, but because they had Jewish wives or husbands. Statistics would suggest that some of these were veterans of 'Gräfin Cathleen'. The same year brought Yeats to his seventieth birthday, marked with respectful articles in the

German press and Bethge's effusive letter. The following year brought the case of Carl von Ossietzky, a prisoner in one of the camps also used for Konrad Arndt, and Yeats's refusal to assist. By then, Nazism was able to face down the world. As a minor demonstration of this confidence, they assumed Yeats would never deny their assertions of affinity with him. In this, certainly, manipulation and not just exploitation was manifest.

The situation in late 1933 had been different, even in the relatively unimportant sphere of Hiberno-German relations. While one might dwell on curiosities like the attempt to see the term 'Aryan' reflected in the (botched) Anglicised name 'Erin', or take as eternal truth John A. Costello's proud association (on 5 February 1934) of the Blue Shirts with both Italian Black and German Brown, more light is shed by some considerations of Irish-German trade. De Valera's economic war with Britain produced a surplus of Irish cattle for export, while reinvigorated German industries were keen to follow up Siemens' success in equipping the Ardnacrusha electric power station in the 1920s. To facilitate improved trade relations, the German government now discouraged crude journalistic treatment of Irish internal affairs. Negotiations began in October 1933, and were renewed in December. For many in Ireland, the economic situation was very depressed: James Maxton of the Independent Labour Party in Britain visited Dublin in mid-January 1934 to assess the impact on ordinary working people.[57] Within the Dublin government, misunderstandings placed de Valera under pressure from more vigorous and liberalising ministers (including Sean Lemass) who wished to go beyond the essentially protectionist policy of their leader. High-level talks on 22 January 1934 prompted a temporary euphoria in Irish-German diplomatic circles. Bewley was instructed to keep the Auswärtiges Amt happy while efforts were made to convert shadow into substance. If anyone wished to add a name to the elastic list of Plakette winners, then the moment was ripe to bestow it on an Irish writer already billed in the *Frankfurter Theater Almanach* for a production that very month.

This is not to suggest that the Trade Department stitched things up with the Culture Department. It is, however, a means of indicating that Yeats's double honour in Frankfurt emerged from a variety of political and cultural improvisations as well as from a 'perceived' affinity. These in turn were the product of transitional conditions in the German state, the Frankfurt theatre, even in Irish diplomatic and economic policy.[58] Yeats himself was poised on his decision to undergo a bizarre surgical experiment in London to restimulate his sexual life, which early April duly brought, with convalescence in Rapallo to follow.

Addressed to an actress, the first (surviving) letter he wrote in 1934 simply read 'fatten'.[59] Drama preoccupied him: 'The Words Upon the Window-pane' was to be published by the Cuala Press in April; he was still working on 'The King of the Great Clock Tower'. To Olivia Shakespear he confided, 'I made up the play that I might write lyrics out of dramatic experience, all my personal experience having in some strange way come to an end.'[60] There were other poems, not lyrics; 'Three Songs to the Same Tune' duly appeared in *The Spectator* on 23 February 1934. Contributions to the Blue Shirt cause, he wanted them published fast – no need for proofs.[61] He could not specify the reason for urgency, though the hints he provided were Irish, not German.

Higher concerns included completion of the revised *Vision* (notified to Frank Pearse Sturm on 7 March), and the making of arrangements with Faber & Faber for publication later in the year of *The Holy Mountain*, which Yeats's friend, Shri Purohit Swami, had translated. Throughout these early months of 1934, his health was not good – heavy cold, exhaustion from overwork. These minor physical problems may have been prologues to the swelling theme, reached in Norman Haire's surgery. They certainly were no obstacle to Yeats's phenomenal appetite for diverse commitments. Yet throughout the weeks surrounding the official and public German announcement in *The Times*, the available correspondence shows no awareness of the Frankfurt honour. Not that philosophico-orientalist publications, or even Blue Shirt ballads, had monopolised his attention.

The Irish Academy of Letters had been planning an award scheme for some time (in the event, it honoured the memory of Roger Casement). Cecil Harmsworth had put up money, and the principal task lay in commissioning a suitable token for the winner. During December 1933, Yeats had consulted the English medalist, Maurice Lambert, in London. Academy business necessarily involved the secretary, Walter Starkie, who had been active in the Centre International d'Études sur Le Fascisme. For that reason, or rather from dislike of the Casementalist lobby, George Bernard Shaw refused to act as a judge. On 16 February 1934, two days after his play opened in Frankfurt, Yeats wrote to Patrick McCartan, who favoured naming the award after Casement. McCartan was an Irish-American of decidedly pro-German leanings, who would shortly threaten murder to silence murmurings about Casement's homosexuality. Though Yeats's letter to this willing accomplice discussed at length the purpose of the award, the techniques of making the medal, its size and design, he makes no reference whatsoever to the Frankfurt business, either the production or the Plakette.[62]

Although Yeats met Starkie at least three times between 30 January and 16 February, and was in touch with Maud Gonne and her daughter Iseult throughout February and March, none of these largely fascist-sympathising friends prompted him to make a now-traceable allusion to his sudden fame in the new Germany. Before his letter to Frau Arndt, there is no evidence that he had seen the newspaper announcements, or – and this is even more incredible – that anyone had told him of them. This timetable, however, fits the one that Peter Jochum selected in the Frankfurt archives, the sequence of messages from the Foreign Office in Berlin to the German Legation in Dublin, essentially a March 1934 timetable.

It seems a plausible speculation that Frau Arndt was the first to notify Yeats of his Frankfurt honours, under the guise of sending press cuttings, but also attempting to draw him into visiting Frankfurt.[63] His wider correspondence remained as devoid of references to Frankfurt as before; even the final letter to Oberbürgermeister Krebs (4 June 1934) fails to indicate how Yeats received his Plakette (at the legation? through the post?). The London surgery had begun to fire his imagination; he wrote to Olivia Shakespear about the actress whom he had advised to 'fatten'. Both she and her husband (the dramatist, Denis Johnston) were involved in affairs with others: Yeats played with the idea of the couple being unfaithful to their lovers, and sleeping together in sexual betrayal raised to the power two. Goethe did not figure, Frankfurt had meant nothing to him.

Yeats's standing in the cultural politics of the Third Reich was constructed almost exclusively round 'The Countess Cathleen'. Its themes and idioms are celebrated in the plethora of articles and tributes published to mark his seventieth birthday and the obituaries appearing (some with extraordinary swiftness) after his death in 1939. Yet he never became most favoured Irishman or foreign writer, roles for which William Joyce and P. G. Wodehouse were better qualified. The war was to alter attitudes and reputations, not always with precision. In practice, the Nazis had promoted Friedrich Schiller as the premier classic dramatist, relegating Goethe to an ornamental role. Yeats's dutiful recitation to Oberbürgermeister Krebs of his admiration of *Wilhelm Meister* was already beside the point: more telling was his expressed wish that the Nazi item should become an heirloom in the family, a symbol of the hereditary principle, of patriarchy and of inalienable art-as-property.[64]

It would be wrong to think that the Reich at war became indifferent to obscure literary matters. In January 1940, an excerpt from *On the Boiler* appeared in German translation in the officially produced *Auslese: Internationale Zeitschriftenschau*. Though Yeats's name was listed with scores of other unacceptable artists in 1942, inclusion did not in itself signify condemnation in practice. We know that in 1944 a Munich audience warmly received 'The Land of Heart's Desire' (1894).[65] A late-wartime production of 'The Unicorn from the Stars' (1907) caused disturbances which the director may have deliberately fomented.

As yet incompletely addressed is the question why 'The Countess Cathleen' should have been the play to monopolise Yeats's reception in the German theatre during the 1930s. The Faustian element links it to Frankfurt's preoccupation with Goethe in 1932–34, but there were other theatres in Germany and directors other than Bethge. Evidence for the Nazi years after Yeats's death – that is, the war years – indicates that other (early) plays were known and approved. Nobody seems to have considered Cuchulain a hero deserving to appear alongside Siegfried. The sequence that began with 'On Baile's Strand' (1903) and ended posthumously with 'The Death of Cuchulain' (1939) surely offered possibilities of a *helden* interpretation while underscoring the power of archaic myth. Defending Synge in 1905, Yeats had informed readers of *The United Irishman* that 'Among the audience at the last performance of "On Baile's Strand" there was a famous German scholar who had just edited the old German version of the world-wide story of the king who fights with his own son.'[66] Even this possible debt did nothing to commend Yeats's tragic plays in Frankfurt or Berlin.

Two reasons may have worked against the reception of these pieces – one was the strong attraction of Greek tragedy through which Nazi ideologues took over the long-established love-affair between Romantic Germany and ancient Greece; the second was the brevity of Yeats's Cuchulain plays, a factor unhelpful in building an evening's programme. 'The Countess Cathleen' brought none of these disadvantages, and possessed merits of its own. The more obvious of these have already been noted at length: the folk idiom, the Faustian theme, the blending of nationalism and religion. For modern German readers, Klaus Peter Jochum has provided an analysis of the play's structure, in the context of Yeats's larger contribution to twentieth-century drama. In his treatment of 'The Countess' he gives generous space to a critique of the play made in the early days by a British writer of very different allegiances. Max Beerbohm had observed:

> A sacrifice that turns out to be no sacrifice at all loses most of its pathos, and the beauty of the Countess Cathleen's action is inevitably cheapened for us by the knowledge that she was saved its consequence. Even in the commercial theatre it is no longer necessary for the dramatist to invent at all costs a 'happy ending'. That Mr Yeats has invented one for the 'Countess Cathleen' seems to me a matter of deep irony.[67]

That Dr Jochum can quote the severely donnish T. R. Henn in support of these strictures should persuade us that no mere West End misunderstanding of the Celtic Twilight is at work here. For Beerbohm raises in more considered terms objections also heard from the loud and loutish Frank Hugh O'Donnell. The common element in their distaste for 'The Countess' is its ambivalent relationship to commercialism. Max deplores the play's determination to give a good return on money, to reward the gallery with a happy ending even when this component of popular theatre has been displaced by influences from on high such as Shaw or Ibsen. In other words, 'The Countess' never possesses any tragic potential, for its heroine is guaranteed in advance against loss. Certainly this is the language of the Demon-Merchants themselves, who comment drily on 'the buyer's risk'. Once such an examination of the play's language and texture gets under way, it is difficult to avoid observing that 'redemption' is at once the key term in money-lending or pawn-broking just as it is in Christian salvation. If this is the inner crisis which the play explores, the outer setting – a pub or inn called 'The Queen's Head' – takes on even greater significance. In mundane terms, this sign conforms to the practice of naming taverns and like places after a monarch or local magnate. With a shrine to the Blessed Virgin on or near the premises, it is the Queen of Heaven who is implied, her shrine doubling up as a shop. The lives of Shemus and Mary are dramatically suspended between the low trade in ale and the high trade in souls, with a shortage of foodstuffs as bridge of sighs.

To a German audience both objectively and ideologically conditioned by more than a decade of collective immiseration, the plot was mordantly attractive, the outcome reassuring. Economic depression is abstract, but bread shortages are not. Even inflation, the demon-merchant of Weimar days, achieves concrete form when banknotes prove insufficient at the shop-counter. These conditions had been experienced by millions of Germans after 1918; indeed, for troops in the trenches privations had arrived even earlier. Alfred Döblin's great novel, *Berlin Alexanderplatz* (1929), told the story in great and grim detail. Brecht's *Threepenny Opera* (1928) probed deeper into the underlying causes. Otto Dix and Georg Hirshfeld added graphic and psychologically acute evidence of damage and of danger to come. Over and above these cultural responses to the post-war trauma came the increasingly dominant allegation of foreign treachery – the French were blamed, the Treaty of Versailles was punitive, the reparations unbearable, the Bolsheviks savage subhumans, the Jews everywhere. There was the stab in the back, and the enemy within.

Friedrich Bethge epitomises many of these anxieties and bogus analyses. From a respectable home, educated if already restless before the war, severely wounded and demobbed into chaos, he had shifted between the ledger and the truncheon in an effort to get a grip on things. Clerk, street-fighter, poet, married man, political functionary, dramatist, Gauleiter, bestower of the Plakette, winner of the Plakette – a giant among dwarves, a Robert Gregory writ miserably small in Black-Letter, Hugh Selwyn Mauberley psychotically back from the dead. Or, in another perspective, Bethge was banality itself, the ordinary reduced to unimportance. For eyes like these, 'The Countess' was less mystery-play than miracle, a fable to be enacted as a benefit concert for the entire Schauspielhaus, by February 1934 *Judenfrei*, or near as dammit. It was the petit-bourgeois dream come true, recovery without painful heroics, risks loudly bemoaned and then 'honourably' disowned, thanks to a leadership obligingly swept off to Heaven. After Hunger, the Brown excitements; after the excitements, business as usual.

Shortly after Yeats's death, when Germany's business went on the offensive, the resignation-with-dividends theme became irrelevant. In any case, there never had been a revival of Bethge's 1934 production, merely a series of retrospections to mark Yeats's seventieth birthday and his death. There is aptness in Wagner's choice of 'The Mask'; a transitional piece, of little depth in itself, the poem marks the development of a far more complex dramatic theory than that employed in 'The Countess', a theory embracing character, history and the world of spirit, a theory discovered through poetry and occultic practice. It would be impossible to render 'At the Hawk's Well' (1916) – when Yeats first used masks on stage – petit-bourgeois. Though Yeats strongly turns after 1928 towards political and aesthetic pathways on which the signposts to fascism are clearly visible, the poetry and drama he wrote thereafter had little 'take-up' with the master-race. (The eugenicist and violent prose of *On the Boiler* was another matter, in which a willingness to predict 'tragic' crisis outbid any ability in specifying it.) During the Second World War, George Orwell classified Yeats as a writer who reached fascism by the aristocratic route, having commenced his quest at an early date. 'The Countess' suits Orwell's argument, while complicating the timetable of Yeats's reception in Germany.

Like the ordinary people in paintings by the Great Masters in Auden's poem, 'Musée des Beaux Arts', ordinary Germans were going about their business as best they could, relieved that the secrecy enveloping the concentration-camp system disobliged them from condemning it. At least in parts of the country. Few foresaw with any accuracy their own grossly lesser but consequential suffering. The trumpet blew, the panzers rolled, Paris fell, London nightly trembled. But then the Führer, of whom Yeats had once (only once) felt emulous, chose in high summer of 1941 to blow eastwards as well as westwards. Millions died on the Russian Front, victims of the despised Bolsheviks or of that unappreciated commander, General Winter. Numbers made it home to a nonexistent homeland. One Luftwaffe conscript, an instructor in communications, begot while on leave in March 1944 a daughter. At birth, she was spirited to a barn near Bamberg in December 1944. He too takes his part in the casual tragedy. She lies awake night after night fearing she never gets the answers right, despite two weeks at the Yeats Summer School, 1967.

To the west, the Main joins the Rhine some distance downstream from Frankfurt, far from the Lorelei rocks and the Wagnerian temptresses. Yeats was ever the passive partner in the strange but unquestionably conscious relationship he had with some ideas and practices behind the Nazi parade. While he is morally assisted by ideas of artistic detachment, taken over (incomplete) from the Romantics, more often he makes sense if seen to practise a cynical 'need-to-know' economy of truth. In his play, the heroine saves rather than tempts; in Eliot's 'Murder in the Cathedral' (1935), the spiritual vanity of seeking martyrdom is painstakingly analysed. If the occasion of the Frankfurt celebrations found Yeats at home in Riversdale with his wife, it also found him posing in correspondence with two former lovers – Shakespear and Gonne. Similarly, he did not need to know about the Frankfurt honours (the production, at least) until Frau Arndt was persuaded to write. This entwining of political and sexual allure is characteristic, and the multiplicity of his emotional commitments is to a degree mirrored in his political interests also. Whereas two- (or three-) timing is a familiar enough sexual phenomenon among men, Yeats is distinctive in that he can 'flirt' with fascism while remaining 'true' to eighteenth-century politics. The analogy does not stand up to examination, of course. Politics implies action, physical and mental and social – and being in just one place at a time.

The Nazi prize befell Yeats (we are to believe) just as German measles might have done. His translator had been active as early as 1925.[68] After February 1934, Ernst E. Stein published other Yeats pieces in translation, including 'On Baile's Strand' in November 1934 (though without any consequent stage-production). Because of his initials, he must be a candidate for authorship of the obituary that appeared on 2 February 1939 in the *Berliner Börsenzeitung*. This startlingly detailed and prompt tribute carries no Nazi overtone, yet its appearance is testimony to Yeats's acceptability in the Germany of 1939. In 1951, Yeats's bibliographer thanked 'Mr E. E. Stein' for checking translations, from which we may conclude that he survived the war a committed Yeatsian.[69]

Yeats's behaviour challenges the accepted distinction between 'active' and 'passive', unless one accepts that, in relation to Nazi Germany, he was mentally active and physically passive – an unsatisfactory interim solution. Dublin opinion in the 1930s accommodated more than a modicum of culturalist passive anti-Semitism and, later, some of the more vocally active kind. Coin of the realm, in Tom Garvin's phrase, though it would be a mistake to excuse Yeats on the grounds that 'they were all at it'. Studied neglect of the poet's undeniable interest in the fascist regimes is a post-war phenomenon, taking its place in a Cold War realignment of Communism v. the Democratic Rest of Us. A greater neglect relates to the very early textual occasion through which the SS-Dramaturg sought to engage with Yeats. To understand February 1934 one needs to look back through that episode towards 1892.

Intrusive Ghosts

A puppet in Turkish attire and with a hookah in its mouth sat
before a chessboard placed on a large table. A system of mirrors
created the illusion that this table was transparent from all sides.
Actually, a little hunchback who was an expert chess player sat
inside and guided the puppet's hand by means of strings. One can
imagine a philosophical counterpart to this device. The puppet
called 'historical materialism' is to win all the time. It can easily be a
match for anyone if it enlists the services of theology, which today,
as we know, is wizened and has to keep out of sight.

Walter Benjamin, 'Theses on the Philosophy of History', 1940

I make the truth.
'The Death of Cuchulain', 1938

Swift, Parnell and Some Anglo-Irish Others

The Tower (1928) is perhaps Yeats's greatest collection, whether
judged by the quality of individual poems or by the capacious and
symphonic arrangement of the whole. The opening line of the
opening poem themes the entire enterprise: 'This is no country for
old men.' (Yeats turned sixty-three that year.) Then the dominant
title-poem opens its concluding section: 'It is time that I wrote my
will.' His own death preoccupied the poet, even as his homeland
chose the national grid over the national being. 'The Tower' looked
to the past, including the Irish eighteenth century, its 'people of
Burke and of Grattan'. These exemplary political figures, each in his
own way a spokesman for liberal attitudes towards difference of
religious belief and ethnicity, appear at the close of the 1920s. But
facing which way?

Yeats's next full collection, *The Winding Stair and Other Poems*,
was published on 19 September 1933, bringing together work much
of which had appeared in interim slim volumes. The title alludes to a
central feature of the Norman tower at Ballylee, County Galway,
which the family had taken their final leave of in the summer of 1929.
Architecture casts a long shadow over these poems: 'great windows

open to the south', then 'the broken, crumbling battlement', and – most poignantly prophetic – the 'shapeless mound'. As the collection moves towards the sequence of Crazy Jane poems that close it, Swift is inscribed in the stone of epitaph. Destruction and madness are held at arm's length, but the struggle may prove unequal. If there is a moment of recovered confidence and spiritual well-being, it occurs in the fourth section of the sequence, tellingly named 'Vacillation'.

Dialogue with the eighteenth century has been sustained in 'Blood and the Moon' and 'The Seven Sages'. The voice of Jonathan Swift finally dominates 'The Words upon the Window-pane', which Yeats wrote in 1930 and saw into print at his sisters' Cuala Press in January 1934. But this is a dead Swift, or a quickened spirit who intrudes on a 1920s' *séance* to curse the day upon which he was born. The play is remarkable in a dozen ways, not least in its uncanny theatrical power. The central (absent) voice protests that he has something in his blood no child must inherit – 'attacks of dizziness ... worse things' – and for that reason he cannot marry. But a latter-day student at the *séance*, named John Corbet, translates Swift on eugenics back into late eighteenth-century politics: 'He foresaw Democracy, he must have dreaded the future. Did he refuse to beget children because of that dread? Was Swift mad? Or was it the intellect itself that was mad?'

In the course of this exposition, the student has described Swift as 'the chief representative of the intellect of his epoch'. His view has been taken over by Elizabeth Cullingford in her whitewashing of Yeats on the issue of fascism, despite the absurdity of anyone who resists democracy being set up as a 'representative'. Yeats ascribes to Corbet that weasel word, as a warning against easy acceptance of the student as the poet's own mouthpiece. To little avail. In Cullingford's exposition, the tragic crux of Yeats's engagement with the eighteenth century turns into a convenient alibi, Swift displaces Hitler, and history is smoothly ironed into a straight, exclusively Irish line. But Yeats had said otherwise. Writing to Thomas McGreevy in April 1932, he proposed a far-from-straightforward analysis of his own play: 'One of the characters gives what he supposes to have been Swift's point of view[,] that is all. Swift the arrogant, the exclusive, appears or speaks to common people at a common seance. To me, mediumship is the antithesis of the highly developed, conscious individuality, you may even call it democracy in its final form. I always dramatise, even in my essays; every truth has a counter-truth.'[1]

Perhaps this convenient doubling sanctioned Yeats's neglect of Swift's vehement hatred of warfare.

Irony quickly challenges the academic ironing out of these complexities. Hidden in the clothes cupboard is a name-echo possibly without significance. In 'The Words Upon the Window-pane', the medium's 'control' is a spirit called Lulu, a little girl who died when she was five or six; she it is who will describe Swift as a bad old man who does not know he is dead. While Yeats was working on the play, he stayed at Glendalough occasionally, dining with Francis Stuart while Iseult was visiting Maud Gonne in Dublin. The occasion varied. 'Frances Stuart always agrees with me or pretends to & that is very dull & he has a young art student with him called "Lulu" who never opens her mouth.' A few days later the situation improved: the student missed dinner, having got wet while fishing – 'Lulus absence & Iseults presence made all the difference.'[2] Together with echoes of horse-talk among some of the *dramatis personae*, which reflected Stuart's current preoccupations, the name of silent Lulu who is Iseult's undeclared rival moves between the play and the couple with whom Yeats had a most intense paternal relationship. Its intensity preoccupies the next chapter.

More compelling evidence supports the notion that 'The Words Upon the Window-pane' secretly explores the playwright's own emotional history. The name John Corbet, to whom the play's superficial account of Swift is attributed, lies close to Yeats's own family tree. The poet's nearest brother was Robert Corbet Yeats (1870–1873) and the sister who effectively ran the Cuala Press was Elizabeth Corbet Yeats (1868–1940), usually known as Lolly. The recurrent Christian name came into the Yeats line from Jane Grace Corbet (1811–1876) who married the poet's grandfather-namesake in 1835.[3] We shall meet more Corbets in the sweet by-and-by of the past.

Yeats's parlour-drama of 1934 brilliantly brought eugenics, the eighteenth century, mediumship and his own ancestry into disputatious play. What is ultimately suppressed in the play-script is the Victorian source – Sheridan Le Fanu's fiction – which Yeats drew upon for his setting and its vulgarised metaphysics. The resulting clash of Augustan and Free State Irelands is great fun, especially for those who have always taken Punch's side in his battering of Judy. As far as Yeats's dramatic canon is concerned, the succeeding plays manifest a strange coarsening of action and idiom, with decapitation centre-stage in 'A Full Moon in March' and 'The King's Threshold' (both 1935), and suggestively offstage in 'The Death of Cuchulain' (1938). In the poetry, this development is accompanied by the emergence of heroes more recently dead than Jonathan Swift and Edmund Burke. Pre-eminent among them is Charles Stewart Parnell. Though the Chief had died in 1891, Yeats's great concentration of writing about Parnell dates from the 1930s. At the time of the funeral at Glasnevin, the young poet had published a decidedly impatient tribute – 'Mourn, and Then Onward' – which (as Conor Cruise O'Brien pointed out in 1965) was an early triumph of cunning over passion.[4]

When Yeats resumes interest in the dead Chief, the title is 'A Parnellite at Parnell's Funeral'. Yeats had not been a Parnellite in the 1880s and early 1890s: on the contrary, he cleaved to the John O'Leary school of nationalism, which eschewed bombs and voting lobbies with equal fastidiousness. We can accept the title has a dramatic dimension, without implying that Yeats was revising his own political history in this particular regard. The issue is complicated by the intermittent publication of the various materials that eventually cohere in the canonical text, 'Parnell's Funeral'. The first sighting occurred in the introduction to Yeats's play 'Fighting the Waves', as published in *The Dublin Magazine* of April–June 1932, where what becomes the third stanza was printed. While the exercise of composition and revision deserves the closest attention from students of Yeats's poetic method, here we can be satisfied with noting the intermingling of poetry, drama and expository prose in *The King of the Great Clock Tower, Commentaries and Poems*. Thematic variety is no less astonishing, for this extraordinary volume, issued by Lolly Yeats from the Cuala Press in December 1934, brings decapitation, Parnell and the Blue Shirts within a single gathering.

Parnell had died of natural causes in Brighton more than forty years earlier: the tragic possibilities had to be worked up through association, contrast and intensification. Like Swift, he was to be mobilised through hocus-pocus rather than historical research. The Cuala Press format was not fully sufficient for this transformation of Parnell from dead politician into pagan god. Macmillan of London issued *A Full Moon in March* on 22 November 1935, which, despite its title, included a great deal more than the title-play. The two decapitation plays occupy the opening pages, followed by 'Parnell's Funeral and Other Poems'. This sectional heading powerfully associates the retrospective Parnell material with contemporary Irish politics and occultic vision, for what follows are 'Three Songs to the Same Tune', 'Alternative Song for the Severed Head in "The King of the Great Clock Tower"', 'Two Songs Rewritten for the Tune's Sake', 'A Prayer for Old Age', 'Church and State' and 'Supernatural Songs'. The hand which in 1928 crafted the elegiac Tower collection has clenched itself.

Textual evolution may not immediately convey excitement, but in Yeats's case the shaping of these books from the early 1930s constituted sustained acts of self-interpretation simultaneously aesthetic, erotic, paramedical, political and spiritual. Other recent heroes are evoked from time to time, for example in 'The O'Rahilly', where a minor figure from the list of nationalist fatalities in Easter 1916 is briskly commemorated. The case of Roger Casement (1864–1916) was to prove far more problematic.

Toller and O'Casey: Non Anglo-Irish Others

Yeats advanced Irish nationality, and in politics Irish nationalism, as a system of purifying filters through which grosser external matter might not contaminate his thought or exhaust his resources. Thus to Ethel Mannin in 1938 he would loftily declare that no Irish nationalist of the John O'Leary stripe ever meddled in international politics: the stripe, of course, was a very narrow band, and others meddled profitably in (for example) American politics.

At right angles to this selective procedure, Yeats employed a second – social class, fairly simply defined. His antagonism towards Bolshevism was unremarkable, being shared by virtually everyone except members of a communist party. His more local animus against any kind of Labour militancy became pronounced once the Irish Free State was established, and reached its most critical phase in the years when the Abbey Theatre depended on Sean O'Casey (1884–1964) for a revival of its fortunes. As a native of Dublin (and indeed a baptised member of the Church of Ireland), O'Casey came within Yeats's circles of approval and support. But as a proletarian with increasingly committed attitudes towards international socialism (and communism), O'Casey lay outside the Pale.

Ernst Toller (1893–1939), whom we have met in connection with the Ossietzky case, poses other problems for the biographer of Yeats. It is not that he was wholly a stranger to Irish literary circles. As early as 1923, he was named in a hostile article in the Dublin-based Jesuit magazine, *Studies*, and identified as the restless, neuropathic, Byronic 'poet and orator of International Peace'. Ireland then was still experiencing the final spasms of civil war, and the reasons for Father Lambert MacKenna's aversion to International Peace have to be sought internationally. In the same manner, it makes more sense to introduce the German dramatist fully, rather than commence with his apparently sudden intrusion into the correspondence of Yeats and Ethel Mannin or his earlier unfortunate featuring among Erich Gottgetreu's heroes during the lunch-table fracas in Coole Park. The son of a moderately prosperous Jewish merchant, Toller had been born in Samotschin, in present-day Poland. (Some relatives may have heard Yeats browbeat them at the London PEN Club in December 1933.) Education had taken him to the University of Grenoble in France just prior to the opening of the Great War. Seeing himself as patriotic German, Toller enrolled in a Bavarian artillery regiment from which he chose to transfer in a front-line unit to escape the anti-Semitic animus of his comrades. Appalled by the slaughter he witnessed at Verdun, he suffered near-total collapse and was declared unfit for further military service.

Now enlisted at the University of Heidelberg, he met the founder of modern sociology, Max Weber, with whom he developed a close friendship. When his anti-war and anti-nationalist activities resulted in expulsion, he moved to Munich to help Kurt Eisner (assassinated 1919) organise a munition workers' strike. Imprisoned and committed to a psychiatric clinic, by late 1918 Toller was well prepared to participate in the German revolution of October/November. Berlin's Spartacus revolution of January 1919 stimulated a more drastic response, resulting in the murder of Eisner, Karl Liebknecht and Rosa Luxemburg. As the revolutions collapsed, Toller was charged with high treason, though, partly through the testimony of Max Weber and Thomas Mann, he was not sentenced to death. Serving five years in prison, he turned to playwriting so successfully that 'Masses and Man' was performed widely throughout Germany with the author still behind bars. His literary reputation even reached Dublin, where the Jesuit Father MacKenna found it advisable to warn his readers that Toller had also distinguished himself as President and Food Commissioner for the Munich Soviet and later as strategist of the Red Guards.[5]

The left in Ireland knew no such moments of victory and

annihilation. The new state was, however, an object of great interest abroad. Though Toller never succeeded in reaching Ireland, he met the novelist Peadar O'Donnell and the dramatist Denis Johnston in England. He had written a film-script on Lola Montez (1818–1861), the Irish-born dancer whose relationship with Louis I of Bavaria obliged the king to abdicate in 1848. If one admired the martyrs of Easter 1916, then surely Toller had something to recommend him. Like James Connolly and Francis Sheehy-Skeffington, he was an advanced socialist and an anti-imperialist – a Marxist like Connolly and a pacifist like Sheehy-Skeffington. Like Pearse, he had briefly been head of an insurrectionary government and, like Thomas MacDonagh, was a playwright. But as the Free State consolidated itself, celebration of the 1916 martyrs was rigorously editing their allegiances and interests, to concentrate on the nationalist agenda at the expense of more radical objectives. Unlike them, Toller was un-Irish and dangerously alive.

In January 1925, maintaining its commitment to world theatre, the Dublin Drama League staged 'Masses and Man', which opened up possibilities of a closer and more dynamic relationship between German Expressionism and the Irish movement. This was probably the poor production that Yeats invoked in writing to Mannin in the 1930s to explain his attitude. For his part, Toller was impressed by Sean O'Casey's 'Juno and the Paycock'; both O'Casey and Denis Johnston absorbed elements of the German's approach to drama, controversially so in the case of O'Casey's 'Silver Tassie', which Yeats in effect vetoed for the Abbey in 1928.

Yeats of course remains offstage throughout Toller's developing Irish phase (such as it was). If he acknowledged the great debt which the Abbey Theatre owed O'Casey, and accommodated himself for that reason to O'Casey's proletarian ways, there were limits, quickly reached. He was adamantly opposed to 'The Silver Tassie' and while confusion persists as to how, exactly when and by whom this innovatory anti-war play was rejected in the Abbey, Yeats left no one in any doubt about his views. In a letter that O'Casey predictably released to the newspapers, Yeats admonished him:

> you are not interested in the great war; you never stood on its battlefields, or walked its hospitals, and so write out of your opinions. You illustrate those opinions by a series of almost unrelated scenes, as you might in a leading article; there is no dominating character, no dominating action, neither psychological unity nor unity of action.[6]

This was a Toller argument in everything but name. He and O'Casey shared strong left-wing views, and the Irish dramatist was now adopting the German's general approach to drama. If Yeats spoke the literal truth in declaring that O'Casey had never stood at Verdun or on the banks of the Somme, it was no more than a literal truth. The older writer's attempt at flattery in describing the earlier plays – 'you moved us as Swift moved his contemporaries' – was strangely inappropriate given the Dean's lifelong detestation of war. Likewise his explanation of delay in responding to the new script (mistakenly sent on to him at his Rapallo address) underlined the political differences between them. There was therefore a sequence of theatre crises in 1928 – rejection of 'The Silver Tassie', a consequently nervous reading of Denis Johnston's anti-heroic play about Robert Emmet, even the squabble with Gottgetreu – which underscored Yeats's increasingly assertive and authoritarian position. The O'Casey business hit the headlines, but the common denominator was provided by Toller at a distance.

If Toller was dangerous in the eyes of a new Irish establishment in the mid-1920s, the coming to power of Nazism placed him at extreme risk. Joseph Goebbels, who controlled theatre as well as other opportunities for propaganda, lost no time in denouncing the pacifist of 1916. Two million German soldiers, he declared, rise from the graves of Flanders and Holland to indict 'the Jew Toller'. That was on 1 April 1933: by September, Toller was in London seeking assistance. O'Casey and Yeats made up in the mid-1930s, and Yeats came to speak well of Toller. The context, however, was another crisis at the Abbey. Yeats certainly recommended Toller's 'Mrs Eddy' to his fellow-directors, even though he thought it trivial and superficial compared to 'Hoppla' (1927) or 'The Blind Goddess' (1932). Strong plays were needed to reassert the theatre's supremacy in Dublin's cultural life. Yeats was prepared to stage O'Donnell's 'Wrack' to support an innovative programme.[7] Here was an indulgence of the left if ever there was one. But was there one? Ernest Blythe in retrospect elaborated a strange opinion of Yeats's to explain the ultimate *non*-production of 'Mrs Eddy'. Yeats, he alleged, voted against staging Toller's play because 'he was not going to have a play performed in the Abbey which would offend the susceptibilities of Christian Scientists, however few of them might see it'.[8] For this reason or some other, 'Mrs Eddy' never reached the Abbey stage, and Yeats's undertaking to Toller and Ethel Mannin came to naught. But 'The

Silver Tassie', being Irish, was finally admitted into the repertoire. It filled the stalls and coffers in August 1935, and was followed by O'Casey's 'Within the Gates'. Yeats's doctrinaire attitude towards pacifism was thereafter channelled into the business of excluding Wilfred Owen and the English war poets from his eccentric *Oxford Book of Modern Verse* (1936). Owen's summary of his seventh hell or final resting place – 'I have not been to the Front, I have been in front of it' – may lack Yeats's sangfroid. If Yeats had read Toller's *I Was a German* (1933), with its harrowing account of a French soldier's protracted dying cries on front-line barbed wire, he might have revised his contempt for Owen's 'passive suffering'. But who is to say that he did not read it?

Casement and Wellesley

When Yeats introduced Casement's name into his argument against supporting the Ossietzky petition in 1936, he compounded a private problem of artistic conscience, because Casement had been implicated in German wartime affairs, fatally so. British colonial officer turned Irish cultural nationalist, he had travelled in 1914 to Berlin in search of military support for the Irish Republican Brotherhood and their planned insurrection. His execution for treason followed his arrest on Good Friday 1916 when he returned to Ireland, though the ultimate imposition of the death penalty resulted as much from rumour-mongering to destroy his moral character as from the court's judgment. Casement, it was averred, had been a promiscuous homosexual.

According to Mannin, writing at the end of the 1930s, Yeats had signed the petition aimed at saving Casement's life in the summer of 1916, but only at Maud Gonne's instigation.[9] The implication was that her influence – that of an old lover still ardently sought for – had pushed him across a line he would not (for Ossietzky's sake) cross a second time. In fact Yeats had not signed such a petition, and Mannin's testimony is faulty.[10] But there is more. Casement was not just a historical precedent, to be cited and then laid aside; he was a matter of urgent, contemporary concern. Between 1930 and 1940, at least ten books about him were published, together with a good deal of commemorative journalism in 1936.[11] That year alone saw the publication of at least three lengthy books. Only one appears to have caught Yeats's attention. *The Forged Casement Diaries* was published in Dublin, its author a naturalised American medical doctor, William Joseph [Marie Alois] Maloney (1882–1952).

The earlier studies of Casement included two by Denis Gwynn, whom Yeats knew as the son of Stephen Gwynn, a Protestant Home Ruler of Ulster origins. Denis, however, had converted to Catholicism and his many scholarly publications reflect his attachment to Rome as well as his nationalism. He and Yeats met to discuss the biography of Edward Martyn. In his 1936 edition of *The Life and Death of Roger Casement*, Gwynn quietly filleted the lengthy introduction that had opened the first edition of 1930. What he removed, in effect, was his discussion of the forgery question. And though it was Maloney's book that excited Yeats, Gwynn's original introduction had contained matter scarcely less controversial.

In 1917, Gwynn had been invalided home from the Western Front and posted to the Ministry of Information in London. There he had met a Scottish-educated Englishman, George Herbert Mair (1887–1926), who:

> made no secret, among the wide circle of his friends, that it was he who had been responsible for having [Casement's] diary copied. He claimed to have read it, and I remember that he referred to one passage describing an incident in London. I regret now that I made no further inquiries about the matter at the time. Mair – who was closely in touch with several Liberal Cabinet Ministers – told me also (whether this was accurate or not I cannot say) that the Cabinet had seriously considered whether they would drop the prosecution for High Treason and make him the centre of a second Oscar Wilde trial instead, in order to discredit him finally in Ireland.[12]

Mair had one unique claim on Yeats's attention, quite unconnected with Casement. Shortly after the death of Synge in 1909, the future master of propaganda had married Molly Allgood, the Abbey actress to whom Synge had been engaged. Whether Yeats read Gwynn's 1930 Introduction is impossible to establish, but in 1936 the entire discussion of Casement's sexuality and the use made of diaries was excised from the second edition. This did not prevent Maloney from quoting the Gwynn of 1930, or from waxing sarcastic at Mair's expense.

Not only Gwynn (who had met Casement occasionally), but Geoffrey Parmiter (who died as recently as 2000), issued a biography in 1936. At one level, these were further acts of commemorative politics, exactly twenty years having elapsed since the trial and execution. But Yeats nowhere featured in the record, not even as the signatory of a petition for clemency or as the author of a letter to the Home Secretary. If Gwynn and Parmiter gave unintended offence by ignoring Yeats, injury was inflicted in Maloney's opening pages where the journalist, Wickham Steed, was belaboured for his support of the Czech patriot, Thomas Masaryk, during the Great War: the same Wickham Steed was currently leading the Ossietzky campaign, an irritant in Yeats's life. From Hone (1943) onwards, it has been assumed that the ballads 'Roger Casement' and 'The Ghost of Roger Casement' were positively inspired by Maloney's book. It may make more sense to read them as acts of retaliation, prompted by unease rather than conviction.

To Mannin, in a letter of 15 November 1936, Yeats wrote in anger about the purveyors in 1916 of Casement's (allegedly forged) diaries:

> Casement was not a very able man but he was gallant and unselfish, and had surely his right to leave what he considered an unsullied name. I long to break my rule against politics and call these men criminals but I must not. Perhaps a verse may come to me, now or a year hence. I have lately written a song in defence of Parnell [. A]bout love and marriage less foul lies were circulated . . .[13]

To Dorothy Wellesley he made more extensive comments, beginning (as far as we can judge) on 28 November 1936. The dates are significant because the manuscripts of the resultant poems ('Roger Casement' and 'The Ghost of Roger Casement') are dated October/November and October respectively.[14] Yeats was not above falsifying the date appended to a poem in print, but here he seems to be either concealing from his correspondents the early date of his response to Maloney's book or deceiving himself (and subsequent editors) by pre-dating the manuscripts. In either case, a degree of nervousness is present.

The correspondents concerned were of divergent sexual tendencies, Mannin quite voraciously heterosexual, Wellesley a lesbian: both were married. Though letters between Yeats and Wellesley – as published – make no reference to genealogy, her husband was heir apparent to the dukedom of Wellington. (He duly succeeded in 1943.) The original duke had been an Irishman by birth, but had distinguished himself as the victor of Waterloo in 1815 and later as saviour of the Tory party. Fortunately for Casement, the Iron Duke did not intervene mediumistically in Yeats's exchange with the future duchess on the subject of homosexuality and republicanism.

It is a remarkable fact of Yeats's *Letters,* as selected by Allan Wade in 1954, that all references to Casement date from November 1936 to February 1937 and involve no other individual recipient but Mannin and Lady Wellesley.[15] Correspondence with the latter had first been published in 1940 – that is, in the early days of the war – and the texts show evidence of diplomatic editing, especially in the discussion of Casement. We know that John Kelly's great edition will multiply the number of available letters by a vast factor, and improve the texts, but Wade's edition retains a representative value of its own. It efficiently demonstrates the way the ghost of Roger Casement intruded abruptly on Yeats in 1936, just as the Insurrection had itself intruded twenty years earlier.

In the first letter to Wellesley alluding to the Casement business, Yeats went out of his way to note the sexual ambivalence between them, 'when you crossed the room with that boyish movement, it was no man who looked at you, it was the woman in me. It seems that I can make a woman express herself as never before. I have looked out of her eyes. I have shared her desire.' Ten days later he admitted that, in responding to Maloney's book, he had 'got into a blind rage & only half read the passage' that prompted an allegation he now conceded was false. All his life, he continued, he was the subject of 'these fits ... in this case I lost the book & trusted to memory. I am full of shame.' Two days later he was reporting to Wellesley the growth of the Catholic Front in Ireland and its threatened violence towards Yeats's Academy of Letters; the same letter oddly reports 'an outbreak among the young in favour of the king' – that is Edward VIII, shortly to abdicate. The period was characterised by an emotional crisis, the first cause (of five) of which Yeats mechanistically identified as 'Casement forgeries (rage that men of honour should do such things)'. The correspondence with Wellesley persisted into the New Year, as did Yeats's sense of desolation. On 28 January 1937, he provided his correspondent with a résumé of his experiences:

> Something happened to me in the darkness some weeks ago. It began with those damned forgeries – I have the old Fenian conscience – death & execution are in the day's work but not that. Everything seems exaggerated [*sic*] – I had not a symptom of illness yet I had to take to my bed. I kept repeating the sonnet of Shakespeare's about 'captain good' – I felt I was in an utter solitude. Perhaps I lost you then, for my part of my sense of solitude was that I felt I would never know that supreme experience of life – that I think possible to the young – to share profound thought &

then to touch. I have come out of that darkness a man you have never known – more man of genius, more gay, more miserable.[16]

On 2 February 1937, 'Roger Casement' was printed in the *Irish Press*, a paper owned by the de Valera family and doggedly loyal to the ruling Fianna Fáil party that Yeats detested. His preferred place of publication had been the Protestant-owned and (for that reason supposedly) pro-British *Irish Times*. Quite why he thought the *Times* would take such a poem is unclear, but the ultimate appearance of 'Roger Casement' in de Valera's *Irish Press* indicates a degree of calculation on Yeats's part – the ballad was to be popular, it demanded a mass circulation, it conformed to a republican belief in British perfidy. (Never mind Edward VIII for the moment.)

Yet alongside these cunning manoeuvres, one traces Yeats's profound uncertainty and inner disturbance. Casement drew together themes that might otherwise be held safely apart – nation and sexuality, nativism and foreign service – or be paired off in approved combinations of strictly limited application, John Bull v. Mother Ireland. Yeats's own involvement with Wellesley obliged him to recognise contradictions between his national credentials and his relationship with English high society. The frisson of this might be intensified creatively by the ambivalence of their sexuality as a couple. Suddenly intruding into this *ménage à deux*, the dead Casement pointed to the fatal consequences of altered or transgressed loyalties. What is more, Casement's commitment to a German alliance on behalf of the Irish Republican Brotherhood was now, in the 1930s, reactivated with respect to the new Nazi regime. Irish republicans were in cahoots with Berlin, and the Reich had its assiduous agents at work in Dublin. Maud Gonne assisted this undermining of the Free State. The director of Ireland's premier museum, with an office in Kildare Street, beside parliament, headed the local Nazi cadre. Others, ranging from subversive Clissmann to shabby Moylett, play their parts.

There were parallels between Yeats and Casement that provoked reflection. Both had been born on the southern shore of Dublin Bay – Yeats in Sandymount, Casement in Sandycove – within ten months of each other. Both had immediate Ulster Protestant backgrounds, though in one case (Casement's) this fact has been emphasised to a high degree, and in the other (Yeats's) it has been suppressed to a similar extent. Both came from a stratum of society characterised by uncertainty of status: were they rural gentry, were they middle-class or professional people, were they part of some 'Protestant Ascendancy' elite of supposedly historic cultural achievement? Both families had suffered genteel impoverishment and the humiliation of necessitous living in English cities – Liverpool in Casement's case, London in Yeats's. In both cases, steps had been taken to compensate for these social dislocations: Casement had been baptised a Catholic in what was in effect a secret childhood ceremony, while a rather older Yeats had joined himself to a secret revolutionary brotherhood. Both men were offered knighthoods by the Crown, Casement accepting, Yeats declining the honour.

We have only Mannin's word for it that Maud Gonne featured in Yeats's liberal defence of his non-support of Ossietzky. She too became a convert to Catholicism and, in a sense, a renegade from her (English) class origins. As far as Yeats was concerned, Gonne's sexuality was not voracious and her relationship with her husband (the drunken vainglorious lout of 'Easter 1916') did little to commend heterosexual coexistence. Yeats had other outlets – or inlets – and never took his infatuations to the point of an exclusive fidelity. As for Yeats's efforts on Casement's behalf, evidence is difficult to trace: his own *Autobiographies* and *Memoirs* are silent; none of the early Lives document a commitment on his part, and indeed we have to wait for Brown (1999) for any perceptive biographical comment.[17]

At the time of Casement's celebrated exposure of South American brutality in the rubber industry, Yeats wrote to Augusta Gregory describing a London hack who had been advised to publish stories about business executives. 'Now he is writing up the Rubber atrocities.'[18] There is no reference to the living Casement, and no sense that either Gregory or Yeats took any interest in his campaigns. A year later, in 1914, Yeats's circle had their view of Casement, though it rarely – if ever – broke forth in speech or public print. George Russell described someone 'with no heavy mentality to embarrass him in his actions'; John Butler Yeats thought him 'like a very nice girl who is just hysterical enough to be charming and interesting among strangers and a trial to his own friends'.[19] Prejudicial judgment did not prevent both men liking Casement, but they had their reservations. When the moment for action occurred in the summer of 1916, Yeats had made his representations to Herbert Asquith, the Prime Minister, and to Herbert Samuel, the Home Secretary, but he made them privately, writing from Calvados in Normandy. (As it happened, Yeats knew Asquith quite well and got on with him socially.) It was left to more straight-forward aggressive personalities such as Arthur Conan Doyle and Bernard Shaw to fight the public fight. Maybe Yeats had doubts about Casement, not merely his practical abilities but his private conduct. This would not have been a moralistic reservation – after all, Yeats had championed Wilde and continued to do so; after all, he liked the boy in Dorothy Wellesley. But Yeats had also noted the suffering caused to Wilde's friends by his exposure, and if he suspected Casement of being homosexual – and the rumours were of promiscuous and prolific homosexuality – he may well have decided to look no closer. It was easier and nobler to stand by a convicted traitor than a suspected renter of underaged boys. To Wellesley he reported Irish public opinion, and then went well beyond it:

> there is a demand for a production of the documents & their submission to some impartial tribunal. It would be a great relief to me if they were so submitted & proved genuine.[20]

Yet as all the Casement biographies silently demonstrate, Yeats had not ostentatiously stood by Casement in 1916. His poem, 'Sixteen Dead Men', is generally taken to allude to the fifteen leaders of the Insurrection who were shot in Dublin, with Casement as the implied sixteenth at best: some of the Dublin leaders are named, Casement is not. 'Easter 1916', a much finer poem, names four of the fifteen and clearly refers to others without disguise or ambiguity. But there is no allusion to Casement, unless – as Brian Inglis half-hints – it comes in the phrase about 'excess of love'. His role in the Easter events had been an abortive attempt to call off the Insurrection at the last minute, and Yeats (who remained cautious of publishing the poem for years) may have worried about how Irish history would judge Casement in the light of this attempt.

Dr Maloney's book in 1936 sought to eliminate all questions of doubt or merely reluctant veneration. Against the advice of G. B. Shaw, the American published his lengthy accusation of forgery, directed at the British authorities. It nowhere mentions Yeats, except for a passing remark of Casement's in a letter of 1911 to Mrs Alice Stopford Green, when he quotes 'The Lover Tells of the Rose in His Heart' (1892):

> The wrong of unshapely things is a wrong too great to be told.
> I hunger to build them anew and sit on a green knoll apart.

This was not the poetry Yeats in 1936 would have chosen to

represent him. Apart from its pathos and passivity, which he had manfully striven to overcome, these poems of *The Wind Among the Reeds* had been addressed for the most part to Maud Gonne. Reading half the poem ramblingly reinscribed into Maloney's book, the poet cannot but have recalled Gonne's pressing him to sign the petition for reprieve in 1916. Maloney's book did not inspire Yeats to defend Casement once again; it provoked him to do with excess what he had done with diplomatic indirection in the first place.

The intensity of this self-authentification through repetition can be judged from the letters to Wellesley, notably that of *c.* 28 January 1937. Yeats had taken to his bed, though scarcely ill. He recalled Sonnet 66 by Shakespeare, without citing its ninth line ('And art made tongue-tied by authority'), but ended his talking cure by emphasising how he feared that he had lost the ability to 'share profound thought & then to touch'. This experience he associated with youth generally, and by implication with heterosexual intimacy, despite the ambivalence of the sonnets. By way of conclusion, he has become 'a man you have never known – more man of genius, more gay, more miserable'. But a man, rather than the woman in him to which he had referred in the letter of 28 November 1936. This had not been self-authentification after all, but male-remaking.

The two-month crisis of sexual identity was prompted by Maloney's book about Casement: 'it began with those damned forgeries ...' The expletive is unusual in Yeats's correspondence. 'Damnable' would have been better judged if the behaviour of the forgers was his target. But 'damned' carries with it an acknowledgment of the intractable reality of the documents, whether forged or authentic. His declaration that he had the old Fenian conscience leads on curiously to 'death & execution are in the day's work but not that'. It has been assumed that 'that' is forgery or blackmail-through-forgery – which is to say Yeats condones killing and would accept execution in a good cause, but not the manufacture of false and damaging evidence of 'unnatural practices'. Paraphrased in this way, his declarations carry little weight. But the assumptions just referred to all arise *after* the triumph of the forgery theorists. What if 'that' alluded to the practices themselves? Does Yeats's letter to Wellesley reveal a suspicion that Casement had indeed been a paedophile?

The retrospective republicanism that Yeats achieved by publishing his Casement ballad in the *Irish Press* exemplifies several characteristics of his personality, not least the political cunning to which Cruise

O'Brien drew attention in his 1965 essay. At a deeper level, it also enacts a historical movement within the poet's deliberately sculpted (auto-) biography. Whether from his occultist enquiries, or from more mundane considerations, he learned early to resist linear models of development. Neither civilisation nor the individual life moved to a 'Forward March' tune. Within his own biography, events, that substantially occurred in the summer of 1916, significantly occurred in the late autumn of 1936. For Yeats, Casement was always a dead man, a ghost.

In keeping with such logic, at least one member of the Blood Kindred maintained contact with Yeats after January 1939. Indeed, Dorothy Wellesley went to the trouble and expense of publishing their correspondence, at once posthumous and one-sided. *Beyond the Grave* (c.1950) is a patchwork of extracts from letters she apparently directed to her dead friend throughout the war years and after, together with some extraneous matter by S. T. Coleridge or about English flowers. There are also references to Sappho and Lesbos, as if in this ghostly non-exchange the truth might be published. Given the author's delicate mental health, quotation from a privately printed volume may seem intrusive, but Wellesley's determination to publish was matched only by the sheer perversity of her expressed political views. Hers is the only known case of a living person haunting a dead one.

Towards the end of June 1942 (a busy month), she informed him that she was a Tory Democrat, not an impossible combination, despite a further declaration that she was a Romantic-Realist. A week or so earlier she called Stalin 'that man of genius', while Hitler was 'fundamentally a second-rate man'. These views may be unexpected in one who, in the mid-1930s, had thought Hitler morally better than Mussolini. Her admiration of Uncle Joe, on the other hand, was a suitably classless phenomenon throughout wartime Britain. Of more immediate concern to Yeats in Vichy France was the virtual head of the collaborationist government. In her eyes, Pierre Laval (1883–1945) was 'the corrupt Jew', a bitterly and unintended ironic comment in mid-1942 when Britain was struggling with its conscience about accepting refugees from France. (Britain won.) Just as the villain's fault is his alleged Jewishness rather than his collaboration with the Nazis, so it is not entirely clear what 'side' Wellesley approves in her account of the north African campaign:

Germans once again taking the offensive, owing without doubt to the distracted actions of the French under the corrupt Jew, Laval. Impossible to believe that the French nation can submit to such humiliation except under semi-starvation. No use to judge, to record.[21]

Conventionally, Wellesley was a loyal British subject. But her communications with the dead Yeats allowed her to speculate on a post-war future in terms less clear-cut. 'Some horrific belief is beginning to grow in my own mind, a belief that almost total destruction of our present civilisation is the only solution.' To some extent, she had already experienced a preview. 'I have watched the faces of the Uneducatable Mass well enough to know that.' So much for Tory Democracy. Some of this, she acknowledged, sprang from her rereading of On the Boiler, Yeats's contribution to the carnival-carnage of autumn 1939. He had urged the need for war.

Personal frailties notwithstanding, the author of Beyond the Grave provides a unique account of political and ethical confusion expressly linked to Yeats's thinking. While there are comic aspects – she transcribes for the dead poet his own 'Prayer for My Daughter' – there is also a bizarre combination of acute and obtuse foresight. 'I do not think the real holocaust has yet begun,' she writes in June 1942. Yet even after the liberation of Dachau (in which her son-in-law took part), she holds Jews responsible for much of the trouble. They now monopolise the Idle Rich and are behaving disgracefully in Israel, as if Belgravia and Bethlehem divided the world's attention. When photographs from the concentration camps were exhibited in London, 'a large part of the British public believed them to be faked. I saw them myself, but could not stay.'[22] It is difficult to avoid the conclusion that she questions the evidence of anti-Semitism on the Nazis' part.

Walter Benjamin and the Lady from 'Purgatory'

Beyond the Grave contained the disjecta membra of Wellesley's relationship with Yeats, the parts that could not be admitted by Oxford University Press into Letters on Poetry (1940), a wartime publication widely reviewed – by R. P. Blackmur, Cleanth Brooks, Alan Tate and some other, less conservative admirers. That Yeats's literary friendships should first be commemorated and publicised in the particular case of Dorothy Wellesley does more than expose the dubious politics which they shared: it also draws attention to the poet's very limited circle of intimate friends in the later 1930s –

friends, that is, with literary achievement or talent of the first rank. Death had taken Augusta Gregory, who had been more than friend. There was Ezra Pound, of course, but in 1940 Pound was in Rome vociferously supporting the Axis powers. His name was not to be given prominence in any wartime celebration of Yeats. The younger Irish writers – Austin Clarke, Patrick Kavanagh, Louis MacNeice, Frank O'Connor, Sean O'Faolain, Francis Stuart – had either chosen to write in prose, or in other ways distanced themselves from the master. Some had been scared off by Yeats, or were offended by his exclusion of them from his *Oxford Book of Modern Verse* (1936). Those Irish writers whom Yeats encouraged – Oliver St John Gogarty, F. R. Higgins and Stuart – scarcely constituted a band of brilliant devotees.

The ageing Yeats's literary friends were distinctly mediocre as writers: they were also predominantly English and female. Ethel Mannin, Margot Collis and Dorothy Wellesley doubled up as the poet's lovers, augmented later by Lady Elizabeth Pelham (a spiritualist), and the journalists Hilda Matheson and Edith Shackleton Heald. Matheson was in fact Wellesley's lover but, through her BBC activities and her association with the Royal Institute for International Affairs, she also appears to have had links with the British intelligence services. Evelyn Marriott, who drove down with Heald for the last days in southern France, was sister to an MI5 man. Behind Wellesley's near-madness there may have been active a degree of careful method on somebody else's part, to ensure that the dying prophet of war did not overstep the limits of British tolerance. After all, Sean Russell's bombs were already setting a likely scene for declarations from 'the old Fenian conscience'.

If the British authorities were worried about Yeats's potential for embarrassment, they had failed to note how his complex and multiple entanglement with English women had involved its own transgressive element. This was not national but sexual. He had transcended the conflict between England and Ireland, converting it into an aristocratic union of individuals. Pelham and Wellesley were top-drawer, and if the others were unmistakably middle-class, the lesbianism of several provided its own version of a privileged minority, a coterie of shared and intense feeling beyond comprehension by the Uneducatable Masses. Nothing of the kind could have been found in Ireland.

But Ireland dominated the imagery of those plays through which Yeats made his final contribution to a theatre he had virtually invented. His last play, 'The Death of Cuchulain' (1939), is not widely approved, but its frankness repeats the more subtly treated plot of murder in 'Purgatory' (1938). Both plays intimately relate violent death and sexual generation, one through the use of heroic myth, the other through allusions to recent history. The radical separation of myth from history is itself a noteworthy feature of the late drama, as if bringing them together might prove unmanageable even for Yeats. Cuchulain is the supreme hero of Irish saga and myth, the defender of Ulster against invasion from the west and south. Mortally wounded, he is confronted by the principal women in his life – his faithful wife, his guileful mistress, and a figure whom Roy Foster classifies as Cuchulain's 'avenging love-object'. Aoife is more properly the woman who bore Cuchulain's son, the son he found himself obliged to kill through heroic allegiance to his king. At midpoint in the play it seems that Aoife will kill Cuchulain, to repeat and cancel the death inflicted on their child. This would have given a Greek complexion to Yeats's last tragedy.

The play veers into a more abstract resolution, perhaps indicative of tragedy's unavailability to him. Cuchulain having suffered six mortal wounds, he has gone one better than Christ, a point Patrick Pearse might have appreciated. Certainly, the dying hero's injuries are dramatically suggestive of a typology, including Shakespeare's Julius Caesar (and perhaps St Sebastian) as well as Christ. The analogy with Caesar – 'see what a rent the envious Casca made' – foregrounds the conflict between ambitious authority and the conniving many. That with Sebastian is visualised in Cuchulain's dying posture, tied to a rock with his own belt, tied indeed by Aoife whom he thinks may deliver the *coup de grâce*. He is not, however, to be killed by a woman. The intervention of a supernatural figure, the Morrigu, allows for a stylised climax with music, curtains, dances and (later) fairground noises.

After this stage business, the audience sees six wooden parallelograms, emblemising the six mortal wounds or (more likely) the six who wounded Cuchulain. The crow-headed Morrigu holds up a seventh block of wood, announcing that it is the head of Cuchulain. As numerologically the wounds are equated with the wounders, so the block is the head. This last move effects a drastic metonymy, by which the exact place or receptacle of decapitation becomes the head (or in Latin *caput*). It thus elides the act of killing, just as the agent of death is now drawn from among supernatural beings, not humans. It would be silly to proclaim Yeats's curtain scene 'the aesthetising of murder on stage', and promptly to conclude that such theatre is fascistic. Yet it is no less unforgivably myopic to ignore its celebration of violence.

Yeats very nearly steers the play into the present. Ragged (which is to say, impoverished) street-singers occupy the brightened stage. There is no indication as to the sex of these singers, nor apparently do records survive to indicate how the parts were cast in the first production – by Austin Clarke in 1949. The Singer may recall that 'there are some living / That do my limbs unclothe', but in a ragged figure who ascribes strong combinations of words – 'adore and loathe' – to men, while also employing them in the first person, the effect is far from conclusive.[23] This indeterminedness renders the play powerfully ambivalent, bringing to the ancient Irish material something of the frisson Yeats nurtured at Penns in the Rocks and Steyning. His last two plays were written in the houses of his English women friends, far from Sligo and Dublin's Post Office.

'Purgatory', which takes its title from Christian theology, had ended with an invocation of the Almighty unusual in Yeats's work, 'O God, / Release my mother's soul ...' Less obviously, 'The Death of Cuchulain' also echoes a religious idiom. 'No body like his body / Has modern woman borne ...' reads like a fusion of Lamentations 1:12 with the traditional view of the Virgin Mary's unique suffering at the death of her son. In the Old Testament passage, the (female) city of Jerusalem cries out, 'see if there by any sorrow like unto my sorrow'. In Handel's *Messiah* (Dublin, 1741), the passage is translated into the masculine third person ('any sorrow like unto His sorrow') as part of the predictive narrative of Jesus in fulfilment of Old Testament longings. These longings, it hardly needs to be said, arose from foreign domination and exile.

Perhaps this textual finessing could have been reserved for another occasion, were it not for the urgency of re-establishing some historical sense of the play, aesthetically unsatisfactory though it may be. Yeats was ever the product of Victorian Ireland, and the Dublin origins of *Messiah* were compounded when Ebenezer Prout (1835–1909; professor of music at Trinity College) edited the music for nineteenth-century ears. Cuchulain as Christ-and-Caesar hand-in-glove with Sebastian may seem a portmanteau martyr, but Yeats's entire dramatic oeuvre had been dedicated to wresting poetic drama out of euphemistic Victorian piffle, everything Joyce meant when he

interesting

referred to Lawn Tennyson. If a biblical echo, also an echo of Handel, is detected in the lyric that ends 'The Death of Cuchulain', then it is another intrusive ghost, a cold updraught from the playwright's Victorian past.

The nineteenth century is everywhere evident in 'Purgatory', so much so that readers have wondered what deeper meaning lies below the surface. During the first production in August 1938, Father Terence Connolly, a Jesuit priest from Boston College, raised the issue of allegory in the play. Professor Donald Torchiana was inclined to find instead a 'theory of the symbolic tragedy of the eighteenth century'.[24] Yeats, in reply to Connolly, invoked the fate of Coole Park (without naming it) and the sale of its contents after Augusta Gregory's death in 1932. But surely Foster goes too far in local piety when he insists that 'these Irish obsessions drive *Purgatory*, rather than any ill-digested notions about Nazi legislation'.[25] If the play is driven, then something more than differences with Margaret Gough, Lady Gregory's daughter-in-law, are accountable. Yeats said so. 'The problem is not Irish, but European . . .' citing Nazi legislation.

The least Protestant of magicians, Yeats had nonetheless inherited and never lost an anti-Catholic prejudice with roots in the Penal Laws, the struggle for and against Emancipation (1829), and the resultant loss of monopolies and privileges among members of the Irish Church Establishment, especially in borough towns (1840). Yeats was a grandson and great-grandson of that clerical Establishment. To Dorothy Wellesley, he relayed an account of his tiff with Father Connolly: 'After a week of clerical conspiracy I understand the satisfaction a Spaniard finds in raping a nun.'[26] Unknown to Connolly, Yeats's early drafts for the play indicated that the 'groom' whom the lady of the Big House married was thought of as a Catholic, thus rendering covertly sectarian the declared theme of social miscegenation. Something of the same kind will characterise manuscript versions of 'The Death of Cuchulain'.[27]

Completing his plays, Yeats had bigger fish to fry than such obsessions. 'Purgatory' had folkloric as well as theological sources, and its organising principle – that the dead dream back through their earthly experiences – had already been put to powerful dramatic use in 'The Words Upon the Window-pane'. Linking the two plays is a pervasive concern with heredity: the Swift who haunts the earlier play fears that, begetting a child, he would pass on a mental condition that he never quite defines; the Old Man of 'Purgatory' kills his son in order to prevent the transmission of 'pollution'. Between 1930 and 1938, undefined madness is replaced by a 'pollution' strongly defined in terms of blood, the mixing in marriage of blue blood with blood closer to the soil. If this bears any resemblance to the *Blut-und Boden-literatur* favoured in Germany before and after 1933, it is a resemblance at a very high level of sophistication. The Goethe-Plakette award of 1934 had brought Yeats and one such German writer (Hermann Stehr) together on paper or in bronze; the play produced on that occasion, 'The Countess Cathleen', utilised an older Teutonic motif, the Faustian bargain. 'Purgatory' is neither a blood-and-soil novelette nor a drama pitting humanity against supernatural and/or Satanic powers. On the contrary, the disturbing factor lies exactly in its insistence on keeping blood and soil apart – no Antaeus myth will serve. Even more eerie is the exclusively human spectrum within which a mechanistic spiritual process works itself out. A man has killed his father and must now kill his son; pollution involves no elements of moral, social or cultural transmission; it is a kind of mediumless contagion. This is to summarise what the Old Man declares and enacts on stage; what Yeats believed may be different, but he has made it difficult to detect the difference.

At the head of this chapter the coexistence of Yeats and the German philosopher-critic, Walter Benjamin (1892–1940), may have raised eyebrows. The Irish poet is highly unlikely to have heard of Benjamin, who remained an obscure figure for many years after his suicide. He, however, was aware of Yeats's dramatic and other writings, naming him among certain 'great artists and exceptional theoreticians' who fail to understand the concept of allegory as Benjamin understands it.[28] Though Yeats was known only to a small following in Germany – unlike, say, Shaw or even Joyce – his significance has been appreciated by scholars of Benjamin and his associates. The pianist-critic, Charles Rosen, lists *A Vision* (1925) as one of the central texts of an age of esoteric literature, commencing with Eliot's *The Waste Land* and Joyce's *Ulysses* (both 1922) and including Rilke's *Sonnets to Orpheus* (1923) and Benjamin's unpublished dissertation of German baroque tragic drama. At a deeper historical level, he names Benjamin, André Breton and Yeats as the three foremost in a twentieth-century tradition deriving from a specific strand of Romanticism which negotiated creatively between the twin imperatives of religious feeling and secularisation.[29]

This is not the excellent European company in which Yeats

normally finds himself nowadays. In the cautious terms of Roy Foster, Yeats was right-wing in his politics, an authoritarian of purely Irish concern. Remote from localised preoccupations, Benjamin is best known as a Marxist, though one given to flying in the face of party and proletariat. In keeping with these familiar characterisations, the epigraphs above contrast with each other. Considered more closely, 'The Death of Cuchulain' might be shown to resemble the curious machine described in the first of Benjamin's 'Theses on the Philosophy of History'.[30] The Old Man is director not only of the play that succeeds him onstage, but also of his own performance, after which he disappears (as it were under a table that is apparently, not actually, transparent). The speeches of the three women who have dominated Cuchulain's life are determined by their prior roles, yet they take possession of what seems autonomous life. To leave that life, the hero is by paradox strapped to a standing stone. Yeats, who had not only rapped tables, but set the main (invisible) action of 'The Words Upon the Window-pane' around or above one, was sceptical of the occult to which he devoted himself.

Among the women who contributed to his exuberant old age, Ethel Mannin was the privileged recipient of more insights than Wellesley or the unfortunate Margot Collis. Mannin was a proclaimed communist, less air-borne than Benjamin, but also less consistent in the long run. Mild contradiction leavened the corre-spondence between poet and novelist. He told her of his membership of the oath-bound Irish Republican Brotherhood, which disapproved of both communists and Englishwomen. This followed on an earlier, perhaps teasing, certainly ungrammatical declaration that 'my politics are my secret'.[31] Was she Aoife, a vengeful feminist, or Ethne Inguba; how did Emer back in Rathfarnham feel about these London liaisons? Yeats tried to avoid political discussion, at least partly because he knew of their divergences of opinion. But there were other, far more profound reasons. Beyond or behind *A Vision* (then undergoing revision), Yeats disclosed that he also possessed a 'private philosophy' (his quote marks). This had come in the same manner as the 'public philosophy' that went into *A Vision*, but it dealt with 'individual mind', as distinct from the historical whirlygigs of his published system. He had not attempted to publish the private thought because he only half-understood it himself. His letter to Mannin then proceeded to discuss Rilke and his conception of death, adding:

In my own philosophy the sensuous image is changed from time to time at predestined moments called Initiationary [sic] Moments ... One sensuous image leads to another because they are never analysed. At The Critical Moment they are dissolved by analysis & we enter by free will pure unified experience. When all the sensuous images are dissolved we meet true death.[32]

While Yeats was willing to sketch this private belief for Ethel Mannin, it is clear that what she got was no more than the most elementary outline. He drew the discussion into more familiar paths, with references to Blake and (without naming him) the contemporary German philosopher Georg Simmel, whose book on Rembrandt he was apparently reading. There is some suggestion that the course from one sensuous image to another involves (perhaps by way of mere illustration) different national characteristics or experiences, but the letter does not sustain the theme. Nevertheless, sufficient new terms and names are divulged in this brief correspondence to indicate that Yeats in 1938 was turning his attention, his private attention, in unexpected directions. In 1934, he had confessed to the Frankfurt authorities that he knew little or nothing of German culture beyond Goethe and Jakob Böhme. Now he was reading about Rilke, and even delving into German philosophical art history. Simmel (1858–1918), who was Jewish, had taught Benjamin in the University of Berlin.

The term 'analysis' is almost as unexpected, though the context of Initiationary and Critical Moments makes it clear that nothing straightforward is meant. The previous year, however, Yeats had employed the term in a manner that linked childhood (or earlier) experience and political attitude:

I say to myself, 'I feel' this or that – I 'hate' something or 'like' something. I thus analyse my feeling, relate one feeling to another and so on until I say 'Yes, I must always have believed that or known that.' AE says ... that by similar analysis he traced his experience back to a pre-natal condition and was filled with terror as if about to approach some act nature desired to keep hidden. No reasoning forward ever gives me a conviction. My analysis has a result the opposite of AE's, mine dissolves terror. Two days ago while trying to analyse my periodical outbursts of political hatred, I remembered how I had deliberately exasperated a friendly audience. I found it was from fear of a theme they were thinking of; now that I have got rid of this fear by finding its root in my general conception of life I shall keep my temper better. If one is afraid of looking into a face one hits the face.[33]

This is certainly not what was meant by analysis in Vienna, though the role played by infantile or pre-infantile experience is one 'the Jewish science' would have thought deserving of refinement. If Yeats had no time for Freud, this did not prevent him from approving a plan three months later to have Lennox Robinson psychoanalysed with a view to treating his chronic drunkenness.[34] One of Robinson's more able drinking cronies was Georgie Yeats, the poet's wife.

Even if the friendly audience cannot be identified conclusively as the Jews and Indians of late 1933, several topics of major biographical interest arise from the letter of May 1937, as if from sunken seas. Belief, or firmly held knowledge, is generated for Yeats through the analysis of feelings. Belief thus generated is retrospective, at least as far as the conscious mind is concerned. The working from feeling through analysis to belief brings relief, dissolves terror. The analysis of feeling, as a mental practice, may suggest a primitive or lay form of psychoanalysis, though it also recalls that coldness we found analysed in Baudelaire's account of Delacroix. In any case, and this case is limited by the single letter in which the matter is discussed, Yeats's named feelings are only three, or at most four, in number: hating, liking, and the feelings of terror and fear. Not forgetting the brevity of his exposition, we find a very narrow band of emotional 'feelings' disclosed by this semi-private Yeats. Compared with the rich expressiveness of the poetry, and the variety of the dramatic characters, it is heart-stopping in its implications.

Seven months later, just before Christmas 1937, Yeats offered a different perspective to Mannin on the question of political utterance. He was off to Monte Carlo and, as if to mollify that admission made to an active communist, he reminded her that he had never discussed his political opinions with her – or 'with anybody'. This was arrant nonsense, scattered like primroses en route to the everlasting boiler:

> The other day I discovered that I must increase the income of the Cuala Press by about £150 a year & decided to issue a kind of Fors Clavigera. I must in the first number discuss social politics in so far as they affect Ireland. I must lay [?] aside this pleasant path I have built up for years & seek the brutality, the ill breeding, the barbarism of truth. Pray for me my dear, I want an atheist's prayers, no Christian can do me any good.[35]

There is no obligation to take Yeats's proclaimed commercial motive as explaining the *content* of the resulting publication, except to note that he evidently felt his views would sell. (In the event, they didn't.) Likewise his description of a sustained refusal to proclaim his views as a pleasant or undemanding path can be read as tailor-made for his immediate left-wing reader/lover. The genuine Yeatsian tone is unmistakable in the undertaking 'to seek the brutality, the ill breeding, the barbarism of truth' – with perhaps a hint of irony in the simplified concept of 'truth'. Nevertheless, the phrase is mightily ambiguous. Alliteration bounces along from brutality to barbarism, using the touchstone value-term 'breeding' as its fulcrum. Is truth ill-bred, and thus to be best avoided as a kind of philosophical vulgarity behind which a private credo may be preferred? Questions shed light, even in the absence of answers, and it is possible that Yeats here suggests a grave necessity (masquerading as financial need) to seek truth, even if it involves what in the social domain one regards as *mésalliance*, ill-breeding, a stable-groom tupping a gentle lady. Though the tone is different beyond description, such an undertaking, together with its implications of brutality and barbarism, shares certain preoccupations with the metapsychology of Freud. While one registers a sense of Yeats's reluctant embarking on a new political quest in his last year or two, and so registers also the possibility of nuanced uncertainty (even downright confusion), the comparison with Freud opens up chasms of divergent assumption. From early in his career as psychoanalyst, Freud had recognised the violence (brutality) at work in the human personality, in human relations and in society. From shortly after the Great War, he recognised the growth of destructive patterns in European political and social life, pathological drives every bit as powerful as the instinct towards self-preservation and species-survival. For Freud in the 1930s, however, the imperative was for man to attend to brutality in order to avoid barbarism. Yeats suggests a more one-sided approach, closer to dicta of the Goncourt Brothers in *fin de siècle* Paris than to the cultural theories of post-war Central Europe.

In keeping with this reversion to nineteenth-century habits of thought, Yeats duly prepared his highly personal version of Ruskin's *Fors Clavigera*. Only a single number of *On the Boiler* ever appeared (posthumously), as if to underline the anachronistic nature of its model and the drastic ethical divergence between model and message. It contained the first printing of 'Purgatory', together with rantings on eugenics, rantings against education, rantings in favour of war, which have done so much to cloud Yeats's reputation. The correspondence with Mannin discloses a kind of logic – or 'analysis' – generating the frenzied propaganda and the chilly, mechanico-spiritual formality of the play.

We should return to 'Purgatory'. Beliefs similar to the Old Man's were ten a pfennig in Europe. In the autumn of 1931, Yeats had been reading (in translation) Ludwig Fischer's *Die Natürliche Ordnung*.[36] If Yeats differed crucially in any respect, the alternative doctrine was evidently still withheld for the Private Philosophy. While reading Simmel on portraiture, and thinking about Rilke, Yeats collected pamphlets outlining these beliefs in accessible English summaries of Nazi doctrine. That is to say, he did not dispose of them when they arrived, solicited or otherwise. Bad money drives out good, though the same may not hold true for beliefs generated from feelings. He disapproved of German legislation that encouraged large families, preferring quality to quantity: the Nazis differed from him in wanting both (as they defined these things). Large and small numbers of offspring provided one way of telling Catholic from Protestant families in Ireland. Yeats's views on progeny do not reduce to this basic sectarian observation, but they accommodated it.

Then there is 'The Death of Cuchulain'. The Old Man who plays producer cannot remember the name [*sic*] of his parents, though he suspects he may be the son of Talma 'and he was so old that his friends and acquaintances still read Virgil and Homer'. As a name, Talma has the ring of someone out of Macpherson's forged Ossianic poems, though the reference books point at François Joseph Talma (1763–1826), French classical actor and (as it happens) political radical.[37] On the other hand, let us not forget Sir Lawrence Alma-Tadema (1836–1912), a successful Victorian painter while Yeats's father habitually plunged. These ancestral sigla precede the drama of Cuchulain and his women, and take us no further back than the early nineteenth century.

If Cuchulain bears the wounds inflicted by six men who never appear in the play except as black parallelograms, the all-male cast of 'Purgatory' is dominated by an unseen woman. This is the Lady who married beneath her, bore a son who was father to the son we see onstage. Her absence is the ghostly intrusion that sets the play alight. Torchiana obligingly has calculated that 'the scenario has the Old Man begotten some sixty-three years earlier than the time of the play ... [and the house burned] close to the death of Parnell in October 1891'[38]. While this approach runs the risk of turning 'Purgatory' into a *drame-à-clef*, it rescues it from Plato-and-Rainewater interpretations in which the departed soul displaces any living human as the focus of dramatic action. The two males have more palpably displaced the woman, though it is her purgatorial suffering which is at the removed heart of the play.

She deserves some attention. First, she is never named. (Indeed, the only proper nouns are October, the Curragh, 'Aughrim and the Boyne', London, India, Latin, Tertullian, Adam, God – a notable hierarchy.) Second, her social status is only very obliquely indicated: no title or rank, no surname. Third, she is principally identified in terms of sexual relation – mother (repeatedly), and grandam (once) – or by reduction 'she' (insistently). Fourth, and this point seems to have escaped most commentators, her death is identified as simultaneous with the birth of her one son, the Old Man of the play. This is a typal or parabolic biography, not a historical or social one. Despite the severely constructed and finely enunciated plot, there has been no shortage of proffered identifications with actual family chronicles in Ireland. Hone's biography preserves a lengthy account of a story told by Yeats himself some time before the Great War. In the manner of traditional story-tellers, he had begun, 'Centuries ago there lived in a castle in Ireland ... ', and the narrative covered at least four generations. Other sources in Yeats's own writings include *The Celtic Twilight* (the edition of 1902) and *Reveries Over Childhood and Youth* (1914), in which latter Yeats specified Castle Dargan and Castle Fury in County Sligo, property owned by distant relatives. Strictly speaking, we should regard these as precedents rather than sources of the play, though both relations may obtain.

Now Roy Foster, in the second volume of his definitive biography, records how Yeats and Lady Gregory had discussed 'madness, how it destroys a family, brings them down, as the Parnell family'. This conversation took place a decade before the play was begun. Not satisfied with a jab at the previously sainted Parnells of Wicklow, he reveals that 'the core of the story comes from a ... Galway estate, Tyrone House, on a lonely peninsula beyond Ardrahan, owned by the St George family'.[39] One motive behind the search for historical sources is of course to set up digressions from the contemporary explanation offered by Yeats himself plainly in terms of Nazi legislation as well as Irish marriage patterns.

A consideration of these plentiful tales and sources might suggest that the basic action of 'Purgatory' reflects a widespread and long-established Irish social deviant practice. Somerville and Ross had drawn on the St George saga in *The Big House at Inver* (1925), and there are elements of the same to be found in stories by Sheridan Le

Fanu (1814–1872). What Yeats adds in assembling the materials for his play is the sense of ineradicable guilt in sexual generation across class (and perhaps religious) boundaries. It is in this sense that he can assure Father Connolly and others that he founded his play on an exceptional case. Foster is (in my view) demonstrably wrong in linking it closely to Yeats's loss of access to Coole Park: 'the park and its trees, with the owner returning to see the May blossom, are famously evoked' in the play. Perhaps, but they are *sardonically* evoked, as evidence of a condescending attitude towards the house typical of nineteenth-century proprietors. Land legislation and land war, intervening between this idyll and Torchiana's speculative date for the Old Man's burning of the house, had sharpened attitudes towards possession, inheritance and blood. Of the St George family, the novelist Violet Martin reported in 1912 that 'a very grand Lady Harriet St Lawrence married a St George ... and was so corroded with pride that she would not allow her daughters to associate with the Galway people. She lived to see them marry two men in the yard.'[40] Prompts towards Anglo-Irish marital downsizing included peacock pride and obsessive bad judgment. Such a notion of class amounted to a biologically isolatable thing, like a laboratory culture on a dish, and such notions intensified when land and money fell prey to dispersal. There were those who chose to marry outside the pale and for good reason – Yeats himself had been one of them. But Yeats had never belonged to the landowning class, though he elegised it, and thus in the dishonest decade felt all the more keenly the final disappearance of a hereditary substance his family had never possessed. He was not the last to bolster personal security by the awkward manoeuvre of a lateral equality-by-association with his social superiors.

The spectral lady of 'Purgatory' whom the audience does not 'spectate' is the betrayer of her class, yet it is towards her that the degenerate Old Man extends his sympathy. What we know factually of her is conventionally admirable, at least outside Tyrone House and its likes. Moral responsibility in marrying the stable-yard groom, combined with natural instincts – 'she is mad about him' – suggests a degree of social coherence absent from the rake-hellish tales of shooting and drinking available in Yeats's earlier prose writings. Both the Old Man and Yeats beg to differ. Her son is not impressed by the history of social responsibility; in so far as he offers a different morality (deploring the misalliance), he does so through the brilliantly dramatised envisioning of his own pre-natal experience: to the visibly empty, spiritually occupied window, he addresses these urgent retrospective injunctions:

> Do not let him touch you! It is not true
> That drunken men cannot beget,
> And if he touch he must beget
> And you must bear his murderer . . .
> But there's a problem: she must live
> Through everything in exact detail,
> Driven to it by remorse, and yet
> Can she renew the sexual act
> And find no pleasure in it, and if not,
> If pleasure and remorse must both be there,
> Which is the greater?

By the larger forms and movements of the play, Yeats has evidently decided against social coherence, and opted for a purity in blood that had its advocates outside Ireland in the 1930s. It also had its advocates inside Ireland, not excluding Adolf Mahr, the Austrian-born director of the National Museum, and one of the directors of the Abbey Theatre, Walter Starkie. Nazi propaganda quietly infiltrated corners of the Irish press, deftly manipulated by the charming but ruthless Helmut Clissmann. Maud Gonne gave ear. Unfortunately Harold's Cross had not yet given Dublin a Georg Simmel or a Walter Benjamin. Indeed, the lamentable thinness of Yeats's political utterances in the late 1930s is matched by the transparency of everyone else's. As for the worst, full of passionate intensity, it seems unrealistic to conclude that Yeats heard nothing. If he found comfort and security from time to time with Dorothy Wellesley, he certainly acquired a tolerance of erratic prejudice, *folie de grandeur* and more than a little racism.

The argument that Yeats was authoritarian (but not fascist) has some validity in terms of strict definition. He was never a member of a fascist party or movement, and he never endorsed all (or even the majority) of those crucial areas of policy and practice that characterised fascism. The comparison, however, is falsely constructed, for authoritarianism never in itself formed and defined a party. Where a political movement was marked strongly by authoritarian attitudes and values – for example, in Portugal or Austria – the course of the 1930s demonstrated how impossible it was to hold a line which did not have to compromise with the reality of fascism either at home or in the international arena. The French right wing was perhaps the example with which Yeats was most familiar. While his expressed views on French affairs declined quantitatively after the excitement of a possible Action française breakthrough in the mid-1920s, we find no occasion on which he distinguished between an authoritarianism still uncontaminated by the business of Nazi subversion (on the one hand) and the proclaimed fascism of Rome and Berlin.

The experience of Austria illustrates with brutal economy the inexorable relationship between traditional authoritarianism and the new movements. During a brief civil war in 1934, right-wing forces defeated Austrian socialism by such civilised means as bombarding a Viennese workers' housing complex. The bishops and the party that tragic story made. Four years later, Hitler annexed the country, despite attempts by Chancellor Dollfuss (murdered by the Nazis) to maintain independence and by his successor (Schuschnigg) to organise a referendum to support national integrity. These events, culminating in the *Anschluss* of 1938, occurred during Yeats's lifetime and during the months in which he prepared *On the Boiler*.

As for racism, of which Yeats is almost universally found innocent, it was not in the early Italian experiment a key element of fascism. But there was always a dynamic pushing the ultra-nationalism of Mussolini towards a more categorical and doctrinal statement, which not only lauded the nation but also systematically denigrated specific other groups according to their merits. After 1933, it was difficult to avoid the conjunction of racism and ultra-nationalism, so triumphant and hate-filled was the Nazi creed. Nor was fascism ever a passive element in this relationship. As the example of Austria demonstrates, it sought by violent and manipulative means to shape nationalist and authoritarian movement to its own purposes, either by allegiance or sometimes by annihilation. The fascism considered by Yeats's admirers in connection with Yeats is an oddly inactive, distant evil – Legionnaires' Disease on Mars – of which, of course, the great man can be declared immunely innocent.

The defence offered on Iseult Gonne's behalf is worth considering in relation to Yeats himself. Anna MacBride White has written:

> It must be remembered that at that time very many people in Ireland were pro-German on the old principle that England's enemy was Ireland's friend. Also, like Yeats, Iseult believed in the aristocracy of thought and what she saw as the promise Germany had to offer the

world. Her friendship with the Hempels recovered gradually from the diplomatic debacle of Goertz's arrival and deepened, becoming one of the most crucial things in her life. As with Goertz Iseult shared with them a common cultural European background with a shared vision of Germany as a power destined to ennoble and purify the world.[41]

Before dismissing this as poppycock, one should note exactly what has to be omitted from its highly self-censoring account of the 1930s: the name of Adolf Hitler, the existence of concentration camps, the persecution of Jews (indeed, Bethel Solomons nowhere appears in this apologia, though he saved Iseult's life in 1920), the operations of Helmut Clissmann, the anti-Semitism of both Maud Gonne and her daughter.

What we can be certain of is Yeats's silence, if not his innocence.

Part Two
Family Matters

Marital Politics and the House of Stuart

> Are we, that fore-know, the actual or potential traitors of the race-process? Do we as it were forbid the ban[n]s when the event is struggling to be born?
>
> To Olivia Shakespear, July 1927

> Both dieties – Zeus, the ravisher of Persephone, and Dionysus, her son – were also called Zagreus, which in our language means 'mighty hunter'. I shall later say more of this matter, but the stories of the Daktyloi and the Kabeiroi have already made it plain that father and son could be identical.
>
> Carl Kerényi, *The Gods of the Greeks* (1951)

In his autobiographical account of 'The Tragic Generation', written during the Irish Troubles of 1920–22, Yeats sought to create a distance between himself and lesser figures of the 1890s, while paying tribute to a few noble spirits, J. M. Synge in particular. The volume closes with seven vignettes in the present tense, as if the author could not quite commit them to history. Samuel Mathers dominates two, accoutred in anecdotes about women and their strange tastes. A young Jewish scholar with a ring of alchemical gold occupies the fifth, while the last is given entirely to Alfred Jarry and his food-obsessed meta-satirical play, 'Ubu Roi'. Yeats concludes:

> I am very sad, for comedy, objectivity, has displayed its growing power once more. I say: 'After Stéphane Mallarmé, after Paul Verlaine, after Gustave Moreau, after Puvis de Chavannes, after our own verse, after all our subtle colour and nervous rhythm, after the faint mixed tints of Conder, what more is possible? After us the Savage God.'[1]

Yeats had good reason to predict in this fashion, or good reason to record his prediction after a quarter-century. War had slaughtered millions in Europe, including 40,000 from his own small remote island. Brutal, if limited, post-war civil conflicts persisted in the Baltic States, in parts of Germany and Russia, in Ireland and Italy. Yet the implications of his prophecy are not fulfilled in the roll-call of deaths, or in any other merely negative assessment of the early twentieth century. The sub-text of Yeats's oracular closing remarks on the era of his birth strongly suggests the necessity, the aesthetic desirability, of the Savage God.

These radically changed allegiances – from Mallarmé to Mussolini, if one likes – are traceable on several levels. In addition to the artistic and political, personal appearance comes to act as a revelation of Yeats's powerful inner drives. One gets a glimpse of him in middle age from the recollections of a man who met him in a London tobacconist's shop before the Great War. Father Desmond Chute (1895–1962) became a very minor artist who sketched Yeats in Rapallo and later left a brief account of 'a figure in a dressing gown, sitting motionless in the winter sunshine. Only a hand moves, writes, from time to time, with a gold fountain-pen in a leather-bound book. Are we present at the generation of an immortal?'

Yeats's first biographer, who also accompanied him to Mussolini's Italy, was not loath to praise the poet's appearance:

> There was a search for elegance in his silver-buckled shoes, in the wide black riband, attached to his tortoise-shell-rimmed glasses, which fell like a bar across his face; and in the gold ring worn on his little finger. But more marked than these accessories was the elegance of his bearing, the noble carriage of his head, the harmony of his gestures; something of the ease and grace of a *grand seigneur* in his manners.[2]

As Hone observed, not many years had elapsed since George Moore had compared the poet to a folded umbrella, left behind at a picnic. The alteration to Yeats's appearance stemmed from many sources – biological, economic and sociological. But the subject's vanity should not be underestimated, and the dignity conferred on him by nomination to the Irish Senate was likewise transformed into an instrument of domination. Amid the crippled deformities and deranged amputees observed by writers such as Alfred Döblin and Bertolt Brecht in Germany, physical beauty came to embody an attitude towards power and history. British writers were more discreet, and when they failed to maintain sufficient discretion (as with Owen), they earned Yeats's rebuke. Roy Foster has reported from his explorations among the papers preceding *A Vision* that 'One of the enduringly obscure areas of the developing theory remained the relation between physical beauty to the creation of beauty in the work of (for instance) Keats and Shelley'.[3] In due course, Yeats might advance a class analysis, based on his observations of the Abbey's *corps de théâtre*. In 1918, the body – at least as viewed for a moment by admirers – might pre-shadow Unity of Being, a phrase first recorded in that year. Lesser mortals looked their parts.

Isolde without Tristan

The bodies of others posed different problems. The beauty of women, the awkwardness of ill-bred actors, the dashing features of a crippled hero – all required a magisterial response. Yeats's occult idealism is easily contrasted to the materialism of his age, whether one defines this in relation to Marxist philosophy or the gross appetites of western European high society. However, the occult sought to renegotiate relations between spirit and matter, not simply to abolish the latter. Bodily manifestation played a central role in the rituals he observed, while sexual and narcotic pleasure provided physical avenues to insight, illumination and hocus-pocus. From early days, Maud Gonne had shared in these pursuits. His celebration of her is well known through such poems as 'The Lover tells of the Rose in his Heart' (1892), 'No Second Troy' (1908) and 'Her Praise' (1915). Though her physical beauty is more implied than described, the effect is never less than moving.

Less well known is Yeats's relationship with Gonne's daughter, who played a deeply ambiguous role in his emotional and political life. At the time of the Easter Rising, Iscult complained that she found herself to be nameless. Her passport consequently provoked suspicion among the authorities as she tried to move from wartime France, through London, to rebel Ireland.[1] This condition stemmed from the mother's reluctance to concede that Iseult was in fact her daughter – the girl was usually introduced as 'Madame's niece' or sometimes even her 'cousin', a description that erased the generational difference between them. Behind the euphemism was the further embarrassment that Maud Gonne had separated from the man – Lucien Millevoye (1850–1918) – who was Iseult's biological progenitor, and had married another man – John MacBride (1865–1916) – whom she had divorced and who had now been executed by the British for his part in the rising.

Far from robbing Iseult of ancestral dignity, these circumstances loaded her with a compensating symbolic power. Neither a Millevoye nor a Gonne nor a MacBride, she was uniquely and incontrovertibly Iseult. In an age that still rang with the sonorous leitmotifs of Richard Wagner's music dramas, mythological fate was her identifying inheritance. That the operatic heroine was the victim of an aged king's infatuation as much as she was victim of a romantic collusion between Eros and Thanatos can hardly have been lost on Yeats, her senior by more than thirty years. Wagner, as nasty an anti-Semite as genius could sponsor, stood pre-eminent among those giants of German *Kultur* for which the Great War was being fought, at least in the eyes of thoughtful and patriotic Thomas Mann. Since her childhood, Yeats had taken the closest interest in this nameless, essential Iseult, sending her books when she was four, cherishing a picture of her, and remarking at length on her beauty at age thirteen. Yet she remained outside his frame of literary reference, except in a very few poems. One of these, 'Michael Robartes and the Dancer', is a playful dialogue on the theme of woman's commitment either to beauty of body or to thought, education and opinion.

Born on 6 August 1894, Iseult Germaine Lucille was a desired conception for whom these tributes were bizarrely ordained. Maud had lost her first child by Millevoye, and in an effort to establish some occult link with the dead boy (Georges), she had succumbed to the French adventurer's renewed embrace in the very mausoleum where their infant was buried. The result was predictably, if prosaically, anarchic, further aggravated by a family belief that daughters among the Gonnes bore ill-luck. Iseult described herself as 'a wild gutter cat' at one point, undeserving and demanding.[5] That had been in 1909. Now, as the new decade unfolded, the designer child was about to become a designing woman.

The initiative, however, was repeatedly taken by Yeats. He indulged, and sometimes encouraged, the notion that Iseult was his daughter, either in biological fact or in some even more satisfactory occult sense. Although this fancy was in part an aspect of his extended relationship with Maud Gonne, it also contributed to a series of highly masculinist exchanges between Yeats and his friends W. T. Horton and Ezra Pound. Even his denials that she was *really* his daughter suggested that in some superior sense she really *was* his daughter. When he introduced her to the Indian writer Rabindranath Tagore in 1913, he commenced a pattern of actions which constituted her 'coming out' into the high society that mattered to him – a bohemian, artistic world in which the possibility that he (a bachelor approaching fifty) had a child was acceptable. Less delicately, he repeatedly made Augusta Gregory auditor of his desires and anxieties, bombarding her with letters and enquiries at awkward moments.

Iseult's illnesses and her horoscopes took up equal time. Just into her teens, her dislike of modern-dress plays evidently won his approval, and encouraged further intimacy. His pride in the growing girl's interest in St John of the Cross was only one example of a literary and spiritual relationship that bore strange fruit.[6]

At the time of the Easter Rising, Iseult was twenty-one, employed with her mother in a Normandy hospital where wounded French soldiers were treated, far away from the battlefields. MacBride's death brought a well-earned private sense of vindication, for Yeats had taken Maud Gonne's side in the divisive arguments preceding her divorce from the 'drunken vain-glorious lout'. This had not endeared him to the ultra-Fenians. Yeats was badly shaken by the rising and by the ruthlessness with which it was suppressed. His emotional life was equally unsteady, and when he travelled to France, his motives in seeking out Maud Gonne and her daughter were confused. His proposal of marriage to the older woman is well known, but the transfer of his plans on to the daughter constituted an audacious, not to say foolhardy, determination to settle down at this most unsettled moment.

While the complex marital uncertainties would persist even after Iseult's own marriage to Francis Stuart in 1920, the immediate political context of their discussion had its odd features. Maud Gonne was resolutely anti-English, but love of France had resulted in her dedication to the Allied cause through medical aid. The death of her former husband brought an opportunity to adjust her relationship with Fenian opinion, by announcing that he had died for Ireland, redeemed himself and made her a heroic widow. Writing in May 1916 some weeks after the executions, Yeats employed a distinctly military image to convey his sense of Iseult's adult maturity – she has become 'a commanding person'. But the political solution to which he looks is still the old, essentially Parnellite one. When the present crisis is over, 'there will be a new Ireland to build up'. The prospect 'does really look like Home Rule almost at once'. Yeats's reasoning was as weak as his prophecy. Assuming that the Prime Minister would soon find himself involved in a peace conference with the Germans, Yeats argued that Irish Home Rule would strengthen his hand with the defeated invader of gallant little Belgium. No peace talks were imminent, and by year's end Asquith was no longer Prime Minister. Behind the reliance on old models for a domestic solution, and the faulty predictions about international affairs, Yeats nonetheless reveals a calculating side to his assessment of matters in Dublin. He told Maud Gonne of rumours now spreading that the British had used poison gas to suppress the rising: these he knew to be false, but their circulation might yet be helpful.[7] Here is a secret politics, maintained below the neo-Parnellite predictions. Within it, Iseult may achieve a commanding position already evidenced in her maturing beauty.

Six weeks later, on the heels of rejection by Maud Gonne, Yeats pursued a hidden dialectic of the private and public. To Augusta Gregory, he gave the impression that Maud felt marriage with him would disrupt the important, different work of each. He wished her to abandon the propagandist agitation at which she excelled, but the bargain as outlined did not cast him simply as a poet at risk in a transformed household. He conceded that she would find it hard to give up politics; on the other hand, he had given her 'a written statement of my political creed'.[8] The difference between them lay less in a conventional juxtaposition of politics with art and more in an occult emphasis on his written – that is, coded – politics over and above her hectoring vocal performances. In keeping with this prioritising of the undisclosed creed, Yeats was simultaneously selecting from Iseult's manuscripts, with a view to publication. So far as we know, nothing came of his efforts. Just as Iseult remained out of sight in his poetry, so her writings remained hidden from the public eye.[9]

Despite his editorial attention to the daughter, and his exchanges with the mother, hopes of marriage with Iseult had not been abandoned. The wish for some understanding with her kept him away from Coole Park in August, a time of year normally spent there in perpetuation of a relationship uniting the literary and personal as no other ever did.[10] Horton would shortly intervene with some 'impression' he had about the relationship with Iseult, prompting Yeats to arrange a meeting at which he wished to be told the date (important for astrologers) on which the impression had arisen.[11] A year after his regretful abstention from Coole's quiet hospitality, the position remained unchanged. 'Iseult and I are on our old intimate terms,' he wrote to Augusta Gregory, 'but I don't think she will accept.' An added factor was the completion of a play, 'The Dreaming of the Bones', which drew the approval of mother and daughter alike because – Yeats hinted – it contained some popular aspect beyond the limited appeal of his earlier experiments in the Noh style. The new work employed dancer and zither, mask-resembling make-up and unfolding curtain, but the emotional crux centred on lovers who could not kiss.

Enter George

Behind the sexual manoeuvres in Normandy, Yeats's friends were keen to arrange a suitable marriage, a story ably told by Brenda Maddox in *George's Ghosts*. Georgina Hyde-Lees became Yeats's wife a few months after the latest *pas-de-trois*, in anticipation of which he admitted candidly 'all this will seem strangely cold & calculating'. The arrangements with mother and daughter now included a 'kind of guardianship' under which Yeats would look after Iseult's interests, though Maud (best placed to know the truth) became increasingly convinced that Iseult was Yeats's child.[12] In parallel, the quasi-supposed father wrote to Gregory at Coole presenting the fact of Iseult always having been 'something like a child' to him as an explanation for being less upset than he might have been at her latest rejection of him as suitor.[13] Yeats married Georgina Hyde-Lees on 20 October 1917, and soon commenced transforming her pet name Georgie into the masculine form, George (or in French Georges, like Iseult's dead brother).

The relationship with Iseult remained important. Though as male he had taken the leading role, she had not been passive. Indeed Yeats told Gregory that Iseult had wanted to marry him in 1912 – she at eighteen, he forty-seven – and that the feeling lasted with her for two years. Her stated reason for contemplating such a step lay in shared qualities of what Iseult termed race ('You were the only person of my own race I had met'), though he was inclined to gloss this for Gregory to mean the only person of culture she had met.[14] Given her biological father's predilections, and the company her mother kept, this latter was probably true. Recourse to the word 'race' may be idiosyncratic, mixing Victorian notions and French usage, but it will surface in the passionate, unconsummated love between the dead in 'The Dreaming of the Bones' (1917). Largely written in the Gonnes' house in Normandy, the play carried forward Yeats's complicated feelings for Iseult, even as he may have seen it as transcending them, purged of any personal motivation. 'George' Hyde-Lees understood her role as wife to an extraordinary man, accepting the notion of his guardianship.

He was aware that, being beautiful and captivating, Iseult had received many proposals. He must have known too that she had lost her virginity, having slept with (amongst presumed others) his friend Ezra Pound. Yeats's own physical relations with her, in her youth and perhaps as late as the 1930s, remain suitably masked. Marriage provided a basis for external social contacts to flourish. In 1918, Yeats arranged for her to sub-rent his old rooms in Woburn Buildings, while she worked as a library assistant-cum-student at the School of Oriental Studies, a position he engineered while she lost or stole a good many utensils from the apartment. In August he recalled the years during which she had been to him 'like a very dear daughter' and asked (rather ambiguously) if she could not be that once again. His business-like postscript – 'Send me your work' – offered a different kind of patronage, as buffer or link.[15]

The efforts were substantial. Iseult acted as Yeats's secretary in his attempt to understand a new 'school' of French poets: Charles Péguy (1873–1914), Paul Claudel (1868–1955) and Francis Jammes (1868–1938). They exemplified a trinity of political virtues for Ireland in flux – a Dreyfusard socialist turned martyred patriot, a right-wing or royalist Catholic, a celebrant of peasant life. (No Apollinaire, no Valéry.) The immediate object was a lecture Yeats planned to give at the Abbey Theatre – in effect, a piece of war propaganda, though he could not admit this. There was, of course, another side to Péguy: Tzvetan Todorov finds 'a French theoretician with a pithy turn of phrase' for whom 'the Republic is one and indivisible' and 'in time of war there is only one rule, and it is the rule of the Jacobins'; or (climactically) 'woe betide the party that does not eliminate its internal enemies'.[16] For the moment, Yeats dwelt on the martyr rather than the cause. Later there was to be a proposed book by Iseult on the same subject. She refused to allow Yeats to publish certain little compositions of her own, objecting to any display of her feelings and beliefs. With spectators in the soul, she held, nobody can be sincere – a theme explored in 'one of her most curious little essays'.[17] The book about Catholic poetry was proposed by Yeats as an alternative to the self-revealing publication of her own work. Nothing came of it.

Catholicism was not a theme at which Yeats shone. Too many inherited social prejudices had survived the extinction of any Protestant belief. Irish Catholicism was an inherent part of Irish folklore which, fortunately, displayed redeeming elements of paganism. Little of that leaven was to found in the plain fare of organised nationalism, which – apart from a few exceptional figures drawn from the upper middle classes and a few déclassé aristocrats – was Catholic to a man. Maud Gonne's conversion to Rome had been largely a conversion to Irish Catholicism, with the unapproved retention of exotic beliefs in astrology, fairies, reincarnated siblings and the like. Her mental indiscipline perturbed Yeats, who genuinely worried for her state of mind. Thus at the beginning of 1918 he sought Iseult's aid in getting her mother to read papal encyclicals by Leo XIII and Pius X, together with books on Catholic economics. 'Help me to keep her orthodox, for that will keep her sane.' Hostile to the Church's demand of total obedience, Yeats accepted (in the context) the encyclicals as 'the fundamentals of spiritual belief applied to social questions'. For his own soul, he was committing ever more thoroughly to the revelations emerging from under George's automatic hand. A new Cuchulain poem had resulted, 'full of this new philosophy', which he longed to explain to Iseult, but it was 'all so vast & one part depends upon another'.[18] By May 1918 he was applying himself to Catholic economics more as a means of acquiring arguments than convictions.

As Yeats occasionally admitted, Iseult's life was unhappy and disturbed. She suffered from an exaggerated sense of inadequacy and guilt, and was prone to melancholia. Minor physical illness, compounded by a powerful addiction to cigarettes, also afflicted her. In August 1916, she was 'dying of self-analysis', and everything had become food for accusations of sin, with John of the Cross as adviser. Part of the problem lay in the bohemianism into which she was invited by various parties, including her own (biological) father. Millevoye had insisted that the role of an Aspasia was the most powerful and happy life a woman could find, at which Iseult refused to see him ever again. According to Yeats, burdening as ever the ear of Augusta Gregory, Iseult had forsworn all bohemian options 'because of her birth'. Instead, he had introduced her to Lady Cunard in London, who raved about the young girl's complexion, and to William Rothenstein, who promised to paint her.[19] In London it was called high society; in Paris the *demi-monde*.

The politics of genteel La Bohème altered with the sudden emergence of a radical challenge to the economic and social order of Western Europe. Revolution in Russia explicitly promised to export itself to the more advanced capitalist countries. Those who had been amused to *épater les bourgeois* now found the Bolsheviks committed to a more extensive programme. While spiritualism had offered alternative views of the Great War, and of the loss of sons and husbands, it seemed a worthless defence against Lenin and Trotsky. The automatic writing, which Yeats developed with his wife on their honeymoon, led him to confront the Russian upheavals just as (by a pleasing corollary) it also put him in touch with titled supposed ancestors. In May 1919, he wrote at length to his old friend from art-school days, George William Russell, assuring AE that Iseult disliked Russian communism as much as he (Yeats) did. A veritable credo, adapted for changing times, followed:

> What I want is that Ireland be kept from giving itself ... to Marxian revolution, or Marxian definitions of value, in any form. I consider the Marxian criterion of value, as in this age the spear-head of materialism & leading to inevitable murder. From that phase follows the well-known phrase 'can the bourgeois be innocent?'[20]

Not innocence but survival was the issue at stake, not just of the individual, but of an entire way of life, which might be termed class society without risk of cliché. The quickened pace and altered direction of Irish politics in the earlier part of the century had alerted Yeats to the values encoded in great houses and hereditary rights. His commitment to the Irish cause might require adjustment or qualification in the light of that realisation. The useful distinction between national and international affairs, invoked whenever embarrassing claims were made on his political credit, could not be an absolute in theory, even if it was presented as one in practice and in public. Murder might now be inevitable, thanks to the universal anti-bourgeois commitment of Moscow. But the double murder of Rosa Luxemburg and Karl Liebknecht in May 1919 at the hands of Germany's 'Black and Tans' was not to register in Yeats's radical-reactionary tally of world politics, while the anti-communism of Rome and Berlin could rely on his silent indulgence.

May 1919 had its local intensities in Ireland, as the renewed Troubles gave every evidence of building to a final conflict between nationalism and the imperial government in London. 'Nineteen Hundred and Nineteen' is Yeats's meditation on the recrudescence of tumult and violence, in which allusions to ancient witchcraft and 'violence upon the roads' are conjoined. His investigations through automatic writing led him to see the present scene in a broad context which acknowledged historical detail and yet also supposed a psychic-spiritual reality beyond mere incident and individual. Iseult was one of his intimates for whom he sought horoscopic and related assurances. Her 'good mask' was serenity, her 'bad mask' self-distrust. (These seem like observations any decent doctor might have made.) But, Yeats continued, her evil genius is 'terror' (the quotation marks are his own) caused by the subconscious memory of a deepening vision-haunted loneliness from which a related spirit might begin a kind of Agony in the Garden.[21] These observations remained theoretical in August 1918. When they found some equivalent in the world of action, Yeats responded in ways that showed him as outraged father rather than the justified astrologer. What was the relationship between the personal and political, terror in Phase 16 and revolution in Munich?

While Ireland braced itself for a war of independence, Iseult was drifting, with some involvement in a film project that came to nothing. She had, it seems, committed herself as a way of getting new clothes.[22] The distance between Dublin and London was greatly intensified by the political and military conflict, and Yeats's earlier haunts – whether those shared with Ezra Pound or those more shadowy retreats of magicians and hashish-eaters – became to a degree inaccessible. The Parnellite era, in which a gentleman had led a nationalist lobby, had disappeared for ever and with it any dream of Home Rule. But some of the older myths and ambitions were transmutable into newer and harder metal. Samuel [McGregor] Mathers (1854–1918) had been a youthful comrade in the Order of the Golden Dawn, though his increasingly outlandish behaviour led to a breach. Mathers claimed to excel in ritual magic and military training, but Yeats wearied of his obsession with kilts and sword-dances. Dying as the Great War ended, Mathers unwittingly bequeathed his eccentric Jacobitism to the post-war survivors. The politics of 1890s Jacobitism had united sentimental antiquarianism with a desire for traditional authority, something that would approximate to the Divine Right of Kings possessed once by the Stuart monarchs. (Sentimentalism is here defined along Joycean lines as emotion enjoyed without payment in the coin of experience.) Among the better-connected victims of war were the Romanovs and Habsburgs in which that theory persisted, not to mention Hohenzollern upstarts whose overreaching had (in British eyes) provoked war in the first place. The fall of the Romanovs registered in Yeats's first experiments with automatic writing, and would reverberate in the 1930s. Russian communism gave offence, not simply on economic grounds, but on the fundamental basis that it destroyed the last vestige of the Divine Right. Whereas most western philosophers and historians had seen the emergence of a secular order, distinct from the religious, as occurring at the time of the Renaissance, it was possible by a kind of long-sighted myopia to convert Nicholas and his luckless family, the dupes of a deranged monk, into paradigms of traditional sanctity and loveliness. To do so involved a massive and deliberate neglect of the evidence showing the consequence of in-breeding among 'the best'.

Yeats's summary of the Russian threat in May 1919 contained one element already noted in his assessment of the Irish situation in May 1916. Propaganda, or at best partisan judgment, affected virtually every topic requiring discussion. Iseult had been inclined to believe AE's figure of 400 executed by the new Russian government. For that reason Yeats advised his old friend otherwise:

> that is why I sent you certain Russian comments on that figure, as well as on the figure of 13000 which was published some time ago as coming from the Russian government itself. There are financial reasons why American comment is just now sometimes biased. Thomas said in the House of Commons a couple of weeks ago 'Every responsible representative of English labour is convinced, owing to information come into their possession that the present Russian government is worse than that of the Autocrasy'.[23]

The danger lay in the Irish tendency automatically to oppose England and, while the Americans might manipulate facts for their own purposes, it was necessary even to 'believe' English Labour in the higher cause of opposing Marxian economics. Propaganda was whatever presentation of ideas obstructed Yeats's own considered interests. In October 1922, he endorsed an official Abbey Theatre submission to the new Irish government appealing for state patronage. 'The Comédie Française is one of the glories of France, the famous Moscow Art Theatre is subsidised by the Soviet Government. Germany possesses scores of national municipal theatres. These countries believe that a theatre which is not dependent for its existence on the caprice of the public can play a great part in the education of a nation.'[24]

A Very Young Pretender

Iseult's future husband, Henry Francis Montgomery Stuart, emerged into these debates – the public as well as the cabbalistic – as if from nowhere. While a pupil at Rugby School, the Australian-born son of Ulster parents had been stirred by news of the Bolshevik Revolution with its promise of total destruction for the capitalist world. Stuart's immediate family background was dysfunctional to the -nth degree; his alcoholic father had committed suicide in pathetic circumstances, and his mother remarried disastrously to an alcoholic cousin. A pipe-toking aunt in trousers sent up smoke-screens of normality. Just as bad in Yeats's eyes, the Stuarts and their Montgomery kin hailed from Ulster. At the age of seventeen, and looking like a gormless Adonis, Stuart blundered into a circle that included the Gonnes and Lennox Robinson. On 30 January 1920, he was received into the Roman Catholic Church. By April he had married Iseult. A wordy letter of Maud Gonne's suggests that Yeats had encouraged Iseult: 'She certainly took your advice of taking no notice of what I might think or advise.'[25]

In the ensuing domestic crisis, much was made of the fact that Yeats had not met the young man for, in the Gonnes' eyes, it gave the poet licence to act as magisterial arbitrator. To confuse matters, they also felt that Stuart could be (or become) Yeats's 'spiritual child'. Iseult wrote to her former admirer suggesting that her very young husband was perhaps even more his (Yeats's child) than she was.[26] Yeat's position was complicated by material factors. Delayed renovations to his medieval tower at Ballylee, County Galway, had resulted in his removal as far as Oxford. Thus mured above local difficulties, he learned in July 1920 of intimidation and threats in the district, including some directed against his English wife: these emanated from the fringes of a political movement he generally endorsed. Nevertheless, when summoned by Maud Gonne in late July to intervene in her daughter's marital difficulties, Yeats quit Oxford for Dublin, having at the age of a frail fifty-five to sleep on the floor while crossing the Irish Sea by ferry. All he knew was that horrible family trouble had broken out. With a genealogist's acumen, he quickly established from Robinson that 'Francis Stuart's mother is an untrustworthy romantic minded woman & that she was most anxious for the marriage.'[27]

The month of August 1920 established an occultist enquiry into an Irish marriage unparalleled in the record-books. Yeats was in touch with his old friend Gregory on 29 July, announcing his departure from Oxford for remote Glenmalure in Wicklow to sort out Iseult's troubles. Only his wife and sister Lily, together with Robinson, knew of his motives in returning. His immediate objective appears to have been to send the young woman to Coole, but the presence there of the recently widowed Margaret Gregory made that plan impractical (if, indeed, Lady Gregory would have entertained it). The journey was marred by an encounter with Lord and Lady Dunsany at Euston Station – the couple were arguing – by a general search for arms in the luggage at Holyhead, and by overcrowding on the boat. Once in Dublin, he put up at the St Stephen's Green Club, where he was visited the next morning by Robinson. The latter's recruitment to the conspiracy resulted from his prior knowledge of Francis Stuart's family, otherwise unknown. Sending back his address to George in Oxford, he gave it as 'c/o Madame Gonne' with the local Wicklow details, rather than Madame (or even plain Mrs) Stuart. The older lovers of the 1890s were united in their efforts to rescue a woman who was the daughter of at least one of them. Robinson had smelt violets during his conversation that morning, a supernatural signal in Yeats's view that their mission would prosper.[28] Robinson, however, was also in love with Iseult, despite a reputation among Dubliners as a homosexual in denial. The Yeatses had briefly considered pairing off Lennox and Iseult, and were now reaping a whirlwind.

It did not take long to size up the situation. Iseult had been systematically denied sleep and food by her young husband. His objective was apparently to get her to leave Ireland, where her friends disliked him. Yeats's objective was a formal settlement which certainly involved money, but did not apparently envisage divorce. Before July was out, Iseult consented to enter the Ivanhoe Nursing Home because, in addition to her privations, she was pregnant. 'Iseult is still in love with him & defends him always & always gets back to his longing for power (by this she means power over her).'[29] Yeats formed the opinion that Stuart was 'a criminal lunatic', even before meeting the young man. The tiny isolated cottage accommodated the poet and two women, both of whom he had proposed to less than four years earlier.

As Iseult was inclined to excuse her husband, the principal narrative of her sufferings was provided by Maud Gonne. He had thrown her out on the country roadside in her nightgown and burned her other clothes with paraffin. He had also deprived her of food, and set her onerous tasks while he lay abed. Though Glenmalure was cut off from regular communications by lying effectively at the end of a seven-mile cul-de-sac, there were witnesses to some of Stuart's behaviour. Yeats was keen to interview a neighbour – a retired ladies' maid. He had already collected a deposition from a young art student who had given Iseult food when she had not eaten all day. His departure for Dublin to make arrangements at the nursing home was frustrated by Maud's need to attend Mass in distant Rathdrum or Greenane, the latter village mentioned more than once in Synge's Wicklow plays.[30]

The dead Synge breathes ironically over these events. The cottage in which Stuart and his wife were staying had provided the setting of 'In the Shadow of the Glen'. The play showed the efforts of a young woman to escape a loveless marriage to an older man, though at the climax she chooses a homeless tramp rather than her diligent and timid declared lover. Yeats was not sympathetic to any romantic or sacrificial arrangements in real life. Stuart he now thought to be a sadist, a term reserved exclusively in his correspondence for Iseult's husband. Stuart's poetry seemed to confirm the diagnosis for, as Yeats reported to his wife, in one of the poems he imagined himself crucifying a woman. (The poem also borrowed heavily from Yeats, a point not reported to George.)

Stuart's behaviour was inexcusable, but it was hardly inexplicable. Even A. N. Jeffares, among Yeats biographers the most hostile to Stuart, has conceded that in 1920 he was an 'unawakened adolescent'.[31] His extreme youth as Irish husband, a damaged upbringing that had probably involved sexual abuse by his stepfather, and his infatuation with the Gonne circle did not make for uxorious *sangfroid*. If Stuart imitated Yeats's work, and besought an introduction to the master, he also took seriously the penitential severity of the Catholic saints to whom Iseult was devoted. If she was afflicted with self-accusations of sin, he was at hand to assist in her redemption. Back in Dublin by 4 August, Yeats began to contemplate the spiritual side of the delinquent husband. 'He asked a series of naïve questions, and made a series of naïve statements suggesting an extreme simplicity till she at last said to herself "he is a blessed angel," – plainly she was hoping for "Gods Fool."'[32] Consequently Yeats assigned him to Phase 14 of his evolving philosophico-historical system. This at least obviated the need to examine who amongst his elders might be responsible for Stuart's imitative behaviour as unawakened adolescent.

The letters of August 1920 are directed to Augusta Gregory at Coole, George Yeats in Oxford, and Bethel Solomons (1885–1965), the gynaecologist whom Yeats consulted in Dublin. There is one surviving letter to Iseult herself, written on 1 September when most of the drama was over. Letters to Maud Gonne do not survive, either because she and Yeats were under the same cottage roof for most of the crucial period, or because of a general destruction of her papers which occurred in the civil war. Three dominant topics emerge; these, in tight alphabetical order, are Madness, Magic and the Saving of Money.

That Francis Stuart was insane was presumed at the outset. Victorian notions of hereditary madness were encouraged by the discovery that his father died in a lunatic asylum '& his mothers father died of drink with the result, as I think, that he is a Sadist & cannot love without torturing'.[33] Dr Solomons was not to be rushed into such conclusions, and while reciting the same family chronicle to another correspondent, Yeats admitted 'there is a chance'. Later in the month, and citing the advice of Gregory, he reported that 'a doctor in lunacy' might be consulted, with a view, presumably, to having Stuart declared mentally incapable and with a possible further view to having the marriage annulled or dissolved in some fashion.[34]

Apart from Stuart, all the major actors were committed believers in some form of exoteric spiritualism. This included Mrs Yeats in Oxford, who cannot have relished the prospect of an Iseult returned to heroic spinsterhood. During the early days of his efforts on Iseult's behalf, Yeats intended to consult the College of Arms on matters of genealogy raised in the course of his enquiries into the spirit world, but kept postponing the visit. On 7 August, he asked his wife if she would consider casting Stuart's horoscope: 'he was born at Sydney on April 29 between 4 and 8 A.M. He was 18 on his last birthday.'[35] By 1 September he was able to give Iseult a detailed account of the astrological context in which the clothes-burning and starvation had been effected – 'this should mean that the worst is over'. The word 'fool' circulated in these heavens also, for Yeats could assure Iseult that 'no fool, no person without a possible future of spiritual importance has ever had an "initiatory moment"' of the kind she had experienced in Glenmalure.[36] The argument was two-edged, for both husband and wife were Phase 14, circumstances that required clever elucidation.

Iseult's pregnancy impressed Yeats with the urgency of his mission, for his wife had already suffered a miscarriage, and indeed endured a second 'mishap' in the course of the month. Solomons may have been chosen for Mrs Stuart because he had advised Mrs Yeats. He was unlikely to have been Maud Gonne's natural choice, being Jewish. Yet Yeats manifestly trusted him and indeed relied on him, perhaps because zodiacal signs played no part in good medicine. There is no mention of Solomons's fees, which may have been absorbed into Yeats's account with him. Nursing-home charges, on the other hand, must fall on the young woman's mother, who (Yeats assured Gregory) 'is very poor'. After the wedding, Maud Gonne had given £50 to Iseult, who had an income of £100 per annum in her own right, no princessly dowry. Stuart, on the other hand, had about £350 a year. The financial issues were sharply etched in Yeats's letters to his wife and to Gregory, where the annual incomes were fiddled somewhat, to Stuart's moral disadvantage. Accordingly, Madame Gonne – the 'madame' was a republican affectation – could not afford to keep her daughter in a nursing home for more than a few days, whereas Stuart had obliged his new wife to sign the lease for their first apartment and generally wasted her substance. The contrast was more than a little contrived, as Stuart was in fact too young to sign a binding legal agreement, and Gonne owned at least two houses in Ireland, with property elsewhere. The Glenmalure cottage had been bought in autumn 1919 from the proceeds of selling Iseult's house in Normandy – Sean MacBride got a seven-seater car. But the contrast was contrived by Yeats to extort charity, or bed and board, from one or other of his correspondents. 'The marriage was brought about & settlements prevented by certain machanations [sic],' he added darkly.[37] None of these was darker than the plan to match Iseult with Robinson.

In practical terms, he sought an agreement by which Stuart would settle money on Iseult and on the expected child, to protect them against any recurrence of his impositions. Stuart replied grandly that it was 'unbeautiful to speak of money', though he went on to offer £150 per annum to Iseult, provided there was no legal document involved.[38] As the money was dependent on his mother's good faith – another fool, according to Yeats – the Gonnes rejected it and proceeded to consult expensive lawyers. It says a great deal for Yeats's capabilities as a negotiator that any agreement was reached: the Stuart marriage lasted, in its fashion, until Francis left Ireland for Berlin on the eve of the Second World War.

From the outset, Yeats had based his strategy on the argument that, as he had never met Francis Stuart, he would be regarded as an impartial broker. Given the youth's naïvety, this was wisely judged, though Stuart cannot have been unaware of Iseult's former relations with the poet. An unexpected consequence arose when Yeats began to read Stuart's poems and, while keeping apart, to assess him more objectively. Initially, his tasks as assigned by Maud Gonne included dealing with the Stuart family, but gradually he disencumbered himself. Iseult insisted that her husband possessed 'charm & certain gifts of poetical phantasy'. While seeking to persuade his wife that they should take in Stuart temporarily – after a settlement, of course – Yeats wrote, 'If he comes to Oxford I beleive [sic] I shall be able to find these qualities & to keep them before my mind sufficiently to make it possible to become his friend.'[39] A capacity to empathise with a sadist just out of Rugby did not blind Yeats to other heroic possibilities in the situation. A day after his Oxford proposal he fused the hope given by a reading of Stuart's poem with the recollection of phantom violets smelled by Lennox Robinson in the St Stephen's Green Club. 'I have been able to work without anger & indeed almost without emotion of any kind. I am glad of one thing which is that Maud Gonne & I are very good friends now.'[40]

A second letter to his wife on that same day maintains the theme, though with a sting in its tail. 'I am even gay as if I were hunting some beast ... It is precisely because I am not deeply moved that I am useful.' These words may have been designed to reassure George. He then reverted to College of Arms business, and to the threats issued against her in the vicinity of Ballylee. Returning to Iseult by way of the interpretive system that would become *A Vision*, he suddenly turned like an animal on his earlier sympathy and characterisation:

> I wonder if her husband is not a [Phase] 14, whose vanished primary has left a hole which a wild beast has chosen for its lair. Then too I notice this, 14s ... commonly marry 14s, & according to a communication of a year ago a woman falls in love with a mans antithetical. As anti[thetical] of 14 is the Fool, all 14s should be in danger of marriages with deranged or deficient persons ... His poetry suggests 14.[41]

Literature and the occult, literature and politics – the events of summer 1920 moved in a magic circle. Among the reasons given for Stuart's assaults on Iseult were disagreements about poetry and her complaints about his prose-style. She had been passive during much of the ordeal, and maintained a high degree of composure even when relating her story to Yeats. Only once did she show indignation, when she told Yeats that Stuart liked Walter de la Mare's poetry, which she considered second-rate.[42] In keeping with his imagery of the hunter and the wild beast, Yeats concluded one of his reports to Augusta with a sigh of regret and the line from 'Two Songs of a Fool': 'Alas "The horn's sweet note and the tooth of the hound."'[43]

Conjunctions of sweetness and violence recur in Yeats's descriptions of the human state, the one redeemed from its crassness by the other, in his philosophy. There was a further level of ominous literary paralleling to set in place before his summer correspondence about the Stuarts could end. This focused on Iseult's unborn child, whose imminence had been confirmed by Bethel Solomons against the horoscopic findings of George Yeats, who thought the pregnancy a false one – she had detected 'deception & entanglement of all kinds'.[44] Certainly, emotional transference was building up in the small cottage where the principal actors were confined. George in Oxford was suffering her second miscarriage, and thus her attitudes towards Iseult's pregnancy were vulnerable to unconscious motivation or projection. Yeats, for his part, magnificently slipped in a letter back to George, 'I wonder if Maude [sic] is still in love with him' – that is, Francis Stuart.[45] Editors might pause before replacing Maude with Iseult; might it not be equally possible that, at some level, Yeats wondered if Maud was still in love with him [Yeats]? For George, a greater worry linked her husband with the younger woman.

These were the ingredients of Greek tragedy. An ageing man, who entertained the thought that he was father of a young woman now at odds with her husband, and who had also proposed marriage to her, finds himself appointed to negotiate with the young man's family for a separation. Add to this domestic scene the national conflict in which all the individuals were deeply committed, despite their diverse origins: Maud Gonne, the English-born daughter of a colonel; Iseult, the French-born daughter of a right-wing adventurer; and Yeats, the child of unsettled Protestant Ascendancy. The birth of Iseult's daughter – christened Dolores Veronica, lest happy times befall her – brought Yeats back into Francis Stuart's personal life. Writing to the mother from Shillingford in Berkshire, he proposed (with some jocularity) that when the girl was seventeen or eighteen long consultations should take place to see 'what is to be done to make her marriage lucky'. The age specified was exactly that at which the fool Stuart married Iseult and, as if to obstruct any repetition of that 'tragedy', Yeats suggested that 'perhaps we may marry her into my family'.[46] Regal successions can hardly have been planned with greater promptness, and if Yeats was in part merely jesting, the underlying urge remained powerful to achieve in the next generation what had proved impossible in his own. A dynastic alliance might constitute a dialectics of blood, at once distancing Yeats from Iseult and uniting their lines. A measure of sophisticated obtuseness closed his letter to her on the question of the infant Dolores's horoscope. His wife, imminently expecting their second child, chafed to be in Ballylee, but her condition and the condition of Ireland (he told Iseult) made him wary of rural Galway. The lines now ran parallel in his correspondence.

Dolores died of meningitis in July 1921. Yeats was told promptly in a long letter from the distressed mother, with heart-breaking details of the infant's fingers closing round her own fingers when 'it was ill'. He felt that better doctors might have been employed – he distrusted Kathleen Lynn ('a violent woman'), who was a friend of Maud Gonne's. Physicians were able only to reckon with disease, and Mrs Yeats had concluded months earlier that the child would not live. In addition to her horoscopic methods, there was the evidence of high mortality among female Gonnes – a fate that had exempted Maud. 'Perhaps it is well,' Yeats confided to Augusta Gregory, 'that a race of tragic women should die out' – at least before any real prospect of one marrying into the Yeats line. His report to Coole Park continued the theme of succession and generation. A nurse was expected the following day, to help George in her second confinement.

Names for the new arrival had been debated. Their first child, Anne (born in February, 1919), had been so named to perpetuate a line, more automatic writing than verifiable pedigree, with Anne Hyde, a seventeenth-century Duchess of Ormonde. If the second child were another girl, it was to be distinctively named Stuarta – if a boy, William Michael. Lady Gregory can hardly have swallowed explanations of this choice. Another girl, Yeats told her, 'will be a blow to George made all the worse because [her mother] says that all the Stuartas in her family have been "corkers" & the probable horoscope does rather suggest a "corker"'.[47] The obvious affinity of names was with Iseult Stuart or Francis Stuart rather than any 'Erskine line' as proposed by Mrs Yeats's biographer.[48] The aristocratic pretensions evident in the naming of Anne Yeats could be traced into the second nomination, if a nod to the House of Stuart were perceived in Yeats's odd choice. But the only female of that royal line who achieved fame was Mary, Queen of Scots, beheaded by her cousin in 1587. Though the German poet Friedrich Schiller wrote a tragedy based on the life and death of Mary Stuart, the later Jacobite cause had petered out by Walter Scott's time, to be commemorated for its gorgeous futility in his novel of 1814, *Waverley*.

'A Hair Divides the False & True'

Yeats's general account of August 1920 placed his Glenmalure interventions in perspective. 'I believe that ever since my return from America I have had a need of action & that this activity has been very good for me.'[49] There was no shortage of action in Ireland and, while seeking the advice of Darrel Figgis and Desmond FitzGerald about intimidation near Ballylee, he demonstrated an astute sense of the national mood. But this was not a stage upon which he performed any central part: he was an observer and a director in strange combinations. From recognising that a profound need for action had been filled through his efforts to sort out the Stuarts' marriage problems, there immediately followed those metaphors of wild beast and of hunting, already noted. His mood of blood-sports gaiety he traced back to a different emotional response: 'I think it came when I pitied Francis Stuart, though I do not know why that should be. That night I preyed [*sic*] to be given enough harshness to act strongly.'[50] Yeats's inability to spell the difference between praying and preying, linked to vagueness as to whom or what he might address his preyers, inscribes a chilling record of his emotional oscillations.

The Irish literary context in which he sought to resolve the marital crisis of the Stuarts was pregnant with historical self-consciousness, its hour come round at last. The dead Synge haunted the Glenmalure cottage, having dramatised sexual choice based on fancy and on indifference to property. Alive in Paris, Joyce was finishing *Ulysses*, a novel of modern urban life which – being set 'sixteen years since' – was already becoming historical. The Citizen of 16 June 1904 was about to take up office as Minister for This or That. Within eighteen months, Yeats would consider such a role for himself. These thoughts were sufficiently practical to be classified by Roy Foster as 'minister-ial ambitions' not be wrecked by undue concern for his British Civil List pension, which might be forgone. Had he taken up such an offer, Yeats would have invoked German practice in 'the application of art to industry' and sought an inquiry into the German example.[51] In the event no such ministry was established, and Yeats supported the new regime, but remained unbound by it. His position might be compared to that of the renowned liberal Whig, Henry Grattan (1746–1820), who (in the eyes of his opponents) indulged in severe criticism of government without ever having known the constraints and rigours of office. Yeats invoked Grattan's name in 'The Tower'. Eighteenth-century political sentimentality had been the object of Walter Scott's richly informed analysis in *Waverley*, but there was no Scott in latter-day Ireland to warn of the dangers implicit in any renewal of the Jacobite attitude, any radicalising of the tradition invoking higher authorities than those of realisable politics.

There was Joyce, whose view of the Irish past was not wholly un-Scott-ish, but Yeats did not have *Ulysses* at his disposal when he saved the house of Stuart. There was also Ezra Pound, best man at the Yeatses' wedding. In August 1920, while the business of ensuring Iseult's safety was still unfinished, Yeats wrote from Oxford about 'Hugh Selwyn Mauberley', Pound's angry elegiac response to the Great War. What Yeats admired in the poem was 'style which is always neighbour to nobility when it is neighbour to beauty, a proud humility, that quality that makes ones hair stand up as though one saw a spirit'.[52] The final phrase reveals how difficult he found it to think outside occultic protocols, while the general tenor of his criticism is distinctly antique in its choice of virtues – Tennysonian or worse. Disgust at the horrors of war and the incompetence of Britain's governing classes acted as compost for *revulsions towards* earlier forms of authority, or rather it gave rise to a dangerous 'sport' – radicalised tradition. Mathers had handed over the torch at a time conducive to the cultivation of a new Jacobitism. Francis might yet prove to be the Young Pretender. As if to advance the cause, his cash-strapped mother-in-law bought a bogus castle in Laragh where Iseult later entertained Hitler's envoys.

The summer of 1920 brought a publisher's enquiry. Macmillan of New York wanted 'an impartial history of Ireland' and sought Yeats's recommendation of an author. His first choice would have been Standish O'Grady, as near an approximation to unreconstructed Anglo-Irish Protestant Ascendancy Romantic Jacobitism as one could hope for. But, Yeats realised, the author of *The Coming of Cuchulainn* was 'past the work now'. Knowing that the publishers wanted 'a Gentleman & a Scholour', he wondered if Mrs Alice

Stopford Green did not fit the bill – 'the obvious selection'. Or, perhaps, Lennox Robinson. The latter was taking the apparent survival of Iseult's marriage badly, and so might welcome 'an oppertunity [*sic*] for expression of conviction & impression – "impartial" is of course all nonsense'.[53] Yeats's own attitude to Robinson's brandy-doused gloom was conveyed in a letter back to George, 'I am so busy that the tragedy is lightened for me.'[54]

While Yeats set his cottage of sexual confusion in order, reconciling his own 'spiritual' children to a sort of incest, the country was drawn deeper into the cruelties of civil war, liberation struggle and counter-insurgency. He had found 'action' in his role at a time when the word came increasingly to denote military conflict: enemy action, men killed in action, etc. Yeats knew other technical kinds of action all too well – stage action as distinct from dialogue, libel actions, etc. In 'Ego Dominus Tuus' he had employed the word – rare in his poetry – to link 'those who love the world' and those who 'paint or write'; both do so 'in action'. The poem finally appears as a species of dedicatory text to *Per Amica Silentia Lunae* (1918), a prose volume that also contains a Prologue and Epilogue dedicated to Iseult. Roy Foster valuably traces Yeats's interests in the work of Sigmund Freud and Carl Gustav Jung behind Section II as finally published, without specification of their names. Though *Per Amica* pre-dates the Irish Troubles and the marriage of Iseult to Francis Stuart, it constitutes Yeats's principal philosophical statement for the years leading up to the work later published as *A Vision* (1925). The elision of Freud's name, by which Yeats's preference for an idealist theory of dreams and memory is assisted, is but one stage in the gradual overcoming of all obstacles to the creation of a psycho-philosophy of history in which the individual is subordinated to determined cyclical move-ments of immensely slow periodicity. A second comes with 'the need to override the passivity induced by Romantic doctrines of "sincerity and self-realisation"', as Foster puts it. The third stage is in short the doctrine of masks, of seeking opposites and cultivating the anti-self. 'Override' is one of those supple English verbs which are less comfortable if translated into Nietzschean German where, if it avoids the physicality of *übergehen*, it is in danger of acquiring the dialectical voltage of *aufheben*. By such overriding, tragedy might be lightened, or transferred to another to become, in the after-effect, second-hand.

By an action being at once domestic and (analogically) military, the classic western tradition of politics (affairs of the *polis*) is doubly eclipsed. In Glenmalure Yeats brilliantly achieves the Home Rule lost amid the rush to arms in 1914: equally real men, however, will have to fight it out from Balbriggan to Solaheadbeg, from 1919 to God Knew When. The apogee of this kind of 'action' Yeats ultimately finds in a transmitted version of Indian philosophy. In a later letter to Olivia Shakespear, he wove an elaborate account of political, domestic and literary activity in which a curiously impersonal psychology emerges as a strength:

> I shall be in London on April 10. I had meant to go rather sooner as my gardener says I should not miss this garden in April. You can apply much of the Swami thought to our life if you translate it. 'Act and remain apart from action'.
>
> During the last few days I have been in conflict with certain people in the govement [sic] about the Abbey. I had to risk its future; only yesterday did I get the decission [sic] I wanted. I watch myself with interest. I found that once I had a clear idea, & knew I was not acting from temper, I did not seem to be personally involved. I looked on as if some stranger was doing it all. I had an hours [sic] interview with De Valera. I had never met him before & I was impressed by his simplicity & honesty though we differed through out. It was a curious experience, each recognised the others point of view so completely. I had gone there full of suspicion, but my suspicion vanished at once. You must not beleive [sic] what you read in the English papers. They decide moral questions in the interest of their parties & express their decissions [sic] with a complacency that rouses other nations to fury. Here I think we are generally troubled about right & wrong, we do not decide easily. The hungry mass is nearer to the saint than the full man. 'A hair divides the false & true' – one should never be satisfied in any contravisy [sic] until one has found the hair – one is liable to think it must look like a ship's cable.[55]

One should not quarrel with a biographer over the use of 'override' as a metaphor treating successive literary attitudes to sincerity or anything else. Nor should I single out Roy Foster for comment in relation to a book title universally received in the passive voice. Yeats's first choice for what became *Per Amica Silentia Lunae* was 'An Alphabet', but – as Foster puts it – 'the chosen title, suggesting reflections in the friendly silence of moonlight, is more apposite'. While Yeats's Latin source remains unexamined, the illusion remains unbroken. But the phrase comes from Virgil's account of the military strategy leading to the destruction of Troy – the wooden horse on the shore, the departure of the fleet (but only to the island of Tenedos), and then a stealthy return of the deceitful Greeks 'by the friendly silence of the quiet moonshine' to seize the city, aided by agents hidden within the horse.

From 'The Rose of the World' (1891) to the marching songs written for Ireland's fascist Blue Shirts, Yeats deployed the familiar image of Troy, a classical allusion greatly re-energised by the excavations of Heinrich Schliemann in the 1870s, proving the existence of an historical city. It came to signify an eternal pattern of abduction, conquest, rape, destruction and cultural renewal. But *Per Amica Silentia Lunae* is a rare-for-Yeats reference to the cunning of Ulysses, whose abandonment of the foreshore and taking to the reflective waves is the basis of Latin civilisation. Yeats's response to the home-seeking warrior stands in striking contrast to Joyce's pre-*Work-in-Progress* work in progress.

Morbus Démocraticus: (1924-25)

As for propaganda, our servants will do that for us.
                              Augusta Gregory to a journalist, 1928

In 1912, Yeats had been short-listed for membership of whatever
Irish Senate might emerge from the Home Rule proposals then
looking feasible. The House of Lords thought otherwise about these,
and in due course 1916 brought an even more absolute veto. In 1922,
when the first native government was set up, Yeats considered the
possibility of taking a ministry with responsibility for the arts. Power
attracted him, and his growing reputation as poet and playwright did
nothing to diminish a mutual attraction. But the political situation as
it emerged from the War of Independence was not one that he found
congenial. A Home Rule Senate would have been created by
nomination, at least for the first few years. By 1921 elective politics
had superseded the older conventions, despite the new threat of
militarism.

Jephson O'Connell and the National Army Mutiny

The problem for all revolutions is consolidation. After a short but
brutal civil war (1922), the Irish Free State found itself burdened with
a standing army of more than 50,000 men which, in times of
recession, it could not afford. Official attempts to encourage
retirements or a more general demobilisation were matched by the
growth of lobbies or factions within the army itself. Three groups,
none of them clearly definable, may be identified. One was a
reconstructed Irish Republican Brotherhood, designed to secure by
the old conspiratorial means the gains made under the Treaty of 1921.
The second termed itself the Irish Republican Army Organisation
(hereinafter IRAO), a covert yet petitioning body of officers
disgruntled by the prospects of unemployment and by suspicions of
favouritism and corruption. The third, particularly detested by the
second, was a number of officers and men who had served in the

1. Probable location of the Armstrong home at Hawkswood, County Cavan, home of Grace Armstrong who married William Corbet in 1791.
2. Sandymount Castle, Robert Corbet's house in the Dublin suburbs, c. 1860. *From left to right*: Grace Yeats, Mary Wise (née Yeats), Jenny Yeats; Robert Wise and Michael (the servant); Uncle Robert Corbet; a Beatty cousin (standing); Ellen Yeats (seated beside Corbet) and Isaac Yeats.

3. Memorial tablet in the parish church, Tullylish, County Down, honouring William Butler Yeats, the sometime absentee rector, grandfather and namesake of the poet.

4. Victorian industrial buildings in the parish of Tullylish, County Down.

5. A contemporary photograph of Ashfield Terrace, Terenure, where the Yeats family lived (much to the poet's shame) while a pupil at the High School.

6. Iseult Gonne *c.* 1918.

7. W. K. Magee (John Eglinton), from a drawing by J. B. Yeats who regarded his subject as excessively sympathetic to English values. (Date unknown).

8. Austin Clarke in old age at Templeogue, County Dublin. He directed *The Death of Cuchalain* in 1949.

9. The 'demon-merchants' in Friedrich Bethge's Frankfurt 1934 production of Yeats's 'Countess Cathleen' in German translation.

10. Dermot MacManus (still in British uniform, on the extreme left) with other officers of the Irish National Army, 1923.

11. Roger Casement, from a series of Irish political woodcut portraits made by Harry Kernoff.

12. Helmut Clissmann *c*. 1940.

13. Winners of the Goethe-Plakette, including a draft-list of nominees for 1934.

(*Detail*) The last four names are Hermann Stehr, Ernst Krieck, W. B. Yeats, and Josef Goebbels.

14. Yeats's German producer, Friedrich Bethge (centre), with Adolf Hitler, Joseph Goebbels, and others.

Edward Hempel, German Minister to Ireland gave this book to W. B. Yeats in remembrance of an unforgetable afternoon he spent with him in September 1938.

15. Eduard Hempel's inscription to W. B. Yeats on a presentation copy of *Germany Speaks* (1937).

British forces at some time prior to their rallying to the Irish flag. The IRAO strongly suspected that some government ministers were secretly encouraging the new IRB, while others (notably O'Higgins) resented and feared the persistence in peacetime of military attitudes disrespectful of civil authority.

One Monday evening in January 1924, Desmond FitzGerald had been unable to gain entrance to the Yeatses' house on Merrion Square for the customary weekly gathering. Attendance had become sparse, and Yeats felt free to abandon the arrangement and go out to dinner instead. News of the efforts made by the Minister for External Affairs prompted him to apologise because he was 'particularly anxious to see you about something', which could not be committed to paper.[1] The Monday evenings were not exclusively literary occasions, and some discreet politicking was always possible. The army row broke in March 1924. In the skeletal-biography that prefaces John Kelly's magnificent edition of Yeats's *Collected Letters*, nothing is indicated for the year prior to 6 May. In practice, the recently invested Nobel laureate was closely in touch with several of the conflicting factions. In December 1922, he had been appointed to the Irish Senate, in consequence of which bullets had been fired through his windows. If his loyalties remained with W. T. Cosgrave's government, Yeats made himself available to awkwardly oppositional views. As early as September 1923 he entertained O'Higgins (who was Minister for Home Affairs, not for Defence), Commandant Dermot MacManus and Colonel Jephson B. O'Connell in his Merrion Square home, to facilitate their discussion of army discipline and morale. Both of the officers became close associates of Yeats in his political development; both belonged (in one sense or another) to Group 3 among the army factions of 1924. O'Higgins, after his assassination in 1927, became a sublime point of reference in poems such as 'Death' and 'Parnell's Funeral'.

Among Yeats's papers in the National Library of Ireland there survives a copy of *The Truth about the Army Crisis*, issued anonymously by the IRAO with a preface by Liam Tobin. The envelope in which it was kept bears notes relating to later poems, including 'The Municipal Gallery Re-visited' and the rumbustious 'Colonel Martin'. There are also scribbled names of army officers from 1924, an indication that, when O'Higgins and O'Connell withdrew for private discussion, Yeats did not drop the topic of army politics. O'Connell was an ordained Catholic priest of an English diocese, no longer exercising his vocation.[2] He was obsessed with immorality among his troops and the spread of venereal disease, while O'Higgins was concerned about incidents of sexual assault by men already implicated in civil-war atrocities of an indefensible kind. The Irish Army was not a pretty picture. Whether a *coup d'état* was feared, or envisaged, is less clear. With the government divided, even as the army was, the new Senator obliged a minister not responsible for the army and an officer complaining of his superiors' conduct.

During January 1924 Yeats wrote many letters to acknowledge congratulations on his Nobel award and his speech in Stockholm, though he was also concerned for his sister, Lily, ill with tuberculosis in a London hospital. On balance, cheerfulness won. He assured Augusta Gregory that life in Dublin was reviving after the conflict – 'a new genuine society is being born'. To the painter Edmund Dulac, he sketched out a more paradoxical image, 'Politicians want to be artistic, and artistic people [want] to meet politicians.' Quite where Yeats fitted into this dialectic remained to be decided. 'In the Senate I speak as little upon Politics as is possible, reserving myself for the things I understand.'[3]

The meeting of late September 1923 evidently faded in his memory for, when MacManus sought to check details in May 1924, neither Yeats nor his wife could quite confirm the date. The intervening time had been largely pleasant, involving a stately voyage across the North Sea towards the Royal Academy in Stockholm. January having proved to be an in-tray of congratulations, February became a steady flood of correspondence despatched outwards to agents, publishers, translators and other literary professionals. One society hostess of loosely Anglo-Irish background, the Marchioness of Londonderry, attempted to bag the laureate for a salon, but got in return a nugget of political fantasy: 'I wonder if we shall end by the spectacle of a high Tory Ireland – North & South – face-to-face with a socialist England.' Within a week or so, Yeats was reminding a tired dramatist of the Abbey's sacrifices during 'the national war and the civil war', as if Toryism were as remote from his thoughts as Tory Island. His opinions should sometimes be read as the products of the mirrors they were aimed at.[4]

While continuing to work on *A Vision*, Yeats had two immediate preoccupations in March. The proofs of his *Essays* required correction and prompt return (via his agent, A. P. Watt) to the publishers, Macmillan and Co., in London. The volume brought together discursive prose work dating from early in the century and some new material, mainly footnotes to 'Per Amica Silentia Lunae' (1916-17): it formed the fourth volume of Macmillan's authoritative *Collected Edition of the Works*, and suitably marked the poet's acknowledgment in Sweden as a true master of contemporary literature. For all the arcane thinking of the essays, Yeats readily appreciated the professional services of his agent in maximising income and maintaining efficient relations with publishers, translators and others. Like the punter in 'The Words upon the Window-pane', he combined an interest in the occult and a compound interest in the bank. The Nobel funds had been invested at 5 per cent.

Even more worldly affairs pressed upon him at the Abbey Theatre. 'Juno and the Paycock', Sean O'Casey's first full-length play to reach the stage, had opened on 3 March. Its tragic-comic juxtaposition of civil war and domestic betrayal disturbed an audience unused to such an analysis of recent political and military events. As the historian John Regan has observed, 'about an hour and a half after the curtain came down on the penultimate performance, [President W. T.] Cosgrave was handed an ultimatum in Government Buildings from the IRAO which made clear that a section of the army was in revolt'.[5] Among the immediate consequences was the military descent on a government minister's home in pursuit of mutineers. Depending on definitions, Yeats's guests of September might have featured on such a warrant. Kevin O'Higgins was obliged to make a semi-coherent justification of the government's position, while concealing the extent to which minister was daggers-drawn with minister. A semblance of restored order came with the appointment of Eoin O'Duffy as Inspector-General of the army, thereby projecting that figure one step further on his headlong career towards fascistic excess. On the other side of the city, O'Casey's 'Captain' Jack Boyle rolls on his feet in the final act of 'Juno', observing that 'the whole worl's ... in a terrible state o' ... chassis!' Only a month earlier Yeats had repeatedly emphasised the same diagnosis. Endorsing authoritative government as if it were inevitable, he asked his *Irish Times* interlocutor, 'What else can chaos produce even though our chaos has been a very small thing compared with the chaos in Central Europe?'

Yeats's forgetfulness about the September meeting with MacManus and O'Connell was probably genuine. (He once enquired in a hotel whether or not he had already eaten the soup, for he couldn't quite remember ...) The events of March isolated the two officers for, while they shared IRAO's hostility to what they saw as an IRB lodge within the army, a secret society patronised by the Minister for Defence (Mulcahy), they also were linked with Group 3, those with previous British Service. O'Connell's service had been (briefly) to the Catholic Church in Salford but, by acquired instinct, he manifested a not-wholly native Irish intellectuality. MacManus had served with the Inniskillings in Gallipoli, where he had been severely wounded.[6] Yeats, who had probably forgotten whether he had ever taken an IRB oath, was never close to that new element in the politics of 1924. Liam Tobin and Emmet Dalton, the more publicly recognised leaders of IRAO, were scarcely to his taste, though Dalton eventually became a significant contributor to the development of film. Yeats was rubbing shoulders with the ex-Brits, in the company of a politician who would soon propose a dual-monarchy. 'Authoritative government' was a kite, not a flag.

Jephson O'Connell was determined to redress any debits in Yeats's memory of him, and sometime before 20 May 1924 a lengthy statement was despatched, drawn up earlier for his appearance before a Cabinet Committee of Inquiry. Cross-examined by Richard Mulcahy, he had provided 'no names except those given in my document', and so he could assure Yeats that 'the two Senators and my primary source are still unknown'. It is clear that the second senator was Andrew Jameson, a distilling magnate and so (by Irish logic) a representative of the old Anglo-Irish gentry. What O'Connell had been discussing or planning with the two senators has yet to be established, but the 'primary source' was glossed by Mrs Yeats as 'a man who was appointed by IRA to spy on IRB [but] reported to J O'Connell instead!' Mrs Yeats's enjoyment of this conspiratorial frisson is unmistakable, and she came to regard O'Connell as an ideal visitor when she and the poet travelled to Italy.

Of the two, MacManus in practice became closer to Yeats. The various papers and pamphlets about the Mutiny that reached him included a lengthy summary of the limping swashbuckler – 'he was appointed Acting Director of Mountjoy Prison at a critical moment of its history, and it was mainly through his stand for stern Military discipline that the prisoners' morale was broken'. If the temporal suspensions of the Blood Kindred were to be relied upon, MacManus could have sprung from the pages of Elizabeth Bowen's novel of 1949, *The Heat of the Day*, in which Great War victimage and disgust at democratic folly lead Robert Kelway into active sympathy with the

Nazis. More traceably, MacManus stands behind the throne when Yeats in the 1930s looks towards Central Europe.

Yeats's pronouncements in the *Irish Times* raise an issue that bedevils assessment of his politics, the distinction between prescriptive and descriptive statements. It is one thing to describe a situation in terms of the authoritative government observed therein; it is another to prescribe authoritative government as a desirable solution. Nothing in the state of Irish affairs early in 1924 could be described as authoritative: government ministers were at odds on fundamental matters, the army was murmurous, the economy slumberous. The party in power had difficulty in finding candidates for by-elections, and the 'opposition' was scarcely legal. Following on his grand Stockholm thoughts, Yeats desired for Ireland what manifestly did not pertain. The philosophico-historical system under elaboration as *A Vision* provided a means of asserting that authoritative government would inevitably come (round). But for lesser readers, content with the *Irish Times*, the rhetorical question must suffice. 'What else can chaos produce . . . ?' Yeats's politics never excluded literature and the arts; it was in a double sense dramatic. If his newspaper interview of 16 February 1924 did not reflect realities as they existed in the cabinet and the mess-room, it adroitly anticipated and countered O'Casey's moving plea for a politics of compassion, 'Take away our hearts o' stone, and give us hearts o' flesh . . .' The play's larger irony is played out in miniature when Mrs Boyle speaks these words, borrowed from Mrs Tancred of Act Two, O'Casey having borrowed the name for 'a very old woman obviously shaken by the death of her son' – a republican to be buried 'like a king' from Walter Scott.[7]

L'Action française

Though at home the civil war brought danger and enforced sequestration in the Tower, Yeats did not have long to wait for an opportunity to express his commitments in foreign politics. At the Irish Race Convention, held in Paris as the civil-war divisions were opening up, he and his brother, the painter Jack Yeats, participated in the cultural 'fringe' events. While the convention functioned as an offstage performance by the principal actors in a civil war about to open at home, for Yeats it brought him back to the scene of his principal foreign experience as a young man – Paris. The week-long event was tense with imminent conflict, as Eamon de Valera (bitter opponent of the Treaty) presided at many sessions. Both brothers spoke on Monday, 23 January 1922, the poet's topic being the lyrics and plays of modern Ireland. In Dublin, writers and politicians had believed they were in perennial communion, for that was the nature of the Irish character, wasn't it? But Easter 1916 had revealed how the militants were capable of pursuing their own course, which broke upon sedentary men with traumatic effect. Here in Paris, on the world's stage, Yeats and de Valera visibly shared the action, though they vied for Maud Gonne's attention.[8] Anti-Treatyites used the convention to liaise with supporters from overseas, for it had been long planned. Constance Markiewicz, whose imprisonment Yeats marked coldly with the poem 'On a Political Prisoner', was present, well to the left of the men. Leading members of the pro-Treaty party chose to stay at home, consolidating the position won by a majority vote in Dáil Eireann. While Yeats politically supported the settlement with Britain, his role as the leading representative of Irish culture allowed him to associate with de Valera, who (for the moment) rejected democratic decisions and so initiated the civil war.

The occasion not only provided the opportunity for him to observe soon-to-be-warring factions among the Irish delegation, but also to assess the issue of nationality and race in the context of post-war France. Back in the 1890s he had conspired with Maud Gonne and others in Paris in exile, though differing from her in the crucial matter of Captain Alfred Dreyfus's alleged treachery. The issues personalised round the figure of Dreyfus had never been as limited as that stigmatising suggests; in the aftermath of – ultimately – victorious war in 1914–18, they assumed their full proportions. In 1923, L'Action française of Charles Maurras (1868–1952) opposed the holding of parliamentary elections, due the following year. But, by February 1924, the movement had been obliged to change course, deciding to run candidates in four Paris constituencies while seeking alliances on the right in others. What caught Yeats's attention was the possibility 'that a Royalist coup d'état may come in France any day'. Near the end of the 1920s, the Centre International d'Études sur le Fascisme counted L'Action as an important French ally in the struggle to globalise the Duce's doctrines and practices.[9]

On 17 February 1924, a play by Paul Claudel was produced by the Dublin Drama League. In the aftermath of Easter 1916, when he was staying with Maud Gonne in Normandy, Yeats had read some of the new Catholic literature of France, assisted by Iseult. The day before

'L'Otage' opened in Dublin, he published an interview in the *Irish Times*, deftly publicising the play and linking it to his own current political concerns: it was headed 'Paul Claudel and Mussolini – a New School of Thought'. Much of the article is presented in Yeats's own words, though the interviewer or typesetter occasionally mistakes the point. From the outset, he insists on linking French literature and Italian fascism. Though he only names Claudel and Charles Péguy (killed in the war), Yeats declares that these writers 'are giving expression in literature to the same movement that has brought Mussolini into power in Italy, and that threatens France'. The sentence is nicely poised between implicit approval of Roman fascism and an apparent concern that France might be *threatened* by something similar. The treatment of Péguy is particularly cavalier, for the latter had been an ardent socialist (turned mystical patriot under gunfire). Of his Joan of Arc trilogy, Yeats declares that 'we find in these plays the same emotions which give Mussolini his great audiences in Italy'. Driving home this historical point, he observes that 'Charles Maurras, the political philosopher of the movement in France, had already written his principal works' before 1914. In both of the cases he advances, a historical dimension to fascism is positively emphasised – Maurras is not some post-war phenomenon, and Péguy celebrates medieval French resistance to the English.

Files of the newspaper, *L'Action française*, for the period indicate that the movement was certainly attentive to foreign affairs – the rise of Ramsey MacDonald to power in Britain (23 January 1924) and the early struggles of Adolf Hitler in Munich (sentenced on 1 April to five years in jail; released 20 December 1924). The English had succumbed either to *suicide voluntaire* or to *Morbus Démocraticus*, while – Maurras declared in a signed article – France was 'kaput' (20 February). Amid the gloom, Jeanne d'Arc burns brightly and redemptively (see issue of two days earlier). Yeats in the *Irish Times* plays down Maurras' current, stylish but extreme writings in favour of the literary mediaeval, August 1914 serving as the end point of that happy era. His interest in L'Action française, expressed linked to Claudel and Péguy, is inseparable from the influence of Iseult Gonne, though endorsement of the arch-anti-Dreyfusard Maurras testifies to altered attitudes towards Maud Gonne also. Maurras applauds Mussolini (as Yeats does), and does not fail to miss the brown stirrings in Munich. The movement was not nationalist in any restrictive sense. On 11 May, the French Left defeated the national bloc, and Maurras disappears from Yeats's *à la carte*. On 10 June, the Italian socialist leader was murdered by the fascists, the Opposition quit the Chamber, and Mussolini remains on Yeats's list of recommendations.

Movement is a broad term in Yeats's use of it here, as if he were careless about precision. On the contrary. Cunning is everywhere evident in the interview, as he balances Mussolini's boasted trampling on Liberty's corpse with the socialists' alleged mirror-dance. Readers are invited to consider fascism 'without admiring Mussolini or condemning him'. But his approval of a French royalist *coup d'état* is evident enough, and his comment about Mussolini on the decomposing body of Liberty was repeated in August at a public dinner, without any show of even-handedness.[10] For the present, Yeats in February 1924 was happy to announce, 'I see the same tendency here in Ireland towards authoritative government.' Not only see, but encourage. If he and Jephson O'Connell were anxious to prevent a certain element in the National Army from seizing the political initiative, they were not averse to secret political manoeuvres of their own.

Setting the pattern for later biographers, Hone and Ellmann frame these outbursts as if they were provoked by the pettiness of life in provincial Ireland, rather than considering them collectively as evidence of a consistent – if also cautious – philosophy of violence. In Hone's case, there was a shared interest in fascist Italy for, having reported the approval of Mussolini in August 1924, two months after Matteotti's murder, he reserved for another chapter Yeats's holiday in Italy three months later. In February 1925, Hone teamed up with the Yeatses in Rome.[11] The pattern essentially ensured that political matter, and especially continental interest, never achieved critical mass.

Though Hone at the time (and Ellmann in retrospect) may have felt a need to orientate their comments on the actually existing Irish Free State, Yeats himself surveyed the world in his *Irish Times* interview. Not only the possibility of a French coup, but also the death of Lenin in January 1924, caught his attention. Thus, on the heels of his royalist predictions, he observed that 'in Russia the very contrary opinions have gone even further from democracy – there are 100,000 Communists controlling one hundred million who are indifferent or hostile'. Distance from democracy was the measure of political virtue. In so far as de Valera's republicans flouted Irish parliamentary and electoral decisions, even they won a measure of grudging respect. Crisis could be defused through recourse to the higher cynicism. To Olivia Shakespear he wrote, 'All those of us here who are in the secret are laughing over a government enquiery [*sic*] which has just been held into the state of our army. One man was "convicted of manslaughter & condemned to be very severely reprimanded". If you were an active member of society I would not dare write that to you for fear Lady Lavery would report me to the President [i.e. W. T. Cosgrave]. The whole enquiery [*sic*] is a comment on democracy which may have historical effects, if the facts get out.'[12]

Control is the crucial verb in Yeats's politics, democracy the dreaded noun. His fear of the mob – whether it be attached to Bolshevism or the Catholic Front – is matter for psychological enquiry on another occasion, but in applauding L'Action française he was capable of subtle discrimination, describing Maurras as a figure 'whom one can admire as a thinker without admiring his practical politics'. Indeed, a major distinction between Yeats's embrace of authoritarianism in 1924 and in mid-1934 should be constructed round his later abandonment of subtle discrimination in favour of unguarded endorsement and callous indifference. Perhaps the observation made to Maud Gonne in 1927, that we may judge acts but not individual persons, should be read as a 'turn' of emphasis.

Terror, *A Vision* and Joseph Hone

A biography of Joseph Maunsel Hone (1882–1959) would illuminate a great deal about Yeats's political interests. *The Arch-Poet*, Roy Foster's second and concluding volume, ably demonstrates the arts of avoidance in this connection. By a close reading of the index, it is possible to learn that Yeats considered the establishment of 'a new political party' in the late 1920s. The biography proper has little more to say. While Yeats and Hone were in Italy early in 1925, *A Vision* was being completed. Alongside, the two men discussed 'the formation of a distinctly undemocratic party in Ireland'. The reader is told nothing of substance about their specific objectives: instead, an elliptical account of the system resumes: 'The message of *A Vision* may [*sic*] be aristocratic as much as determinist, but it certainly expects "irrational violence" and totalitarian government to replace a decadent democracy. This may [*sic*] mark a stage towards "unity of being", but that desideratum seems far away ... Selectively quoted, and read in retrospect, "Dove or Swan" is an ominous text.'[13]

It is not clear how one might read any part of *A Vision* except in retrospect, nor is it possible to quote from a text non-selectively. Between the ominous and the retrospect, not much is revealed. The hazard lights that surround treatment of the Italian plans for an Irish anti-democratic party never illuminate any document relating to specific politics or economics. Instead, there is a digressive footnote about Yeats's view of Charles Dickens. Perhaps this is intended to draw the sting from his remark (vis-à-vis *A Vision*), 'I think the dead are our emotions & by their senses I pray that when I am dead I may look out upon our world through young mans eyes.' Selectively quoted, this may impress readers as plum-loco bunkum – to speak in homespun. As the new chapter about to commence deals with *The Catholic Bulletin*'s sustained diatribe against Yeats, any doubt about his grip on things becomes a benefit.[14] But underlying the bunkum is a confidence in (other people's) transcendence of individual death, which thoughtful analysts from Arthur Koestler to Roger Griffin have detected at the heart of the fascist psyche, even in the case of passive fellow-travellers.[15]

The political initiatives considered by Hone and Yeats cannot be wholly distinguished from the philosophical bunkum. If 'the dead are our emotions', then which particular emotions bear the names Luxemburg and Liebknecht or (for local effect) Noel Lemass and Dolores Stuart; which emotions stand in for the nameless poor of workhouse graveyards? Even in hyperbolic form, the notion profoundly affects conceptualisation of both 'emotion' and 'death'. If one can say that perhaps it was as well a race of tragic women should die out, is the victim of meningitis redeemed from such callousness by use of the word 'tragic'? Confronted by the imminent deaths of importunate strangers, is one proof against the consolation that they shall take their place amongst one's own angelic future emotions? The hyperbole may be reined in by a re-naming of Yeats's view as determinist: it is, however, a very odd determinism that allows for two-way traffic across the death-bed. Neither Marx nor Spengler found room for such liberties in their left- and right-variant Determinisms. Consequently, it is better for the Arch-Poet if the matter is taken up in a different chapter.

In the context of the *Bulletin*'s campaign of mockery, Yeats can legitimately be seen as taking up his political position 'in the group of senators who included Andrew Jameson, James Douglas, and other representatives of land, money, and the remnants of Ascendancy'. Several hundred pages separate this from the endnote which establishes that Joseph Hone acted as secretary to this group and as a sort of spokesman airing policy in the *Irish Statesman*. If, as Augusta Gregory's private journal seems to confirm, one proposal was a 'dual monarchy', together with a new National Unionist Party, the suppression of the *Irish Times* and the Freemasons, and the repatriation of Henry Grattan's remains from Westminster Abbey, one would expect the historical biographer to analyse these radical proposals. Instead, the endnote observes, 'not all of these ideas may have been ironic, but none of them was carried very far'. Under cover of this deflating balloon, it is conceded that 'the Italian example was specifically invoked'.[16]

Recourse to the *Irish Statesman* of 27 June 1925 will lead to modification of these findings. For a start, the article (entitled 'How to Revive the Irish Unionist Party') appeared above the pseudonym, Gael. Joseph Hone was no more or less a Gael than Yeats himself: on his father's side he came of Ulster Presbyterian stock, which had conformed to the Church of Ireland by the nineteenth century. Famous as painters in the landscape tradition, the Hones were also represented among the Established clergy: indeed, W. B. Yeats's biographer had a forebear who served with the Revd W. B. Yeats in the diocese of Connor. Why Joe Hone felt the need to secrete his political prospectus under so misleading a *nom de guerre* is a question deserving some consideration – once the meat of the matter is digested.

Yeats's name featured no more than Hone's. Indeed, the article is austerely impersonal. There is a side-swipe at 'the ex-Ascendancy, so-called', though it is not clear to which side the swipe is aligned. The objective is 'to seek a vital foundation of doctrine' in politics – a phrase as redolent of the new ideological forum of ideas as 'bread and circuses' was of the old. This might well involve 'even the necessity to suppress the *Irish Times* and other local defeatist activities [*sic*]', an appalling vista that reveals decidedly un-local perspectives. Freemasons were to be excluded – not generally, as Gregory had supposed, but merely from the new party's councils – and this as a gesture of anti-sectarianism. The new party, presented in terms ranging from 'imperialist' to 'national', is conceived as a reconciliation of all classes, a new deal between Britain and Ireland, and a shrewd jigging of

North and South to outwit Labour. 'In external policy National Unionists will be anti-democratic, but in a progressive and modern sense.' (For 'progressive' might one read 'more and more' – as in 'more and more anti-democratic'; for 'modern', read 'Italian'?)

The *anti*-democratic basis of the new party – not merely an *un*democratic one – is crucial to its vitalist energy. (Of course, no party emerges, but its component proposals can be traced in Yeats's thinking for fifteen years.) The actually existing parties pay lip service to 'democracy, parliamentarism, pacifism, equality' and other vices. Hone-the-Gael may have been reading Carl Schmidt, whose *Politische Romantik* had appeared in the Yeatsian *annus horribilis* of 1919, a proto-fascist who admired Patrick Pearse's 'decisionism' as a precedent for the Hitlerite real thing. Or Hone-the-Gael may have stuck to D'Annunzio, the putsch-poet of Italian fascism. 'There is no peace except in war and through war,' Hone intoned, without naming his authority. Worse had followed 1919, and Yeats had displayed great personal courage in defending the aged and politically vulnerable Augusta Gregory in the civil war. Fratricide suspended, nobody in June 1925 wanted renewed violence except diehard republicans whom de Valera was busily shafting and the group for which Hone was secretary or sectarist. 'A lack of real conflict' was Hone's complaint in 1925: in 1937, Yeats echoed this, shouting, 'Conflict, more conflict' when asked by an Indian visitor what his (Yeats's) message for India was.[17]

Gregory's journal informs us that these ideas were floated by Yeats and his associates in July 1925. She thoroughly disapproved of the Grattan repatriation, which was Yeats's pet scheme, though her objection appears to have rested on fears that St Patrick's Cathedral might be handed over by the Church of Ireland to the Catholics (and Grattan with it!). What Yeats planned was a 'demonstration' at the reinterment, and the prospect of a Roman-style cult of the hero doubtless offended her sensibilities. As late as 1927, some of these notions were still buzzing: at one of Yeats's 'Monday Evenings' on 13 February, General Jephson O'Connell aired his 'semi-confidential' proposal to have George V proclaimed King of Ireland in a version of the dual-monarchy scheme. Gregory, though weak with influenza, still thought the idea unwelcome and had sharp things to say of O'Connell. 'The Priest turned warrior,' she called him, 'who was in some of the Army troubles a year or two ago.' Kevin O'Higgins sat behind the proposal, intended to ease North–South tensions, but

Gregory was unwilling to contemplate 'any more direct domination by King George than we already have'.[18] Yeats evidently took a different view.

Dual monarchy did not necessarily imply authoritarianism, let alone anything stronger. In Irish eyes, however, it was invariably linked with the example of Hungary within the Habsburg Empire, and Hungary in the 1920s possessed the nearest thing to a fascist government outside Italy. George V was no Habsburg but, as a newly proclaimed head of state – proclaimed by whom? – he could in the future become a rallying point for those on the right disaffected with electoral politics. His eldest son, Edward VIII, featured in just such a manner at his abdication in 1936, earning Yeats's approval. The old Fenian conscience tolerated monarchs better than democrats.

Visiting Coole in July 1924, Yeats aired his new convictions. For inspiration, he leafed through books by W. E. H. Lecky (1838–1903), a historian who had combined modern scholarship and sympathy for Irish grievances with his officially Unionist politics. Gregory read aloud from Anthony Trollope's novel about an Irish MP, *Phineas Finn* (1869).[19] In the background, controversy over interpretations of Sir Hugh Lane's will, and the ownership of his French Impressionist paintings, continued to rumble. Yeats feared that his long immersion in philosophy might have damaged his poetic genius, but Gregory's conversation inspired a line or two (duly unacknowledged) for work in progress. She also turned the Grattan scheme to better ends by suggesting that a speech about the Abbey Theatre might compare its nurture of drama to the oratory of the eighteenth-century parliament. Yeats's disenchantment with the new regime took the form of comparing himself to 'a young English officer who went into the Post Office to buy a stamp at the beginning of the Rising in 1916 and was kept there for a week'.

These country-house fantasies are not wholly unconnected to the plans laid down in Capri earlier in the year when Hone holidayed with the Yeatses. In an unpublished letter of 22 May 1925, Hone evidently summarised their political speculations – the National Unionist Party would work towards a constitutional reform of relations between Britain and Ireland aimed at achieving 'a status like that before 1800'. A good deal of confusion or selective ignorance informs these schemes: the eighteenth-century Irish parliament was notoriously corrupt; Grattan remained in perpetual opposition exercising an influence that was often moral rather than political; and no Catholics could be elected. Perhaps Gael's article had been a spoof or a kite, though a Francis Jervois in reply identified defence against Bolshevism as a more than adequate justification of strange schemes. Catholics would be crucial to the success of the National Unionist Party, the right kind of Catholics of course – Jacobites sworn to defend George V and civilisation.

In this context, Yeats's involvement with the short-lived magazine *To-morrow* makes more sense than anyone has yet detected. Two issues were published, in August and September 1924, printed in Manchester in an attempt to outwit censorious Irish opinion. Offence was particularly focused on a short story by Lennox Robinson, 'The Madonna of Slieve Dun', deemed to have insulted the doctrine of the Virgin Birth. Another fictional contribution, Margaret Barrington's 'Colour', dealt with the love of a black man and white woman, while Yeats's poem 'Leda and the Swan' pursued the sexual theme into realms the common reader thought bestial (or more correctly, avian). The desire to shock was paramount. In Augusta Gregory's opinion, the enterprise had been set up 'for no purpose ... but to fill the Stuarts' idleness'. She believed that Robinson was a disciple of a German named Hartmann, who was 'anti-church', and feared that the government intended to suppress the paper. Both Francis Stuart and Iseult had recently been in jail for their republican activities, and both now contributed to a higher form of opposition. Under the name Maurice Gonne, she had written 'The Kingdom Slow to Come', a meditation on mystical questions, for the first issue; as Iseult Stuart, she added a short story, 'The Poplar Road', to the second and final issue.

Iseult's thoughts on Jakob Böhme harmonised with the editorial 'To all Artists and Writers' appearing in the August issue. Though signed H. [i.e. Francis] Stuart and Cecil Salkeld, the piece was acknowledged to be Yeats's work from the outset. The first three words indicate why Yeats did not want to put his name to it:

> We are Catholics, but of the school of Pope Julius the Second and of the Medician Popes, who ordered Michaelangelo and Raphael to paint upon the walls of the Vatican, and upon the ceiling of the Sistine Chapel, the doctrine of the Platonic Academy of Florence, the reconciliation of Galilee and Parnassus.[20]

What followed gave well-distributed offence, condemning the literary style of Irish bishops along with 'the art and literature of modern Europe', while also asserting the immortality of man's soul.

Certainly Iseult Gonne knew French poetry, and Cecil Salkeld German. *To-morrow* published two poems in German by O. J. Fleck, otherwise unknown. If Gregory's suspicions about Lennox Robinson's tutelage to German anti-church attitudes do not fit the picture perfectly, much depends on identifying Hartmann more closely. Was he the critical Kantian Eduard von Hartmann (1842–1906) with no known Irish links? Hardly Dr Hans Hartmann, Celtic scholar and sometime member of the National Museum staff in Dublin, who later headed up the Irish Section of the Nazi propaganda radio service?[21] Gregory was puzzled by the scatter-gun offensiveness of *To-morrow*, sexually risqué in the first issue and due in the second (she had heard) to recommend the surrender of St Patrick's Cathedral. Here was a stray detail from the secret politics of an embryonic National Unionist Party. Authoritarianism in the Church was attractive to Yeats, Hone and perhaps even the former Catholic priest Jephson O'Connell, *provided* it was proven through the good aesthetic taste of the Medicis: a Catholic authoritarianism appealed as a means of keeping down a democracy whose majorities would inevitably be based on voters who were Catholics in religious practice. If the latter could be persuaded to foreground (religious) authoritarianism and relegate democracy to the background, then a political picture might emerge in which Ireland would embrace 'national union' under enlightened leadership. If the emergent-Nazi Hartmann perhaps lurks outside the picture, one should note the presence of the Jewish poet and critic, Con Leventhal, among *To-morrow*'s editors, and the more ambiguous reconciliation of religious Galilee with Hellenic literary inspiration.

Usually dismissed as a damp squib ('Leda and the Swan' apart), *To-morrow* makes more sense when considered in the evolving 'turn' of Yeats's politics. The editorial echoes things he had written as early as 1896, but it provokes crisis and confrontation in an Ireland exhausted by civil war. 'Leda and the Swan' does more than beef up sexual provocations offered by Barrington and Robinson; it reorients the theme in terms of establishing a new reality. That outcome will be the virtual refoundation of western civilisation conceived as synchronous with 'some movement, or birth from above, preceded by some violent annunciation'. This certainly makes Edmund Burkean authoritarianism look like a Young Conservatives' bring-and-buy. In the editorial, in the famous poem, in the echoes of National Unionist aspiration, *To-morrow* was a Yeatsian project with attitude. His tactical deployment of high Catholicism was renewed in September 1929, when he chose to confront government infringements on what he regarded as freedom of literary expression in an article provocatively entitled 'The Censorship and Saint Thomas Aquinas'.

In his very old age, Yeats opined that 'the danger is that there will be no war'. This was not the anti-appeasement of Winston Churchill, or even that ascribed to Dorothy Wellesley. A civil war between the masses and 'the skilful' was predicted, though the belligerent parties are not further identified. History is, however, invoked to provide a clue. 'During the Great War Germany had four hundred submarine commanders, and sixty per cent of the damage done was the work of twenty-four men.' If now, in 1938, the skilful attempt nothing, 'European civilisation, like those older civilisations that saw the triumph of their gangrel stocks, will accept decay.' Politically, this is about as confused as things can get, but in terms of morality Yeats is insistently clear on the desirability of war. When he was writing *A Vision*, he continues, he had constantly impressed upon him the word 'terror' – though who or what was doing the impressing is lost in the grammatical style he chooses for his report. Because of 'that indefinable impression', he made Michael Robartes (the fictional character who plays a role in the philosophical work) say: 'Dear predatory birds, prepare for war ... test art, morality, custom, thought, by Thermopylae, make rich and poor act so to one another that they can stand together there. Love war because of its horror, that belief may be changed, civilisation renewed ...'[22] Thinking of Hans-Wilhelm in Hamburg, the Steinbergs of Kenilworth Park did not appeal to the author of this violent, corporative meta-morality – nor he to them.

When was Yeats first 'impressed' by terror? In *Reveries over Childhood and Youth* (1916), the first volume of his *Autobiographies*, he first described the sequenceless isolated memories through which he can reach back to his infant years. Though the experience is common enough among those who try to organise their earliest recollections, Yeats's sense was 'as if time had not yet been created, for all thoughts are connected with emotion and place without sequence'. This, though convincing as an account of infancy recollected in maturity, also describes the spiritual geometry through which he later sought to relate events among the dead with those of present-day social life. The childhood scene, we should note, is London, not Sligo. Through a Fitzroy Road window, he sees a number of boys at play, including a uniformed telegraph boy. A servant tells the young Yeats that the telegraph boy is going to blow up the town, 'and I go to sleep in terror'. With only a paragraph break, the *Reveries* continue: 'After that come memories of Sligo.'[23] The sequentiality of events is now highly significant, for the reader has been placed in a biography of the poet, shaped by himself. But the entry to sleep, in the prior world, has been coincidental with terror. Sleep, perchance to dream.

Surfaces

I have now with much Pains and Study, conducted the Reader to a period, where he must expect to hear of great Revolutions.
Jonathan Swift, *A Tale of a Tub* (1704).

Profundity is irrelevant, because it lives in depth, underground.
Denis Donoghue on Jonathan Swift, 1969

How did a man of Yeats's intelligence, sensibility and knowledge of human affairs come to hold such reprehensible views? One answer is advanced here: it refers to the absence of any inherited or immediately acquired theory of public life available to one of Yeats's peculiar background in Ireland. Another, referring to a theory of limited moral liability, awaits the reader of later chapters.

Victorian Britain was notoriously prolific of sages – Arnold, Bagehot, Carlyle, Mill, Newman, Ruskin etc. – whose views of contemporary society were broadcast and debated widely. In addition, two important Prime Ministers – Disraeli and Gladstone – could be classified as intellectuals, albeit of contrasting type. Victorian Ireland possessed nothing comparable at home, and contributed no figure of comparable stature to the larger debate. Only in 1876, with the arrival of George Bernard Shaw (1856–1950) on the London scene, did Irish intellect take up the metropolitan challenge. Before and after this date, Ireland's political leaders were effective, but in ways that precluded reflective or abstract thought. Daniel O'Connell and Charles Stewart Parnell were tacticians of the highest order, and each contributed significantly to the practice of democracy in the United Kingdom. Neither could be regarded as sage, neither left a testimony that his successors could read, mark, learn and inwardly digest.

There was of course a radical side to the picture, with Shaw (and, while he lived, Oscar Wilde) in sympathy. James Fintan Lalor (1807–1849), Michael Davitt (1846–1906) and the young James Connolly (1868–1916) preached a proletarian sermon unpalatable to

244

Yeats. John Mitchel (1815–1875) was more to his taste, but Mitchel proved all too easily reducible to the physical force nostrums of Fenianism. If Yeats found this general inheritance unhelpful in guiding him to an adequately complex sense of Irish public life, how did others of his generation, and others still younger, respond? On the whole, public opinion acknowledged the legitimacy and efficacy of electoral politics, returning members to the imperial parliament and extracting from it reforms of local government that further extended the practice of democracy. Davitt and Connolly were by no means convinced of the adequacy of these procedures, and each harnessed agitational and trade-unionist activities to the conventional parliamentary vehicle. Among the Blood Kindred, Patrick Moylett (a degenerate Fenian perhaps) would deplore in his memoirs Davitt's support for the admission of Jewish refugees to Dublin. 'The cause of Labour is the cause of Ireland, and the cause of Ireland is the cause of Labour,' Connolly declared. Yeats did not concur, but he had little by way of public argument to substitute for the divine gospel of discontent (James Larkin's phrase).

One could trace occultic sources for Yeats's alternative or secret politics. Indeed, at the close of 'Some Paper Tigers' above, an examination of Fechner's *On Life After Death* (as annotated by the poet) made plain some very direct connections. It may be that Seamus Deane's pronouncement that fascism is the political form the occult takes is a shade too absolute. But few can deny that Yeats's recognition of his own thought in Spengler's *Decline of the West* reveals a philosophy of history that is at once irrational, elitist, catastrophic and occult. Though Plato can be invoked as an Idealist, an aesthetician and occasionally as a political philosopher – his banishment of poets from *The Republic* was unfortunate – there is little or no evidence in Yeats's writings of any familiarity with the classics of western political thought from ancient Greece to the late Renaissance. The exception, Castiglione's *Book of the Courtier*, which he discovered in 1903 through Lady Gregory, is remarkable precisely because it obscures and (ideally) cancels Machiavelli's *Prince*. Roy Foster is surely right when he relates Yeats's study of *The Courtier* to his belief (vis-à-vis Iseult Gonne) that 'spectacular good looks might be a creative achievement in themselves', but remiss in failing to note the absence of any mediation between the conditions in which Castiglione (1478–1529) wrote and those in which Miss Gonne smoked.[1] Yeats as a philosopher of history had a strange contempt for the passage of time and the mundane changes it wrought.

More substantially, he manifested little interest in Aristotle. The neglect is all the more obvious if one reads his younger contemporary, James Joyce, whose fiction (up to and including *Ulysses* in 1922) is suffused with varieties of Aristotelianism, some transmitted through his Jesuit education and reading of St Thomas Aquinas, others acquired from adventurous heterodox private study. At one level, the contrast between an art-school training and the abstract disciplines of scholasticism deserves notice, especially in relation to someone who will pontificate on education, its deleterious effect on the lower orders and its magical ability to protect the gentleman from any risk of declension on the social ladder. More locally potent is education as the measure (indeed, the means) of Irish Catholic preparation for nationhood and state-building, as against the reliance on inherited tradition, custom and deference which continued to characterise Yeats's political responses. In 1926, he spoke of new acts of energy 'for the creation of tradition'.[2] Before that, long years were devoted to a rearguard defence of a culture that took education for granted. His insouciance had its conservative ambitions. Cullingford advises us that 'Yeats valued "the courtesy that makes our cottages as courtly as the palace"', but fails to reflect on the questionable use of 'our', a possessive adjective that substantiates neither possession (in the larger sense) nor occupation (of the smallholding).[3] A politics based on this reading of Castiglione was fated to be no more than compensation for loss of that landownership with which the Yeatses were in any case only modestly endowed.

The Senator and the Censorship

The establishment of the Irish Free State brought more solid opportunities. If Yeats lacked any sophisticated theory of action as might have been derived from Aristotle, he had earned recognition as a cultural activist of unrivalled literary accomplishment. Few aspects of his public life have won more positive approval than his membership of the Senate established under the new government. The politicians who conceived the idea, Oliver St John Gogarty who reputedly stiffened their resolve, and the poet who accepted the offer in December 1922 achieved a remarkable harmony of purpose. The result was six years of visible achievement, especially in areas associated with education and the arts. In practical terms, Yeats led three important committees of the Senate: that dealing with Gaelic Manuscripts (1923/24), with the design of Ireland's Coinage (1926–28) and a less successful committee to devise a Federation of the Arts along the lines of Sweden's Royal Academy. As this record demonstrates, if Yeats brought neither statesmanship nor academic political science to the Senate, he applied those skills as a chairman and lobbyist which he had acquired through innumerable literary controversies. His equally practical concern for the material fabric of school buildings contributed to the making of 'Among School Children', perhaps the poem most closely linked to his work in the Senate.

The coinage, designed by an Englishman called Percy Medcalfe, was superb in its elegant simplicity and rhythmical stillness, essential qualities in tokens to be used endlessly in the daily commerce of millions. Yeats's views did not go unaugmented by those of other members on the committee, and in his published commentary he went so far as to admit his mistake in thinking at first that the work of several artists might be included in the set finally approved. 'What We Did or Tried to Do' is unique among Yeats's senatorial utterances in revealing his informedness on the new Italy. Among seven designers invited to submit (three of whom were to be Irish), Yeats was especially interested in the work of Publio Morbiducci (1889–1963), designer of the fascist emblem as represented on Mussolini's coins. For any parallel expression of approval, one looks not to the public record of Senate debates, but to a speech delivered on 30 November 1925 to the Irish Literary Society.

As the editor of Yeats's parliamentary contributions recognised, this was the public expression of views that informed the Senator as he went about the business of visiting educational establishments round the country. It commenced with praise of Dublin's new enthusiasm for music, under the baton of Colonel Fritz Brase (later discovered to be a Nazi unlikely to have taken in Moses Slager), head of the National Army's school of music. In this context, the word 'discipline' is repeated in tandem with the 'plastic and receptive' condition of the Irish public, for whom 'education in the most common and necessary subjects' is urgently needed. Starting thus, Yeats launched into a detailed and damning account of the country's primary schools, their insanitary condition and inadequate size. Repeatedly the Italian example is recommended, with reference to introducing young children to new subjects, to inculcating a knowledge of classic texts, and to correlating all areas of study as 'one lesson'. Some of this could be distinguished from any specifically fascist policy; Montessori methods of teaching infants have their own professional integrity. Other aspects of Yeats's rhetoric can be ascribed to his belief that Giovanni Gentile, the Italian Minister for Education, was a philosophical descendant of George Berkeley, Yeats's favourite eighteenth-century anti-materialist. But all of it can be readily established as incontrovertible evidence of his informed engagement with fascist Italy as a model for (gradual or discreet) Irish emulation. Reaching for the imperative mood that will increasingly deliver his political opinions, he said:

> Feed the immature imagination upon that old folk life, and the mature intellect upon Berkeley and the great modern idealist philosophy created by his influence, upon Burke who restored to political thought its sense of history, and Ireland is reborn, potent, armed and wise.[4]

Behind the imperative-mood verb lies a scarcely concealed insistence that the two levels of cultivation – 'immature imagination' and 'mature intellect' – should remain apart; they are, by implication, social classes. In this context 'the great modern idealist philosophy' is fascism itself, ideally represented by Gentile, 'the most profound disciple of our Berkeley', but of necessity delivered by Mussolini's Black Shirts. The lecture mixes admirable concern for the welfare of children with a political programme extending much further. It goes well beyond the occasional endorsement of 'authority' with which he marked L'Action française and the French elections of early 1924, and anticipates the emphasis on armament to be made in *On the Boiler* (1939). Members of the Irish Literary Society were urged to use their influence in the press, an institution for which Yeats had limited use, thinking it vulnerable to the kind of manipulation he was at that moment encouraging. But above all, 'The Child and the State' constituted a semi-public obverse to the coinage of senatorial rectitude now celebrated. In the course of three interventions in the Conditions of Schools debate of March–April 1926, he diligently cited statistics and practices drawn from a study of Denmark, Northern Ireland, Norway, Scotland, the United States, 'Catholic Austria' and (just once) Italy.

This record of widely informed liberalism features Divorce on the A-side, with Censorship occupying most of the B- or flip-side, topics upon which Yeats consolidated his place in his own pantheon of

Anglo-Irish heroes. A Senate debate on divorce seemed inevitable in the spring of 1925, when the Dáil (or lower house) adopted a resolution in favour of prohibiting the dissolution of marriages. For procedural reasons, the upper house never had an opportunity to discuss the matter, but Yeats sent 'notes' to his friend George W. Russell; these, or rather his polished draft speech, were published in the *Irish Statesman* on 14 March. Again Italy was a point of reference, with Yeats poking fun at the Catholic Church's vain opposition to Italian unity. Warming to his theme, he quoted some member of an illustrious house which had produced cardinals and (perhaps) even a Pope, to the effect that indissoluble marriage went hand-in-hand with tolerance of illicit relations between the sexes. (Balzac supplied further evidence of the good sense in this.) This was not an argument likely to placate Irish ecclesiastical opinion, which inclined to the view that sex was at best the Creator's least admirable invention.

When the issue of divorce (or rather the prohibition of divorce) finally reached the floor of the Senate in June 1925, Yeats largely abandoned his Italian analogies. But, *pace* the claim that he had little interest in European matters, he substituted references to the legal status of divorce in America, England, France 'and the Scandinavian countries'. The speech appalled Senator Colonel Maurice Moore, who greeted with 'No, no' an early and mild instance of Yeats's determination to be aggressively sectarian. Taunting the Catholic absolutists, he suggested they 'study the morality of countries where marriage is indissoluble – Spain, Italy, and the South American nations'. In apparent contrast are listed the heroes of so-called Protestant Irish patriotism – Burke, Emmet, Grattan, Parnell, Swift – and, assimilating himself to this heterogeneous list, he concluded that 'we have created most of the modern literature of this country. We have created the best of its political intelligence.' At least, the chairman's intervention suggests that a conclusion had been reached which, however, proved temporary under reply of fire. Finally, Yeats at full throttle offered to explain 'the extreme immorality of my mind a little further', denying there was 'any statesman in Europe who would not have gladly accepted the immorality of the renaissance if he could be assured of his country possessing the genius of the renaissance. Genius has its virtue, and it is only a small blot on its escutcheon if it is sexually irregular.'[5]

This has been admired and deplored by the parties thus parodied. Its absurdities deserve some attention, not least the fatuous question about a latter-day politician choosing or not choosing the fifteenth-century Renaissance, which (to a degree) was a concept not fully developed until the nineteenth century. If 'we' had created the best of Ireland's political intelligence, 'we' had done it a painfully long time ago: Parnell, the only half-recent name, divided the country like no other. Perhaps Yeats was bent on the same end, speaking not to persuade but to offend. Behind the scenes and the senatorial rhetoric there was the little cabal minuted by Hone-the-Gael with its plans to repatriate Grattan and turn that most Whiggish of Whigs into a hero of the National Unionist Party.

Yeats's Senate speech in defence of divorce is thus notable for its offensiveness. Perhaps no outcome other than the prohibitive one then freezing into position was at all possible. But an argument could have been made in measured style, aimed at keeping majority and minority in dialogue with each other. In strictly denominational terms, at least one Protestant bishop was opposed to permitting divorce, and in symbolic terms Yeats (as we have seen) was not averse to presenting himself in the Catholic colours of a suitably remote Medicean papacy. But these cross-party positions were never to be the basis for any reconciliation, if such involved compromise. National unity was to be forged in the heat of conflict. Swift's hatred and Burke's 'gothick side', these alternative configurations were taken up in the 1930s, with 'the people of Burke and of Grattan' ('The Tower', 1928) serving as an elegiac bridging section in the complex development of Yeats's retrospective politics.

Yeats's last senatorial battle revolved round censorship. This was an issue on which he had honed his talents as a controversialist many years earlier, but especially in 1909 during a series of disputes with the British authorities. His sincerity as an opponent of literary censorship cannot be questioned. But writing in *The Spectator* on 29 September 1928, he revealed an element of deliberate provocativeness which I have suspected in his earlier peroration on divorce: 'There are irresponsible moments when I hope that the Bill will pass in its present form, or be amended by the Republicans [i.e. Fianna Fáil], as some foretell, into a still more drastic form, and force all men of intellect, who mean to spend their lives here, into a common understanding.'[6] These words were never spoken in the Senate, from which, on 18 July 1928, he in effect withdrew due to sudden ill health. Yeats had already indicated his decision not to seek re-election by government, and subsequent discussion of the proposed censorship took place without him. His opposition was not a parliamentary one, though it lacked neither vigour nor detail.

Yeats's health dictated that he should spend the winters abroad, and to this end he moved in early November to Italy, where of course censorship flourished. Before this, however, two articles appeared, both already noted. In addition to the piece in *The Spectator*, there was 'The Censorship and St Thomas Aquinas', published in the *Irish Statesman* on 22 September 1928. He did not formally cease to be a Senator until 28 November, on which day he took possession of a new apartment in Rapallo. No one could complain about an ailing man's failure to attend the Senate during his last few weeks as a member: Yeats had diligently voted on bills to drain the River Barrow, advocated independent inspection of the prisons, chaired his committees with great success, and generally acquitted himself excellently as an ageing but devoted Senator. There is of course the suspicion that his non-senatorial political expression came closer to his heart's desire, however impractical that might have been.

Yeats being a writer, censorship was both a political and a personal matter. Nevertheless, his opposition was less than total. As far as books were concerned, he remained unmoved when *Manhattan Transfer* (1925), a novel by the American socialist John Dos Passos (1896–1970), was banned. Censorship did not earn his general condemnation. Only when the pressure was directed locally did he respond with his full powers. Prohibition of Liam O'Flaherty's *The Puritan* in 1932 led to an interview with the *Manchester Guardian* while, on the political front, Yeats revived his earlier Federation of the Arts project in the form of an Irish Academy of Letters, which would defend literature (but not necessarily any other form of expression) against government prohibitions. To this end, he set up the gourmet fascist Walter Starkie as secretary to the academy.

Yeats's attitude to newspapers was increasingly coloured by his condemnation of propaganda. As on most topics, he reserved the right to contradict himself. Thus, in November 1938 when the Abbey was rejecting a new play by Paul Vincent Carroll and planning a revival of his own 'Purgatory', Yeats wrote to F. R. Higgins in the following terms:

> Send Carroll those extracts from my letter if you wish. They are logically incomplete without the statement that the play might endanger the future of the Abbey. We obviously would not have rejected it merely because it was propaganda considering the excellence of its kind. I recognise,

however, that you may not think it wise to draw his attention to the peril in which the Abbey might be, as we cannot explain our present relation to the Government.[7]

This does not read like a manifesto of artistic independence, but, in the global scheme of things, it was hardly a headline issue.

The course of world events after 1930 provided matter for report, which gave more than ample scope for complacent ignorance, distortion, partisan comment and downright lying. Manipulation of the press during the Great War (by George Mair, amongst others) has sometimes been blamed for the decline in standards that persisted through the post-war diplomatic struggles, the Wall Street Crash and into the low dishonest decade. But a newspaper is a complex thing, written by many hands, overseen by competing authorities (editors, proprietors, shareholders, advertisers) and depending on circulation in a public market that is very rarely unifocal, and never unifocal on all issues. To damn even a single issue of a newspaper as propaganda is like damning the rainbow because it is red.

Manipulation of the news certainly bothered Yeats. He knew, however, that during the Black and Tan war the English press had done more to publicise official atrocities and general brutality than most politicians in Westminster. The English journalist Hugh Martin worked in the knowledge that forces of the Crown had sworn to kill him. When the Irish Free State was established, some members of the new Establishment came to dislike the variety of news carried in imported British papers. Desmond FitzGerald was particularly disturbed by reports of crime involving sex; others looked to the small-ads column where details of birth-control methods were publicised. Beyond the Establishment, republican sympathisers recognised the wiles of Perfidious Albion. Periodic attacks on the distribution of English papers in Ireland emphasised an underlying violence of opinion on issues affecting religious or political identity. Though the Yeatses practised birth-control, and the poet avidly read crime novels (not necessarily with a sex content), he made no general defence of press freedom for these reasons or better. Instead, he informed his English readers that Irish government ministers did not wish for the powers they were about to confer on themselves: these resulted from special interest lobbies, of a clericalist kind. It is true that, in *The Spectator* article of September 1928, he mocked those who 'think that if they could exclude English newspapers, with their police-court cases which excite the imagination . . . innocence would return'.[8] His general comment on newspapers increasingly featured a blanket jeremiad against manipulation. Echoing words from his *Spectator* article, *On the Boiler* went further in 1938/39:

> I beg our governments to exclude all alien appeal to mass instincts. The Irish mind has still, in country rapscallion or in Bernard Shaw, an ancient, cold, explosive, detonating impartiality. The English mind, excited by its newspaper proprietors and its schoolmasters, has turned into a bed-hot harlot.[9]

It took time to reach this pitch of censorious enthusiasm. The press in post-war Britain had come under the control of 'barons' who tried to use their papers as political forces. Rothermere and Northcliffe wielded more influence than the average government minister, who had but one voice in cabinet and was constrained by the protocols of the civil service. Dublin-born Cecil Harmsworth of the *Daily Mail* was a prime example: Yeats was on dining terms since 1926 and, though the paper was positively pro-Nazi in the 1930s, nothing inhibited Yeats from approving a Harmsworth Prize for his Academy of Letters – the impartial Shaw refused to act as a judge. The purpose of the prize was manifestly political and designed to forge links with Germany – the honouring of Roger Casement. Nor was Yeats deterred from consulting Lord Harmsworth in May 1938 on the future of the Cuala Press.

A Postscript on Jack Yeats

In listing the Blood Kindred, or at least a representative group of them, we have strangely ignored the claims of blood-kinship. Among the extended Yeats family there were a few individuals who shared some of his ideas about the supernatural, the occult and the realm of the dead. On the surface, the person to whom he publicly alluded in this connection was George Pollexfen (1839–1910), who joined the Order of the Golden Dawn, concerned himself with his nephew's plans for a Celtic Order of Mysteries and was finally buried with full masonic honours. Pollexfen's clairvoyant servant Mary Battle (d. 1908) had mediumistic abilities together with a vast repertoire of folk legend; there was, however, no blood-link between her and the Pollexfens or Yeatses. As the poet often stayed at Thornhill, the Victorian semi-detached house in Sligo where she looked after her employer, Battle might be regarded as one of a domestic circle, but not 'kindred'.

Her dreams of horsemen on the mountains enclosing Sligo have been taken as material reflected in some of Yeats's late poems, including the 'Three Songs to the One Burden'. Susan Mary Yeats (1866–1949, known as Lily) was the older of his two sisters, who recounted dreams which the family took as evidence of otherworldly existences. Despite the comparative intimacy between these two, the women of Yeats's household – mother and sisters – play a very minor role in the psychic-drama he systematised in *A Vision*. Blood, it might even be suspected, precluded kindredship. For obvious reasons, much the same might be said of the two siblings who died in infancy – Jane Grace Yeats (1875–1876) and Robert Corbet Yeats (1870–1873) – though we will have reason to turn to the last-named before *Blood Kindred* is finally laid to rest.

For the moment, however, the decks are cleared for a classic encounter of brother with brother, Shem with Sean. At what other point in a biography of William Butler Yeats should one introduce his younger brother, the painter John (Jack) Butler Yeats (1871–1957)? In a book organised more conventionally on chronological lines, the two children would appear together in the early pages, gradually diverging as they choose their vocations, and then by agreement leaving the ground solely to the principal subject. With politics as the organising theme, and with the Blood Kindred serving as Greek chorus, this neat arrangement (flattering of the principal subject) does not apply. Jack Yeats disagreed with his brother on political issues, and their differences provide a means of judging the poet's relationship to family origins. When their father died in February 1922, the younger son paid him a tribute that (unwittingly, no doubt) reflected on the elder's choice of art. 'Like most fine talkers, I think he had a simple nature which flowed on. Talking is not such an usurpation as writing, which becomes mortised into a man's soul. Truthfully painting does nothing but reveal.'[10]

In the early 1920s, the two supported opposing sides in the civil war, Jack providing 'safe-house' accommodation for Republicans, and Willy decorating the Free State Senate, consolidating the socially conservative rule of W. T. Cosgrave and his cabinet. A comparison between 'On a Political Prisoner' (the poem of 1919) and 'Communicating with Prisoners' (Jack's picture of 1924) involves a larger time-span than the civil war, and serves to underscore the extent and nature of fraternal conflict.[11] The picture presents an image of friends and relatives attempting to signal to prisoners in high jail windows:

isolation and community seek each other in the grey light of war. The poem is a chilly reflection on the incarceration of Countess Markiewicz, though inspiration came from the similar plight of Maud Gonne with whom Yeats was briefly feuding. An ability to transfer his focus from one unmanageable female revolutionary to another sheds its own light on questions of sincerity, inspiration and aesthetic tactics.

The Spanish Civil War polarised opinion in Europe. W. B. Yeats's response was ambiguous, hating as he did socialism and politicised Catholicism with impartiality. Jack's position has to be inferred from less firmly mortised evidence.[12] At home, the latter's friendship with the Jewish painter Estella Solomons, with the Sinclair family and their kinsman Samuel Beckett, kept channels open to continental influences, as did the devout Catholic critic and poet, Thomas MacGreevy. Beckett and MacGreevy were part of the Joyce circle in Paris, and the development of the Yeats brothers' work suggests that Jack Yeats and James Joyce employed increasingly fluid techniques, with rhythm and colour ebbing and flowing within confident formal structures. The poet acknowledged this similarity in 1930, comparing Jack's book, *Sligo*, with *Work-in-Progress*.[13] Willy's own late style, in contrast, emphasised a strong line, often preferring the beat to the rhythm, and (in grammar) favouring the imperative mood.

At the end of the 1930s, when the poet was in full spate against democracy – 'muck in the yard' – Jack Yeats was moving in quite another direction. Forebodings of war's disclosures break like anxiety lines in 'The Tinkers' Encampment', also known as 'The Blood of Abel' (1941), its double-name encapsulating a local culture intimately known and an international catastrophe. According to MacGreevy, the picture was based on Christ's denunciation of those who had rejected the prophets and wise men, 'that upon you may come all the righteous blood shed upon the earth, from the blood of righteous Abel unto the blood of Zacharias, son of Barachias, whom ye slew between the temple and the altar (Matthew 23:35)'. Inspection of the canvas certainly confirms the accuracy of the alternative title, through the depiction of horses, canvas-covered vehicles and ragged figures. Blood-shedding was thought by the settled community to be a common pastime among tinkers (now known as Travellers), a verdict reached without factoring in its own crusades, persecutions, wars and capital sentences. Jack Yeats brings the tinkers in from the margins, as his friend Synge had done in a play – 'The Tinkers' Wedding' –

deemed too immoral for Dublin in the early twentieth century. He also historicises the Christian perspective on violence and exclusion. So far from being bloodthirsty, the Christ to whom MacGreevy directs us is the reluctant seer who would rather 'have gathered thy children together, even as a hen gathereth her chickens under her wings, and ye would not!' The brother-poet's adoption of John Mitchel's prayer invites comparison.

In March 1922, as the civil warriors were girding their loins, Jack Yeats wrote to Joseph Hone in tones of mild admonishment, 'No one creates ... the artist assembles memories.'[14] Brother William was at work on *A Vision*, that is, on creating unknown experience. Soon, he would commend the creation of tradition. The Romantic ideology of artistic creativity proved singularly inappropriate in the mid-twentieth century, when unprecedented orgies of human destruction occurred, and not without warning. Some who believed they could create were willing to deny the destruction.

Behind the brothers lay their father, the splendidly erratic and cussed John Butler Yeats (1839–1922), who spent his final years as a permanently short-term exile in New York. 'Old JB', as he tended to become in the exasperated talk of his many friends, was the antithesis of dominating patriarch in that he was himself a rebel against inherited values and beliefs. An artist, an agnostic, an incorrigible non-finisher of tasks, he provided little provocation to Oedipal rebellion in his sons, thus frustrating what Freud at least would regard as a foundational element in the modern male's psychology. His influence on Willie and Jack differed in each case, but it is relatively easy to chart his determined resistance to his elder son's opinions, while admiring his success. 'The men whom Nietzsche's theory fits are only great men of a sort, a sort of Yahoo great men. The struggle is how to get rid of them, they belong to the clumsy and brutal side of things ...' Thus Old JB in 1906, before he had left for America. Later, after the hegira, and wishing Willie well with 'The Player Queen', he took delight in relating his son's longed-for success in the theatre to the claims of democracy. 'Democratic art is that sort which unites a whole audience ... I am sure that in Ancient Greece drama was democratic ... In these thoughts I think Lady Gregory ought to agree with me – she has a democratic fibre.'[15] This was not the only aspect to the Prodigal Father's mind, but it was one against which his elder son could revolt.

Blood

We know that ghosts cannot speak until they have drunk blood;
and the spirits which we evoke demand the blood of our hearts. We
give it to them gladly; but if they then abide our question,
something from us has entered into them; something alien, that
must be cast out in the name of truth.

Tycho von Wilamowitz-Möllendorf, *Greek Historical Writing*, 1908

Though Yeats was in important ways Robert Lowell's great precursor
as public poet, on questions of blood they differed in strikingly
simple ways. The older of the two could intone, 'Send war in our
time, O Lord', and do so when the Almighty had little choice but to
comply. Lowell (1917–1977), a puritan convert to Catholicism and
pacifism, came to poetic maturity through mental confrontation with
the Second World War, the blasphemous answer to Yeats's prayer. It
might be possible to argue – at least for a moment or two – that
remarks like Yeats's should not be taken literally. After all, the phrase,
occurring in the third section of 'Under Ben Bulben', is attributed to
the nineteenth-century Irish rebel, John Mitchel, and (in any case)
parodies the Book of Common Prayer. Aggressive rewriting of a
Protestant liturgy is noteworthy in both Mitchel and Yeats, the
former the son of a liberal Presbyterian in County Down and the
latter the grandson of an absentee rector hostile to his Presbyterian
counterpart in the same county. Yet when we read Yeats's interview
with the *Irish Independent* of August 1938, it is difficult to maintain
this distinction between what is said and what is meant. War has a
sublime pedigree as poetic metaphor – in Milton, in Blake, for
example – but it is hard to see how a specific endorsement of Nazi
legislation can be read as the image of something less lethal, more
liberal. Vegetarians have derived little comfort from the example of
Herr Hitler.

Despite Yeats's prominent attribution of his 1938 prayer to John
Mitchel, it is likely that the source lay closer to hand. In *John Bull's
Other Empire*, Roger Casement had invoked similar sentiments in

relation to a world war in which he sought German support against Britain; on the eve of a second war, Yeats performed yet another of his exercises in editing history, omitting the avowedly pro-German Casement to invoke Mitchel instead, a sea-green incorruptible of remoter times. Mitchel's war had been fought and lost back in 1865, between Confederate America and the abolitionist northern states. Mitchel had supported the Confederacy, and Negro slavery with it. Largely forgotten in Irish nationalist commemorations, the American Civil War had been in several ways the first truly and terribly modern conflict, involving technology (especially railways) on an unprecedented scale and heralding the even greater slaughter of combatants in 1914–18. The social and cultural scars inflicted by Union and Confederate are traceable like a Braille text in twentieth-century American literature, not only that written by southerners like William Faulkner and Flannery O'Connor, but in Hemingway, Lowell and Norman Mailer. More abstractly and practically, von Clausewitz's celebrated but outmoded dictum was in the process of cynical revision; from now on, war was to feature as the advancement of science by other means.

On the Boiler (1939), with a Digression on Canaries

Yeats's last pronouncements were highly political, and they embraced topics ranging from education to warfare. Woven throughout his distinctly transgressive opinions was a concern with science unsuspected by many of his close readers over the years. Officially Yeats detested science, though he studied alchemy and magic, with which seventeenth-century scientists like Isaac Newton (1642–1727) had maintained a dialogue. Throughout his life he engaged with various kinds of science and pseudo-science, including parapsychology and eugenics, but preferred to call them by other names. Yeats was not the only member of his generation to revere alchemy: August Strindberg (1849–1912) engaged more practically with the notion, but Strindberg (unlike Yeats) has been recognised as clinically insane at times. When Yeats followed up the ideas and experiences of friends with tenacity, the results were sensibly classified with other 'metaphors for poetry'. The high-arch time-span implied through figures like Newton and John Locke (1632–1704) is visible in a few sardonic lines in 'Fragments' [1], of 1931:

Locke sank into a swoon;
The Garden died;
God took the spinning jenny
Out of his side.

Although the imagery of this is ironically drawn from everything
Yeats detested, the few lines may suggest a rereading of his larger
philosophical position as Magic Darwinism, an outlook or cultivated
social habit that concedes the projectory of modern science while
substituting irrational terms. His intermittent enthusiasm for 'the
new', together with a naïve recourse to pseudo-sciences such as
biologist eugenics, and his more impressive citations of geometry,
slowly amount to a ghost-rationalism. More locally and politically,
Yeats's rejection of Victorian positivism and physicalism might be
recognised as his means of overlooking the long decades and centuries
that lay between the time of his family settlement in Ireland and the
moment of his own conception, bodily and spiritually, as a child of
displacement. Even the spinning jenny, which he contemptuously
relates to Eve as a product of Adam's spare rib, can look strangely
like an allusion to the linen industry from which his grandfather fled.

Yet science, even those lesser popularising discourses of daftness,
will take its revenge on Yeats for his casualness. His sources for
oracular remarks on intelligence and biology in *On the Boiler* (1939)
are second-hand at best, and largely unexamined. At moments like
these, one becomes aware of how much in arrears Yeats could fall in
his subscription to Idealism. Nevertheless, if he struts vertiginously
towards a totalitarian, potentially racist, position in this regard, his
persistent attachment to an imagined past distinguishes him from the
German conservative revolutionaries (Martin Heidegger, Ernst
Jünger, Carl Schmitt, etc.) for whom only a well-regimented
Armageddon held out any prospect of *Kultur*. That attachment
nurtured images of human community, efficacious intelligence, even
content and fulfilment in the individual. But the period of Yeats's
devotion to that vision does not extend into his last decade, or at least
not very far into it. In the posthumously published work one finds
him abandoning the distinction between his own aggressive caution
and the headlong decisionism of the Germans. In that context, it may
be timely to recall Oscar Wilde's comments on activity and reflection:
'There is always something peculiarly impotent about the violence of
a literary man. It seems to bear no reference to facts, for it is never
kept in check by action.'[1]

In Yeats's case, two networks had served to hold these explosive tendencies together – almost to the end. One was a remarkably articulate, if selective, ideology of the family: 'those who had power in Ireland', as he rather touchingly expressed it in 1914. There is a blurring in his formulation of these important precursors, a blurring between kindred in some strict ancestral (or biological) sense and (on the other hand) kindred in the sense of social affinity or mental agreement. Power, it seems, authorises such blurring. Or, to be more critical, the blurring allows power to present itself as authority. We see much of this in his treatment of ancestors:

> When Huguenot artists designed the tapestries for the Irish House of Lords, depicting the Battle of the Boyne and the siege of Derry, they celebrated the defeat of their old enemy Louis XIV, and the establishment of a Protestant Ascendency [sic] which was to impose upon Catholic Ireland, an oppression copied in all its details from that imposed upon the French Protestants. Did my own great-great-grandmother, the Huguenot Marie Voisin feel a vindictive triumph, or did she remember that her friend Archbishop King had been a loyal servant of James II and had, unless greatly slandered, accepted his present master after much vacillation, and that despite Episcopal vehemence, his clergy were suspected of a desire to restore a Catholic family to the English throne [?]. The Irish House of Lords, however, when it ordered the Huguenot tapestries, probably accepted the weavers [sic] argument that the Battle of the Boyne was to Ireland what the defeat of the Armada was to England. Armed with this new power, they were to modernise the social structure, with great cruelty but effectively, and to establish our political nationality by quarrelling with England over the woolen trade, a protestant monopoly.[2]

In the sentence where he acknowledges the modernising role of his Protestant ascendancy, he instances the Irish woollen trade. That is, he instances the commercial nexus – textiles – from which the pedlar Jarvis Yeats launched the family's social ascent. In the 1760s, the spinning jenny revolutionised what the Huguenots had set in place, and the way lay open for the conversion of small-scale craft monopolies into a mass industry linked to increased democratisation of the lower classes. With *On the Boiler*, Yeats repudiates that historical development, root and branch.

The problems with which Yeats was struggling in the late nineteenth century were by no means unique to Ireland, nor was nationalism the only solution proposed. Traditionally, nationalism has been presented as a Great-Chain-of-Being-Irish, unbroken and uniform from the arrival of the Celts to the departure of everyone else. His play of 1919, 'The Dreaming of the Bones', is based upon just such a popular notion, and his even more cryptic phrases about preserving the ancient deposit mobilise it. ('Ancient' in turn becomes a favourite adjective of the biographer.) But nationalism is a relatively recent phenomenon, and its terminology has been used in a variety of ways. For Yeats certainly, and for others less consciously, late-nineteenth-century nationalism was not necessarily a form of democracy, a revolt of the Irish majority against external rule; it was embraced precisely because it articulated minority and because it valorised minority at a time when mass society was growing exponentially. His rebuke of John Eglinton in 1901 had signalled the merely relative value and strategic place of 'nation' in Yeats's cultural politics. A speech on Home Rule is exceptional which, by its un-Yeatsian concessionary rhythms, proves the rule. In this sense, the sudden turning upon democracy in 1923 and 1924 is no contradiction of his earlier devotion to the Irish people, their literary tradition and their political cause. At the end of his life, he could write, 'I am no nationalist, except in Ireland for passing reasons.' The preceding sentences indicate the extent to which he had embraced the ethics of 1870:

> When I stand upon O'Connell Bridge [Dublin] in the half-light and notice that discordant architecture, all those electric signs, where modern heterogeneity has taken physical form, a vague hatred comes up out of my own dark and I am certain that wherever in Europe there are minds strong enough to lead others the same vague hatred rises; in four or five or in less generations this hatred will have issued in violence and imposed some kind of rule of kindred. I cannot know the nature of that rule, for its opposite fills the light; all I can do to bring it nearer is to intensify my hatred.[3]

It is at such points that one recalls the immediate response of Archibald MacLeish who emphasised Yeats's isolation, being in Ireland, and Yeats's demonstration of this isolation in mistaking the American's meaning. 'A General Introduction for My Work' (1937) conducts its hatred under the highest auspices – those of transcendental idealism – 'the world knows nothing because it has made nothing, we know everything because we have made everything'. This may be fine as *Spätstil* but, in terms of poetry and politics, it strongly echoes his response to the murder of the 'strong man' of Irish politics, Kevin O'Higgins, ten years earlier:

> Nor dread nor hope attend
> A dying animal;

A man awaits his end
Dreading and hoping all;
Many times he died,
Many times rose again.
A great man in his pride
Confronting murderous men
Casts derision upon
Supercession of breath;
He knows death to the bone –
Man has created death.

Here Berkeley and Heidegger stare in puzzlement at each other across the politician's grave. Yeats's idealism, deriving as much from the nineteenth-century revival of Berkeleyanism and from the British school of Bradley and Bosanquet as from the arcane ancients whom he prefers to cite, proves itself to be synonymous with brutal cynicism and the glorification of death. Perhaps that is precisely why the nineteenth-century mediators of the idealist tradition are given short shrift in Yeats's account of his philosophy. In the same way, he acknowledges Parnell and the consequences of Parnell's fall, but does so in the context of his own acknowledgment by the Nobel Committee and its acknowledgment in turn of Irish independence as embodied in him. In other words, Parnell's place as the culmination of a nineteenth-century political process is silently denied. There is certainly now a counter-case to made, arguing that Yeats's conservatism – to use a mellow term – stands in direct continuity with the Toryism of Parnell's predecessor, the young 'Orange' Isaac Butt and his colleagues in the *Dublin University Magazine* of the 1830s, colleagues whom it has been repeatedly averred included the Revd W. B. Yeats. Not the least of these young Tories was the Platonist, William Archer Butler (1814–1848), whose early death was greatly lamented by some who looked for a revival of philosophical politics in Ireland.

As we have seen, Yeats consciously inherited no tradition of political discourse. Instead of a philosophical politics, the poet provided as the lesser of his contributions to Irish culture a politicised history. He was by no means its only begetter. But the brilliance of his expression and dramatic ordering of the material has eclipsed lesser figures, so that it is they who linger under the accusation of tendentiousness while he works *per amica silentia lunae*. A first stage of the process concentrated on the creation of an Irish canon of literature, initially discounting the eighteenth century and strongly representing the recent Victorian past; a second stage, implicit in the first, reversed these evaluations. Historians would of course dispute many of Yeats's assumptions; most recently the notion that Protestant Ascendancy could be traced earlier than the 1780s has been effectively exploded. But veracity is not the issue at stake. Instead, what we find is that, through the central image or event of death, family history and national history are refashioned in each other's image, the Yeatses and the century of ascendancy finally achieve congruence, not without a little chivvying help from the *Catholic Bulletin.* The poet's later interest in eugenics, in the family as the basis of civilisation, is inevitably read through his authoritarian politics. But his historiography, whether in relation to the fall of Parnell or the achievements of the Irish eighteenth century, is of a piece with this. Yeats has, in a multiplicity of textual revisions, projected into history his own notion of a precursor culture in which the social experience of his Victorian forebears featured – at the most – intermittently. In this special sense, he makes himself, like a man editing his own appearance in *Burke's Landed Gentry.*

Two recent contributions to the *Yeats Annual* have helped to clarify the relationship between this poetic undertaking and the role of sexuality in modernist literature. In the first, the poet's dedication to the female muse of classical tradition is considered, particularly in relation to the late plays where a violent struggle between her and the male author is repeatedly enacted. Tim Armstrong is concerned to relate this theme to Yeats's vasectomy in 1934, to the ensuing affairs with younger women, and to what he terms 'the sexualised text'.[4] If the overall objective of these endeavours was to give birth to oneself, then the implications were not solely personal. Self-begetting must eliminate all progenitors, all ancestors, from whom Yeats now no longer seeks – or can no longer hope for – 'pardon'. The sexual theories that he practices in the 1930s deny his real, immediate ancestry, with the imagined community of Protestant Ascendancy substituted instead, together with touching detail of Swift's association with shadowy Voisin relatives and the absurd notion of Swift as ancestor to the poet Wellesley. The historiography implicit in Yeats's sexual theories combines with a contemporary politics; for the Steinach operation (in effect a vasectomy) not only prefaces a renewal of poetic creativity, but also coincides with acceptance of the Goethe-Plakette, and inaugurates the engagements with Nazism which are implicit in the Ossietzky affair in 1936 and the approval of German legislation in August 1938. Finding the Blue Shirts inadequate to his needs, Yeats empowered himself within the conventional or traditional sexual roles of poet and muse, and found that the endorsement of a more violent politics followed by necessity.

The second article relevant to this aspect of his thought politely corrects the impression, given in Cullingford's standard treatment of Yeats's politics, that his interest in eugenics was comparatively innocent. David Bradshaw has gone further than any previous enquirer in demonstrating how Yeats's involvement with the Eugenics Society aligned him with a particular faction within the movement, one that stressed hereditarian (or 'biologist') rather than environmental explanations of 'degenerate' human beings. While the reform eugenicists were anxious to dissociate themselves from developments in Germany after 1933, the member whose work Yeats explicitly cites in *On the Boiler* – Raymond B. Cattell – was of a different persuasion. In *Psychology and Social Progress* (1933), Cattell had declared that 'the country which first adopts eugenic measures of a strongly positive kind will be the first to pull itself out of the universal decline and, if it can devise methods to protect itself from destruction in the crash of neighbouring states, it has every prospect of inheriting the earth'.[5]

Yeats joined the society in November 1936, and his principal topic of interest was the measurement of intelligence among the leisured classes (which he had at last joined). His concern was not the engendering of a large, healthy population – as was the case among French eugenicists and, with a different emphasis, among German exponents of selective breeding. Where France and Germany could complain that the Great War had decimated the population and left the State undermanned, Ireland's experience (though less recent) had been of dangerous overpopulation at the time of the Famine. This was a formative trauma for John Mitchel, and it even surfaces momentarily in the exclusively urban world of Joyce's *Dubliners*. A threatened repetition of the calamity provides a motive of Faustian proportions in 'The Countess Cathleen'. Irish nationalism, as valorised minority, offered an ideal basis for an experimental escape from demographic Whiggery. To this end, the mature Yeats was concerned to reduce the size of families as well as to breed selectively for 'intelligence'. 'The Quality', not quantity, was his desire.

With Yeats's diverse activities, it is important to note the coincidence of events. Membership of the Eugenics Society was effected in the same month that Ossietzky belatedly won the Nobel Peace Prize. The latter event had been carefully planned, with an increase of press coverage in the weeks before the final announcement (24/25 November 1936) in Stockholm. Given the furore in Claridge's Hotel when Mannin and Toller had tried to recruit Yeats to the Ossietzky campaign, he cannot have forgotten the German prisoner when he paid his fees to the Eugenics Society. But contention rapidly ensued. Cattell's next publication was effectively disowned by the society, not least for his disturbing blend of military similes and applause for the German government's 'being the first to adopt sterilisation together with a positive emphasis on racial improvement'.[6] It was this publication, *The Fight for Our National Intelligence,* which Yeats endorsed in On *the Boiler,* where military simile veers sharply towards military planning. As with the Blue Shirts in the early 1930s, Yeats parted from questionable company by moving to a more – not less – extreme position. In the very late 1930s, any remaining element of hesitancy in Yeats's decisionism was suddenly reduced, like a drop below zero in the moral temperature.

He was in possession also of material emanating from Nazi Germany, and published in English. In his copy of *German Education Today,* he would have read how, since 1933, the government had decreed that more time should be spent on 'the literature, history and geography' of Germany and on 'ethnology, heredity, racial hygiene, genealogy, and population policy'. Since December 1935, special education had been provided for those destined 'to prepare the future *Erbhofbauer* (owner of a hereditary farm) for all those tasks which the Reich hereditary farm law has imposed upon him'.[7] Whether *German Education Today* was his principal source or not, this latter provision was part of the legislation that Yeats approved in the *Irish Independent* interview of August 1938. The intent of these laws was to dispossess non-Aryans, among whom the Jews were pre-eminent.

If Yeats's reading of this booklet remains an unverifiable/unfalsifiable matter, there are areas where concrete conclusions may be reached. The reassembling of Yeats's commitments for November 1936, dispersed as they have been by apologists for his 'liberal anti-whiggery', must go a long way towards laying the foundation for a fuller appreciation of his engagement with German politics and the issues of race and medicine implicated in fascism. Yet perhaps the most telling aspect of Bradshaw's article is his publication of some preliminary drafts for *On the Boiler*, which refer back to the nineteenth century. These are fragmentary and gnomic, but from their cancelled lines there emerges an unlikely name – that of John Stuart Mill. The argument is itself like a palimpsest, with one statement all but obliterated under another. Nevertheless, textual excavation below the record of Yeats's excitement in reading Cattell uncovers the earlier excitement caused by William Morris's translation of *Sigurd the Volsung*. The interplay between contemporary controversy and ancient saga is a familiar Yeatsian motif, and it is replicated in the drafts through allusion to a letter in the *Eugenics Review* commending Robert Burton's *Anatomy of Melancholy* (1621). Yeats's renewed interest in baroque melancholia is paralleled and contrasted in the work of Walter Benjamin, whose *Ursprung des Deutschen Trauerspiels* (1928) proposed a subtle taxonomy of literary genres in which Yeats himself find a niche.

The nineteenth century is the faithful unbarking dog in Yeats's night-thoughts, his dark and private philosophy of history. In biographical terms, a crucial encounter remains that between Yeats and his father, the progenitor whom any theory of self-begetting must eliminate. While the draft cited by Bradshaw says that 'Mill & Ruskin were not the cause of our quarrel', the passage persists in reciting the principal items of the great nineteenth-century debates – young Yeats had berated 'the English government because of Ireland' and now saw his father as having been 'like Walt Whitman a mystical democrat'. Unable to reconcile his own attachment to Ireland with the implied rejection of democracy, he concludes, 'I gave myself up to a dream of the best bread [*sic*] from the best.' Here is something close to an admission that self-begetting is at best a private dream, at its unspeakable worst a political nightmare from which millions did not awaken.[8]

This is not a meretricious reading of *On the Boiler*. In a sentence that has escaped lengthy analysis, Yeats refers to a Negro girl who lived near Sligo in his childhood. She possessed the rare ability to discover plovers' nests, but despite this affinity with nature she is classified 'among those our civilisation must reject'. Is Yeats here momentarily re-enacting Mitchel's endorsement of American slavery or, even less palatably, enlisting in the school of Rosenberg and Goebbels? The word 'must' appears with extraordinary frequency in these late writings, finally dominating the three-point statement on eugenics and psychical research, dated 23 December 1938. If the girl must be rejected, there will be little finessing about the manner in which she and her kind are to be disposed of. And yet, if there was a mind to, a 'liberal' reading could be attempted. It would run along lines like these: the Negro girl, like the poet, possessed a heightened affinity with nature and, for that reason, she like him lies outside what is (by this reading) 'our civilisation'. The latter phrase has to be ironically inflected if the liberal reading is to stand, and the effort to ironise the passage will prove insupportable. Why? Because Yeats begins first to assimilate the girl to a class he condescended to revere but never remotely belonged to – the peasantry, in whom a similar affinity to nature is assumed – and then, second, substitutes for her Negroness an Asian affinity dreamed up from a German Idealist nowhere. 'Among these peasants, there is much of Asia, where Hegel has said every civilisation begins.' Yeats's editors struggle to gloss this, while his biographers give it the cold shoulder. In the end, 'we must hold to what we have that the next civilisation may be born, not from a virgin's womb, nor a tomb without a body, not from a void, but from our own rich experience'.[9] In this version of Yeats's replacement of Christianity by some new dispensation, a Germanic ideology specifically linked to the elimination of a racially defined person is unmistakable. If allusion to William Morris had been played down in Yeats's published account of Cattell, it emerges here as the climactic of his rejection of the Negress: *Sigurd the Volsung* (1876) is quoted exactly at that point where the ultimate White Teutonic hero (aka Siegfried) is born, who now in Yeats's text of 1939 effaces the black 'Asiatic' Christian dispensation most recently noted in the independent Ethiopian kingdom lost to Mussolini. The particular victim cited as an example is, potentially at least, identifiable to the historical biographer, for she was a resident of Rosses Point perhaps more permanently than Yeats was, a subject of Queen Victoria as he was, if not an apple of Maud Gonne's eye.

The Negro is a point of reference more economically traced in Yeats's correspondence than abstract and variable terms like 'hatred'. The association of the girl at Rosses Point with wild birds may have arisen in his mind through an intermediary reference in his correspondence with Olivia Shakespear, mother-in-law of Ezra Pound. Having despatched *The Trembling of the Veil* to his publisher in the summer of 1922, and placing undue confidence in a civil war truce, Yeats was inclined to digress happily:

I interrupt my letter at intervals to watch my canaries in their big cage

where there are two nests [–] one, which disturbs George, is the nest of a
half caste, a bird that looks half sparrow & it threatens to abound in
young. It is the American negro question & all the worse because
George's energetic mind has conceived a project of selling canaries
through the newspapers. Who will want half castes?[10]

Perhaps this was an isolated jest between former lovers, and
perhaps its racialist flavour comes under the 'culturalist' rubric, which
Jurgen Habermas found adequate in the case of Heidegger and the
Jews. But it is a flavour that biographers have not developed in
confecting Yeats's attitude towards race.

The same discretion doubtless explains their neglect of the poet's
gleeful account of Nancy Cunard living in a 'negro hotel' in Harlem,
New York's black district, an account duplicated in letters to his wife
and Olivia Shakespear.[11] This was in May 1932, when the European
debate about race was warming up in German streets. Two years
later, and pursuing a mentally unstable actress, Yeats took up the
digression once more. At a loss how to proceed with a poem for
Margot Collis, he sought vigorous male company. Gogarty was not
available, so he made do eventually with Dermot MacManus, at
whom we will look more closely in due course. Hour by hour,
MacManus diverted Yeats with 'astonishing stories of North Africa[n] Negroes'. The letter does not specify what characteristics of
these people astonished Yeats, who records no astonishment at the
suggestion that there *were* Negroes in North Africa. But the pen-
portrait of the raconteur indirectly says a lot. Described by Yeats as a
lame ex-British officer and Free-State general [*sic*], MacManus had
suffered wounds in the Great War that 'had given him my inhibition
and several others' now cured by oriental meditations:

> Every morning he stands before his mirror and commands himself to
> become more positive, more masculine, more independent of the feelings
> of others. Six months ago he was ordered off the hunting field by a
> political enemy. He turned his horse and rode the man down. If he goes
> on with those meditations he will be murdered. His hobby is Asia and
> North Africa.[12]

Perhaps this was an isolated jest between new lovers, though the
'inhibition' that afflicted Yeats without any origin in the Great War
remains near-inscrutable. (Brenda Maddox diagnoses impotence.[13])
What is plainly clear is that, in Yeats's language, Negro means sex.
This does not make him a virulent racist but, together with the

chicken-butcher-as-paedophile, it makes his Vision of the Blood Kindred a less liberal reception committee.

'Coole and Ballylee, 1931': Augusta Gregory as Victim

It is fitting that the commentator who pre-emptively acquitted Yeats of any fascist inclinations should also commend his feminism. In each case, evidence may yet jeopardise her achievements. Just as the nameless little black girl of Victorian Sligo obtrudes into Yeats's post-Abyssinian reminiscences, so the celebrated name of Augusta Gregory carries with it a concealed history – a textual history, in this case, through which one finds the poet borrowing from personal accounts of surgery endured under local anaesthetic.

One of the most serviceable clichés employed to describe literary Modernism specifies montage as a characteristic device. Perhaps the idea, as a critical response to the bewildering internal prolixity – and odd, concomitant poverty – of texts by Joyce, Mann, Pound and others, derives from the visual arts where the example of Georges Braque provided dozens of instances. For montage essentially depends on the ability of the viewer to see the physical effects of juxtaposing material from an external source together with the inner texture of the composition in question. To an extent, then, montage cannot be fully reproduced as a literary technique and must always slide towards being a form of allusiveness, to be apprehended in different degrees by different readers. The tactile fact of a border existing between the two kinds of material employed, obvious enough in a picture, has no equivalent in a written composition.

This ambiguity of structure is related to a more pervasive ambiguity of conception. For, in discussing 'literary montage', one is constantly uncertain as to what is original. Does one distinguish between the original material and the newly effected composition? In this sense, the original has been defined in terms of temporal or historical priority. But perhaps one instead distinguishes between the second-hand material, obtained from some prior source, and the original composition now being achieved by the latter-day artist? In this sense, origins and originality relate to the activity of the arranger – to some creative faculty which (however) can employ the non-original.

Among the great modernists Yeats does not usually figure as a major practitioner of montage. Eliot's *Waste Land* (1922), Joyce's

Finnegans Wake (1939), Thomas Mann's *Doctor Faustus* (1947), Ezra Pound's *Cantos* (1925 onwards) spring to mind, but not *Four Plays for Dancers* (1921) or *The Tower* (1928). Yeats was of the first generation of modernists and the examples of montage just cited are late for the most part. In the case of Joyce and Mann, one could also invoke their irony as an aspect of their relationship to literary tradition. Yeats is not often ironic in this way, though he and Pound share a savage kind of ironic disillusion. It may be then that, by virtue of his age and of his emotional temperament, Yeats was exempt from the temptations that led to the widespread practice of montage.

Yet the concurrence of age and temperament is not an easy proposition in Yeats's case. As an old man he was flamboyantly unsettled, randy and extreme in his opinions. We are in a position now to appreciate also how his behaviour in the 1930s relates to the mid-nineteenth-century period of his parents' youth and his own begetting; how – so to speak – his old age and the age into which he was born can be seen as a historical structure with its particular, vengeful tonalities. The relationship of the low dishonest decade to the stuffiness of Victorianism is less significant than the apogetic movement of knowledge and experience, straining towards knowledge without experience, experience without knowledge.

How does anything of this manifest itself in the poems or plays? Let us take a well-known couplet from 'The Man and the Echo' (1938):

> Did that play of mine send out
> Certain men the English shot?

It has been customary to read these lines as evidence of Yeats's unease on the topic of his responsibility for events in the world of politics and anger. In the context of his having it both ways – the passion and cunning noted by Conor Cruise O'Brien – nothing could be more convenient than a conscientious anxiety about whether a kinetic relationship exists between words and deeds. Thus the customary reading generates an image of the poet as a man worried by the consequences of his own literary work. The grammatical form which this worrying takes – a question – appears to underline the motif of uncertainty, as if nothing indicative could be proposed on such a topic. The sense of poetic uncertainty can then be contrasted to the certainty of men whom the English shot. For the adjective in the second line nimbly suggests both the specificity of those men –

Patrick Pearse and Thomas MacDonagh, etc., and not just the ragtag-and-bobtail of unknown volunteers – and their certainty in doing what they did. This certainty of theirs counterbalances the implication of passivity in their featuring in the poem simply as victims. Certainty indeed mediates between the twin vulgarities of action and passion, the imposing of violence and the endurance of suffering.

The poem from which the lines are taken has its own rhetorical form, that of quasi-dialogue between 'Man' to whom the majority of lines are assigned and 'Echo', who simply repeats the last three or four words of successive utterances. These echoes undoubtedly have their ironic effect, undercutting the rhymed couplets with hollow fragmentary repetition; yet they also mimic an imperative mood – 'lie down and die' – which the principal speaker has not attained. The poem divides its attention rather than concentrates it.

For this reason, or others, little attention has been paid to the claim of the speaker to 'that play of mine'. Just as no one drastically distinguishes between the Man and Yeats himself, so all are agreed that the play in question is 'Cathleen ni Houlihan' (1902), in which Maud Gonne had originally starred. But it has long been recognised that Yeats's claim to the play cannot go unchallenged. From the early 1970s onwards, a succession of critics – Daniel J. Murphy, James Pethica, Lucy McDiarmid and Maureen Waters – have demonstrated the central role of Augusta Gregory in the writing of 'Cathleen ni Houlihan', to the point where the play is now included in her *Selected Writings* (1995). This is not to reject Yeats as author or co-author, but simply to insist on the fully cooperative nature of the writing, a point he conceded in private.

Gregory returned to the play later in life. In 1919, on the day before St Patrick's Day, she reluctantly agreed to stand in for Maire Walker when it went into rehearsal at the Abbey Theatre. That evening she had difficulty reaching the theatre, due to the crowds gathered in Dublin's O'Connell Street to cheer Constance Gore-Booth (the Countess Markiewitz), released from Holloway Prison in London earlier in the month. Gregory's Journal records a curious detail of the scene – 'Madame Gonne followed in another waggonette, but was not cheered' – curious because the second released prisoner had been the original player of the part Gregory had just opted to perform in the revival of 'Cathleen ni Houlihan'. There is an idiom of theatre people generally that such an actor or actress had 'created' the part, in that it had become famous as a result of their playing it in the first productions; in the specific Irish case, there are several rival 'creators': Gonne and Gregory as players, Gregory and Yeats as authors. In the event, the reluctant stand-in got two curtain calls each night. Nothing could more palpably demonstrate the close interaction of drama and politics than the roles of Gregory and Gonne that week, and later in the year certain and uncertain men would be shot on a far greater scale than anything seen in Dublin since 1916.

As the war of independence wore on, Gregory maintained her Journal and even published anonymous excerpts from it in the London-based magazine, *The Nation*. With the cooperation of the editor, H. W. Massingham, she was able to confront English public opinion with the realities of Black and Tan conduct in Ireland, especially in the case of Ellen Quinn's murder on 4 November 1920. Yeats drew on this particularly brutal incident – Mrs Quinn was pregnant when she was shot – in the fourth stanza of 'Nineteen Hundred and Nineteen':

> Now days are dragon-ridden, the nightmare
> Rides upon sleep: a drunken soldiery
> Can leave the mother, murdered at her door,
> To crawl in her own blood, and go scot-free;
> The night can sweat with terror as before
> We pieced our thoughts into philosophy,
> And planned to bring the world under a rule,
> Who are but weasels fighting in a hole.

As Yeats was based in Oxford at this time, his debt to Gregory was direct and uncomplicated. The opening phrase of the poem's last section may also draw on her Journal, though in a less open fashion. Repeatedly she had noted the warning of local people that the Black and Tans assaulted women; 'don't let your Misses walk on the road, they are out for drink and women'. This prominence of the road in the terrorising of the district (and many other districts) in part derived from the habit of country people of using roads for social promenading in the evenings; it had little to do with any direct engagement of insurgent Volunteer units. Thus the first half-line of Section VI – 'Violence upon the roads:' – sustains the poem's focus on the contemporary scene. The remainder of the line – 'violence of horses;' – develops and intensifies a related but retrospective theme, for the section and poem conclude with the famous evocation of Robert Artisson and fourteenth-century witchcraft. The violent conflict of 1919–22 was the first Irish exposure to the internal combustion engine as an instrument of war – the Rising of Easter 1916 had been an infantry affair on the rebels' part, with a few last chivalric charges by British cavalry on the other. A technology, in part accelerated by the Great War and in part based on the local availability of private motor-cars, initially gave the government a major advantage without any agreed code of conduct to ensure that the advantage did not obliterate generally accepted rules of engagement. The Black and Tans were mobilised and motorised; commandeered lorries and private cars, together with Crossley tenders, gave them the ability to move rapidly across extensive areas of the countryside, shooting with impunity from fast-moving vehicles, raiding individual houses without notice to rape or molest women from whom they could depart on the instant, and (in one notorious case near Coole) executing prisoners by dragging them behind the vehicles. Thus Yeats's 'violence upon the roads' at once catches and drops the idiom of contemporary slaughter, missing its socio-sexual implication and rapidly substituting the horses of an outmoded military code.

Yeats vigorously denounced government violence at a meeting of the Oxford Union, and it is intended as no disparagement of his anger that it was augmented by the fact of his own absence from Ireland. We have already noticed one curiously displaced treatment of the motorised violence so strikingly characteristic of the period in Yeats's correspondence with H. J. C. Grierson. Writing in the autumn of 1922, all but two years after the Gregory Journal entries just cited, Yeats remarked on the violence of the Black and Tans 'in my own neighbourhood', and he specifically mentioned the murder of two brothers named Loughnane who were dragged behind lorries: 'There was nothing for the mother but the head.' This displacement in time, with its deliberate coolness of tone, is balanced by an intimacy of placing; the incident is presented as having occurred in Yeats's immediate vicinity, though he was out of the country at the time, lacked Gregory's personal knowledge of the people concerned, and had only taken possession of his Norman tower-house in 1917, then uninhabitable. Thoor Ballylee had once been part of the Gregory estate, made available to him through the distribution of land by the Congested Districts Board, and so but a tenuous base upon which to erect claims to 'my own neighbourhood'.

In the old days, one might at this point have summarised part at least of this evidence in some remarks on Yeats as *arriviste*. His status as landowner depended on the dismemberment of the Gregory estate, whose condition he would simultaneously lament as tragic. The agency of his promotion was a government board officially charged with the redistribution of land to smallholders. These awkward details would then have merged with the embarrassment of his absence in Oxford, and this might have been contrasted with Gregory's dogged persistence in staying at Coole. In the old days, of course, attention to class was rarely matched by any comparable interest in women's contribution to the literary movement. Fortunately, the more recent emphasis on the politics of textuality allows for a comprehensive examination of Yeats's debt to Gregory.

In the matter of 'Cathleen ni Houlihan', Yeats effectively monopolised the public existence of a play which they had jointly written. In 'Nineteen Hundred and Nineteen' (and later in the play 'Purgatory') he made use of details from her Journal without acknowledgment. If one were to compare in parallel columns a passage from the journal and the opening stanza of 'Coole Park and Ballylee, 1931', the implications of what might politely be termed intertextuality go beyond mere detail:

FROM ENTRY FOR 2 SEPTEMBER 1926	FROM STANZA ONE, FEBRUARY 1931
. . . And next morning at quarter to eleven (after preparations from 6 o'c. on) I was laid on the table, no chloroform, just the local anaesthetic – it lasted about 20 minutes. I had not much pain, though feeling the knife working about made me feel queer. But I fixed my mind upon a river, the river at Roxborough, imagined it as it flows from the mountains through the flat land from Kilchreest – then under the road bridge, then under the Volunteer memorial bridge; through the deerpark, then deepens; sallys and bulrushes on one side, coots and wildfowl making their nests there – on the other, the green lawns; past the house, past the long line of buildings, stables, kennels, dairy,	Under my window-ledge the waters race, Otters below and moor-hens on the top, Run for a mile undimmed in Heaven's face

the garden walls; then, narrow and deep here, it turned the old mill-wheel supplying water also for the steam engine that helped the saw-mills work. Then the division the parting of the waters, the otters' cave, the bed of soft mud which we children used to make the little vessels that never went through the baking without cracks; the dip of the stream underground, rising later to join its sunlit branch; a rushing current again, passing by Ravahasey, Caherlinney, Poll na Sionnach [,] Eserkelly, Castleboy, bridges again and then through thickets of laurel beside a forsaken garden – (A sting of pain here from the knife, but I only make a face and hear a voice say, 'Put in another drop') – And then by a sloping field of daffodils – and so at last to the high road where it went out of our demesne. (Some pain again) and for a moment I think of the river that has bounded my second phase of life rising in the park at Coole, flowing under the high poplars on its steep bank, vanishing under rocks that nature has made a bridge; then flowing on again till it widens into the lake. But before I had come to its disappearance at Inchy only to appear again as it mixes into Galway Bay, the Surgeon told me the knife had done its work. And presently the flow of warm blood was stopped with straps and bandages, and I was given praise for courage and told that I was 'very good' and there was but a slight feeling of faintness and then I was carried upstairs.

Then darkening through 'dark' Raftery's 'cellar' drop,

Run underground, rise in a rocky place

In Coole demesne, and there to finish up

Spread to a lake and drop into a hole.

What's water but the generated soul?

One consequence of paralleling the two passages is an enhanced awareness of duration. Gregory tells us that her operation – for the removal of a lump in her breast – lasted twenty minutes. This mundane detail provides a basis of plausibility for the itinerary she mentally followed as a means of distancing herself from the distress of surgery under limited anaesthetic. With nine places named, and others requiring no name, her mental experience can be appreciated as a measured endeavour to endure the passage of worrying and painful time. These places are duly populated with animals or imagined in their customary foliage: bulrushes, coots, otters, daffodils, poplars and so forth. But the dominant trope of the passage is the motion of rivers above and below ground, which mutely stands in for the flowing of her blood and the penetration of the surgeon's knife. Indeed, the business in hand only surfaces at the beginning and end: meanwhile the imaginary tracing of rivers almost monopolises the passage. Three related binary fractions can be set out:

$$(1) \qquad\qquad (2) \qquad\qquad (3)$$

$$\frac{\text{knife}}{\text{blood}} \qquad\qquad \frac{\text{image}}{\text{pain}} \qquad\qquad \frac{\text{sunlit river}}{\text{buried stream}}$$

Of these, the first fraction is the most mobile, for the knife is initially above the surface of the skin and the blood below it, then their position is reversed throughout the operation. The second is stabilised to a great extent by Gregory's concentrated will; only rarely does she concede that the imagined scene is invaded by pain. The third is structurally secure and integrated, in that the water is at all times the same river, known to the patient who evokes it deliberately and who deals with the knife and blood by these means.

To this model, we should add two further factors: Gregory's voluntary submission to the operation, and the continued anxiety about cancer, which persisted even after surgery had been successfully completed. Or, perhaps, add a third factor. In her journal, she makes it clear that Yeats had spent 'that dreadful hour before I was taken downstairs' in the nursing home with her; he too was 'very good', acquiring from her an approving epigraph bestowed in turn upon her by the surgeon.

I am aware of certain predictable objections. The two most fundamental of these cancel each other out. One argues that I am engaging in a form of prurience by relating a passage of one person's poetry to another's account of intimate experience. The other reminds me that Gregory was in the habit of leaving her journal on view in Coole, so that a privileged guest like Yeats was implicitly encouraged to read it. What these arguments share is a concern with the ethics of transposition from source to art-work, from prose to poetry. What they fail to admit is that the crucial polarity is that of body/soul (rather than prose/poetry) and that body is metonymically present as blood – which is to say, it is present in a state brimming upon absence, or spillage. On the poetic side of this delicate balance, blood has been miraculously transformed into water, but (in compensation) water is now all emblem, is declared to be nothing less than 'the generated soul'.

Like 'Coole Park, 1929', this poem commemorates a truly remarkable figure in Yeats's life. Gregory had indeed possessed 'powerful character', had occupied for many decades a role combining that of pupil and patron, or of silent collaborator and conscientious objector. In his emotional life, none contributed so much while demanding so little. There was more. Whether in relation to the Abbey, the civil war, the Lane pictures or the rehabilitation of de Valera, Gregory's political sense guided Yeats at times when his own acumen was threatened by increasingly authoritarian habits of reaction. As she moved slowly towards death, he began to write about her in the past tense, as with Synge twenty or so years earlier. Poets polish their lines, and elegists find rehearsal time at awkward moments, but the dry-eyed compositional procedures behind 'Coole Park and Ballylee, 1931' bespeak attitudes towards death that will look very different in 1939 from their first inscription in 1909. In so far as Yeats countenanced advisers during his final hieratic decade, he found none with Gregory's qualities.

Two or Three Small Wars

Pity the planet, all joy gone
from this sweet volcanic cone;
peace to our children when they fall
in small war on the heels of small
war – until the end of time
to police the earth, a ghost
orbiting forever lost
in our monotonous sublime.

Robert Lowell, 'Waking Early Sunday Morning', 1967

Begotten by a dissident Literary Revival, the conservative Irish Free State lacked cultured institutional progeny of its own body for reassurance in the face of sterile political fact. On 26 July 1928, four men met in the office of the Minister for Finance to discuss the possible establishment of a new Irish Academy. Of these, AE (that is, George William Russell) had best (though not unblemished) claim to be regarded as the literary conscience of the Free State. Yeats, a Senator soon to retire and a world-renowned Nobel laureate, was by far the best known. The other two were men of affairs, with secondary interests in literature. Walter Fitzwilliam Starkie (1894–1976) taught Romance languages at Trinity College and conducted musicological field work among Europe's gypsies. The minister was Ernest Blythe (1889–1975), an Ulster Presbyterian by birth and an early member of the Sinn Féin movement, who published several volumes of reminiscence in Gaelic.

Let us note two less local occurrences. A few days after the ministerial meeting, the English novelist Percy Wyndham Lewis (1882–1957) sent Yeats a copy of *The Childermass*, so inaugurating an exchange of letters and opinions of considerable ideological force. The 'turn' towards post-mortem politics was under way. Yeats identified the first hundred pages of the novel as an account of 'the first condition of the dead according to the manner of [?ghosts] all over the world'.[14] Lewis published his *Hitler* in March 1931, a pre-emptive strike on behalf of neo-conservative revolution, which the Führer admired – Yeats owned a copy. Pound was already working on behalf of Mussolini, and it remained for Irish associates to find bit-parts as best they could.

Three days after initiating his correspondence with Lewis, Yeats at Coole Park met a 'stupid' German who infuriated his hosts at lunch by praising Charlie Chaplin, Ernst Toller and Upton Sinclair. With a letter of introduction from AE, he had travelled to discuss modern theatre, in which he was passionately interested. Lady Gregory reportedly declared, 'As for propaganda, our servants will do that for us', the intended ironic allusion to Villiers de l'Isle Adam rebounding Greek-fashion upon her. Her own journal suggests that she tried to play a moderating role in the clash of world-renowned poet and obscure journalist.

On Thursday, 15 August 1928, the servants in question were away at a sports event in Kilcolgan, it being a holy day in the Catholic calendar. Consequently Gregory took the young man into the garden where she was plucking cress. She gave him nectarines to eat, 'then to the house and showed him books and answered questions, and when Yeats came down we had lunch'. So far no sign of conflict. But Yeats 'bristled up' at the mention of Chaplin, Sinclair and Toller, and emitted a 'stream of invective' at the visitor. Sinclair was an American novelist irredeemably socialist in outlook, Toller, the German dramatist (about whom the visitor might have rights to an opinion), while Chaplin was the piteous star of films that Mrs Yeats greatly enjoyed – even Gregory admitted some approval of the little man. Having added 'a soothing word now and again' during the meal, she finally took her guest off to see the lake. Hours later, when the continental intruder had left, Yeats after dinner was 'still breathing threatenings and slaughters against him and against A. E. for sending him'.

Why the fury against this piddling visitor? Did mention of Toller prompt recollection of Yeats's and Gregory's rejection of O'Casey's new and Expressionistic play earlier that summer? Did the fact that Yeats and Gregory were, that very day, vetting another playscript with Expressionist leanings (Denis Johnston's 'The Old Lady Says "No"') render the arrival of a Toller-groupie particularly unwelcome? And who was he? Erich Gottgetreu (born in Chemnitz, 1903) was a Jewish writer who later escaped from Central Europe to Palestine/Israel in 1933, relatively unbruised by his experiences among the founders of Irish drama – Gregory condescending but kind, Yeats disproportionately outraged at a twenty-five-year-old Jew's enthusiasms. Before his flight from *Kultur*, Gottgetreu worked for the Social Democrats' press service in Berlin, and later was a correspondent for *La Bourse Égyptienne*. But, as Yeats's behaviour signalled, a 'turn' was certainly under way in his attitude to political matters.[15] For his part, Gottgetreu omitted any reference to the incident in his subsequent volume of travel-reports.[16]

Blythe's fame in Irish political history rests on his decision to *reduce* old-age pensions by 10 per cent. Later he was a major figure in the Blue Shirt movement, a journalist *provocateur* of ambition who consulted with Yeats on issues of anti-democratic action. When de Valera came to power, he appointed the former minister to the board of the Abbey Theatre, at one stroke neutralising a creative theatre and a cantankerous opponent. For thirty years Blythe exercised a narrowly restrictive control over productions, tours, budgets – the entire life of the National Theatre. But he was a man of the hard right, when a fascist dawn was brightening over Ireland – a false dawn, as it proved, through no fault of Blythe's. While a member of Dáil Eireann, he sat for the constituency of Monaghan where Eoin O'Duffy had been born and in which the present writer lives.

Gregory died in May 1932. During 1933 Blythe wrote a series of articles about the Blue Shirts under the name 'Onlooker', as apt a *nom de plume* as Hone's Gael. No mere observer, Blythe was a major activist among Blue Shirts, and his journalism demonstrates the talents of a self-fulfilling prophet. The Army Comrades, he argues, 'will be obliged to run the political parties'; within months, and with Blythe's assistance, O'Duffy is head of Fine Gael. In this detail he was merely adjusting for Irish circumstances Mussolini's edict of February 1928, when the fascist party was authorised to 'designate' public representation. Addressing the nation's young people, as Starkie had advised, Blythe commends them for thinking dismissively of politicians while 'the best men in the community' find no place in public life. This echo of 'The Second Coming' – where the best lack all conviction – neatly turns Yeats's apprehension into an endorsement of the rough beast.[17]

Walter Starkie was more malleable: Dublin's dirtiest joke (to date) suggested that his conception stemmed from a wet dream, rescued by a spoon. Appointed to the Abbey board in 1927, Starkie had found himself in Rome when Kevin O'Higgins was assassinated that July, in Rome and on the eve of a personal audience with the Duce.[18] The next year he did the Abbey directors some service in their dispute with Sean O'Casey and their rejection of *The Silver Tassie* in 1928. When Yeats began to plan his Irish Academy of Letters, he conceded a place among the founding members to Starkie, the author of some entertaining travel books and little else. His defence lay in the man's secretarial ability and his knowledge of European institutions. As Yeats's proposed institution resembled the Académie française much as a pub resembles a salon, Starkie's alleged experience among national academies counted for little, for all it might impress yokels like Frank O'Connor and Fred Higgins. Fieldwork among Spanish and other gypsies apart – Gerald Brenan thought it worthless – Starkie's European credentials were minted by the Centre International d'Études sur le Fascisme, a far-from-impartial think-tank based in Brussels and Lausanne. He allegedly edited its annual journal.

I have only traced two *annuaires* of the centre, those of 1928 and 1929. In each case, the preliminary or editorial matter is signed by H.

de Vries de Heekelingen. The first issue contains two articles of Irish interest: one by the Hungarian-born Odon Por, with whom AE had associated at the beginning of the 1920s; the other by Starkie, under whose influence Por had come to Irish attention.[19] Por's theme remained cooperativism, which he commended to the corporative spirit of Italian fascism. In a frenzy of impartial scruple, the *annuaire* of 1928 described Por not as a fascist, but as a 'Guildman'. Its contents were rigorously organised, opening with two articles on the history of the Italian 'revolution', three articles on 'reforms' successively introduced within the established system, three (including Por's) on specialist topics, and finally three contributions assessing the prospects for fascism in France, Germany and Ireland.

Starkie's article, '*L'Irlande s'orient-elle vers le fascisme?*', describes a new state burdened by its post-revolutionary legacy. Given Italy's later contempt for the League of Nations, it is ironic that he should date the maturity of the Free State from its admission to the league in September 1923. Politically, the article is resolutely anti-republican, even mildly pro-British. Much attention is given to literary and theatrical matters, with references to Stephen Gwynn, AE and Sean O'Casey (but not Yeats). The presence of a younger generation is stressed, for it is they who will determine in what political direction Ireland will face. Starkie's opening epigraph from Machiavelli declares that when men are well governed they do not search for novel liberties. The assassination of Kevin O'Higgins – '*aussi noble dans sa mort que dans sa vie*' – is presented as symbolic of a horror that might further expand if Ireland lacks direction. This is a Yeatsian theme, though the poem 'Death' (written in September 1927) has not yet been published.

Literature is represented by theatre, theatre by the Abbey, the Abbey by O'Casey, '*l'auteur dramatique du jour*'. Given O'Casey's communistic leanings, it is an odd emphasis, not incompatible with fascist ethics. O'Higgins's assassination in July 1927 helps to date Starkie's composition of the article with an unhelpfully early *terminus ad quem*, and so it remains impossible to decide whether, in describing O'Casey as he does, he wrote in the knowledge that 'The Silver Tassie' had been rejected (May 1928) by Yeats and himself, together with the other Abbey directors. Certainly, Starkie gives no indication to readers of the fascist *annuaire* that O'Casey was experimenting with German-style Expressionism or responding to the example of the left-wing Ernst Toller. On the contrary, O'Casey is implicitly condemned for lacking any conception of '*un monde nouveau inondé de lumière*' in his Dublin 'Troubles' trilogy. Hope is to be the big thing (we hope). The example proposed is Gabriele D'Annunzio (1863–1938) because '*le patriotisme du passé est sterile*'.

Recommendation of Mussolini's court jester was in many ways admirably irresponsible in Starkie. Though the activist-dramatist was a loyal party man, his record included casting a Jewish woman as the Christian martyr Sebastian – he liked her legs – and showering the city of Vienna with poetry dropped from an aeroplane. (There was also the attempted coup in Trieste.) Nevertheless, Starkie's citation of Machiavelli and criticism of O'Casey provide a neat synopsis of the fascism towards which Ireland might direct itself. Avoiding novelty in political freedom while inundating a new world with light, Irish society would transform itself into a veritable work of art, like D'Annunzio abolishing distinctions between the political and the dramatic.

If this may have appealed to Yeats in certain moods, Starkie's concluding remarks worked in a very different direction. The influence of the newly established Société de la Royauté du Christ (*anglice*, The Society of Christ the King) was particularly notable in Dublin for, like fascism, it combated every form of naturalism, egoism and agnosticism (not to mention democracy). There is no evidence that Starkie had been involved with the Medicean Catholics of *To-morrow* in 1924, and his Trinity professorship proclaimed a degree of snobber-class distance from conventional Irish Catholic attitudes. Yet, when it came to selecting members for his Irish Academy of Letters in 1932, Yeats listed the Irish *sociétaire* of the Centre International d'Études sur le Fascisme among the founders. His motives were practical, likewise his reservations. Writing to his wife for advice, he confessed, 'I told Shaw that Starkie could only be justified by his utility as secretary. Do you think him impossible in that capacity?'[20] For all her acuity in political matters, Mrs Yeats did not prevent the Duce's Dubliner from further advancing himself.

Starkie and Blythe at the Abbey, not forgetting Adolf Mahr in the National Museum, provided ideological backbone in Dublin's flabby arts-administration (a concept then happily unknown). Mahr dutifully promoted fellow-travellers – Hans Hartmann from Germany and Liam Gogan from Dublin. The later arrival of Clissmann provided a publicity agent for the ideas of these men, especially the Nazis, though a central feature of his work was to influence Irish opinion (the MacBrides and Stuarts, Peadar O'Donnell, etc.) without drawing too much attention to the apparatus of subversion. The Italian Legation also had its agents at work, including one in Trinity College. It was seen by W. J. Maloney as a fount of support during his 1936 campaign to prove Casement's diaries to be British forgeries, with the knock-on effect of commending a pro-German policy. Yeats exploited the dead Casement, but dodged Maloney, who may have been a British agent provocateur. Some of this ideological mapping of 1930s' Dublin highlights things that scarcely bore upon the lives of ordinary citizens, but Yeats was no ordinary citizen. Blythe he connived with intensively during the Blue Shirt period, and continued to meet in the Abbey's directors' box. With his Spanish wife, Starkie occasionally dined with the Yeatses, as well as stiffening resolve on the board. International events of the mid-1930s provided notable opportunities for the refining of an anti-democratic and pro-fascist sensibility.

Perhaps the first of these – the Austrian Civil War of 1934 – was too small an affair to impact on Ireland, though it brought into existence a clerical-fascist regime attractive to a few on the Irish right. Violent destruction of Viennese housing districts and suppression of the Social Democrat party were signs of the coming times, observed in passing by one poet, W. H. Auden. Later in 1934, Yeats deliberately made contact with Auden in connection with a London theatre season for which he thought including 'the poetical left' was advisable.[21] In 1934/35, he was engaged in a veritable (if short-lived) Popular Front among writers, encouraging Auden in England while restoring his old alliance with O'Casey in the Abbey. This did not bring any discernible acknowledgment of the international crisis. Auden, for his part, agreed to marry Thomas Mann's daughter Erika as a means of providing her with non-German citizenship – at such times 'what else are buggers for?'

Abyssinia scarcely registered more clearly than Austria on the seismograph of Irish public opinion in the 1930s. While Leonard and Virginia Woolf tuned in apprehensively to the BBC on 4 October 1935 to catch the first responses to Italy's invasion, the chronology of Yeats's activities for the period between 20 September and 12 October is blank. He had turned seventy in June of that year, and was fêted in the German press. This blatant act of colonial, or imperialist, expansion drew no rebuke from the old Fenian and latter-day post-colonialist icon, though it had been predicted and threatened for years. Woolf, for those who descried Woolf, had done so in his *Empire and Commerce in Africa* (1920). Aldous Huxley thought it 'a war of unparalleled meanness of brutality'.[22] The League of Nations, in which Ireland was now playing an ever more important role, condemned the invasion. De Valera was resolute, but Irish public opinion was inclined to judge the matter partly on grounds of religious sympathy – the Italians, though fascist aggressors, were Catholics. Under cover of the mob, Yeats kept quiet.

It was as late as 11 December 1936, more than a year after the war began and at a time when he was seeing Starkie, when Yeats offered Ethel Mannin an explanation of his attitude. His letter began with reassurances that he did not hate England, though he hated matters relating to 'a financial policy the people so little understand'. If a celestial visitor told him English financial policy was right, he would say, 'Because you are an angel I must believe what you say. But what am I to do? Certain things drive me mad & I lose control of my tongue.' Yet on the question of Italy's African campaign, his tongue had most certainly been held, while it now and nonetheless could proceed to assure his red-in-the-bed correspondent:

> All through the Abyssinian war my sympathies were with the Abyssinians but those feelings were chilled by my knowledge that the English government was using those feelings in myself & others to help an imperial policy I distrusted. To the wife of a Cabinet minister who had discoursed to him on England's noble attitude, the monk, Shree Purohit Swami said 'There cannot be two swords in one scabard' & said no more.[23]

Yeats had said less. His silences were contradictory, and his eventual explanation was worthy of Frank Richard's schoolboy hero – 'Bunter, are you there?' Reply from Bunter, 'No'. This is to risk trivialising, for want of a comprehensive metaphor, a question of life and death. Perhaps Yeats's lesser interest in Ethiopia reflected at a political level the judgment later recorded in *On the Boiler* (1939) about that black girl near Little Belfast – just one of those 'our civilisation must reject'. Yeats's non-racism was a relative matter, with Indians always likely to win his approval over Negroes. The lofty citation of the Swami marks her contrast with ancient and approved civilisations. In December 1932, Yeats rebuked an American scholar for calling the people of present-day Sri Lanka 'blacks'. 'I remember Lord Salisbury getting into no end of a mess through calling some Indian a black man.'[24] There is also the influence of Walter Starkie to be considered, who wrote in the local newspapers to support the invasion.

The 1930s has become in retrospect a ski-slope of ever accelerating catastrophe on which individual rumbles, stumbles, tumbles were (it now seems) both inevitable and imperceptible. Who can be blamed for failing to read Hitler's seizure of the lost Rhineland territories as an omen? Who can be blamed for missing the Austrian Civil War, which, in any case, was tidied up by the *Anschluss* of 1938? As for the April 1937 bombing of Guernica, an undefended civilian town in the Basque country, is it not enough to say that Picasso eventually did the right thing on our collective behalf? Yeats will allude to bombs in drafting 'Under Ben Bulben', but they will have no reference to any actual bombs, whether those of Sean Russell or the Luftwaffe's Kondor unit.

Instead, Yeats's Spanish Civil War has been configured for recent consumption through a single unverified statement of support for the republican government. The happy discovery of Pablo Neruda's *Memoirs* allowed Elizabeth Cullingford to present a liberal Yeats to the world, one whose attitude on this issue evidenced a wider commitment to anti- and indeed post-colonialism.[25] In point of fact, Neruda only claimed that Yeats had 'replied', quoting nothing from the reply, but implying that by this in itself Yeats 'rallied to the defence of the Spanish Republic'.[26] The Swedish novelist Selma Lagerlöf (1858–1940) is the only other writer whom Neruda mentions in this connection.[27] Fortunately for Cullingford's conclusions, there was no public statement from Yeats in the mid-1930s to parallel 'From Democracy to Authority' of 1924. The direction indicated in the earlier pronouncement on Mussolini and Maurras, together with everything known of Yeats's attitude towards democracy, should have advised caution. The untraced 'reply' – Neruda's request is likewise untraced – has been tentatively attributed to early February 1937: on 7 February, the philosophical fascist and convert-Catholic, higher-Hindu Dermot MacManus called on Yeats to discuss the Spanish war, an adviser unlikely to have approved of collaboration with the communist Neruda or to have opposed condemnation of Mussolini's adventures. Undaunted by these embarrassments, the late Edward Said incorporated Cullingford's conclusions into a Field Day pamphlet-essay. Even Roy Foster, in writing of Yeats's local difficulties in 1937, embroidered on Cullingford's wishful thinking: 'later that year he [Yeats] would lend his name to a letter of support for the Second International Writers' Congress being held in Madrid, as a gesture of solidarity with the Republic'.[28] Solidarity does not sound like authentic Yeats – or authentic Foster.

If Yeats had wished for anything of that kind, the legitimate Spanish government's presence at the World Fair in Paris provided a readily accessible forum from July 1937 onwards. Picasso's 'Guernica' ensured that the pavilion was not neglected. In contrast the (2nd) International Writers' Congress was a largely Stalinist affair, trumpeting its anti-fascist credentials in a manner that an erstwhile Blue Shirt laureate could scarcely have embraced. The missing 'reply' alluded to by Neruda has itself been embraced in the even more obvious lack of any corroboration. Perhaps it is time this myth of Yeats's support for the legitimate Spanish republic is acknowledged as the tissue of unsubstantiated and uncorroborated wish-fulfilment which it has become in the minds of its sponsors.[29]

Local issues in Ireland unquestionably affected Yeats's attitude to the great crisis of the mid-1930s. 'Spain' was seen by many as a crusade against communism, a holy war in the name of the Catholicism beloved of the majority in Ireland. On the left of the IRA there was a significant enrolment of volunteers to fight for the government side, together with a few genuine communists such as Michael O'Riordan. With more flamboyance than efficiency, General O'Duffy rallied the remnants of his Blue Shirts in support of Franco and the fascist rebels. This was the O'Duffy with whom Yeats had fraternised in 1933, writing songs and contributing money to a cause that disappointed in its timidity and its conventional piety. The songs were replaced by other commitments, Indian philosophy and sexual rejuvenation among them. But they were not cast aside; on the contrary, they were recast in more precious oriental metals; 'to get rid of the bitterness, irritation & hatred, my work in Ireland has brought into my work I want to make the last song sweet & exultant, a sort of European Geeta, or rather my Geeta not doctrine but song'.[30] The *Bhagavad Gita* was not exempt from the history in which it was studied, but it provided a higher register for the concerns Yeats had taken down into the muck-yard of Irish popular opinion.

In March 1937, Yeats had been obliged to recognise once again a crisis on his doorstep, or that of the Abbey Theatre:

The political situation here is unexpected & threatening. De Velera [*sic*] introduced his bill to stop volunteers [travelling to Spain] – the opposition promised support & then in twenty four hours everything changed. Cosgrave went to bed, & the opposition turned against the bill & demanded the recognition of Franco. Cosgrave stayed in bed. De Velera [*sic*] carried his bill against the most violent opposition, his own party doubtful. The reason was that it was suddenly realised that vast numbers of the people believe that Franco is a Catholic fighting against paganism. I have it on good authority that he [i.e. de Valera] has been alarmed for months at the growth of what is called the 'Catholic Front'. I have noticed an ever increasing bigotry in the little pious or semi-literary reviews. I am convinced that if the Spanish War goes on, or if it ceases & O'Duffy's volunteers return heros [*sic*] my 'pagan' institutions, the theatre, the academy, will be fighting for their lives against combined Catholic & Gaelic bigotry. A friar or monk has already threatened us with mob violence.[31]

Quite apart from threats to the fledgling Irish Academy of Letters, Yeats was moved to some degree by an inherited fear of popular Catholicism. He always postulated his nationalism on: (i) a folk element that could be seen as pre-Catholic, or (ii) a high cultural stratum that could absorb Catholicism with the bad weather, or (iii) a Fenian allegiance to trump the Church (but only in limited circumstances). His close friends among Irish Catholics were not numerous. Kevin O'Higgins was dead. Desmond FitzGerald, though fearfully anti-Bolshevik, was also moralistic. Jephson O'Connell was likewise preoccupied with the sexual hygiene of the nation's warriors and tedious detail of national accountancy. With whom could Yeats associate and consult on the Spanish question?

Dermot Arthur Maurice MacManus bid fair to be Yeats's ideal renaissance man – a soldier and a folklorist, a Catholic and a gentleman. His family background lay in County Mayo where, on what became the MacManus estate, the Gaelic poet Antony Raftery (*c.*1784–1835) was born at Killeaden, then owned by the Taafes. Originally Catholic and Gaelic themselves, the nineteenth-century MacManuses adhered to the Church of Ireland and intermarried with the Strongs: West Indian properties provided substance, though members of the new clan dissented from the anti-black prejudices of colonial settlers. The novelists Charlotte Elizabeth MacManus (1853–1944) and L. A. G. Strong (1896–1958) brought the family names before the reading public. Yeats first met Miss MacManus in London at a centenary commemoration of the 1798 rebellion. She inclined to a Wilde Goose or Jacobite view of Irish affairs. Strong took the bold step of dedicating his biography of Thomas Moore to Yeats, and got away with it.

Leonard Strong MacManus, father of Yeats's adventurer, was a medical man. The elder son (Desmond) followed suit, as did a daughter Emily, who became matron of Guy's Hospital in London. Dermot entered Sandhurst to become an officer in the 1st battalion of the Inniskilling Fusiliers. Having served in India (where he converted to Catholicism), his regiment moved to the Dardanelles, and in that military disaster he suffered shell-damage to both feet. After the war, he briefly studied astronomy at Trinity College Dublin, holding an ex-serviceman's bursary.[32] During this period, and probably in 1920, he met George Yeats, through whom he came into contact with her husband. Magic, Hinduism and folklore were among their shared interests. (An intermediary may have been Lennox Robinson, later credited with advice on *The Middle Kingdom*, MacManus's 'history' of Irish fairies.[33]) In the same year he married Kathleen Thompson, the daughter of Sir William Thompson, a leading figure in Dublin's medical kingdom. The wedding, to solemnise a mixed marriage between Catholic groom and Protestant young lady, was a hole-in-the-corner affair, conducted in working-class Ringsend. Later the couple lived at Woodville, near Lough Gowna in County Longford. No longer having Coole to visit, the Yeatses stayed in the house for eight days in September 1933, when Mrs MacManus took in paying guests to make gentry ends meet: 'A lovely place, blue shirts on[e] side of lake, I.R.A. on the other, no railway station within nine miles.'[34]

MacManus's war injuries and astronomical studies do not appear to have prevented him from claiming a place in the struggle for independence. The nature and extent of his contribution are difficult to establish with precision, though by 1924 he was a commandant (or, perhaps, captain) in the National Army, conniving with Yeats and a few others at the time of the threatened mutiny. His loyalties were always liable to erosion amid his more numerous interests. In the early days of the Second World War, Irish Army Intelligence worried about his associations with the veteran IRA leader, Dan Breen, though investment in the same business firm (and not politics) had put the two men in touch. G2 was also inclined to deny that MacManus had ever been officially attached.[35] In 1942, as the Vision of Blood Kindred dispersed, MacManus was collecting on behalf of a 'Poles in Russia' fund. Only a slight adjustment of the Yeatsian lens would have revealed a different figure – eccentric, unreliable, extreme, a fantasist. For that reason amongst others, MacManus may offer a surer guide to the poet's thinking about Spain than Pablo Neruda. In 1936, the two were meeting privately at least once a week to discuss Hindu philosophy and Spanish politics, a combination of interests unlikely to accommodate the Chilean Stalinist.[36]

Between 1924 and 1939, Dermot MacManus played a significant role in Yeats's political life, drawing him into the higher councils of the Blue Shirts and advising on military aspects of the Spanish Civil War. In May 1933, Yeats chose to send MacManus three guineas for the Army Comrades, which otherwise he would have given to Cumann na Gael; 'one cannot be non-political in Ireland'. In the accompanying letter, he praised Lawrence's *Lady Chatterley's Lover* – 'beautiful and moving' – and described protests to the Department of Justice at the banning of Shaw's *The Adventures of the Black Girl in Her Search for God*. 'The Minister said it was the pictures they minded upon which I unrolled before his plainly astonished eyes a large photograph of the ceiling of the Sistine Chapel & pointed out that there were not even fig-leaves.'[37] From these details, MacManus emerges as no puritan Catholic, but one of the Medicean kind praised by *To-morrow* in 1924. At that time Senator Yeats, Commandant [*sic*] MacManus, General O'Connell and Senator Jameson had met privately to discuss a matter not to be mentioned in correspondence. Efforts to present Yeats's involvement with the magazine as part of an anti-censorship campaign not only ignore his other activities in 1924, but also underestimate his tolerance of censorship where the censors can be relied on.[38]

Nine years after *To-morrow* and the Army Mutiny, MacManus was taking initiatives in his dealings with Yeats. In the poet's account to Olivia Shakespear, the whole business was a political comedy:

Act I. Capt Macmanus [*sic*], the ex British officer I spoke of, his head full of vague Fascism, got probably from me decided that Gen O Duffey [*sic*] should be made leader of a body of young men formed to keep meetings from being broken up. He put into O Duffey's head – he describes him as 'a simple peasant' – Fascist ideas and started him off to organise that body of young men. Act II. some journalist announced that 30,000 of these young men were going to march through Dublin on a certain day (the correct number was 3,000). Government panic. Would not O Duffy, who had once been head of the Army and more recently head of the police, march on the government with 30,000, plus army & police. Result marshal law – in its Irish form – armoured cars in the streets, & new police force drawn from the I.R.A. to guard the goverment & O Duffy organisation proclaimed. Act III. O Duffy is made thereby so important that Cosgrave surrenders the leadership of his party to O Duffy & all the opposition unites under him.[39]

Perhaps Yeats favoured political tragedy, but for the moment he had paid his money and was watching the show with interest.

By mid-1935, the Blue Shirt business had dropped from the headlines, though Yeats still attended to MacManus's needs. A letter of introduction to the Swami stressed the former British officer's sympathy with Indian aspirations: 'he was wounded in the war, & then came to Ireland where he took an active part in the war against England ... a daring determined man'.[40] Within less than a year, relations between the two men cooled. Yeats's entanglement with the unfortunate Margot Collis suddenly absorbed all his energies, while the course of the war in Spain led to differences of political emphasis between poet and adventurer. 'I am sorry but I cannot do what you ask,' Yeats wrote. 'A month or so ago I refused Ethel Mannin's most urgent request that I should take similar action for a victim of Hitlers. I said, & this is quite true, that I had always refused to have any part, however slight, in international politics. Once I began there would be no end.'[41] Roy Foster assumes that MacManus here was enlisting Yeats's support 'probably regarding Mussolini's flouting of the League [of Nations] over Abyssinia', but the paralleling of the new request with Mannin's appeal on Ossietzky's behalf makes this unlikely. Was MacManus one to oppose the Duce? Is there any evidence of MacManus protesting at anything, independent of Yeats's refusal?

The end of 1936 saw Yeats throw himself into the controversy over Roger Casement's allegedly forged diaries, aligning himself with nationalist opinion in Ireland while a Catholic Front was growing in influence.[42] Writing to Dorothy Wellesley in England after a period of illness, he complained that all politics was foul lying:

Last night being at last no longer infectious I had MacManus in. He is the gun man I have told you of ... He says that in England the educated classes are politics-mad but that the mass of the people have free minds whereas it is the opposite with us. Certainly I never meet anybody who seems to care which side wins in Spain or anywhere else. Yet we are not ignorant – MacManus knows more about military conditions in Spain than anybody I have met.[43]

It is impossible to see the Blue Shirt prophet of 1933 as a defender of the Spanish government in 1936 or 1937, or the fairy-researching convert to Catholicism as an ally of Reds and anarchists. Yeats had evidently refused some request of his friend (not necessarily linked to Abyssinia) – consistent in this, even if he continued to admire military know-how and the authority of the few.

A letter of three days later to a woman of different political outlook reflected a different view of MacManus. To Ethel Mannin, Yeats described 'an Irish revolutionary [who] fought in the great war & then though crippled with wounds, became one of Michael Collins' men':

> I know no man who in the service of his political convictions has lived a life of such danger. I see him almost every week – we constantly discuss the war in Spain, in which he is deeply learned because all war interests him. The last time I met him I suddenly remembered that I did not know on which side were his sympathies & he did not know on which side mine were, except that neither of us wanted to see General O'Duffy back in Ireland with enhanced fame helping 'the Catholic front'.

In the usual sense of the phrase, MacManus was never 'one of Michael Collins' men', the squad of hardened guerrillas who executed fourteen British intelligence officers on 21 November 1920 and inaugurated Ireland's first Bloody Sunday. MacManus's badly damaged feet, encased in surgical-steel boots, were not fleet enough for such activities. Yeats's phrase is part of his sexual braggadocio in writing to Ethel Mannin. In 1920, MacManus was studying astronomy in Trinity College and astrology with George Yeats. The claim that, after weekly discussions in 1937, neither MacManus nor Yeats knew which side the other supported in Spain likewise needs decipherment. As Mediceans, they could lament the prospect of Rough O'Duffy's triumph, but indifference towards each other's commitment arose from a shared interest in wider and deeper things than Irish factionalism. When Yeats had put MacManus in touch with Swami, he was attending to the former soldier's Indian background. The *Bhavagad Gita* had appeared late in 1935 in the Swami's translation, with a lengthy dedication to Yeats on his seventieth birthday. At the heart of this Hindu text is the recommendation of a philosophical attitude towards war. For Mannin's benefit, Yeats weaves Indian and Irish nationalism together, though one can detect through the knotted strands a glint of pro-Franco-ism and a gleam of that concern with international finance that often masked anti-Semitism:

> I don't know on which side a single friend of mine is, probably none of

us are on any side. I am an old Fenian & I think the old Fenian in me would rejoice if a Fachist [*sic*] nation or government controlled Spain because that would weaken the British Empire, force England to be civil to India perhaps to set them free, & loosen the hand of English finance in the far East, of which I hear occasionally. But this is mere instinct. A thing I would never act on.

The first sentence of this is manifest nonsense. As for the impact of a Franco-ist victory on the British Empire, it did not in the end prove decisive. But Yeats's disinclination to act should not be read as caution or restraint. The Geeta's message (now attributed to the Swami) was 'act and remain apart from action'.[44] It allowed Yeats to conclude his account of European politics with a mixture of general complacency and specialist indignation: 'All Germany on one side & kept there by rhetoric & manipulated news; & all England on the other side & kept there by rhetoric & manipulated news.'[45] No differences between Penn in the Rocks and Dachau are acknowledged. Suspension of judgment on international affairs, based on the disappearance of 'the old reliability of news in our Press' after the Great War, was a stock right-wing response to the unpalatable in the 1930s.[46]

After the weekly discussions in 1936/37, MacManus seems to have dropped down the ladder of Yeats's advisory men of action. Others were partly eclipsed. Though Joseph Hone continued to assemble material for his biography, Yeats was inclined to be mildly satirical about the former Gael and secretary to a cabal of senators and army officers, describing him as 'the most lethargic man I know'. There was a whiff of scandal to excite Dorothy Wellesley, for it was said that a son of Hone's 'some little time ago inherited a small property. He sold it for £2000 & has come to Ireland to blow the money. He has brought a wife & several very beautiful young men. In his bed-room there are three beds, one for the wife, one for Nat, one for the selected beautiful young man. When the three get into one bed (which seems to me the milk of human kindness) the wife says she does not like it because she is always put next the wall.'[47] Yeats was choosing English and female heroes to replace MacManus and O'Connell, though Patrick McCartan in America remained a useful fund-raiser.

Biographies, especially those with a tendency to move backwards in time, should be loath to propound model lessons in historical research. Nevertheless I cannot help juxtaposing the few primary texts of Yeats referring to the Spanish war – these several letters, just cited – with Neruda's late report of an apparently irrecoverable secondary source. The letters are far from chiming in unison on the Spanish theme, and therein lies an indication of their authenticity as aspects of Yeats's politics. They lie even further from any verification of Neruda's claim. By late 1937, Yeats had given up thinking of Spain because the Catholic Front threat in Dublin had receded. Once again, Edmund Burke's good man had done nothing.

Beyond the conventional emphasis on verification there arises a possibility of arguing the value of biography as a way of assessing a person's political attitudes towards an issue on which s/he makes few or no public statements. I do not suggest that the biographer of Yeats best answers questions about his attitudes towards Spain: instead I suggest that at least mini-biographies of Hone, MacManus and Starkie are required if the question of the poet's position is to be fully understood. Equally helpful would be accounts of Yeats's female friends in these closing years.

Ceremonies and Innocence

There is no bloodless myth will hold.
Geoffrey Hill, 'Genesis', 1952

Alfred Nobel and Peace

Yeats's winning of the Nobel Prize for Literature in 1923 has rightly been regarded as at once a well-earned acknowledgment of his achievement and a remarkable encouragement to a writer who went on to eclipse that achievement in collections such as *The Tower* (1928). For the record, one might note that he first thought of the possibility that the award might come his way as early as 1909, when negotiations were afoot to secure for him a British Civil List pension.[1] His apprehensions about the latter were fixed on the question of an Irish recipient's continuing freedom to speak his political mind. A few years later, he was delighted by Rabindranath Tagore's winning the award, partly because it upset Edmund Gosse (who championed Thomas Hardy) and partly because the publicity would increase the appeal of Tagore's play 'The Post Office', which the Abbey Theatre was planning to stage.[2]

In many ways the eventual award to Yeats revealed a dynamic potential in the prize itself. The citation made it clear that, in honouring Yeats, the Swedish Academy's committee was also giving formal recognition to Ireland as one of the newest nation-states in Europe. Such political dimensions were not at odds with the founder's intentions. In his will, Alfred Nobel (1833–1896), an engineer who had written poetry and drama, looked forward to the abolition or at least the reduction of standing armies, and his prizes for physics, chemistry and physiology/medicine were flanked by more humanistic awards in literature and the area now covered by the Peace Prize. There were inevitably some who felt that the whole scheme sought to compensate for the terrible consequences of Nobel's most famous invention – dynamite – in 1866. It is worth devoting a moment to the thought that, without him, neither *The Tower* nor the dynamitard faction within Fenianism might have happened. The worldwide Nobel enterprise was represented in Ireland at the time of the Troubles by a Tipperary man who fronted an import agency with Patrick Moylett as cover for the supply of arms to Michael Collins. It was never an Olympian affair.

Despite the Irish references in the official citation, Yeats's award was processed through the English committee of the Swedish organisation, and the British Ambassador was on hand. To some extent, these circumstances arose from the undeveloped state of Ireland's diplomatic corps, but they also accurately reflected the country's formal status as a British dominion. (G. B. Shaw is invariably listed as a British winner of the prize.) In recent years, complaints of political bias have occasionally arisen in response to specific awards, or to the studied neglect of writers like Graham Greene who offended powerful interests. Some attention to the official history of the Nobel prizes reveals that a political dimension has always been present. During the Great War, the committee sought to honour writers through whom they could endorse 'literary neutralism'. One consequence was a temporary preponderance of Scandinavian laureates, with Knut Hamsun in 1920 marking the end of that pattern. The next decade was devoted in practice to honouring 'the grand style'. Yeats in 1923 and Thomas Mann in 1929 certainly met that criterion, and indeed *both* writers demonstrated the strength to continue that was provided by such recognition.

Though the English committee was responsible for advancing Yeats's case through the Nobel and academic bureaucracy, the nomination proper had been the work of Per Hallström (1866–1960), an enthusiast for his work who was both President of the Nobel committee and a member of the Swedish Academy. Erik Palmstierna (1877–1959), the Swedish Ambassador in London, was also an admirer of Yeats's work and shared his spiritualist interests. On at least one occasion in 1923 (presumably before the Nobel announcement), he visited the Yeatses in Merrion Square. Yeats, who was only the second Anglophone writer to win the Literature Prize, was remarkably well connected.[3]

In strictly literary terms, he and Thomas Mann meet on just one occasion, the very late poem 'Politics', with which Yeats intended to close his last collection and which carried an epigraph (unique in Yeats's *Collected Poems*) from Mann. Just as poem and title exist in tension, so do Yeats and Mann appear as an odd couple. I find only one prior reference to Mann in Yeats's published work, and this occurs (as we would expect) in a prose context. In the final section of the *Autobiographies* entitled 'The Bounty of Sweden' (1925), he summarised events and circumstances leading up to his winning the Nobel Prize:

> Early in November [1923] a journalist called to show me a printed paragraph saying that the Nobel Prize would probably be conferred upon Herr Mann, the distinguished novelist, or upon myself. I did not know that the Swedish Academy had ever heard my name; tried to escape an interview by talking of Rabindranath Tagore, of his gift to his School of the seven thousand pounds awarded him; almost succeeded in dismissing the whole Reuter paragraph from my memory. Herr Mann has many readers, is a famous novelist with his fixed place in the world, and, said I to myself, well fitted for such a honour: whereas I am but a writer of plays which are acted by players with a literary mind for a few evenings, and I have altered them so many times that I doubt the value of every passage. I am more confident of my lyrics, or of some few amongst them, but then I have got into the habit of recommending or commending myself to general company for anything rather than my gift of lyric writing, which concerns such a meagre troop.[4]

Here is the poet at his most publicly feline; in private correspondence with John Quinn he is far more direct: 'I see I have a chance of the Nobel prize' – this in the postscript to a business letter.[5] The essential contrast, which Yeats draws between himself and the novelist, relates to fixity. Mann has his fixed place in the world; his work is (so to speak) stabilised by his many readers. The plays through which Yeats refers to his own accomplishment undergo perpetual change, however, and depend on performance for a few evenings. Superficially, Yeats argues that he refers to his drama as a form of decoy, being more confident of his lyric writing. But as the latter is emphatically characterised as appealing to 'such a meagre troop', the distinction is hardly categorical. Mann, it is powerfully suggested, exists in a solid prose world; Yeats, according to himself, is a man of protean poetic textuality. Here we find another of those intrusive disjunctions which hold apart the text of the poem 'Politics' and the title itself. Of course, the same disjunction might be flattered with a philosophical description whereby world and mind, or body and soul, appear as antagonists. Yeats often subscribed to such an idealism, but he was also prone to fall into arrears with his subscription.

Another disjunction arises when one compares Yeats's anticipation of the Nobel award with his account of travelling to Stockholm a few weeks later. The journey was made in several stages, from Dublin to England, then from Harwich across the North Sea to Denmark, and finally from Copenhagen to Stockholm. In *The Bounty of Sweden* (1925) he devoted several pages to these superficial preliminaries, before climaxing with the text of his lecture before the Royal Academy of Sweden. His account of the journey works to establish two themes: one, of his *being seen* as the Nobel Prize winner; two, of the political opinions expressed by various persons whom he encountered in travelling. The Danish boat carried numerous commercial travellers but, after some time, the Yeatses are recognised because somebody had 'a newspaper with my portrait'. At dinner, a man who represented a Danish exporter in Ireland talks to them, commenting on Irish farmers' failure to make winter butter and their pathetic reliance on government initiatives. An elderly Swede kisses Mrs Yeats's hand, earning a Dane's displeasure at Frenchified gallantry. A distinguished (but unnamed) poet meets them at Esbjerg; at Copenhagen they are met by journalists. There is much discussion of Danish education, and some advance praise of the Swedish royal family. Someone predicts a socialist government, and Yeats wonders 'what Denmark will make of that mechanical eighteenth-century dream; we know what half-mediaeval Russia has made of it'.[6] If he was truly attending to Lenin's Soviet experiments, it is difficult to reconcile the practice with the definition: a more obvious 'mechanical eighteenth-century dream' to which he soon referred repeatedly was Swedenborgianism.

Yeats chose to underscore his familiarity with two Scandinavian writers – the mystic engineer, Emanuel Swedenborg (1688–1772), and the alchemist-playwright, August Strindberg (1849–1912). At a banquet in Stockholm, he was quizzed by a woman who knew about his psychical researches. Intending to explain himself, Yeats runs into difficulties:

> We are going to change the thought of the world, I say, to bring it back to all its old truths, but I dread the future. Think what the people have made of the political thought of the eighteenth century, and now we must offer them a new fanaticism. Then I stop ashamed, for I am talking habitual thoughts, and not adapting them to her ear, forgetting beauty in the pursuit of truth, and I wonder if age has made my mind rigid and heavy.[7]

History does not record the Swedish lady's response to the

proffered fanaticism, but, if she followed Yeats's development, she was not in doubt as to his serious intent.

Yeats's address to the Swedish Royal Academy on 13 December 1923 – he called it a lecture, in publishing it – generously paid tribute to J. M. Synge and Augusta Gregory as his co-workers. In doing so, he inevitably drew attention to the dramatic side of his own creative work, though the Nobel committee had sought to reward his great lyric genius. There were questions of protocol to be considered: he could hardly sing the praises of any writer who might have been a rival in the committee's eyes or who might become a candidate in years to come. Consequently, the dead Synge and an ageing woman prose-writer posed no threat to the ceremony. Joyce's name is notably absent from his account of the Irish literary movement. If Yeats's field of activity were defined more broadly, one could speculate on the opportunity he had to celebrate the modern movement generally. *Ulysses* and Eliot's *The Waste Land* had both appeared the previous year, and Lawrence's *Women in Love* one year earlier still. But Yeats chose not to present himself as a modernist or as a participant in international literary movements: he was an Irish cultural nationalist.

This note was struck in the second paragraph with the declaration that Ireland's disillusion with parliamentary politics, at the time of Parnell's death, begat its modern literature. But Yeats's language is not merely political; it is biological. Referring to the Anglo-Irish war (his term) of 1919–21, he declared that 'the race began, as I think, to be troubled by that event's long gestation'. The term 'race' here clearly does not mean family, in the way that Yeats had used it in his early autobiography, and 'gestation' emphasises the biologist model for his representation of military/political change in Ireland. A few pages later there occurs an anecdote about Willie Fay, one of the actors on whom the Irish dramatic movement had relied in its early days. Fay had toured:

> in a theatrical company managed by a Negro. I doubt if he had learned much in it, for its methods were rough and noisy, the Negro whitening his face when he played a white man, but, so strong is stage convention, blackening it when he played a black man.[8]

Though Yeats had referred to the Afro-American R. B. Lewis on an earlier occasion (never of course naming him), the Swedish Royal Academy was the first audience to be entertained with the detail of a black actor blacking up to play a black character. It is a harmless enough detail, were it not for the teller's subsequent classification of blacks 'among those our civilisation must reject, or leave unrewarded at some level below that co-ordination that modern civilisation finds essential'.[9] In a final rhetorical flourish, he compared Sweden to his own emergent country in distinctly political terms, once again conjoining race:

> I think most of all, perhaps, of that splendid spectacle of your Court, a family beloved and able that has gathered about it not the rank only but the intellect of its country. No like spectacle will in Ireland show its work of discipline and of taste, though it might satisfy a need of the race no institution under the influence of English or American democracy can satisfy.[10]

This is Yeats in uncharacteristically pessimistic mood: the conjunction of rank and intellect will *not*, he insists, come about in Ireland. Nevertheless the virtues and vices of his political taxonomy are plainly stated – family and race on the credit side, democracy the great debit. The mood is that of December 1923, the time of his address to the Swedish Academy: by the time he will publish these words in July 1925, he will have drawn strength from his Nobel honour and committed himself to the pursuit of some such conjunction through the less-than-ideal facilities provided by the Irish Senate. 'From Democracy to Authority', published in the *Irish Times* of 16 February 1924, marked a staging post. The Army Mutiny, occurring shortly afterwards, was an occasion for secret politics, and *To-morrow* a platform for more public, if short-lived, provocations. At a deeper level, however, Yeats slowly engaged with Thomas Mann in an undeclared struggle. Their rival-identical aims were to define education as a cultural activity of high worth, to see development (*Bildung*) pitted against old truths, or to deny all but the most basic instruction to the majority of men and women.

Between Balzac and Freud: 'A Prayer for My Daughter'

Dublin thought Yeats had overdone his fawning to the Swedish royals. More exactly, Yeats admired the hierarchical arrangements of court life in Stockholm as they interacted with family. In December 1923 these interactions were greatly to the fore: the widower Crown Prince had just married Louise Battenberg (1889–1965) in London as his second wife. Their homecoming merged with the Nobel events on 11 December to give a heightened sense of general celebration.

Crowns had fallen since November 1918, and with them some heads: Habsburgs, Hohenzollerns, Romanovs, and lesser immortals. Noble blood meant a good deal to the commoner in Yeats, who had devoted much ingenuity to the pursuit of titled supposed ancestors. Blood bid fair to be another metaphor for poetry, provided of course its opposite – the disembodied spirits of dead persons – were also admitted to the creative process. As truth is enhanced for Yeats by the validity of counter-truth, so bloodshed is counter-balanced by leaks from the psychic reservoir. Much of this thinking is concentrated in 'If I Were Four-and-Twenty', published in August 1919 some months after the birth of his daughter: the hero throughout is Honoré de Balzac (1799–1850).[11]

Automatic writing, which led into his pursuit of titled ancestors, had been the gift of an understanding wife. Psychic fruitfulness was matched by sexual, though not without the trauma of miscarriage and alarm. The Yeatses' first child was born on 26 February 1919 and named after a seventeenth-century Duchess of Ormonde. In keeping with this desired pedigree, her father horoscopically identified the astrological conditions of her moment of birth: apparently it was 'the passing of the objective historical circle of Christianity or democracy'. He did not achieve this insight, however, until the summer of 1934 when, as it happened, he was once again commending Balzac to the public. In a letter transmitting the new intelligence on Anne's birth to Olivia Shakespear, he also recalled his Stockholm triumph, prompted by a remark recently made by a Swede to George Yeats, 'Our Royal Family liked your husband better than any other Nobel prize winner. They said he has the manners of a Courtier.'[12]

In 1934, Nobel Prize winners were being hounded out of German universities to face contumely, domestic eviction, violence at the hands and feet of the SA. Yeats maintained the dignified silence of a courtier, preferring in Mussolini's Rapallo to contemplate verses in which 'a monk reads his breviary at midnight upon the tomb of long dead lovers on the aniversary [sic] of their deaths for on that night they are united above the tomb, their embrace being not partial but a conflagration of the entire body & so shedding the light he reads by'. It is tempting to dismiss Gothic emissions of this kind as the sort of thing which – to quote Philip French – gives bad taste a bad name. It accords oddly with a respect for family and the courts of Battenberg and Bernadotte. Yet the letter turns back upon itself, as though seeking its own counter-truth: 'Strange that I should write these things ... when if I were to offer my self for new love I could only expect to be accepted by the very young wearied by the passive embraces of the bolster.'[13] Yeats as chicken-butcher, but in the mind only?

In violation of counter-chronology, we have run ahead of ourselves. The moment had been 'when Mars and Venus were just past conjunction' – that is, two minutes before 10 a.m. on Wednesday, 26 February 1919. One month earlier, the father-to-be had spoken on 'Socialism and War' in Trinity College, a text strangely un-uncovered by scholars in that institution. It is worth considering if the conjunction of Mars and Venus meant nothing more than a date in 1918 when, while the Great War continued lethally to rage, the Yeatses fruitfully made love. *His rebus gestis*, he began writing 'A Prayer for My Daughter' on 1 April 1919, a fine civil poem.

In 'If I Were Four-and-Twenty' Yeats offered a number of mentors to Irish youth. These were without exception literary, though the context was political. From France, he recommended Paul Claudel, Francis Jammes and Charles Péguy – the Catholic/nationalist triumvirate whom he had studied under Iseult Gonne's direction during the Great War – together, climactically, with Balzac, France's greatest novelist and author of the vast fictional panorama known as the *Comédie humaine*. This last was a lifelong enthusiasm, commencing in youth when his father proposed that he should read the entire works of Balzac – which Yeats did, on several occasions, in English translation. John Butler Yeats was not alone among denizens of Victorian London in admiring the *Comédie* – Karl Marx was also a keen and appreciative reader. But in 1919 Yeats the poet had decidedly anti-Marxian objectives. He was prepared to recommend a modified version of neo-platonic-cum-Celtic Christianity to scotch the socialism inspired by James Connolly, which was then influential in the Labour and nationalist movements.

As Roy Foster has noted, 'If I Were Four-and-Twenty' contains some of Yeats's most original thinking on politics. Commencing with the self-command, 'Hammer your thoughts into unity', and looking towards 'Unity of Being', he invokes a myriad of authorities, qualified at time by 'perhaps'. Drawing on what he believed Balzac's vision of society was, Yeats conceives order in terms of 'two struggles': between family and family, between individual and individual. If individualism proves less influential than bourgeois-dynasticism (my term), society will insist on privilege, but above all on 'the rights of property'.[14] This last concept is distinctly modern, being no older than the French or American Revolutions: before the eighteenth century property was regarded as both God-given and natural, dependent on no abstract theory of rights. Yeats intervenes in a contemporary debate, regarding it as perhaps more urgent than it really was. Connolly's successors in the Labour movement were not thinkers of the same calibre, nor did the international situation encourage revolutionary change in the manner of 1916. British governments had effectively abolished the old system of landowner-ship. Yeats's fear was that any emergent Irish government might take the process a stage further and, under socialist influences, abolish private property *tout court*. As he soon discovered, W. T. Cosgrave had no such ambitions.

Examining 'If I Were Four-and-Twenty', we find Yeats's own thought divided between two struggles, even while insisting on the convergence of literature, politics and philosophy. To use medical metaphors, these were diagnosis and prescription. He was to prove better at the former than the latter. When confronted by the undeniable portends of social change under de Valera's Fianna Fáil, his cocktail of political pills mixed native Blue Shirtism with the *Bhagavad Gita*. Even when he concluded that de Valera was not a communist, he still commended Nazi legislation. During earlier crises, his professional advice was less extreme, though marked by exaggeration and counsels of strategic despair: consider the Army Mutiny, the civil war and the Anglo-Irish conflict. Perhaps the most acute dichotomy had arisen in 1916 when, rightly perceiving that all had changed, he looked forward to modified Home Rule, while scores of thousands were slaughtered in France. If one were to seek a bridge across these divided responses, it might be found in Yeats's complex attitude towards blood. Blood is a multivalent symbol or metaphor because it can be used to indicate life and death almost indistinguishably and because it encodes restriction and succession equally well.

Or, in other words, Mars and Venus. A few weeks before Anne Yeats's birth, the opening shots of the War of Independence were fired by the emergent Irish Republican Army. The infant's earliest months were paralleled by the growth of violence in the country and the disillusion of figures like Augusta Gregory. The poet-father's concern was less immediately political. He was anxious to understand the full significance of his daughter's naming. The Instructors who worked through George Yeats's automatic writing suggested that the child was the reincarnation of the seventeenth-century duchess. One of these Instructors, by name Ontelos, demanded that Yeats 'fully grasp the meaning of your having been Anne's lover & now her father & the husband of her child who is now her mother'.[15] One can only hope that Yeats did, for surely few others have. The wonder is that the poem composed during these early troubled days of the child's life is as clear as it is.

Its clarity derives in part from Yeats's decidedly one-sided reading of Balzac. Though Marx admired the thoroughness with which the *Comédie humaine* recorded and analysed French society in the nineteenth century, Yeats preferred to emphasise Balzac's interest in spiritualism, in sexual aspects of paranormal behaviour, and in the life and teachings of Swedenborg. (Swedenborg features briefly in one of Balzac's most exotic *contes*, 'Séraphita', where the main interest focuses on the interchangeable gender-roles of angels. For good measure, Yeats addressed Alick Schepeler, a spiritualist lady-friend of 1915–16, as Séraphita.) The Great War changed Balzac, as it did much else in the heritable past. In the 1920s, attitudes towards Balzac were becoming polarised in France. Proto-fascist royalists in L'Action française venerated him less as the chronicler of an avaricious and vulgar bourgeoisie and more as the elegist for lost authority, for the elegance and apparent stability of the *ancien régime*. It is no coincidence that, in tandem with this revaluation of Balzac, there arose a school of historiography hostile to the revolution of 1789. Yeats was part of the reactionary reading that appealed in France after the Great War, and his responsiveness to these continental earthquakes of opinion should be borne in mind when he subsequently declares himself uninvolved in European affairs.

The Balzac whom Marx read had been under no illusions about the stability of the old world: he was its pathologist, not its cosmetician. A 'left' version of Balzac has been influential in the last half-century, through the (very different) approaches of György Lukács and Roland Barthes. A protean novelist, his 'message' was not to be monopolised by one party. Not that Lukács was any model of consistency, even after his adoption of Marxism. His *Theory of the Novel* (1920 in German) and *The Historical Novel* (1937 in Russian) differ in their approval of Balzac, the latter heavily influenced by the ideological struggle in Central Europe. In addition to Yeats and Lukács, Balzac had in Sigmund Freud another and differently distinctive loyal reader. After Freud had left Vienna for London, he devoted much of his final days to rereading *La Peau de chagrin*, confirming in it anticipations of his own *Todestrieb* (death drive) theory explored in *Beyond the Pleasure Principle* (1920), written in the year of 'A Prayer'.[16]

'A Prayer for My Daughter' shows blessedly little debt to its author, the Duchess of Ormonde. Perhaps the South Californian side of the poet's imagination had been on holiday during the poem's composition. It is nonetheless linked to the previous item in *Michael Robartes and the Dancer* (1921) as by an umbilical cord. 'The Second Coming' closes on the word 'born', having revealed (through the automatic scripts) that two millennia were now 'vexed to nightmare by a rocking cradle'. And the succeeding poem opens, 'Once more the storm is howling ...' Thus placed in the collection of 1921, Yeats's prayer for his daughter takes its more significant place in his prophetico-political system. It is also a sexual-political code, as the poem proceeds to differentiate the girl from two women whom her father has loved: Maud Gonne and her daughter, Iseult.[17] She is to be her mother's daughter – that is, Georgie Yeats's. That a prayer should be required to achieve this end gives some indication of the power exercised in the poet-father's imagination by the other women, and the events of a year later in Glenmalure prove how enmeshed with them he remained.

The drive of the poem might be identified in these terms as one directed towards establishing the child's independent life. Yet the virtues sought for her quickly disclose restrictions within the burgeoning natural imagery. Courtesy is all very well, especially as glossed in the lively manner of Castiglione, but this courtesy is to be acquired by learning. The child is to become a flourishing *hidden* tree and, within that, her thoughts are to be linnet-like, engaged (perhaps caged) in a purely internalised business of 'dispensing round / Their magnanimities of sound'. By the end of Stanza 6, she is to live 'like some green laurel / Rooted in one dear perpetual place'. In a poem rich with classical allusion, the laurel is not only a growing (but immovable) tree, it is the plucked leaf decorating the victorious male's brow.

Thereafter, hatred begins to trespass in the blessed retreat, its signature to be found in four successive stanzas. On this occasion, Yeats does not endorse it. His dismissal of it, however, is achieved at the price of conceding that the linnet is immovable artifice, like the 'form' that Grecian goldsmiths make in the final stanza of 'Sailing to Byzantium':

> If there's no hatred in a mind
> Assault and battery of the wind
> Can never tear the linnet from the leaf.

There follows the renowned stanza about Maud Gonne and the 'old bellows full of angry wind' (her husband). On this high horse, Yeats seems well set to draw his prayer to a fruitful conclusion, 'all hatred driven hence'. Yet the need to reiterate the word sounds a note of warning. If Stanza 9 celebrated the self-generating and self-sustaining world of art, what has become of the daughter? The next and final stanza sends in a bridegroom who will bring to her a house 'Where all's accustomed, ceremonious'. Good. But hatred intrudes yet again, as if hawked by some revenant salesman invading the ordained space:

> For arrogance and hatred are the wares
> Peddled in the thoroughfares.
> How but in custom and in ceremony
> Are innocence and beauty born?
> Ceremony's a name for the rich horn
> And custom for the spreading laurel tree.

Read in a certain light, 'A Prayer for My Daughter' is one of Yeats's most moving poems. But the light we read poetry by is never static. It is naturally affected by our own age and experience, or is subject to illumination from other texts, or becomes prone to shadows cast by non-texts, brute events. In 'A Prayer's' final stanza, the cluster of abstractions rendered stately only serves to expose a marmorial texture in the whole poem's emergent imagery. Reversing the familiar dictum about Michelangelo's 'David', this work of art shows the human figure growing back into rhyming marble. Indeed, stone insistently dominates the collection in which 'A Prayer' appears as the third item from the end. It is an altar-piece in the opening title-poem; it is stubbornly disruptive in 'Easter 1916'; there casually enough in 'Towards Break of Day'; transformed to a lofty rock in 'On a Political Prisoner', etc. But from 'The Second Coming' to the book's close, the poems trace a petrification finally and literally achieved in 'To be Carved on a Stone at Thoor Ballylee'.

The book consists of fourteen items, written between November 1914 and November 1919, with 'A Prayer for My Daughter' as its nearest approach to celebration. The immediate successor on the page, 'A Meditation in Time of War' (9 November 1914), appears to draw on the later-written poem by utilising 'the old wind-broken tree'. 'A Meditation' is one of Yeats's doctrinal poems: for a moment he

> knew that One is animate
> Mankind inanimate phantasy.

The fate outlined in 'A Prayer for My Daughter' signally omits any reference to her generative future as woman. The bridegroom stanza was an afterthought, replacing three in which she is imagined walking in Coole Park (by 'the stony edges of the lake') after the poet's death. Her birth prefigures no future birth, no generative life, no family continuity. She has been artfully placed beyond the pleasure principle.

Yeats reread Balzac while facing down Freud. While at work on 'Per Amica Silentia Lunae' (1917), he had looked into *The Interpretation of Dreams* (1900). The Freud whom he now approached in 1919 as the author of 'A Prayer for My Daughter' was not the professional analyst of dreams or individual neurosis, but the reluctant philosopher of cultural atrophy and, more immediately, the death instinct. In one of the discarded stanzas, Yeats has the young woman cry out to him (being dead) that all is well. The substitution of a walk-on bridegroom for this dead father marks a critical moment in the textual tussle to close the poem. In an even more gauche (discarded) detail, her cry is likely overheard by a labourer or common man. This awkward intrusion relates more to the collection as a whole than to the individual poem from which it was easily expunged. Elsewhere in *Michael Robartes and the Dancer*, a figure similar to the one expunged from 'A Prayer' appears at the end of 'Under Saturn' (an un-stony poem in the collection), where he 'had served my people' near Sligo. More tendentiously, this labouring man recognises the Saturnine poet after twenty years, but serves also to imply connection with 'a red-haired Yeats whose looks, although he died / Before my time, seem like a vivid memory'. The redhead, of course, was not a native of Sligo as frequently celebrated by the poet, but a resident in unchronicled County Down and Sandymount Castle, a stray in the legend of family which the poet arduously constructs, but cannot project now that he had reached his own daughter's cradle.

The futures for Anne lie behind her in the ancestral – more

specifically, great-grand-paternal – past. 'Under Saturn' had ended with 'a child's vow sworn in vain':

> Never to leave that valley his fathers called their home.

The insistence, in 'If I Were Four-and-Twenty', on original sin derives from no theological commitment to Christian orthodoxy, though the doctrine supplies as a powerful metaphor for an ancestral innocence that cannot be regained. In keeping with this strong, if purely formal, belief, Yeats substitutes the bridegroom and suppresses what Freud would call a retrograde drive. If Freud seems obtrusive here, one should note in the earliest pages of *Beyond the Pleasure Principle* his acknowledgment of a debt to 'a small work' by G. T. Fechner, whom Yeats and his wife were reading in the earliest days of their marriage. It is not the same small work in their case, but the occurrence of Fechner's name in Berggasse and Thoor Ballylee serves to underline the decisive choices the poet was making in these years – opting for the life-after-death aspect of Fechner's thought, and avoiding the implications of Freud's new insight into death-after-life.[18]

Bones of Contention

'Under Saturn' had been written for George Yeats to explain how the poet was not brooding for Maud Gonne, but for Blood Kindred. A minor piece, it is one of several occasional poems diplomatically establishing his new life. The crises of 1916/17 had not been resolved in a sunburst of recovery, private or public. The sudden insurrection, followed by the steady routine of court martial and execution, shocked Yeats, partly because it did not fit into any pattern of known behaviour, political or military. It underscored his isolation from the realities of advanced Irish opinion, and even suggested a degree of naïvety. 'Easter 1916' conveys a quality of abashed self-realisation that is rare in his work.

The creative life responded anxiously to the events of Easter. In poetry, the great tribute emerged very slowly, with the result that Yeats has been suspected of calculation in the timing of its publication. But what there is of calculation in 'Easter 1916' measures the painful, and ultimately scrupulous, calibration of the poet's awkward relationship with the men executed, 'the old bellows' included. From these, however, the poem excluded Roger Casement, the only one who might have claimed some class affinity with Yeats. There were other reasons why Casement fails to gain entrance to the implied pantheon of the poem – he was the only one of the rebel leaders to be tried in a civilian court, the only one to be hanged; he was executed in England (not Ireland), and his final weeks and days were dogged by persistent rumours of an exotic homosexual career. On all counts, Casement differed from the straightforward 'martyr for old Ireland' pattern, nor did he win the honour of a military execution.

In drama, the response was more direct and more remote. 'The Dreaming of the Bones' preoccupied Yeats while he was staying with Maud and Iseult Gonne in Normandy during the late summer of 1917. Having been rejected by both women when he proposed marriage to them the previous year, he knew the personal as well as political significance of his plot – a Volunteer fleeing from the General Post Office has reached County Clare, where he has an unsought, visionary encounter with Dervorgilla and Dermot whose twelfth-century illicit passion had 'brought the Normans in', and Ireland's long humiliation. The collocations of person and place were certainly difficult. Staying in Normandy, Yeats wished to invoke the Norman invasion, the *fons et origo* of Irish suffering. And as for the women, he said of Iseult at this time that she 'has always been something like a daughter to me'. Indeed, he offered this as a rationale for his not being too despondent at her rejection, while Maud Gonne, her mother, was 'in a joyous & self-forgetting condition of political hatred'. This Yeats found additionally helpful as he worked on his play under their roof. Though the completed work is among the most dramatically effective of his Noh-type plays, it is infused with autobiographical anxiety.

His distance from the leaders of the rising, in advance of their military action, would be touchingly acknowledged in 'Easter 1916'. In the play, distance is dramatised in the Young Man's having fled from Dublin, after that action, with a view to escaping to the Aran Islands; the dramatic action occurs as he awaits a boat to take him on the final leg of his journey. Anticipating Beckett, Yeats dramatises an impasse. It is unlikely that any member of the GPO garrison embarked on such a dangerous and pointless westward undertaking. Its significance may be taken as symbolic, but only within a literary and not a political context. Escape to the far west could be interpreted as keeping faith with the pure cultural imperatives that lay behind the rising, at least in Patrick Pearse's formulation. Had not Yeats directed J. M. Synge to the Aran Islands twenty years before the rising, thereby inaugurating a successful theatre for Ireland? There was no practical benefit to be won: the far west had failed effectively to 'rise' in its proclaimed support of Sinn Féin.

Nevertheless, suspects in Galway were arrested in 1916, and their internment contributed much to their subsequent political development. One of them, Frank Hynes, later recorded that there had been close on a thousand troops in the mid-Clare village of Tulla searching for local rebels (Liam Mellows was among them).[19] This was far from the coastal isolation of 'The Dreaming of the Bones'. There was, however, one instance of an agrarian radical who would do something similar to the young volunteer of Yeats's play. Laurence Ginnell (1854–1928), sometime MP for Westmeath, went to convalesce on the islands after his imprisonment in May 1919, breaking his journey westward to stay with the Moylett family in Mayo.[20] While in prison, he had been succeeded as Sinn Féin's Director of Publicity by Desmond FitzGerald (1888–1947), a poet and a friend of Ezra Pound. Yeats could not have had Ginnell in mind two years earlier, and the MP – a proponent of the Ranch War and of cattle-driving – was not the kind of rebel of whom Yeats approved. Like Maud Gonne or Constance Markiewitz, Ginnell would 'hurl the little streets upon the great' – but without her sex or redeeming class credentials. Nevertheless, Ginnell's conduct (rather than example) provides us with the opportunity to reconsider the Volunteer's role in 'The Dreaming of the Bones'.

A general resemblance of the plot, or dramatic situation, to that of Synge's 'Playboy' deserves notice. A young man is seeking shelter, having struck a blow against patriarchal authority. Christy Mahon's prototype had fled from the mainland to Aran, though Synge, for his own reasons, confines the action to the western seaboard. Despite his heroic initiative, the young man in each case is fearful not simply because he may be caught by a vengeful father (biological or ideological), but because the zone of transition from danger to safety in which he hides is said to be rife with spirits, 'the walking dead' in Synge's phrase. Yeats's play seeks to turn Synge's savage comedy into gnomic tragedy. In the course of the stately, highly stylised action, the Volunteer gradually emerges as more than the shadow of a gunman. But is he the privileged witness of spiritual agony which most productions and interpretations imagine? Or, to take a non-

Yeatsian parallel, is he akin to Marlow, narrator of Conrad's *Heart of Darkness*, a traveller with tales of another world, beyond the rules of ordinary men and women? The Syngean parallels are finite, and Yeats's play contains a strong narrative drive which sanctions a comparison with novel or novella. Both figures wait by the margin of the ocean, with listeners eager to be informed or entertained. Both reveal histories of invasion, rapine and exploitation – Conrad's being contemporary, Yeats's distantly historical. 'The Dreaming of the Bones' remains a quizzical text.

There is a third reading permitted by the shadow of Ginnell (aged sixty-two at the time of the rising) behind the Volunteer. The act of flight from the battle cannot be easily presented as heroic, but for the most part Yeats's protagonist is thought of as taking a sensible course of action, reuniting himself with the Gaelic west in defeat. But what if one were to consider him as guilty and cowardly, a deserter of the cause and not its dramatic representative? That such feelings existed, the playwright knew in his heart – feelings of inadequacy, unpreparedness, lack of courage in the raw. Disliking Ginnell's form of radical action, and indeed unconscious of Ginnell's example, Yeats creates a spokesman for the 1916 rebels who is marked by Yeats's own shortcomings and preferences as a sedentary man of fifty-one. Thus 'the Young Man' is already a projection into the past, even before he encounters twelfth-century ghosts.

Yeats might equally see himself in the dilemma of the two lovers condemned to exclusion from bliss until forgiven by one of their own race. The term is awkward in the context. If it is assumed that Dermot and Dervorgilla are – 'racially' speaking – Celts or Gaels, they can never be forgiven by that vast component of the Irish people descended from Normans, Old English, New English, Huguenots or more casual dwellers in Mountmellick, Mount Pottinger or Mount Melleray. Of these groups within the mongrel stock, the Normans are very large indeed, including most folk whose name begins with Fitz (-gerald, -gibbon, -maurice, etc.), not to mention the Burkes (including Edmund and the more recent Mary), Devereux, Laceys and other housekeepers of the nation. But the Norman-descended most particularly cannot assist, for it was they (as an invasive force) whom the lovers were responsible for introducing into Ireland. More broadly, no Barton, Brugha, Casement, Childers, de Valera, Emmet, Figgis, Gonne, Gore-Booth, Gregory, Lemass, Pearse, Shaw, Synge,

Wilde, Wolfe Tone or Yeats will do. Of course, the stipulation is a dramatic one, without historical provenance.

The dramatist certainly dwelt on the question for, at the time of Kevin O'Higgins's murder in 1927, he enquired of Olivia Shakespear, 'Are we, that fore-know, the actual or potential traitors of the race-process [?] Do we as it were forbid the bands [*sic*] when the event is struggling to be born[?]'[21] Whether the dyslexic Yeats here means 'swaddling bands' or 'wedding banns' is not clear, though in either case an offence against procreation is implied. Race-process, though indubitably the kernel of the play's concern, is hard to pin down with any particularity. Yeats's recourse to metaphors of generation was long-standing: the Swedes had listened to a similar message in 1923. In 1927 it had its own embarrassment, even for Yeats. Sean MacBride was among those tearaway IRA men suspected of O'Higgins's murder, on which basis he had been arrested by the government and held in Mountjoy Prison. As the son of Major John MacBride, the young man was well qualified to forgive the lovers in Yeats's play. As the descendant of eighteenth-century Gonnes of Dublin, he was disqualified from performing the rites of absolution. His half-sister, Iseult, was even less well placed to assist. The daughter of Lucien Millevoye might even have been a Norman herself; certainly she was a Normandy landowner and, like Sean, had the additional burden in her blood of English-originating Dubliners. Yeats's ideas were, of course, occasional rather than consistent. While keeping Olivia Shakespear abreast of developments in the O'Higgins case, he provided early news of the row soon to break over Sean O'Casey's new play, 'The Silver Tassie'. 'Ideas go to the heads of these uneducated men – while they are content to observe I feel all is well.'[22] Ideas of race-process were permitted, even from one who could not spell 'shugger' otherwise.

The immediate personal unease apparently revived memories of an earlier emotional and visionary crisis, albeit one that had ended in hope. Working on 'The Dreaming of the Bones', Yeats cannot have forgotten the Vision of the Archer which occurred on the night of 14/15 August 1896 for, in 1920 when he came to reconsider this richly symbolic dream as an autobiographer, he referred to the incident as 'the stirring of the bones'. His subsequent note for the cryptic text is remarkably explicit:

The conception [*sic*] of the play is derived from the world-wide belief that the dead dream back, for a certain time, through the more personal thoughts and deeds of life. The wicked, according to Cornelius Agrippa, dream themselves to be consumed by flames and persecuted by demons; and there is precisely the same thought in a Japanese 'Noh' play, where a spirit, advised by a Buddhist priest she has met upon the road, seeks to escape from the flames by ceasing to believe in the dream. The lovers in my play have lost themselves in a different but still self-created winding of the labyrinth of conscience. The Judwalis distinguished between the Shade which dreams back in the order of their intensity . . .[23]

And so on, with further reference to 'the folklore of all countries'. What Yeats does not invoke in his apologia is the Swedenborgian statement of similar beliefs. This he had encountered in Sheridan Le Fanu's collection of tales, *In a Glass Darkly* (1872), which Yeats read as a child. Based on the papers of a fictional Dr Hesselius, Le Fanu's insistent enquiry into guilt was too close to the bone for admission to the rationale of 'The Dreaming of the Bones'. It indicted Yeats's own class in too unmistakable a fashion to allow for the subtle dramatic cruxes and nuances of his dialogue. Instead, he invented a constitutive fiction of his own – the papers of one Michael Robartes, an antitype of the poet, a rough man-of-action.

In keeping with its metaphysical claims, the play moves between the dramatist's past and future. In November 1894, Yeats had stayed in Lisadell, the Gore-Booths' house outside Sligo, officially to speak to the Revd Fletcher Le Fanu (the local rector, 'a relation of the great man of that name') on matters of folklore. Unofficially, notions of proposing marriage to Eva Gore-Booth arose in his mind. As he recognised, 'this house would never accept so penniless a suitor', and wisely held his tongue.[24] Fletcher Le Fanu had earlier entertained similar ambitions but, when attempting to jump over a cow couchant to impress the girls, had unfortunately fallen from his horse. Yeats in those days was miserably unhappy, ambitious, timid and shrewd – he sent books to Mrs Fletcher Le Fanu for parochial fund-raisers. His beloved, he noted, was known to local people as Miss Gore, for they disdained the commercial side of the family encoded in '-Booth'. His pennilessness was thus converted into a form of social honour. Eva turned out to be a lesbian; Roger Casement appears to have been the only man she was emotionally moved by. Michael Robartes, whom Yeats mobilised in accounting for 'The Dreaming of the Bones', had first appeared during the love-lorn 1890s; after 1917 he took on decidedly more aggressive airs; in the 1930s, Yeats sought a real-life counterpart for his hero in Patrick McCartan, Dermot MacManus and Eoin O'Duffy. To judge by their surnames, they were qualified to absolve Dermot and Dervorgilla. The occultic play swivelled between *fin de siècle* and proto-fascist tonalities.

There were other, biographical pressures at work when the piece was shaped. Augusta Gregory had already written (1907) a play based on Dervorgilla, concentrating on 'the swift, unflinching, terrible judgment' of young Gaels upon the old woman who (in her youth) had brought the foreigner into Ireland. Gregory's 'Dervorgilla' was set at Mellifont, a Cistercian monastery in County Louth and the place where Dervorgilla died in 1193. (She was, correctly, Derbforgaill, widow of Tigernán ua Ruairc.) The medieval details are just so much chronicle, and reflect the party-interest of the compilers and their patrons, until (in the nineteenth century) nationalism seizes on the tale as central to the origin myth of Irish grievances against Britain. Gregory follows the pattern adding, however, a touching treatment of youth and age ill-placed to understand each other. Yeats and Gregory knew such differences of perspective in their own relationship.

Mellifont is a suitable site for these meditations: a religious house belonging to a great continental order (the Cistercians), it had been built by a native Gaelic Archbishop of Armagh, Malachi, on land provided by a native king. It stood, in the first instance, as a demonstration of Gaelic Ireland's direct contact with European culture. Architecturally, it contained buildings regarded as transitional between the Romanesque style of the early Celtic Church and the Gothic style associated with the invading Normans. Its most celebrated surviving structure is the lavabo, where monks symbolically washed their hands. Add to all of these 'inter-cultural' details Mellifont's frontier position between Ulster and Leinster (or medieval Meath), and one gains a sense of its richly mixed connotations.

Yeats's Dervorgilla play is set on the other side of Ireland, near another Cistercian abbey, Corcomroe in County Clare, again an example of Gaelic royal patronage resulting in a continental religious house. It is not entirely clear when he decided on this setting, with its symbolically powerful closeness to Aran, residual Gaelic culture and (in 1916) security from immediate armed retribution. On the back of an envelope Yeats informed Augusta Gregory, 'have almost decided to place my Dergovilla [*sic*] play in the neighbourhood of Mellifont. If so I will go to Armagh.'[25] Beyond the day and month (8

November), editors are unsure when this note was written, probably in 1918. If Yeats switched his setting from the historically appropriate Mellifont to the dramatically effective Corcomroe as the guns fell silent on the Western Front – or indeed, if he momentarily considered substituting the Ulster frontier location – then the political implications are mighty.

They are also deeply personal. Corcomroe lies a short distance inland from Lady Gregory's summer house at Mount Vernon, County Clare. The final choice of that setting may have involved a respectful avoidance of a setting she herself had used in her 'Dervorgilla' of pre-war times. It also distanced the play from the Gonnes amongst whom it had been conceived, and the natural landscape of County Clare stands in sharper contrast to Normandy than the well-watered fields of Mellifont. The late date for adoption of a western setting does not quite accommodate Laurence Ginnell, but it does affect the preference of a non-Ulster setting, or at least a setting in which the contemporary tensions of Ulster society do not impinge. Not only in the Volunteer's quitting Dublin for Aran, but in the playwright's struggle to fix on a setting, is Yeats's argument with modernity inscribed.

Parapsychology and the Great War

W. B. Yeats was an exceptional poet. In gravity of matter, in rhetorical control and power, in range of tone, he and John Milton are well matched. Like the author of *Paradise Lost,* Yeats mixed learning, politics and religion into his Parnassian dough, often transforming unleavened prose sources into near-miraculous poetic utterances. Where these sources are his own notes, one bows in admiration; where they derive from other private sources, one also trembles for his temerity. But the declension from the king-killing seventeenth century down to the mass-murdering modern age witnessed parallel vulgarisations of thought and belief. Yeats was not always above these, though he soared impressively. What W. H. Auden termed the south Californian side of his genius was inseparable from the poetry, for good or ill.

The impact of the Great War on the imaginative, cultural and political worlds in which Yeats lived can hardly be exaggerated. Yet it was an event to which he paid a curiously oblique attention. The relationship between literary Modernism and the slaughter of

1914–18 has been thoroughly explored, also the more local question of Irish separatism as a mid-war and post-war phenomenon. Recent research by historians has drawn attention to the Irish contribution *to* the war, as distinct from the more familiar reaction away from it. In all of these enquiries, Yeats would appear to be a marginal figure: nothing that he wrote has the same powerful dialectic of relationship to the Western Front as Shaw's *Heartbreak House* or Lawrence's *Women in Love*, nor do his political initiatives of the war years (cf. his defence of Casement in 1916) refer directly to the conflict or Irish involvement in it.

A sub-division of the Blood Kindred could be recruited to fill the gap. If victims of the war are required, then Thomas Kettle, Henry MacCormack and William Redmond might answer well. Among notable figures in the Irish campaign for independence after 1918, a significant number were drawn from the ranks of disenchanted front-line British Army officers. The best known of these were Robert Barton, Erskine Childers and David Robinson – all relatives, as it happens, and so potential illustrations of a Yeatsian theory about family. But there were others. One of Patrick Moylett's objections to the shadow 'native' administration emerging under de Valera's leadership before 1921 was the prominence of ex-British elements. Certainly, the three former officers just named played distractingly unpredictable roles in the years immediately following. Barton signed the 1921 treaty in London and then opposed it back in Dublin. Childers, who was secretary to the Irish delegation, became director of publicity for the republicans who launched the civil war. Robinson, a less political but more 'dashing' figure, strangely failed to be adopted by Yeats for his pantheon of Anglo-Irish swashbucklers.

The most notable of these was MacManus, whose war experiences cannot be verified. Another psychologically damaged veteran, whom Yeats kept on a very long finger, was William J. Maloney. MacManus shared Yeats's belief in the primacy of an eternal spirit world, compared to which foot-rot among the lance-corporals was of little concern. Yeats admired MacManus's stylish courage in overcoming his injuries of body and libido, but one cannot help feeling that admiration was grounded in a shared commitment to the irrational. For the soldier, the war may have been a primary cause as he sought some explanation of unparalleled human folly in a superhuman dimension. For the poet, the war had never physically impinged. In a

strangely elusive document, written before April 1916, Yeats summarised his position:

> I only know very vaguely what Mr Pearce [*sic, recte* Pearse] has written
> about politics, but I understand it is some sort of anti-Englishism or anti-
> recruiting. If this is true I am as vehemently opposed to Mr Pearce's
> politics as I am to the Unionism of the Provost [of Trinity College]. I
> have friends fighting in Flanders, I had one in the trenches at Antwerp,
> and I have a very dear friend nursing the wounded in a French hospital
> [Maud Gonne]. How can I help but feeling as they feel and desiring a
> German defeat?[26]

Even if this were digitally enhanced, or flattered under the heading
'vacillation', it would still amount to no more than flim-flam. It may
have been written for delivery at Trinity College's Gaelic Society in
November 1914, at a meeting banned by the Provost (J. P. Mahaffy)
because of Patrick Pearse's intended presence. What is disingenuous
about the passage (as we have it) is its studied exclusion of Yeats's
cardinal rule in assessing the war – the spiritualist rule. Early in 1914,
Yeats had looked forward to visiting Transylvania, less in pursuit of
his fellow-Dubliner's villain (Dracula) than in search of a wider
enquiry into the paranormal. His likely companion for the trip was
Everard Feilding, of the Society for Psychical Research, who had
been asked by the Vatican to investigate an alleged miracle in France.
In the event, the guns of August put an end to the scheme. This was
not a new area of enquiry; through folklore and other less venerable
sources, the spirit world had been rapping on Yeats's door for
decades. The society, which he joined as an associate member in 1913,
offered a more systematic framework for his interests. However, as
Roy Foster has put it, Yeats veered from a 'scientific' to a 'spiritist'
approach, and back again.

In down-to-earth terms, he was living at Stone Cottage at
Colman's Heath in Sussex, sharing with Ezra Pound. The early part
of 1914 was devoted to magic, mediumship and related topics while in
England; for all of February and March he was in the United States
on a treadmill of lectures about 'The Theatre of Beauty'. Throughout
he laboured at lines that would conclude *Responsibilities* (1914), lines
at once bitter, convoluted and reminiscent of his *fin-de-siècle* past.
'While I, from that reed-throated whisperer . . .' he begins, as if in the
1890s, but ends in a new ferocity, recognising that all the poet's
priceless things 'Are but a post the passing dogs defile'. The new tone
would prove apt to coming events.

Before war, there was a trip to Paris with Feilding to investigate a miracle, and numerous *séances*, mainly unsuccessful. Maud Gonne accompanied the investigators to Poitiers where a religious picture had begun to bleed. The English summer provided more *séances*, lunch with the Asquiths, and the final passage of the Irish Home Rule Act. The model of an eccentric Anglo-Irish gentleman, Yeats left for his customary August at Coole Park. The Great War began on 4 August. September was almost entirely unproductive. In October he wrote prose. On 9 November, he began to write 'A Meditation in Time of War'.

As with the concluding poem of *Reponsibilities*, there is a strong contrast of styles, even within the five lines of the finished piece. The first line catches a unique spiritual pulse, a moment of insight; lines 2–3 sketch a familiar western landscape of elemental stone and tree (old in each case); the remaining lines are:

> I knew that One is animate,
> Mankind inanimate phantasy.

We have already seen how this poem, not collected until 1920, contributes to the stony final pages of *Michael Robartes and the Dancer*. We now see it at its moment of composition in November 1914. Some months earlier, Yeats worked at an essay entitled 'Swedenborg, Mediums and the Desolate Places', which was eventually published in 1920 as an introduction to Lady Gregory's *Visions and Beliefs in the West of Ireland*. By the time of publication, much had changed in the west of Ireland, and the image of that region projected in the book wholly fails to register the impact of war, rebellion and guerrilla warfare. Of course, traditional beliefs are said to be impervious: but believers are not. Even more antique was Yeats's introduction, which, having finished it in the autumn of 1914, he left unaltered.

In many ways it remains one of his most approachable essays on supernatural affairs. Its account of Swedenborg includes amusing stories:

> There went on about Swedenborg an intermittent 'Battle of the Friends' and on certain occasions had not the good fought upon his side, the evil troop, by some carriage accident or the like, would have caused his death, for all associations of good spirits have an answering mob, whose members grow more hateful to look on through the centuries.[27]

This of course was taking place 'on the other side', after some exchanges with the Blood Kindred. The bellicose language – battle, fought, troop, mob – is in keeping with the Swedenborgian theory of the afterlife repeating in reverse or obverse what had occurred in the earthly life. But it also carries distinctive echoes of contemporary affairs in France and London. Of the newly declared conflict, Yeats has only one reference to make:

> Today while the great battle in Northern France is still undecided, should I climb to the top of that old house in Soho where a medium is sitting among servant girls, some would, it may be, ask for news of Gordon Highlander or Munster Fusilier, and the fat old woman would tell in Cockney language how the dead do not yet know they are dead, but stumble on amid visionary smoke and noise, and how angelic spirits seem to awaken them but still in vain.[28]

About a year later, Maud Gonne wrote to Yeats in not dissimilar terms:

> The thousands of Irish soldiers who have been killed are being drawn together in this wild reel time I have been hearing. They are dancing to it, some with almost frenzied intensity & enthusiasm while others seem to be drawn in unwittingly not knowing why, but the rhythm is so strong & compelling they have to dance. It is leading them back to the spiritual Ireland from which they have wandered & where they find their self-realisation & Perfectionment & to whom they would bring their strength.[29]

By 1918, spiritualism would become a desperate last resort for many widows and bereaved parents anxious to 'hear from' soldiers who had disappeared into the Western Front. Even hard-headed scientists like Arthur Conan Doyle took up the chase. Yeats and Gonne differ from these searchers by the strong confidence that they already have found the truth about death in battle. Yeats, indeed, had found it even before the first phase of the war was over. Those who were liquidised under shell attack, or ripped to shreds in an alchemy of barbed wire, bayonets and bullets, did not know they were dead. Which is to say they mistakenly thought they were alive. In commencing the business of 'dreaming-back', how much spiritual time did each spend (again) on the wire, under fire, or plain in agony? Yeats does not say, because – *pace* Pound – Yeats's abundance of emotions found no room for compassion.

The style of 'Swedenborg, Mediums and the Desolate Places' makes this ornately plain. Describing in October 1914 certain Polish experiments and their communicators, Yeats commends their success in making:

> one imagines, from some finer substance than a phosphorescent mud ... images not wholly different from themselves, figures in a galanty show, not too strained or too extravagant to speak their very thought.

Discussing more unruly spirits in the succeeding paragraph, Yeats goes on to remark dolefully that 'all these shadows have drunk from the pool of blood and become delirious'.[30] The question of Yeats's poetic style will be taken up towards the end of *Blood Kindred*: here we pause over prosaic effects. Certain phrases act as a species of insurance policy – 'one imagines ... not wholly different' – according to which he is not absolutely committed to belief in the actual success of the Polish experimenters. 'Their very thought' may seem to belong in the same camp, though second thoughts may be advisable. As a phrase, the 'phosphorescent mud' surely radiates a consummate, if unconscious, indifference to the conditions in which Gordon Highlander or Munster Fusilier (Gonne's 'thousands of Irish soldiers') were wallowing even as he wrote. The same stylistic unconscious governs the precious 'galanty show', a phrase that just avoids stumbling on gallantry. This is of a piece with 'their very thought' – except that, in retrospect, the last phrase now emerges as paralleling:

> Often now among these faint effects one will seem [*sic*] to speak with the very dead.

Again the small-print or insurance clauses should be closely studied. If Yeats does not fully accept the experiments, the communicators and conversations with the very dead, then the indifference displayed towards fellow-men caught in the Battle of the Frontiers, the Battle of the Marne, and finally the terrible trench-warfare that persisted for four years, is all the more callous. In more than five years elapsing between completion of the essay (14 October 1914) and its publication in 1920, he did not think to revisit the phosphorescent mud. Blood for the ghosts was a venerable classic trope, and the Great War certainly generated a new assessment of Greek tragedy, 'pity and terror', and the prospects for a contemporary tragic literature. In 1926, Yeats chided Sean O'Casey for dramatising war-effects he had never witnessed. Yeats had prepared himself for this confrontation with the saviour of the Abbey's finances by advising (himself), in papers contributing to *A Vision* (1925), 'we should not attribute a very high degree of reality to the

Great War'.[31] In 1936, banishing the war poets from *The Oxford Book of Modern Verse*, he damned pity and 'passive suffering'. Back in 1914, he turned from the prologue to these universal themes to recall from the Sligo of his childhood a stable boy who condemned his late master to haunt a lighthouse and, in turn, was sacked by the widow.[32]

Several ways of proceeding suggest themselves. The first would compare Yeats's position at the commencement of war (only the 'One is animate') and at war's end ('Hammer your thoughts into unity'). By this means, the impact of the slaughter might be measured in the coarsening of his thought, the growing reliance on violent imagery and the coincidence of his self-disciplining programme with the rhetoric of early Italian fascism. A second approach would search for additional commentary on the war, its casualties and its impact on culture: there is little. In a diary of 1909, however, he had recorded a conversation with a daring amateur mountaineer, Edward Evans:

> On the way back E[vans] said, 'There is so little life now. Look at the modern soldier – he is nothing – and the ancient soldier was something – he had to be strong and skilful, they fought man to man.' I said, 'There are some books like that – ideas as wonderful as a campaign by Moltke, but no man. The plan of campaign was not so impressive in the old books, but all was human!' He answered, 'When races cease to believe in Christ, God takes the life of them, at last they cease to procreate.'[33]

The great German general was long dead by 1909, but one is struck by how Yeats's recourse to books (rather than individual soldiers) is in turn qualified by his respect for grand strategy – and victory. Evans's diagnosis of terminal decline is a well-turned period effect, more 1890s than Edwardian, but still recognisable as a commonplace among deep thinkers. Yeats's distinctive, perhaps unconscious, stylistic contribution is of course his adoption of the Victorian Irish political slogan 'The Plan of Campaign' (which linked agrarian agitation to nationalist in a withholding of rents) to depoliticise and restore it to the general vocabulary of military tactics.

The third approach to Yeats's decidedly marginal comments on the Great War focuses on the conclusion of Section VIII in 'Swedenborg, Mediums and the Desolate Places', where the fat old Cockney woman had confirmed that the dead in Flanders do not know they are dead. After Polish and historical allusions, Yeats drew the section to a close with reference to the stable boy in Sligo, dismissed for condemning a ghost to haunt so difficult a station as the local lighthouse. This movement, the introduction of a youth from the period of Yeats's own childhood, should be read as a substitution. A comparable moment occurs in the earliest pages of his first autobiography, *Reveries Over Childhood and Youth*, written in 1914, where a telegraph boy in a London street is recalled as a dangerous passing figure in Yeats's recollections of passive infancy. The Victorian past is a resource which he was niggard in drawing on for major effects, but to it he assigned a number of surrogates as if they might occupy identity where he found little that fitted.

Fighting with a School Friend

William Kirkpatrick Magee (1868–1961) was a Dubliner of Presbyterian background educated at the High School and Trinity College. For nearly a quarter of a century he worked on the staff of the National Library, earning his place in Episode 9 ('Scylla and Charybdis') of Joyce's *Ulysses* (1922). After the foundation of the Irish Free State, he emigrated to England, dying in Bournemouth at an advanced age. His reputation today is not high, with touchy combativeness serving as his most memorable characteristic. A pseudonym, 'John Eglinton', allegedly taken from Elizabeth Barrett Browning's *Aurora Leigh* (1856), does not assist efforts at rehabilitation.

Nevertheless, Eglinton/Magee deserves attention in any biographical study of Yeats. With Fred Gregg, Charles Johnston, Charles Weekes, Claude Wright and W. B. Yeats, he formed a theosophical 'militant tendency' among the otherwise placid pupils at the High School in the mid-1880s. Both Magee and Johnston had brothers who also participated, with the result that the city had a nucleus of irrational intellectuals any Black Forest town would have envied. That this group emerged in the High School, rather than in some other establishment of secondary education, is not surprising. Catholic schools like Belvedere (Joyce's Alma Mater) were better protected from heterodox religious speculation, as *A Portrait of the Artist* amply testifies, while lower down the social scale the Christian Brothers catered for Paddy Stink and Mickey Mud without benefit of heresy in the playground. For the Established, and former-Established Church, St Columba's School provided a good replica of the English public-school milieu directly under Church of Ireland management: here the occult seemed vulgar, if not faintly Roman, in its easy traffic between the physical and spiritual. High School was new, founded in 1870 in tandem with the disestablishment of the Church of Ireland. It catered for the middle classes in their commercial rather than professional aspect, though bishops and professors rose from its benches in time. More particularly, it provided education for the sons of families where the commercial future was imposed, not chosen. It was as if designed for those who, fearing they might some day lie in the gutter, resolved to study the stars.

Yeats found Eglinton (as Magee gradually became) a difficult fellow. In the *Autobiographies* he is introduced – rather late, one might think – as George Russell's friend, one of the Ely Place vegetarian theosophists. And that is the last time his name appears in Yeats's published personal writings. As far as private correspondence is concerned, the man disappears in 1906/07 when Eglinton was translating 'Oedipus' for the Abbey. Despite this apparently truncated friendship, the crucial articles which reveal the relationship between 'early' Yeats and 'mature' Yeats are devoted (antagonistically) to the literary journalism of Magee. In *Two Essays on the Remnant* (1894), Magee's (or rather Eglinton's) objective had been a learned and cultured 'remnant' of a people, which might come out from its debased surroundings in materialist society and thus preserve the higher values and eternal verities. Though the author was an agnostic, the Judaic or biblical vocabulary was deliberate.

Yeats's response is significant, not only because it endorses notions of an elite as the saviours of civilisation, but because it records his break with Fabianism and guild socialism. Though Morris is acknowledged as one of 'the Remnant', Yeats more emphatically links utopian projects with the names of dead artists: 'I have known two or three men of philosophic intellect like Wilde or Beardsley who spent their lives in a fantastic protest against a society they could not remake.'[34] As neither exemplar had reached years of discretion, Yeats's case is hardly a universal one. And in any case, Eglinton was keener to abandon modern society than to change it. Without quite saying so, his antagonist wishes to take up an activist position while rejecting the metropolitan world *tout court*. The only available grounds for this was nationalism of the primitivist kind, as distinct from – say – the contemporary Hungarian effort to wrest the Hungarian economy (industry included) from imperial hands.

Redefined to meet these needs, Ireland would shed much of east Ulster, especially Belfast and the Lagan and Bann valleys.

Ideologically speaking, Yeats's option was self-endorsing within cultural nationalism. It remains to be seen whether a psychological motive, subconsciously to edit the family past, predisposed him towards the primitivist camp. He had not been born to the plough, the homespun jerkin, bacon smoked over the open fire. These were images to be sought, whether in the past or present or even some future land of heart's desire. Certainly, within the larger nationalist enterprise, his particular school (that of John O'Leary) helpfully combined a hard doctrinal line with a relaxed programme of implementation. No dynamite, no parliamentary compromise. Yeats's lifelong search for radical innocence involved a selective engagement with the past, launched from a selective disengagement from the filthy modern tide. The desired 'edition' involved both annotation and elucidation; what's more, in another sense of the verb to edit, it involved the reduction or emendation of the past. The deeply ambiguous nature of this undertaking is well caught in Yeats's prefatory lines for the collection, *Responsibilities* (1914): 'Pardon, old fathers ...'

What Yeats seeks pardon for emerges only after twenty lines devoted to listing his forebears – he seeks pardon for having no child. Here, as in the debate with John Eglinton, the dead are identified as exemplary mentors. When they are also artists, they are found to possess philosophical or intellectual power, and thus Yeats's Swift of the 1930s is already implicit in these manoeuvres of the late 1890s. Eglinton, however, is not admitted to the same league. With deliberately cumbersome effect, Yeats imagines a dialogue between Eglinton and one of the more militant among the Remnant. The latter declares – gratuitously – that he hadn't 'a country clergyman among [his] ancestors for ten generations, nothing but soldiers', and announces that he wants 'to pull down Totenham [*sic*] Court-road, and to build it nearer to the heart's desire'. Here indeed is verbal condensation at work, for the title of Yeats's early play ('The Land of Heart's Desire', 1894; cover design by Beardsley) drew on the same passage from Omar Khayyám, which also featured in the motto of the Fabians. The dialogue essentially arraigns the imagination against the sword as modes of transformation, but it shifts gear abruptly to declare:

The truth is that John Eglinton is too preoccupied with English literature and civilisation to remember that the decadence he has described is merely the modern way, because it is the English way, because it is the commercial way. Other countries only share it in so far as they are commercial. Here and there over Europe there are countries that preserve a more picturesque and elastic life.[35]

This is not Yeats at his most rigorous, but there is a compensating frankness. Whereas his own land of heart's desire has been aligned with an impossible utopianism, England (it is conceded) is not the eternal or inevitable enemy – commerce is, commerce as the medium or agent of modernisation. However, Eglinton has been foolish enough (in Yeats's view) to 'turn from all National ideas and see the hope of the world in individual freedom'. Eglinton, however, had a sophisticated view of the limits within which it was possible to invoke ancient literature as a model for the present. Though he shared Yeats's detestation of what we would now call consumer society, he had no illusions as to the *reality* of what modern life was. Things did exist for him, independent of his mind. Yeats, on the other hand, took this occasion to express with particular clarity his own anti-humanist view of inspiration – 'Nobody can write well ... unless his thought, or *some like thought* [emphasis added], is moving in other minds than his, for nobody can do more than speak messages from the spirit of his time.'[36] The individual mind operates at a purely subsidiary level.

This was but the climax of a longer onslaught on the old school friend. The earlier stages had been orchestrated with some care on all sides. Late in 1898, Yeats and his associates were anxious to interest the public in questions about national drama, even though the curtain on the Irish Literary Theatre project had not risen. Using an article by Eglinton as a pretext, Yeats deliberately launched an exchange of views in the Dublin *Daily Express*. Not only Eglinton, but also George Russell and the folklorist William Larminie, joined in. At one level, the public disagreement was a sham, engineered to manipulate newspaper readers and to prepare the ground for a long-planned initiative. But at other levels, distinct differences of opinion between the conspirators could be detected. Wordsworth recurs as a topic of disagreement. Eglinton, quoting William Blake's 'fear that Wordsworth loves nature', added that, as a philosopher if not as a poet, Yeats 'would no doubt sympathise with that solicitude'.[37] Quoting Yeats's beloved Blake, he tellingly distinguishes between two schools of English romanticism, and aligns himself with Wordsworth.

Later, George Russell, acting as a benign umpire, found it necessary to argue that a 'mystical view of nature' – though it is a national characteristic in Celtic Ireland – is 'peculiar to but one English poet, Wordsworth'.[38] The differences were not simply those of literary pedigree. Russell's contribution moves nervously through a consideration of Decadence as the source of present needs and aspirations, even suggesting that 'because a spiritual flaw can be urged against a certain phase of life' the latter should not 'remain unexpressed'. There are asides about 'psychology', and the whole piece exemplifies the incoherence that Yeats found so infuriating in his arts-school friend.

By comparison, Yeats is the practised polemicist, moving adroitly to polish off his secondary-school friend with the assistance of temporary allies. There were serious differences between the two men. In a manner that Yeats could never approve, Eglinton even endorsed invention as a modern form of imagination:

> The facts of life with which poetry is concerned are not the complex and conventional facts, but the simple and universal. This age cannot have a realistic poet, as it fondly dreams, because poetry is ideal and not realistic. The kinematograph, the bicycle, electric tramcars, labour-saving contrivances, etc, are not susceptible of poetic treatment, but are, in fact, themselves the poetry, not without a kind of suggestiveness, of a scientific age, with which the poetry of Greek and Hebrew tradition vainly endeavours to vie.[39]

This too has its ounce of incoherence; or rather, it states two propositions, both compelling but also mutually incompatible. Joyce will be master of the second, releasing the utensils of Mr Bloom's domestic life into fabulous dialogue with Stephen Dedalus's Hellenic thoughts. Synge will practise a related art, ironically lodged in the colder side of peasant life. If Eglinton aspired to be the mentor of this tendency, Yeats was determined to kill him off, and with him any objective philosophy of history.

It is hardly a coincidence that a crucial moment in the dispute occurred when Yeats was unhappily absorbed in western themes. In October 1898, he was stricken with a heavy cold, leading on to a month or more of depression. His psychic experiments with George Pollexfen were not going well; indeed, he felt the two of them were under attack by lunar powers. On 24 October, he commenced his own attack with correspondence to the publisher, Elkin Mathews, about cover designs, and on 29 October published 'John Eglinton and Spiritual Art' in the *Daily Express* (Dublin). Through this period

Yeats is based in Sligo, commencing the month of November with a further (unpublished) attack on Eglinton's aesthetic ideas and – when he finally returns to Dublin – assailing the assistant librarian in Kildare Street. Underlying these rural-urban tensions was Yeats's unresolved relationship with Maud Gonne. The day after his row with Eglinton in the National Library, Yeats told Maud how he had dreamed that she kissed him. They visited John O'Leary, and later in the evening she kissed him for the first time on the lips. One cannot help feeling that Eglinton and his ideas were punch-bags in Yeats's preparation for greater engagements and conflicts.

The row between them touched on many crucial issues. These include: a) the extent to which (limitations within which) ancient tragedy or epic can provide models for emulation; b) the tension between an idealist aesthetic and decisionist 'ideas of good and evil' which might somehow be implemented; c) the concept of an elite; d) universal as distinct from particularist values. Those who have already read Yeats's thumping approval of 'individualist Italy' may be surprised by this earlier turn of events, but there is another logic at work. What Yeats wants, in November 1901, are 're-arrangements of life and thought which make men feel that they are part of a social order, of a tradition, of a movement wiser than themselves'.[40]

It is not the individualist, but the corporative spirit that is at work here. In a high and sublime sense, there is no individual for Yeats apart from himself. In part, this follows from his philosophical position, for in the Yeatsian version of idealism a material object exists only in relation to a greater entity, Mind: discrete existences are not permitted. This self-centredness is given complexity through his elaborate dialectic of Self and Anti-Self: it is very far removed from selfishness. Yet if Yeatsian individualism can be glossed as a version of philosophical Idealism, we have to note the very different cultural and historical conditions in which – say – George Berkeley had lived, and those of the twentieth century. Who, it might be asked, was about to effect those 're-arrangements of life' for which Yeats yearned? His dismissal of Eglinton's individualism, even when it was linked to the elitism of a Remnant, may be related to his development of a tragic vision.

Tragedy in the twentieth century, tragedy written in the future tense, cannot simply be identified with the ancient Greek practice. Sybilline divination cannot be tapped on the Ravenhill Road, nor is primeval ceremony a 'thing' like replica furniture. A great deal of moral ambiguity surrounds the application of tragic vocabularies to mass-executions, industrialised warfare and extermination camps. Eglinton possessed his own modicum of divination, suggesting in May 1899 that if 'the approaching ages on the Continent are to be filled with great social and political questions and events which can hardly have immediate expression in literature then it is quite likely that literature, as it did once before, would migrate to a quiet country like Ireland, where there is no great tradition to be upset or much social sediment to be stirred up, and where the spectacle of such changes might afford a purely intellectual impulse'.[41]

Eglinton in the twenty-first century is more remote from sympathetic scrutiny than yesterday's man, yet in such observations he demonstrated a sense of unfolding history which at least matched Yeats's. In both *The Remnant* and *Literary Ideals*, he also touched on what would become Europe's 'Jewish Question' in a way that illuminates Yeats's avoidance of the anti-Semitic component in fascism and Nazism when the poet came to approve other aspects of these ideologies. For Eglinton (citing Ernest Renan), the Jews exemplified a nation which, while politically weak, was ordained to revolve spiritual truths in its bosom; considered in 1899, Ireland seemed fitted for the same high destiny. The biblical notion of 'the remnant' provided a framework for such thought, while the philo-semitic ideas of the so-called Plymouth Brethren – founded in Dublin and Wicklow in the 1830s – added a recent and eloquent vindication of historic Israel. The Synge family had nurtured Brethrenism from the outset, and its influence can be traced in J. M. Synge's work, especially 'The Well of the Saints' (1905).

Yeats found Synge easier to mould to Yeatsian ends than Eglinton, but Synge died conveniently young. Even before Synge's plays had reached the stage, Yeats had moved to counter Eglinton's influence. *Literary Ideals in Ireland* (1899) was followed by *Ideals in Ireland* (1901), a volume edited by Augusta Gregory and conforming more closely to a Yeatsian agenda. Of the eight contributions, two came from Yeats's own pen, two from that of Douglas Hyde, with support from AE, Standish O'Grady, George Moore and D. P. Moran. While these could generate their own quarrelsomeness, and were not always respectful of Yeats's authority, only Moran lay outside the pale. Eglinton was banished, and obliged to forge his own weapons of response in *Dana*, a short-lived journal favoured by Synge, but to which Yeats never contributed.

By the beginning of the twentieth century Yeats had discarded all those early friends who had gathered together as the Dublin Hermetic Society in June 1885, the High School gang. Eglinton had been defeated in more or less open warfare; Johnston went to New York where he found the company of John Butler Yeats more congenial; Charles Weekes moved to England from where he acted as amateur legal adviser to Maunsel & Co.; and Claude Wright devoted himself so exclusively to theosophy that even Yeats fell out of view. Only AE survived in good standing, largely because he was a reliable foil.[42] Also departed to America was Frederick Gregg. In obvious ways, this was the natural dispersion of a youthful group into the wider world. It was, however, Yeats's *only* youthful group and its break-up is striking for the way in which he succeeded in holding the ring while others left. The elder Yeats was inclined to rebuke his son for this clearing of the decks. On 14 April 1909, he mentioned seeing a letter to Johnston: 'It seemed to me rather laconic and cold written to an old friend and a good friend. Mrs Chas Johnston told me that they both worked very hard for you before you arrived.'[43]

Part Three
Origins and Responsibilities

Victorian Kindred

The old wound in my ass
has opened up again, but I
am passed the prodigies
of youth's campaigns, and weep
where I used to laugh
in war's red humors, half
in love with silly-assed pains
and half not feeling them.
I have to sit up with
an indoor unsittable itch
before I go down late
and weeping to the storm-
cellar on a dirty night
and go to bed with the worms.
So pull the dirt up over me
for Old Billy Blue Balls,
the oldest private in the world
with two ass-holes and no
place to go to for a laugh
except the last one. Say:
the North won the Civil War
without much help from me
although I wear a proof
of the war's obscenity.
Alan Dugan, 'Fabrication of Ancestors for Old Billy Dugan, Shot
in the Ass in the Civil War, My Father Said'

When the dead communicated with Yeats, they underwent some
process of social grading which, in effect, eliminated men with less
than one-thousand-a-year or the basics of genteel education. Uncle
Mattie, for example, died in 1885 and remained out of touch,
embarrassed by the state in which he had left the fragmentary Yeats
lands in County Kildare. Even more eloquently silent in death was
Susan Yeats (née Pollexfen), the poet's mother who died in 1900,
though some of her male kinsmen were among Yeats's most

encouraging occult sponsors. Between these two instances, one could deduce a principle of sorts: spiritual communications recognise social hierarchies of class and gender. If this seems to give the advantage to elder sons of the well-to-do, one should note (without scorn) how tentative Yeats can be in assuming that his progenitors remain attentive in death. If the Blood Kindred can accommodate congenial minds not related biologically, then a law of compensation insists that the blood-line does not automatically toe the party-line.

Countless Kathleens

In the 1880s and '90s, Yeats had several futures ahead of him. His theosophical interests prompted poems on Indian themes; his curiosity about the theatre led to experiments as different as the play 'Mosada' (1886) and the dramatic-poem 'The Wanderings of Oisin' (1889). With legitimate hindsight, we can now see that the latter pointed forward. Nevertheless, one can imagine alternative lines of development. The insular Irish might have become more cooperative, with the Scottish and Welsh, in a pan-Celtic Revival. When Sir John Rhys (1840–1915) published *Lectures on the Origins and Growth of Religion as Illustrated by Celtic Heathendom* (1888), Yeats considered writing a review of it, but did not in practice do so. The Scottish scholar and man of letters Andrew Lang (1844–1912) demonstrated the importance of folklore for an understanding of cultivated mythology, but, to young Yeats's chagrin, failed to see the merit of 'The Wanderings', though the poet was a regular contributor to the *Scots Observer*. Nor was England wholly beyond the pale. Alfred Trübner Nutt (1856–1910) – like Lang, a Londoner by residence – edited the *Folklore Journal* and assisted in the establishment of the Irish Texts Society in 1898. The English Folk Song Society is a testimony to the influence of demotic art on the music of Vaughan Williams (1872–1958) and other composers of that generation. Williams composed an opera based very strictly on Synge's 'Riders to the Sea'.

There was, of course, a central paradox in the notion of a London-based Celtic Revival. Even if William Morris's efforts to align English tradition with the Nordic past had prospered, and if Yeats had been able to forge an alliance between the two movements, the metropolis could never be home to a new literature founded on myth and folklore. In the last years of Victoria's reign, London's vastness was beyond compare, its imperial grandeur unavoidable. The logic of withdrawal to the Celtic periphery was perfect, and only Ireland provided insular security and a related political consciousness. In 1898, the foundation of the Irish Text Society was for many observers lost behind the fireworks in rival commemorations of the United Irishmen and their insurrection one hundred years earlier.

In Yeats's *Collected Plays*, 'The Countess Cathleen' is dated 1892, 'with seriously misleading pedantry'.[1] Its origins lay in early spring 1889 when drafting and sketching began. The first version to reach print was entitled 'The Countess Kathleen' (August 1892) – that is, within ten months of Parnell's death. On 6 May 1892 there had been a copyright performance in Shepherd's Bush, but this hardly constituted public theatre. Between the commencement of work and the coy premiere, two events blending politics and sex had affected Yeats's creative life – the controversy (December 1889 onwards) over Parnell's relationship with Katherine O'Shea and his own meeting with Maud Gonne. Eros brought calamity in one case, promised unknown returns in the other. In February 1889, Yeats had written vaguely to John O'Leary about ambitions to write a poetic play: 'I have long been intending to write one founded on the tale of "Countess Kathleen O'Shea" in the folk lore book.'[2] That the folk original should have revolved round a figure bearing virtually the same name as Parnell's married mistress (she was Mrs William O'Shea) is both striking and largely unreported. Though Yeats's letters confirm that he noted the name as given above, the (French-language) source actually names the countess as Ketty O'Connor.[3] A Parnellite Unconscious was at work.

Even after Yeats completed the play, he not only took advantage of every opportunity to amend it, but also began to distinguish between a 'reading text' and a stage-text. The alterations were prompted by experience with theatre productions, but they involved drastic surgery. In 1963 Peter Ure constructed a five-column chart to illustrate the main changes made between 1892 and 1934. These include the renaming of characters, the altered spelling of the heroine's name, the introduction and subsequent removal of additional spirit-characters, the expansion and subsequent reduction of a robbery scene, and so on. Even the formal structure was changed from a five-scene sequence to a more conventional (though unconvincing) three-act one. Three years after Ure, Russell Alspach published his *Variorum Edition of the Plays*. Here one finds a collation of twenty-seven different printings. Amongst these, Alspach identifies 'the Tauchnitz version of 1913 [as] the earliest almost-final version of the play', and prints some of the (dreadful) lines that Yeats excised for this German cheap edition:

> *Fifth Spirit.* To think of all the things we forget.
> *Sixth Spirit.* That's why we groan and why our lids are wet.

Substituting Kitty O'Shea for Ketty O'Connor, Yeats was thinking of one of the things he had simultaneously forgotten. In his own emotional life, Maud Gonne (to whom the play was dedicated) utterly eclipsed other young women. Amongst these, Katharine Tynan (1861–1931) made her own contribution to the complicated background to his play, its sources and motivations. In her *Ballads and Lyrics* (1891), she had printed 'The Charity of the Countess Kathleen'. Described in an endnote as 'an authentic folk-story of the West of Ireland and ... perhaps the only instance in legend of one who sold her soul for the Love of God', the poem revolves round a Kathleen *O'Hea*.[4] We have therefore Cathleens and Kathleens, a Kitty and a Ketty, an O'Connor, an O'Hea and two O'Sheas.

The history of 'The Countess C/Kathleen' will be exhaustively traced in Warwick Gould's textual biography of the poet/dramatist. Its generic status is itself a doubling of what might be uni-textual. The great English director and translator of Ibsen, William Archer, thought it fine as verse but unactable onstage, a considered professional opinion dismissed many years later by Peter Jochum. When a note appeared in the journal *Folklore* of June 1895, seeking clarification of the plot's 'true source', the headline specified 'Mr W. B. Yeats's Poem [*sic*] of *Countess Kathleen*'. The story had been printed 'many years ago in an Irish newspaper as a piece of Irish folklore', though there was reason 'to think it is French or Breton'.[5] Frank Hugh O'Donnell (1848–1916), Yeats's most virulent opponent, purported to believe it 'a nightmare yarn found in some German magazine'.[6] Play or poem, Breton or German, French or Irish, Cathleen or Kathleen, 'The Countess' defied classification.

Of course, there are scholarly procedures that reduce the apparent options. The name O'Shea enters the printed sources in the 1860s, when a journalist of that denomination preferred it before the O'Connor he found in his French source. Yet to 'correct' Yeats on this point would be to travesty the contemporary significance of his accepting that the legendary countess and the mistress of Ireland's

Dead King (Parnell) bore the same name. Catalogued under one heading or another, 'The Countess Cathleen' pulses with late-Victorian angst. Fear of renewed famine in Ireland is only the most obvious, its emotional force for Yeats resulting mainly from Maud Gonne's involvement in political agitation on the issue. Other distinctly Irish anxieties concern the relationship of an aristocratic individual to the impoverished masses, in which connection the play can be seen to reflect obliquely on Parnell's anomalous position as a landlord leader of a peasant-cum-petit-bourgeois radical movement.

As in 'The Playboy of the Western World', Synge's masterpiece of 1907, the action opens in a public house, a setting that seeks to negotiate the role of commercial activity within an agrarian, even primitive society. Or rather, this contemporary society advances contradictory images of itself which the drama explores: Yeats to the end of confirming a traditional-transcendental concept of reality, Synge to something far less clear-cut or reassuring. With this aspect of the scene in mind, one regards 'The Countess Cathleen' as a nervous but penetrating enquiry into the spiritual conditions underpinning modernity.

One detail of the play that outraged O'Donnell more than any other was the breaking and kicking of a shrine to the Blessed Virgin, accompanied by remarks about the inefficacy of divine power. This was an offence against what he called 'the Irish Catholic religion' – that is, against the homogenised ideology of nation and Church, politics and theology. Yeats can hardly have been surprised that Cardinal Logue took offence and publicly condemned the play. There was a broader confluence of ideas and forces upon which 'The Countess Cathleen' bobbed and dipped, broader than the local Irish mixture of religion and nationalism. However crudely staged, Shemus Rua's assault on the machinery of veneration – statues, shrines, etc. – was an attempt dramatically to test a metaphysical rumour then current in Europe. God is dead, Nietzsche's Zarathustra had declared in the market-place, leading Joyce's Dedalus ironically to define this vestigial/contemporary deity as 'a shout in the street'. More cautious thinkers alluded to a withdrawn god (*deus absconditus*), invoking the Old Testament itself as an authority for this undermining of its authority. Writers as irreconcilable as Joris Huysmans, György Lukács, Max Nordau, Bram Stoker, Max Weber, Oscar Wilde and Yeats joined hands round the immaterial corpse. The Dubliners among this ill-assorted crew are at odds with each other no less than their more exotic fellows. In its determination to relate eros and blood-lust, Wilde's 'Salomé' (1893/94) challenges the legal limits of dramatic representation with regard to biblical or divine persons. In its incidental but symptomatic travesty of Eucharistic theology, Stoker's *Dracula* (1897) desperately seeks a counter-magic to nail the undead.[7] Yeats's poem/play shies from these extravagances, yet offers parodic versions of the transcendental in answer to the contemporary crisis.

O'Donnell provides little insight into the work he so completely denounces. Nevertheless, in *The Stage Irishman* (1904) he touches on an aspect of dramatic representation that goes to the heart of 'The Countess'. Invoking commercial London ironically as the antithesis of Yeats's Celtic quest, he declares that 'Tottenham Court Road never turned out anything quite so obvious in Old Baronial Furniture.'[8] Collapsing the play into a *précis* of its stage props, he uncannily adverts both to the Gothic fashions of the 1790s and to the question of historicism generally. More soberly, Michael McAteer has recently drawn attention to the several historical backgrounds discernible behind the several versions of 'The Countess C/Kathleen'. These might be backlisted as 1880, 1845 and 1798, with a leap then to the late sixteenth century, and a greater leap to the borderline between pagan and Christian Ireland. This last cannot be tied to a date because, as Yeats never ceased to remind his readers, vestiges of paganism survived in nineteenth-century Irish devotional practice and reflection. In short, the play was and is agog for multiple interpretation. McAteer's objective is a Marxist analysis of the souls = gold dimension to the play and, in pursuing this, he further demonstrates how sensitive to contending ideologies 'The Countess' was and is. Or, to put it in terms of the heroine's social origins, she is indeterminedly 'an emblem of an old Gaelic order or [of] the Anglo-Irish ascendancy which displaced [it]'.[9] Friedrich Bethge in 1934 may have been reviving the play's pre-emptive anti-modernism; doing so in the first year of the Thousand Year Reich, he testified to its malleability in the dreadful cauldron. This was one of the futures awaiting the *fin-de-siècle* Yeats.

Just as the Great Famine of 1845–47 is a necessary source for 'The Countess Cathleen' – and the 1880s' scarcities merely an occasion, charged with libidinal material – so the Frankfurt honours of February 1934 relate to the Decadence that Yeats was at once opposing and exemplifying in his first excursion onstage. The

Nazified Goethe celebrations were a mere opportunity to draw in the Irish dramatist: no two-way or reciprocal relationship had previously existed. Indeed, the late-Victorian Yeats had been somewhat scornful of Goethe as a 'utilitarian' writer.

The roots of fascism have been traced well into the nineteenth century – into the hyper-rapid growth of mass society, the proliferation of racialist theories, etc. – even if the Great War remains the catastrophic bugle-call to reaction. These causes were not restricted to Italy and Germany; indeed, the two cases are very different, seen from the aetiological point of view. There is an understandable but, in the last analysis, unacceptable tendency to define fascism by reference near-exclusively to successful fascism, to those instances where fascist movements acquired governmental power. Hence the general ignorance about fascism in Denmark or Switzerland. The tendency also exempts some painful cases from further scrutiny – Hungary, Portugal, Romania and Spain being the main beneficiaries.

By a conjunction of these two perspectives, we should now be able to see that, even in the United Kingdom of Great Britain and Ireland, some of the conditions for the growth of what in the 1920s became continental fascism were in existence before the end of the nineteenth century. Other conditions proved more powerful; yet rapid industrialisation, exposure to cultural difference, the eclipse of traditional elites and religious disenchantment occurred in more ways than resulted simply in the British Labour Party. Regional differences marked the smaller island off from the larger; inside each, more local differences gave rise to distinctive Scottish developments, already conditioned by Scottish historical consciousness. In Ireland, the rival ideologies of nationalism and unionism oddly shared a common interest in downplaying difference. Yet by 1880, Ulster had in practice broken several moulds. It remains for me to show how Yeats inherited the stresses and fractures of that history.

Ulstermen and Alfred Dreyfus

A little-remembered electoral occurrence in the year of Yeats's birth saw an already disgraced Liberal defeated in Lisburn, County Antrim. Two years earlier, John Doherty Barbour had outpolled his Conservative rival, only to be unseated as the kidnapper of some thirty electors in the town. Like other inheritors of the Whig tradition, Barbour (a linen baron) drew on a political constituency that defined itself in part by looking to 'survivors and descendants of the Belfast United Irishmen'.[10] Industrial growth, and shifts in population, contributed to realignments in south-east Ulster politics to be observed in the 1860s. On the other side of the bi-partisan fence, Toryism was also undergoing sea-changes. In February 1868, a bankrupt County Down landlord, William Johnston (1829–1902), pleaded not guilty to charges of breaching the peace in a manner likely to cause sectarian violence. More than one hundred similarly charged had bowed to the law's mild justice, but Johnston was determined on a sentence of martyrdom amounting, in the event, to just one month's imprisonment. Shortly afterwards, 'Johnston of Ballykilbeg' was a force in the land, an Orange firebrand, implacable foe of Popery and – in time – an MP. His second son, Charles, was a close school friend of the poet. Yeats visited Ballykilbeg in east County Down during July 1891, when young Johnston briefly had the place to himself as his father was touring the Orange lodges of Canada.

The friendship had been established at the Erasmus Smith High School, Dublin, where both had been unorthodox pupils in an establishment founded to improve Protestant Ireland's upper-lower-middle-class boys. John Butler Yeats had a studio in nearby York Street, while the Johnstons lived a little to the suburban south on Leinster Road, Rathmines. The school's origins lay in provisions of Erasmus Smith (1611–1691, army contractor and 'Turkey merchant') for Protestant education in Ireland. One consequence was the establishment of elementary education in scores of so-called English schools across Ireland, including one (fl.1841–1903) at Drumcliff, County Sligo, under the patronage of Owen Wynne (not the up-and-coming Gore-Booths.) The Dublin High School was a Victorian final dividend from the profits of seventeenth-century land confiscation in Tipperary. Its buildings incorporated the town house of John Hatch (d. 1797), shadowy ancestor of J. M. Synge.[11] The site is now occupied by a large urban police station.

Yeats spent two and a half school years behind the railings (1881–83), later associating it (inaccurately) with a house near Harold's Cross to which his family did not move until the spring of 1884. In his *Autobiographies*, he bitterly recorded how they 'lived in a villa where the red bricks were made pretentious and vulgar with streaks of slate colour, and there seemed to be enemies everywhere.'[12] When his star was approaching its zenith, he still recalled with horror 'that

Rathgar villa where we all lived when I went to school, a time of crowding & indignity ...'[13] For the boy, the High School was to deprive him of that education away from home which, by the 1880s, contrived to induce gentility by separating the child from local (and increasingly confident) influences. The financial embarrassment of John Butler Yeats was partly self-inflicted through a quietist devotion to painting, but partly the result of a collapse in rents from small inherited properties in County Kildare. (William Johnston's difficulties were of the latter kind, uncompromised by art.) It was young Yeats's canny sense of changing social realities to substitute a different locality (Sligo) and to argue an identification of an elite gentry with folk tradition.

Charles Johnston (1867–1931) had studied for the Indian civil-service examinations, served briefly as a magistrate, but returned to Ireland in 1890 on grounds of ill-health. His father lobbied Lord Salisbury for a consular post, but the son was too young for the service. In 1888, he married a niece of Madame Blavatsky in Moscow, thereby sacrificing a Mahatmaship that required celibacy. High School in the early 1880s was home to several future adepts in the occult.[14] In addition to Yeats and Johnston, we have met Charles Weekes (1867–1946) and Frederick James Gregg (1864–1927), less dedicated in later life but part of a schoolboy intelligentsia that meant a lot to the unhappy Yeats. It is significant that their early reading included the Evolutionists – Haeckel, for example – for behind Yeats's adult pursuit of the occult lay a desire for scientific rigour. In the Victorian mind, the pursuit of an evolutionary science was compatible with ideas of an Aryan race, if not seven or more Aryan races. Of a related 'Anglo-Irish will to power' – just recently rediscovered – one can only note how little came of it, unless Cuchulain was its avatar.[15] If Yeats was the only real genius to spring from the Harcourt Street school-yard, Johnston became a respectable scholar in the craft. Credit for initiating the hermetic friendship is invariably granted to Yeats. However, as Lewis and Ada and Georgiana Johnston were adepts alongside their better-known brother, it may be wondered if the Johnstons did not possess a collective aptitude equal to any individual.

The earlier past demands attention too in the search for an originary crisis. While the infant poet yet slept in the lee of Sandymount Castle, 'Johnston of Ballykilbeg' had found himself promoted as 'the working man's friend', not only in his own county of Down, and in Belfast, but as far north as Ballymoney. In March 1868, a Protestant Working Men's Association was founded with the object of getting him into parliament to disrupt the patronage system of the established parties. Johnston played the independent with some brio, declaring himself 'free from aristocratic, democratic or any other shackles'.[16] The linen trade was experiencing a downturn, after the prosperity generated by civil war in America. Johnston's politics essentially fastened Protestants in the northern working class to the Conservative party, by winning for them the virtual right to nominate one MP. The rhetoric was democratic, but it was also sectarian. The effect was to convert Protestants in the northern working class into 'the protestant working class', thereby assisting in the magical ethnogenesis of the Unionist People of Ulster.

In so far as scholars of Yeats trouble with Irish Toryism, they have concentrated on Standish James O'Grady (1846–1928), novelist, historian and controversialist. Michael McAteer has rightly emphasised his importance in the making of 'The Countess Cathleen'.[17] O'Grady detested populism; Yeats venerated O'Grady, and so it has seemed unnecessary to go further. But when the young poet visited his theosophical friend at Ballykilbeg, he was returning to a county in which the name Yeats was inscribed in stone. The Revd William Butler Yeats had been rector of Tullylish, on the River Bann, where from the 1830s onwards linen had transformed the landscape and the inherited patterns of social behaviour. The factory-village had hosted an anti-Repeal rally, disturbing evidence that mass oppositional politics breeds a mass counter-opposition. Thus Yeats's temperament was very different from that of William Johnston, just as the moment of his flight southwards differed in every way from the opportunity later seized by 'Ballykilbeg' in 1868. Yet their sons, embracing the systematic irrationalism of occultic and theosophical wisdom, shared in a cultural compensation sought for loss of traditional authority and income. Johnston's many children displayed a collective impulse gratefully to embrace Asia, its spiritual and administrative openings. For the poet, an important element in the compensation package was the right (self-authorised) to discount his family origins in the industrial north and to substitute a western provenance.

The Famine of 1845–47 totally altered Irish social relations, embittering political attitudes towards Britain and widening the economic gap between under-developed and developing regions, between landless peasants and factory operatives. Its more abstract offspring – the terrible twins of emigration and populism – found contrasting sponsors in American ethnic-identity politics and Disraelian electoral reform. The latter proved to be the swifter in its domestic impact. The two great manifestations of Irish populism occurring in Yeats's 'prentice years were – first, opposition to Home Rule (1885–86) and, second, the divisive response to Parnell's embroilment in divorce proceedings (1891).

The earlier of these saw vast demonstrations in Belfast and other Ulster centres, in a campaign in part at least orchestrated by the revived Orange Order. Working-class numbers, headed by a quasi-traditional leadership, characterised the threat to Gladstone's proposed devolution for Ireland. Johnston of Ballykilbeg was the principal organiser of a huge rally held in the Ulster Hall, Belfast, on 22 February 1886, with Randolph Churchill as principal speaker. In 1891, however, opinion was mobilised more indirectly – through newspapers, sermons, by-election meetings and the pre-existing nationalist lobbies which now threatened to split. Yeats's first publication (in the *Dublin University Review*) appeared in March 1885, his first book (*Mosada*) in October 1886. The poetic drama was never reprinted by Yeats after 1889, its passionate-cynical Spanish Inquisition hero, and its Moors-for-Protestants substitution, best forgotten. By the time of Parnell's death in October 1891, he was a more cunning writer. 'Mourn – and then Onward!' appeared punctually (and anonymously) in *The United Irishman*, while the following month he published his first work of (pseudonymous) fiction, *John Sherman and Dhoya*.

To be exact, he published two fictional texts between the same covers. The second of these ('Dhoya') involves mythological figures to balance the contemporary and social focus of 'John Sherman'. In their contrasting ways, both fictions rebuke the mob, reject the noise of urban life, replace secularism with a shy religion of the heart. None of this was very remarkable in theme: it was Yeats's collecting the mythological and the contemporary together (but not conjoining them) which gave edge to the little volume. Psychologistic critics might detect an underlying Oedipal conflict in these tales.[18] A useful point of ingress can be found in the early pages when Sherman replies to the accusation that he is vegetating in small-town Ballah:

No, I am seeing the world. In your big towns a man finds his minority and knows nothing outside its border. He knows only the people like himself. But here one chats with the whole world in a day's walk, for every man one meets is a class. The knowledge I am picking up may be useful to me when I enter the great cities and their ignorance.[19]

Ballah is recognisably Sligo, at the time of its Little Belfast reputation, yet nowhere admitting the clash of the sash. How man fits the world, that grand theme of nineteenth-century fiction, crystallises in Yeats's all-too-brief experiment. In Malthusian-demographic terms, it pervades Dickens's explorations of English poverty, the break-up-and-down of family, the corrosive work of pride and greed. In terms at times sociological and at others occultic, it animates Balzac's *Comédie humaine*. Tolstoy's anarcho-Christianity addresses some of the same problems – *How Much Land Does a Man Need?* With the notable exception of Anthony Trollope, English novelists born into the United Kingdom avoided the western island, where native-born writers largely avoided urban, congested settings. George Moore's *Drama in Muslin* (1886) tracked from an English girls' school, through Dublin's débutante balls and hotel lobbies, to the grim struggle on western estates. The same author's *Parnell and His Island* (also 1886) originated in articles written in French for a Paris newspaper.[20] We have to look to James Joyce and *Dubliners* (1914) for the first imaginative prose meditation on post-Parnellite Ireland and its urban dynamics. By then Yeats was king of the cats.

His ascent to this eminence, capped with Swinburne's death in 1909, involved a period of foreign service in France. The literary avant-garde put grit in his native Celtic pap, with Jarry's *Ubu Roi* (1896) stimulating Yeats to acknowledge the Savage God. Paris offered a home to Oscar Wilde after his imprisonment; indeed, the city of light combined harsh illumination and soft drugs in proportions satisfactory to the cutely outrageous Yeats. It also was home to Maud Gonne, with whom he had become infatuated during his 'Countess Cathleen' phase – home likewise to her adventurer-lover Lucien Millevoye. Paris, it seemed, was the one place where man fitted the world, spiritually and bodily.

French politics, as Millevoye and his Boulangist friends determined, was no Platonic symposium. Conspiracy and corruption were rife. The symptomatic crisis first broke in 1894 when an army officer, Alfred Dreyfus (1859–1935), was tried *in camera* for treason and transported to Devil's Island. The charge alleged secret communication with the Germans on defence matters; the accused was Jewish. When the prisoner's family gained evidence pointing to a different villain, a campaign to vindicate Dreyfus got under way, dividing

French society into pro- and anti- factions. The novelist Émile Zola (1840–1902) espoused the Dreyfusard cause, his public letter *J'accuse* (1898) leading to imprisonment, escape to England and a hero's return. Yeats was Dreyfusard, Gonne anti-Dreyfus. It was not until 1906 that the prisoner was finally cleared in a civilian court.

Contrary to sentimental opinion, the divisions over Dreyfus were not congruent with the established right/left polarities of French politics since the revolution. There were anti-Dreyfusard socialists, and Dreyfusard conservatives. But the *Affair* gave concrete shape to two powerful motive forces in European society on the brink of the twentieth century – militarism and anti-Semitism. Some who condemned the prisoner to extended confinement in his tropical cell knew (even admitted) him to be innocent; for them, the Army's honour transcended individual rights to justice. That Dreyfus was Jewish was perhaps the irreducible heart of the matter, yet his origins in part-Protestant Alsace gave further evidence of dubious nationality. As the name hinted, he had gone over to the enemy of 1870; the whole three-footed tribe was ambivalent, not to be trusted, by its nature guilty in advance of the facts. *À la lanterne!*

Anti-Semitism was taken by the conventional French mind to deal with Freemasonry, free thought, revolutionary politics and illuminism. Some items on this menu already appealed to Yeats, who had been introduced to the arcana of the Irish Grand Lodge by Pollexfen relatives in Sligo and who (with Charles Johnston, John Eglinton and AE) had met the Home Rule crisis of 1885 by founding the Dublin Hermetic Society.[21] That was in York Street, a run-down part of Georgian Dublin owned largely by the Synge family. One could stay within the laager, see visions, and yet feel the constrictive power of ascendancy, the *vigor mortis* of old mastership. Paris for Yeats was, on the other hand, a big town in which he found his minority and learned to value it. Though the Dreyfusards were numerous, their characteristic modes of thought and action were not 'popular'. This in itself commended the captain to Yeats, who had no inherited anti-Semitism to inhibit his allegiance. The Gallican Church, on the other hand, revelled in a blood-guilt theology of Jewish responsibility for the crucifixion, while also exemplifying 'France for the French' nationalism of the day.

Yeats had not been a Parnellite in the years before the Chief's death. 'Mourn – and then Onward!' was an opportunistic move, so untypical that in later years sensitive readers like Arland Ussher would deny that the Nobel laureate could have written it, so useful (on the other hand) that it was remobilised in 1922 to commemorate Arthur Griffith. Dreyfus was an admirable substitute for Parnell, because he represented nothing but himself, strove for nothing but his integrity and his right to pursue his quiet career. He was supported by lodges and cells, and by the opponents of crass materialism. He had no following – an ideal leader.

Unionist opposition to Home Rule awkwardly combined minority rejection with the assertion of mob power. The mob was not just urban but industrial, doubly removed from the springs of nature and the landscape of myths and ghosts. The Johnston affair of 1868 was an early sign of Protestant mass power, prefaced in 1859 by widespread manifestations of hysteria, arising from (sometimes leading to) evangelical revivalism: the areas affected lay primarily in east Ulster, both rural (north Antrim) and urban (Belfast and environs). Socially, those involved came from the lower end of the scale, with the linen industry providing a context where women responded to harsh working conditions through ecstacy. Theologically and ecclesiologically, the Great Revival was unsustainable. A few years later, Disraeli's Reform Act (1867), enfranchising artisans – the men, at least – provided a means of referring Ulster energies from the spiritual back to the political domain. In Britain and for other reasons, Reform saved the Tory party; in Ireland it transformed the old Reformation-based antagonisms between Catholic and Protestant into a faith-and-factory struggle, where employment, 'ethnicity' and denominational 'identity' rotated as trumps. Home Rule, a notion conceived by John Butler Yeats's friend Isaac Butt (a rogue Orangeman and improvident barrister) was quickly renamed Rome Rule by its opponents.

Belfast became the cockpit of the new politics, though areas outside Ulster manifested impressively. From Bandon in County Cork ('even the pigs are protestant') to Sligo (or Little Belfast), small towns and manufacturing areas hosted the contest. Before Reform, even before the Famine, County Down had undergone massive social change, transforming village and parish into industrial estates with tied schools, health care and back-to-back housing. This was a world Yeats officially abjured, even though he stayed at Ballykilbeg for some weeks while Parnell's campaign of survival ran its gauntlet of church-gate meetings, railway station riots and editorial frenzy. Within three months, the Chief was dead, escorted back to Ireland by

Maud Gonne wearing deep mourning for her dead infant whom she would seek to reincarnate. There was to be no reincarnation of Parnell, and (for Yeats) no return to Ulster. Instead of dead certainties, 'Ireland was to be like soft wax for years to come.'[22]

Tara's Halls Uprooted

In June 2003, a medical doctor living in County Donegal effected the return to Ethiopia of a religious relic looted by British troops in 1868. Ian MacLennan had identified in a London bookshop a tabernacle representing the lost Ark of the Covenant in which the ancient Israelites had taken the Ten Commandments out of Egypt. Newspapers inevitably compared the bespectacled doctor to Indiana Jones of Hollywood, while in less global terms he took his place in a longer history of Irish-Jewish comparisons.

Ancient historians acknowledge the central importance of Tara, a hilltop site on the plains of County Meath, in accounts of Ireland during the transition from paganism to Christianity. But, as their mentor expresses it, 'the mythological material is so rich and varied that not even the most assiduous monkish synchroniser nor the most diplomatic fabricator of pedigrees could bring complete order into this chaos'.[23] Recent topics are not wholly immune to the same fate. Tara, however, occupied a central place in the evolving discourse of modern Ireland precisely because it suggested a centralised authority in ancient times, a factor which (the argument goes) proved modern Ireland's entitlement to statehood. Antiquarian and archaeological interest accelerated during the nineteenth century, with the work of figures as eccentric as Charles Vallencey and William Wilde. By coincidence, so to speak, Tara lay reasonably close to Dublin (a Viking settlement) and also within reach of what was emerging as the frontier between industrialising Ulster and the more traditional south. A suitable crisis arose at Tara in the dying days of Victoria's reign. At this point, the poet Yeats became involved in the politics and mythology of place.

His first intimation of trouble seems to have arisen while he was attending a mesmeristic session in Madame Blavatsky's London home. Everyone present looked to Ireland for spiritual teaching in 1888. A second-sighted man, who spotted Yeats's rheumatism, announced that the Ark of the Covenant (lost when the Temple was destroyed) was buried at Tara. 'But he's a fool,' added Yeats.[24] By the early summer of 1899, a British-Israelite pilgrimage or search-party had arrived, with the approval of a local landlord, Gustavus Villiers Briscoe. Far from maintaining the parallel history of ancient Ireland and national Israel, this quasi-religious group held that the pure British-Israel race had been driven out by Gaels (aka Canaanites). Fortunately the Ark, which they had spirited out of Jerusalem, was safely concealed on the island. Where else? Certainly, there was a visible attachment to the Ark in the iconography of prominent Irish organisations, most notably the Orange Order. Freemasonry also played its part, and the attachment of such movements to the British Empire made clear the latent hostility between the pilgrims and the advocates of Irish cultural nationalism.

Opponents of the expedition included Arthur Griffith (anti-semitic editor of *The United Irishman*), Maud Gonne, T. W. Rolleston, and whomever they could recruit to the cause. There was also a body of emergent archaeological professionalism, which blenched at the thought of pilgrims with picks guided by the Bible. Tara under threat brought together an unlikely alliance of the zealously anti-Masonic Griffith with scientific excavators like George Coffey (1857–1916). Gaelic scholars including Douglas Hyde rallied in the face of intrusive ignorance, and the literary movement was seen as a valuable ally. Based for much of the time in Paris, where she still rode with the anti-Dreyfusards, Gonne was a hammer unto British Israel.

Despite the second-sighted man of ten years earlier, Yeats kept his distance. As the initial controversy waxed and waned, excavations were abandoned some time in 1900. By the early summer of 1901, he was revising his introduction to a selection of William Blake's poems, first published in 1893, a simple tasking complicated by his not having a Bible to hand for references. On 20 June he left Sligo to see Gonne in Dublin. The two were planning a mystical order of Gaelic heroes, to be based at Castle Rock in Lough Key, County Roscommon. As further distraction from the world of Blake, Yeats arranged to be shown over Sandymount Castle, a small suburban neo-Gothic pile in the shadow of which he had been born. Once owned by his Corbet relatives, it was now a school. The two castles emblemised conflicting aspects of Yeats's life, the mystical and socio-respectable, the rural and urban. One was always yet to be built; the other had never really existed, its turrets a fashionable simulacrum.

In its first issue of the new century, *The United Irishman* had carried a clamorous article, signed with the initials M. Q., and almost certainly written by Maud Gonne. 'Tara of the Kings shall be free,' the author promised, 'but first the river of blood shall flow.' In this rhetoric, Tara was simultaneously Christian and pagan, like C/ Kathleen; it was the site of ancient buildings and also a verdant green hill. Twice blessed in these regards, it was a more attractive *locus* than the Castle of Heroes or Sandymount Academical Institute (as the Corbet home had become). Having seen over the castle where his grandfather had lived in retirement, Yeats donated a copy of his *Book of Irish Verse* inscribed pointedly 'To Sandymount Castle School Library'. Work resumed at Tara in June 1902, and the literary divisions were called up to support Gonne, Griffith and the other protesters. With Hyde and George Moore, Yeats visited the site; jointly they reported their findings and feelings in a letter published in the London *Times* on 27 June 1902. The work of destruction, it was averred, would leave many bitter memories behind.

Amidst these disputes and desecrations at Tara of the Kings, Queen Victoria had died (January 1901). That in itself did not trouble Yeats. But later, recalling the Ark controversy in secluded Coole Park, he wrote of it in letters and in verse. To Wilfrid Scawen Blunt (1840–1922), English anti-imperialist and lover of Augusta Gregory, he reported the locals' indignation at the Tara excavations and their belief that what was sought was not the Ark, but 'the Golden Plough and the Golden Harrow which are fabled to be buried there'.[25] Here was evidence of a folk preference for pagan myth rather than Judaic. In a poem entitled 'In the Seven Woods' written in August 1902, he wove together more subtle themes of past and present regal authority:

> I have heard the pigeons of the Seven Woods
> Make their faint thunder, and the garden bees
> Hum in the lime-tree flowers; and put away
> The unavailing outcries and the old bitterness
> That empty the heart. I have forgot awhile   5
> Tara uprooted and new commonness
> Upon the throne and crying about the streets
> And hanging its paper flowers from post to post,
> Because it is alone of all things happy.
> I am contented, for I know that Quiet   10
> Wanders laughing and eating her wild heart
> Among pigeons and bees, while that Great Archer,
> Who but awaits His hour to shoot, still hangs
> A cloudy quiver over Pairc-na-lee.

Edward VII may not have recognised himself in this commoner's description, but his succession (lines 6–7) is used to mark yet another declension from past dignity and power. In his place, the poet awaits an ancient authority whose weaponry is poised in natural guise above a place itself disguised in a dying language Yeats recognised but did not know. So much is relatively clear, even if his way with capital letters and Gaelic can look like inflationary rhetoric. But there is a simple grammatical question about 'In the Seven Woods' which (for this reader at least) defies answering. What is the 'it' of line 9? Or to ask a more abstract question: why should whatever is 'alone of all things happy' be representable only by the neutral pronoun?

Yeats the poet returned to Tara on two occasions, quickly in 'The Two Kings' (October 1912) and after much delay in 'In Tara's Halls' (June 1938). Both involve intense and inscrutable sexual conflicts, the earlier poem utilising a Tennysonian narrative that infuriated Ezra Pound, the late poem invoking the Golden Plough beloved of Meath folk in 1902. The two kings are brothers and mortals, set at odds by the intervention of a god and his 'unnatural majesty' (line 149). Returning to his wife after a wasteful war, one brother is lured into conflict with a supernatural stag, described with much homoerotic detail; the other, wasting inexplicably at home during the war, is tempted into desire of his brother's wife. The poem ends with the woman's insistence on a human and mortal ethic, more Browning-esque than Tennysonian:

> Never will I believe there is any change
> Can blot out of my memory this life
> Sweetened by death, but if I could believe,
> That were a double hunger in my lips
> For what is doubly brief.

Here the anguish implicit in a Vision of Blood Kindred is rejected, but without total conviction.

According to one typescript version, 'In Tara's Halls' dealt with a king whom Yeats chose later to style simply a man. (By 1938, kings were ever commoner than Edward VII, though Edward VIII had won the poet's approval for, like Parnell, he had loved his lass.) The origins of the piece are obscure, though, in July 1932, Francis Stuart admitted that he had contributed some 'horsey dialogue' to an otherwise unknown script called 'Tara Hall'. Mary Manning had some part in this, and the whole thing sounds like a lampoon or satire. Yeats's poem that followed six years later was far from satiric. 'In Tara's Halls' relates the death of a man aged 101 who, though he had loved God and woman, never asked for love in return. The final speech of this patriarch is delivered 'between / The golden plough and harrow', instructing workmen to prepare his grave, whereupon he 'Lay in the coffin, stopped his breath and died'. Invoking Bronze Age Ireland, and its fabulous instruments of fertility, the 'king' achieves a modern triumph of the will.

In the reign of Edward the Common, the poet's father had railed against Pound's misreading of 'The Two Kings'. John Butler Yeats, painter and intellectual pugilist, insisted that it possessed qualities much sought after by Tennyson, but never attained – 'splendour of imagination, a liberating splendour, cold as sunrise'. With the king of 'In Tara's Halls' having declined to ask for love, and with this sharper appreciation of 'The Two Kings', we encounter unmistakably that quality discerned by Baudelaire in Delacroix. The cold-eyed Yeats was more obviously the author of 'The Cold Heaven' (1912). But did the poet remember his father's praise when, years later in June 1914, he imagined in 'The Fisherman' an ideal audience, an ideal solitary listener of whom he cried:

> Before I am old
> I shall have written him one
> Poem maybe as cold
> And passionate as the dawn.

Passion and coldness often collocate in Yeats's work, not least in those patterns where early and late concerns are conjoined. 'Father and Child' (1926) is officially explained as arising from a remark by the poet's daughter Anne (then aged seven!), though it seems more likely to encode Yeats's rebuke of Iseult Gonne, who against advice had married Francis Stuart whose 'hair is beautiful / Cold as the March wind his eyes'. The proponent of the Anne-theory, A. Norman Jeffares, provides by way of compensation a crucial detail buried in the sources of 'The Two Kings' – that when King Eochaid dug up the mounds (at Tara) in search of Edain (taken by the god), 'he was gulled into accepting her identical daughter as his wife'. Compare Yeats on Maud and Iseult.

Tara and its 'immedicable' mound (line 129) stood foursquare between volcanic emotional regions of Yeats's mind. In some private symbolism an incurable *mons*, Tara's protection in 1902 was not simply a patriotic duty in the face of zealous fundamentalism. The politics of his involvement went deeper, and his return to that locus testified to its almost inadmissible significance. But if Tara held nature and culture apart, it was also a point where they bordered each other, where they met. If Maud Gonne was the Muse who added intensity to a patriotic motive, she was also the mother of Iseult, whose father Yeats sometimes 'thought' he might be. Amidst the waxing-and-waning controversy, two deaths occurred that marked new frontiers between past and present. The less important was that of the Queen (22 January 1901); just over a year earlier, the poet's mother had died, also in London (3 January 1900).

Susan Yeats (1841–1900, née Pollexfen) is one of the silences in Yeats's work and, until very recently, likewise in his biographers' work.[26] She had borne John Butler Yeats six children: the poet on 13 June 1865 in Sandymount, County Dublin; Susan Mary (or Lily) on 25 August 1866 in Sligo; Elizabeth Corbet (or Lolly) on 11 March 1868 in London; Robert Corbet on 27 March 1870 in London; John Butler (or Jack) on 29 August 1871 in London; and, after a lull of exactly four years, Jane Grace on 29 August 1875 in London. Robert and Jane both died in infancy. If we include Jane Grace, three of the children were given secondary forenames to signal the Yeatses' attachment to their Corbet kin. This was an inheritance at once grand and ungainly, especially if one looked at the gain aspect of ungainly. The hill of Tara usefully obscured several views of the past that haunted the poet, not least because it lay between the city of Dublin and the frontier of Leinster with Ulster. The controversy functioned as what Freud called a screen-memory in an essay of 1901. Sharply etched but of little real significance, it blocked out less palatable material, not necessarily earlier, but linked with the construction of earliest identity.[27]

Bleaching History

In official genealogical terms, Yeats's proclaimed Irish ancestor was Jervis Yeats. The first paragraph of the first biography presents this figure as 'the old merchant' referred to in the introductory verses in *Responsibilities* (1914), where Yeats begs:

> Pardon, old fathers, if you still remain
> Somewhere in ear-shot for the story's end ...

In fact, both Yeats and his biographer err in these details, and the former must take some responsibility for the latter's compounding of the error. These details aside, the historical record states unambiguously that, in December 1700 when his son John was baptised in St Michan's Church, Dublin, Jervis Yeats was entered as a 'pedlar'. The social distance between pedlar and merchant was not as great then as the words now suggest: but even if we rewrite the baptismal entry, so that it identifies a commercial traveller or door-to-door salesman, we are left with someone less readily assimilated into the Protestant Ascendancy as traditionally conceived.[28] At the baptism of an earlier child, Jervis Yeats was described as a soldier. The poet was descended from the soldier-pedlar's other son, Benjamin.

What is significant here is not the rapidity with which the demobbed Protestant soldier of c.1690 was able to rise through the ranks of pedlars to become a wholesale linen merchant and freeman of the city. It is rather the way family history – at a time of the breaking of nations, the lamps going out all over Europe – becomes an arena in which latter-day visions of the past are substantiated. A good deal of Yeats's first volume of autobiography, *Reveries Over Childhood and Youth* (1914), relates miscellaneous stories of 'ancestors or great uncles [who] bore a part in Irish history'.[29] This is still flippant stuff in which one can detect – though it is not stressed – the presence of Yeats's ancestors in Ireland at a date long preceding Jervis the pedlar. Nevertheless, Yeats singles out a 'great-great-grandfather, who had married a certain Mary Butler', and describes a silver heirloom cup with the Butler crest and the date 1534 engraved under the lip. Mary Butler was the daughter of one John Butler, who was (in Lily Yeats's words) 'many years first clerk in the bar office' at Dublin Castle: her husband was Benjamin Yeats (d. 1795), grandson of Jervis.[30] This eighteenth-century alliance with the Butlers brought the Yeatses into complex and repeated contact with branches of officialdom associated directly or indirectly with the maintenance of law and order. The Dukedom of Ormonde, which the poet preferred to invoke, lay out of sight.

Mary Butler brought 626 acres of land in County Kildare to the family, a property that was finally slipping out of Yeats's hands at the end of the nineteenth century. Her son, John Yeats (1774–1846), was educated at Trinity College Dublin, took holy orders and became rector 'long years ago' of Drumcliff parish, County Sligo. Pastor John married Jane Taylor, whose father (William Taylor, 1747–1817) was chief civil clerk in the Chief Secretary's office in Dublin Castle.

(There are, consequently, on the poet's direct ancestral line, two marriages into or within the castle apparatus.) George Yeats (born 1784) married Jane's sister Sarah, and George's niece (Mary Jane Terry) married yet another Taylor offcut, and thus reinforced the stitching between two families.

It has been recorded that 'one of the Taylors was employed by the government "to know the history of every person of prominence in Dublin," and at his death the government claimed and took five thousand pounds in "secret service money" found in his desk'.[31] Few have paused to consider where such conduct fits into a Yeats family tradition blending occasional rebelliousness with unremarkable loyalty. Did William Taylor play a part in destroying Robert Emmet, for example, or did he pay the informers McNally and Armstrong, who betrayed United Irishmen comrades? When Taylor died on 3 July 1817 in his seventieth year, he was extensively eulogised in the *Dublin Evening Post* for his fidelity to government, though that government (through functionaries like Taylor) systematically suborned and corrupted the city's newspapers with secret payments and lavish patronage.[32]

There is a second connection to Emmet, perhaps no more to be proven than the possibility that an ancestral Taylor connived to trap the traitor. In the *Reveries*, Yeats mentions 'the notorious Major Sirr, who arrested Lord Edward Fitzgerald' as 'godfather to several of my great-great-grandfather's children; while, to make a balance, my great-grandfather had been Robert Emmet's friend and was suspected and imprisoned but for a few hours'.[33] The godfathering might be traceable if someone were ever to find Henry Charles Sirr (1764–1841) worth the full biographical effort. The friendship of the Revd Mr John Yeats with Emmet (1778–1803), on the other hand, is potentially verifiable through a dozen biographies of the young patriot. None of them has any reference to John Yeats, not even Ruan O'Donnell, the most encyclopaedic of the professional historians among Emmet's biographers.

This is not to say that Yeats in the *Reveries* is caught in pure invention. His remark about imprisonment for a few hours very likely descends from the Visitation conducted in Trinity College by Chancellor John Fitzgibbon and Patrick Duigenan to root out subversion. That occurred in April 1798, involving the forcible detention in the Examination Hall of students, resident graduates, staff, Fellows and others, with the subsequent interrogation of suspects – Thomas Moore was a particular focus of attention. If the

Visitation provided descendants of Pastor John Yeats with a 'what-did-you-do-during-the-Rebellion?' pretext for sentiment, Victorian families found other ways to link themselves back to the young 'martyr'. Emma Dobbin, mother of the novelist Sheridan Le Fanu (1814–1873), nurtured the memory of her father attending Emmet's execution in his official capacity as a Dublin clergyman: the Emmet biographers are as silent about Dr William Dobbin as they are about Pastor John Yeats.[34] The poet Yeats's autobiography is, as most recognise, a creative work.

Whatever Taylor's relation to the business of spying and suborning, it was in the Taylor apartments in the castle that William Butler Yeats (1806–1862) was born. Like his father, he went to Trinity and entered the Church; in due course he became rector of Tullylish in County Down. The parish was an unremarkable one, though, among earlier rectors, one notes George Synge in 1634. The Revd W. B. Yeats's wife was Jane Grace Corbet (1811–1876). The grandson of his clerical namesake, the poet chose more often to allude to his *great*-grandfather, the rector of Drumcliff in Sligo. Lily Yeats's notebook of family lore, from which it is likely her brother borrowed some phrases – he certainly looted his father's correspondence – begins with ancestors no more remote than Jervis; apart from the Butler link (established in 1773 and venerated retrospectively), most of her findings relate to the late eighteenth and nineteenth centuries. Alternating family history with horoscopes for living relatives, Lily's notebook uncannily anticipates 'The Words upon the Window-pane', just as Augusta Gregory's journal fed 'Coole Park and Ballylee, 1931'.

Other names deserve attention also. The Yeatses' link with the Armstrongs commenced when William Corbet married Grace Armstrong (d. 1861) 'of Hackwood', County Cavan in 1791, the celebrant being the Revd Richard Brooke. The Armstrongs were an old family of military habit, the Corbets were virtually unknown, and Hack-(or Hawkes-) wood near untraceable. Lily Yeats found that William's father, Patrick Corbet (d. 1790, 'an eminent law agent'), was the earliest of the line she could or would trace, though the surname was well represented in 1790s' Dublin. Significantly, it was also well represented in County Down, was the dominant surname in the parish of Dromara, and lent itself to numerous place-names near Tullylish – for example, the village of Corbet and nearby Corbet's Lough.

None of William and Grace's sons married 'so we have no relations of the name'; others died young and overseas. For the Yeatses, the most significant was Robert Corbet (b. 29 July 1795; d. 1872), the owner of Sandymount 'Castle'. Two Victorian Yeatses were given the names 'Robert Corbet' at baptism: both died in childhood. Writing his *séance* play in the early 1930s, Yeats named the principal expository character, John Corbet. It is only in a few very late poems and one play that he refers to this branch of his tree.

Compared to his eventual acknowledgment of the terminal, but Dublin-based, Corbets, the poet paid little or no attention to the extensive records in Lily's notebook of the wider family's place in eighteenth-century Ulster, not only in Cavan, but shortly in County Down also. Laura Armstrong he had loved when they were still children, a suitable end to an unpromising infra-family intimacy. One of her forebears, Letitia Armstrong, had married the Revd Thomas Beatty in 1797, and it was he who presided when the young Revd William Butler Yeats married Jane Grace Corbet in 1835. The Beattys were a Down-based clerical family, and the Yeatses were in some measure their dependants, at least in the matter of livings in Ulster. John Beatty was rector of Tullylish in 1775, Thomas Beatty in 1813.

The famous consolidation of Sligo as Yeats family territory is facilitated by selective amnesia in relation to commitments or obligations in Ulster. Tullylish is located in north-central Down, on the River Bann, between the larger towns of Portadown and Banbridge. County Armagh lies close to the west, Belfast not far to the north-east. In the 1790s parts of the county were organised by the United Irishmen: on 13 June 1798, the rebel army was defeated at Ballynahinch. Flax-growing and linen provided the stable source of income in rural Armagh and Down, but across Ulster the structure of the industry was changing in the early decades of the new century. South Ulster towns like Ballybay, or smaller villages like Rockcorry in County Monaghan, were unable to maintain their place in an increasingly mechanised and centralised industry. Manufacture shifted north-eastwards. Political and economic development inter-acted with demographic patterns of confessional allegiance. Within County Down, Tullylish was part of a mixed area. According to Lewis's *Topographical Dictionary* (1837), it contained 'with the post-town of Gilford' just over 10,000 inhabitants. Many of these would have lived in or near the town, which became a parish in its own right thirty years later. The vicar had a tithe income of c. £230 per annum, and his residence stood in a glebe of forty acres about a mile from the church.[35]

Having graduated from Trinity College Dublin, the Revd Mr W. B. Yeats took up his first living as curate of Moira, County Down, in 1835, where Thomas Beatty was now rector. A year later, he moved as rector/vicar of Tullylish, a living which until then had been taken by the deans of Dromore. In fact, Beatty had (*ex officio* as dean) held the rectory of Tullylish before taking that of Moira: before him, his father John Beatty had been for two years (1775–77) rector there also. It was Beatty turf. Of the elder cleric, the poet Yeats provides an intriguing account in the first volume of his *Autobiographies:*

> He was a connection and close friend of my great-grandmother Corbet, and though we spoke of him as 'Uncle Beattie' in our childhood, no blood relation. My great-grandmother who died at ninety-three had many memories of him. He was the friend of Goldsmith and was accustomed to boast, clergyman though he was, that he belonged to a hunt-club of which every member but himself had been hanged or transported for treason, and that it was not possible to ask him a question he could not reply to with a perfectly appropriate blasphemy or indecency.[36]

From this we can deduce that, blood relation or not, Yeats's clerical career was launched in Down on the strength of a family 'connection'. Such arrangements were quite normal at the time; what is striking is the neglect of northern links and place-names in W. B. Yeats's account of his ancestry. We have already noted that the rector had been born in Dublin Castle; four of his siblings were born, however, in Gilford, County Down between 1808 and 1811, a pattern that would suggest a strong family attachment through the Beattys, or possibly on the Taylor side.[37] Of such a pattern nothing is discernible in the poet's account of his family.

Some clue as to the forces at work behind this silence may be deducted from the poet's treatment of Uncle Beattie [*sic*]. The tribute arises from recollection of a portrait 'too harsh and merry for its company' of miniatures. These had taken his fancy as a boy, and now as a mature writer, 'perhaps it is only fancy or the softening touch of the miniaturist that makes me discover in their faces some courtesy and much gentleness'. One of the two is less than half-identified ('a great-great-grandfather') – and the other turns out to be 'too harsh and merry'. The aesthetic frame only partly assimilates its human material, and the intransigent Beatty is then doubled as uncle and non-relative, friend of Goldsmith (he of the 'honey-pot' mind) and also a rake-hellish associate of (future) rebels. The association probably took place in Volunteer clubs during the early 1780s, though oddly Yeats misses this opportunity to claim a patriotic bonus. Additionally or alternatively, there are traces existing in folk-songs of transportation resulting more from social than politico-military offence: the most famous of these songs, 'The Boys of Mullaghbawn' relates to the area of south-east Ulster where Beatty and Yeats rode.

Within a year or two of arriving in Tullylish, the Revd Mr Yeats saw a resolution passed at a vestry meeting 'that in future no person but a Protestant of the Established Church be placed on the poor list of this parish'.[38] Published accounts of the family concede that the rector did not get on affably with his Presbyterian neighbours, but an exclusion of their poor (also the Catholic poor) from parish relief was to prove an error of judgment. The local dissenting minister, John Johnston, had been appointed back in 1811; a formidable preacher and leader of his flock, he remained in Tullylish till his death in 1862. Attached to what was tellingly named Civiltown Presbyterian Church, he became a patriarch of reviving Presbyterianism.[39] Socially, Johnston evidenced contradictions that his Establishment counterpart found unpalatable. The minister's wife was Frances Jackson, of Crieve House, Ballybay, whose well-to-do family had been a major force in the linen trade of County Monaghan. From her adopted manse, she became known to locals as Lady Johnston, as if in defiance of the official nobility.[40] Yet in 1836 the Civiltown church in Tullylish was a very plain building with an earthen floor to the aisle, housing an average attendance of 800. Famine in the mid-1840s drove small numbers of depressed Catholics in from western districts and further complicated the patterns of denominational allegiance and economic in/dependence. The number of Catholic burials in Tullylish jumped by close on 400 per cent in the years 1846–47.[41]

Across the island, the period of Yeats's settling into the Tullylish glebe-house was characterised by the introduction of a national system of poor-law unions. The parish was divided between the unions of Lurgan and Banbridge, but in the records of neither does the new rector feature. Administration was overseen by a Board of Guardians made up almost exclusively of resident gentry and a few of the aristocracy. Colonel William Blacker (1777–1853) was the principal active landlord: he had been active earlier at the Battle of the

Diamond (1797), becoming a founder of the Orange Order. In practice, lesser mortals ran the dormitories, schools, dispensaries and other services. Men of the cloth were recruited as chaplains, usually three in number – for Catholics, Presbyterians and members of the Church of Ireland/England among the inmates of the Union. Even in the last capacity, there was no role for someone of W. B. Yeats's standing. Too much the gentleman to be a mere chaplain, and yet lacking the landed qualification that might have put him among the Guardians and their circle, he gradually found himself on the outside of a social administrative system of ever-increasing importance. When Tullylish elected two residents to serve as Guardians in 1843/44, it chose George Phelps (gentleman) and Samuel Mills (linen manufacturer) in dual recognition of the parish's changing economic life.

The early years of the Banbridge and Lurgan unions saw contributions from men with names associated with the rector and his family – Armstrong, Beatty, Corbett, and so forth. Despite his previous connections in the area (mainly through the Beattys), Yeats was alone of his name. Professor William Murphy's chart of the family lists eleven siblings, for six of whom no date of death can be assigned. None of the eleven seems to have married.[42] As a family man and a holder of public (clerical) office, he was also alone in his generation. Both Blacker and the rector were contributors to the *Dublin University Magazine*, the former credited with a number of popular, highly sectarian compositions – 'The Protestant Boys', and another (about Cromwell) containing the famous line 'So put your trust in God, me boys, and keep your powder dry'. The distance between the author's place in society and the audience he addressed constituted a frontier, an inhibition to culture which W. B. Yeats, for one, was unable or unwilling to cross.

There were other impediments. From the outset, the unions became a fairground for shows of strength between rival denominations among the paupers housed in its buildings. The Lurgan Union's Catholic chaplain, Father O'Brien – his Christian name eluded the minute-keeper – complained about books circulated for religious reading, about the provision of furniture to serve as an altar at Mass, and about arrangements for his care when the Established Church provided instruction. Hamilton Dobbin, the Presbyterian chaplain, is not known to have had difficulties. In 1842, the suspicion arose that paupers of the Established Church had been buried without a funeral service being read over their graves.[43]

Whatever laxity may have characterised management of the union, it still represented a timely innovation in social services when Ireland was on the brink of disaster. Tullylish was only one electoral district 'feeding into' the Lurgan and Banbridge unions; there the rector lived in a dilapidated old house, preached in an even older and more ruinous church, the whole surrounded by new industrial and residential structures. It was not a good living. Nothing prepared him, or the majority of his fellow-clergy, for the horrors to come. Early in 1846 – the first spring of famine – officially appointed visitors to Lurgan Union recommended 'that the Old Men & Womens Dormitories be ceiled [sic] to prevent the effluvia of these apartments ascending to the injury of the health of the Paupers in the Apartments above'.[44] Neither the building of external fever sheds, nor the substantial weekly provisions (e.g. 2,800 lb of bread, more than 1,000 gallons of milk, 500 lb of 'coarse meat' and ten barrels of lime for hygiene) can represent the scale of human suffering in mid-Down during the famine. Death rates there were lower than in the south and west of the country, much lower than – for example – in Schull (County Cork), where J. M. Synge's grandfather succumbed to famine fever helping 'benighted papists' in mortal distress. What did his fellow-director of the Abbey Theatre have by way of family tradition?

In January 1847, the Revd W. B. Yeats described to the Lord Lieutenant how a relief committee had bound itself by such stringent rules 'as to prevent us from giving [free food] to any parties, but such is the distress of the people this rule must be relaxed' – after eighteenth months of abject distress.[45] Joseph Hone, in his 1943 biography of the poet, tells us that, 'at the time of the great famine', the rector 'went with another Irish clergyman to collect relief in England'. No explanation of this external and indirect mode of support for his parishioners is provided, nor does the area's local historian advert to any such fund raising.[46] Instead Hone, whose own family roots could be traced in Tullylish, proceeds with a disquieting conjunction:

> [Yeats] disliked Presbyterians ... and could never come to an under-standing with the aggressive North, because his Evangelicalism belonged to the cultivated classes, and instead of being a hatred of human nature was 'an intense pity mixed with an affectionate and human delight'.[47]

What diminishes this as testimony is its own patent impatience with northern dissent, aggravated in 1943 by the violent and divisive events that had partitioned Ireland, formally in 1920–22, informally but effectively several decades earlier. When the Revd W. B. Yeats abandoned Tullylish and 'retired' to Dublin, he was effecting a retreat similar in its orientation to the processes of division which marked off Ulster from the rest of the island in the last quarter of the nineteenth century. To appreciate the point, one has to look more closely at the localities involved and the manner in which they too were changing with the times, independent of the famine crisis.

According to the Ordnance Survey memoir of 1834, Tullylish possessed nine bleaching greens, two flax-scutching mills, one spinning mill, one vitriol works, three corn mills and a flour mill. Drawing power from the river that flowed just below the church, the area was at the time of Yeats's arrival well on the way towards a further, traumatic stage of industrialisation. If the official focus of that development was Gilford, where a model industrial village named Dunbarton was built in the 1840s by linen magnates Dunbar & McMaster, the impact was registered on older, so-called traditional perspectives and boundaries elsewhere in the parish. Gilford's population rose from 643 to 2,892 in the twenty years from 1841 to 1861, with a 'truly fantastic growth' between 1851 and 1861 (when the Revd Mr Yeats was still for the most part a resident). If the conventional view has been that the poet's grandfather opted for metropolitan comfort rather than rural isolation, nothing further from the truth could be devised.[48]

The new industrialisation of the parish brought with it challenges to the Established Church. Some time before 1827, glebe-land at Seapatrick had been acquired by William Hayes to establish his third son in power-spinning and weaving. By 1835 young Frederick Hayes (1802–1853), a contemporary of the rector's, was producing linen and cotton union cloth with one hundred power-looms at Seapatrick on land ordained to support God's deputy.[49] As early in the Yeats rectorship as 1839, Hugh Dunbar (d. 1847) was employing 1,700 handlooms at Huntley Glen, Tullylish. By contrast, on the local estate of Sir William Johnston (d. c.1841), there were only sixty-nine tenants.[50] Dunbar was a Unitarian whose paternalistic enterprises included provision of land for a new Catholic church. While the McMasters supported the Established Church personally – 'noblesse' oblige – their activity in business was a different matter, wholly independent of the allegiances that informed the very notion of a church establishment. In November 1841, the company built a new thread factory; at the formal opening, 800 hundred people sat down to tea; dancing followed, with singing by some of the 'operatives'. This expansion of business was not only celebrated, but balanced by the opening of a reading room and library. Local worthies were present – no sign of the rector – but so were ladies and gentlemen from Belfast, now palpably nearer since canals and railways brought the factory system into rural Ireland. The factory even supplied hospital facilities for its workers housed in a complex new village augmenting the older town. New churches sprang up through the 1840s, emphasising the isolation of the old parish church upstream.[51] By 1846, when the 'effluvia' of famine victims was threatening the health of paupers in the union, a factory inspector could rate the Dunbar McMaster mill among the largest in Ireland.

These changes were accomplished by an acceleration or intensification of existing methods. Where landlords had accumulated capital, and indeed tenant farmers had done likewise through trade or speculation, no new financial institutional changes were formally put in place. But, as linen in the Bann valley came not just to augment farming, but virtually to dominate and redirect it, so the resulting manufactories, mills and other concentrations of labour and investment were organized through joint-stock companies or partnerships.[52] In the Revd W. B. Yeats's immediate view were numerous instances. Hugh Dunbar was variously a director of Dunbar Thompson & Co., Dunbar McMaster & Co. and Dunbar Dickson & Co. Separate companies were often formed to specialise in different activities, but in all a fundamental purpose was to protect the principal shareholders from risk of loss. Joint-stock companies did not have denominational loyalties, even if they were directed by men who allowed such concerns to affect their short-term activities. Where land and religion found common ground in the very concept of parish, the new wealth had no attachment to value, tradition or belief. A Quaker bleach-green owner known casually as Ben Hutton (1781–1866) became obliterated by Benj. Haughton & Co. Individual identities, likewise familiar landmarks, were transmogrified. By means of the Bann Reservoir Act (1836), mill owners along the river were empowered to raise funds through £50 shares to build three reservoirs, one of these effectively turning nearby Corbet or Corbet's Lough into an artificial lake.[53] For the moment, we do not know what kinsman of Mrs William Butler Yeats had been accommodated in that place-name.

All this is remote from the poet – surely? Yes, and the task must be to measure the remoteness, account for it in terms of social relationship as well as the poet's pet theories of family. Of the business of partnerships, Yeats perhaps knew more than might first strike one in the Celtic Twilight. His mother's family had established themselves in Sligo when William Pollexfen (1811–1892) married Elizabeth Middleton in 1837 and became a partner in his brother-in-law's business. Shipping and milling formed the basis of their small-town prosperity. The actual Sligo relationships upon which the young Willie Yeats relied as a child – as distinct from the rectorship of an earlier century – were contemporary with the capitalisation of Tullylish. These were Pollexfen links, not Yeatsian ones. Sligo may have been thought a Little Belfast for its sectarian animosities, but Tullylish was Near Belfast in its commercial development.

Pre-famine Ireland experienced phenomenal population growth, and a fertile area enjoying good natural sources of power, close proximity to ports and markets and entrepreneurial leadership was perhaps bound to thrive. In 1834, the researcher for Lewis's *Dictionary* had already noted that plans were afoot to enlarge the parish church in Tullylish, built in 1698 on the outer defences of an ancient fort. In 1827, a square tower and an outer aisle were added, and 'the church is now about to be again enlarged, to enable it to afford sufficient accommodations for the still increasing numbers of the congregation'. By contrast, the old rectory in which the rector's first child was born in 1839 'very soon after became a ruin'.[54] Nothing came of the planned enlargement of the church until 1859 when a local landlord chose to lobby the Ecclesiastical Commissioners in Dublin.

Alexander John Robert Stewart (b. 1827), related to the Londonderry family and holding lands in Donegal, was High Sheriff of County Down in addition to his role as master of the estate; his agent George Bowen lived in Laurencetown House, formerly the home of the Laurence family. Indeed, one of the other changes occurring in Tullylish during the 1830s and '40s is the replacement of old (relatively small) landowners, who had given their names to places, by new occupants, some of them already well connected, and others still energetically planting themselves on the social map. This, together with the growth of evangelicalism among Presbyterians, extends the pattern of rapid change in the rector's territory.

Nor were property and dissent at odds in early Victorian Ulster.

Quakers were of course long renowned as enterprising capitalists who stood apart from Church and Army, title and fashion. Other groups in the area produced their exceptional men. Despite humble origins, the Revd John Johnston was no bothy preacher. He was the principal figure in Irish Presbyterianism calling for the revival that suddenly swept through the eastern counties of Ulster and beyond in 1859. On 29 June, he presided at a gathering of nearly 40,000 people in Belfast's Botanic Gardens. The Ulster Revival was the latest in a series of turbulent upheavals in Anglophone Protestantism, in which the Scots-Irish played a leading role not only in the British Isles but also in America. Contention between lay and clerical members had obvious implications for the theory and practice of church government generally, while the hysterical manifestations that accompanied the 1859 revival identified new areas of sensitivity, where women and industrial labour came together in ways already challenging traditional authority. It has been argued that revivalism broke the sturdy independence of the Presbyterian Church, but it also posed major problems, theological and pastoral, for the Establishment.[55]

A man who, when Macaulay's *History* came out in 1848, 'threw the parish to his curate and went to bed until he had read all the volumes', was no match for the 'patriarch of open-air assemblies', a phenomenon now not of frontier dissent, but of urban mass-politics.[56] Revivalism could not be sustained theologically without its becoming a mere habit, but it fed the mobilisation of Ulster Protestant opinion when the Home Rule question began to take shape a decade later. The Revd W. B. Yeats was gone out of the north by 1859, and the physical fabric of the church he left behind was decaying. The aid that A. J. R. Stewart sought in Dublin had been for a new building, and not simply for repairs or extensions. The situation he sought to remedy was not parochial decay, but the vulnerability of the episcopalian establishment newly challenged for leadership by the local Presbyterian minister. Initially Stewart was disappointed, but the threat of independent funding for a new church appears to have persuaded the authorities that the Establishment should not be embarrassed by private enterprise.

On 15 March 1861, a foundation stone was laid, the weather on that occasion earning the most fulsome treatment in the *Belfast Newsletter*. Rural Tullylish was now city news, 'and while the rich and great of the neighbourhood were present, not the least pleasing scene amongst the entire assembly was the presence of some 400

Sunday School children and their teachers, dressed in holiday attire ... [together with] the High Sheriff's large staff of halberd-men, dressed in their handsome liveries, which attracted so much attention in Downpatrick during the assizes.' Public reporting of the children in their Sunday best was not simply Victorian sentiment; it signalled the press's recognition of the parents as readers, or potential readers, whose contribution to social harmony was valued. Curates did the spiritual honours, with the landlord, his agent and the building contractor attending to the rest. George Bowen listed the benefactors, among them 'the Rev. William B. Yeats, our esteemed and worthy rector, whose absence from among us this day from ill health we must regret'. The Dean of Dromore 'proceeded at some length to show what great privileges Protestants enjoyed more especially in possessing liberty of conscience, the right of private judgment, and the free use of the Scriptures of Truth'. It was a thoroughly modern occasion, with debts and the evils of popery vying for damnation.

The rector was by now in his fifties, and set in Sandymount ways. The consecration of his Bannside church took place on 31 October 1862, and he died later that year. Perhaps it was unlikely that he should attend the ceremony; in any event his absence again was politely noted. The *Belfast Newsletter* recorded that 'the site on which the new church stands is very picturesque, being distant from the busy hum and bustle of the other manufacturing town of Gilford, in rather a secluded spot over the banks of a pretty large river ...'[57]

The withdrawal of the Revd W. B. Yeats from Ulster in the face of industrialisation and Presbyterian resurgence does not in itself demand ponderously symbolic interpretation. Some facts, however, might be ventured. Tullylish was the hub of a major industrial revolution in Ulster, and hence in Ireland as a whole. Belfast, as a commercial centre, as a port, and as a larger manufacturing town in its own right, cannot be gainsaid. Yet in the distinctive industrialised countryside of Yeats's parish, modern patterns of living were well established. Newspapers have been already noted, going about their urbanising business. The role of women as factory workers was crucial, altering so-called traditional notions of family structure. Terrace-housing, sometimes very cramped but on the whole well designed as to hygiene, privacy and self-help factors like garden plots or yards, broke down multi-generational co-habitation to encourage 'the nuclear family'. Education, provided by employers rather than Church or State, included the provision of adult (night) classes, with traceable effects on literacy. On the dark side of the moon, child labour had certainly been exploited, but the rise in prosperity (interrupted by the famine) eliminated further need of that lamentable practice. The disciplining of a fresh labour force, linked to rudimentary 'welfare', encouraged inter-class harmony, but did so (as far as the old order was concerned) at the price of admitting proletarian voices to civil society's conversation. The old order of landlord and tithe-supported rector was obsolete and, in places like Tullylish, visibly so.

It should be said of Tullylish's absentee that his preoccupations were less worldly and vain than those of many colleagues in the Victorian Church. W. M. Murphy's exhaustive biography of the painter John Butler Yeats (son of the rector, father of the poet) projects convincingly the image of a learned, kindly and pious man, with sufficient private means to forgo his clerical income, or at least part of it. This may not tell the whole story, for in 1849 the Revd Yeats found it expedient to borrow £999 in cash through the Royal Exchange Assurance Co., the debt to be charged 'upon the estate and lands of Thomastown and Clareduff as also the Rectory of Tullylish and the tithes or composition and Glebe lands thereof'.[58] As befits an Irish-American, the biographer is not indulgent of Ulster Protestant foibles, but rather is prone to assume that Tullylish was 'a lonely place' in 1839 when the painter was born, and that it remained so during his father's ministry. It is on such grounds that the Revd W. B. Yeats consequently gains his sympathy in his clash with 'Presbyterianism and its gloomy puritan doctrines'.

The poet's streamlining of his ancestry to set up a polar opposition between Sligo and Dublin, country and city, west and east, has thus affected the latter-day commentary that claims to authenticate his insight. The marginalising of County Down forms part of a broader reconsideration of the Irish regions, reducing the complexity of an eighteenth-century pattern to the two-dimensional conflicts institutionalised today. For example, not only was the Revd John Beatty an associate of Goldsmith, but so was Thomas Dawson Laurence, a local poet in Tullylish. A network of school acquaintances, marriages and clerical appointments might be traced from Down in the east, through Armagh, Monaghan, Cavan, Roscommon and Westmeath, to Sligo in the west. In part, this pattern depended on the diocese as a significant *social* organisation; in part, it reflected the non-centralised form of late-eighteenth-century life in Ireland, at least among the minor gentry who did not fix ambitious gaze on the Dublin parliament. Yet details of family history can readily be cited to substantiate the pattern at several levels of social activity. Yeats's predecessor as rector of Tullylish was W. H. Wynne, whose family owned Hazelwood House in Sligo. And though 'Uncle Beattie' was declared by the poet to be no blood-relation, his son the Revd Thomas Beatty married a sister of Yeats's mother-in-law. In 1865, when the poet was born in Sandymount, Dublin, the doctor in attendance was another Thomas Beatty, of the same family.[59]

Between the rector's appointment in 1836 and his namesake/ grandson's birth just thirty years later, the relationship to each other of the regions and districts of Ireland, its rural enclaves and urban centres, had changed markedly. Doubtless the change had begun earlier, and was to accelerate later. In the course of the nineteenth century, the structure of Irish society and that of Denmark (for example) diverged in ways sufficiently distinct as to underline a need to examine precisely what the Irish pattern was. The paradigm of these changes was to be partition, which graphically illustrated a network of more pervasive alterations from diversity and complexity towards a binary schematism. Ideological constructs played their part in preparing the ground for the essentially political act of partition. As far as the later emergence of Protestant Ascendancy in the mid-to-late nineteenth century is concerned, one important development was the incorporation, into the Church of Ireland, of individuals and families with hereditary attachments to other, non-established branches of Protestantism. For example, the Hones were Presbyterian when they arrived in Ireland, the Bewleys Quakers. Here again, a moment of comparative analysis can facilitate a better understanding of the social construction, in Ireland, of the modernist generation. The lower nobility of Austro-Hungary admitted Jews to its ranks in the course of the nineteenth century, thus setting up patterns in which cosmopolitan culture, estate ownership and confessional difference altered drastically in Magyar-speaking Hungary. The ultimate failure of this assimilation (compared to that embodied in 'Protestant Ascendancy') is reflected in the extreme tensions of Hungarian communism and modernism.[60]

Untroubled by these exotic influences, and yet profoundly affected by industrialisation, the parish of Tullylish conveniently brings together a Hone and a Bewley who served as curates in the Established Church. Accommodation with the Church of Ireland may have been sought as a form of social advance, or it may have been effected through altering patterns of education. In terms of its ecclesiastical personnel, and its experience of industrialisation, Tullylish illustrates significant change; it even – given the growth of population and the participation of its Presbyterian minister in mass-revivalism – illustrates traumatic change. Whatever the broader context, the Yeats rectorship in County Down straddles a crucial period of modernisation in Irish society. Cuchulain in 'On Baile's Strand' runs at the waves with his sword; a South Ulster man by birth, he might be less resonantly and more accurately described as fighting 'the filthy modern tide' of steam-powered mills, limited liability and mass meetings.

Corbet's Lough or Castle Corbet

To what, then, did the rector retire? The answer in simple terms is Sandymount Castle, the Dublin home of Robert Corbet, his brother-in-law. But as neither the home nor the brother-in-law was quite conventional, the Revd Yeats's retirement is less simple than it might seem. What is at issue is not just some scene from an Irish clerical life, but a fundamental aspect of the poet Yeats's construction of his personal, familial and (as he might have said on occasion) racial past. The *Autobiographies* contain a passage wonderfully weaving together quite distinct elements of the poet's ancestry, allowing the reader to confuse one grandfather with another and to merge Sligo and Sandymount as if they were virtually identical. Speaking initially of the Corbets, and then shifting to a village on Sligo Bay, he proceeds as follows:

> One great-uncle fell at New Orleans in 1813, while another, who became Governor of Penang, led the forlorn hope at the taking of Rangoon, and even in the last generation of all there had been lives of some power and pleasure. An old man who had entertained many famous people in his eighteenth-century house, where battlement and tower showed the influence of Horace Walpole, had but lately, after losing all his money, drowned himself, first taking off his rings and chain and watch as became a collector of many beautiful things; [*sic*] and once, to remind us of more passionate life, a gunboat put into Rosses, commanded by the illegitimate son of some great-uncle or other.[61]

The semi-colon in this oddly links Corbet (and 'the last generation of all') with a distaff relative clearly more able in mastering the sea.

For, in the story retailed by the poet, Corbet had committed suicide by jumping off a ship in Dublin Bay. The bachelor master of Sandymount Castle was the last of his line, a terminal condition that Yeats celebrates in other heroes from Swift to Synge. The eighteenth-century house hardly connotes antique dignities in a man born in that century and, as for the influence of Horace Walpole, readers may judge for themselves by studying the one surviving photograph of Sandymount Castle. The exchanges between Sligo and Dublin, Dublin and Down, which are partly subliminal in this passage, can be illuminated in comparative terms. In the very early years of the Revd Yeats's settling in to Tullylish, Sir Robert Gore-Booth was building Lissadel House some miles north-west of Sligo town. He was grandfather to Constance Markiewicz, just as the County Down rector was grandfather to her poetic admirer and political critic. In the best-known poem celebrating the Gore-Booths, Yeats refers to the house as 'that old Georgian mansion', though strictly speaking it was Victorian or (at best) datable to the brief forgotten reign (1830–37) of William IV. While it may seem unremarkable that Lissadel should be aligned with Georgian houses (Coole Park, notably), the process once again involves the repression of nineteenth-century origins and the promotion of eighteenth-century associations. By marriage to the Gores, the Booths had become a cut above their commercial origins in early modern Sligo, a process Yeats also renders timeless.[62]

Nineteenth-century social mobility was never a one-way traffic. The account of the Corbets of Sandymount provided by Yeats's father differs in a number of respects from that inscribed in the poetic history. In confirmation of the eclipse suffered by Robert Corbet, the Dublin postal directories indicate that his residence shifted to Upper Mount Street c.1868. Yet it is difficult to establish a solid basis from which to measure this decline and fall. If we seek his pedigree, it is not possible to go back more than two generations without resorting to guesses. (His father, William Corbet – d. 1824 – had been a solicitor who acquired an official post; his father Patrick – d. c.1790 – had been a more humble law agent.) Robert Corbet was a second son, with little inheritance. Nor has any landed estate come to light. To what extent was his Victorian wealth an Irish Sea bubble? To what extent were the Yeats properties, complicated from the outset by the will of 1777, entangled in Corbet's own affairs to the detriment of both parties? Certainly Robert Corbet looks less and less like Croesus, the more one learns of his circumstances. Comparisons with Gregorys and Persses, which Yeats will press in 1930, are perverse. His brother, Arthur, remained a bank clerk, a position which did not do justice to the man's self-esteem. Despite an appalling stammer, Arthur Corbet went over to Bible Christianity towards the end of his life.

What one derives from J. B. Yeats's account of life in the two-story castle is a vivid image of Victorian eccentricity, wounded family pride and impracticality. A settlement between Jane Grace Corbet and the Revd W. B. Yeats refers to her as being 'of Sandymount Castle', whereas her brother is simply 'of Sandymount in the Co. of Dublin', a distinction which may have disguised Robert Corbet's less-than-absolute possession of the Gothic residence on which his Yeats relatives later doted.[63] From c.1849, the rector of Tullylish lived next door or closer, and despite at least one severe attack of rheumatic fever, his health does not appear to have given cause for anxiety before his sudden death after a good lunch in the castle in November 1862. The inheritance of property in Dublin City and County Kildare in 1846 doubtless had given some impetus to the withdrawal from Ulster, though mortgages reduced the income from these properties. In 1862, when John B. Yeats inherited the same house and lands, he promptly appointed his impractical Corbet uncle as agent; he may have had no alternative, given Corbet's prior role in negotiating on the rector's behalf with the Royal Exchange Assurance Co.

Corbet finance remains something of a mystery, despite W. M. Murphy's industrious research. Robert Corbet made his professional debut as 'stock broker' in the Dublin directory of 1832. According to the poet, he had served in the Peninsular Wars; according to the poet's sister, he had joined the 69th Regiment of Foot in 1815, and was on half-pay the next year. (Another version limits Corbet's military career to sharing rooms with a French prisoner of war in Hastings.) By 1837 he is a solicitor, following in his father William's footsteps. William Corbet (married to Grace Armstrong) was a solicitor in the Irish courts of Chancery and Exchequer. And thus it was that young Robert obtained a minor post later transformed by the Encumbered Estates Act (1848) into a conduit through which purchase money passed, with consequential large fees for Corbet. The disaster of the famine, resulting in part from the growth in population, was a great fillip to the Corbet finances. In addition, Robert Corbet had held (since May 1832) an agency with the Royal Exchange Assurance Co. This provided a sound commercial basis for suburban existence, but it brought little in the way of elevated status in early Victorian society. Proposed in April 1840 for membership of the Grand Masters' Lodge, some time before the end of March 1841 he was initiated into that blue-chip division of Irish Freemasonry.[64]

As a doughty old Tory and a conventional adherent of the Established Church, it was Corbet's lot to flourish and to fall while the major presuppositions of his social existence were swept aside. A steady invasion of the professions by middle-class Catholics, the abolition of protestant monopoly in local government, the impact of the famine on landed estate, and the complex changes in Irish culture that led to the disestablishment (1869) of the Church of Ireland rendered highly perilous the insouciant course Corbet was disposed to follow. He had already acquired his castle by the mid-1830s, and it is reasonable to conclude that his social attitudes were well formed before the Municipal Reform Act of 1840 destroyed the exclusive privileges of Dublin's Protestant minority. The Corbets were then on intimate terms with Isaac Butt – also, since February 1842, a Freemason who had pleaded the cause of the unreformed Corporation at the bar of the House of Lords back in 1840. John B. Yeats leaves his readers in little doubt about uncle Corbet's social attitudes: 'If he suspected his Catholic neighbours, all the same he liked them.' Or, more broadly, 'his sympathies were extremely narrow'; and, in generous conclusion, Corbet had hoped to die 'in the odours of a well approved and well-tested worldliness'.[65] By the time he died, his erstwhile friend Butt had become the defender of Fenians, the prophet of Home Rule, and the father of several bastards.

The consequences of this detour into the suburban avenues of Yeats's family history are not limited simply to counteracting the poet's tendency, which increased as he grew older, to celebrate ancestors 'who had power in Ireland'.[66] It is difficult to classify the Corbets among these, however kindly their attitude even to Catholic neighbours. And having placed the Corbets actually rather than potentially, one can see that the family doctor who supervised the birth of the poet existed not solely as a relative and a descendant of churchmen: he also took his fees as a director of the Dublin Oil Gas Lighting Company. If one notes Robert Corbet as an agent for life assurance rather than a gothic baron; if one remembers the factories of Gilford and the new larger church at Tullylish; if one accepts the Pollexfens and Middletons as small-town business people, millers and ship-owners in a middling way of trade, local agents for the mercantile insurers; and – finally – if one observes that the Yeats entry in *Burke's Irish Families* frankly lists 'Henry, emigrated to USA, where he disappeared ... Edwin, emigrated to Toronto, Canada, where he worked in a bank ... Isaac Butt [Yeats] Sec[retary] Artisan Dwelling Co ...', then the mundane reality of the chronicle can be registered alongside the poet's mythologised version. The great gazebo, which the speaking 'we' invokes behind 'In Memory of Eva Gore-Booth and Con Markiewicz', was a gimcrack Victorian fabrication.

Unfortunately for Yeats, there were some who retained a strong sense of his mixed social origins. The best-known satirist of his pretensions was George Moore who, in the third volume of a wicked autobiography, described how his erstwhile friend 'began to thunder like Ben Tillett against the middle classes, stamping his feet, working himself into a great temper, all because the middle classes did not dip their hands into their pockets and give [Sir Hugh] Lane the money he wanted for his exhibition of French paintings. And we asked ourselves why our Willie Yeats should feel himself called upon to denounce his own class.'[67] That was written in 1914, just after Yeats had returned from an American tour. An earlier, private vignette, composed by someone of the class to which Yeats aspired, presented him as 'a cross between a Dominie Sampson and a starved R. C. curate'. The writer was Violet Martin, the date 1901.[68] In a sense, class was not the sole objective, even if commonness was Yeats's constant fear. Elevated status had its attractions, and aristocracy represented one form in which that might be achieved. But the word 'status' in itself compounds the difficulty, because it implies not only social position, but also an outer perspective in which status would appear. Status could provide only an exposed kind of authority, and was notoriously distinct from power. Coterie, on the other hand, promised exclusivity, secret knowledge and a dramatic forum for action. The transactions of literary modernism frequently took on the appearance of conspiracy, and the conditions of Irish society helped to blur the distinction between appearance and reality. Thus John Eglinton's Remnant could be made to resemble a Fenian cell, a masonic lodge, a company of the Calvinist elect. Readers of the Eglinton/Yeats quarrel who discern in Yeats's position a blueprint for the aristocracy of his later political utterances are too precipitous. What is desired is a protected and empowered smallness of numbers – a desire which in time takes on specifically eugenicist overtones. But so long as Ireland remained a victimised part of the grossly commercial and disgustingly populous United Kingdom, there was no reason for further retreat.

Independence brought its own problems, even if membership of the Senate conferred a degree of elevation and authority. By 1922 Yeats was constantly under attack from clerical quarters. For those keen to play down his own predilections, it has been convenient to underline the extreme right-wing opinions of hostile magazines like the *Catholic Bulletin*, in whose editorials Yeats's name frequently appeared. Yeats and his Catholic tormentors had several things in common – a conjoined interest in education and fascism, for example. Swift and Berkeley were the subject of pleasing articles or the source of allusions in issues of the *Bulletin*, whereas 'Senator Pollexfen Yeats' was repeatedly mocked. His winning of the Nobel Prize in 1923 provoked some exceptionally virulent remarks about 'the Stockholm dole', in accepting which he endorsed 'the lunatic drivellings of Swedenborg'.[69]

Behind the cheap journalese lay a not wholly lunatic appreciation of Irish social history. The *Bulletin*'s sarcastic incorporation of Pollexfen into the string of Yeats's names and titles – by February he was 'Senator William Butler Pollexfen Yeats' – was very likely prompted by its hatred of Freemasonry. Contrary again to a silence maintained by the poet, he was not the only member of his family to sit in the Irish Senate in the 1920s. Arthur Jackson had been made a member of the first Senate in 1922; husband of Alice Jane Pollexfen (1857–1928, sister of Yeats's mother), Jackson was a Belfast man taken into the firm of W. G. T. Pollexfen & Co. on his marriage.[70] The *Catholic Bulletin* was jibing at a kinship lobby in the Senate, though Yeats preferred to associate himself with Andrew Jameson, and a group of wealthy industrial magnates and bankers than with his uncle (by marriage). Seemingly the stereotypical Ulster businessman, Jackson had become managing director. He long protected George Pollexfen from the unpredicted consequences of that astrologer's financial incompetence, and (most galling for the Yeatses) had signed the annual Christmas cheque which had kept the household of John Butler Yeats in decently festive style throughout the 1880s and '90s.[71] Yeats's attitude towards Jackson replicates the sensitised folly of Thomas Mann's Buddenbrook family in its later generations, aloof from the mercantile world in which a living is made, and not unaligned with destructive aesthetic forces.

Far more comprehensive, however, was the *Bulletin*'s repeated denunciation of Yeats and his circle as the New Ascendancy.[72] In 1924, Yeats had not yet taken up the notion of Protestant Ascendancy; his vindication of eighteenth-century Ireland would only achieve full articulation in these terms some ten years later when the *Bulletin*, in aligning itself with pro-Franco opinion, almost dissuaded him from endorsing the fascist revolt. Moreover, the editor (Father Timothy Corcoran) repeatedly associated the 'old' ascendancy with anti-Catholic bigotry in the 1790s, and not with Swift and Berkeley in the early eighteenth century. In so far as Yeats's later elaboration of an Irish augustan cultural elite, invoking these great names and styled as the Protestant Ascendancy, can be compared with Father Corcoran's splenetic apostrophes, an argument about basic historical veracity might not go against the editor.[73] What is damaging to Yeats in any comparison is not so much a greater degree of crude accuracy in Father Corcoran's dating, but rather the extent to which Yeats accepts the terms of the *Bulletin*'s challenge. His response is distinctly reactive rather than constructive. The splendid coterie that he imagined in the 1930s, as a bulwark against the historiography of independent Ireland, derived in part at least from his opponents. If, as now seems generally accepted, Yeats's historiography was an oblique statement of contemporary political needs, then he seceded from the generation of 1870 only to associate himself with an eighteenth-century elite mediated to him through diverse channels – including the *cloaca* of scurrilous journalism.

A longing to rise above the filthy modern tide was never wholly to be realised. Permanence was for ever vitiated by process. In more local terms, some busybody could always conjure up the irredeemably commercial Pollexfens or the Bible-thumping of other relatives too close for comfort. Romantic transcendentalism, according to which the entire combustible world might be changed utterly, had not outlived the generation of Blake and Shelley. Utilitarianism had won the day, even in the eyes of those who aligned themselves with the defeated. It was possible to retreat into a tapestried Tennysonian world and, while Yeats appreciated the attractions of this option, he came to prefer a hesitant decisionism or calculated irrationalism. As admonitory precursor, the Revd W. B. Yeats is part of the pattern moving, in the face of growing industrialisation in his parish or on the doubtful strength of his inheritance and the mushroom affluence of his brother-in-law, from County Down to suburban Dublin. In the mass of scholarly comment provoked by his grandson and namesake, he has been politely saluted as a gentleman of the old school, then bundled aside. If he had been a benign nullity, the poet's passing over a phase of history which the rector embodied might be allowable. His absence from the poetic mythology is suspicious. The specific circumstances of his career now argue for some such assumption. Moreover, his son's biographer has cautiously published evidence to suggest that the Revd Yeats had not been popular in Tullylish, that the son admitted his father had 'made such a mess of his life'.[74] On an inner wall of the new church at Tullylish, a plaque commemorates the rector who did not attend its consecration. The wording is conventional, even affectionate: but instead of the usual biblical text, there is only a biblical reference – to St John's Gospel, the sixth verse of the tenth chapter. There diligent research will reveal how his parishioners had remembered the Lord's anointed rector – 'I am the way, and the truth, and the life; no one comes to the Father but by me'. The castle in Sandymount, its gothic porch and chained eagle, its masonic suicide, can hardly be read either as devotion to duty or as innocent retirement.

In 'The Words Upon the Window-pane', we have noted the presence of a Corbet, a living character whose role is to identify the voices of the dead. But it would be a mistake to assume any positive affinity between character and playwright on the basis of their shared access to the name Corbet. Writing to the poet Thomas MacGreevy in 1932, Yeats dealt sharply with the play. 'One of the characters gives what he supposes to have been Swift's point of view ... To me, mediumship is the antithesis of the highly developed, conscious individuality, you may even call it democracy in its final form.'[75] Seen in this light, the play's John Corbet resembles the Young Man in 'The Dreaming of the Bones': both are immature or incompetent commentators on spiritual conflicts of the highest significance, though the conflicts have taken place in lamentably debased (even democratic) circumstances. Yeats had early been frightened at a *séance* and, though he persisted in attending many during his middle years, his own account of 'The Words Upon the Window-pane' emphasises that 'Swift the arrogant, the exclusive appears [*sic*] to common people at a common séance.'[76]

Among these common people, the most obviously named is Dr Trench. The minor poet Frederick Herbert Trench (1865–1923) may be implicated as a contemporary of Yeats's much influenced by the Celtic Revival, whose *Deirdre Wedded* (1901) anticipated Yeats's own play. Surely the real thrust hits Wilbraham Fitz-John Trench (1873–1939), who in time had the temerity to die in the same year as Yeats but who, for the moment, is significant as the poet's successful rival in 1913 for the chair of English in Trinity College. The fictive 'Dr Trench' is in part a caricature of what Yeats might have become, had he won the academic contest: a stolid enquirer, keen to see fair play, otherwise unremarkable. There is no need to suspect that Yeats was aware of the incipient politics of Trench's sons – Patrick (a communist) and the Germany-befriending Chalmers ('Terry'). But Dr Trench complements the Young Man of the play, John Corbet, in providing a silent framework of historico-personal allusion. Both names reach back into the Victorian past – Corbet through Yeats's own Sandymount origins, and the doctor through Richard Chenevix Trench (1807–1886), effective founder of *The Oxford Dictionary of the English Language*.

Alerted again to those forgotten biographical details, the reader of the play finds the seemingly minor character of Abraham Johnson suddenly transformed. This Johnson is from Belfast; he is, in his own words, 'by profession a minister of the Gospel':

> I produce considerable effect by singing and preaching, but I know that my effect should be much greater than it is. My hope is that I shall be able to communicate with the great Evangelist Sankey. I want to ask him to stand invisible beside me when I speak or sing, and lay his hands upon my head and give me such a portion of his power that my work may be blessed as the work of Moody and Sankey was blessed.[77]

American revivalist preachers Ira David Sankey (1840–1908) and Dwight Lyman Moody (1837–1899) sought to recreate the massive spiritual turmoil of the 1859 Ulster Revival. Such upheavals had disturbed the more traditional Church of Ireland clergy on theological and social grounds (not least because of their impact among the Belfast proletariat, mill-girls especially) while they also occasioned mass meetings of a potentially political direction. In an early draft of the play, a further remark of Abraham Johnson's underlined his northern background: 'A woman in Belfast, a fortune teller who has a great gift with the cards, a woman in every way comparable to one of the ancient sybils, told [me] that I would be able to speak to Mr Sankey if I came to Dublin.'[78] This Johnson of the play is seeking to acquire a power once exercised by a Johnson of history, or to be precise – Johnston. The Revd John Johnston of Tullylish had in effect driven the Revd Yeats to *this* house, where now the tables are to be rapped and turned. The Belfast woman comparable to one of the sibyls is repressed in the canonical text, for it is not Johns[t]on who must seek spiritual renewal in Dublin, but his rival Yeats. Sibyls may have been as out of place in the Tullylish manse as they were in the dingy rooming-house near Dublin. And Belfast might be more aptly represented by young thrusting managers like (Senator) Arthur Jackson than by any nameless sibyl. But in another of the poet's revisions, affecting the motive for Mrs Mallet's attendance at the *séance*, Yeats changed the cause of her husband's death from a modish air accident to drowning, the fate that befell a less successful manager of the family's interest, a Corbet who cannot be sworn.

Robert Corbet, who indubitably died by drowning in 1870, is not however the most touching absence from the Yeatsian chronicle. There was, or had been, his namesake who entered Trinity College Dublin in May 1758 aged 19 years, listed as the son of a *decanus clericus*. Though the father's name is not given, other records strongly imply that he was Francis Corbet, treasurer of Saint Patrick's Cathedral, and then dean in (at first, disputed) succession to Jonathan Swift in 1745. It is this Dean Corbet who is absented from the Yeatses' family notes. He had been a valued colleague of Swift's, entrusted with certain textual problems in *Gulliver's Travels*, and appointed executor of Esther Johnson's will. Later he became a major actor in the implementation of Swift's posthumous arrangements for the establishment of a mental hospital in Dublin. Why should the poet be disinclined to invoke these namesakes of his traceable Dublin ancestors, especially when he was at work on a play about Swift and Stella, involving a wholly fictitious latter-day John Corbet (1688–1775)? The Dean's son walked the streets of Dublin, when Yeats's earliest-declared Corbet ancestor died in the city. Eager to create blood links with remote Butlers and countesses of Ormonde, Yeats is strangely neglectful of a likely kinsman in daily contact with Dean Swift whom Yeats wishes to set up as a spiritual ancestor.

The existence of a decomposed and redistributed family history in the text and proto-text of 'The Words Upon the Window-pane' can no longer be doubted; linked with Jonathan Swift, just as Yeats's prose energetically links his own family with the Dean of St Patrick's, the play acquires its political aura also. Loss of faith, the familiar explanation of modernist anxiety in terms of a search for surrogate beliefs, colours the surface of the play. An underlying and persistent attention to the structure (especially absent structure) of family aligns

'The Words Upon the Window-pane' decisively with the eugenicist concerns of Yeats's last decade.

Second-Hand Tragedy, or
'Are You Content'

He that in Sligo at Drumcliff
Set up an old stone Cross,
That red-headed rector in County Down
A good man on a horse,
Sandymount Corbets, that notable man
Old William Pollexfen,
The smuggler Middleton, Butlers far back,
Half-legendary men.
                              'Are You Content', 1938

Yeats's aesthetic and political interests in the years after the Great War were of a kind associated with a projected Conservative Revolution (Hugo von Hofmannsthal's phrase). Difficulties arise in arguing the case in any further detail. First, between 1928 and 1934 Yeats was preoccupied with events in Ireland, not merely mentally so preoccupied, but actively engaged in the political and literary life of an isolated island. In the later analysis of Archibald MacLeish, the Irish poet was hampered by a provincial inheritance despite the sophistication of his mind and imagination. Of course some recent historians have come to classify the 'Troubles' of 1919–22 as leading to a conservative revolution in Irish politics, but they scarcely take Hofmannsthal's project as a measure of W. T. Cosgrave's politics. Second, if Yeats's problematic arises in 1933 (or at any rate after the 'turn' of 1928–30) then, strictly speaking, the Austrian's project is already a thing of the past for Hofmannsthal died in 1929. The Conservative Revolution was either greatly embarrassed by the rise of Nazism, and the groundswell of populist anti-Semitism that Hitler used to gain power, or it accommodated itself to the new realpolitik. Stefan George decamped for Switzerland in 1933, as a practical demonstration of his attitude.

Nevertheless, the Conservative Revolution has been a convenient way of gathering together names which borrowed more strength from each other than any one possessed alone. F. R. Curtius bracketed Hofmannsthal, T. S. Eliot and Charles Maurras under the description in 1929. The combination was admirably international, and the virtues celebrated distinctly imperial, at once German and Greek or (less fancifully) 'Romanic-German substance, as an ancestral heritage'. Curtius did not have 20,000 storm troopers in mind, gathered under the eagle, nor did they pay much attention to him when their time came. Yeats stood outside this arena of catastrophic misjudgment, emulous of it at times.[1] In 1965, Josephine MacNeill claimed that Yeats had told her of Stefan George's writing to him, though nothing to this effect has been proven.[2]

Commentators have zealously confined him to an external relationship with fascism, perhaps suspecting that Yeats tarred with a black shirt would be a less marketable commodity. The practice is not confined to admirers of him alone, for comment on Eliot, Wyndham Lewis, Pound and other 'authoritarians' among the Modernists is likewise rich in kindly befuddlement. Jeffrey Meyers argues that 'though Lewis' [sic] book was pro-Hitler, it cannot be said to be pro-Fascist. *Hitler* revealed not that he sympathised with Fascism, but that he grossly misunderstood its true nature.'[3] Jason Harding's defence of Eliot and *The Criterion* frequently takes the form of punching Tom Paulin or David Bradshaw slowly on the nose, while ignoring the manifest contradiction of Eliot's 'argument for the priority of ethics over politics' when placed beside his 'reasons of race and religion [which] combine to make any large number of free-thinking Jews undesirable'. Eliot's public statement to this effect had been made in the year of Hitler's triumph: it appeared in print the following year when Nazi policy towards the Jews was unmistakable. There is neither distortion nor exaggeration saying that the latter was an implementation of Eliot's view, nor did the Christian who 'felt inclined to approach public affairs from the point of view of a moralist' feel inclined to comment. Eliot had a secret politics based on the dubious ethics of secrecy. When he read Montgomery Belgion's *Epitaph on Nuremberg* in 1947, he praised the book in a private letter to the author, but reserved the right to disagree (publicly).[4]

Compared to Eliot's hand-washing, Yeats's behaviour is straight-forward. Nevertheless, biographers have mimicked the silence of lambs. Those who immediately followed on Hone's heels (Ellmann and Jeffares) ignored the Frankfurt footnote, despite Ellmann's Jewishness and despite Jeffares having visited Nazi Germany in 1936 as a High School (Dublin) sixth-former.[5] Cullingford in her response to Cruise O'Brien diplomatically suppressed Yeats's commendation of Nazi legislation in August 1938. Cruise O'Brien, silently revising his own argument for republication, deleted his account of Yeats's support for Sinn Féin in February 1921 when speaking at the Oxford Union. More recent biographers, while grasping other nettles, have decided to overlook Yeats's gleeful telling of his experiences at the London PEN Club and his fantasia that 'every woman there was a Britannia and was suckling a little Polish Jew'. In keeping with this, they pass over Yeats's gloss of Jewish chicken-butcher as child-molester, while one adroitly noted Ulick O'Connor's whitewashing of Gogarty on the general anti-Semitic issue. Also omitted is the remark about nun-raping in republican Spain, which Yeats rather fancied. These are minor matters and their exclusion might be explained on the basis of good taste. There is no room for good taste in good historical biography.

In a damaging remark that Roy Foster treats very openly, Yeats compared the Irish and German political scenes in 1933: 'There is so little in our stocking that we are ready at any moment to turn it inside out & how can we not feel emulous when we see Hitler juggling with his sausage of a stocking[?]'[6] The sentiment is unmistakable, yet its expression is clumsy. To feel emulous is to fail in emulation or to recognise one's failure in some regard. Awkwardness in Yeats's struggling to express his view of Hitler is a failure of literary style, unimportant perhaps in a private letter, yet significant in the wider discussion of his political views. It remains to be seen whether the broader occurrence constitutes a veil or curtain between poet and political topic or whether, in counter-distinction, the elimination of this failure is achieved by his interposing such a veil between himself and the 'action' of politics. What is certain is this: we cannot settle for a solution modelled on Meyers's Wyndham Lewis, in which Yeats's mistaken views of fascism are taken as proof positive of their unimportance. Those who mistook fascism were amongst its most useful instruments.

The Tendencies of Yeats's Late Style

One does not usually think of George Orwell as a critic of poetry, though he was acute to linguistic change. In the middle of the Second World War, he broadcast a talk under the title 'The Meaning of a Poem' – the poet in question being Gerard Manley Hopkins. That was on 14 May 1942; later in the same BBC series, his topic was 'Literature and Totalitarianism'. If Hopkins was an unlikely first choice of individual poet for Orwell, the absence of reference to any individual writer (bar Shakespeare and Tolstoy) in the second programme is even more surprising. Orwell held views on D. H. Lawrence and T. S. Eliot (positive), Pound (negative), and on literary Modernism generally. But wartime was not the moment to investigate too carefully or publicly what relations existed between Anglophone writers and totalitarianism. Better to point out how easy the Nazi regime in France had found it to accommodate intellectuals, 'even when they were "decadent"', or to predict how totalitarianism 'is going to be world-wide'.[7] T. W. Adorno, using a different lexicon and scarcely aware of Orwell's existence, would soon agree.

In January 1943, Joseph Hone's biography was anticipated by a study from remoter parts, V. K. Narayana Menon's *The Development of William Butler Yeats*. Orwell, reviewing it for *Horizon*, posed a question that remains as unanswered as it is unavoidable. To be fair to those who have failed in one or both regards, Orwell strictly makes a statement, though its challenge surely begs an answer:

> One thing that Marxist criticism has not succeeded in doing is to trace the connection between 'tendency' and literary style ... In the case of Yeats, there must be some kind of connection between his wayward, even tortured style of writing and his rather sinister vision of life.[8]

Perhaps 'tortured' is both the clue and the solution – at least Adorno's meditation of Beckett's *Endgame* would support such a view. Pouncing closely on Orwell's use of a word, one surely mimics a procedure that will be central to any search for the connection between style and political tendency. Yet what does he mean by 'tendency'? Does he mean an inbuilt, ever-present bias (as in a bowls-player's bowl), or does he mean something more active and less given, a thing responsive and changing like a shuttlecock in turbulent air? Metaphors drawn from sport may seem trivial, but none lies beyond damaging criticism.

Orwell takes us further along the path of his unanswered question, observing that 'translated into political terms, Yeats's tendency is Fascist. Throughout most of his life, and long before Fascism was ever heard of, he had the outlook of those who reach Fascism by the aristocratic route.'[9] Given that Menon's endeavour was to gauge 'the great poetry of Yeats's last days' against *A Vision*, Orwell has most usefully turned the argument into an historical direction. Yeats's tendency preceded fascism, he says, without quite committing himself to the extreme view that the poet was a fascist *avant la lettre*. Instead, he discriminates between the various routes to fascism, Yeats having travelled on or close to the aristocratic one. Again, Orwell's caution is evident in his choice of words. For Yeats was no aristocrat, and could only have travelled *in the style* of one. We need our Victorian history to confirm this location of the poet and his origins in some class-calculus.

David Pierce, no indulger of fascist proclivities, oddly nominates 'Beautiful Lofty Things' as 'the nearest Yeats got to writing a fascist poem of merit'. Much earlier, and writing under Orwell's influence, Donald Davie had opted for 'Blood and the Moon'. These choices illustrate the fallacy of assuming that 'the tendency' finds expression in 'the poetry'. Pierce's approach is most informative when he notes that 'Beautiful Lofty Things' had first been drafted on the flyleaf of Yeats's copy of Sacheverell Sitwell's *Canons of Giant Art: Twenty Torsos in Heroic Landscapes* (1933), which Sitwell himself regarded as ultimately written 'in praise of Fascist Italy'.[10] This textual pathway is one we have observed Yeats to use on other, broadly similar occasions. An extreme case is 'Under Ben Bulben' in draft, with its children dancing under the bombs and its armed philosophers seeking each other; by the time the poem is completed, at least these grossnesses have been purged. By the same token, however, it seems that the grossness was a necessary stage: grossness is purged, not critiqued. Yeats himself had explored the matter in 'Ancestral Houses', the first section of 'Meditations in Time of Civil War'. In the fourth stanza, 'Ancestral Houses' moves towards the interrogative, using as its phrasal engine a formulaic 'what if . . .' structure. The grammar of this is obscure, but the consequent considered is that we must 'take our greatness with our violence'. The poem of seventeen years later, with its drafts, has reversed priorities and abandoned the interrogative: in the Ben Bulben material, we must take our violence with, as bonus, whatever greatness we command.

A lesser case was considered by William Empson in 'The Variants for the Byzantium Poems' (1965), where he classified certain drafts as 'not boss shots but extra material' that Yeats finally excluded on grounds of technique. Though these particular poems dealt with purification, the process of writing did not involve purification, but rather selection and arrangement. Empson was writing at a time when (he claimed) 'English and American critics interpret Yeats as implying

Christian doctrine whenever that is possible . . .' Thus he was tickled to find among the drafts for 'Sailing to Byzantium' the following line about the speaker's first youth:

For many loves have I taken off my clothes
For some I threw them off in haste, for some slowly and indifferently
And laid down on my bed that I might be . . .

The textual-pathway approach is unlikely in this case to contribute much to the issue of Yeats's politics, but it raises some general questions that might eventually suggest general principles. Taking the third line as laid out above, the reader surely must consider the sexual identity of the speaker (what is sometimes called the gender). The passivity implied in the line suggests a conventional female waiting for her male lover, and the plurality of loves admitted to could suggest a Gaelic source, the medieval (ninth-century) poem of regret for lost youth and pleasure, generally known as 'The Nun [or Hag] of Beare'.[11]

Against this passivity as a stereotyped gender 'position' eventually abandoned along with the Gaelic nuances, one might look at an aspect of Yeats's grammar that is not only active but imperative. A benign instance concludes 'The Municipal Gallery Re-visited' (1937), with lines I have used in the dedication of *Blood Kindred*:

Think where man's glory most begins and ends
And say my glory was I had such friends.

'Think . . . say . . .' These imperatives have been modulated in advance by clear identification of the addressee – 'You that would judge me . . .' – as perfectly ordinary, a human being who can 'come to this hallowed place' to study portraits of Yeats's friends. In several senses 'The Municipal Gallery Re-visited' is one of Yeats's *civil* poems. But in others, the addressee is less easily identified, the imperative grammar unmistakable. Of the twenty *Last Poems* (1939), four commence in this manner: these are 'Under Ben Bulben' (the first poem in the collection), 'The Black Tower' (the last poem Yeats completed), 'Three Marching Songs' (originally written for the Blue Shirts) and 'Long Legged Fly' (where speaker and auditor have Caesar as 'our master'). Much has been made of 'The Black Tower' as a poem about political propaganda, of which I can only say that it seems to me muddled prose technically and, in substance, a thing acceptable among the *Stahlhelm*.

Last Poems includes work central to any recognition of Yeats as a very great poet: 'Cuchulain Comforted', 'The Statues', 'A Bronze

Head', 'The Apparitions' (a personal favourite) and 'The Circus Animals' Desertion'. Editors defend Yeats's weaker performances by treating them as complementary to (necessary to?) the masterpieces. Thus David Albright explains the oddly titled 'Are You Content' as contrasting with its predecessor in *New Poems* (1938), 'The Municipal Gallery Re-visited'. The better-known poem invites (or commands) judgment on the poet in the context of his friends and contemporaries; the lesser relates him to his ancestors.

One example of parallel phrasing in the two poems opens up a larger concern. In 'The Municipal Gallery', Yeats's most distinguished fellow-dramatist is referred to in the last stanza:

> And here's John Synge himself, that rooted man.

The word 'himself' could be arrested on suspicion of loitering without intent, being a filler, especially as it also looks like an unlicensed use of Hiberno-English emphasis in a poem otherwise grandly Anglo-Irish and innocent of dialect. But we have another, lesser poem to consider. In 'Are You Content' we have a similar epithet divided over two rough-hewn lines listing ancestors:

> Sandymount Corbets, that notable man
> Old William Pollexfen.

The last-named had been Yeats's grandfather, who became a partner in the Middleton business in Sligo and married into the Middleton family. Whatever had been Pollexfen's genius, it scarcely deserved to be measured so obviously with J. M. Synge's in the immediately preceding item of *New Poems*. Yet Albright is right in saying that Yeats had long felt his inadequacy by the standards of his ancestors, for 'Are You Content' half interrogates him(self) on the issue. The theme, and not any isolatable fact, is significant. On genealogy and hereditable property, Pollexfen had been more pathetic than heroic, believing his family descended from the Phoenicians and he himself wrongly cheated of a manor in Devon, a picture of which hung in perpetual memory on his bedroom wall.

'Are You Content' does not quite interrogate the poet on these matters – an absent question-mark from the title gives the game away early. But it does turn the question of blood kindred into a retrospective suddenly populated by figures to whom Yeats had made little, if any, reference in earlier work. In the only question posed:

> Have I, that put it into words,

Spoilt what old loins have sent?

The next stanza then lists those who, with 'eyes spiritualised by death', can judge. They include 'That [sic] red-headed rector in County Down / A good man on a horse / Sandymount Corbets . . .' and so on. It is deplorable verse. But at last the canon of his poetry, as he very consciously shaped it in his final months, absorbs or releases the name of the place and family to which ancestor-namesake ('a good man in a verse') had fled from the bright satanic mills of Tullylish. The opening of the last stanza surely echoes the earlier W. B. Yeats's Sandymount retreat: 'Infirm and aged I might stay / In some good company . . . Smiling at the sea.'

Perhaps the emphasis has by now shifted away from Yeats's tendency and towards his late style which, drawing on Edward Said's general description, we find to be transgressive. Is Yeats's 'flirtation' with Nazi legislation, later in the year of his discontent, transgressive in some purely stylistic sense? Do 'The Lover's Song', 'The Chambermaid's Second Song', 'The Lady's Third Song' – with their smug-smutty ventriloquism – come under the same heading? If the songs of 1936 attempt something abandoned in the earliest drafts for 'Sailing to Byzantium' (1926), are there other significant movements of thematic *ritorno*?

Among the *Last Poems*, 'The Black Tower' has its distinction. Nobody (whom I have read) has related it to Louis MacNeice's *The Dark Tower* or rather to MacNeice's source in *King Lear* (Act III, Scene 4), where loyal Edgar invokes the ballad line 'Childe Rowland to the dark tower came'. Cullingford divines in the drafts a schema with 'the Irish solicited by an unspecified foreign power', to which one can only say that the Irish are unspecified in the draft also.[12] Relentlessly justifying accounts of Yeats dodge the uncomfortable bits and, in doing so, diminish his stature and the awefulness of his dilemma. 'The Black Tower' no more rhymed or predicted de Valeran neutrality than Churchill's 1940 outburst called for a tidier foreshore. Both look for war, Yeats's timetable being infinitely more relaxed than the new Prime Minister's, but war-vigilant none the less.

It is also homoerotic, masochistic and accoutred in neo-medieval trappings. The first line of the draft reads (as far as the best editor can suggest), 'I speak for the greyed garrison.'[13] The addressees in line 4 'are not of our kin' and are dismissed in line 9, 'Begone you are not oath bound'. By the time the poem was put to rest on 21 January 1939 (a week before Yeats's death), the opening had adopted the familiar imperative mood – 'Say that the men of old black tower' – which, if acted upon, would ensure that 'Those banners come not in'. Some readings would have the banners represent newspaper propaganda – surely a knee-jerk bow to the conveniently adjacent (but external) idiom 'banner headlines'. Albright is closer to making sense when he sees it depicting 'an attempt to outwait an imbecile civilisation – as if *antithetical* heroism and magnificence had dwindled down to a single Black Tower, a frontier outpost where soldiers, stiffened almost to icons, stoically await their king's resurrection'.[14]

In 1938 the western democracies deserved round condemnation on grounds of political strategy, but they hardly constituted an imbecile civilisation. (Had they not given us Yeats and Joyce in Ireland, Hardy and Eliot in England, to go no further?) Yeats's judgment, which deserves Albright's summary, was wildly exaggerated, as his recent comparison of hereditary 'problems' in Ireland and Nazi Germany shockingly demonstrated. In Nazi Germany, they had ways of dealing with individual imbeciles and, as just a few months would confirm, of dealing with neighbouring states also. One further line from the earliest draft points the way back to an earlier text for illumination: 'The Gods have brought us milk & flesh'. The phallo-iconic oath-bound soldiers may even be dead; certainly, the italicised 'chorus' lines declare *There in the tomb stand the dead upright*', and these lines offer a secondary, impersonal statement to complement that of the speaker (or speakers). But the Gods have brought food just as, in Yeats's first play of 1899, food was supplied to famine victims by Cathleen's willingness to risk her immortal soul. In the final scene, the Countess is rescued by *armed* angels, though 'their armour is old and worn, and their drawn swords dim and dinted'. By 1939, the guardians are not even armour-bound, just oath-bound, yet there remains a glimmer of 1890s Celticity: *There in the tomb drops the faint moonlight.*' The Victorian play anticipates stoic but enfeebled vigilance, just as the poem of 1939 looks back to fey theatricality for its effects. Early in 'The Countess Cathleen', the First Merchant (in the market for souls) advises how his Master:

> at the end
> Shall pull apart the pale ribs of the moon
> And quench the stars in the ancestral night.

It is an odd eschatology which sees the last and satanic things as being engulfed in the *ancestral*. Yeats was almost as fond of this adjective as his biographer, but one should not overlook its significance here when early and late (so to speak) converge. As his working concepts of politics, history, philosophy and (on occasion) theology were elaborated over forty years, family and blood became their shorthand terms. These were not symbolic terms. William Pollexfen eventually is 'that notable man' just as truly as Synge had been 'that rooted man'. My choice of tenses is deliberate, because Synge can be assigned to the past in a way that ancestral Pollexfen (and Corbet, and Middleton, and 'that red-headed rector in County Down') will never be *assigned*. Strong valorisation of family/blood cannot automatically be regarded as part of an authoritarian politics, for forms of such politics are possible without it. The same can be said of death, for death is in a sense a medium for the transmission of family through blood. But in 1939 no one could avoid recognising in the German version of fascism a politics in which race/blood (and unavoidably family/blood also) was a central ideological category. Likewise death.

Rilke's Conception of Death

Yeats was not an avid reader of contemporary foreign literature, partly because linguistic ability restricted him to French and partly because the European temper of the age was not to his taste. Even reading authors such as Claudel and Péguy, he needed or certainly sought the help of Iseult Gonne. Never keen on literary criticism, his tolerance of such secondary matter declined further in the excitement of his closing months. Consequently the interest he took in a collection of essays about the Prague-born German-speaking poet, Rainer Maria Rilke (1875–1926) was exceptional. In the summer of 1938, William Rose, a London-based scholar, sent Yeats in Dublin a pre-publication copy of *Rainer Maria Rilke: Aspects of His Mind and Poetry*. Glancing at it, Yeats noted one essay by Rose that annoyed him, and departed for England. He told Dorothy Wellesley that he annotated the margin of the essay with lines containing what would become his self-epitaph:

> Draw rein; draw breath.
> Cast a cold eye
> On life, on death.
> Horseman pass by.

The cold eye that Yeats cast on Rose's essay was not, however, a final judgment. For the moment, he was more eager to record for

Lady Dorothy his violent response to a Jesuit's criticism of his play, 'Purgatory', which premiered that month in the Peacock Theatre. 'After a week of clerical conspiracy I understand the satisfaction a Spaniard finds in raping a nun.'[15]

Two days later, on 17 August 1938, and writing now to the learned Germanist, Yeats thought better of Rilke. He had read Rose's own essay first; that is, he had deliberately chosen the topic of death from among several discussed, influenced perhaps by the fact that he had met Rose some time earlier. At first 'repelled by the brooding on death ... a theme foreign to our Irish literature', he came to realise that he needed to study the relevant poems through competent translations. The marginal lines already disclosed to Dorothy Welles-ley were once again written into the record, a curious emphasis given that Yeats's copy of *Rainer Maria Rilke; Aspects of His Mind and Poetry* does not carry these marginalia. One must suspect that the essay on Rilke provided an opportunity for Yeats to try out lines already composed (at least in his head) and which never made it into the margin. The letter to Rose concludes quite warmly, 'I thank you very much for what may become important to me.'[16]

Yeats gives the impression that he has been at first annoyed and then intrigued by allusions to the theme of death in some poems by Rilke. In fact, Rose's essay refers extensively to a lengthy prose work, a novella with autobiographical undertones. Though he does not specify it, Yeats was alluding to the text now known as *The Notebook of Malte Laurids Brigge*. Published in 1910, *Die Aufzeichnungen des Malte Laurids Brigge* was first translated into English in 1930 as *Journal of My Other Self*. This Yeatsian title is well earned by the opening pages in which the reclusive German poet, a willing dependant of aristocratic patrons, evokes the squalor of Parisian streets that Yeats had walked in the 1890s. The poor live close to death; even a pregnant woman whom Brigge observes leaning against the wall of a *maison d'accouchement* is close to it. In sanatoria, people 'die from one of the deaths assigned to the institution'. Rilke's poetic evocation in prose captures a moment in history where death is changing: for many, it is or will be a mechanical experience, an end-product (so to speak) of mass society.

Rose nowhere mentions Yeats in his essay, though *The Notebook* in some ways resembles *Reveries over Childhood and Youth*, the first volume of Yeats's autobiography. Rilke's hero, or mask, is a young Dane visiting Paris, but recalling the decay of his ancestral, landed home at Ulsgaard. The atmospherics of the fiction are palpable, especially in the account of old Chamberlain Brigge's death, evoking desolate servants, empty rooms and a ravished landscape. Though Yeats would later attempt to fabricate such a landed and titled ancestry for himself, the family sketched in the *Reveries* had been a number of scattered individuals, one allegedly a friend of the rebel Robert Emmet, another kinsman to the police bloodhound who broke the United Irishmen in Dublin, and others (like the Corbets) colourful nonentities. What *Rilke: Aspects of His Mind and Poetry* did for Yeats in the summer before he died was to confront him with a unified image of death and inheritance, of social decline and integrated literary sensibility. It was a counterpoint to eugenics and *On the Boiler*, all the more poignant for being German in origin, like the hate-loaded Terramare pamphlets he also preserved. In August 1938 the Nazis mobilised, with Rilke's Prague, their target. Yeats could nonetheless publicly declare on 13 August that 'in Germany there is special legislation to enable old families to go on living where their fathers lived' – unless of course they were Jews like Stefan Zweig, who now, in an introduction to the Rilke essays, referred ironically to 'we of the German tongue', a stateless, persecuted literary intelligentsia for whom Yeats had no word to offer.

Roy Foster regards Yeats on the Nuremberg Laws as 'at best – unforgivably myopic', which 'strikes an ominous note in retrospect'.[17] In August 1938, no one had to wait for retrospection. Paris and London were home to thousands of refugees; nor were the newspapers mute. Closer to the bone, Maud Gonne, Iseult and Francis Stuart were clamouring against the admission of Jews to Ireland, and Yeats (in Burke's phrase) did nothing. His reading of a book about Rilke awkwardly demonstrates his present awareness of German culture and German barbarism, while the satisfaction of imagined nun-raping gives little indication of a fine political sensibility.

The Denmark of Malte Laurids Brigge prompted memories of 'Hamlet'. Yeats's attitude towards Shakespeare was never as brusque as Bernard Shaw's, but it took the approach of death to draw out his accumulated views. The poem 'Lapis Lazuli', written in July 1936, had been published earlier in 1938 than his encounter with the dead Rilke. 'There struts Hamlet, there is Lear, / That's Ophelia, that Cordelia,' the poem had declared to support its thesis that gaiety is the proper response to catastrophe. Yeats's emphasis on the positive value of being gay in the face of death is surely no less aridly theoretical than his supposedly theoretical (by implication, limited) commitment to the Blue Shirts, fascism and Nazi legislation. Such a sense of tragedy is – at best – one remove from experience. The sense is generated by rapid-fire literary reference. The suicide of Ernst Toller, on the other hand, may have been the work of an inferior dramatist.

Writing to Toller's friend, Ethel Mannin, on 9 October 1938, Yeats reverted to Rilke and claimed that the German poet instanced Hamlet to illustrate his 'conception of death': 'According to Rilke a man's death is born with him & if life is successful & he escapes mere "mass death" his nature is completed by his final union with it.' This was a tricky issue, given Yeats's own affair with Mannin, and Toller's desperate attempts to avoid mere mass death in one of Hitler's camps. Yeats's initial annoyance at the Rilkean view of death may have arisen from a feeling that it punctured the breezy view of Hamlet advanced in 'Lapis Lazuli'. Characteristically, he was unsure how to spell Rilky's name aright and was unable accurately to cite William Rose's article. This had been 'Rilke and the Conception of Death', a title which implied that death itself is conceived in tandem with life.

In his last years, Rilke had accepted a commission to translate from French the long poem 'Anabase' by Saint-John Perse (Marie René Alexis Saint-Léger Léger, 1887–1975). Taking its title from the ancient Greek narrative of Xenophon, and its account of Cyrus's invasion of Asia Minor, the poem relates how a conqueror amidst his new territories breaks off to explore an inner world closer to the self. In the event, Rilke was unable to proceed with the project; through Hofmannstal the task of translator was conferred on the German-Jewish Marxist philosopher-theologian, Walter Benjamin (1892–1940). This was a world wholly unknown to Yeats, despite his friend Eliot's translation of the *Anabasis* in 1930. International, inter-cultural, inter-linguistic activity did not 'come easily' to him, except in what might appear deliberately exotic commitments to Indian or Japanese ideas and forms. Even these might be accused of orientalism. Europe was Paris, with holidays in Rapallo and Majorca. Thus, when a European crisis of unprecedented proportions opened at the end of the 1930s, Yeats had no professional artistic perspective upon it. The seemingly principled declaration that he never meddled in interna-tional politics, while it adhered to Irish nationalist orthodoxies (of the strict observance), might be cabbalistically interpreted as an admission of provincial ignorance. It is one horn of a tragic dilemma.

The other emerges from any extended comparison of Yeats's apprehension of the common life with that of Rilke in *Malte Laurids Brigge*. Both poets loved a lord or (better, in Yeats's eye) a lady, both appreciated the embrace of castle-walls and esoteric spirits. But *Malte Laurids Brigge* effortlessly conveys a sympathy with the urban masses and the abandoned individual difficult to match in Yeats, except where – in contrast – he extols Irish peasant endurance. If his upbringing, both inherited and nurtured, left him unfitted to judge the condition of Central Europe, or the state of the ghettos, or the value of translated contemporary literature, he also chose to distance himself from local instances of roughly comparable experience – the slums, the dialects of Ulster and the pitifully few refugees who slipped into Dublin. The general and the particular, the European and the national, were alike remote. Instead, one got Remoteness itself valorised through table-tapping, automatic writing and selective use of the Eugenics Society.

His tragic dilemma, then, placed Yeats between great personal qualities which cancelled rather than complemented each other. Committed to Irish politics (if any), he was blind to the cultural crisis in Europe. Committed to a hieratic view of culture, he sneered at the 'misshapen bodies' of new actors joining the Abbey Theatre, praised illiteracy, and worked against parliamentary democracy. Some have concluded that these are proof of Yeats's reactionary (not fascist) politics. But in the 1930s, to be a reactionary was to give fascism benefit of the doubt. The fascist cause would have been no better off if Yeats had openly declared himself an unqualified supporter.

Comparing William Faulkner

In many ways, William Butler Yeats and William Faulkner (1897–1962) appear as contrasting figures in the annals of literary Modernism. They devoted themselves to very different genres, and pursued very different modes of living. Not even the formidable team of Lennox Robinson and Mrs Yeats could have out-consumed Faulkner in whiskey-drinking. Towards the end of his life, the Mississippian took up fox-hunting in classier Virginia, as if in mockery of the Irish poet's sedentary celebration of a good seat. The University of Virginia remained unimpressed by Faulkner's unsouthern attitudes towards 'race' and 'colour' in the era of Civil Rights. Bodily excess is not a mere personal foible in the novelist's behaviour:

it constitutes a social registration of official themes and covert preoccupations which structure the fiction, even while it features only shadowily by way of indirect allusion. By contrast, nothing in Yeats's public behaviour approximated to a 'porter-drinker's randy laughter'.

Having said that, we should acknowledge the resemblances that make the contrast. Some of these may seem trivial or marginal. Consider Faulkner the unofficial American attaché in Japan in 1955, and compare Yeats who earlier acted as his country's self-appointed cultural ambassador *in absentia* and whose interest in Japanese history went beyond anything Faulkner worked up. What both writers appreciated was the dignified *manners* of Japanese people, their preservation in the mid-twentieth century of traditional courtesy and speech. In each case, the admiration sprang from disappointment at the decline in 'standards' that had taken place at home – in the American South and in the Irish Free State. Yeats and Faulkner are profoundly elegiac writers, whose evocations of the past mix celebration with clear-eyed and critical judgment. Their political attitudes are expressions of a historical sense at once aesthetic and ethical.

A resemblance between Faulkner's society and that which produced the Irish Literary Revival was first noticed by the short-story writer Sean O'Faolain in a Princeton lecture series of 1953, three years after the American had won the Nobel Prize. He was concerned mainly with the power of provincial self-confidence in both regions, 'the same feeling that whatever happens in Ballydehob or Jefferson has never happened anywhere else before, and is more important than anything that happened in any period in any part of the cosmos'.[18] Certainly, Yeats was afflicted by assumptions of his own universal centrality. The resemblances extend beyond locale to the social structure. Robert Corbet's bizarre career would not be out of place in a temperate-zone version of *Sartoris* (1929), Faulkner's fictional account of an ancestor. The nineteenth-century family boasted of colonels and paraded masonic uniforms, in a Mississippi slowly recovering from the civil war. Though comparisons are invidious, Ireland's catastrophe had been the famine of 1845–47 which, through emigration generally and the career of John Mitchel specifically, impacted on the American conflict. If disgruntled and displaced Irishmen enlisted in the Yankee battalions, the Confederates were supported by volunteers from the Scots-Irish (also known as Ulster Scots) settlers of the Carolinas and Georgia. In the United Kingdom, sympathy with the southern states was in part based on older resentments of Bostonian separatism, and in part on economic rivalry. More locally in Ireland, uniforms for the rebel army were manufactured in Limerick. As a journalist, Mitchel's unique blend of anti-imperialism and pro-slavery fed back into the political legacy that Yeats invoked and refined from the 1880s until his death.

Thus the defeated South in which William Faulkner's forebears sought to define their eminence in society was tinged, however mildly, with Irish pigmentation. His own people had come from Scotland and, in early fiction, he touched on themes of Jacobite defeat and futile resistance to modernisation. No more than the Yeatses in seventeenth-century Ireland were the Falkners (as originally spelled) pioneers, but followers of English rule. During Reconstruction and after, the dignity of smallish landowners, railway builders and educated semi-professionals sought protection in a myth of planter aristocracy to which retrospective affiliation could be effected. William Clark Falkner (1825–1889) – 'the Old Colonel' and the novelist's great-grandfather – was of this class, with hard-fact violence to his credit also. Yeats, by contrast, had to romance about 'Uncle Beattie', the drinking companion of men transported or executed for treason (or less), declining (for political reasons) to investigate the closer forebear who maintained secret-service payments for informers.

The wider context in which the two family histories converge is necessarily very broad. Ireland within the United Kingdom after 1801 must seem the obverse of the new republic led by Washington, Jefferson and other decolonising heroes. But nineteenth-century western society at large underwent rapid processes of industrialisation and urbanisation, differing in degree but not in essence from country to country. England had set the course much earlier, as Adam Smith (with Karl Marx in scornful concurrence) testified. In Germany, the political centralisation required to direct the process occurred late, with a consequent acceleration of delayed development. Civil war in America may not have brought centralisation, but it was prompted by – while also generating – the mobilisation of vast industrial resources in nature. Against such a global horizon, the famine in Mayo, the Lagan valley's linen mills, and the fortunes of the Yeats and Corbet families appear insignificant. In origin a natural catastrophe, the Great Famine was politicised through government (in)activity and (rather later) by nationalist propaganda. All of these factors distinguished it from contrasting economic conditions in east Ulster, though even Tullylish felt the effects of the crisis to the west and south.[19] But taken together, linen and famine achieved a massively increased concentration of commercial, social and cultural activity on the eastern seaboard. The Irish west became a forcing house of compensatory myth for Victorians, even as the Old South reshaped its Confederate legends and chivalrous rapists.

In age Faulkner could·have been Yeats's son. But after the Great War, the generations were mixed and mingled by decimation of the young and by the mental anguish of those old enough to have prevented the folly ever starting. As Sean O'Casey demonstrated in 1926 and again in 1928, the violent events of 1914–18 were themselves resistant to suppression. The 1920s restaged the war; Nijinsky expressed the onset of his madness by declaring that he would *dance* the Great War. Faulkner's United States had arrived on the Western Front in time to take the curtain call, but Faulkner himself was compelled to invent a war record and to survive imaginary injuries. (Yeats, as we have seen, was absent, having sought blood from a stone statue.) What the war did for these artists, as for millions of unknown participants, was to provide a general, almost a universal, language of dislocation. Walter Benjamin was the radical philosopher of this loss, even as his abstraction re-enacted it. More specific geographies – from Ben Bulben to Yoknapatawpha, from a few revisited *loci* of medieval saga to those mapped in modernist fiction – serve only as accessible, tolerable sub-sets of the unimaginable destruction of experience in total war.[20]

Unlike Eliot, Wyndham Lewis or Pound, the Irish poet and American novelist knew and made known extensive topographies. Perhaps their common point of reference was Thomas Hardy, who had given up fiction before Faulkner was born but, as a poet, lived till 1928 when Yeats published *The Tower* and Faulkner was completing *The Sound and the Fury*. What unites Yeats and Faulkner across their differences is their concern with blood. One can read blood in several related but distinct idioms – blood as pedigree, as race, as life, as the hymen, as menstruation, as death. At the risk of appearing trivial, I could point out that Faulkner's mother came of good blood; she was Maud Butler, every item of her name a trophy in the Yeatsian cabinet. But as the poet's spirit instructors appear to have missed this collocation of Miss Gonne's Christian name and her would-be lover's second Christian (or ancestral) name, the visionary pursuit was not taken up in Mississippi. Nevertheless, inherited blood became a touchstone of class, especially for those who had to work hard for their patrician ancestry. Such an inheritance was inalienable, unlike landed estate or railway shares. It was of course susceptible to more shameful kinds of damage, through miscegenation, misalliance and other mistakes of the night.

These themes are trumpeted in *On the Boiler* (1939). Ten years earlier, Faulkner published *The Sound and the Fury*; indeed, it appeared in the same year as his historical novel *Sartoris*, with its evocation of great-grandfather William Clark Falkner. Shakespeare's *Macbeth*, from which the more famous novel derives its title, revolves round an act of heightened, even sacrilegious, patricide. Very late in the play, the regicide's wife reflects on his deed: 'Who would have thought the old man to have had so much blood in him?' (V: 1: 42). Their guilt is commingled, just as her senses are confused and her language debased, even in thoughtless confession. Faulkner's story is in part told by an idiot but, like Lady Macbeth's rambling speech, it signifies something.

'April Seventh 1928', the first and most experimental chapter of *The Sound and the Fury*, is narrated by Benjy Compson, for whom the passage of time has little reality and in whose thoughts past events and present coexist indistinguishably. One technical source of this radical technique was Freud's account of the unconscious mind, though Faulkner was also an avid admirer of Joyce's *Ulysses* (1922) and its stream-of-consciousness interludes. The second, 'June Second 1910', is narrated by Benjy's brother, Quentin (a profoundly disturbed student in Harvard), who commits suicide in the aftermath of his narration. 'April Sixth 1928' proceeds from the mind of Jason Compson, a third brother, and provides an account of local life in a southern town where the Compsons have fallen in status and are obliged to work for a living. Jason's narrative is strewn with racialist and anti-Semitic venom. With an exact prescience, Faulkner fictionalises the impact of the Wall Street Crash (October 1929) on small-time speculators, while also demonstrating the cotton-growing South's predicament as an 'internal colony' within the US economy. Narrated from an objective if hardly omniscient point-of-view, the final chapter explores the social world of the Compsons' black servants and provides detail which the reader requires to complete his or her understanding of the preceding narratives.

In its timing of action and publication, *The Sound and the Fury* joins with the major work of Yeats and Heidegger to mark a 'turning' in cultural interpretation and apprehension. If, as Hillis Miller has persuasively argued, Heidegger's philosophy eloquently employs boundaries and bridges as metaphors for structures of being, then these are abundant in Faulkner's fiction, especially in Benjy's narrative where fences and doors provide him with physical support and definition in his turbulent mental vacuum.[21] The idiot's apparently empty mind contains, even preserves, experiences which his university-based brother cannot endure. Sexually impotent and burdened with family secrets, Quentin kills himself in the year when his sister marries (and then bears a daughter who is christened Quentin). In Benjy's simplified mind, he (Benjy) is or can be the father of any child his sister gives birth to, while Jason – Faulkner thought him the nastiest character he had created – insists that the little girl could never know who her father was, because her mother could never be sure which the father was. These four siblings, and their intimate antagonistic desires for each other, square the circle of blood kindred from actual suicide to imagined incest, with even more dysfunctional generations represented in the pathetic Mrs Compson and the promiscuous Miss Quentin.

In some ways, *The Sound and the Fury* resembles Hardy's *Return of the Native* (1878) in its investigation of ill-advised sexual choice within a threatened and enclosed community. But more fundamental is the attitude of both novelists (and Yeats) to the question of tragedy. George Steiner concluded nearly half a century ago that the modern age was, in a strict sense, incapable of producing a tragic art, whether on the stage or on paper.[22] Much, though not all, of his argument reflected the impact of totalitarianism and of the Holocaust on human sensibility. When Yeats had sailed into his rest, all the necessities of that catastrophe were in place and, in outline certainly, discernible to the dying poet. In October 1938, when war seemed inevitable but was averted, he expressed relief, adding that he 'should not have lived to see the end of its dark tunnel'.[23] The image was not exclusively Yeats's. In her novel of London under the Blitz, Elizabeth Bowen would evoke 'the lightless middle of the tunnel'.[24] In contrast to his published utterances, including the endorsement of Mitchel's prayer for war, Yeats's late correspondence reveals deep disquiet about the coming crisis. As ever with him, even the disquiet is divided. If war was a *dark* tunnel, and one so long that he would not live to see its end, the metaphor ultimately suggests light, however distant and achieved at whatever price.

In this divided mood, Yeats as dramatist was preoccupied with the possibilities of writing tragedy for the contemporary stage. Settled in southern France for the winter of 1938/39, he was seeing 'Purgatory' into print, while revising 'The Death of Cuchulain'. The first of these one-act plays was peculiarly concerned with Faulknerian issues of misalliance and violence, while the second sought to conclude a cycle of hero-plays which he had commenced in 1903. As a dramatic device, The Fool of 'On Baile's Strand' may derive from Shakespeare, but in terms of an evolving Modernism, he will find kith and kin among Faulkner's holy defectives. Even the domestic scene of bread-making, which provides a foil to the offstage tragic encounter between Cuchulain and his son, has its counterpart in the final chapter of *The Sound and the Fury*, when the Negro housekeeper, Dilsey, cooks, sings and caresses Benjy's head. Both the first and last play in Yeats's Cuchulain cycle deal with the hero's death – that is, both seize upon the central and climactic event of tragic action. 'On Baile's Strand' presents offstage an implied death, as Cuchulain fights with the ungovernable tide. 'The Death of Cuchulain' more than thirty years later finds it necessary to use a narrator to explain the dramatic enterprise, which may conclude with an implied coincidence of hero's death and author's death.

At the middle point of this long-sustained engagement with contemporary theatre, Yeats wrote a manifesto in the form of a letter to Lady Gregory. As quoted by Raymond Williams, it endorses the ideals of 'a people's theatre', which rejects both naturalism and regionalism while still making articulate 'all the dumb classes each with its own knowledge of the world'.[25] More fully considered, 'A People's Theatre' (1919) sets out reasons why Yeats and (he hopes) Lady Gregory should *alter* their relationship to the original theatrical movement. In many ways, it is a political statement about the relationship between class and representation, issued at the height of the Irish 'Troubles' when invocation of 'Red Terror' could hold an audience anywhere in Europe. Williams chose to ignore this dimension to the piece, just as his treatment of Yeats's drama of the 1930s ignores all political considerations. Indeed, what he omits from his citation of 'A People's Theatre' is exactly Yeats's reservation; the passage continues:

... dumb classes each with his own knowledge of the world, its own dignity, but all objective with the objectivity of the office and the workshop, of the newspaper and the street, of mechanism and of politics.[26]

Instead, Williams quotes a much earlier pronouncement of the poet-dramatist to the effect that the 'idiom of the Irish-thinking people of the West . . . is the only good English spoken by any large number of Irish people today'. Whether Yeats in 1904, or Williams half a century later, was in a position to judge the different English 'idioms' spoken in Donegal or the Glens of Antrim (or even Kerry) is doubtful. Further, neither gives any thought to the historical condition of this idiom of the Irish-thinking people, its emergence from Gaelic into English, its coexistence with (say) folk-song in Gaelic and commercial activity in standard English, its transitional and dynamic qualities and characteristics. What emerges instead from the mono-aural valorisation of western speech thus hypostatised is an acceptance of the notion that theatre must recall words 'to their ancient [sic] sovereignty'. From this important and potent decision, Yeats moves to create a ritual drama in which death necessarily is the ultimate and supreme human 'experience'.

So much is indisputable and admirable, were it not for the problems so oddly neglected by Williams, the Marxist: those of class and representation. With regard to the latter, it may be asserted that only that death which is violent, or is at least placed in relation to power, can be integrated into a dramatic action. Power may be sexual rather than military or executive, and it may take the form of chronic illness (as in Ibsen's 'Ghosts'), but it nonetheless retains its social determinants. In the days of Sophocles or Aeschylus, so great a gap (of time, metaphysical status, etc.) divided the audience from the characters depicted onstage that this larger sense of death was both recognisable and credible. Any attempt at modern tragedy was to find itself addressing audiences so much closer imaginatively to any stage character that the classic reactions of pity and terror were likely to be confused. Yeats was not to be daunted by these obstacles, despite his acute awareness of the historical and (so to speak) religious factors at work. But, in the second chapter of *The Sound and the Fury*, Quentin Compson in Harvard refers elliptically to 'the instant when we come to realise that tragedy is second-hand'.[27]

I say *elliptically* because it is not clear to what extent Quentin is at this point paraphrasing his father's earlier utterance on the issue of male virginity. The theme brings together the Old South's myth of feminine honour and the Compsons' far more immediate sexual inversions. For the young man there are two undeniable and yet incompatible realities – his sexual inexperience and his sense of guilt in incest. Objective fact is not available as a means of reconciling these, or of dissolving one of them. What the novel generates is a high-tension cultural climate within Quentin's distressed mind; part of his difficulty lies in his awareness, not of the closeness of these obsessions and their material, but of their distance from him, their being beyond his reach while also being somehow within him unreachably. Yeats's attitude to 'the idiom of the Irish-thinking people of the west' bears comparison. That idiom results from the impact of social processes with which he must identify – the breakdown of Gaelic society, the introduction of English, the (limited) spread of modernisation. Yet in identifying with the historic cause, he is distant from the cultural effect, to the point that he may desire it as his own, as a means of transcending historical process to reach back to 'ancient sovereignty' in words of no specified language, but indubitably possessing sovereignty. It is a cultural reorientation of breathtaking audacity and intelligence, authorising literary work of extraordinary richness and sensitivity. But there will be a price to be paid.

Yeats's contempt for the middle classes is everywhere evident in 'A People's Theatre'. The extent to which he can retain that notion is exactly measured in his ability to distinguish between 'the people' and the new society of journalists, offices, streets *and politics*. Personally adept at manoeuvring among committees and public servants, Yeats in his vocational aspect deplored such facility. While one can admire the versatility of his attitudes, the distinction upon which they rely is neither ancient nor sovereign, any more than *politics* as such was a novelty in 1919. The distinction is Victorian. In the 1850s and '60s, commercial law introduced the idea of limited liability precisely to protect individuals like Robert Corbet from the consequences of failure in trading enterprises to which they were a party. Alarms in 1866 led to the greater entrenchment of limited liability, despite public disquiet at the fraudulent activities of companies, boards and individual directors. Anthony Trollope wrote his most astringent fiction of contemporary society, *The Way We Live Now* (1873), in the aftermath of such financial and moral crises. Faulkner's *The Sound and the Fury*, with its anticipation of the 1929 crash, examined in Jason Compson the psycho-pathology of petty speculators who project their insecurity into denunciation of elusive Jewish agencies.

Limited liability in the moral domain was a privilege Yeats claimed as a poet, just as it was a price he paid for his brilliance in repossessing an alienated Irish past. No theoretician of finance or, let it be repeated, dealer in anti-Semitic prejudice, Yeats concentrated on what he repeatedly condemns in 'A People's Theatre' as *vulgarity*. It is a strikingly defensive term, almost vulgarly so, to be traced as early as 'The Golden Age' in *The Celtic Twilight* (1893). His fear of the mob, and his nervous allusion to 'Red Terror', smacks more of middle-class insecurity than of any Romanov confrontation with the lesser breeds. There is much fulmination against 'fashion papers', musical comedy and the *Daily Mirror*, in anticipation perhaps of Dr Leavis. This is the puritanical side of Yeats's post-Protestantism, a *rus-in-suburbe* fear of the popular. There is also a more serious distortion of literary history. Shakespeare, Lady Gregory is informed, wrote his best 'when he wrote of those who controlled the mechanism of life'. In support of this selective reading, Yeats invokes but does not specify 'statistics that showed how popular education has coincided with the lessening of Shakespeare's audience'. Against this doubtful pronouncement, one might point out that Yeats's beloved eighteenth century could only face Shakespearean tragedy in modified versions which (for example) restored Cordelia to life. (Ironically for Yeats, the perpetrator was Nahum Tate, a Dubliner.) It would be the democratic twentieth century, in response to a totalitarianism Yeats never abjured, which restored 'The Tragedy of King Lear' to something like its original intensity, its 'ancient sovereignty'. It is fair to say that Yeats's dramatic experiments helped to prepare an audience for a rediscovery of classical and Renaissance tragedy in all its terrors, but the experiments themselves have not been established as tragic drama, however powerful they are as one-act explorations in that direction.[28]

We have looked at two or three plays in some detail, notably 'The Dreaming of the Bones' (1919), 'The Words upon the Window-pane' (1930–34) and 'Purgatory' (1938). In each of these, a degree of spiritual inaccessibility is central, doubling as a mismatch or disarrangement of the bodily senses. Though the eyes of Dermot and Dervorgilla may meet in or after death, 'their lips can never meet' until they are forgiven by 'somebody of their race'. In the *séance*–play, Swift can be heard but not seen, as he curses the day he was born. 'Purgatory' tells of a lady, but never shows her, whose mind in death carries the impression of her low-born husband. Nothing in this drama approaches tragic self-knowledge, unless it is the predicament of the Old Man who kills his son in a pathetic hope of finishing 'all that consequence'.

In other plays, killing is less circumscribed by muddled thinking in the killer. 'A Full Moon in March' (1935) dramatises the encounter of Queen and Swineherd, which ends in her having him decapitated. In a related play of the same period, 'The King of the Great Clock Tower', a Stroller is beheaded because he aspires to dance with a Queen, to sing, and to have her kiss him on the mouth. Both plays close in an erotic dance with the woman embracing the head. A longer and more complicated play set at Tara, 'The Herne's Egg' (1938), finds its erotic dimension in the union of priestess and bird, while violence is enacted with table-legs at a Rabelaisian banquet. One of the contending kings, frustrated by the death of his rival, seeks revenge in raping the priestess, and his followers draw lots to decide the order in which he and they will rape her. She, by way of a happy pre-emptive retaliation, invokes a curse; the king dies on a kitchen spit, only to be turned into a donkey. The play was not produced in Yeats's lifetime.

Commentators have related 'The Herne's Egg' to Alfred Jarry's play, 'Ubu Roi' (1896), and have compared its sexual themes to those of Honoré de Balzac's 'Séraphita' (1835). These venerable French antecedents do Yeats credit, which is why they are cited. Less has been written about the politics of aestheticised murder and gang-rape, or about the beer-hall utensils employed to order matters at Tara. Questions of literary genre are pertinent. In a poem of 1924, Yeats had revived the story of Zeus and Leda. But a dramatic approach to the same myth-citing and myth-making theme necessarily altered the theme by the public and plural audience addressed. Similarly, Balzac's exotic short story remains a text for reflection where a stage-play imposes a kinetic temporal train of reception. Faulkner, in *The Sound and the Fury*, can write of 'Leda lurking in the bushes, whimpering and moaning for the swan, see'.[29] Doubtless, he is alluding to Yeats's poem of two years earlier, but the phantasy is specifically limited to the disturbed fictional narrator, Quentin Compson.

Not only genre but history deserves attention. Dramatisation, even offstage dramatisation, of murder has a long and respectable pedigree; indeed, the religious origins of tragedy lie in such ritual re-enactments. But the enormous changes in human society, which occur between the times of Aeschylus and of Beckett, cannot be ignored.

These include philosophical and theological issues, together with seemingly lesser matters of technology and politics. Firearms, and in particular hand-guns, eliminated the necessity for direct bodily contact of the kind required to execute by sword or axe. In the growth of society, whether calculated simply in numerical terms or more subtly in terms of constitutive engagement, the ancient attendance has been superseded by complex and extensive audiences living, thinking and experiencing in quite different conditions. Secular knowledge, for example, is so increased that even a Coleridgean 'suspension of disbelief' with regard to represented sexual intercourse or death has become highly exceptional.

Thus in the era of the putsch, the concentration camp and the show-trial, staged decapitation or scripted brawling *is* political. The two dramas of decapitation may seek to close the gap, overcome the sensory-spiritual inaccessibility in plays discussed earlier, but by stylising the fatal action they push tragedy further out of reach. 'The Herne's Egg' so drastically adjusts the balance in favour of style as to underline the importance of approaches to, distance from, unmediated death.

The 1930s context, in which Yeats's staged decapitations and the brutalities of closed prison-camps mirrored each other in the darkness, has been advanced as a site for radical reinterpretations of his contribution to literary culture. Let us take the climax of 'The Herne's Egg' and daily routine in Dachau. It is characteristic of the age that two such powerful, if contrastingly scaled, events should be regarded as incomparable: instead, it is acceptable that one compare only like with like, compare one totalitarian system with another, one artist with another artist. The challenge posed by Orwell and V. K. N. Menon remains unmet. Nevertheless, the comparison of Yeats with Faulkner can go some way towards illuminating the relationship between political tendency and literary style.

American public opinion in the 1930s had nurtured a strong current of isolationism. Faulkner haled from a region that enjoyed fewer links with the outside world than, say, New England or California. Personally, he was an immerser rather than a surveyor: he looked into his historical territory with microscopic attention through the right end of a bottle. Yet in the aftermath of the Second World War, Faulkner acknowledged and activated a sense of responsibility with regard to the South and its burden of racialist 'thinking'. As a younger man, he had been friendly with Stark Young, another native of Oxford (Mississippi), who had travelled to Mussolini's Italy in the 1920s and gone over to fascism. But Faulkner steadily resisted the doctrines, for all that he admired the literary interests of his friend.

Service in the armed forces during the war made American blacks deeply conscious both of their national worth and their disadvantageous social condition. Nowhere was this more painfully experienced than in the Deep South. Education, so important a touchstone of culture for both Yeats and Thomas Mann, became the political battleground on which the issue of segregation was to be fought out. Faulkner's pronouncements were not always consistent, nor do they avoid condescension. But, as his biographer puts it, what the novelist did and said was never less than morally courageous. His views cost him a valuable appointment at the University of Virginia, a fabulously Jeffersonian-Yeatsian academy light-years from the rough and tumble of Oxford. His views also made him unacceptable in his home town. In June 1955, he wrote, 'I can see the possible time when I shall have to leave my native state, something as the Jew had to flee from Germany during Hitler. I hope that won't happen of course. But at times I think that nothing but a disaster, a military defeat even perhaps, will wake America up and enable us to save ourselves, or what is left.'[30] The narrator of Mann's *Doctor Faustus* entertained similar treasonable hopes of defeat-as-honour.

Faulkner's motives in supporting integrated schooling may have included a fear of big government (that is, federal) interference in the affairs of his community. His principal values may have been old-fashioned, those of privacy for the most part. But he could fashion a political statement which combined conservatism with the kind of corrective justice that phantasies of race now required as antidote:

> Against that principle which by physical force compels man to relinquish his individuality into the monolithic mass of a state dedicated to the premise that the state alone shall prevail, we, because of the lucky accident of our geography, may have to represent that last community of unified people dedicated to that opposed premise that man can be free by the very act of voluntarily merging and relinquishing his liberty into the liberty of all individual men who want to be free.[31]

By comparison, *On the Boiler* and its attendant expressions of hatred seem juvenile.

Hidden Gods

The comparison of Yeats with Faulkner given above is not the first attempt to see the two writers as comrades in a literary crusade. In a series of lectures delivered in 1955, and published in 1963, Cleanth Brooks devoted successive chapters to the Irish poet and American novelist. His other subjects were T. S. Eliot, Ernest Hemingway and Robert Penn Warren. Despite the Eisenhauerian overtones to Professor Brooks's Christian quest, he chose for his epigraph a passage from Blaise Pascal's *Pensées*: 'every religion which does not affirm that God is hidden is not true – vere tu es deus absconditus'. By what must be coincidence, a very different author, the Romanian-born French Marxist Lucien Goldmann, published a study of Pascal and Jean Racine in 1959 under the title, *Le Dieu caché*: this reached the English reading world in 1964 as *The Hidden God*.

Like *The Unicorn* (1954), Virginia Moore's earlier study of Yeats's 'search for reality', Brooks's chapter laboured hard to provide an account of the poet as Christian in some heterodox, yet positive, sense. Innocent of feminism, and having access only to Yeats's published work, Brooks expressed little or no interest in the poet's drama and hence in any tragic dimension to his world-view. Goldmann, on the other side of the Atlantic, saturated himself in seventeenth-century French theology while officially committed to the revolutionary potential of the working class. If they could be brought together, the two *Hidden Gods* might offer a model for the consideration of Yeats as a religious writer, with especial reference to his tragic or would-be tragic drama.

Goldmann's immediate master was Lukács, with whom he shared a Central-Eastern European background. His largely Hegelian concept of world-view also owes something to the Swiss psychologist Jean Piaget (1896–1980), from whom he in part derives his genetic structuralism.[32] His choice of Pascal as a founder of modern dialectical thought was in part based on the need to counter in France the influence of Cartesian rationalism. These diverse sources and strategies might not look like the credentials of a single-minded Marxist, but then Goldmann's objective was to provide a comprehensive rebuttal of single-minded thinking. Yeats's venerated mentor would have concurred: 'without contraries is no progression' in The *Marriage of Heaven and Hell* or, less generally, in the verse 'Letter to Thomas Butts' (1802):

May God us keep
From single vision and Newton's sleep![33]

What Goldmann offers to Yeatsians is a means to recover William Blake historically. Just as Balzac had become contested between the left and right in Europe, so from the mid-Victorian years onwards Blake had been commandeered first by the Pre-Raphaelites, and then by Yeats in the 1890s. With each step of this transformation of Blake's legacy, the revolutionary context in which he had written – *for* which he had written – faded like the Cheshire Cat. Politically, a stage of the recovery was effected in 1954 by the American scholar David V. Erdman in *Prophet Against Empire*.

Goldmann's emphasis on tragic vision and on the theological concept of a hidden god is not matched in Yeats's case simply by a historical argument which recovers Blake's political radicalism. Within Anglophone literature, Yeats's place in the long and discontinuous transformation of Romanticism into Modernism relates specifically to a crucial shift of substance and tone. Instead of metaphysics as the motor of Abstract Idealism, he invokes the supernatural. This is a substitution of profound significance, not only for Yeats and the specific social relations in which he worked, but also within the broader European context, where it aligns itself with other optings for the irrational. In place of romantic nationalism linked to the advance of the middle classes came pseudo-scientific discourses of race from the pen of J. A. Gobineau and others in France and (later) Germany. As Irishman, Yeats stood outside their immediate sphere of influence; as European, he stood in their margins. One characteristic of race-influenced thinking is its inability to accommodate contraries. And where it entertained notions of 'progression', these were of a strongly deterministic and biologistic kind.

Blood Kindred has sought to see Yeats in a comparative framework – nay, several comparative frameworks – where he can be seen both as Irish and European, poet and political thinker. It is important to formulate as similar a pairing of terms to account for his positions with regard to *belief*. The temptation is to concede that – adapting the formula just used – 'he can be seen both as committed to a reality proven by the senses and to a reality postulated by metaphysics'. Instead, Yeats is a supernaturalist with all the strange biology *séances*, ectoplasm and the rest that his late-Victorian gear entails.

If I am sympathetic to the kind of philosophy practised by Lukács and Goldmann (not omitting Freud), why should I be concerned to lament Yeats's preference for the supernatural over metaphysics? Had not Marx abolished metaphysics when he stood Hegel the right way up? In answering these questions, I should not dodge the brutal applications and cynical distortions of Marxism which have contributed to the unparalleled lethalness of the twentieth century. These have already been acknowledged in *Blood Kindred* through condemnation of Stalin's anti-Semitism, though the charges do not end there.[34] The shame and the challenge may coincide in a manner that specifically illuminates the life and work of W. B. Yeats.

It is entirely reasonable to retain a commitment to metaphysics while rejecting belief in any reality beyond human apprehension. Humans are unique in their knowledge of their own finitude – which is to say, in their pre-experience of death, of non-existence. In a fundamental and ineradicable sense, metaphysics is central to our knowledge of ourselves. While a biography does not allow for adequate exploration of theoretical questions, it is already evident to readers of *Blood Kindred* that Yeats was a writer and thinker much preoccupied with death. As an intensification of this concern lies the tragic mode he confronted and explored in some of the most accomplished poems and plays in the modern language. But it would be inaccurate and misleading to add the conventional phrase 'written throughout his life'.

In short, the tragedian is a twentieth-century figure, to some extent self-begotten out of a decadent late-Victorian figure. The sexuality implicit in this briefest of genealogies recurs in a peculiar compound of inversion and exhibitionism in Yeats's correspondence with Dorothy Wellesley, his comments on Roger Casement, and his recourse to a dramatised symbolism of decapitation, rape and ritualised killing in his plays of the 1930s. The recurrence is a good example of an uncaused effect or, to cleave to a more appropriate psychological vocabulary, of an auxiliary moment. In one of the finest studies of Yeats's tragic thought, Daniel T. O'Hara has taken these features as a meta-commentary on the writing itself: 'The violence, discordance, and crudity (if not coarseness) of Yeats's deeds of interpretation belie all his claims to being genuinely open and forgiving.'[35] This analysis is based on Yeats's autobiographies – at the earliest of which the poet worked in the months leading up to the outbreak of war in August 1914 – that is, when he was already fifty years of age.

The collection *Responsibilities* (published in May 1914), and the poem 'Upon a House Shaken by the Land Agitation' (written in August 1909), have been identified as the textual emergence of a 'modern' Yeats, untrammelled by 1890s' trumpery. James Longenbach has traced the longer transformative process effected when Yeats and Pound shared Stone Cottage in Sussex for three successive winters (1914–16) and found there the well-developed seeds of their later fascist interests and commitments.[36] If the 'turn' towards fascism has been discerned in the late 1920s that claim has as much to do with the chronology of fascist expansion beyond Italy as it has with Yeats's thought. The preliminary orientation happened earlier, even if it did not occur on the hereditary, aristocratic path suspected by George Orwell. The tragic tone, and the fascist inclination, come into view retrospectively, but were near-simultaneous in their origins.

The point could never be demonstrated with precision. But we might look at a cluster of minor events taking place in May–June 1913. Yeats was considering the chair of English at the Trinity College Dublin, vacant since the death of Edward Dowden. Though in ill-health, he was pursuing a busy schedule of disappointing *séances* in London, while also keeping an eye on the Abbey Theatre's affairs. Poems in progress include 'Beggar to Beggar Cried'. On 13 May, he received £249 9s. 1d. from the £50,000 estate of George Pollexfen (d. 1910). Two weeks later he had a symbolic dream of the Middleton house at Rosses Point, Sligo. Two weeks later again, he became agitated by fears that he had impregnated Mabel Dickinson and would have to marry her. Two dangerous career options (the academic life, the shotgun marriage) are interfiled with two intimate but contrasting family experiences (a very modest inheritance, a compensating homely dream). The poem displays these topics in a remarkably raw fashion.[37]

Old John Butler Yeats was exasperated by his brother-in-law's failure to privilege the hard-up Yeatses in his will. There had been several years of legal wrangling before the pay-out, and the final result saw the family business pass into the hands of Arthur Jackson, a northerner. Belfast had come to Little Belfast with the prospect (as Jack Yeats believed) of 'harsher rule now – Belfast rule' for the employers. Both brothers had indulged in nostalgia at the time of the funeral, a grandly masonic affair, with Jack adding a wreath of flowers in the late lamented's racing colours.[38] For the poet, the modest dividend intensified the urge towards mythologising the Pollexfens and Middletons, while preferring the voice of beggars and hermits in his poetry. Small-town mill- and ship-owners were about to be transmogrified into an unofficial aristocracy or at least 'gentlemen to the backbone', as an earlier rhapsodist classified a grade of Irish rural society. Neither in Irish nor British terms was 1913 the ideal moment for reinvention of the patriarchal country squire. Decades of land legislation had stripped the real out of Irish real estate. In the 1910 novel by E. M. Forster (which Yeats appears to have ignored), commerce occupied Howards End, an English country house that Margaret Schlegel married into 'to keep the soul from sloppiness'.

The notion of a hidden god hardly indulges the soul; rather it requires discipline to the point of self-denial. 'The Countess Cathleen' explored the theme using an inherited plot and a recognisably contemporary social context. Katharine Tynan had claimed that the old (or not so old) tale of the legendary countess was unique as an instance of one sacrificing her soul for the love of God. This absurdity, which has no resemblance to negative theology, the *via negativa*, or to any other of the dialectical theologies of post-Reformation Europe, may well explain why God hid or what He hid from.

Demob

Ah! When the ghost begins to quicken,
Confusion of the death-bed over, is it sent
Out naked on the roads, as the books say, and stricken
By the injustice of the skies for punishment?
                                'The Cold Heaven', 1912

On 6 February 1939, the Yeats family issued a list of those from
whom they had already received telegrams or other messages of
sympathy. Leaving aside collective bodies like the Abbey Theatre's
Board of Directors, there were eighty-three individuals, including at
least one Catholic priest and one Jew (Bethel Solomons).[1] The
Germans were Margarete and Gerhart Hauptmann, and Eduard
Hempel, with no apparent showing by the Clissmanns.[2]

It had been an axiom of Yeats's spiritual geometry that particular
places constituted spiritual values in themselves and could be
expected to host events or visitations of an appropriate kind.[3] In his
youth, he had earnestly sought to transmute the Sligo of casual
sectarianism into a faery landscape and a noble domain. With Maud
Gonne he had dreamed of establishing a magical order on an island in
Lough Key, east of Sligo, in County Roscommon.

Eventually, these ambitions were addressed by sterner stuff. In
August 1940, the Germans attempted to land Helmut Clissmann and
a radio operator in Sligo Bay. With the help of IRA contacts, they
were to reach England and prepare for the planned German invasion.
Operation Lobster was aborted when the Breton trawler on which
the heroes were travelling developed engine trouble off the Irish west
coast. A year later, Clissmann was involved in another incursion.
Operation Sea Eagle would land a sea-plane on Yeats's and Gonne's
sacred Lough Key, to drop him and Frank Ryan, formerly a left-wing
IRA man. Clissmann was to carry £40,000 for IRA operations in
Northern Ireland, while Ryan talked Eamon de Valera into greater
tolerance of the IRA. Again, nothing happened. Admiral Canaris,
then head of the Abwehr but nowadays suspected of also being in

touch with British intelligence, cancelled the Sea Eagle at an early stage.

Clissmann Among the Danes

Among the Blood Kindred, Leutnant Clissmann deserves a final salute, for he has been the subject of much vague and distorted commentary. Born Ewald Heinrich Helmut Clissmann in Aachen on 11 May 1911, he had visited Ireland in the summers of 1930, 1931, 1932 and 1934. On some at least of these occasions he travelled as part of a so-called 'Young Prussian League' group, which wore grey military uniforms and stunned Dublin with their lavish accoutrements: their host in 1930 was Chalmers Edward Fitzroy Trench, who the following year did a little acting in the Abbey Theatre.[4] Clissmann's arrival in Ireland is thus prefaced by Trench's acquaintance with the duel-scarred Thomsen whom he met in Cambridge. The published account of Clissmann's early life stresses the left-wing orientation of his interests – grey greatcoats notwithstanding – though the anti-left *Deutsche Orden* to which Clissmann almost certainly belonged disappeared into (and not under) the Nazi system after 1933. By the end of 1935, the Irish authorities had misgivings about Clissmann's behaviour: it is some indication of his importance that the German diplomat reporting these to Berlin was reprimanded for not protecting the 'alleged spy'. Shortly afterwards, the diplomat fell from grace.

A place among the Kindred was reserved for Clissmann by virtue of his discretion in not (so far as we know) confronting Yeats in life, instead concentrating on lesser writers such as Peadar O'Donnell and Francis Stuart. But he worked with Minister Hempel, leaving personal possessions in the Dublin Legation that were sold after the war. He was close enough to Iseult Stuart for her to entrust Francis's future to him, and he was an honoured guest among the MacBrides. And he was married to a Sligo woman, daughter of D. A. Mulcahy.

Clissmann's leaving Ireland some months after Yeats's death had been less unfortunate than providential. On 29 August 1939, his wife wrote to him about the departure of other Germans from Dublin, as reported in the papers – 'no names which is just as well'. According to post-war British sources, he had been 'ordered by the German Minister in Dublin to return to Germany', which suggests political rather than routine considerations.[5] From the correspondence of a third party – Rudmose Brown of Trinity College – it can be established that Frau Clissmann was in Copenhagen as early as November 1939, and again in December–January 1940/41. In view of her husband's subsequent career, the choice of rendezvous can hardly have been casual. The years 1940–41 saw the Leutnant attempt his Yeatsian missions in Sligo and Roscommon. The failure of these may have had domestic ramifications. By July 1942, Frau Clissmann and the children were living in the Danish capital.

None of this matches the approved version. The post-war fable of Clissmann's almost accidental recruitment into the Brandenburg Regiment as a foot-soldier does not tally with his presence in Berlin's Technische Hochschule after hostilities had commenced; on the contrary, it bespeaks his continued engagement in subversion under academic colours. Francis Stuart often saw Clissmann in Berlin that summer of 1942.[6] Talk of the family moving into the Reich does not seem to have arisen until the spring, when things were beginning to go seriously wrong for the Nazi war effort. By October 1942, if not a good deal earlier, the Irish Army's G2 unit was fully aware of his role as a German intelligence officer. At the year's end, he was described in the files as 'formerly German gauleiter in Dublin'.[7]

Clissmann maintained his involvement in Irish affairs, having travelled twice to Madrid in an ultimately successful effort to secure the release of Frank Ryan from General Franco's clutches. The late Desmond Williams held that the unfolding German catastrophe in the east ruled out adventures (however small) in the far Gaelic west. Certainly Clissmann's expertise with subversive organisations was applied in practice to the Danish Resistance. His resources were extensive, the bureau to which he was attached having not only Irish but Balkan responsibilities. At some point, he was active in Tunisia, where he directed line-crossing by German agents during the North African campaign.

In the perspective of an Irish historian, perhaps the most significant element in the dossier of offences drawn up by British investigators was Clissmann's involvement in 'a scheme for recruiting Irish [prisoners of war] as possible agents for dispatch to Ireland'. The ghost of Roger Casement was knocking at yet another door. Politically such an operation raised major issues, given Ireland's neutrality and its status as a British dominion. Despite his long apprenticeship in Ireland, Clissmann's most active service was confined to Denmark. Evidence of his movements in 1943 is slight.

By now the retreat from Stalingrad was under way, and the RAF had commenced heavy bombing of Berlin. In Denmark, he answered to Hauptmann Lorentz in the Jutland city of Viborg, though there has also been a claim that he reported to Heinrich Müller (1901–?), head of the Gestapo. Were this confirmable, Clissmann would stand next in line to one of the fifteen bureaucrats who, at Wannersee in January 1942, planned the Final Solution.

We must settle for less awful perspectives. At Christmas 1943, the Clissmann family entertained Frank Ryan in their Copenhagen home, but the time for Irish initiatives was past. From the summer of 1944 until May 1945, Clissmann worked with the Schiølergruppen (of Danish Nazis) and additionally liaised with the Abwehr and Lorentz. The group had been founded in June 1944 to play 'wehr-wolf' in the event of an Allied invasion. Their initial contact with Clissmann had been established in Münster, where they met him for the first time. However, evidence of Frau Clissmann's visits to Copenhagen from November 1939 onwards, and of the family being settled there by July 1942, strongly argues for long-range planning of Clissmann's involvement in Nazi terrorisation of Denmark, with his Irish peacetime activities constituting a mere boy-scout exercise.

The Schiølergruppen consisted of some fifteen to twenty Danish SS men and others who infiltrated resistance units, tortured saboteurs and waged terror on civilians during the last eight months or so of the war. Clissmann was directly responsible for bombing a Copenhagen café in February 1945 and murdering a suspect member of his own group. Arrested by the Allies, and held at Bad Nenndorf in Germany, he gave evidence in the trial of Danish collaborators in 1946. As he does not appear to have been tried (or even charged) in Denmark, we may take it that his singing was deemed adequate.[8] This cooperation does not necessarily invalidate his own claim to have been beaten up while in British custody, though such a claim served well for a sanitised return to Ireland, effected while Sean MacBride was Minister for External Affairs.

The election of Ireland's first acknowledged inter-party government in February 1948 was quickly followed by two attempts at repatriation of the poet's remains. Ever since Yeats's death in January 1939, it had been intended that his body should be brought back from the South of France for reburial. The outbreak of war made any such scheme impossible, but in September 1948 an Irish naval corvette was despatched by the new government to meet the poet's wishes. Nine years into his death, Yeats was more 'official' than he had been at the time of his demise. A delegation headed by MacBride greeted the cortège in Sligo, and the coffin was laid to rest in Drumcliff churchyard, as directed in 'Under Ben Bulben'. Murmurings to the effect that the wrong body had been exhumed in France have never been taken seriously, nor have they completely faded away.

A similar air of unease blows through the dusty records of the year's other notable repatriation. Clissmann had been released from Bad Nenndorf in 1946, and was living at his family home in Aachen. Subject to the strict rules concerning the mobility of German citizens under the occupying powers, he had evidently expressed no wish to return to Ireland. But the unexpected arrival in power of his old chum, the former IRA chief, altered the picture. There was now no difficulty in obtaining an entry visa (despite Lobster and Sea Eagle), an accomplishment virtually impossible for him while de Valera had been both Taoiseach and Minister for External Affairs. Consequently, in the spring of 1948 the British authorities were approached from several directions with requests for Clissmann's release from restrictions on his international movements. He had been de-Nazified into Category V, reserved for 'the least politically involved Nazis'. Other appeals stressed connections with Ireland through his wife, his having been interned for two years, and the Danes' decision not to prosecute him. C. M. Anderson, who was private secretary to Baron Henderson of Westgate, cited all of these reasons for concluding that Clissmann 'might fairly be considered to have expiated his misdeeds'. That was in August 1948.

But the Commonwealth Relations Office had come to other conclusions, believing that it was 'highly undesirable to allow him to enter Eire ... in view of his past history'. While this initially may have reflected British outrage at Clissmann's propaganda activities before the war, or his aborted attempts to rebuild Valhalla in Ireland's green and pleasant land, there were important non-Irish dimensions. Anderson's opponent, Chitty, had seen 'a detailed secret document', which recorded a career 'so bad that it is quite clear he should not be allowed to leave Germany'. In some quarters, the Category V de-Nazification was proposed for review. The secret document has not yet been traced.

Clissmann's support came through Anderson, who referred to representations received from Ireland, but without naming any of the persons concerned. Anderson's boss, William Henderson

(1891–1984), was a minor Foreign Office minister who corresponded with the odious 'Monty' Belgion (1892–1973), T. S. Eliot's licensed anti-Semite in *The Criterion*. Later, Belgion specialised in denouncing the trial of war criminals. You could be forgiven for seeing a pattern. Less personally driven, Clissmann's release from travel restrictions probably resulted from two very different aspects of his case. First, he had official clearance to enter Ireland, thanks to MacBride, who was simultaneously ensuring that his own brother-in-law (Francis Stuart) was kept out. Second, the authorities in Denmark, where Clissmann had evidently seen most active and questionable service, chose not to prosecute him in return for his evidence in the trial of others. The latter decision effectively left the British without a legal argument to stand on, having 'lent' their prisoner to the Danes for an inquiry into Schiølergruppen crimes. Thus while MacBride greeted a gunship bearing the poet's remains, Clissmann slipped into the country as the ordinary civilian he had extraordinarily become. By one account, his 'repatriation' was effected through Rome, so that he arrived in Ireland in the guise of a returning pilgrim.[9] Once more he was among kindred.

The Cold Eye on Moylett and MacManus

Ireland's recovery from the isolation of wartime was slow. Politically, things returned to normal when de Valera became Taoiseach again with the general election of May 1951. Literary life cautiously tested the entrenched system of state censorship. A new journal, modestly called *Irish Writing*, published the first traces of Samuel Beckett's novel, *Watt*, written while the author was living clandestinely in German-occupied France. The same issue carried a poem by Gogarty: 'Adam and Eve' characterised their Creator as 'a cross 'twixt Hermann Goering / And falutin' Bernard Shaw'.[10]

Dublin rumour suggested that Clissmann's post-war business activities were in part related to the illegal importation of contraceptives, in which case the former Abwehr-man was consistent in subversion. Business continued to preoccupy Patrick Moylett who, however, lost his fashionable address in Monkstown and settled in more modest Rathmines, just round the corner from Yeats's widow in Palmerston Road. In retirement he worked on his memoirs, justifying Arthur Griffith and himself, deploring Michael Davitt, and wholly avoiding the topic of Irish fascism. Robin Dudley Edwards,

Professor of Irish History at University College, was persuaded to read the typescript and even to write a brief introduction for any publisher willing to accept the project. As Moylett seems to have had self-publication in mind, Edwards took the precaution of writing a piece which praised with such audible damnations that its release to the public became impossible. One wonders if Moylett's old comrade in anti-Semitism, Professor Roger McHugh, had any part in seeking Edwards's endorsement.[11]

Though Clissmann returned to Ireland, and Moylett steered an unaltered course, a more intimate chum among the Kindred – Dermot MacManus – moved to Yorkshire where he lived for years in retirement, a victim of painful Great War injuries and accumulated illnesses. At the time of Yeats's death, the widow had urged him to keep in touch, regarding him as one of a very small band of true intimates. It seems that the old soldier later lost his wife and remarried: his second wife, Millicent, came from a background that had been narrowly Wesleyan. Nothing daunted, MacManus kept in touch with Ireland through correspondence with Sybil Le Brocquy, who was writing about Jonathan Swift. Anxious to hear news of his surviving friends – among them Lilo Stephens and Millington Synge – he fought shy of reminiscing about Yeats and categorically refused to sell valuable material in his possession. Instead, he recalled attempts to interest the economic historian George O'Brien in the 'social credit' theories of Major Douglas as approved by Ezra Pound.[12] The correspondence occurred when Northern Ireland was slipping or skipping into renewed sectarian violence, and MacManus's occasional comments about the poet overlap with comments on Bernadette Devlin and Edna O'Brien (is she good, bad or bogus?).

Le Brocquy was sympathetic to the occult side of the Yeats-MacManus story, just as her interest in Swift followed on from speculations made earlier by Yeats and Denis Johnston. MacManus, while reticent, could also be strangely frank:

> A lot of these contacts with W. B. Yeats were of extreme intimacy including one of the most dramatic and important things in his life – a purely occult matter – known, as far as I am aware, only to him, to George [Yeats] and to myself – Gogarty may have had an inkling of it, but I doubt it, though I am pretty sure the Swami was told, and helped him completely.[13]

As with other accounts of the other side that reach those of us moored in the sublunary, much remains unclear. Who was helped by this dramatic thing, Yeats or the Swami? What constitutes being 'helped . . . completely'? More fundamentally, one wants to know the relationship between physical and mental 'contacts'. MacManus appears to have trafficked in the occultic 'rough trade', preferring Scottish witches and Irish fairy forts to the more abstruse topics of Plotinus and the Cambridge neo-Platonists. Correspondence with Le Brocquy led him to approach Kathleen Raine, the English poet and Blakean scholar. Only part of their correspondence is accessible, but from it one gathers that she quizzed MacManus about articles he had published on 'the colour question'.

His reply exemplified his talent at self-centred evasion. 'Now, as to my Negro articles,' he began, 'I have spent a large part of my life voluntarily facing *real* danger.' Summarising his military career, he stressed that his conflict with the Black and Tans had been conducted 'in close co-operation with the real I. R. A. whose leaders were all good conservative patriots, with high standards of courage, integrity and religion'. The emphasis on his attachment to an IRA that had to be identified as the real one, as opposed to the raggle-taggle, raises further doubts about MacManus's Irish war record, doubts audible today among military archivists. But in 1973, and echoing Enoch Powell, he was not 'intimidated by a lot of long-haired, unwashed degenerates in the English Left Wing'. The latter, it seemed, had been perturbed by the Negro articles, in defence of which MacManus now further declared that we [sic] live 'by purity of breeding, in as much as all good horses, cattle, sheep, pigs, grain, potatoes and all else we eat are the product of pure breeding. Why should Man be the only living thing to value being a Mongrel [?]'[14]

What kind of potatoes was he raised on, or what kind of logic? Yet one can risk deducing something of the tone in which he told Yeats 'astonishing stories' about Negroes in 1934. MacManus, like Maloney who wrote *The Forged Casement Diaries* (1936), was a victim of Britain's calamitous Dardanelles adventure in 1915. The psychic damage wreaked on two individuals cannot be taken as representative of post-war manhood, yet innumerable British Legion cottages, and military hospitals, in England and Ireland housed former soldiers incapacitated to one degree or another by the unprecedented intensity of their traumatic experience. Historians agree that fascism was in part a result of the Great War, and that the Second World War was in many ways merely a resumption of hostilities. In local Irish terms, Elizabeth Bowen's fiction certainly makes the connection, notably in

The Heat of the Day (1949). Yeats's dismissive attitude towards the Great War, his preference for higher levels of reality than death in the trenches, affected political and cultural attitudes among his colleagues in the Irish literary movement and among the more explicitly ideological disciples – for example, MacManus and Starkie. It also formed the emotional background against which he had conducted his secret domestic politics in 1920.

An Obituary for Francis Stuart (2000)

In June 1999, Francis Stuart defeated the *Irish Times* in an out-of-court settlement. The ninety-seven–year-old novelist's libel action arose from an accusation of wartime anti-Semitism. The proceedings echoed a long and farcical debate at the November 1997 meeting of Aosdána, an academy of Irish writers, musicians and visual artists, founded by the tax-evading former Taoiseach C. J. Haughey. During the proceedings, the poet Maire Mhac an tSaoi (b. 1922) went so far as to murmur the suggestion that Stuart might have been a British agent during the war, a kind of double-stooge. Born in Townsville, Queensland, on 20 April 1902, Stuart was always to be surrounded by controversy. His father, Henry Irwin Stuart, an immigrant from Protestant Ulster, committed suicide in a mental asylum less than four months after the birth, believing himself to be a great criminal. His mother, Lily (née Montgomery), brought the boy home, to grow up shifting between various Irish residences, including Benvarden, a gloomy house on the coast of Antrim. This was a society of collapsing landlordism and diminishing legacies for the next generation, a seedbed of resentment.

On the eleventh anniversary of Henry Stuart's committal as a lunatic, Lily married her first cousin Henry Clements, a retired alcoholic Texan cowboy fond of inviting his stepson to share a bath. Home life for the young Stuart was a hazard of maternal indifference and male irrationality. Apart from the traditional nanny, only an aunt who smoked a pipe and wore men's trousers showed the child any affection. He was sent off first to a prep school in Warwickshire, and then to Rugby, which was brightened by news of the Russian Revolution.

The next logical step was Trinity College Dublin, but Stuart never took it. He was regarded as intellectually dim, a view occasionally endorsed by W. B. Yeats. The great moment in Stuart's drifting life was an encounter with Iseult, daughter of Maud Gonne and Lucien Millevoye, whom Maud subseqently married and divorced. The wife-beating major had been executed after the 1916 Rising, and the beautiful widow (Yeats's inviolate rose) epitomised martyrdom, self-pity and a good deal of racialist bile. Iseult was very beautiful too, and lacked some of her mother's vices.

The young pair eloped to London, but returned to Dublin where they were married a few weeks before the groom's eighteenth birthday. (Iseult, at twenty-five, had already been deflowered by Ezra Pound and, even earlier, had been forced to witness her stepfather exposing himself.) Given his new family's loyalties, Stuart had neither difficulty nor choice in embracing Catholicism and militant national-ism. He supported the republicans during Ireland's civil war of 1922, and was briefly jailed in 1924. A pamphlet-lecture published by Sinn Féin, on *Nationality and Culture*, contained one passage of a decidedly anti-Semitic bias, though by 1970 Stuart said that he had no recollection of either delivering the lecture or seeing the pamphlet: the material in question related to Vienna in the years after 1918 and appears to have drawn on a journey that Stuart made with his wife and mother-in-law. A Gonne sub-text under Stuart's name may have been fabricated.

The marriage was doomed, given his own confused immaturity, Iseult's disinclination towards sex and the interference of both Maud Gonne and Yeats. That it lasted until 1939 is testimony to the strange drifting intensity of two ill-matched loners. The infant death of a daughter, Dolores, occurred in 1921 when Stuart had taken tempo-rary leave of his wife. Yeats, in his astrologer's habit, had declared that the girl should ideally marry into Yeats's own family, as if further to undermine Stuart as a father. In prison a year later he read and wrote, attracted to the visionary work of Dostoevsky. But when Stuart's first book of poems appeared in 1924, its title – *We Have Kept the Faith* – was taken from Rupert Brooke.

While devoid of Yeats's genius, Stuart was something of a ghost-in-reverse for the Nobel Prize winner. The younger man could flirt with Catholicism and violence in a way that Yeats, who ruffled in a manly pose, would not. Their apogee came in the short-lived magazine *To-morrow* (August 1924), for which Yeats wrote a purple editorial above the names of Stuart and a few others. By the end of the 1920s, the Stuarts were living in County Wicklow at Laragh Castle, a British military blockhouse built after the rebellion of 1798. A son, Ion (sometime a sculptor), was born in 1926 and a second daughter, Catherine, or Kay, in 1931 – the latter was suspected by one acute observer of being Yeats's child, not Stuart's, though the poet's ability to achieve an erection during his many 1930s' affairs has been questioned. Lily Clements moved to Laragh also, and the entourage hoped to survive on the profits of poultry farming.

Women and God appeared in 1931. Better fiction quickly followed – *Pigeon Irish, The Coloured Dome* (both 1932) and *Try the Sky* (1933). Yeats was now inclined to be approving, and Stuart became a founding member of the Irish Academy of Letters (1932). He philandered in London, drank everywhere with Liam O'Flaherty, and visited Samuel Beckett in pre-war Paris. As a writer, he was going downhill, too prolific, too undisciplined. He had other preoccupations, notably aeroplanes and horses. Both cost him money. *Racing for Pleasure and Profit* (1937) remains the rarest item for collectors of Stuart, and the passion for breeding and racing also ran strong in his only frankly autobiographical book, *Things to Live For* (1934). At no stage did he interest himself in human eugenics. On the racecourse he was always Harry, always Henry's son, Harry.

During the early 1930s, Yeats was 'flirting' with Ireland's fascist movement, the Blue Shirts, in which Stuart took no interest. 'Send war in our time, O Lord' was to be a death-bed cry of Yeats's, a theme already investigated less noisily by Stuart in a forgotten novel, *The Angel of Pity* (1935). As Yeats's extreme politics developed through an arcane symbolism, so Stuart's complementary role became active and direct. He was to be conscripted as Yeats's posthumous Anti-Self, a literate Moylett. Shortly after the honoured poet died in January 1939, Stuart was invited to give readings in Germany. A month after the invasion of Czechoslovakia, he arrived in Berlin, returning to Ireland for the summer. In late September, he returned to Berlin on a university contract, and with some low-grade IRA contacts. This occurred weeks after the commencement of the Second World War. Clissmann had been central to these plans.

There was no causal relationship between Yeats's death and Stuart's departure, but it fell to the younger man's lot to work out much of what his mentor had preached – the hard, yet bogus, aristocratic credo in an age of mass-murder and ideological hatred. In a document addressed to her husband, Iseult insisted, 'I will not have you look up to imposters of nobility and think their brass is gold.'[15] But it is characteristically unclear if this perceptive comment ever reached his eyes. At thirty-seven, Stuart was either culpably ignorant of what had already happened in Germany or deliberately hostile to humane reasoning – or both. Irish neutrality had an undeniable basis in law, but its defence in moral terms required more energy than Stuart ever expended. He was no democrat, and during four and a half years in the Reich he not only taught its undergraduates (in dwindling numbers), but also wrote and delivered broadcasts on its long-range wireless service.

IRA terrorism in Britain gave Stuart a certain *éclat* in the eyes of the Nazis, and in February 1940 he was asked to write or translate radio scripts. In the words of his poor biographer, Geoffrey Elborn, 'Stuart insisted he would not write anti-Semitic material, and when told this was not required, he agreed.' One broadcast – on 16 December 1942 – certainly praised Hitler, though more were devoted to praising Irish neutrality. The Irish government protested to Berlin twice, on both occasions citing interference in domestic affairs. The issue festers to this day, but none of Stuart's critics has ever taken the trouble to publish transcripts.[16]

Characteristically, Stuart set about complicating his marital and sexual life. First, he took as mistress Nora O'Mara, secretary to Hermann Görtz, who was shortly despatched to Ireland, Laragh and Mrs Stuart's arms.[17] Then he set up with one of his students, Gertrud Meissner. At home, Maud Gonne MacBride assisted in concealing the spy, Görtz, but Iseult was arrested instead, as the collaborator less likely to stir up popular republican support: she was acquitted when tried. Stuart morally sleep-walked through the Reich, until the saturation bombing disturbed his peace. As the Red Army advanced into Germany, Stuart and Meissner set out southwards in mid-September 1944, and spent months shunting about in the chaos of war's end. News of Hitler's death reached them at Dornbirn in western Austria, a few miles short of the Swiss border.

British and French troops were in the area, and in August 1945 Stuart was allowed to travel to Paris. In effect, he was free to go home. Madeleine – as Gertrud came to be renamed – had inspired in him a new kind of Christianity, anarchic and sentimental perhaps, but more attuned to their circumstances than the editorials of *To-morrow*. Back in Dornbirn, the two lived contentedly until, on 21 November, they were arrested by the French authorities. Confusion over Meissner's Christian name added to their difficulties, but, after six months, she and Stuart were released without charge.

They were transferred, however, to a villa in Germany where Stuart was further interrogated; released into the French zone, they lived in relative freedom until October 1946 when he alone was rearrested and detained in Freiburg. Here things got tougher, but he was released once again without charge, though remaining under surveillance well into 1948. The novelist Ethel Mannin described the situation in *German Journey* (1948), though her account was coloured by a desire to re-establish herself in Stuart's eyes, he and Yeats having shared her affections before the war.

Stuart moved to Paris in July 1949, having completed three novels in Freiburg. Of these, two published by Victor Gollancz, *The Pillar of Cloud* (1948) and *Redemption* (1949), remain disturbing, unrivalled novels of physical privation and religious intensity, based more on the author's post-war experience than on the years in Berlin. Madeleine Meissner joined him in August. Although the new novels won some plaudits, an attitude of high caution pervaded the critical response. Basil Liddell-Hart, who had admired some of the pre-war work, corresponded with Stuart, but, until embargoed Foreign Office and Irish External Affairs files are opened, the real nature of their connection cannot be gauged.

The British authorities regarded the Görtz affair as damnable, but it was the Irish State that had been put at risk. At the personal level, Iseult's standing with the British may have been lower than that of her execrated husband, though (unlike him) she had never been a British subject. The Irish made no moves to extradite Stuart, and the UK's 1940 Treachery Act could not be brought to bear on the issue of broadcasts. As for the French, they could not charge a neutral with collaboration. While this analysis of Stuart's escape from retribution is basically legalistic, it remains the case that little substantive evidence of anti-Semitic behaviour or sentiments has been adduced to date. Much the same is true of Yeats.

While Iseult remained alive, it was impossible to bring Madeleine to Ireland, a situation made even worse when Stuart's brother-in-law (briefly an IRA chief) became Minister for External Affairs in 1948. Six years later, Iseult died on 22 March 1954. After her funeral at Glendalough, Stuart returned to London and married Madeleine on 28 April, the day before his fifty-second birthday. In London, later in County Meath, and finally opposite Dublin's Central Hospital for the Criminally Insane, Francis and Madeleine Stuart lived the closest kind of married existence, until her death in 1986. She was his salvation in several regards.

The post-war fiction – in which Madeleine is everywhere recognisable – passed through two repetitions of his 1930s' pattern: good work, followed by a steady decline. Victor Gollancz personally tried to persuade Stuart that his attitude towards Jews should be clarified. The result, *Victors and Vanquished* (1958), is perhaps the weakest of the post-war novels. Soon the author began a long silence broken only in 1970 with *Blacklist*.

Living in a small cottage near Dunshaughlin, County Meath, Stuart had worked on this auto-fiction for more than a decade. A younger writer, Tom MacIntyre, advised cuts which helped to make the book marketable while also eliminating valuable early material. Gollancz was dead. An extract appeared in *Atlantis*. Michael Gill, a Dublin publisher, although keen to have an early viewing, turned *Blacklist* down flat. Southern Illinois University Press, advised by Harry T. Moore (a D. H. Lawrence expert), snapped it up.

Issued in January 1972, it was greeted with amazement and respect, though not with warm enthusiasm. Frank Kermode in *The Listener* was the most perceptive reviewer. The most enduring of Stuart's novels, *Blacklist* provides an unvarnished account of 'H' from childhood confusion to wartime disorientation. The cryptic H is Harry Stuart, son of Harry Irwin Stuart, stepson of Harry Clements, lost son and lost soul. The style is unadorned, at times awkward. But *Blacklist* established Stuart as an Irish writer of rugged, even perverse, independence. Then a third decline in artistic control promptly began.

In the 1970s, the former republican flirted with loyalist organisations in Belfast, but his search for a place among the condemned had little meaning in the new Ireland. There were too many such places. Protesting against Ronald Reagan in 1984, he was an elder statesman of dissent. Everywhere spoken against, yet honoured by Aosdána, the octogenarian Stuart's reputation was fuelled by accounts of an occasional bar-room incident. He married for a third time, to Finola Graham, a painter, in 1987.

No account of Francis Stuart should underestimate the influence of his profoundly dysfunctional family background. Nor was the triangle of Yeats, Iseult Gonne and Maud Gonne MacBride calculated to assist a confused teenager in the early years of marriage, especially as Yeats had wished to marry both Maud and Iseult at different times, and to be husband and surrogate father to Stuart's wife at different times. As a bonus, Iseult expressed the belief to him late in her life that, really, she should have been his mother![18] Emotional disorientation rarely comes from as many angles as Stuart was exposed to – notionally the son of the man who was notionally the father of his wife, who expressed a wish to be mother, not wife. These patterns – incompletely sketched here – do not simply outline a profoundly confused and confusing Family Romance: they too fitted into a larger search for transcendental power.

To see Stuart as Yeats's bad karma is also to acknowledge the serpent-like cunning of the poet's commitment to fascism. Stuart admitted that he made mistakes, but never apologised for his German residence from 1940 to 1945: to have done so would have violated his amoralism. Intermittently vilified in his last years, Francis Stuart served to distract attention from the iniquities of other powerful Irish icons. As in Germany, so in Ireland, the self-proclaimed outcast was manipulated more often than he ever realised. He died at Fenore, County Clare, on 2 February 2000. A death-bed photograph in the *Irish Times* offended many, as did rumours that a much-loved cat was interred or inhumed in the same coffin.

I, the Poet, William Yeats (Ltd); Or, the Good Man Doing Nothing

During a formal conversation in Trinity College Dublin, a leading geneticist remarked that I had written about Nelson Mandela, Máirtín Ó Cadhain and Francis Stuart – a trio he clearly found disturbing. Part of his difficulty lay in the assumption that literary history should stick to good books. Another assumption – doubtless unconscious – may have turned on the suspicion that his discipline had learned no less from the Nazis than Francis Stuart had. During another formal conversation, in another place, a scholar of Celtic studies expressed amazement that I should include Honoré de Balzac in my field of enquiry. What both experts exemplified in these observations was the consequence of our lacking any reflective theory of literature attending to the complexity and difficulty of Irish writing. Instead, what we have had for the duration of the Troubles and beyond has been a version of post-colonialist rhetoric, reliant on spurious claims about Yeats's support for the Spanish Republic and the Irishness of Heathcliff. Macrosoft nationalism.

There has, of course, been no shortage of theorising about the nature of the Irish State, of the Northern Irish policy, and of British policy towards both. Debate has also treated the Union from 1801 onwards, and the relationship between Ireland and Britain before 1800. Yet it would be hazardous to claim that any of these perspectives has put Tullylish in focus, certainly not in a manner that acknowledges high cultural activities like the writing of fiction and poetry as part and parcel of the social reality. In their defence, the economic historians and political scientists could point out that no novelist turned from castle and cabin to narrate the lives of Victorian factory managers and the wives of operatives in the Bann valley. Yeats does raise problems.

No literary theory or other nostrum that banishes the *comédie humaine* can hope to shed light on nineteenth-century Western Europe, even in its Ulster aspect. In 1920 when Yeats was touring the United States and Canada, György Lukács – active in the brief Béla Kun Soviet republic of Hungary – published his pre-Marxist *Theory of the Novel* in Berlin. Derived generally from Hegel, and more locally from Goethe's concept of the daemonic, it sought to classify the novel into historical phases, as the modern successor to ancient tragic drama and archaic epic. In Homer, in Dante and in the Upanishads, epic had reflected an integrated world where gods and men moved in their assigned spheres, but not exclusively. Zeus raped Leda and, after the battle of mythic heroes, Troy fell and Homer composed the *Odyssey*.

From a disadvantage point at the opening of the twentieth century, it could seem that everything went rapidly downhill after Troy. Classical tragedy masked the frenzy of Greek religion, Renaissance imitation scarcely survived into the seventeenth century, and the Enlightenment proved a disappointment. Nietzsche offered only eternal return. Freud pointed to the Oedipal in all of us. The symbolic no longer shone in its own self-evidence to man, but taunted with elusive intimacy, oppressive distance. Though Iseult Gonne and Francis Stuart had featured as 'spiritual children' of the poet, during the years surrounding his courtship and marriage, Yeats left two children of his own body – a daughter Anne (1919–2001) and son Michael (b. 1921). Apart from one appearance as an unnamed dunce, Stuart never made it into the *dramatis personae* of the poetry, while his wife (never named) pervades the work of more than a decade and a half.

The two poems written to celebrate the births of Yeats's actual, not just symbolic, children differ in quality, largely because the first-born monopolised certain themes that could not simply be repeated on the second occasion. Nevertheless, the inferior quality of 'A Prayer for My Son' (written in December 1921, published in *The Tower*, 1928) augured ill for relationship of father-and-son thus inaugurated. It is no family secret that the young Michael Yeats did not much like his father. At school, the boy was teased with the words 'Bid a strong ghost ...', being the opening words of the poem written for his protection, a poem in which he was said to be at risk of murder (like the infant Christ). In maturity he chose a path in public life which distinctly marked him off from the paternal model; in politics he joined de Valera's party, Fianna Fáil, and if this resulted in his sitting (like his father) in the Irish Senate, the performance differed greatly in tone. Michael Yeats deplored his poem -'verse of maudlin sentimentality'.[19]

By contrast with 'A Prayer for My Son', Anne's poem (written and published in 1919) envisaged her in a series of natural relationships protecting her from the hatred that is repeatedly observed by the poet-father:

> O may she live like some green laurel
> Rooted in one dear perpetual place.

The final stanza of the poem was to be disappointed. No bridegroom brought her to a house 'where all's accustomed, ceremonious'. Michael married Gráinne, daughter of P. S. O'Hegarty (1879–1955), a former member of the Irish Republican Brotherhood, civil servant and bibliophile. Together son and daughter administered the affairs of their father's literary estate, with a degree of affable good sense unparalleled in the post-mortem annals of other high modernists. Few literary properties have thrived exponentially as Yeats's has; no other property as the consequence of deliberate generosity.

Let us note in conclusion two other groups of two poems. First, there are two six-line poems commemorating great poets: 'Swift's Epitaph', written in 1929–30 when Yeats was embarking on the 'turn' in his outlook, and 'To be Carved on a Stone at Thoor Ballylee', written more than ten years earlier. More could be said about this pair, their near-identical syllabic structure and rhyme pattern, and the implied linking of the Augustan poet long dead and the Modernist poet with twenty years to live. But the other pair of poems demands attention also. This second group links 'To be Carved ... ' with

'Michael Robartes and the Dancer', by appearing (respectively) as the last and first items in the collection *Michael Robartes and the Dancer* (1921). The dancer, one need hardly add, was Iseult Gonne, later Mrs Stuart. There is thus elicited from a consideration of these poems in their several places and shapes a triangular relationship of Jonathan Swift, Iseult Gonne and 'I, the poet William Yeats' (the opening words of 'To be Carved . . .').

Not quite an eternal triangle, the configuration carries strong historical and mytho-political resonances. Swift's young woman had been Esther Vanhomrigh: she and the older Esther Johnson divided his affections and inspired some of his most memorable poetry. Two hundred years later, Iseult had for older rival her own mother, a political hater less polished than Swift, but scarcely less loved by the poor than the Dean in mid-eighteenth-century Dublin. If these women figured as the Muse for their poets, the result in each case was very different. Swift's poems addressed to women could praise, but they could also reprimand. Mrs Johnson's own poems were highly accomplished. The Muse is a difficult role to play and, with the possible exception of Maud Gonne, none of the four women sought it, though their poet-beaux invoked it. Yeats did so particularly in correspondence with another woman, Dorothy Wellesley, to whom, in 1936, he made the remarkable claim that (the celibate) Swift was 'our ancestor'.[20] Only a sexless process of generation, imagined or desired, could establish that lineage.

'To be Carved on a Stone at Thoor Ballylee' was written after Yeats's marriage, but before the conception of his first child. Its concern is with real-estate and with continuity sought through private property: the building may become a ruin *once again*; it shall be or shall have been the property of 'my wife George'. The inscribed lines may escape ruin, but, if they endure, they do so through the perpetuation of ownership: in a literal sense they are literary property. The first line (used to entitle this section of my last chapter) is also a remarkable assertion of a singularity of person that Yeats rarely conceded. No Mask, no Anti-Self: it moves from the ego-pronoun to the compacted name through a proud vocational statement. The poem is a lapidary inscription, intended to survive even the building upon which it is to be placed, and to survive also both the poet and his wife (and inheritor). Human characters will be succeeded by engraved characters, with a just-discernible play upon the grave. Though the poem foresees ruin and death, and makes no allusion to progeny, it also assumes the persistence of words. These words are to be inscribed not only in lines and rhymes, but also in wills and testaments, titles and readings, words in perpetuity.

Yeats is strong on inheritance, and regards poetry as a form of spiritual and national legacy, which is to say that *poetry* (for him) is also a form of *property*. Indeed the two words, when placed together, mirror each other in a troubled fashion. This may seem difficult to apprehend, or may seem an observation more useful to the compiler of crossword puzzles than to the literary historian. If a third word, *propriety*, is introduced, it acts as a link between them, between the accustomed and ceremonious values of art and the dear perpetual place these might be proper to. Such a mode of verbal argument – argument about words and not just about what they signify – can bear one final extension. Commencing with a term common in American usage (real-estate), one can see how the legally technical term *realty* is a compact version of familiar *reality*.

Not that, for Yeats, reality was familiar or easily accessed. In 'Vacillation' (1932), a conventional contrast is drawn in the course of a dialogue between Heart and Soul: 'seek out reality, leave things that seem'. In 'Ego Dominus Tuus' (1915), it is averred that art, which must itself be striven for with great labour and intelligence, 'is but a vision of reality'. In 'Meru' (1934), he refers to 'the desolation of reality', meaning (we have always assumed) that reality is a desolation, but perhaps allowing also as a sub-meaning that reality will suffer desolation. In all three poems, it is implicit that ultimate reality is only knowable (if at all) by a series of elaborate mediations, whether philosophical or spiritualist, religious or artistic.

Not everyone held such opinions, and Yeats did not always hold them. In his revolutionary youth and in 'September 1913' he celebrated the tradition of Theobald Wolfe Tone (1763–1798), who had memorably committed himself to 'the men of no property'. In less urban circumstances, Yeats had also revered the Irish peasant, those custodians of a folk tradition which, while anchored to place, had little grip on real-estate. As many critics have noted, his attitudes changed, and 'Upon a House Shaken by the Land Agitation' (written in August 1909) registers fears that the emergent occupier/ownership system will not bring cultural distinction. Yeats's politics from the occasion of the Bolshevik Revolution always found time for a

denunciation of communism, socialism and Labour militancy, unem-
barrassed by memories of 1913 and the cause of Dublin's poor. What
has failed to emerge is any clear account of the poetry in the light of
this property-politics.

The course of nationalist politics in the nineteenth century had
taken in various alliances between nation and class, between the
possessors and 'the men of no property'. Deliberate vagueness as to
the ultimate entitlement of the latter characterised political utterances
from the days of Wolfe Tone to those of Parnell; the era of
independence brought no greater clarity and but little charity.
Michael Davitt's radical perspectives on land, likewise Connolly's
Marxism and Larkin's trade-union militancy earned scant approval
from Yeats, except in so far as these could be re-presented as aspects
of the nation's travail or the struggle against English materialism. Yet
none of this analysis reaches the kind of understanding promised in
Lucien Goldmann's homological structuralism.

Steps towards such an understanding are undertaken tentatively. As
one relatively low-level proposition, let us consider if the Yeatsian
doctrine of masks, or more particularly the binary pairing of Self and
Anti-Self, is not an abstraction *from* the political and economic
structure of the United Kingdom of Great Britain and Ireland *into* a
realm at once aesthetic and metaphysical. This is not to pretend that
the nature of the UK was a sufficient or sole cause. On the contrary,
all complex aesthetic works have multiple and complex 'causes'; what
one is saying in the case of Yeats is that the material and social causes
should not be overlooked always in favour of others.

Since 1801, the state into which Yeats was born sixty-four years
later had been both a unified structure and a binary one: unified at the
levels of sovereign and legislature, but at many sub-levels of executive
marked by divergent patterns on one island (Great Britain) and the
other (Ireland). These divergences were not simply the legacy of
historical difference (before 1801); they were often developed within
the United Kingdom in contradiction to, and yet in implementation
of, its unitary structure. Oliver MacDonagh has detailed some of the
most important of these in *Ireland: the Union and its Aftermath*
(1977), with the significant additional emphasis on the development
of innovative institutions in Victorian Ireland (cf. policing, mental-
health provision, primary education) where established practices were
perpetuated in Great Britain.

Ireland was thus, at certain points, both a retarded and an advanced component of the whole. Whereas England (not the larger component, Britain) presented itself and was widely regarded as representative of the United Kingdom, this status was only possible if England were also not-representative of other small component parts – Kerry, or Carmarthen, or indeed Scotland (which retained its own legal system). This argument does not just re-version the Irish nationalist complaint that the United Kingdom exploited Ireland in order to develop England. It is a 'structuralist' one in which attention is drawn to the coexistence of unitary and binary systems, and to the relationship between oppositions and contradictions.

Historically, the testing moment for the United Kingdom arose in 1845 with the onset of the Irish Famine coinciding with the death of Daniel O'Connell. We have looked at the impact of that trauma in County Down, where Yeats's grandfather observed the combined work of industrialisation and agricultural crisis from the mouldering windows of his parsonage. From that date modern Irish nationalism effectively commenced, less in reaction to English (or British) political policy than to the introduction of Free Trade and the creation of a single (unified) market across the Kingdom. The emotive power of a literature invoking the famine is best demonstrated in Yeats's 'The Countess Cathleen' with its Faustian plot supported by a tapestried backcloth of famine-induced death, deprivation and social collapse. The play's many changes between 1892 and 1934 merely emphasise its exceptional plasticity as a historical drama, its power to evoke the recent present through archaic images.

In the manner of a Theodor Adorno, we could read this Yeats as Baudelaire turned upside-down; from John Mitchel on, the famine was thrust forward as the gross reality and grim mirror of Anglo-Irish relations.[21] The publication of John O'Rourke's *History of the Great Irish Famine* (1875), followed as it was by three bad harvests and widespread agricultural depression (1877–79), lent an air of permanency to what was, for most people living in Ireland, the memory of a crisis – moral as well as physical – *which they had survived*, and from which they had (however indirectly and impersonally) thrived through reduced competition, government reform and ideological compensation. Yeats's domestic history hopped round the Hungry Forties as if the decade were a relative of dubious legitimacy: he was born in 1865, and his notable precursor was rector in Drumcliff 'long years ago'; what lay in between was adverted to in a few carefully phrased declarations. The truth was that the Yeatses 'had a good Famine', just as certain fortunate army officers 'had a good war' in 1914–18. But psycho-economically, the famine transformed the United Kingdom by providing the resentment upon which the contradictions were reduced to being oppositions; similarly, the unitary system came to resemble a disguise masking a two-tiered reality behind parliamentary show and royal absence. There are certainly poems by Yeats which bravely and ingeniously aspire to present a vision of that reality.

Arguments of self-exculpation were advanced on behalf of the United Kingdom, but in a voice recognisably British, even English. Anthony Trollope, whose fiction Lady Gregory read aloud to Yeats when he stayed at Coole, was one of the better-known architects of such argument. As the shift of metaphor suggests, the question increasingly involved the *characterisation* of Ireland – Paddy, the simian peasant, the happy idiot, the intimidating skeleton, the invisible dynamitard. From this, it was but a step to the representation of relations within the United Kingdom *as a dramatic dialogue*. And what immediately strikes one about Yeats's early work, seen against the background of political images from the 1870s and '80s, is its strong preference for the dialogic even in pieces (like 'The Wanderings of Oisin', 1889) that are far from being dramatic. Only through two-ness can one-ness be sought. Of course many of his early and immature poems are meltingly Irish, though their unifocal quality lies more in the particularities of place rather than in the (at times languid) dynamics of movement towards place, a dynamics that implies a second and different place. 'I will arise and go now, and go to Innisfree ...' ploddingly resolves three times to move.

The doctrine of masks follows later, owing much to Nietzsche. But the exotic source should not distract us from considering if Yeats's complex oppositions cannot also be read politically as replicating, in apparently aesthetic terms, some of the structuring relations of the United Kingdom. At a lower, more intensive, level of generalisation, I also would revert to the mid-Victorian legal invention of 'limited liability partnership' as an economic correlative to the equally central doctrine of political disinterestedness. By the terms of legislation passed in 1862, the partners in businesses based on this concept were immune to claims on their purse over and above their formal investment in the partnership or company. Introduced to encourage and protect entrepreneurs, limited liability had unavoidable ethical consequences when considered in the abstract. One was no longer his brother's bookkeeper. All wealth abstracted from the business became inaccessible to persons who had dealt with it. Had Great-Uncle Corbet been protected by such arrangements, he might not have gone overboard in 1870.[22] The death of Robert Corbet and the birth of Robert Corbet Yeats closely together narrate blood kindred, with the poet's infant brother then threatening all succession by dying in infancy. Without these deaths, what name would the priggish expositor of 'The Words Upon the Window-pane' bear? By what agency would Swift's 'tragic' politics be downloaded for the Revd Mr Johnston of Belfast?

Of course I am using Robert Corbet here in a symbolic way, knowing that no statement of mine can establish him as a cause of any literary work written by his younger kinsman. Literary history, or for that matter biography, is condemned to the fallen post-Homeric world bewailed by Lukács and Yeats in their different ways. It is not, however, condemned to adopt the immaterialism and irrationality of the *séance*. One can only lament the indulgence sometimes shown towards forms of modern magic, which Yeats himself never fully embraced nor wholeheartedly endorsed. In a less arcane example, Roy Foster usefully describes a dream that haunted Yeats the day after he had written in his diary about the legacy of Swift and Burke for the Irish Free State: in the dream, Sandymount Castle and Coole Park merge 'into decline and ruin. His own identification with Ascendancy Ireland could not be clearer.' Of this one can only ask, 'Could he have been any more thoroughly confused?'[23] Likewise *The Arch-Poet* is replete with factual details of Yeats's interest in automatic writing, his wife's practice of that art, and their joint pursuit of the revelations disclosed. As many fine poems and plays, not forgetting *A Vision* in its two versions, derive from this practice, the Yeatses' automatic writing has its unchallengeable literary importance. But, quite distinct from the poetic *oeuvre*, automatic writing is a historical phenomenon subject to the procedures of the historian's craft.

These are instances of second-degree blurring. The Yeatses' automatic writing needs to be read in the after-light of the Great War, which Yeats, of course, was inclined to play down. The Ascendancy Ireland ruinations relate to 'The Words Upon the Window-pane' in which the voice of Swift is heard, and (one suspects) to the ruined parsonage in Tullylish. Foster quotes Yeats quoting Swift quoting the Bible: one wishes one of the three could quote accurately. More

serious are the similar indulgences extended towards Yeats's 'flirtation' with fascism. 'To an extent perhaps unrecognised, WBY's
affinity with fascism (not National Socialism) was a matter of
rhetorical style; and the achievement of style, as he himself had
decreed long before, was closely connected to shock tactics.'[24] Even if
the details of Yeats's actual links with Nazi Germany had been
enquired into diligently, there remain problems of understanding,
which the above judgments fail to acknowledge.

George Orwell's observations on Yeats, when they are cited, are
now usually condensed into the question about political tendency
and literary style. As we have seen, the topic is clarified when restated
in terms of politics and grammar. Orwell's second and equally potent
remark, to the effect that the poet had reached fascism by the
aristocratic route and by a date much earlier than any with which
fascism is generally linked, deserves equal attention. The linking of
insurance-man Corbet to Lady Gregory is an 'aristocratic route' to be
negotiated with care. In practice, few commentators have given the
general topic more than a passing glance, relying on the metaphor of
flirtation to explain their not taking it seriously. A dangerous erosion
of distinctions and procedures occurs in this context. For, if fascism
was of no great importance in Yeats's life and thought, it does not
follow that fascism is of little importance to his biographer. One
notices with fascination Roy Foster's repeated insistence that his
subject was no Nazi, or ever indebted to such ruffian sources.[25] The
repetition is at risk of cancelling the message, especially when
ancillary arguments – like Yeats's medieval knees – lack health.

The difference between Orwell and Foster is more real than
apparent. The former holds that the poet's politics could (ideally at
least) be understood through an analysis of his style. The latter
suggests that the style (understood as a superficial end-in-itself) is all
that the politics amounts to. It is in this context that the need to argue
real relationships between (say) law and literary form or (to be more
radical) between economics and dialogic structures becomes urgent. It
does not have to focus on limited liability or on 'The Countess
Cathleen'. Yeats's publishing practices afford an accessible subject for
note, especially after 1900 when he arranged to have his literary affairs
overseen by the literary agent Alexander Pollock Watt (1837–1914).
What is striking is not just the Pollexfen-like concern with money,
but the combination of this modern third-party managerial practice

with a private-press mode of publishing through his sisters' Cuala Press in imitation of William Morris's guild socialist ideas.[26]

The best royalties with the best typography cannot be a bad ideal. Yet through limited editions transcended in UK and US contracts, Yeats's publishing history provides a major instance of his practising that limited liability already referred to. At one level, this is merely to repeat in other language that the poet was a shrewd businessman. At another, however, we begin to encounter an ethical derogation which takes on the gravest political aspect from the early 1920s onwards. Perhaps it is cynical to date this practice from the establishment of fascism in Italy; perhaps it is closer to the movements of Yeats's mind to date it from the imperfect but permanent establishment of an Irish national state round the same time. Certainly the two are interconnected. It is only after Irish nationalism has achieved power (the power to take human life, as he carefully specifies) that he begins to use that nationalism as an explanation of his non-availability in other political spheres. It is equally true that it is with reference to authoritarian or fascist politics that he declines to act, citing the Irish nation as his one and only loyalty. Edmund Burke's good man starts doing nothing. As a moral, intellectual or political figure of recognised authority, Yeats cannot be drawn on; the articles of agreement in his self-contained partnership limit his liability while leaving him free to accept Frankfurt honours after office hours. This practice provides a second explanation of why Yeats held the reprehensible views about class, blood, education and warfare that he did. He was licensed to hold them by the provisions of Victorian legal concepts raised into spiritualist doctrines; under a different partnership, he wrote poetry. To be fair, Yeats never actively condoned fascist violence; he was never looking in that direction at the material time. To be fair, we no longer accept Voltaire's too-flattering dictum that, (only) as long as people believe in absurdities, they will continue to commit atrocities. But anything can be condoned, preferably in silence.

Was Yeats a fascist? Does the answer to that question determine one's sense of his political behaviour from early manhood to the end? The first question is too crudely constructed, for a positive answer consigns him to a category of people – he becomes a member of a 'class', as the logicians would put it. In this connection, it is only fair to make psychological as well as political observations. Yeats possessed great courage, and at times confronted formidable opponents. But his way of dealing with an opposing power, or with violence directed towards him, was to combine resistance with a form of covert negotiation. He moved between positions, was altered by what he opposed, and never underestimated the enemy. Part of him was the enemy.

Better perhaps to ask: was Yeats fascist? – to prefer the adjective over the noun. In this shape, the enquiry allows answers relating to individual specific events and occasions. Personally, I think the answer is that he was fascist on (for me) too many occasions. Perhaps the hurtfulness of this judgment should be tempered by the qualification that, on many of these, he was fascist *by doing nothing*. Although Roy Foster, to whom I am indebted many times over, hardly intended to provide me with a way of resolving the issue, he did so when he wrote that attempts to identify the Frankfurt episode as recognition by the Nazi State of 'a distinguished fellow traveller' have been comprehensively rebutted.[27] That is precisely what Yeats was, *on occasion*. He did not travel early, and he did not travel often. But, to paraphrase the law of treason, he gave comfort to democracy's enemies, to decency's enemies, to the enemies of art and culture. It was not a cause without effect, a victimless inaction. I am reminded of Robert Browning's Duke, he of the 900-year-old name: 'all smiles stopped together'.

I hope that readers will give serious consideration to my argument that roots of Yeats's effective behaviour should be traced well before his date of birth in 1865, to – more exactly – the famine years in County Down. What is significant is not just his grandfather-namesake's career in Tullylish, and not just his quitting the factory-town when he did. It is the unique, yet characteristically Victorian, interaction of that trajectory with the office-and-suburbs existence of Robert Corbet. I hope also that my account of Yeats's intervention in Glenmalure will convey an appreciation of his courage in the troubled Ireland of 1920, just as it should also indicate the damage done, alongside the rescue effected, within Iseult Gonne's marriage to Francis Stuart. Yeats's dealings with Joseph Hone, Dermot MacManus and Walter Starkie are still incompletely known, but at least none of them is to be further cast as a colourless or selfless disciple. I apologise (somewhat) for my fiction of Yeats's personal Blood Kindred – Clissmann, Moylett and Co. – but he who believes absurdities is open to being taken seriously.

I would like to end by emphasising a striking but uncommented-upon aspect of Yeats's last days. The company on the Riviera was not few – there was of course his wife, George, in residence; nearby were Edith Shackleton Heald, Hilda Matheson and Dorothy Wellesley; at a further remove the Irish painter Dermod O'Brien and his wife, likewise the Australian-born poet Walter Turner and his wife; and beyond that circle, it seems that the Austrian pianist Artur Schnabel and his Jewish wife were at hand. Also, it would appear, a nameless German who very shortly would write an extremely up-to-the-minute obituary for the Berlin stock-exchange's *Literary Gazette*. The list goes some way towards justifying Wellesley's recollection of German and Austrian acquaintances, as detailed in her otherwise baffling post-obituary in *The Times*. What were those 'new ideas'?

The striking absences are Yeats's own blood relatives – sisters, brother, son, daughter. For one who venerated nationality, race (in whatever sense), inheritance and family, he died abroad among strangers, none of the strangers native to the place. Mabel O'Brien did not even know the names of his English lady friends when she set about writing home to the poet's sister. Unusual coldness in the southern French weather had set off his angina, an external implacably real coldness with no Baudelairean nonsense or correspondence about it. Auden notes the significance of this – 'And snow disfigured the public statues.'

Canon A. D. Tupper-Carey, the Church of England's man in Monte Carlo, did the honours. The old Fenian conscience was buried in a temporary grave, almost a communal fosse. Sean MacBride would ferry him home, after the Holocaust.

Notes

In the Catacombs

1 George Mills Harper and Walter Kelly Hood (eds), *A Critical Edition of Yeats's* A Vision (1925). London: Macmillan, 1978, p. 222.

2 Roy Foster remarks that the additional fact of Yeats's having quoted Il Duce with approval 'cannot be ignored'. In practice, of course, it is ignored by being incorporated into a depoliticising narrative; see R. F. Foster, *W. B. Yeats, a Life: II, The Arch-Poet*. Oxford: Oxford University Press, 2003, p. 291. The passage from *A Vision* is found in *A Critical Edition*, p. 215.

3 Edward W. Said, *Freud and the Non-European* (introduction by Christopher Bollas, response by Jacqueline Rose). London: Verso, 2003, pp. 28–29. Said's engagement with Yeats began with his pamphlet, *Nationalism, Colonialism; Yeats and Decolonisation*. Derry: Field Day, 1988.

4 R. M. Kain, *Dublin in the Age of William Butler Yeats and James Joyce*. Norman: University of Oklahoma Press, 1962. See K. P. S. Jochum, *W. B. Yeats: A Classified Bibliography of Criticism* (2nd edn). Urbana & Chicago: University of Illinois Press, 1990, p. 189.

5 Samuel Beckett, *Disjecta*. London: Calder, 1983, p. 97.

6 For a detailed account see Adrian Lyttleton, *The Seizure of Power in Italy* 1919–1929. London: Weidenfeld & Nicolson, 1973.

7 The best treatment of the general problem is Roger Griffin, *The Nature of Fascism*. London: Routledge, 1993 (2nd edn), see especially the first two chapters. Other recent studies include A. James Gregor, *Interpretations of Fascism* (New Brunswick: Transaction, 1997) and Renzo de Felice, *Les Interprétations du fascisme* (Paris: Syrtes, 2000, trans. from the Italian edition of 1971) and Eugen Weber, *Varieties of Fascism* (New York: Van Nostrand, 1964).

8 See Lucien Goldmann, *Towards a Sociology of the Novel* (trans. Alan Sheridan). London: Tavistock, 1975.

9 See Nicholas Allen, *George Russell (AE) and the New Ireland* 1905–30. Dublin: Four Courts, 2003, esp. pp. 116–143, 154, 156.

10 W. B. Yeats, *Later Essays* (ed. W. H. O'Donnell). New York: Scribner's, 1994, p. 210. In 1933, under Hitler's orders, a 'New German Evangelical Church' had been established, with a view to purging assimilated Jews from the ranks of the German clergy. This provision was designed promptly to carry out in terms of personnel what Yeats contemplated at a more abstract and futuristic level. In 1935, he described the AE of *c.* 1896/7 as 'a German Christian born too soon'. See introduction to *The Mandukya Upanishad*. London: Faber, 1935.

11 In correspondence with Sybil Le Brocquy, MacManus in old age gave his birthday as 22 November 1891, though the year might be read as 1892; see NLI: Ms. 21,677.

12 Robert Fisk, *In Time of War, Ireland, Ulster and the Price of Neutrality 1939–1945*. London: Deutsch, 1983, p. 374.

13 Mrs Griffin did not exaggerate: the party's attitude to Irish citizenship was modelled very exactly on that of an early Nazi programme of 1920, made available in English in G. Feder (trans. E. T. S. Dugdale), *Hitler's Official Programme*. London: Allen & Unwin, 1934, see p. 22. References in this chapter to Irish police (Garda Síochána) and National Army

intelligence are taken from files (G2) preserved in Cathal Brugha Barracks, Dublin; due to the physical nature of these, a page or folio reference per item is not always practical.

14 Carey had his moment of fame in August 1941 when he was vigorously warned (and perhaps even beaten up) by the police to desist from anti-Semitic sloganising and attacks on Jewish businesses in central Dublin.

15 W. B. Yeats, *Autobiographies* (ed. W. H. O'Donnell and D. N. Archibald). New York: Scribner, 1999, p. 92.

16 WBY to Augusta Gregory, 1 March [1922], writing from Oxford. Access No. 4082.

17 National Archives, Dublin: Foreign Affairs 2003/17/1.

18 Quoted in Dermot Keogh, *Jews in Twentieth-Century Ireland*. Cork: Cork University Press, 1998, p. 125.

19 National Archives, Dublin: Foreign Affairs 102/229.

20 Yeats's endeavour to recruit relativity to his occult philosophy of history was doomed to failure; on the differences between 'the usually reversible time of theoretical physics and the irreversible times of thermo-dynamics and of human consciousness', see Kenneth Denbigh, *Three Concepts of Time* (1981). In any case, Yeats did not persist in his endeavour.

21 For a recent, if clumsy, study of the minister, see John P. Duggan, *Herr Hempel at the German Legation in Dublin 1937–1945*. Dublin: Irish Academic Press, 2003. A retired Irish Army officer, Duggan makes no reference to *Germany Speaks* and seems unaware of Hempel's meetings with Yeats. His book is dedicated 'to the memory of Eva Hempel', rather as one might dedicate an objective life of Hitler to Eva Braun.

22 *Irish Times*, 29 June 1965.

23 WBY to Dorothy Wellesley, 4 May [1937]. Access No. 6922.

24 Duggan, *Herr Hempel*, p. 19. See also Robert Greacen's review in *Books Ireland* in February 2004, p. 19.

25 Military Archives G2/X/1091 (docket 381). The report dates from December 1943, when Nazi fortunes were low.

26 On Elpis and O'Sullivan, see Military Archives G2/X/1091 (dockets 101, April, and 160, July 1942); on the Brughas' hospitality, see Duggan, *Herr Hempel*, p. 201. Rory Brugha junior (born 1917) later became a sanctified member of Fianna Fáil.

27 For an account of Evola in the eyes of one poet who remained in Nazi Germany, see Hans Thomas Hakl, ' "Die Alder Odhs fliegen den Adlern des Romanischen Legion entgegen": Gottfried Benn und Julius Evola' in Benn Johrbuch I (2003), pp. 100–31.

28 Richard Ellmann, *The Identity of Yeats* (2nd edn). London: Faber, 1964, p. 8.

29 A. Norman Jeffares, Anna MacBride White and Christina Bridgwater (eds), *Letters to W. B. Yeats and Ezra Pound from Iseult Gonne: a Girl Who Knew All Dante Once*. Basingstoke: Palgrave, 2004, p. 153. (Hereafter cited as *Knew Dante*.)

30 Duggan, *Herr Hempel*, p. 237 n.38, records British Foreign Office evidence which surely reveals Hempel's earlier political loyalties. The cryptic card-entry 'DVP 28–33' is best understood as his membership of the Deutschnationale Volkspartei for the five years leading up to Hitler's accession.

31 For some comment on Hempel's own difficulties in transmitting letters – he had no 'diplomatic bag' facility – see Carolle J. Carter, *The Shamrock and the Swastika: German Espionage in Ireland in World War II*. Palo Alta: Pacific Books, 1977, p. 38.

32 Ted Honderich, *Philosophy, a Kind of Life*. London: Routledge, 2001.

33 WBY to Edith Shackleton Heald, 12 September [1938]. Access No. 7303.

34 Jon Stallworthy, *Vision and Revision in Yeats's Last Poems*. Oxford: Clarendon Press, 1969, pp. 148–149.

35 WBY to Dorothy Wellesley, 15 August [1938]. Access No. 7290. Yeats reports that, in response to the essay he disliked, he wrote in the margin of the book four lines resembling what will become the closing lines of 'Under Ben Bulben'. However, his copy of W. Rose

and G. C. Houston (eds), *Rainer Maria Rilke: Aspects of His Mind and Poetry* (London: Sidgwick, 1938), contains no such draft.

36 James Pethica (ed.), *Last Poems: Manuscript Materials by W. B. Yeats.* Ithaca, London: Cornell University Press, 1997. See pp. 2–47 for matter relating to 'Under Ben Bulben'.

37 The words scored through here for clarity are in fact cancellations in the original.

38 Elizabeth Cullingford, *Yeats, Ireland, and Fascism.* London: Macmillan, 1981, pp. 144–145.

39 Stallworthy, *Vision and Revision*, p. 160.

40 Kiepenheuer (1880–1949) had published Bertholt Brecht's 'Baal' in 1922; his interest in publishing Franz Kafka's posthumously available writings was stifled by the Nazis.

41 The most extensive account is in Diana Souhami, *Gluck 1895–1978*. London: Pandora, 1988.

42 The writer subsequently altered his article when gathering it into a large collection of his own writings. Mc Cormack, 'The Historian as Writer or Critic?' *Irish Historical Studies* vol 30 no. 117 (May 1996).

43 Introduction to the never-published Scribners 'Dublin Edition' of his works; see William H. O'Donnell (ed.), W. B. Yeats, *Later Essays.* New York: Scribners, 1994, p. 216.

44 Elizabeth Cullingford (*Yeats, Ireland and Fascism*) cites Yeats's support of Home Rule in 1912 and notes his later desire to 'win' Ulster for the Irish State, but declines to comment on the frailty of these positions.

45 St John's Gospel, the sixth verse of the fourteenth chapter.

46 If the even more turbulent Middle East seems unconnected with those European legacies, it is important to recall that the state of Israel results from the Holocaust, as from other causes including the Balfour Declaration which Yeats tacitly approved. Edward Said's recommendation of a post-colonial Yeats arose from his own experiences as a Palestinian displaced by the Israelis.

47 A dangerously late-remaining victim of these provisions advertised in the columns of the London *Times* on Saturday, 11 February 1939, 'Head gardener, German Jew (32), formerly own large farm, well experienced in all duties and willing to be useful anywhere, seeks employment in England. Write Herbert Stern, Siegen-in-Westfalen, Emilienstr. 16.' Dorothy Wellesley's post-obituary of Yeats had appeared two days earlier.

48 13 August 1938, *Irish Independent*, p. 9. I believe the first academic citation of this dates to 1966, when it appeared (p. 358) in Donald T. Torchiana, *W. B. Yeats & Georgian Ireland.* Evanston: Northwestern University Press, 1966. Later, it was reprinted (in part, but including the German reference) in E. H. Mikhail, *WB Yeats; Interviews and Recollections.* London: Macmillan, 1977, vol. 2, pp. 231–232. Its neglect in Cullingford's work of 1981 can hardly be due to ignorance.

49 See *The Times* of 17 September 1935, cited by Andrew Sharf, *The British Press and Jews under Nazi Rule.* London: Oxford University Press, 1964, p. 45.

50 Joseph Hone, *W. B. Yeats 1865–1939.* London: Macmillan, 1942 (*recte* 1943), p. 467.

51 Michael Butler Yeats, *Cast a Cold Eye: Memories of a Poet's Son and Politician.* Dublin: Blackwater, [n.d.], p. 20.

52 Quoted in Max Weinreich, *Hitler's Professors; the Part of Scholarship in Germany's Crimes Against the Jewish People* (2nd edn, first pub. 1946). New Haven: Yale University Press, 1999, pp. 81–82.

53 *The Times*, 9 February 1939. The footnotes in *Letters on Poetry from WB Yeats to Dorothy Wellesley* (Oxford: Oxford University Press, 1964) are initialled in the same way, confirming Dorothy Wellesley's authorship of this obit. As an example of the discretion employed by Yeats's professional admirers, Roy Foster wholly ignores the second *Times* obituary; see R. F. Foster, *W. B. Yeats, a Life: I, the Apprentice Mage.* Oxford: Oxford University Press, 1997. pp. 165–166.

54 'I see small difference between Communism and Fascism, both being tyrannical. On the whole Hitler a better human being perhaps than Mussolini.' Dorothy Wellesley to WBY, 27 January 1937; see *Letters on Poetry*, p. 122.

55 See F. R. Gannon, *The British Press and Germany, 1936–1939*. Oxford: Clarendon Press, 1971, pp. 139, 263–264.

56 Obituaries also appeared in the *Blätter der Städtischen Bühnen*, the *Deutsche Rundschau*, the *Frankfurter Zeitung*, the *Frankischer Kurier* and the *Münchener Neueste Nachrichten*.

57 Stefan George is referred to also in Dutch obituaries for Yeats; see Roselinde Supheert, *Yeats in Holland*. Amsterdam: Rodopi, 1995, pp. 129, 227.

58 Or, at the very least, was in the confidence of a person to whom Yeats had given such access. The initials E. S. appear at the end of the obituary. Ernst Stein, whose translation of Yeats's early play, 'On Baile's Strand', was published in *Die Neue Rundschau* in November 1934, may well have been the unnamed German acquaintance referred to in Wellesley's obituary. His translation was used for the Bethge-Meissner production of 'The Countess Cathleen' in February 1934.

59 And there are plenty of these. As the second millennium ended, 'lives' of Yeats fell upon each other like starving refugees in search of bread. A. N. Jeffares published *W. B. Yeats; A New Biography* in 1988, his first contribution to the genre having appeared in 1949, just ten years after the poet's death; the new biography went into a second edition in 2001. Alastair Macrae and William Murphy published in 1995; Keith Aldritt, Stephen Coote and Roy Foster in 1997; Brenda Maddox and Terence Brown in 1999.

60 Cf. Mrs Rooney's 'This dust will not settle in our time'; Grey's remark became familiar after the publication of his memoirs in 1925.

A Troubled Mirror

1 Seamus Heaney, *Preoccupations: Selected Prose 1968–1978*. London: Faber, 1980, p. 107.

2 WBY to Katharine Tynan, [18 November 1887]. John Kelly (ed.), *The Collected Letters of W. B. Yeats: Vol. 1 1865–1895*. Oxford: Clarendon Press, 1986, p. 41.

3 See Seamus Deane, *Celtic Revivals; Essays in Modern Irish Literature 1880–1980* (London: Faber, 1985); *A Short History of Irish Literature* (London: Hutchinson, 1986); and especially *Strange Country; Modernity and Nationhood in Irish Writing Since 1790* (Oxford: Clarendon Press, 1998).

4 *Irish Times*, 10 June 1965. 'Bend Sinister', Denis Donoghue's review of A. N. Jeffares and K. G. W. Cross (eds), *In Excited Reverie: Centenary Tribute to W. B. Yeats 1865–1939* (London: Macmillan, 1965) had appeared on 5 June.

5 *Irish Times*, 16 June 1965.

6 *Irish Times*, 17 June 1965.

7 WBY to Olivia Shakespear, 13 July [1933]. Access No. 5915.

8 Joseph M. Hassett, *Yeats and the Poetics of Hate*. Dublin: Gill and Macmillan, 1986, p. 1; see also pp. 75–79 for discussion of Yeats and the collective unconscious. For a brief account of Jung's compliance with Nazi requirements in 1933–34, see Yosef Hayim Yerushalmi, *Freud's Moses: Judaism Terminable and Interminable*. New Haven: Yale University Press, 1991, pp. 48–49.

9 See Foster (2003), p. 708 n. 64.

10 W. B. Yeats, *A Vision* (revised edn). London: Macmillan, 1962, p. 8.

11 Elizabeth Cullingford, author of *Yeats, Ireland and Fascism* (1981).

12 See pp. 408–22.

13 Jurgen Habermas, *The New Conservatism: Cultural Criticism and the Historians' Debate* (ed. and trans. Shierry Weber Nicholson). Cambridge: Polity Press, 1989, p. 158. The article quoted here was originally published in 1988; it appears on pp. 140–172. On Heidegger's politics, see Victor Farias, *Heidegger et le nazisme* (n.p.: Verdier, 1987); and Richard Wolin, *The Politics of Being; the Political Thought of Martin Heidegger* (New York: Columbia University Press, 1990).

14 W. B. Yeats, *The King of the Great Clock Tower; Commentaries and Poems*. Dublin: Cuala Press, 1934, p. 37.

15 Habermas, *The New Conservatism*, p. 154.

16 Ibid., p. 148, original emphasis retained.

17 Hartmut Buchner (ed.), *Japan und Heidegger*. Sigmaringen: Thorbecke, 1989. This was a celebratory collection of essays published in conjunction with the philosopher's home town to mark the centenary of his birth.

18 WBY to Maud Gonne, 16 June [1938]. Anna MacBride White and A. Norman Jeffares (eds), *The Gonne–Yeats Letters 1893–1938*. London: Hutchinson, 1992, p. 451.

19 Z. Zajderowa, *The Dark Side of the Moon*. London: Faber, 1946. Eliot was in effect the publisher of the book, in addition to his role as sponsor.

20 Christopher Ricks, *T. S. Eliot and Prejudice*. Berkeley: University of California Press, 1988. In *The London Review of Books*, 9 May 1996, Tom Paulin reviewed Anthony Julius, *TS Eliot, Anti-Semitism and Literary Form* (Cambridge: Cambridge University Press, 1995).

21 See letter to Mrs George Yeats [18 November 1932]. Access No. 5781.

22 See Edward Said, *Orientalism*. London: Routledge, 1978, pp. 118–119.

23 '*Delacroix était passionnément amoreux de la passion, et froidement déterminé àchercher les moyens d'exprimer la passion de la manière la plus visible*' (from 'L'oeuvre et la vie d'Eugène Delacroix'), Charles Baudelaire, *Selected Critical Studies*. Cambridge: Cambridge University Press, 1949, p. 205.

24 WBY to Ethel Mannin, 26 October [1936]. Access No. 6682. This letter also illustrates Yeats's concern to distinguish between emotion and action. Suggesting that he and Mannin should not meet until after he had finished revising *A Vision* and completing his work on the *Upanishads*, he wrote, 'I think we have been working towards the same position, we have the same hatred of the built & mechanical, a hatred that sees no expression in action, perhaps the most we can discover is what we must not do.'

25 WBY to Ethel Mannin, 15 November [1936]. Access No. 6716.

26 Yeats, *Autobiographies* (1999), p. 115.

27 WBY to Edmund Dulac, 13 May [1925]. Access No. 4728.

28 T. S. Eliot, *The Metaphysical Poets* (*Times Literary Supplement*, 20/10/1921).

29 See Martin Heidegger, *An Introduction to Metaphysics* (trans. Ralph Mannheim). New Haven: Yale University Press, 1979, esp. pp. 42, 45, 50, 199, etc. Originally published in 1953, and first translated in 1959 by Günter Grass's future translator, the text had been delivered as lectures in 1935.

30 Ella O'Dwyer, *The Rising of the Moon: The Language of Power*. London: Pluto Press, 2003. This work originated in a doctoral thesis written under the qualified supervision of Professor R. A. Welch at the University of Ulster.

31 Edward Said, *Culture and Imperialism*. London: Chatto & Windus, 1993, p. 284.

32 Richard A. Kaye, *The Flirt's Tragedy; Desire without End in Victorian and Edwardian Fiction*. Charlottesville: University Press of Virginia, 2002, p. 14.

33 Foster (2003), p. 465.

34 Georg Simmel, *On Women, Sexuality and Love* (trans. G. Oakes). New Haven: Yale University Press, 1984.

35 Louis MacNeice, *The Poetry of W. B. Yeats*. London: Oxford University Press, 1941, p. 133.

36 WBY to Augusta Gregory, [5 June 1900]. Warwick Gould *et al.* (eds), *Collected Letters of W. B. Yeats; Volume II 1896–1900*. Oxford: Clarendon Press, 1997, pp. 536–537.

37 WBY to Florence Farr (Mrs Emery), [16 February 1906]. Access No. 349.

38 WBY to Olivia Shakespear, 12 January [1928]. Access No. 5062.

39 WBY to Desmond FitzGerald, 30 March 1933. Access No. 5853.

40 WBY to T. Sturge Moore, 12 February [1928]. Access No. 5076.

41 WBY to Olivia Shakespear, 24 July [1934]. Access No. 6072.

42 WBY to Ethel Mannin, 4 March [1935]. Access No. 6194.

43 WBY to John O'Leary, [8 August 1889]. *Collected Letters I*, p. 180.

44 WBY to the editor, *The United Irishman*, 30 December 1893. *Collected Letters I*, p. 373.

45 WBY to Sir Edward Marsh, 20 August [1916]. Access No. 3024.

46 WBY to Clement Shorter, 17 May 1918. Access No. 3441.

47 WBY to the organisers of Warriors' Day, 21 January 1921. Access No. 3850.

48 Quoted in Foster (2003) p. 257, as evidence of Yeats's 'ancient genius' for impartially irritating all shades of opinion.

49 WBY to unknown, 9 September 1933. Access No. 5938.

Some Paper Tigers

1 It is possible, even likely, that Auden intended *The Winding Stair and Other Poems* of 1933, which gathered together the 1929 volume and two sequences of 1932. Whichever is intended, the poems pre-date the era of aggressive international fascism.

2 See Edward Mendelson (ed.), *The English Auden; Poems, Essays and Dramatic Writings 1927–1939*. London: Faber, 1977, pp. 389–393.

3 For the bombing campaign, etc., see J. Bowyer Bell, *The Secret Army; the IRA 1916–1979*. Swords: Poolbeg, 1989, pp. 145–167.

4 Richard Ellmann, *Yeats, the Man and the Masks* (2nd edn). Oxford: Oxford University Press, 1979, p. xxv.

5 *Constructive Democracy*. London: Allen & Unwin, 1938. The accession date-stamp on the copyright deposit copy in the library, Trinity College Dublin, indicates that the book was in circulation in February 1938, eleven months earlier than Wellesley's relating it to Yeats's political views.

6 Bonn (1873–1965) published *Die Englische Kolonisation in Irland* (1906), and later adverted to his Irish travels in *Wandering Scholar* (1949).

7 For an extensive discussion of Mann's early statement of a political position, see Chapter 5 ('Unpolitics') in T. J. Reed, *Thomas Mann; the Uses of Tradition*. Oxford; Clarendon Press, 1974, pp. 179–225.

8 I am grateful to Professor Martin Pugh for his discussion of this issue.

9 Originally published in the Dublin University journal, *Hermathena*, the article has been absorbed into Mc Cormack, *From Burke to Beckett: Ascendancy, Tradition and Betrayal in Literary History*. Cork: Cork University Press, 1994, pp. 386–391.

10 K. P. S. Jochum, 'Yeats and the Goethe Plakette: An Unpublished Letter and its Context', *Yeats Annual* No. 15 (2002), pp. 281–287. See also Jochum, *W. B. Yeats, A Classified Bibliography of Criticism* (2nd ed). Urbana and Chicago: University of Illinois Press, 1990.

11 George Mills Harper and Walter Kelly Hood (eds), *A Critical Edition of Yeats's* A Vision *(1925)*. London: Macmillan, 1978, p. 214.

12 Hone (1943), p. 403n.

13 Foster (2003), p. 468.

14 See *Irish Independent*, 13 August 1938, p. 9, and the titles cited above where this material is rereprinted.

15 De Bosis also edited *The Golden Book of Italian Poetry*. London, New York: Oxford University Press, 1932.

16 Gustav Theodor Fechner *On Life After Death* (trans. Hugo Wernekke) 3rd ed. Chicago, London: Open Court, 1914. pp. 36, 43.

17 Ibid., p. 54.

18 Ibid., p. 53.

19 I quote from John Kelly, *A W. B. Yeats Chronology*. London: Palgrave, 2003, p. 284 (29 March 1933).

20 Fechner, *On Life After Death*, p. 75.

The Unspeakable Question

1 T. S. Eliot, *After Strange Gods; a Primer of Modern Heresy*. New York: Harcourt, Brace, 1934, p. 20. Originally delivered as the Page-Barbour Lectures at the University of Virgina in 1933, the book was never reprinted by Eliot. Among the modern heretics whom Eliot condemns by quotation in his Appendix are Herbert Read and John McMurray.

2 See Jason Harding, *The* Criterion; *Cultural Politics and Periodical Networks in Inter-War Britain*. Oxford: Oxford University Press, 2002, pp. 143–144. On evidence supplied by Mrs Valerie Eliot, Harding attributes the review in question to Montgomery Belgion (1892–1973), writing for Eliot as editor. At the end of the war, Belgion sought to play down Jewish suffering in Nazi Germany in displays of insensitivity which shock even Jason Harding. For Paulin's observations, see 'Undesirable', *London Review of Books* (9 May 1996), pp. 13-15.

3 For comment on the book's general reception, see Andrew Sharf, *The British Press and Jews under Nazi Rule*. London: Oxford University Press, 1964, pp. 76-77.

4 Harold Marcuse, *Legacies of Dachau; The Uses and Abuses of a Concentration Camp 1933-2001*. Cambridge: Cambridge University Press, 2001, p. 22.

5 *The Criterion*, vol. 15, no. 61 (July 1936), pp. 759–760. As a matter of fact, only one chapter of *The Yellow Spot* is devoted to the concentration camps. The reviewer's innumeracy may have been induced by the 'sensationalist' account of one prisoner, the poet Erich Mühsam, whose thumbs were broken to prevent him ever writing. Further to this end, Mühsam was then murdered on 9 July 1934 in Oranienburg.

6 WBY to Ethel Mannin, 6 April [1936]. Access No. 6530.

7 WBY to Ethel Mannin, [6 April 1936]. Access No. 6530.

8 See *The Collected Works of W. B. Yeats; Volume 5, Later Essays* (ed. W. H. O'Donnell). New York: Scribner's, 1994. The reference to Toynbee occurs in Yeats's introduction to a (never issued) Dublin collected edition. For Irish philo-Semitism, see W. J. Mc Cormack, *Fool of the Family; a Life of J. M. Synge*. London: Weidenfeld, 2000.

9 Yeats, *Later Essays* (1994), p. 29.

10 Cited in Foster (2003), p. 165.

11 Terence Brown, *The Life of W. B. Yeats; A Critical Biography*. Oxford: Blackwell, 1999, p. 238.

12 WBY to Maud Gonne, 25 December [1933]. *Gonne–Yeats Letters* 1992, p. 449. The mother of Sabina Wizniak had fled Berlin in 1936 for the comparative safety (and the squalor) of Warsaw's Ghetto, only to be murdered by the invaders (her fellow-countrymen) in 1939 or shortly afterwards. A daughter, aged about fifteen in 1939, died later in a concentration camp.

13 See, for example, *The Persecution of the Jews in Germany*, a 52-page pamphlet issued by the Board of Deputies of British Jews in April 1933 and made up principally of excerpts from German and British newspapers.

14 Military Archives (Dublin), G2/2278. The sales figures derive from Eileen Walsh, writing to Gonne on 22 November 1943 and citing Weiland as her authority: Walsh had just returned to Dublin from Germany at a date suggesting remarkable dedication.

15 Ibid. Gonne to Pfaus, 20 August 1939.

16 Yeats, 'The Irish Censorship', first published in *The Spectator*, 29 September 1928; reprinted in J. P. Frayne and Colton Johnson (eds), *Uncollected Prose by W. B. Yeats*, vol. 2. London: Macmillan, 1975, p. 480.

17 Austin Clarke was so damaged by his relationship with Lia Cummins that he was promptly confined to St Patrick's Hospital for several months. The experience is finally refracted in his long poem, *Mnemosyne Lay in Dust* (1966). Cummins was the granddaughter of John Ronayne, a Home Rule MP for Cork City in the 1870s. Educated at various posh convents, she went to Vienna to study medicine, but never completed a degree. Her capitulation to

Nazism may have psychological origins, but it also indicates one strand of Irish society capable of attaching itself to totalitarian and racialist politics. She died in 1943.

18 WBY to Dorothy Wellesley, 19 May [1937]; the passage quoted was silently omitted from the letter as printed in *Letters on Poetry from W. B. Yeats to Dorothy Wellesley* (1940), an omission perpetuated in the 1965 edition.

19 For a more extensive discussion, see James Knowlson, *Damned to Fame; the Life of Samuel Beckett*. London: Bloomsbury, 1996, pp. 275–281.

20 I owe this point to Jackie Blackman, who is working on Beckett's debt to Judaism.

21 See Anon., *Museum Judenplatz for Medieval Life in Vienna*. Vienna: Pichler Verlag, [n.d., c.2000], p. 114.

22 MacNeice (1941), p. 196.

23 WBY 'A General Introduction to My Work', p. 212

24 Ibid., p. 211

25 *Gonne–Yeats Letters*, p. 449.

26 Yeats, *Later Essays*, p. 212.

27 The threat to exterminate (*auszuroten*) was quoted in the *Manchester Guardian*, the *Daily Telegraph* and the *Daily Herald* (all 23 November 1938), and indeed a leading article in the *Daily Telegraph* of 28 June had already used 'extermination' as the desired end of Nazi policy. The *Sheffield Telegraph* of 6 August asked, 'must the Jews of Germany perish in the wilderness as a million Armenians did when deported by the Turks? . . . To the advocates of racial purity remorseless thoroughness is always justified.' (See Sharf, *The British Press*, pp. 96–97.) Yeats was working on proofs of *On the Boiler* early in December, having already reached the South of France (though hardly out of touch with world news) – see his undated letter to F. R. Higgins, Access No. 7354.

28 Yeats, *Later Essays*, p. 210.

29 In a footnote to *On the Boiler*, Yeats cites page numbers in Edmund Husserl's *Ideas: General Introduction to Pure Phenomenology* (in German 1913; trans. W. Boyce Gibson, 1931). When Martin Heidegger became Rector of Freiburg University, he barred his former mentor, Husserl, from using the library on the grounds of his Jewishness.

30 See *Daily Telegraph*, 6 July 1938, p. 15, quoted in F. R. Gannon, *The British Press and Germany 1936–1939*. Oxford: Clarendon Press, 1971, p. 193.

31 See David Bradshaw, 'British Writers and Anti-Fascism in the 1930s: Part Two, Under the Hawk's Wing', *Woolf Studies Annual* 4 (1998), pp. 41–66.

32 K. P. S. Jochum, *W. B. Yeats; A Classified Bibliography of Criticism*. [London:] Dawson, 1978, p. 510; Allan Wade, *A Bibliography of the Writings of W. B. Yeats*. London: Hart-Davis, 1951, p. 359–360.

33 Thomas Mann, *Diaries 1918–1939* (trans. Richard and Clara Winston). London: Clark, 1984, p. 196. British sympathisers sent Adrian Stephen to Germany in a vain attempt to gain direct access to the prisoner.

34 Kurt Pfeister, 'Der irische Dichter William Yeats', *Frankfurter Zeitung*, 14 February 1934, p. 1.

35 See Bradshaw, 'British Writers' pp. 45, 48, 58, etc.

36 See *What Was His Crime? The Case of Carl von Ossietzky* (London: printed by Camelot, 1937); Berthhold Jacob, *Weltburger Ossietzky* (Paris: Carrefour, 1937); Felix Burger and K. D. Singer, *Carl von Ossietszky*. (Zurich: Europa, 1937).

37 Brenda Maddox, *George's Ghosts; A New Life of W. B. Yeats*. London: Picador, 1999, p. 277.

38 Ethel Mannin, *Privileged Spectator*. London: Jarrolds, 1939. Quoted from E. H. Mikhail, *W. B. Yeats; Interviews and Recollections*. London: Macmillan, 1977, vol. 2, p. 273.

39 Geoffrey Thurley, *The Turbulent Dream; Passion & Politics in the Poetry of W. B. Yeats*. St Lucia: University of Queensland, 1983, p. 201. English-born, Thurley had taught briefly in

Trinity College Dublin in the 1960s, but was refused tenure. He subsequently and unsuccessfully applied for a chair in University College.

40 See Allan Wade, *The Letters of W. B. Yeats*. London: Hart-Davis, 1954, p. 834.

41 See Patrick O'Neill, *Ireland and Germany: a Study in Literary Relations*. Frankfurt: Peter Lang, 1985, p. 272; Heinz Kosok, 'Yeats in Germany' in A. N. Jeffares (ed.), *Yeats the European*. Gerrards Cross: Smythe, 1989, p. 260.

42 For the canonical text, see Yeats's *Poems*, p. 472; for the draft as sent to Dorothy Wellesley, see *Letters on Poetry from W. B. Yeats to Dorothy Wellesley*. London: Oxford University Press, 1964, pp. 180–181.

43 Ibid., p. 163.

44 Archibald MacLeish, 'Public Speech and Private Speech in Poetry', *Yale Review*, vol. 27 No 3 (March 1938), p. 544.

45 Ibid., pp. 544–545.

46 *Letters on Poetry*, p. 173.

47 MacLeish 'Public Speech', p. 545

48 Ibid., pp. 545–546.

49 Cullingford (1993) suggests that Yeats's attitude to Mann is ironic (see p. 2).

50 *Yale Review*, vol. 25 (1936), p. 21.

51 See Thomas Mann, *Reflections of a Nonpolitical Man* (trans. W. D. Morris). New York: Ungar, 1983.

52 Thomas Mann, *Order of the Day; Political Essays and Speeches of Two Decades*. New York: Knopf, 1942, pp. 125–126.

53 Yeats, *Later Essays*, pp. 239–240. The primitivist contempt for education may well have come from the German racist and archaeologist Leo Frobenius (1873–1935) whom Yeats had been studying in the spring of 1929. See WBY to Thomas Sturge Moore, 17 April [1929]. Access No. 5238.

54 Hone (1943), p. 467.

55 O'Shea (1985), p. 101.

56 Bradshaw (1992), pp. 206–207.

57 Foreign Affairs 216/303. 'The Refugee' by Emil Slotover originally dramatised the escape of a German Jew to Austria and his account of the concentration camps. After Hempel's intervention in 1943, the hero had become Hungarian and there were no concentration camps, at least not German ones. Of course, one wonders how the Minister heard of the original script before its first performance.

58 Ray Rivlin, *Shalom Ireland; A Social History of Jews in Modern Ireland*. Dublin: Gill and Macmillan, 2003, p. 109.

'My Frankfurt Honour'

1 Joseph Hone, *Ireland Since 1922*. London: Faber, 1932, pp. 9, 6.

2 Yeats, *Autobiographies* (1999), p. 244. The editors cite *Eckermann's Conversations with Goethe* for the date of 7 April 1829.

3 For a detailed account of the various Goethe awards in Frankfurt and elsewhere, see Eva Dambacher, *Literatur- und Kulturpreise 1859–1949; Eine Dokumentation*. Marbach: Deutsche Schillergesellschaft, 1966, pp. 57–64, etc. On the pre-1933 mayor, see Dieter Rebentisch, *Ludwig Landmann, Frankfurt Oberbürgermeister der Weimarer Republik*. Wiesbaden: Steiner, 1975.

4 For the record, the winners of Der Goethepreis der Stadt Frankfurt am Main from 1927 to 1945 were as follows:

1927 – Stefan Georg (writer);
1928 – Albert Schweitzer (medical doctor and philosopher);
1929 – Leopold Ziegler (philosopher);
1930 – Sigmund Freud (psychoanalyst);

1931 – Ricarda Huch (writer);
1932 – Gerhart Hauptmann (writer);
1933 – Hermann Stehr (writer);
1934 – Hans Pfitzner (musician);
1935 – Hermann Stegemann ('der Schriftsteller', writer);
1936 – Georg Kolbe (sculptor);
1937 – Guido Kolbenheyer (writer and philosopher);
1938 – Hans Carossa (medical doctor and writer);
1939 – Carl Bosch (industrial chemist);
1940 – Agnes Miegel (writer);
1941 – Wilhelm Schäfer (writer);
1942 – Richard Kuhn (medical scientist);
1945 – Max Planck (physicist).

The last-named was honoured by the post-Nazi authorities. From 1946 onwards, the award has been given in most, but not all, years. Distinguished recipients have included Karl Jaspers (1947), Thomas Mann (1949), Walter Gropius (1961), Ingmar Bergmann (1976), Raymond Aron (1979), Ernst Jünger (1982) and Sir Ernst Gombrich (1994). This information has been supplied by the Presse- und Informations amt der Stadt Frankfurt am Main. Professions (*Dichter, Arzt*, etc.) have been translated.

5 Thomas Mann, *Diaries 1918–1939* (trans. Richard and Clara Winston). London: Clark, 1984, p. 195.

6 These lists are preserved (with some correspondence) in the Institut für Stadtgeschichte, see Magistratsakten (47/69) 8.640.

7 See Dambacher, *Literatur- und Kulturpreise*, p. 59; Ernst Klee, *Das Personenlexikon zum Dritten Reich* (Frankfurt: Fischer, 2003, p. 341); Rolf Wiggershaus, *The Frankfurt School; its History, Theories and Political Significance* (Cambridge: Polity Press, 1994, pp. 128–129). The Institute for Social Research, which had an external association with the university, was also raided by the SA, and closed down: as a consequence T. W. Adorno and others of the 'Frankfurt School' went into exile. Robert C. Holub provides a detailed account of the committee discussion leading to the 1930 Goethe-Preis award in a web-based paper, 'From the Pedestal to the Couch: Goethe, Freud and Jewish Assimilation', in the course of which he quotes the Nazi paper, *Volkischer Beobachter*, to the effect that 'the anti-Semitic Goethe would turn over in his grave if he knew that a Jew had received a prize that carries his name', 29 August 1930, p. 2.

8 See Hugo Ott, *Martin Heidegger, a Political Life* (London: Harper/Collins, 1993, pp. 254–255, etc); Richard Wolin, *The Politics of Being; the Political Thought of Martin Heidegger* (New York: Columbia University Press, 1990, pp. 97–98). For a different perspective, see also *Lettres Choisies de Martin Buber 1899–1965*. Paris: CNRS Editions, 2004. (Especially pp. 196–212.)

9 Magistratsakten (47/69) 8.640 f.15v, also f.73. Several problems arise here: 1) where notable Nazis were in receipt of the Plakette (cf. Krieck), the correspondence in this file is minimal, thus paucity in the Goebbels discussion is not in itself evidence that he did not get his Plakette; however – 2) the first fifty or so recipients in 1932 were for the most part diligent locals, hardly in the same heroic mould as the Reichsminister for Propaganda, and consequently we might conclude that he declined the honour; finally – 3) the objects themselves were by now in short supply: a decision to reorder twenty is recorded (f.88) in October 1935, of which 10 per cent stayed in-Haus (Meissner in 1938, Bethge in 1941), with two significant awards to Paul Walden (like Yeats a non-German) in 1942 and the wily physicist Otto Hahn in March 1944. On the evidence here, it seems reasonable to conclude that Goebbels was duly chosen for the next Plakette after Yeats, though his receipt of this remains to be confirmed. (NB. Yeats papers are ff.63–72, and the second reference to Goebbels is f.73.)

10 *Das Literarische Echo*, Heft 7, April 1934, p. 427. I am grateful to Denis Tate for finding this reference. The Magistratsakten file gives 7 May for Krieck's award, indicating that discrepancies between dates may arise through confusion of a decision to award, with notification of the award, or actual presentation (or despatch) of the award. In Krieck's case, the publicity preceded the actual awarding.

11 See *Dokumente zur Geschichte der Frankfurter Juden 1933–1945*. Frankfurt-am-Main: Waldemar Kramer, 1963, pp. 80–81. I am grateful to Michael Lenarz for drawing my attention to this source. Herbert Graf published 'Memories of an Invisible Man' in *Opera News* (1972).

12 Much detail in this paragraph derives from Bettina Schültke, 'The Municipal Theatre in Frankfurt-on-Main: a Provincial Theatre under National Socialism', in Günter Berghaus (ed.), *Fascism and Theatre; Comparative Studies on the Aesthetics and Politics of Performance in Europe 1925–1945*. Oxford: Berghahn Books, 1996, pp. 157–171.

13 The official announcement is a major instrument of confusion on this issue. Referring to the manner in which the plaque/plakette is 'now given only in exceptional cases', it implies a lengthy prior history of bestowing the award which, in fact, was less than two years old. It was the Goethe-Preis, established by the left-liberal Jewish Oberbürgermeister Landmann in 1926, which could boast of a distinguished past.

14 Her father, Ernst Stünz (a master-carpenter), founded the Workers' Sports Movement; her mother Karoline (née Prinz) was the daughter of the Red Prinz, co-founder of the SPD in Frankfurt. Frau Arndt's husband died on 13 November 1940. During the Nazi years, Betty Arndt worked as bookkeeper in her father's business. Her son Güntar Arndt, is not persuaded of this identification.

15 Telegram from the German Legation, Dublin, to Foreign Office (Berlin), 14 March 1934, quoted in the original German and this translation in K. P. S. Jochum, 'Yeats and the Goethe-Plakette: an Unpublished Letter and its Context', *Yeats Annual* No. 14 (2002), pp. 282–283. The telegram had been sent by Georg von Dehn Schmidt.

16 Winter got the repeat orders in 1935, but an artist named Schiffers had made some twenty-two Plaketten in 1932, including those of Hauptmann and Mann. For the record, one should note that the early examples came in two distinct forms, first a round Plakette, and then a '*viereckige*' (four-sided or lozenge-shaped) model. Yeats seems to have got the second, Winter's work.

17 WBY to Friedrich Krebs, 4 June 1934. Access No. 6056. This was also the period leading up to the Night of the Long Knives (30 June 1934).

   Chastising David Pierce, who had confused a Preis with a Plakette, Jochum tells us that the award given to Yeats had been 'established in 1931, two years before Hitler and the Nazis took over the German government'. This would not seem to be true, for the earliest correspondence in Frankfurt is dated 19 May 1932. If the date of institution was 1932, it is important to note that the Nazis were the largest party in the Reichstag by July 1932, with Hitler already wielding considerable power, even if he was not yet Chancellor. The presence of the city's police chief among the organisers is some indication of the pressures acknowledged in launching the scheme.

18 Jochum, 'Yeats and the Goethe-Plakette', p. 284.

19 See Klee, *Das Personenlexikon*, p. 337.

20 Bettina Schültke, *Theater oder Propaganda? Die Städtischen Bühnen Frankfurt am Main 1933–1945*. Frankfurt: Waldemar Kramer, 1997, pp. 242–243, and more generally pp. 230–256.

21 Bethge is not mentioned in Thomas Nevin's sympathetic *Ernst Jünger and Germany: Into the Abyss 1914–1945*. London: Constable, 1997.

22 Joseph Wulf, *Theater und Film im Dritten Reich*. Gutersloh: Mohn Verlag, 1964, pp. 199–204.

23 See ibid., pp. 228–229, for reproductions of a '*Gutachten*' (or Testimonial) written by

Bethge in October 1933 on stationery of the Frankfurt municipal opera house and theatre bearing his additional stamp as Chefdramaturg Gau-Kulturwart für Hessen-Nassau. Bethge's promotion is recorded on p. 371.

24 See Julius Pokorny, *A History of Ireland* (trans. S. D. King). Dublin: Talbot Press, 1933. Pól O Dochartaigh, *Julius Pokorny 1887–1970*. Dublin: Four Courts, 2004. Pokorny survived the war, lived to the age of eighty-two, and died when knocked down by a tram. In 1967, and by now professor in Munich, Pokorny gave a student, Cecilie Roppelt, a text in Old Irish to assist her travels as a tourist in Ireland.

25 *Letters*, pp. 808–809.

26 On Rosenberg's anti-Irish journalism, see Mervyn O'Driscoll, *Ireland, Germany and the Nazis; Politics and Diplomacy 1919–1939*. Dublin: Four Courts, 2004, pp. 99, 114.

27 Conversation with Terence Brown, 9 March 2004.

28 See Magistratsakten (47/69) 8.640 f.94 for a typed copy.

29 For an incisive treatment of Bethge, Krebs and the politics of literary awards, see Björn Schaal, 'In Goethes Namen, von Goebbels' Gnaden: Der Frankfurter Goethepreis 1933–45', in *Frankfurter Rundschau*, 24 August 2002, p. 19. The title roughly translates 'In Goethe's Name, by Goebbels's Favour'.

30 Heinz Kosok provides much useful information in 'Yeats and Germany' in A. N. Jeffares (ed.), *Yeats the European*. Gerrards Cross: Smythe, 1989, pp. 258–271. Note also that Stein's translation of 'The Countess Cathleen' had been printed in Hellerau by Jakob Hegner in 1925. It can hardly have inspired the decision to stage the play in 1934, unless, that is, the translator personally proposed it. Stein's translations of 'On Baile's Strand' and 'The King's Threshhold' were published in November 1934 and October 1935 in *Die Neue Rundschau*.

31 *Frankfurter Theater Almanach 1919–1920*, p. 117. Plays by Gregory, Shaw, Synge and Yeats were performed.

32 See Kosok, 'Yeats in Germany', p. 260.

33 WBY to Frau Arndt. Access No. 6024.

34 W. B. Yeats, *Collected Plays*. London: Macmillan, 1957, p. 4.

35 See brief obituary in *Frankfurter Zeitung*, 3 November 1970.

36 Verhoeven later teamed up with the temporarily *un-deutsch* Fritz Peter Buch in the film *Jakko* (1941), for which Buch was scriptwriter and director. Their efforts were appraised in the *Völkischer Beobachter* on 13 October 1941. The second actor, Franz Schneider, had previously been at the Landestheater, Darmstadt; he is not to be confused with a namesake, a Frankfurt journalist who was associated with the Gruppe 47 (Gunter Grass *et al.*).

37 Schültke, *Theater oder Propaganda?*, p. 450. See also Ludwig Wagner, *Der Szeniker Ludwig Sievert; Studie zur Entwicklungsgeschicte d. Bühnenbildes im letzten Jahrzehnt*. Berlin: Bühnenvolksbundverlag, 1926. Carl Niessen (ed.), *Der Szeniker Ludwig Sievert; Ein Leben f. d. Bühne*. Cologne: Wallraf-Richartz-Museums, 1959.

38 See Wilhelm Merides, *Hermann Stehr: Leben und Werk*. Würzburg, [1964].

39 'Über Goethes menschliche Grösse (1933): Ansprache anlässlich der Entgegennahme des Goethespreises der Stadt Frankfurt a. M.' in a volume (pp. 76–82) of speeches, writings and diaries, *Das Stundenglas* (Leipzig: List, 1936).

40 Hone (1943), p. 403 n.1. For a Marxist reading of the play, see Michael McAteer, 'A Currency Crisis: Modernist Dialectics in *The Countess Cathleen*', in Betsy Taylor FitzSimon and James H Murphy (eds), *The Irish Revival Reappraised*. Dublin: Four Courts, 2004, pp. 187–204.

41 On Pinkus, see Walter A. Reichart, *Ein Leben für Gerhart Hauptmann*. Berlin: Schmidt, 1991, pp. 47–48.

42 See 'An Irishman's Diary, *The Irish Times*, 16 February 1934; the announcement dutifully described Clissmann as 'the young lecturer who replaced Dr Bauersfeld last year'.

43 Quoted in O'Driscoll, *Ireland, Germany and the Nazis*, p. 129. There is no evidence to

suggest that Bewley was present at the Frankfurt ceremonies (letter from Stadt Frankfurt am Main, Institut für Stadsgeschichte, 22 September 1993, to the present writer).

44 WBY to the editor of *Time and Tide*, [27 May 1933]. Access No. 5884.

45 Thomas Nevin, *Ernst Jünger and Germany; into the Abyss, 1914–1945*. London: Constable, 1997, pp. 142–143.

46 Binchy's article appeared in the March 1933 issue of *Studies*, a respected Jesuit periodical circulating widely.

47 'Once is as Good as Never' in Walter Benjamin, *Selected Writings; Volume 2, 1927–1934*. Cambridge, Mass.: Belknap Press, 1999, p. 741.

48 For some reason, Jochum claims that nothing can be recovered to provide further details of Wagner; but see *Frankfurter Biographie; Personengeschictliches Lexikon*. Frankfurt: Waldemar Kramer, 1994, vol. 2, p. 528. Wagner was a Dramaturg, like Bethge.

49 *Braune Blätter der Städtischen Bühnen Frankfurt am Main*, vol. 6, no. 19 (1939), pp. 225–228.

50 John London (ed.), *Theatre Under the Nazis*. Manchester: Manchester University Press, 2000.

51 See Barbara Panse, 'Censorship in Nazi Germany: The Influence of the Reich's Ministry of Propaganda on German Theatre and Drama 1933–45' in Berghaus, *Fascism and Theatre*, pp. 140–156.

52 Yeats, *Autobiographies* (1999), p. 344. The conversation, probably taking place on 23 Janaury 1909, included Augustine Birrell and John Henry Bernard. The topic developed from a consideration of wealth as an influence on knowledge and culture, with Birrell citing the example of Darwin's personal circumstances as a positive factor in the researching and writing of *On the Origin of Species*. Earlier in the month, Yeats had been examining the Yeats family's Ancestor Book with his sister's aid, and looking to reread novels by Balzac. Meanwhile, his friend J. M. Synge was a few months short of death.

53 See WBY to T. Sturge Moore, 23 February [1928]. Access No. 5080.

54 See Schültke, *Theater oder Propaganda?*, pp. 232–236.

55 George Bernard Shaw to Ashley Dukes, 3 January 1939; see Dan H. Lawrence (ed.), *Bernard Shaw, Collected Letters 1926–1950*. London: Max Reinhardt, 1988, p. 523. See my Introduction to a new edition of *Plays Pleasant* (London: Penguin, 2003).

56 WBY to Olivia Shakespear, 27 February 1934, *Letters*, p. 820.

57 See *Irish Times*, 17 January 1934. Maxton was familiar with Ireland from civil war days, if not earlier: he had been in contact with the youthful Sean MacBride at a time when the latter was reluctant to be seen associating with a notorious Clydeside Red. During these secret rendezvous, Maxton stayed with my aunt in Kilmainham.

58 The Institut für Stadgeschichte records provide quite extensive documentation concerning two expatriate Germans – Henry Janssen and Ferdinand Thun, industrialists/businessmen in the United States involved with the influential Carl Schuz Memorial Foundation. Janssen visited Germany in the summer of 1937, and corresponded with Krebs from the Kaiserhof Hotel in Bad Nauheim about Goethean hardware. He cited Ernst Beutler of the Goethehaus as an intermediary. In the supporting documentation, it is stated that SS Standartenführer Legationrat Dr Scholz at the German Embassy in Washington had been at work on the inclusion of the two men in some award scheme. Though the episode, which reached a positive conclusion, occurred three years after Yeats's initiation, it indicates the role of SS staff in legations and embassies, and also Krebs's interest in attracting non-residents to accept the Plakette. For these papers, see the second foliation sequence in Magistratsakten (47/69) 8. 640 ff.1–38 (esp. f.19), and also the first sequence f.123. The second sequence contains a list of Plakette winners to date, not including Yeats, while Anlage 3 details 'new Plakettes' issued after 1932 to seven individuals, including two with oriental names (Tai Chi Tao and Dr Ting). Perhaps this is evidence of racial liberalism on Krebs's part. I am especially grateful to Sylvia Goldhammer for her assistance with this material.

59 WBY to Shelah Richards, 1 January 1934. Access No. 5987.

60 WBY to Olivia Shakespear, 21 January [1934]. Access No. 5998.

61 See letter of 18 February 1934, to the editor of *The Spectator*. Access No. 6006; see also No. 5993.

62 WBY to Patrick McCartan, [16 February 1934]. Access No. 6004.

63 Yeats's letter to Frau Arndt is preserved in Pennsylvania State Library, and is now part of an autograph collection illustrating literary relations with Germany. It is a wholly isolated item, purchased in 1968, and no evidence of Frau Arndt's identity is attached. I am grateful to Stella Stelts for this information.

64 WBY to [Friedrich Krebs], 4 June 1934. Access No. 5056.

65 See Kosok, 'Yeats in Germany', p. 261. These occurrences, in print and onstage, scuttle Roy Foster's reliance on an implication in Klaus Peter Jochum's article, that Yeats was placed on a list of prohibited writers soon after February 1934.

66 WBY to the editor of *The United Irishman*, [28 January 1905]. Access No. 106.

67 Max Beerbaum, 'In Dublin', quoted by Klaus Peter Jochum, *Die dramatischen Struktur der Spiele von W. B. Yeats*. Frankfurt-am-Main: Athenaeum, 1967 [*recte* 1971], pp. 30–31.

68 Ernst E. Stein should not be confused with the literary critic, Ernst Stein (1915–1967), who worked in the Johannes R. Becher Archive in the DDR.

69 Allan Wade, *A Bibliography of the Writings of W. B. Yeats*. London: Hart-Davis, 1951, p. 13.

Intrusive Ghosts

1 WBY to Thomas McGreevy, 23 April 1934. Access No. 5648.

2 WBY to George Yeats, 11 July and 14 July [1932]. Access Nos 5699 and 5703.

3 Foster (1997), p. 20.

4 I have discussed Parnell in the context of 'Yeats's Gothic Politics' in Mc Cormack (1993), pp. 193–205; see also pp. 217–219.

5 Lambert MacKenna, 'The Bolshevik Revolution in Munich', *Studies* vol. 12 (1923), pp. 361–377. See Joachim Fischer, 'Ernst Toller and Ireland', in Richard Dove and Stephen Lamb (ed.), *German Writers and Politics 1918–39*. London: Macmillan, 1992, pp. 192–206. And Richard Dove, *He Was a German; A Biography of Ernst Toller*. London: Libris, 1990.

6 WBY to Sean O'Casey, 20 April 1928. Access No. 5101.

7 See WBY to Lennox Robinson, 23 March 1935. Access No. 6213.

8 Ernest Blythe, 'The Yeats I Knew', reprinted in Mikhail, vol. 2, p. 387. One of the few Irish Christian Scientists likely to have attended such a production was Douglas Gageby, later an Irish Army intelligence officer detailed to keep tabs on some members of the Blood Kindred.

9 Yeats did not sign the general petition, but chose to lobby the Prime Minister, Herbert Asquith, whom he knew personally. No letter to this effect has been traced. He did, however, write to the Home Secretary, Access No. 3002.

10 See Montgomery Hyde (ed.), *Famous Trials 9: Roger Casement*. London: Penguin, 1964, pp. 187–195.

11 Denis Gwynn, *The Life and Death of Roger Casement*. London: Cape, 1930. Carl Spindler, *The Mystery of the Casement Ship. With authentic documents*. Berlin: Kribe, [1931]. Robert Monteith, *Casement's Last Adventure*. Chicago: privately printed, 1932. Balder Olden, *Paradiese des Teufels, das Leben Sir Roger Casements*. Berlin: Universitas, [c.1933]. Mario Borza, *La Tragica Impresa di Sir Roger Casement*. [Verona]: Mondadori, [1934]. Denis Gwynn, *The Life and Death of Roger Casement*. London: Newnes, [1936]. Geoffrey Vincent de Clifton Parmiter, *Roger Casement*. London: Barker, 1936. W. J. Maloney, *The Forged Casement Diaries*. Dublin: Talbot Press, 1936. H. W. Guenther-Franken [pseud., i.e. Walther Guenther Schreckenbach], *Roger Casement. Ein Leben für Irlands Freiheit. (Von England verraten.)* Berlin: [1940]. Francis Stuart, *Der Fall Casement. Das Leben Sir Roger*

Casements und der Verleumdungsfeldzug des Secret Service. Hamburg: Hanseatische Verlag, [1940].

12 Gwynn, *The Life and Death of Roger Casement*, p. 20.

13 *Letters*, Wade, pp. 867–868.

14 Jeffares (1984), pp. 384–387.

15 Earlier references can be found in the as-yet-unpublished complete correspondence, but these add little to our understanding of Yeats's acquaintance with Casement. A letter written to Augusta Gregory as late as 13 December 1914 indicates that neither he nor she had met Casement. Beyond this date, Casement was in America, Germany or the Tower of London.

16 WBY to Dorothy Wellesley, *Letters on Poetry*, p. 123. Warwick Gould, in conversation, offered the diagnosis that Yeats was suffering from acute depression, and cited letters of Mrs Yeats from some years earlier. I think this is a plausible and humane view, but still wonder why he went into depression at this moment of Maloney's publication, which raised, in a very sloppy fashion, questions of politics and sex.

17 Cf. the appropriate period (1916) in Hone (1943), pp. 299–304; Ellmann (1948), pp. 216–219; Jeffares (1949), pp. 186–190; see also Brown (1999), pp. 227–231.

18 WBY to Augusta Gregory, 24 January 1913. Access No. 2073.

19 See Murphy (1978), p. 424.

20 WBY to Dorothy Wellesley, *Letters on Poetry*, p. 128.

21 Dorothy Wellesley, *Beyond the Grave; Letters on Poetry to W. B. Yeats.* Tunbridge Wells: C. Baldwin, printer, [n. d.].

22 Ibid., p. 55.

23 'The Death of Cuchulain' displays evidence of incomplete revision and of decisions made that death rendered final. The lyric quoted here originally featured as two, quite separate moments in the play; one feels that Yeats's merging of them was incompletely effected. That still leaves a lot of 'gender' indeterminedness. See Phillip L. Marcus (ed.), *The Death of Cuchulain; Manuscript Materials, Including the Author's Final Text.* Ithaca: Cornell University Press, 1982, pp. 105–165.

24 Donald T. Torchiana, *W. B. Yeats and Georgian Ireland.* Evanston: Northwestern University Press, 1966, p. 351. The chapter devoted to 'Purgatory' forms what is virtually an epilogue or appendix to Torchiana's account of Yeats's engagement with Swift, Burke, etc; the phrase quoted is in some respects an attempt to justify the inclusion of the chapter – a valuable analysis – in a book that does not wholly suit it.

25 Foster (2003), p. 629.

26 WBY to Dorothy Wellesley, 15 August [1938]. Access No. 7290.

27 See Marcus (ed.), *The Death of Cuchulain*, p. 109. The line 'I have heard it said in chapel' is written above a draft of the lyric with which the play ends; the same line also appears in drafts of the poem 'John Kinsella's Lament for Mrs Mary Moore'. The term 'chapel', with its implication of a small-scale or humble church building, was used throughout the Irish countryside to denote a Catholic church.

28 Walter Benjamin, *The Origins of German Tragic Drama* (trans. John Osborne). London: New Left Books, 1977, p. 162.

29 See Charles Rosen, 'The Ruins of Walter Benjamin', in Gary Smith (ed.), *On Walter Benjamin; Critical Essays and Recollections.* Cambridge (Mass.): MIT Press, 1991, pp. 152–153, 170.

30 Walter Benjamin, *Illuminations* (trans. Harry Zohn). London: Cape, 1970, p. 255.

31 WBY to Ethel Mannin, 30 November 1936 and 27 September [1936]. Access Nos 6733 and 6654.

32 WBY to Ethel Mannin, 9 October [1938]. Access No. 7312.

33 WBY to Ethel Mannin, 24 May [1937]. Access No. 6940. It is possible that Yeats was recalling his speech to the London meeting of PEN in December 1933, though other

occasions on which he enraged a potentially sympathetic audience may well have arisen in the intervening three and half years.

34 See WBY to Edith Shackleton Heald, 10 August 1937. Access No. 7037.

35 WBY to Ethel Mannin, 17 December [1937]. Access No. 7135.

36 See WBY to Mario Rossi, 8 October 1931. Access No. 5519.

37 There is an apt, if serpentine, logic to the Old Man's being descended from the French actor. Apart from theatrical continuity in being producer of a play, the Old Man introduces an action that recalls Talma's famous performance in Voltaire's 'Brutus': the play deals with the fatal conflict of father and son, and Talma shocked Parisians by appearing in a Roman toga.

38 The over-particular dating of the actions is, in fact, based on an inaccurate placing of the Irish Party's rejection of Parnell, which occured in December 1890 and not in 1889 as Torchiana would have it.

39 Foster (2003), p. 618.

40 Gifford Lewis (ed.), *The Selected Letters of Somerville and Ross*. London: Faber, 1989, p. 294.

41 Jeffares, MacBride White and Bridgwater (eds), *Knew Dante* (2004), p. 153.

Marital Politics and the House of Stuart

1 Yeats, *Autobiographies* (1999).

2 Wade (1943), p. 367; see also Desmond Chute in Mikhail (1977), vol. 1, p. 140.

3 Foster (2003), p. 111.

4 See WBY to Augusta Gregory, [18 May 1916]. Access No. 2955.

5 See *Letters*, vol. 2, p. 368. There is a good account of the difficulties and terrors of Iseult's upbringing in the prologue to Jeffares, MacBride White and Bridgwater (eds), *Knew Dante* (2004), p. 30.

6 WBY to Augusta Gregory, [4 May 1910]. Access No. 1346.

7 WBY to Maud Gonne, [21 May 1916]. Access No. 2958.

8 WBY to Augusta Gregory, [3 July 1916]. Access No. 2996.

9 These have now been discussed in *Knew Dante*, pp. 150–176.

10 WBY to Augusta Gregory, 19 August [1916]. Access No. 3022.

11 WBY to W. T. Horton, 8 September [1916]. Access No. 3255.

12 WBY to Augusta Gregory, 22 September 1917. Access No. 3328.

13 WBY to Augusta Gregory, 8 September [1917]. Access No. 3320.

14 WBY to Augusta Gregory, 14 August [1916]. Access No. 3017.

15 WBY to Iseult [Gonne], 18 August [1918]. Access No. 3472.

16 Tzvetan Todorov, *Hope and Memory: Lessons from the Twentieth Century*. Princeton: Princeton University Press, 2003, pp. 247-248. For a more extended treatment, see Chapter 2, 'The Beautiful Community: the Fascist Legacy of Charles Péguy', in David Carroll, *French Literary Fascism; Nationalism, Anti-Semitism and the Ideology of Culture*. Princeton: Princeton University Press, 1995.

17 See WBY to Augusta Gregory, 12 August [1916]. Access No. 3016.

18 WBY to Iseult [Gonne], 9 February [1918]. Access No. 3408.

19 WBY to Augusta Gregory, 25 May [1916]. Access No. 2964.

20 WBY to G. W. Russell, [c. 5 May 1919]. Access No. 3603.

21 WBY to Iseult [Gonne], [18 August 1918, writing from the St Stephens' Green Club, Dublin]. Access No. 3473.

22 See WBY to Lennox Robinson, 18 October [1919]. Access No. 3663.

23 WBY to G. W. Russell, [c. 5 May 1919]. J. H. Thomas (1874-1949) was a leading moderate in the Labour party and trade-union movement, subsequently obliged to quit the party and deprived of his pension by his union. Access No. 3603

24 See Access No. 4198.

25 Maud Gonne to WBY, June [1920], *Gonne–Yeats Letters* (1992), p. 402.

26 See *Gonne–Yeats Letters*, p. 402; also *Knew Dante*, p. 118.
27 WBY to George Yeats, [30 July 1920]. Access No. 3750.
28 WBY to George Yeats, [30 July 1920]. Access No. 3750.
29 WBY to George Yeats, [31 July 1920]. Access No. 3751.
30 WBY to George Yeats, [1 August 1920]. Access No. 3752.
31 See *Gonne–Yeats Letters*, p. 402.
32 WBY to George Yeats, 4 August [1920]. Access No. 3761.
33 WBY to George Yeats, 1 August [1920]. Access No. 3754.
34 WBY to George Yeats, 10 August [1920]. Access No. 3768.
35 WBY to George Yeats, 7 August [1920]. Access No. 3764.
36 WBY to Iseult Stuart, 1 September [1920]. Access No. 3775.
37 WBY to Augusta Gregory, 3 August [1920]. Access No. 3756.
38 WBY to George Yeats, 7 August [1920]. Access No. 3764.
39 WBY to Augusta Gregory, 3 August [1920]. Access No. 3756.
40 WBY to George Yeats, 4 August [1920]. Access No. 3760.
41 WBY to George Yeats, 4 August [1920]. Access No. 3761.
42 WBY to George Yeats, 1 August [1920]. Access No. 3754.
43 WBY to Augusta Gregory, 3 August [1920]. Access No. 3756.
44 Quoted in Foster (2003), p. 175.
45 WBY to George Yeats, [1 August 1920]. Access No. 3752.
46 WBY to Iseult Stuart, 10 April [1921]. Access No. 3901.
47 WBY to Augusta Gegory, 9 August [1921]. Access No. 3960.
48 Ann Saddlemyer, *Becoming George; The Life of Mrs W. B. Yeats*. Oxford: 2002, p. 278.
49 WBY to George Yeats, 4 August [1920]. Access No. 3761.
50 WBY to George Yeats, 6 August [1920]. Access No. 3763.
51 See Foster (2003), p. 208.
52 WBY to Ezra Pound, 22 August [1920]. Access No. 3771.
53 WBY to Lennox Robinson, 1 September [1920] Access No. 3776.
54 WBY to George Yeats, 2 August [1920]. Access No 3755.
55 WBY to Olivia Shakespear, 9 March [1933]. Access No. 5836. I give the text as available in the electronic edition.

Morbus Démocraticus

1 WBY to D. Fitzgerald, 23 January 1924. Access No. 4456.
2 According to a three-page typescript about Jephson O'Connell (NLI Ms. 22,103 (iii)), written by his fellow-officer Dermot MacManus, the former had been a British Army chaplain who attached himself to Tom Barry's flying column in the early days of the Troubles: though he acted solely in a spiritual capacity, O'Connell was disciplined by the Catholic Bishop of Cork. MacManus cannot be taken as a wholly reliable witness, and the typescript is remarkably vague when discussing more important aspects of O'Connell's career.
3 WBY to Augusta Gregory, 26 January 1924. Access no. 4461; WBY to Edmund Dulac, 28 January 1924. Access No. 4462; WBY to John Quinn, 29 January 1924. Access No. 4464.
4 WBY to Londonderry, 9 February 1924. Access No. 4473. Also to Thomas Nally, 28 February 1924. Access No. 4489. Nally was a playwright whose work had been held over for years.
5 John M. Regan, *The Irish Counter-Revolution 1921–1936*. Dublin: Gill and Macmillan, 1999. pp. 182–183.
6 The *Connacht Telegraph* of 31 July 1915 reported, 'Lieutenant Dermot A. M. MacManus who has recently been severely wounded at Gallipoli is the second son of the late Dr Leonard Strong MacManus, of Mayo House Wandsworth Common, London, and Killeaden House Co. Mayo. Lieutenant MacManus entered Sandhurst in February 1911, and

was gazetted to the 1 Battallion Royal Inniskilling Fusiliers in March 1912.' I am grateful to Anthony J. Jordan for this reference.

7 Sean O'Casey, 'Juno and the Paycock', in John P. Harrington (ed.), *Modern Irish Drama*. New York: Norton, 1991, pp. 253–254, 234.

8 See Bruce Arnold, *Jack Yeats* (New Haven: Yale University Press, 1998, pp. 211–212) for the Yeatses in Paris; Charles Bewley, *Memoirs of a Wild Goose* (Dublin: Lilliput, 1989, pp. 83–85) for a colourful account of the Race Convention and de Valera's manipulation of his female supporters.

9 See Homen Christo, 'L'Esprit fasciste en France', *Centre International d'Études sur le Fascisme Annuaire No.* 1 (1928), p. 177. Yeats's Abbey Theatre co-director, Walter Starkie, was a leading light in the centre.

10 Ellmann (1948), p. 245, quoting an unpublished speech; see also Hone (1943), pp. 364–365.

11 Hone (1943), pp. 365–367; by a comparable strategem, Jeffares (1949) manages to postpone reference to Mussolini until treating the Yeats of 1931.

12 WBY to Olivia Shakespear, 21 June [1924]. Access No. 4570.

13 Foster (2003), p. 291. See p. 793 (column 1) for the index reference.

14 In his review of *The Arch-Poet* for the *Times Literary Supplement* (26 September 2003), Declan Kiberd rightly chides Foster for a degree of inherited Yeatsian anti-Catholicism, though it suits neither Foster nor Kiberd to admit that *The Catholic Bulletin*'s analysis of the poet's social origins and class position was crudely accurate; see Mc Cormack, *From Burke to Beckett: Ascendancy, Tradition and Betrayal in Literary History*. Cork: Cork University Press, 1994, pp. 311–319.

15 For Koestler, see *The Ghost in the Machine* (1970); see Griffin, *The Nature of Fascism*. London: Routledge, 1993 (3rd edn), p. 186, etc.

16 Foster (2003), pp. 299, 719 n.16.

17 See Hone (1943), p. 459. The visit (by Professor Bose) is not included in John Kelly's *A W. B. Yeats Chronology*. London: Palgrave, 2003. Hone's article appeared in the *Irish Statesman*, 27 June 1924, pp. 491–492. On 11 July, a letter of support from Francis Jervois was published (p. 558).

18 Augusta Gregory, *Journals*, vol. 2. Gerrards Cross: Smythe, 1987, p. 169. See also Terence de Vere White, *Kevin O'Higgins* (first pub. 1948). Dublin: Anvil Press, 1986, p. 225, for O'Higgins's 1926 initiative in this regard.

19 See the present writer's Appendix, 'Lecky, Mark Twain and Literary History' in Donal McCartney, *W. E. H. Lecky, Historian and Politician, 1838–1903*. Dublin: Lilliput Press, 1994, pp. 195–207; and his Introduction to A. Trollope, *Phineas Finn; the Irish Member* (ed. Hugh Osborne and David Skilton). London: Everyman, 1997, pp. xvii–xxxv.

20 See John P. Frayne and Colton Johnson (eds), *Uncollected Prose by W. B. Yeats: Volume Two*. London: Macmillan, 1975, pp. 438–439.

21 See Robert Fisk, *In Time of War; Ireland, Ulster and the Price of Neutrality 1939–45*. Dublin: Gill and Macmillan [n.d.], pp. 385–386, etc. Mahr's Hartmann would seem too young to have been Robinson's guru, having been born in 1909 and only reaching Ireland in 1937. The philosopher, on the other hand, is already long dead, though he had an Irish disciple in John Henry Bernard (1869–1927), successively Dean of St Patrick's Cathedral, Archbishop of Dublin and Provost of Trinity College: see 'Estrangement' in Yeats's *Autobiographies*.

22 See 'On the Boiler' in Yeats, *Later Essays* (1994), p. 231.

23 Yeats, *Autobiographies* (1999), p. 41.

Surfaces

1 *Foster* (2003), p. 111.

2 See 'Judges's Costumes' in Donald R. Pearce (ed.), *The Senate Speeches of W. B. Yeats*. London: Faber, 1961, p. 126.

3 Cullingford (1981), p. 71. This author's preference for paraphrase over criticism obscures Yeats's own tendency to take belief for observation, as in the matter of courtly cottages.

4 'The Child and the State', first published in the *Irish Statesman*, December 1925, reprinted in Pearce (ed.), *The Senate Speeches*, p. 172.

5 Pearce (ed.), *The Senate Speeches*, pp. 95–96, 99, 102.

6 Ibid., (appendix V), p. 179.

7 WBY to F. R. Higgins, 7 November [1938]. Access No. 7327. The play was 'The White Steed', dealing with clerical intolerance in rural Ireland. For comment of limited plausibility on the theatre's attitude, see Earnán de Blaghd, 'The Yeats I Knew', collected in Mikhail, vol. 2, pp. 389–90.

8 Pearce (ed.), *The Senate Speeches*, (appendix V), p. 179.

9 Yeats, *Later Essays* (1994), p. 243.

10 Jack Yeats to John Quinn, 21 February 1922; quoted in B. L. Reid, *The Man from New York: John Quinn and His Friends*. New York, 1968.

11 W. J. Mc Cormack, 'Communicating with Prisoners', in *In the Prison of His Days; A Miscellany for Nelson Mandela*. Dublin: Lilliput Press, 1988, pp. 77–92.

12 See Bruce Arnold, *Jack Yeats*. New Haven: Yale University Press, 1998, p. 249, where the conflict is bizarrely described as 'an unsuccessful republican rebellion in Spain'.

13 'It is a most amusing, animated book, showing more of the true mind & life of Jack Yeats than Jack Yeats' biography will ever show. It is the best of talk & the best of writing and at the top of a fine fashion – I think of James Joyce's linked associations. "My new book is about the night & I have had to put language asleep" he said to me a few days ago.' WBY to Jack Yeats, 18 July [1930]. Access No. 5359. The in-progress collected letters of WBY as yet include only four surviving letters to his brother.

14 Quoted by Hilary Pyle, *Jack B. Yeats, a Biography*. London: Routledge, 1970, p. 128.

15 JBY to WBY, excerpt from a letter of 1906, and JBY to WBY, 1 July 1908; Joseph Hone (ed.), *J. B. Yeats: Letters to his Son W. B. Yeats and Others 1869–1922*. London: Faber, 1944, pp. 97, 108–109. For an exhaustive account, see William M. Murphy, *Prodigal Father; the Life of John Butler Yeats (1839–1922)*. Ithaca: Cornell University Press, 1978.

Blood

1 Oscar Wilde, 'Mr Mahaffy's New Book', in Richard Ellmann (ed.), *The Artist as Critic; Critical Writings of Oscar Wilde*. London: Allen & Union, 1970, p. 81.

2 'Commentary on a Parnellite at Parnell's Funeral', in WBY, *The King of the Great Clock Tower, Commentaries and Poems*. Dublin: Cuala Press, 1934, p. 23.

3 'Introduction' [1937] in Yeats, *Later Essays* (1994) pp. 215–216.

4 Tim Armstrong, 'Giving Birth to Oneself: Yeats's Late Sexuality', *Yeats Annual* No 8 (1991), pp. 39–58.

5 Raymond B. Cattell, *Psychology and Social Progress*. London: Daniel, 1933, p. 410.

6 Cattell, *The Fight for our National Intelligence*. London: King, 1937, p. 141 and p. 134.

7 *German Education Today*.

8 WBY, *Later Essays*, p. 238.

9 'On the Boiler', Yeats, *Later Essays* p. 238.

10 WBY to Olivia Shakespear, 7 June [1922]. Access No. 4135.

11 See Access Nos 5667–5668, both dated 9 May [1932]. The immensely wealthy (and pro-communist) Cunard lived with her black musician lover.

12 WBY to Margot Collis, 26 November [1934]. Access No. 6136. Yeats regularly promoted MacManus up the officer grades of the National Army, perhaps in compensation for MacManus's resignation as early as 1923 when he became governor of Mountjoy Jail in Dublin.

13 Maddox (1999), p. 264. MacManus, when unexpectedly confronted with a published account of this aspect of his life, naturally offered a different view. In 1950, he was shown a copy of

Roger McHugh's edition of Yeats's letters to Margot Collis: in response to the unidentified Church of England curate who had produced the book, he explained the hunting-field incident as occurring when 'an ex-groom' of his had tried 'to raise a riot': see TS copy MacManus to unidentified cleric, 18 October 1970 in NLI Ms. 21,677. By 1968 or earlier, MacManus was living in Harrogate, Yorkshire.

14 WBY to Wyndham Lewis [12 August 1928]. Access No. 5143.

15 See Gregory, *Journals*, vol. 2, p. 306. Gregory (or her editors) gives Gottgetreu's first name as Emil. Erich Gottretreu was born in Chemnitz, 31 July 1903, the son of Adolf and Elsbeth (née Baswitz); educated at Berlin University; married Sara Reznik, 23 June 1934; freelance journalist 1925–28, on the *Volksbote* (Lübeck) in 1929, with the Berlin Social Democrats' press service 1930–33; settled in Palestine late 1933.

16 See Erich Gottgetreu, *Haben Sie gelesen, dass . . . ?* Berlin: Dietz, 1929. Several chapters of the little book deal with Irish encounters and topics, including the Shannon electrification scheme, the crypt in St Michan's Church, Dublin, a visit to G. B. Shaw's birthplace in Synge Street, Dublin, and the moral condition of Adrigoole County Cork in the 1920s. There is no reference to Yeats, Lady Gregory or Coole Park, though theatre and drama recur as personal interests of the author.

17 I draw here on Paul Scott Stanfield, *Yeats and Politics in the 1930s*. London: Macmillan, 1988, pp. 61–62, etc. In keeping with the practice among Yeats 'scholars' of that period, Stanfield plays down Yeats's commitment to extreme right-wing politics, omitting the reference to 'German legislation' when quoting (p. 173) Yeats's exposition of *Purgatory* and its background. Ironists might term this a *trahison des clercs*.

18 See Starkie's unpublished autobiography, TCD Ms. 9193 ff.477–487.

19 TCD Ms 9187 f.343.

20 WBY to George Yeats, [after 27 April 1932]. Access No. 5653.

21 See WBY to George Yeats, [?0 October 1934]. Access No. 6116. These manoeuvres were preliminary to his selection of material for *The Oxford Book of Modern Verse*. For Auden in 1934, see Humphrey Carpenter, *W. H. Auden, a Biography*. London: Allen & Unwin, 1981, p. 69. I am grateful to Gretta Rubik for discussing the civil war situation.

22 Quoted by David Bradshaw in *Woolf Studies Annual* 4 (1998), p. 42.

23 WBY to Ethel Mannin, 11 December [1936]. Access No. 6751. Yeats's lateral thinking on the Abyssinian war strangely resembles Starkie's unpublished account of how Mussolini's adventure distracted him at the moment he should have been attending to Bolshevik subversion in Spain: 'The Abyssinian War monopolised our attention and my ears were deafened by the slogans shouted by militarists and war-mongers. Instead of the Red Star, the Hammer and the Sickle, and the Communist slogans of Red Revolution my ears were deafened by cries of Duce, Duce!' – see TCD Ms. 9193 f.93. Thus, Yeats excuses himself for not defending Abyssinia from colonialist invasion by arguing his suspicions of British interest, while Starkie (after the Second World War) presents Mussolini as a distraction from the more important business of opposing Russian influence in Spain. For evidence of Yeats's contacts with Starkie during late 1936, see George Yeats to Dermot MacManus (ts copy) in NLI 21,677.

24 WBY to Horace Reynolds, 24 December 1932. Access No. 5799.

25 See Cullingford (1981). p. 224, citing Pablo Neruda's *Memoirs* (English trans. 1977).

26 'Priceless replies poured in from all over. One was from Yeats, Ireland's national poet; another from Selma Lagerlöf, the notable Swedish writer. They were both too old to travel to a beleaguered city like Madrid, which was being steadily pounded by bombs, but they rallied to the defence of the Spanish Republic.' Neruda, *Memoirs*. Harmondsworth: Penguin, 1977.

27 The case of Lagerlöf deserves attention in its own right, for it evidences the persistent refusal of Yeats's biographers to verify evidence with regard to his politics. Seven years older than

Yeats, she was certainly unable to travel to Madrid. But her career suggests that sympathy with the legitimate government would have come quite naturally. She had marked the end of the Great War with a pacifist novel, *Bannlyst* (1918), dealing with its baleful consequences. In the 1920s, she was active in the women's movement and, with the rise of Nazism, she assisted German intellectuals and writers to escape from Germany. Specifically, she arranged for the Jewish poet Nelly Sachs to obtain a Swedish visa. Later she donated her gold Nobel Prize winner's medal to a Finnish fund-raising effort during the Winter War.

28 Foster (2003), p. 575. It goes without saying that, when the *Left Review* organised the poll known as 'Authors Take Sides', Yeats did not.

29 While *Blood Kindred* was being prepared for publication, I submitted a summary article – 'Yeats's Politics since 1943: Approaches and Reproaches' – to *The Yearbook of English Studies* (University of Reading), see vol 35, 2005. Referring to the work of Asa Risberg and other Swedish sources, the article demonstrates how the Neruda claim for Selma Lagerlof's support in 1937 is contradicted by primary evidence. Adam Feinstein's *Pablo Neruda: A Biography* (London: Bloomsbury, 2004) makes no claim relative to either Lagerlof or Yeats as supporters of the Spanish Republic. For a detailed account of this phase of Neruda's life, written by a fellow Chilean, see Sergio Macías Brevis, *El Madrid de Pablo Neruda* (Madrid: Tabla Rasa, 2004), esp. p. 151 for the Writers' Congress.

30 WBY to Ethel Mannin, 24 June [1935]. Access No. 6265

31 WBY to Ethel Mannin, 1 March [1937]. Access No. 6835.

32 See Emily E. P. MacManus, *Matron of Guy's*. London: Melrose, 1956. Apart from a mildly anti-Semitic story about Ike Rosenstein (p. 37), the book suggests no ideological hang-up incompatible with the divided loyalties of those middle-class Irish who thought themselves Anglo-Irish. Records in Trinity College indicate that MacManus went on the books in February 1920 and, at the commencement of the academic year 1920/21, was listed as a senior sophister (i.e. final-year) undergraduate. He never graduated. The professor of astronomy's lectures were open to the general public.

33 Ts by MacManus preserved in TCD Library (HIB P 820: 3: 17), 'The Irish Literary Revival 1890–1935', p. 6.

34 WBY to Olivia Shakespear, 20 September [1933]. Access No. 5942.

35 Military Archives, G2/1680, letter of 6 November 1941 to a Garda superintendent.

36 See Saddlemyer, (2002), p. 510. The privacy of their discussions excluded even George Yeats.

37 WBY to Dermot MacManus, 31 May [1933]. Access No. 5886.

38 F. C. Molloy, 'Francis Stuart, W. B. Yeats, and *To-Morrow*', *Yeats Annual* No. 8 (1991), pp. 214–224. See also Access No. 4614.

39 WBY to Olivia Shakespear, 20 September [1933]. Access No. 5942.

40 WBY to Shri Purohit Swami, 11 July [1935]. Access No. 6286.

41 WBY to Dermot MacManus, 23 May [1936]. Access No. 6564.

42 Much has been made by the Forgery Theorists of Yeats's support for W. J. Maloney's *The Forged Casement Diaries* (1936): no copy of the book was to be found in the poet's library two years later. See O'Shea.

43 WBY to Dorothy Wellesley, 8 February [1937]. Access No. 6804.

44 See WBY to Olivia Shakespear, 9 March [1933]. Access No. 5836.

45 WBY to Ethel Mannin, 11 February [1937]. Access No. 6806.

46 See Andrew Sharf, *The British Press and Jews under Nazi Rule*. London: Oxford University Press, 1964, p. 28, quoting 'The Effects of Propaganda' from *The Weekly Review* of 29 December 1938. The *Review* was successor to *G. K.'s Weekly*, a magazine edited by G. K. Chesterton which in September 1933 had dismissed stories of 'the so-called persecution of the Jews in Germany'.

47 WBY to Dorothy Wellesley, 26 February [1937]. Access No. 6827.

Ceremonies and Innocence

1 WBY to Augusta Gregory, [13 December 1909]. Access No. 1242.

2 See WBY to Augusta Gregory, [28 December 1913]. Access No. 2343.

3 See Birgit Bramsback, 'William Butler Yeats and The Bounty of Sweden', *Moderna Språk*, vol. 82, no. 2 (1988), pp. 97–106. The first Anglophone winner of the Nobel Prize for Literature (established 1901) had been Rudyard Kipling in 1907.

4 'The Bounty of Sweden', Yeats, *Autobiographies* (1999), p. 391.

5 WBY to John Quinn, 7 November [1923]. Access No. 4395.

6 'The Bounty of Sweden', pp. 394–395.

7 Ibid., p. 398.

8 Ibid., p. 413.

9 'On the Boiler', *Later Essays* (1994), p. 238.

10 'The Bounty of Sweden', p. 418.

11 See Yeats, *Later Essays*, pp. 34–46. The best introduction to a consideration of Yeats's attitude to Balzac is Warwick Gould, 'A Crowded Theatre: Yeats and Balzac', in A. N. Jeffares (ed.), *Yeats the European*. Gerrards Cross: Smythe, 1989, pp. 69–90.

12 WBY to Olivia Shakespear, 25 August 1934. Access No. 6087. The astrological summary is quoted from Saddlemyer (2002), p. 205.

13 WBY to Olivia Shakespear, 24 July [1934]. Access No. 6072.

14 See Foster (2003), pp. 146–147.

15 Ibid., p. 141.

16 See Edgar Pankow, 'Lecktüre zum Tode: Sigmund Freud und Honoré de Balzac als Leser der letzten Dinge', *Sigmund-Freud Museum Newsletter* 2003, No. 2, pp. 4–16.

17 The allusion to Maud Gonne is clear in stanza 8; in advising the child to be shy of the looking-glass (stanza 3) he reverses advice given in 'Michael Robartes and the Dancer' where the dancer is generally accepted to be Iseult.

18 Sigmund Freud, *Beyond the Pleasure Principle* (trans. James Strachey), in *The Standard Edition of the Complete Psychological Works*. London: Vintage, 2001, vol. 28, pp. 8–10. It is worth noting also that, in 1920, Freud was already studying the *Upanishads* for their fables explaining the origins of human sexuality.

19 Military Archives, Bureau of Military History, Witness Statement No. 446.

20 See Patrick Moylett, Bureau of Military History, Witness Statement No. 767, p. 12.

21 WBY to Olivia Shakespear, [after 10 July 1927]. Access No. 5013.

22 WBY to Olivia Shakespear, 22 May [1929]. Acccess No. 5113.

23 Russell K. Alspach (ed.), *The Variorum Edition of the Plays of W. B. Yeats*. London: Macmillan, 1966, p. 777.

24 W. B. Yeats, *Memoirs* (ed. Denis Donoghue). London: Macmillan, 1972, p. 78.

25 WBY to Augusta Gregory, 8 November [1918?]. Access No. 3523.

26 Quoted by Elizabeth Cullingford, who refers to a typescript 'in the possession of M. B. Yeats' without making any attempt to date the item; see Cullingford, (1981), pp. 86–87.

27 'Swedenborg, Mediums and the Desolate Places' in Yeats, *Later Essays*, p. 53.

28 Ibid., p. 61.

29 Maud Gonne to WBY, 7 November [1915]. *Gonne-Yeats Letters* (1992), p. 363.

30 'Swedenborg, Mediums', p. 63.

31 Quoted in Ellmann (1979), p. 278.

32 'Swedenborg, Mediums', pp. 63–64.

33 Yeats, *Autobiographies*, p. 354.

34 See 'John Eglinton', in John P. Frayne and Colton Johnson (eds), *Uncollected Prose of W. B. Yeats*, vol. 2. London: Macmillan, 1975, p. 257. The piece first appeared in *The United Irishman*, 9 November 1901.

35 Ibid., p. 259.

36 Ibid., p. 257.

37 John Eglinton, 'Mr Yeats and Popular Poetry', in *Literary Ideals in Ireland*. London: Fisher Unwin; Dublin: *Daily Express*, 1899, p. 45.

38 George W. Russell, 'Nationality and Cosmopolitanism in Literature', in *Literary Ideals*, p. 85.

39 Eglinton, 'Mr Yeats and Popular Poetry', in *Literary Ideals*, p. 42.

40 Yeats, 'John Eglinton and Spiritual Art', p. 257.

41 Eglinton, 'What Should be the Subjects of National Drama?', in *Literary Ideals*, p. 10.

42 See Peter Kuch, *Yeats and AE: 'the Antagonism that Unites Dear Friends'*. Gerrards Cross: Smythe, 1986.

43 John Butler Yeats to WBY, 14 April 1909; Hone (ed.) (1944), p. 120.

Victorian Kindred

1 Peter Ure, *Yeats the Playwright; A Commentary on Character and Design in the Major Plays*. London: Routledge, 1963, p. 13.

2 WBY to John O'Leary, 1 February [1889]; Kelly (ed.) (1986), p. 138.

3 Cf. Ellmann, (1979), p. 102; and A. N. Jeffares and A. S. Knowland (eds), *A Commentary on the Collected Plays of W. B. Yeats*. London: Macmillan, 1975, p. 5.

4 Katharine Tynan, *Ballads and Lyrics*. London: Kegan Paul, 1891, pp. 45–50, 153. The library in Trinity College preserves a signed presentation copy from Tynan to WBY dated 'New Year 1892'.

5 E. S. H., 'Mr W. B. Yeats' Poem of *Countess Kathleen*', in *Folklore*, vol. 6, no. 2 (June 1895), pp. 200–201.

6 O'Donnell's assault on the play was concentrated in an anonymous pamphlet, *Souls for Gold!*, published in London in 1899 and consisting of two letters to the newspapers (one of them refused publication). He returned to the theme in *The Stage Irishman of the Pseudo-Celtic Drama* (London: Long, 1904). The 1899 material is now available through appendices added to Augusta Gregory, *Our Irish Theatre: A Chapter of Autobiography*. New York: Oxford University Press, 1972, pp. 261–270.

7 See Seamus Deane *et al.* (eds), *The Field Day Anthology of Irish Writing*. Derry: Field Day, 1991, vol. 2, pp. 831–866, for my discussion of Stoker as pre-emptive anti-modernist.

8 O'Donnell, *The Stage Irishman*, p. 13.

9 Michael McAteer, 'A Currency Crisis; Modernist Dialectics in *The Countess Cathleen*', in Betsy Taylor FitzSimon and James H. Murphy (eds), *The Irish Revival Reappraised*. Dublin: Four Courts Press, 2004, pp. 187–204, esp. p. 189.

10 Peter Gibbon, *The Origins of Ulster Unionism; the Formation of Popular Protestant Politics and Ideology in the Nineteenth Century*. Manchester: Manchester University Press, 1975, p. 105.

11 On Hatch and Harcourt Street, see W. J. Mc Cormack, *The Silence of Barbara Synge*. Manchester: Manchester University Press, 2003.

12 Yeats, *Autobiographies* (1999), p. 92. Though Yeats's intention is to convey the meanness of this accommodation, he still finds it necessary to exaggerate the house by describing it as a villa – it was one in a row of semi-detached houses.

13 WBY to Augusta Gregory, 1 March [1922]. Access No. 4082.

14 The computerised High School records give the following details: Frederick Gregg (born 1864; entered January 1880 till June 1884); Charles Johnston (born 17 February 1867; entered 27 January 1881 till 31 October 1885); Lewis Johnston (entered 27 January 1881 till 31 October 1883); Malcolm Hamilton Magee (born 1866; entered 1 October 1880 till 31 October 1884); William Kirkpatrick Magee (born 1869; entered 30 August 1881 till 31 December 1886); Charles Weekes (born 1867; entered 14 August 1880 till 30 June 1883); William Butler Yeats (born 1865; entered 14 October 1881 till 31 December 1883). I am grateful to the school archivist Alan Phelan for his assistance in this regard.

15 See Edward A. Hagan, 'The Aryan Myth: a Nineteenth-Century Anglo-Irish Will to

Power', in Tadhg Foley and Sean Ryder (eds), *Ideology and Ireland in the Nineteenth Century*. Dublin: Four Courts, 1998, pp. 197–205.

16 On Johnston, see Gibbon, *The Origins of Ulster Unionism*, pp. 99–102, etc.

17 McAteer, 'A Currency Crisis', in *The Irish Revival Reappraised*, p. 189.

18 See Eve Patten's essay 'A Family Romance' appended to Yeats, *John Sherman & Dhoya*. Dublin: Lilliput, 1990.

19 Yeats, *John Sherman*, p. 8.

20 See Carla King's introduction to the edition of *Parnell and His Island*, published by University College Dublin Press in 2004.

21 On the Dublin Hermetic Society, see Selina Guinness, 'Ireland through the Stereoscope: Reading the Cultural Politics of Theosophy in the Irish Literary Revival', in *The Irish Revival Reappraised*, pp. 19–32.

22 Yeats, *Autobiographies*, p. 169.

23 Francis J. Byrne, *Irish Kings and High Kings* (2nd edn). Dublin: Four Courts Press, 2001, p. 52.

24 WBY to John O'Leary, *c.* January 1888: Kelly (ed.) (1986), p. 46.

25 *Collected Letters*, vol. 3, p. 214.

26 But see Maddox (1999).

27 See 'Childhood and Screen Memories', in *The Psychopathology of Everyday Life* (1901), *The Standard Edition of the Complete Psychological Works of Sigmund Freud*. London: Vintage, 2001, vol. 6, pp. 43–52.

28 See *The Registers of the Church of St Michan, Dublin 1636–1700* (ed. H. F. Berry). Dublin: Parish Register Society, [Part II] 1909, pp. 341, 345.

29 Yeats, *Autobiographies*, p. 21.

30 National Library of Ireland Ms 2063. f.6r. This large notebook was compiled during the 1920s by the poet's sister, Susan Mary Yeats, known as Lily, and deals with family history.

31 Lily Yeats's Notebook f.10r. On Taylor, see in particular A. N. Jeffares, *W. B. Yeats; Man and Poet* (2nd edn). London: Routledge, 1962, p. 299 n.17. Some of Taylor's clerkly activities are recorded in a volume of Secret Service accounts preserved in the Public Record Office, Kew (CO 904/3); see Mc Cormack 'Reflections on Writing and Editing' in Charles Benson and Siobhán Fitzpatrick (eds) *A Festschrift for Mary Pollard*. Dublin: Lilliput Press, 2005. See also Thomas Bartlett (ed), *Revolutionary Dublin 1795–1801: The Letters of Francis Higgins to Dublin Castle*. Dublin: Four Courts, 2004, esp. pp 210, 232.

32 On this topic, see Brian Inglis, *The Freedom of the Press in Ireland 1784–1841*. London: Faber, 1954.

33 Yeats, *Autobiographies*, p. 5.

34 W. J. Mc Cormack, *Sheridan Le Fanu and Victorian Ireland*. Oxford: Clarendon Press, 1980, p. 3.

35 Samuel Lewis, *A Topographical Dictionary of Ireland*. London: Lewis, 1837, vol. 2, pp. 658–659; see also vol. 1, pp. 652–653 for an account of the town of Gilford. For a trenchantly sociological analysis of this area and period, see Gibbon's *The Origins of Ulster Unionism* (1975) and, perhaps more important, Sybil Gribben's review of the book in *Irish Economic and Social History*, vol. 4 (1977), pp. 66–72.

36 Yeats, *Autobiographies*, p. 23. Lily Yeats's version of this piece of family lore is decidedly less dramatic, and specifies that Beatty shared his distinction of not being hanged as a rebel with one other member of the hell-fiery club, that one being 'the then bishop of Down'. In the manuscript material which Edward Albert Myles assembled for a parish history of Tullylish, Beatty's association with Goldsmith is authenticated. This material is preserved in the Library of the Representative Church Body, Dublin, and hereinafter cited as Myles Mss.

Biographers of Goldsmith note Beatty sharing a room in Dublin when the two were students (i.e. the latter half of the 1740s) and Goldsmith was formally rebuked for his part in a riot. He appears to have called on the poet once in London, before Goldsmith achieved literary fame. Assuming them to be (roughly) contemporaries in age, Beatty would have been about sixty-eight in 1798, the notable occasion on which treason trials, executions and transportations featured. Yeats is careful to avoid saying that his ancestor's friend (also Goldsmith's friend) was in the club at the time when other members were prosecuted: we may infer that their conviviality occurred much earlier. All in all, the passage exemplifies a literary making much of little.

37 Lily's Yeats's Notebook f.11v, citing 'great grandfather Yeats's prayer-book'.

38 Myles Mss, vol. 2, p. 10l.

39 For an account of Johnston, see the biography of his son; Samuel Prenter, *Life and Labours of the Rev. William Johnston*, D. D. *Belfast.* London: Nisbet, 1895, esp. pp. 1–14; also Anon., *Tullylish Presbyterian Church 1670–1970* (printed Banbridge, c.1970), pp. 21–27.

40 Prenter, *Life and Labours*, pp. 1, 3.

41 Gerard Mac Atasney, *The Famine in Lurgan/Portadown.* Belfast: Beyond the Pale, 1997, p. 117.

42 William M. Murphy, *The Yeats Family and the Pollexfens of Sligo.* Dublin: Dolmen Press, 1971, folding table.

43 Public Record Office of Northern Ireland BG/22/A/2B, p. 399.

44 Public Record Office of Northern Ireland BG/22/A/4, p. 455.

45 Mac Atasney, *The Famine in Lurgan*, p. 38.

46 See Public Record Office of Northern Ireland BG/22/CF/1 for a volume of Lurgan Union's accounts, including treasurer's receipts etc. for 1842–49. The absence of the Revd Yeats's name does not prove his non-contribution, but it does place an onus on historians who wish to cite his contribution to find some confirmation of family lore.

47 Hone, *W. B. Yeats 1865–1939*, pp. 5–7.

48 See *Ordnance Survey Memoirs of Ireland vol. 12, Parishes of County Down III, 1833–38.* Belfast: Institute of Irish Studies, 1992, pp. 1407; and D. S. MacNeice, 'Industrial Villages in Ulster, 1800–1900', in P. Roebuck (ed.), *Plantation to Partition.* Belfast: Blackstaff, 1981, pp. 172–190. See also Marilyn Ruth Cohen, *Proletarianization and Family Structures in the Parish of Tullylish, County Down, Ireland, 1690–1914* (New York School of Social Research, thesis, 1988).

49 Marilyn Cohen, *Linen, Family and Community in Tullylish, County Down 1690–1914.* Dublin: Four Courts, 1997, p. 124.

50 Cohen, *Proletarianization*, pp. 287, 292. See also E. R. R. Green, *The Industrial Archaeology of Down.* Belfast H.M.S.O, 1967.

51 See *Northern Whig*, 22 November 1924, p. 11, and Myles Mss.

52 For a valuable treatment of the broad context, see Martin W. Dowling, *Tenant Right and Agrarian Society in Ulster 1600–1870.* Dublin: Irish Academic Press, 1999, esp. pp. 137–157.

53 Cohen, *Linen, Family*, p. 122.

54 Lewis, *Topographical Dictionary*, vol. 2, pp. 658–659; Lily Yeats's Notebook, f.13v. In 1993, the incumbent informed me of a local tradition that rectors had lived in a house on Whinny Hill, presumably rented when the rectory became uninhabitable. Possibly Yeats had lived here, he added.

55 See Marilyn J. Westerkamp, *Triumph of the Laity; Scots-Irish Piety and the Great Wakening 1625–1760.* New York: Oxford, 1988. Peter Brooke, *Ulster Presbyterianism; The Historical Perspective 1610–1970.* Dublin: Gill and Macmillan; New York, St Martin's Press, 1987.

56 For the story about Macaulay, see Hone, *W. B. Yeats 1865–1939*, p. 5. It might be noted that one of Yeats's curates was the Revd Nathaniel Hone, kinsman of the biographer, and that later in the nineteenth century marriage linked the Yeats and Hone families.

57 Myles Mss, vol. III (unpaged).

58 Registry of Deeds, Dublin: Memorial 1849: 21: 151. It would seem that these securities were already controlled by Robert Corbet who, in effect, participated in this transaction both as private individual and as an agent of the Assurance Co. See Mem. 1847: 15: 231.

59 Murphy (1978), p. 21. It should be added that Murphy's work is invaluable for its attention to the ticklish question of Yeats's family finances. On the Wynnes and Beattys, see *Burke's Irish Family Records,* Myles Mss, and Murphy, *Prodigal Father,* pp. 45, 554.

60 See Mary Gluck, *Georg Lukacs and His Generation 1900–1918.* Cambridge, Mass.: Harvard University Press, 1985.

61 Yeats, *Autobiographies,* pp. 51–52. The 'last generation of all' is illuminated by a parallel passage in Lily Yeats's Notebook where she remarks, 'none of the Corbet sons [i.e. Patrick 1793–1840; Robert 1795–1870; William 1798–1826; and Arthur 1804–?] married, so we have no relations of the name' (f.18v)

62 For the pre-aristocratic history of these families, see Mary O'Dowd, *Power, Politics and Land: Early Modern Sligo 1568–1688.* Belfast: Institute of Irish Studies, 1991, pp. 138, 163 and refs.

63 Dublin Registry of Deeds: Mem. 1839: 6: 19.

64 Lily Yeats's Notebook, f.20v, citing the Corbet family Bible. See also Murphy, *Prodigal Father,* p. 551 n.66; see also the same author's 'The Ancestry of William Butler Yeats', *Yeats Studies* no. 1 (1971), pp. 119. Murphy is inclined to place Corbet's career too late in the century, with the result that his commencement in business before the municipal crisis of 1840 etc. is obscured. His masonic initiation in 1840/41 might be read as a reaction to the loss of Protestant exclusivity in the city corporation, though surviving lodge records do not suggest that Corbet was ever a very active mason.

65 J. B. Yeats, *Early Memories,* pp. 54, 59, 58.

66 Yeats, *Autobiographies,* p. 52.

67 George Moore, *Hail and Farewell* (ed. Richard Cave). Gerrards Cross: Smythe, 1976, p. 540.

68 See Maurice Collis, *Somerville & Ross: a Biography.* London: Faber, 1968, p. 129. Dominie Sampson is a school teacher in Walter Scott's *Guy Mannering.*

69 *Catholic Bulletin,* vol. 14 (1924), p. 6 (January), p. 268 (April).

70 Lily Yeats's Notebook, f.24r. See Yeats, *Letters,* pp. 552–554, for Yeats's positive assessment of Jackson in 1910 at the time of George Pollexfen.

71 Murphy (1978), pp. 175, 204, etc.

72 *Catholic Bulletin,* vol. 14 (1924), p. 7 (January), p. 91 (February), p. 169 (March), etc.

73 See Mc Cormack (1993).

74 See Murphy (1978), pp. 550–551 n.62, citing Ervine's review in the *Spectator,* 11 November 1949. While it is true that Ervine was an unreliable witness on W. B. Yeatsian matters, he was an Ulsterman with access to local traditions of the Tullylish years.

75 WBY to Thomas MacGreevy, 23 April 1932. Letter No. 5648.

76 Access No. 5648.

77 Yeats, *The Words Upon the Window-pane.* Churchtown: Cuala Press, 1934, p. 40.

78 Curtis Bradford, *Yeats at Work.* Carbondale: Southern Illinois University Press, 1965, pp. 231–232.

Second-Hand Tragedy, or 'Are You Content'

1 See Jason Harding, *The* Criterion: *Cultural Politics and Periodical Networks in Interwar-War Britain.* Oxford: Oxford University Press, 2002, pp. 216–217.

2 'He had had a very slight contact with it [Nazism] in the person of the German poet, Stefan George, who was sufficiently Aryan and Germanic to be the poet by adoption of the Nazi leaders. I gathered from Yeats that Stefan George had read some of Yeats's work and had written to him about it. Yeats had read some of George's poems in translation and was interested in him. On the face of it, it might have seemed to Yeats that a Government that had declared affinities in the realms of poetry, music, philosophy etc – as had the Nazis – contrasted favourably with the philistine attitudes of governments in most civilised countries.' Josephine MacNeill in the *Irish Times,* 29 June 1965.

3 Jeffrey Meyers, *The Enemy: a Biography of Wyndham Lewis*. London: Routledge, 1980, p. 189.

4 Harding, *The Criterion*, pp. 189–190, 157; for Eliot's 'ethical' anti-Semitism, see *After Strange Gods; a Primer of Modern Heresy*. New York: Harcourt Brace, 1934, p. 20.

5 Information provided by Alan Phelan, the school archivist.

6 WBY to Olivia Shakespear, 13 July [1933]. Access No. 5915.

7 See 'The Meaning of a Poem', 'Literature and Totalitarianism' and 'London Letter to *Partisan Review*', in George Orwell, *The Collected Essays, Journalism and Letters* (ed. Sonia Orwell and Ian Angus). London: Secker & Warburg, 1968, vol. 2.

8 Ibid., p. 271.

9 Ibid., p. 273.

10 David Pierce, *Yeats's Worlds: Ireland, England and the Poetic Imagination*. New Haven: Yale University Press, 1995, p. 244.

11 Kuno Meyer published a text in 1899, Osborne Bergin in 1914. Readers today are referred to Gerard Murphy, *Early Irish Lyrics* (2nd edn, Dublin: Four Courts, 1998, pp. 74–83) for a scholarly text and prose translation. In 1936, Yeats included Frank O'Connor's very loose version in *The Oxford Book of Modern Poetry* (pp. 398–401) without (apparently) its having appeared in print elsewhere. He had first met O'Connor early in 1927, when work on 'Sailing to Byzantium' had already begun.

12 Cullingford 12 (1981), p. 232.

13 See James Pethica (ed.), Yeats, *The Last Poems* . . . Ithaca: Cornell University Press, 1997, pp. 102–141.

14 W. B. Yeats, *The Poems* (ed. Daniel Albright). London: Everyman's Library, 1992, p. 816. I don't adopt Albright's further suggestion that the Tower is linked to Yeats's Norman tower in Ballylee, though it certainly scotches any idea that the defenders are *resisting* invasion.

15 WBY to Dorothy Wellesley, 15 August [1938]. Access No. 7290.

16 WBY to William Rose, 17 August [1938]. Access No. 7292.

17 Foster (2003), p. 628.

18 Sean O'Faolain, *The Vanishing Hero*. New York: Grosset & Dunlap, 1956, p. 75. See also, T. R. Whitaker, *Swan and Shadow: Yeats's Dialogue with History*. Washington: Catholic University of America Press, 1989, 1989 (especially p. 166).

19 Cohen, *Linen, Family, pp.* 134–155.

20 See Andrew Benjamin and Peter Osbourne (eds), *Walter Benjamin's Philosophy*. London, New York: Routledge, 1994.

21 See J. Hillis Miller, *Topographies*. Stanford: Stanford University Press, 1995. Miller devotes a chapter to Faulkner's *Absolom, Absolom!*, but manifests considerable impatience with the novelist's attitude towards 'southern ideology'.

22 George Steiner, *The Death of Tragedy* (2nd edn). London: Faber, 1995, see esp. pp. 317–318 re. Yeats.

23 W. B. Yeats to Edith Shackleton Heald, 2 October [1938]. Access No. 7307.

24 Elizabeth Bowen, *The Heat of the Day*. London: Cape, 1949, p. 87.

25 Raymond Williams, *Drama from Ibsen to Eliot* (rev. edn) London: Peregrine Books, 1964, pp. 225–226.

26 'A People's Theatre', in W. B. Yeats, *Explorations*. London: Macmillan, 1962, p. 249.

27 William Faulkner, *The Sound and the Fury*. London: Everyman's Library, 1992, pp. 98–99.

28 See Steiner, *The Death of Tragedy*, on the limitations of Yeats's dramatic success.

29 Faulkner, *The Sound and the Fury*, p. 143.

30 Quoted in Frederick J. Carl, *William Faulkner, American Writer*. London: Faber, 1989, p. 902.

31 William Faulkner in the *New York Times*, 13 October 1957, on the Little Rock crisis: quoted in Carl, *William Faulkner*, p. 970.

32 See Mitchel Cohen, *The Wager of Lucien Goldmann; Tragedy, Dialectic and a Hidden God*. Princeton: Princeton University Press, 1994, pp. 133–137.

33 *The Poems of William Blake* (ed. Stevenson and Erdman). London: Longman, 1971, pp. 105, 475.

34 A good example of a Marxist facing the implications of this history is Eric Hobsbaum in *Interesting Times; a Twentieth-Century Life*. London: Allan Lane, 2002.

35 Daniel T. O'Hara, '*Tragic Knowledge*'; Yeats's Autobiography *and Hermeneutics*. New York: Columbia University Press, 1981, p. 127.

36 James Longenbach, *Stone Cottage; Pound, Yeats and Modernism*. New York: Oxford University Press, 1988.

37 Scholarly readers may be intrigued by conflicting exact dates given for this poem. According to John Kelly, editor of Yeats's correspondence, it was written in one sitting on 7 May 1913; in Daniel Albright's edition of the poems, it is dated to 5 March 1913.

38 Bruce Arnold, *Jack Yeats*. New Haven, London: Yale University Press, 1998, p. 170.

Demob

1 The list as published was not a complete record of messages received, though, according to the widow's biographer, only those 'which were most personal' were omitted; see Saddlemyer (2002), p. 567.

2 The published list is given in Pierce (1995), pp. 265–266.

3 The best investigation of this belief, and its importance for Yeats's poetry, is Daniel A. Harris, *Yeats, Coole Park & Ballylee*. Baltimore: Johns Hopkins University Press, 1974.

4 Terry Trench, *Nearly Ninety*, p. 72. The group in 1930 also included Jupp Hoven.

5 See PRO (Kew) FO 940/49. This file is marked 'secret' and 'closed till 1979'. In this chapter all quotations from British material relating to Clissmann come from this source. The business of his 'private property' being 'stored . . . for safe keeping' in the Dublin Legation is noted in Cathy Molohan, *Germany and Ireland 1945–1955: Two Nations' Friendship*. Dublin: Irish Academic Press, 1999, p. 22. It is not without its puzzling aspects: a) Clissmann had Irish relatives through his wife and was not without a domestic base in Ireland; b) he left Dublin before his wife, suggesting that it may have been she who deposited the items in the German Legation when she moved to the Continent. With her Sligo credentials, perhaps Frau Clissmann (née Mulcahy) deserves her own place among the Blood Kindred.

6 According to A. Norman Jeffares and associates, Francis Stuart was teaching in the Technische Hochschule by April 1941; see *Knew Dante* (2004), p. xix. This bit of casual information is all the more remarkable as the editors never once allow the name of Clissmann to fall from their laptops.

7 Military Archives, G2/X/1091, docket 211.

8 See *Højesteretstidende*, vol. 93, nos 21–24 (1949), pp. 634–767; see esp. pp. 639–640, 650, 656, 660–661, 665, 668, 694–698, 718–719, 740, 750, 755, for some indication of Clissmann's role in the events and the trial.

9 See David O'Donoghue, 'Heil Hibernia', in *Sunday Business Post*, 29 April 2001.

10 *Irish Writing*, no. 22 (March 1953), pp. 43–46.

11 It seems that, in 1949, the young bellows of Portobello was kept informed about a Save the German Children Society which harboured admirers of the Third Reich among its members; see *Two Nations' Friendship*. pp. 55 and 122 n.82. However, I have not been able to locate the original of the letter quoted.

12 Dermot MacManus to Sybil Le Brocquy, 22 September 1982. NLI Ms. 21,677. MacManus also invokes Portugal as a political model: see Aoife ní Lochlainn, 'Ailtirí na hAiseirghe; A Party of its Time?' (esp. pp. 199–201 on the appeal of Salazar's dictatorship among Irish fascists in the late 1930s and during the War) in Dermot Keogh and Mervyn O'Driscoll (eds.), *Ireland in World War Two; Diplomacy and Survival* (Cork: Mercier Press, 2004).

13 Dermot MacManus to Sybil Le Brocquy, 12 October 1968. NLI Ms. 21,677.

14 Dermot MacManus to Kathleen Raine, 11 June 1973. NLI Ms. 22,103.

15 *Knew Dante*, p. 150. The editors are unable to date this, though reference to Stuart's fondness for Russian ballerinas suggests it was written before the war.

16 These were published posthumously, see Brendan Barrington (ed.), *The Wartime Broadcasts of Francis Stuart 1942–1944*. Dublin: Lilliput, 2000. See also Damien Keane, 'Francis Stuart to America, 9 June 1940', in *The Dublin Review*, no. 14 (spring 2004), pp. 53–56.

17 I rely on A. N. Jeffares for O'Mara's name, but suspect that the woman was the one known subsequently as Roisín ní Mheara, in her old age author of books about Irish saints on the Continent; see also her remarkable autobiography in Gaelic.

18 In an undated document quoted by Anna MacBride White in *Knew Dante*, p. 150.

19 Michael Butler Yeats, *Cast a Cold Eye: Memories of a Poet's Son and Politician*. [Dublin]: Blackwater, [n.d.], p. 20.

20 The letter (23 December [1936], Access No. 6762) ostensibly deals with the controversy over Roger Casement's diaries: 'When somebody talks of justice, who knows that justice is accompanied by secret forgery, when an archbishop wants a man to go to the communion table, when that man says he is not spiritually fit, then we remember our age old quarrel against gold-brayed [*sic*] and ermine, & that our ancestor Swift has gone where "fierce indignation can lacerate his heart no more" & we go stark, staring mad.'

21 See in particular Adorno's letter of 10 November 1938 to Walter Benjamin, in Gershom Scholem and T. W. Adorno (eds), *The Correspondence of Walter Benjamin 1910–1940*. Chicago: University of Chicago Press, 1994, pp. 579–585.

22 For good detail, see Foster (1997), pp. 9, 545 (n.21).

23 For the diary (9 September 1930) and the dream, see Foster (2003), pp. 409–410.

24 Ibid., p. 483.

25 Ibid., pp. 468, 471, 483, 629, 631.

26 The work of Jerome McGann suggests models on which Yeats's tandem procedures could be investigated.

27 Foster (2003), p. 468.

Text Acknowledgments

The author and publishers are grateful to the following for granting permission to quote from material in copyright.

Poetry, Drama and Prose by W. B. Yeats is reproduced by kind permission of A. P. Watt on behalf of Michael B. Yeats.

Letters by W. B. Yeats are reproduced by kind permission of Oxford University Press.

Quotations from James Joyce's *Ulysses* are reprinted by kind permission of the James Joyce Estate.

Quotation from a letter of G. B. Shaw (3 January 1939) is reprinted by kind permission of the Shaw Estate, administered by the Society of Authors.

Quotations from the work of Iseult Gonne, Maud Gonne, and Oliver St John Gogarty are reprinted by kind permission of Colin Smythe Ltd.

For the use of manuscript material in their care, the author acknowledges the kindness of the Keeper of the National Archives (Dublin), the Director of Military Archives (Dublin), the Trustees of the National Library of Ireland, the Director of the Public Record Office (London) and the Institut für Stadtgeschichte (Frankfurt-am-Main).

'Fabrication of Ancestors for Old Billy Dugan, Shot in the Ass in the Civil War, My Father Said' by Alan Dugan is reproduced from *Collected Poems* (London: Faber, 1970).

Extracts from the work of W. H. Auden are reproduced from *The English Auden* (London: Faber, 1977).

Extracts from Samuel Beckett reproduced from *All that Fall* (London: Faber, 1957) and *Disjecta* (London: Calder, 1983).

Extracts from T. S. Eliot reproduced from *After Strange Gods* (New York: Harcourt Brace, 1934), 'Gerontion' from *The Collected Poems 1909–1935* (London: Faber, 1946).

Extracts from Archibald MacLeish reproduced from 'Public Speech and Private Speech in Poetry' *Yale Review* (March 1938).

Extracts from George Orwell reproduced from *The Collected Essays, Journalism and Letters* (London: Secker & Warburg, 1968).

Every effort has been made to contact all copyright holders. The publishers would be pleased to rectify any omissions or errors brought to their notice at the earliest opportunity.

General Index

Index II – W. B. Yeats

i) HIS LIFE AND THEMES

ii) HIS TEXTS